Great Events from History

The 17th Century

1601-1700

Great Lives from History

The 17th Century

1601 - 1700

Volume 2
1652-1700

Editor
Larissa Juliet Taylor
Colby College

Salem Press
Pasadena, California   Hackensack, New Jersey

Editor in Chief: Dawn P. Dawson

Managing Editor: Christina J. Moose
Acquisitions Editor: Mark Rehn
Research Supervisor: Jeffry Jensen
Manuscript Editors: Desiree Dreeuws, Andy Perry
Assistant Editor: Andrea E. Miller
Production Editor: Kathy Hix
Graphics and Design: James Hutson
Editorial Assistant: Dana Garey
Layout: Eddie Murillo
Photograph Editor: Cynthia Beres

Cover photos: PhotoDisc, Corbis
(Pictured clockwise, from top left: Taj Mahal; 1650 map of the northern portion of the New World; Istanbul; Chateau de Versailles; Il Duomo; statue of Buddha; Jamestown settlement with ships)

∞ The paper used in these volumes conforms to the American National Standard for Permanence of Paper for Printed Library Materials, Z39.48-1992 (R1997).

Some of the essays in this work originally appeared in the following Salem Press sets: *Chronology of European History: 15,000 B.C. to 1997* (1997, edited by John Powell; associate editors, E. G. Weltin, José M. Sánchez, Thomas P. Neill, and Edward P. Keleher) and *Great Events from History: North American Series, Revised Edition* (1997, edited by Frank N. Magill). New material has been added.

Library of Congress Cataloging-in-Publication Data

Great events from history. The 17th century, 1601-1700 / editor, Larissa Juliet Taylor.
p. cm.
Some of the essays in this work were originally published in Chronology of European history, 15,000 B.C. to 1997 and Great events from history : North American series. Rev. ed. 1997.
Includes bibliographical references and index.
ISBN-10: 1-58765-225-0 (set : alk. paper)
ISBN-10: 1-58765-226-9 (v. 1 : alk. paper)
ISBN-10: 1-58765-227-7 (v. 2 : alk. paper)
ISBN-13: 978-1-58765-225-7 (set : alk. paper)
ISBN-13: 978-1-58765-226-4 (v. 1 : alk. paper)
ISBN-13: 978-1-58765-227-1 (v. 2 : alk. paper)
1. Seventeenth century. I. Title: 17th century, 1601-1700. II. Title: Seventeenth century, 1601-1700. III. Taylor, Larissa. IV. Chronology of European history, 15,000 B.C. to 1997. V. Great events from history, North American series. 1997.

D246.G68 2005
909′.6—dc22

2005017362

First Printing

PRINTED IN THE UNITED STATES OF AMERICA

Contents

1650's *(continued)*

1660's

1670's

1680's

1690's

Appendices

Indexes

Keyword List of Contents

List of Maps, Tables, and Sidebars

Africa in the 17th Century

ASIA IN THE 17TH CENTURY

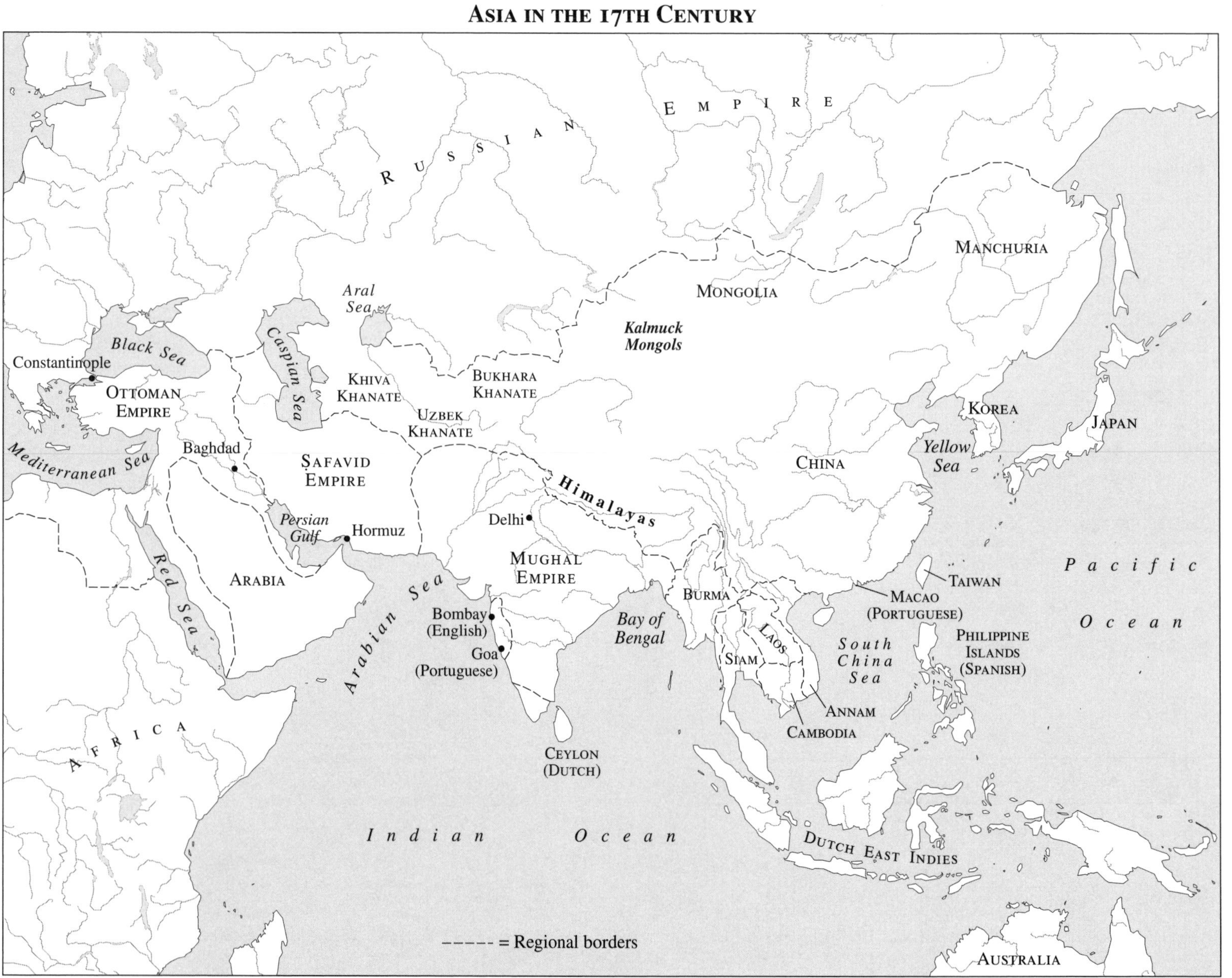

Europe in the 17th Century

European Colonization in the 17th Century

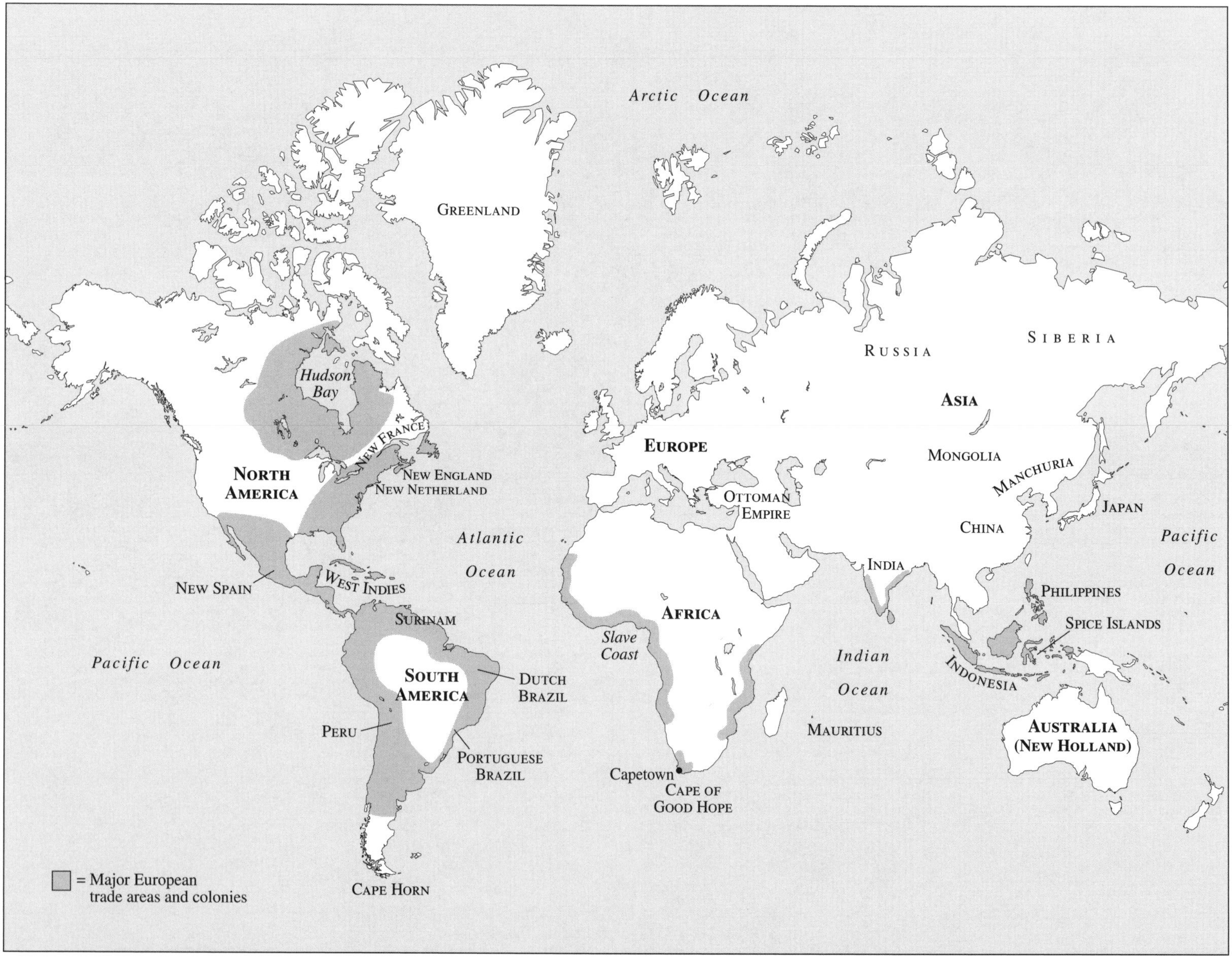

North America in the 17th Century

SOUTH AMERICA IN THE 17TH CENTURY

Great Events from History

The 17th Century

1601-1700

1652-1667
PATRIARCH NIKON'S REFORMS

The leader of the Russian Orthodox Church caused a damaging schism within Russia's major faith by trying to implement controversial reforms in areas such as church administration, clerical training, religious writings, and service rituals.

LOCALE: Russia
CATEGORIES: Religion and theology; organizations and institutions

KEY FIGURES

Nikon (1605-1681), patriarch of the Russian Orthodox Church, 1652-1658, who initiated a sweeping range of reforms
Alexis (1629-1676), Russian czar, r. 1645-1676, who first supported and then opposed Patriarch Nikon
Avvakum Petrovich (1620/1621-1682), Russian priest and leader of the Old Believers, who organized the opposition to Nikon and his religious reforms

SUMMARY OF EVENT

In Russia's development as a nation and organized society, Christianity played a vital role by providing religious values and worship practices that both transformed and united the population. While the fundamental theological dogmas of the Russian Orthodox Church generally remained consistent through the centuries, problems became increasingly evident, calling for clarification and correction. These included relations with Byzantine Orthodoxy, details of religious rituals and practice, and accuracy of religious texts.

A reform movement to restore accuracy to the original forms, both in writing and in practice, emerged in the seventeenth century, notably under the leadership of Nikon, who rose to the high position of patriarch of Moscow. Finding favor with the youthful Czar Alexis, he became the metropolitan of Novgorod, the second most important clerical position in Russia. Upon the death of Patriarch Joseph in 1652, Alexis pressured church authorities to appoint Nikon as patriarch. Using his new authority, and with the Russian monarch's support, Nikon succeeded in undertaking and implementing a series of reforms that were confirmed by church councils beginning in 1653.

These efforts were wide-ranging and had implications for the Russian Orthodox Church. Prior to Nikon's appointment, in the 1630's, a theological seminary had been established in Kiev, a major city in the Ukraine to the south. Its scholars gained a reputation for their careful analyses of religious texts. Nikon encouraged Kievan scholars to review printed materials used in Russia, finding that errors in translation and copying had altered the originals. This process actually began several years before Nikon became patriarch, but he continued his predecessor's reform effort. Nikon's opponents, however, viewed Kiev and its religious scholars as outside the scope of the place they believed to be the center of true Christianity—Moscow—in contrast to the Latin Church in Rome and the Byzantine Church. That some of the Kievan scholars learned Greek and Latin, and used sources in those languages, also made them suspect in the eyes of religious traditionalists in Russia. Their opposition to Nikon's plans also revealed Russian nationalism, opposing ties or cooperation with remote Ukraine, Catholic Poland, or the former Byzantine Empire now under Turkish and Islamic control.

A number of these changes might seem arcane. For example, one reform called for the priest to give the sign of the cross by raising three fingers instead of the traditional two. (The shift referred to the Trinity in the former while the latter signified the divine and human nature of Christ.) In another reform, the form of bowing or kneeling during prayers was reduced from twelve to four, again a change from tradition. Hallelujahs were to be sung three times, not twice, during the service. Prayers that were sung had to be in one tone, not several.

Icons, the two-dimensional representation of Christ and other religious figures, had to follow the traditional Byzantine style rather than the style followed in other countries. Many icons were seized, despoiled, and destroyed. Older guides and manuals used to regulate religious life and ritual were confiscated from churches and homes, sometimes by threats of punishment. Even the route of church processions had to follow new, approved policies, according to the location of the sun. These are only a few of the variations that Nikon sought to impose on religious life.

To fundamental and traditionalist clergy in the Orthodox Church, who had followed for decades practices they believed to be required for their glorification of God and the possible source of salvation, Nikon's changes were heretical. Millions of followers, largely illiterate, also felt threatened by these changes in tradition. Followers became familiar with church traditions and wished that they be retained and practiced as evidence of their

Russian Orthodox Church patriarch Nikon. (Library of Congress)

faith. Reform opponents came to be known as Old Believers, who organized resistance under the leadership of the priest Avvakum Petrovich and other clergy. Avvakum regularly petitioned the Church and the monarch to permit the continuation of traditional rituals, and he opposed relying upon Greek and Latin sources. He also criticized Nikon's methods and wrote a letter to Czar Alexis that read, "Nothing so much engenders schism in the churches as overbearing love of domination on the part of the authorities."

Nikon persevered in these reforms, but he was able to do so because of the approval of church councils that met under his direction. He was determined to control and even destroy Avvakum and the opposition. Nikon generally succeeded in his efforts during a portion of the 1650's, assisted by Czar Alexis and the state in attacking the Old Believers. Large numbers of Orthodox Christians followed Avvakum in resistance to reform, even in the face of threats of religious excommunication or physical injury. By the latter part of the century, thousands of the Old Believers had committed suicide by self-immolation rather than accept the new rules. One estimate places the numbers at approximately twenty thousand individuals. Avvakum, failing to convince the authorities of the error of Nikon's leadership and reforms, was exiled to Siberia. He was executed in 1682.

In the short term, Nikon won the reform battle. However, the Russian Orthodox Church was seriously weakened in the long term. The schism was not only a religious one. Nikon's efforts to increase religious authority—especially the role of the patriarch—called into question the power of the Russian monarchy as well. Nikon sought authority equal to or even superior to the czar. Calling upon several precedents of patriarchal power earlier in the century, he criticized limitations placed on his position and on Church power. His statement could not have been clearer to the czar: "The priesthood is higher than the Tsardom. Unction comes from God, but it comes to the Tsar through the clergy."

This confrontation between the Russian Orthodox Church and the Russian state in the seventeenth century lasted several decades, but the outcome was not seriously in doubt. Relations between Nikon and Alexis cooled, but they sometimes intensified over minor perceived slights and then finally broke when the czar visited and then confronted Nikon in 1658. Alexis criticized Nikon's use of pressure and intimidation to make changes, saying of Nikon that, "he drove men to fast by force, but could not drive anyone by force to believe in God."

In response to what he perceived as personal affronts to him and his lofty position, Nikon left Moscow in July, 1658, and traveled to the distant Voskresensky monastery. Apparently, he hoped the confrontation with the czar would create a crisis that would give him more authority if he was asked to return. The monarch and church officials had had enough, however, and Nikon's efforts during the next several years failed.

There had been no active patriarch between 1658 and 1667, the year a new patriarch was elected to succeed Nikon. Nikon lived in several remote monasteries between 1658 and his death in 1681. A church council in late 1666 condemned and formally stripped him of his title. That same council also declared that Avvakum and the Old Believers were heretics, which further institutionalized the disruptive split in the Orthodox Church in succeeding centuries, a split known as the *raskol* (schism).

Significance

Nikon's confrontation with the czar proved to be his ultimate defeat, but it should not have been surprising. Several European nations in the seventeenth century had been gradually expanding political autocracy, in which primary power resided in the hands of the monarch and secular authorities. Czar Alexis had no intention of being subordinate to Nikon or to Church authority. Alexis's grandson, Peter the Great, continued this trend in asserting total domination over Russia's religious institutions and officials.

No patriarch was appointed after 1708, and Peter abolished the autonomous office of the patriarch in 1721. From that time, the Russian Orthodox Church lost its independence and became a department of the Russian government.

Paradoxically, many of Nikon's religious reforms continued for decades in Russia, showing that most of his reform efforts were successful. His dominating personality and aggressive leadership, though, convinced others that he had to be removed from power.

—*Taylor Stults*

FURTHER READING

Conybeare, F. C. *Russian Dissenters*. New York: Russell and Russell, 1962. Conybeare describes the controversies in the Russian Orthodox Church and provides an entire section on Nikon and Avvakum.

Crummey, Robert O. *The Old Believers and the World of Antichrist: The Vyg Community and the Russian State, 1694-1855*. Madison: University of Wisconsin Press, 1970. One of the most influential and widely cited books in English on the Old Believers.

Kliuchevsky, V. O. *A Course in Russian History: The Seventeenth Century*. Translated by Natalie Duddington. Armonk, N.Y.: M. E. Sharpe, 1994. A classic work by one of Russia's most eminent historians. Chapter 15 deals with Nikon and the schism.

Longworth, Philip. *Alexis: Tsar of All the Russias*. New York: Franklin Watts, 1984. A biography of the Russian monarch who first supported then opposed the reform efforts of Patriarch Nikon.

Lupinin, Nickolas. *Religious Revolt in the Seventeenth Century: The Schism of the Russian Church*. Princeton, N.J.: Kingston Press, 1984. This work covers the religious controversies and their effects in strengthening state power.

Meyendorff, Paul. *Russia, Ritual, and Reform: The Liturgical Reforms of Nikon in the Seventeenth Century*. Crestwood, N.Y.: St. Vladimir's Seminary Press, 1991. A detailed description of religious reforms and their effects.

Michels, Georg Bernhard. *At War with the Church: Religious Dissent in Seventeenth Century Russia*. Stanford, Calif.: Stanford University Press, 1999. Michels assesses the disruptive effects of the religious controversy and focuses on Nikon's opponents.

Millar, James R. *Encyclopedia of Russian History*. New York: Macmillan, 2003. A comprehensive four-volume source that includes entries on Avvakum, Alexis, and Nikon.

SEE ALSO: Apr., 1667-June, 1671: Razin Leads Peasant Uprising in Russia; 1672-c. 1691: Self-Immolation of the Old Believers.

RELATED ARTICLES in *Great Lives from History: The Seventeenth Century, 1601-1700:* Alexis; Avvakum Petrovich; Nikon; Stenka Razin; Sophia.

1652-1689
FOX ORGANIZES THE QUAKERS

George Fox organized the Quakers, one of a number of Christian sects that arose around the time of the English Civil Wars. The sects spread quickly throughout England, despite officially sanctioned persecution of their adherents for their religious beliefs and social practices.

LOCALE: England
CATEGORIES: Religion and theology; social issues and reform

KEY FIGURES

George Fox (1624-1691), first Quaker leader and organizer
Elizabeth Hooton (1600-1672), Quaker missionary and preacher
William Penn (1644-1718), English-born Quaker convert and founder of Pennsylvania
Margaret Fell (1614-1702), Quaker minister and wife of George Fox
Robert Barclay (1648-1690), Quaker theologian
Oliver Cromwell (1599-1658), Puritan general and lord protector of England, 1653-1658
Charles II (1630-1685), king of England, r. 1660-1685

SUMMARY OF EVENT

The Religious Society of Friends, more commonly known as the Quakers because of the tendency of its early members to literally shake with the power of God while worshiping, had its origins in the rugged and sparsely populated counties of northwestern England in the 1640's. Early Quakers, like many Protestants, rejected ritualized forms of worship; unlike Protestants, however, their worship services were not led by ordained ministers and did not involve any recitation of a religious creed. The aim of a Quaker meeting for worship was the direct experience of God. To this end, a Quaker would sit quietly with others in a group, listening for the voice of what they called the Inner Light, the power of God as revealed to a person from within.

Believing strongly in "that of God in every person," many early Quakers were convinced that direct experience of God was possible and enthusiastically witnessed to others in public settings, even interrupting church services on occasion to do so. The name they gave to such ministry was "publishing the Truth." The most famous of the "publishers of the Truth" was George Fox. Born the son of a weaver in the village of Drayton-in-the-Clay, in the English Midlands, Fox began a spiritual search in his late teens that would keep him restless until he began to meet with other Friends to worship. In these meetings, he became convinced, as he reported in his journal, that the "Truth sprang up first to us." As he traveled throughout northern England to preach, Fox became a powerful voice for the early Quakers because of his courage in expressing his religious beliefs and the ardor of his commitment to these beliefs.

A critical point in the development of Quakerism came in 1652, when, having climbed Pendle Hill, a part of the Pennine Range, Fox had a clear experience of being called to gather all people under the name of God. Passionately throwing himself into his ministry, Fox began to attract large crowds, sometimes numbering more than a thousand people, to his preaching. As a result, Quakerism spread rapidly in northern England, as many members of radical Puritan sects, such as the Seekers and the Levellers, became converts.

During the next two decades, the momentum of the movement extended even farther geographically, as Fox and many other Quaker missionaries carried their spiritual message into the southern and more urban parts of England, as well as into Ireland and Scotland. It was during this phase of Quaker growth that such individuals as Robert Barclay and William Penn, both of whom later became prominent Quakers, were converted. Contrary to Puritan practices, women were also included among these missionaries, since Quakers believed that, by virtue of their mutual possession of the Inner Light, both men and women were equally suited to preach the word of God. Three years before marrying George Fox in 1669, Margaret Fell published a defense of women's right to preach under the title of *Women's Speaking Justified* (1666). Along with Elizabeth Hooton, credited with being the first person to preach Quakerism, and Mary Fisher, one of the first Quaker missionaries to America, Fell was one of the many women who helped to spread this new religious movement during the seventeenth century.

The growth of Quakerism came at the expense of tremendous personal hardship to many of its followers, who suffered greatly at the hands of the government for making a public challenge to the established Church of England. During the period of time, following the English Civil Wars, in which Oliver Cromwell established himself as lord protector of England, Quakers and other members of Nonconformist sects experienced some measure of religious tolerance. With the Restoration of Charles II in 1660, however, Parliament acted in 1664 and 1670 to declare all worship services other than those of the Church of England to be "conventicles," or unauthorized services.

While some sects chose to avoid the penalties of the Conventicle Acts by holding their worship services in secret, Quakers worshiped openly. The passage of the Quaker Act in 1662 gave Quakerism the dubious honor of being the only Nonconformist sect to be specifically forbidden by name. As a result of the Quaker Act and the Conventicle Acts, thousands of Friends, including Fox, Fell, and other Quaker leaders, were imprisoned for activities such as participating in worship services, refusing to contribute tithes to the Church of England, or—because Quakers would not swear to tell the truth on the grounds that swearing was expressly forbidden in the Gospel—objecting to the taking of the Oath of Allegiance. Fox himself was imprisoned twice before his Pendle Hill experience and six times after it; his refusal in 1650 to accept a release from prison on the condition that he join the military laid the grounds for the Quaker belief in pacifism, as proclaimed by Fox and Richard Hubberthorne in a declaration to the king in 1661.

George Fox. (Library of Congress)

In some places, such as in Buckinghamshire in 1661, it is estimated that nearly all male Quakers were incarcerated in the course of the year, and at least four thousand Quakers were imprisoned at times during the beginnings of Quakerism. That the sect was able to survive such persecution was largely the result of Fox's efforts to create an administrative structure for Quakerism that united separate Quaker meetings across England into a larger organizational whole. It was Fox's idea to have Monthly Meetings, in which all the meetings of a particular geographical region could participate in order to address specific concerns that Quakers faced. Following his release from prison in 1666, Fox spent the next four years organizing English Quakers into such Monthly Meetings.

Significance

The creation of these meetings, along with Quarterly and Yearly Meetings for business, provided Quakers with the opportunity to take collective action on immediate problems and issues and so to mitigate as best they could the impacts of the sufferings imposed upon them. Through decisions at these business meetings, made by a process of consensus rather than voting, Quaker missionaries and adherents facing hardship as a result of the imprisonment of family members received financial support, and those in prison received visits and special care. Initially, only men participated in the meetings for business, but with the encouragement of Fell and Fox, women's meetings for business also became established among the early Quakers. These meetings provided women with the opportunity to participate in religious affairs—an opportunity not generally afforded them in the seventeenth century.

This decentralized system of organization, pioneered by Fox, in which no one held a position of authority over anyone else in the governance structure, provided Quakerism with a way of maintaining its integrity and momentum despite the lack of religious freedom that dominated England during its formative years and that came to an end only with the passage of the Toleration Act in 1689.

—*Diane P. Michelfelder*

FURTHER READING

Bailey, Richard. *New Light on George Fox and Early Quakerism: The Making and Unmaking of a God.* San Francisco, Calif.: Edwin Mellen Press, 1992. Bailey interprets Fox's meaning of Inner Light, arguing the Inner Light was the celestial Christ who inhabited and made the believer divine.

Barbour, Hugh. *The Quakers in Puritan England.* New Haven, Conn.: Yale University Press, 1964. An insightful treatment of the first few decades of Quaker history and the relationship between Quaker and Puritan beliefs.

Braithwaite, William C. *The Beginnings of Quakerism.* 2d ed. Cambridge, England: Cambridge University Press, 1961. Braithwaite's work is the classic history of this period of Quakerism.

Brinton, Howard. *Quakers for Three Hundred Years.* Wallingford, Pa.: Pendle Hill, 1972. Written by a renowned Quaker scholar, this book is an excellent introduction to the history of the Religious Society of Friends, as well as Quaker religious beliefs and social practices.

Ingle, H. Larry. *First Among Friends: George Fox and the Creation of Quakerism.* New York: Oxford University Press, 1994. A scholarly biography, placing Fox's life within the upheavals of the English Civil Wars, the Revolution, and Reformation.

Mack, Phyllis. "Gender and Spirituality in Early English Quakerism, 1650-1665." In *Witnesses for Change: Quaker Women over Three Centuries*, edited by Elisabeth Potts Brown and Susan Mosher Stuard. New Brunswick, N.J.: Rutgers University Press, 1989. Mack reflects on the women who helped spread the Quaker movement through their missionary work despite religious persecution and discusses the Quakers' own attitudes toward women.

Vann, Richard. *The Social Development of English Quakerism, 1655-1755.* Cambridge, Mass.: Harvard University Press, 1969. Vann's account of the first century of Quakerism focuses on the social context of this movement. Also examines how the denial of religious freedom during the reign of Charles II affected the organizational structure of the Society of Friends.

West, Jessamyn, ed. *The Quaker Reader.* New York: Viking Press, 1962. Reprint. Wallingford, Pa.: Pendle Hill, 1992. Useful anthology of writings both by and concerning Quakers, including selections from a number of classics of Quaker writings.

SEE ALSO: Mar., 1629-1640: "Personal Rule" of Charles I; Oct., 1637-Apr. 15, 1638: Shimabara Revolt; Oct. 23, 1641-1642: Ulster Insurrection; 1642-1651: English Civil Wars; Aug. 17-Sept. 25, 1643: Solemn League and Covenant; Spring, 1645-1660: Puritan New Model Army; 1646-1649: Levellers Launch an Egalitarian Movement; Dec. 6, 1648-May 19, 1649: Establishment of the English Commonwealth; Dec. 16, 1653-Sept. 3, 1658: Cromwell Rules England as Lord Protector; May, 1659-May, 1660: Restoration of Charles II; Mar. 4, 1681: "Holy Experiment" Establishes Pennsylvania; Apr. 4, 1687, and Apr. 27, 1688: Declaration of Liberty of Conscience; May 24, 1689: Toleration Act.

RELATED ARTICLES in *Great Lives from History: The Seventeenth Century, 1601-1700:* Charles I; Charles II (of England); Oliver Cromwell; George Fox; William Penn.

April, 1652
Dutch Begin to Colonize Southern Africa

Dutch colonization of southern Africa began with the establishment of a provisioning station for ships of the Dutch East India Company, thus beginning European settlement in the region. The colony would ultimately displace and dominate the indigenous people of the region.

Locale: Cape of Good Hope, southern Africa
Categories: Economics; expansion and land acquisition; colonization

Key Figures

Autshumao (d. 1663), member of Khoikhoi, or Hottentot, group who acted as interpreter for the Dutch

Doman (d. 1663), Khoikhoi revolt leader against Dutch in 1659

Krotoa (d. 1674), a young Khoikhoi woman who influenced trading patterns between Dutch and indigenous peoples of southern Africa

Simon Adriaan van der Stel (1639-1712), governor of Cape Colony, 1679-1699

Willem Adriaan van der Stel (1664-1733), governor of Cape Colony, 1699-1707

Jan van Riebeeck (1619-1677), first commander of Dutch South African colony, 1652-1662

Summary of Event

European explorers first rounded the Cape of Good Hope in 1487 when Portuguese explorer Bartolomeu Dias sailed into the Indian Ocean. Portuguese explorer Vasco da Gama successfully completed his voyage to India in 1498 and established a direct trade route between Europe and India by sea. This brought an increasing number of ships from many nations to the southern tip of Africa.

During the 1500's, English, Dutch, and French ships stopped at the Cape of Good Hope for food and water on their way to India and on the return voyage. Terrible mortality rates of sailors on long voyages had led Europeans to discover that fresh fruit and meat would improve their health. This made the cape a critical location where they traded with the local Khoikhoi bands who raised cattle and farmed the region.

In 1649, some Dutch sailors who were stranded after losing their ship spent a month at Table Bay near the Cape of Good Hope. Upon their return to Holland, they recommended that the Dutch East India Company annex the peninsula. In 1652, the company sent Jan van Riebeeck and eighty employees to take possession of the territory, which they did in early April. Their purpose was to build a fort and to obtain fruit, meat, and vegetables for Dutch ships. The colony was to be directed by a commander, later governor, and a council of policy, made up of high-ranking company officials. They were subject to the control of the governor-general of the Dutch East India Company in Batavia (now Jakarta, Indonesia). The governor of the Cape Colony could appoint local members to governing bodies, and even church offices were appointed by the governor. This direct control by company officials reflected their desire to support trade to the Indies rather than the establishment of a large Dutch community.

The company directors gave strict orders to maintain peace with the African peoples and other Europeans at the cape. The Dutch commander was to focus on trade. Good relations between the Khoikhoi and the Dutch were maintained through barter, as the Africans were willing to trade cattle and food for iron implements and European manufactures they lacked. Tensions among the various Khoikhoi communities were exploited by the Europeans. One member of an outcast group of Khoikhoi was Autshumao, named Harry by the English who took him to Java in 1631. There, he learned English, and when returned to his people at the cape, he became an important link in the trading network between his band and the English, then the Dutch. Harry's niece, Krotoa, was taken into the home of Commander van Riebeeck. Krotoa was renamed Eva and was raised as a member of van Riebeeck's family. She adopted Christianity and became fluent in Dutch, acting as interpreter as well as an unofficial agent for her people's commerce with the Dutch.

Although van Riebeeck bartered for cattle and grew some vegetables to provision Dutch ships in 1653, the colony was unable to support itself entirely. Staples, such as rice and wheat, had to be imported. The increasing costs associated with the colony led company directors to permit nine employees to be released from their contracts in 1657. Each was given approximately 28.5 acres of land to farm. The company expected to save by reducing salaries and to benefit from the crops they would grow, which would be sold to the company at a fixed cost. These settlers were exempt from taxes for twelve years and permitted to trade directly with the Khoikhoi for cattle as long as they did not compete with the company.

The spectacular Cape of Good Hope, near the location of the first Dutch trade station and the first colony, at Cape Town, in southern Africa. (Corbis)

These first "free burghers," or Boers, whose number had grown to forty by 1662, changed the nature of European settlement in two ways. First, they took land from indigenous peoples and made it unavailable for livestock, on which the local inhabitants depended for their livelihood. Formerly willing to engage in trade with the Europeans, Khoikhoi became alarmed at this encroachment. Doman, a member of the Goringhaiqua Khoikhoi, had been taken to the Dutch East Indies in 1657, where he learned Dutch. He also saw how the Dutch treated the local peoples they dominated. After returning to the Cape Colony, ostensibly as interpreter for the Dutch he rallied the Khoikhoi to attack the farms and crops of Dutch settlers in 1659. Negotiations averted further hostilities but did not permanently resolve the issue of European expansion at the expense of the Khoikhoi. From that moment on, Dutch settlers would continue to expand their control over the land, first around Cape Town, and then throughout all of southern Africa.

The second way in which these Dutch settlers changed the history of South Africa was their need for labor. The first commander of the colony, van Riebeeck, had asked for slave labor as early as 1653. His request was refused. Nevertheless, the growth of the colony and the injunction against enslaving the indigenous peoples made the need for labor increasingly important. The first slaves arrived in 1658 aboard a Dutch ship that had captured a Portuguese slave ship and its cargo. Other slaves were imported from West Africa and Madagascar. Later, slaves came from the East Indies and Southeast Asia, all indiscriminately called Malays. The eventual mixing of Europeans and indigenous populations produced a new group in South Africa that was neither wholly African nor European, and yet would become an important part of South African society.

SIGNIFICANCE

The Dutch colony expanded slowly at first, but the arrival of French Huguenot refugees, Calvinist Protestants who had been expelled from France with the revocation of the Edict of Nantes in 1685, added more than 150 new colonists to the population. By the early 1700's there were nearly three thousand men, women, and children, including slaves and company employees. With the leadership of Governor Simon Adriaan van der Stel and his son Willem Adriaan van der Stel, his successor as governor, farms began to spread outward from the cape. The new settlers extended Dutch settlement and also helped create the image of the Trekboers as pioneers conquering an empty wilderness. For the Khoikhoi, though, European expansion led to the destruction of their way of life. They fought back valiantly but were defeated. The great 1713 smallpox epidemic further decimated the Khoikhoi of the cape area. The various indigenous groups finally lost their clan structure and were thereafter indiscriminately referred to as Hottentots by Europeans.

The destruction of African tribal society was paralleled by the creation of a new society created by European immigrants to Dutch South Africa. French Huguenot refugees were purposefully separated and interspersed among the earlier Dutch settlers to integrate them. The establishment of schools by the company at Stellenbosch in 1686 and Drakenstein in 1691, while educating only a small number of the boys and girls in the colony, did help instill a common background and language among the immigrants. The doctrines of the Calvinist church, shared by most European immigrants, also helped to create a Boer culture that was unique to South Africa. This Afrikaner society, as it came to be called, along with its Dutch-derived local language, Afrikaans, remains an influential part of South African history.

—James A. Baer

FURTHER READING

Boxer, C. R. *The Dutch Seaborne Empire, 1600-1800.* New York: Alfred A. Knopf, 1965. Boxer provides an overview of Dutch expansion worldwide during the seventeenth century. Chapter 9 discusses the Cape Colony.

Elphick, Richard, and Hermann Giliomee, eds. *The Shaping of South African Society, 1652-1840.* Middletown, Conn.: Wesleyan University Press, 1988. A collection of essays that sometimes overlap but provide a complete history of the people of South Africa, including indigenous groups, imported slaves, and Europeans. Also discusses the interaction of these groups.

Giliomee, Hermann. *The Afrikaners: Biography of a People.* London: C. Hurst, 2003. A comprehensive overview of the Afrikaners, from their initial settlement of the country to their role in twenty-first century South Africa.

Readers Digest. *Illustrated History of South Africa: The Real Story.* 3d ed. Cape Town: Readers Digest Association, South Africa, 1993. A massive, colorful, and detailed history of the country from prehistoric to present times. Contributors include many specialists on the region's history. Contains an extensive chronology for the years 1600 through 1800 on pages 40 and 41.

Ross, Robert. *A Concise History of South Africa.* New York: Cambridge University Press, 1999. Ross's discussion includes the Dutch settlement and the later colonial conquest of the country.

Thompson, Leonard. *A History of South Africa.* 1995. Rev. ed. New Haven, Conn.: Yale University Press, 2001. Chapter 2 of this comprehensive history provides an overview of the Dutch colony. Also features information on the Africans who lived in South Africa before European colonization.

Welsh, Frank. *South Africa: A Narrative History.* New York: Kodansha International, 1999. A comprehensive popular history of South Africa, from the Dutch settlement to the end of the twentieth century.

SEE ALSO: 17th cent.: Age of Mercantilism in Southeast Asia; 17th cent.: The Pepper Trade; Mar. 20, 1602: Dutch East India Company Is Founded; 1606-1674: Europeans Settle in India; Apr. 29, 1606: First European Contact with Australia; 1609: Bank of Amsterdam Invents Checks; 1617-1693: European Powers Vie for Control of Gorée; c. 1625: Formation of the Kuba Kingdom; July, 1625-Aug., 1664: Founding of New Amsterdam; Oct., 1625-1637: Dutch and Portuguese Struggle for the Guinea Coast; Jan. 14, 1641: Capture of Malacca; Aug. 26, 1641-Sept., 1648: Conquest of Luanda; 1642 and 1644: Tasman Proves Australia Is a Separate Continent; Mid-17th cent.: Emergence of the Guinea Coast States; Late 17th cent.: Rise of Buganda; 1685: Louis XIV Revokes the Edict of Nantes.

RELATED ARTICLES in *Great Lives from History: The Seventeenth Century, 1601-1700:* Piet Hein; Njinga; Abel Janszoon Tasman.

December 16, 1653-September 3, 1658
CROMWELL RULES ENGLAND AS LORD PROTECTOR

Oliver Cromwell's ascendancy to political power as lord protector paralleled the English experiment with a republican form of government. Cromwell evolved into an autocrat and the monarchy was restored two years after his death, in 1660.

LOCALE: England
CATEGORY: Government and politics

KEY FIGURES

Oliver Cromwell (1599-1658), Parliamentary military leader and lord protector of England, 1653-1658
Richard Cromwell (1626-1712), lord protector of England, 1658-1659
Charles I (1600-1649), king of England, r. 1625-1649

SUMMARY OF EVENT

Until the English political and religious crisis of the early 1640's that culminated in the outbreak of the English Civil Wars in 1642, Oliver Cromwell was a minor figure who had served as a member of Parliament in 1628-1629 and was elected to the Long Parliament in November, 1640. Cromwell came from a family of modest means in Huntington, where he had spent most of his life. He graduated from Sussex College, Cambridge. Initially, Cromwell merely wanted tolerance for Puritan dissenters and for the monarch to recognize the need to govern alongside Parliament, specifically the House of Commons.

After hostilities broke out in May, 1642, between the Royalists and the Parliamentarians, Cromwell demonstrated that he possessed both a strategic and a tactical understanding of military affairs. At the outbreak of the war, Cromwell raised a cavalry force from among his neighbors in Huntington; that force joined the major Parliamentary army at the Battle of Edgehill on October 22, 1642. Through his subsequent successful encounters with the king's forces at Grantham and Winceby, Cromwell's reputation as a warrior expanded. During 1643, Cromwell built a new army, the Ironsides, which played a critical role in the Battle of Marston Moor in 1644. In that battle and later at the Battle of Newbury, Cromwell, serving under the earl of Manchester, led his troops to victory. Cromwell then professionalized these forces during 1644-1645 when, with the third baron Fairfax, he formed the New Model Army.

Cromwell's victory over Charles I at the Battle of Naseby on June 14, 1645, solidified his identity as a major power broker. His success during the later years of the Civil Wars (1645-1651) was based on his control over the New Model Army. Cromwell supported the Pride's Purge of the Long Parliament on December 6, 1648, which resulted in the removal of 140 members and the formation of the reduced Rump Parliament. In January, 1649, Cromwell led the faction within the Rump Parliament that demanded the trial and execution of Charles I. He argued that Charles could not be trusted to cooperate with Parliament and suggested that England should move beyond monarchy to a new form of government that would be centered in the Parliament.

After Charles I's execution on January 30, 1649, the Rump Parliament ruled the nation. It was believed that the king's death was also the death of the monarchy and that a new form of government—the Commonwealth—would constitute the next major phase in the political development of England. At first, Cromwell occupied himself with military matters. He suppressed (1649-1650) an Irish rebellion and then defeated a Scottish Royalist army at the Battle of Worcester in 1651, events sometimes referred to collectively as the Third Civil War.

From the fall of 1651 until the spring of 1653, Cromwell attempted to gain the Rump Parliament's approval for a series of reforms. He proposed measures directed at needed legal, social, and parliamentary reforms. Through political maneuvers and endless debates, however, the leaders of the Rump Parliament managed to stifle all of Cromwell's reform initiatives. Frustrated with the absence of action, Cromwell used his army to expel that Rump Parliament on April 20, 1653. The Rump Parliament was replaced with the Barebones Parliament; Cromwell hoped that it would develop into a "godly parliament" and result in godly government. This experiment failed in a few months, however, and was replaced by the Protectorate, which was established by the first and only written constitution in the history of England, the Instrument of Government (December 16, 1653).

Based on the work of John Lambert, the Instrument of Government established a partnership between the executive lord protector and the legislative Parliament. The powers of the lord protector were restricted: His role as commander of the armed forces was at the discretion of Parliament, and the lord protector had to convene Parliament regularly. He could not alter or repeal laws unless they were in opposition to the Instrument of Government. The document also specified that the lord protector had to have a council of state, and it established the criteria for voting for the new Parliament.

Cromwell became lord protector on the same day that the Instrument of Government was adopted and held that office until his death on September 3, 1658. The Instrument of Government did not survive as long as Cromwell; it was replaced with the Humble Petition and Advice in 1657. Throughout his tenure as lord protector, Cromwell was confronted with threats both from abroad and at home. Catholic powers entered into plots to remove Cromwell and bring about a restoration of a regime that had been more sympathetic to Catholicism and the interests of Catholic powers. Within England, Royalists and conservative Anglicans desired his downfall as well.

Cromwell was a religious Independent and believed in religious tolerance; during his Protectorate, adherents of several faiths, including Catholics, could practice their religions openly. Cromwell's principal problem was working with the Parliament; despite his conciliatory efforts, Parliament proved to be as much an obstacle to him as it had been to Charles. In 1655, Cromwell declared a state of martial law; the country was divided into military districts and generals were assigned to manage the affairs of each district. The local general not only maintained law and order but also served to enforce Cromwell's "reformation of manners"; Cromwell sought to set a moral standard that should be emulated, and he was also eager to eliminate social opportunities for his critics to meet to plot against him.

Oliver Cromwell is sworn in as lord protector of England. (Francis R. Niglutsch)

The lord protector's social program resulted in the end of dueling, the closing of theaters, the suppression of gambling, limiting the number of alehouses, and the enforced maintenance of the Sabbath. Frequently, Cromwell's generals pursued these policies with vigor, resulting in mounting popular dislike of the regime and the military. Cromwell pursued an active foreign policy in which Spain was the principal enemy; his Spanish War (1655-1659) proved to be much more difficult and expensive to prosecute than anticipated, however. It also contributed to the growing public criticism of his government.

To his credit, Cromwell developed the British navy and initiated policies that enhanced Britain's competitive role throughout the world. In June, 1657, the Humble Petition and Advice replaced the Instrument of Government; Cromwell remained as lord protector and had powers that resembled those of a traditional monarch.

Cromwell died on September 3, 1658, and was succeeded as lord protector by his son, Richard Cromwell. Unlike his father in most ways, Richard did not possess the leadership or governing skills to succeed in such a tenuous position; he served from September, 1658, to April, 1659, when he recognized the return the of Rump Parilament. Within eleven months (May, 1660), the Stuart monarchy would be restored with the accession of King Charles II.

SIGNIFICANCE

Cromwell's tenure as lord protector reflected the inherently conservative nature of British politics in the seventeenth century. The English Civil Wars were fought to address grievances that were based upon violations of traditional English liberties in politics and religion, not to establish new ones. Cromwell's Protectorate failed to endure because it was too novel: It did not have the support of the Parliament or the people. In a little more than one and one-half years after Cromwell's death, the son of the beheaded Charles I, Charles II, restored the monarchy peacefully. Cromwell's achievements in foreign affairs and the building of the British navy were more durable, however, and they paved the way for the growth of the British Empire.

—*William T. Walker*

FURTHER READING

Coward, Barry. *The Cromwellian Protectorate*. Manchester, England: Manchester University Press, 2002. An important synthesis of Cromwell and the Protectorate, with emphasis on comparing the aspirations of Cromwell and his associates with what they accomplished; also examines the international impact of the regime in the mid-seventeenth century.

Davis, J. C. *Oliver Cromwell*. New York: Oxford University Press, 2001. Davis examines the paradox of Cromwell—the transformation from the conservative who sought to sustain traditional rights to the religious/political radical of the 1650's; he concludes that the Cromwell was a great historical figure who understood the changing forces of English history.

Gaunt, Peter. *Oliver Cromwell*. Oxford, England: Blackwell, 1996. An excellent introduction to the life and importance of Oliver Cromwell; a valuable annotated bibliography is provided.

Kitson, Frank. *Old Ironsides: The Military Biography of Oliver Cromwell*. London: Weidenfeld and Nicolson, 2004. Biography of Cromwell focuses on his military achievements; generally sympathetic to Cromwell on military matters; readable and useful documentation.

Lynch, Michael. *The Interregnum, 1649-1660*. London: Hodder and Stoughton, 1994. An excellent, student-centered study of this period that includes study/discussion questions and references to current sources. Cromwell emerges as a well-intentioned leader who did not understand the extent and depth of religious and political dissension in England.

Sherwood, Roy Edward. *Oliver Cromwell: King in All but Name, 1653-1658*. New York: St. Martin's Press, 1997. Sherwood argues that not only was Cromwell a "King in All but Name" but that the Cromwellian regime exhibited aspects and practices that were representative of a monarchial government. Illustrated with valuable drawings, useful bibliography.

Smith, David L. *Oliver Cromwell: Politics and Religion in the English Revolution, 1640-1658*. New York: Cambridge University Press, 1991. A very useful book for students who have had an introduction to Cromwell, the English Civil Wars and the Protectorate; provides assessments by historians of different aspects of Cromwell's life and work.

Venning, Timothy. *Cromwellian Foreign Policy*. New York: St. Martin's Press, 1995. Venning argues that Cromwell's active foreign policy, while being pursued with very limited success, was successful because of Cromwell's power, which was based upon his view of his position; Cromwell's foreign policy accomplishments stand up favorably when compared to those of Charles II during the 1660's.

Wheeler, James Scott. *Cromwell in Ireland*. Dublin: Gill and Macmillan, 1999. A scholarly account of the background and development of Cromwell's Irish campaign during 1649 and 1650 and the subsequent impact of its impact on Ireland and Cromwell's leadership during the Protectorate.

SEE ALSO: Mar., 1629-1640: "Personal Rule" of Charles I; Nov. 3, 1640-May 15, 1641: Beginning of England's Long Parliament; 1642-1651: English Civil Wars; Aug. 17-Sept. 25, 1643: Solemn League and Covenant; July 2, 1644: Battle of Marston Moor; Dec. 6, 1648-May 19, 1649: Establishment of the English Commonwealth; May, 1659-May, 1660: Restoration of Charles II.

RELATED ARTICLES in *Great Lives from History: The Seventeenth Century, 1601-1700:* Charles I; Charles II (of England); Oliver Cromwell; Third Baron Fairfax.

1654

PASCAL AND FERMAT DEVISE THE THEORY OF PROBABILITY

Probability theory has become one of the most widely applied branches of mathematics. Two mathematicians, Blaise Pascal and Pierre de Fermat, responded to an inquiry about how to split the stakes from a game, laying the foundations for the subject. Shortly thereafter, the first textbook on the subject was written by Dutch mathematician Christiaan Huygens, who had been thinking about the same issues.

LOCALE: France and the Netherlands
CATEGORY: Mathematics

KEY FIGURES

Blaise Pascal (1623-1662), mathematician, theologian, and philosopher
Pierre de Fermat (1601-1665), mathematician and jurist
Christiaan Huygens (1629-1695), mathematician and physicist

SUMMARY OF EVENT

Probability is the branch of mathematics that assesses how likely certain outcomes are when an experiment is performed. It entered the mathematical literature in the form of questions about games of dice, especially in the work of Gerolamo Cardano (1501-1576). These questions did not seem to have attracted much attention elsewhere, and Cardano's own work suffered from errors. It was not clear at the time how best to define even the basic notions on the basis of which to perform calculations involving events of chance.

Antoine Gombaud, the chevalier de Méré (1607-1684), was a French nobleman with some claim to having done some mathematical work, although his published remains do not provide any basis for judging the quality of his work. He was also a gambler and had investigated two problems. One was that of how to divide up the stakes in a game of dice when the game had to be broken off before it was finished. The other involved the likelihood of throwing a certain number of sixes in a certain number of throws of dice. De Méré knew how many tosses it would take for there to be more than a 50 percent chance of at least one six showing up. He assumed that if he multiplied that by six, he would have the number of tosses it would take for the likelihood of at least two sixes showing up to be more than 50 percent.

Experience showed that this was incorrect (and it had been the view of Cardano, although de Méré was unfamiliar with his work).

Recognizing that he was out of his depth, de Méré turned to the eminent French mathematician Blaise Pascal. Pascal recognized the interest of the problems that had been proposed and initiated a correspondence in 1654 with perhaps the most accomplished mathematician of the period, Pierre de Fermat. It is arguable that this led two of the world's greatest mathematicians to spend their time looking at a problem raised in the context of gambling. Both Pascal and Fermat were able to recognize the mathematical issues underlying the problem, and between them they created the theory of probability.

The nature of their arguments involved a precise analysis of the collection of possible outcomes at each stage of the games being played. Starting with a small number of principles, they could tackle both of the problems raised by de Méré by the use of a process now known as recursion. This involves recognizing at certain stages of the game that the situation is exactly the same as it was at

Blaise Pascal. (Library of Congress)

a previous turn and deriving from that recognition an algebraic equation that could be solved easily. Both Pascal and Fermat felt satisfied with the solutions that they obtained, although the absence of various pieces of the correspondence does not provide a basis for always being able to judge the generality of their arguments.

One of the key ingredients to Pascal's solution was the triangle that bears his name. The triangle starts with a 1 at its apex, has two 1's in the next row, and continues with 1's at the ends of each row and interior elements obtained by adding up the two numbers immediately adjacent to it in the previous row. This particular triangle had been known for many years and went back at least to medieval Arabic mathematicians. What Pascal recognized was the way in which the numbers in a given row corresponded to the coefficients in expansions of a binomial expression, such as raising $a + b$ to the *nth* power. The amount of mathematical ingenuity that Pascal lavished on the triangle was impressive, but more surprising was the extent to which it enabled him thereby to answer questions about probability as well.

Fermat's method of proceeding is less well documented, as is frequently the case with Fermat's work. His inclination was seldom to produce more than the details asked for in a problem rather than the method of proof. His willingness to calculate at length to enumerate all the possible outcomes of an experiment was the basis for his results, which agreed with those of Pascal.

Pascal had a religious conversion shortly after his correspondence with Fermat and gave up mathematics, to a large extent. He made one further contribution to probability, however, which suggested the wider applications of their work. He framed an argument for belief in God that he suggested would be useful in arguing with those who needed to see everything put in terms of games and gambling. The argument used the idea of expectation and has remained an important contribution to philosophy.

The idea of "expectation" is connected with that of "average," and the rise of probability in the seventeenth century was perhaps connected with the availability of large quantities of data coming from national governments and other large bodies, such as municipalities. This notion provided the basis for the treatise on probability put together by the Dutch mathematician Christiaan Huygens (*Libellus de ratiociniis in ludo aleae*, 1657; *The Value of All Chances in Games of Fortune*, 1714). It is not clear how familiar he was with Fermat's and Pascal's work, but he did write the first systematic treatise on the rudiments of probability. From a simple axiom he derived three theorems, and on the strength of those he explained the solutions to a sequence of problems, relying on the same sort of technique that had been used by Pascal. Where Pascal had used the combinatorial ideas embodied in his triangle, however, Huygens just lumbered through long computations. In a way, Huygens's work was a step back, but his casting the ideas of probability in a systematic form helped the subject to get something of a foothold among mathematicians.

Pierre de Fermat. (Library of Congress)

SIGNIFICANCE

Until the time of Pascal and Fermat, there had been a tendency to appeal to arguments from inspiration and authority in many spheres. By the middle of the seventeenth century, the continued hostilities between Catholic and Protestant forces had cooled down to confrontations rather than conflict. In such a setting there was a call for the kind of argument that depended on something that could be accepted by both sides. Mathematics provided such a setting, and so there was a call for the ideas of probability in both Protestant and Catholic Europe.

Although the correspondence of Pascal and Fermat was not immediately available to subsequent mathematicians, the treatise by Huygens provided some impetus for further research. By the end of the century, there was an explosion of interest in probability, and a number of treatments of the basis of the subject took the place of Huygens's original work. Even in the middle of the eighteenth century, however, the leading authority on probability could look back on the subject as having been the creation of Pascal and Fermat. They had not been the first mathematicians to consider questions arising from games of chance, but they were the first to apply enough mathematical systematization to the subject to make sure that they did not fall into the traps that had bedeviled their predecessors and continue to afflict those who assess questions of probability without mathematics.

—*Thomas Drucker*

FURTHER READING

Bernstein, Peter L. *Against the Gods: The Remarkable Story of Risk*. New York: John Wiley and Sons, 1996. A popular examination of the applications of probability to practical issues. Devotes an entire chapter to Pascal and Fermat.

David, Florence N. *Games, Gods, and Gambling: The Origins and History of Probability and Statistical Ideas from the Earliest Times to the Newtonian Era*. New York: Hafner, 1962. This study looks back to various roots for ideas of probability in Western thought and culminates with the generation after Huygens.

Gigerenzer, Gerd, et al. *The Empire of Chance: How Probability Changed Science and Everyday Life*. New York: Cambridge University Press, 1989. This volume primarily looks at how the ideas of Pascal and Fermat about the foundations of the subject affected their successors.

Gonick, Larry, and Woollcott Smith. *The Cartoon Guide to Statistics*. New York: HarperCollins, 1993. This volume not only explains the basic ideas and vocabulary of statistics but also uses seventeenth century France as part of the background.

Hacking, Ian. *The Emergence of Probability: A Philosophical Study of Early Ideas About Probability, Induction, and Statistical Inference*. Cambridge, England: Cambridge University Press, 1975. This is the most sophisticated philosophical examination of Pascal and Fermat and argues that Pascal's religious use of probability is more important than his strictly mathematical work on the subject.

Hald, Anders. *A History of Probability and Statistics and Their Applications Before 1750*. New York: John Wiley and Sons, 1990. The most extensive and technically polished examination of Pascal, Fermat, and Huygens.

Maistrov, L. E. *Probability Theory: A Historical Sketch*. Translated and edited by Samuel Kotz. New York: Academic Press, 1974. This work attempts to debunk some of the stories about de Méré as a gambler contributing to the foundation of probability theory.

Todhunter, Isaac. *A History of the Mathematical Theory of Probability: From the Time of Pascal to That of Laplace*. Sterling, Va.: Thoemmes Press, 2001. A reprint of an 1865 account that tries to reconstruct what Fermat and Pascal wrote to each other by filling in the published record.

SEE ALSO: 1615-1696: Invention and Development of the Calculus; 1623-1674: Earliest Calculators Appear; 1637: Descartes Publishes His *Discourse on Method*; 1673: Huygens Explains the Pendulum; Dec. 7, 1676: Rømer Calculates the Speed of Light.

RELATED ARTICLES in *Great Lives from History: The Seventeenth Century, 1601-1700:* René Descartes; Pierre de Fermat; Christiaan Huygens; Gottfried Wilhelm Leibniz; Blaise Pascal.

1654
PORTUGAL RETAKES CONTROL OF BRAZIL

Expelling Spanish and Dutch usurpers, Portugal reasserted its control of Brazil, which became the richest element of the Portuguese Empire. Brazil exported more sugar and imported more African slaves than any other country.

LOCALE: Brazil

CATEGORIES: Wars, uprisings, and civil unrest; government and politics; expansion and land acquisition; colonization; trade and commerce; economics

KEY FIGURES

Salvador Correia de Sá e Benevides (1594-1688), Brazilian-born governor who was crucial in reasserting Portuguese control of West African slave-trading posts and south Atlantic trade

António Vieira (1608-1697), a leading Brazilian Jesuit orator, writer, and government adviser

António Raposo Tavares (c. 1598-1658), São Paulo official who led numerous, wide-ranging expeditions that expanded colonial frontiers in Brazil

SUMMARY OF EVENT

The Dutch had occupied the northeastern part of Brazil since 1630, but from the mid-1640's until 1654, an alliance of local Brazilian landowners and the Portuguese finally drove the Dutch from what was named New Holland. Portugal had lost its sovereignty in 1580 when the king of Spain, Philip II, became king also of Portugal. The Spanish occupation of the Portuguese throne continued until 1640, when Portugal reasserted its independence.

Portugal regained sovereignty over Brazil in 1654, a country that was much changed since the previous century. Before 1580, Brazil had been a minor component of the Portuguese Empire, the center of which was the wealth of India and Southeast Asia. Incipient sugar plantations, along its northeast coast, was Brazil's only source of wealth for Portugal. Indian slavery failed as a labor supply, but more successful was the importation of slaves from Portugal's advancing possessions along the western coast of Africa, especially Ghana and Angola. Angola provided the greatest number of slaves. "Sugar is Brazil and Brazil is Angola" was a common expression of the time.

The modest but steady prosperity of Brazil's sugar-exporting economy meant that its white immigrant population of about 25,000 people at the beginning of the seventeenth century had grown to almost 100,000 by century's end. Disease as well as defeat by European arms reduced the indigenous population from several million to several hundred thousand, but the African slave population grew most spectacularly. Several hundred thousand Africans were transported to Brazil, arriving at an annual rate of more than one thousand at the beginning of the century to nearly ten thousand by the end of the century.

African slave labor was instrumental to the success of the sugar plantations and mills. Brazil, the largest exporter of sugar during the century, produced more than 1,500 tons at the beginning of the period to almost 400,000 by century's end. Ensuring this success was the more than four hundred sugar mills in Brazil by century's end. Also ensuring success was the huge number of slaves working in the mills, who were "distributed" primarily in three provinces: Pernambuco, Bahia, and Rio de Janeiro. Pernambuco, the richest sugar-producing region, had more than half the mills and plantations. Bahia, the colonial capital of Salvador, was second in the number of mills. However, Rio de Janeiro had developed many more mills, so that by the end of the seventeenth century, Bahia and Rio de Janeiro each held one fourth of the mills. Brazil did not have a monopoly on sugar production. Islands of the Caribbean became major competitors.

The economic preeminence of Brazil within the Portuguese Empire grew steadily. At the beginning of the 1600's, the empire's wealth from Brazil was inferior to that gained from the trade in spices and luxury products from Portuguese colonies in India and East Asia. By the middle of the century, its energy and resources depleted by wars against Spain and the Netherlands, Portugal had lost many of its eastern realms, so Brazil's agricultural wealth became the economic backbone of the empire. Indeed, Brazil became so crucial to Portugal that after 1645, the heir to the Portuguese throne bore the title, prince of Brazil.

Brazil's agricultural wealth was distributed within a rigid hierarchical society. A small number of white plantation owners dominated a mass of enslaved Africans. The owners of the sugar mills were those who owned the vast landholdings known as *latifundia*. These owners were the *senhores de engenho*, the lords of the mills. They dominated Brazilian government and society. Family, slaves, leaseholders of small farms, clergy, and

Slaves from Africa worked in one of the hundreds of sugar mills in Brazil, helping Portugal become the world's leading exporter of sugar by the end of the seventeenth century. (The Granger Collection)

craftspersons were their subordinates. A shortage of white women in early colonial Brazil resulted in abundant interracial coupling among whites, blacks, and indigenous peoples. Brazilian culture was dominated by the Catholic clergy, particularly the Jesuits, whose greatest spokesperson during the period was Father António Vieira, a preacher and scholar.

Brazil's government administration was handled by a Portuguese governor-general, who was located in Salvador. Occasionally, he was referred to as a viceroy, depending on the individual's aristocratic background. The northern coast of Brazil was administered as a separate state, Maranhão, with its capital at São Luis. Dual administration was necessary because the territory of Brazil straddled the equator. Consequently, navigation to and from the country depended on two different sets of ocean winds and currents. In the south, the two most important regions were Rio de Janeiro and, farther south, São Vicente and its satellite city in the coastal highlands, São Paulo. One of the governors of Rio de Janeiro, Salvador Correia de Sá e Benevides, had been crucial in reestablishing Portuguese control in the south Atlantic after he recaptured the African colony of Angola from the Dutch.

São Paulo was to be crucial to the geographic expansion of Brazil. Its residents, called *paulistas*, organized bands of frontiersmen, known as *bandeirantes*. Moving along the rivers of the interior of Brazil that coursed south, west, and north, they raided vast regions of the interior, hunting for indigenous slaves, gold, emeralds, and diamonds. One of the most famous *bandeirante* adventurers was António Raposo Tavares. *Paulistas* moved along a vast area that closely resembles Brazil's modern physical contours (from the Uruguay River in the south to the mouth of the Amazon River in the north). It would be one of the *bandeirantes* who discovered gold in central Brazil in 1695. This discovery led to the largest gold rush in the world in the eighteenth century and also led to the definitive occupation of the Brazilian interior.

SIGNIFICANCE

Brazil was the key element of the Portuguese Empire in the seventeenth century, and its recapture from the Dutch served the empire well. Although sugar production predominated, Brazil also mined gold and diamonds and exported brazilwood (a red dyewood often used for cabinetmaking), cotton, and tobacco. It also exported slaves, and its cattle industry exported meat and hides. Two monopolizing trading fleets thrived, beginning in 1649 with the Commercial Company of Brazil and the Maranhão Company, which formed in 1682. Because of their monopoly, the companies were opposed by many, and they were abolished in the early eighteenth century.

In terms of land, labor, resources, and economy, Brazil was a sociocultural phenomenon that straddled a vast space: the south Atlantic from the coast of eastern South America to the coast of western Africa.

—*Edward A. Riedinger*

FURTHER READING

Landers, Sharon. *An Exploration of the Theory and Practice of Slavery in Seventeenth-Century Brazil in the Writings of Padre Antonio Vieira*. Unpublished doctoral dissertation. Texas Christian University, 1995. Examines the sermons and correspondence of the leading Brazilian Jesuit scholar regarding the theological and social concerns of the rapidly expanding Indian and African slave trade in Brazil.

Marques, António Henrique de Oliveira. *History of Portugal*. 2 vols. New York: Columbia University Press, 1972. Volume one traces the historic development of Brazil, placing that development in the context of the Portuguese Empire in Africa and Asia.

Mello e Souza, Laura de. *The Devil and the Land of the Holy Cross: Witchcraft, Slavery, and Popular Religion in Colonial Brazil*. Austin: University of Texas Press, 2003. This work contrasts the dogma and rites of the official Catholic Church in colonial Brazil to the religious practices of the mixed-race or enslaved population, which amalgamated elements of African, indigenous, and heretical Christian beliefs.

Schwartz, Stuart B. *Sovereignty and Society of Colonial Brazil: The High Court of Bahia and Its Judges, 1609-1751*. Berkeley: University of California Press, 1973. Schwartz examines the key judicial unit for colonial administration of Brazil and the social composition of its magistrates.

SEE ALSO: Dec., 1601: Dutch Defeat the Portuguese in Bantam Harbor; 1608: Jesuits Found Paraguay; 1617-1693: European Powers Vie for Control of Gorée; 1619-c. 1700: The Middle Passage to American Slavery; July, 1625-Aug., 1664: Founding of New Amsterdam; Oct., 1625-1637: Dutch and Portuguese Struggle for the Guinea Coast; 1630's-1694: Slaves Resist Europeans at Palmares; June-Aug., 1640: *Bandeirantes* Expel the Jesuits; Jan. 14, 1641: Capture of Malacca; Aug. 26, 1641-Sept., 1648: Conquest of Luanda; 1644-1671: Ndongo Wars; Mid-17th cent.: Emergence of the Guinea Coast States; Oct. 29, 1665: Battle of Mbwila; Feb. 13, 1668: Spain Recognizes Portugal's Independence; 1670-1699: Rise of the Asante Empire; Beginning 1680's: Guerra dos Bárbaros; Early 1690's: Brazilian Gold Rush.

RELATED ARTICLES in *Great Lives from History: The Seventeenth Century, 1601-1700:* Maurice of Nassau; Njinga; Philip IV; António Vieira.

Summer, 1654-1656
FIRST JEWISH SETTLERS IN NORTH AMERICA

The first documented Jewish settlers in North America arrived in New Amsterdam. They fought for and eventually obtained the right to live and work in New Netherland, despite intense opposition, laying the groundwork for greater religious toleration in the New World.

LOCALE: Manhattan Island, New Netherland (now in New York)

CATEGORIES: Social issues and reform; colonization; religion and theology

KEY FIGURES

Asser Levy (1628?-1682), first Jew to own land and obtain burgher right in New Amsterdam

Dominie Johannes Megapolensis (1603-1670), preacher in New Amsterdam

Peter Stuyvesant (c. 1610-1672), director-general of New Netherland, 1647-1664

SUMMARY OF EVENT

The first Jewish settlers of record in New Amsterdam were Jacob Barsimon and Solomon Pieterson, both of whom came from Holland in the summer of 1654. The next month, twenty-three other Jews arrived, both old and young, refugees from the Portuguese conquest of Dutch Brazil (New Holland), which had been the richest property of the Dutch West India Company in America. After leaving Recife, Brazil, their ship had been captured by Spanish pirates, from whom they were saved by a French privateer, the *Saint Charles*, captained by Jacques de La Motthe. Having little more than the clothes on their backs, the Jewish migrants convinced La Motthe to carry them to New Amsterdam for twenty-five hundred guilders, which they hoped to borrow in that Dutch port. They shortly discovered, however, what Jacob Barsimon and Solomon Pieterson were already learning: There was much opposition to Jews settling in New Netherland.

Their poverty made the Dutch Jews from Brazil especially vulnerable. Unable to borrow the money, they asked La Motthe for extra time to contact friends and receive money from Amsterdam. Rather than waiting, La Motthe brought suit in the City Court of New Amsterdam, which ordered that the Jews' meager belongings should be sold at public auction. Even after all that was worth selling had been sold, the unfortunate exiles still owed almost five hundred guilders. The City Court then ordered that two of the Jews—David Israel and Moses Ambroisius—should be held under civil arrest until the total debt was paid. In October, the matter finally was resolved after the crew of the *Saint Charles*, holding title to the remainder of the Jewish debt, agreed to wait until additional funds could be sent from Amsterdam.

The ordeal of the Jewish refugees was far from over. They wanted to remain in New Amsterdam, but Director-General Peter Stuyvesant complained to the Amsterdam Chamber of the Dutch West India Company. Stuyvesant was against allowing the Jews to stay, as were the city magistrates, who resented "their customary usury and deceitful trading with the Christians," and the deacons of the Reformed Church, who feared that in "their present indigence they might become a charge in the coming winter." Indicating that the colonists generally shared his anti-Semitic views, Stuyvesant informed the Amsterdam directors that "we have for the benefit of this weak and newly developing place and the land in general, deemed it useful to require them in a friendly way to depart." As for the future, he urged "that the deceitful race—such hateful enemies and blasphemers of the name of Christ—be not allowed further to infect and trouble this new colony, to the detraction of your Worships and the dissatisfaction of your Worships' most affectionate subjects."

Despite his vehemence against the Jews, Stuyvesant delayed his expulsion order, waiting instead for guidance from the Amsterdam Chamber of the Dutch West India Company, to whom the unwanted refugees were also appealing. The Jewish community in Amsterdam took up their cause. During the early sixteenth century, the embattled United Provinces—and especially the city of Amsterdam—had become a haven for persecuted European Jews, whose many contributions to Dutch economic and cultural life had brought them considerable religious freedom, political and legal rights, and economic privileges. Not only did Jewish investors own approximately 4 percent of the Dutch West India Company's stock, but also more than six hundred Dutch Jews had participated in colonizing Dutch Brazil. Virtually all of them left Pernambuco in 1654 with the other Dutch nationals, losing practically everything, although the conquering Portuguese had urged them to remain and promised to protect their property. Thus their loyalty to the Dutch republic could hardly be questioned. Moreover, thinly populated New Netherland desperately needed settlers.

On the other hand, Dominie Johannes Megapolensis, one of the leading Dutch Reformed preachers in New Netherland, was especially disturbed because a few additional Jewish families recently had immigrated from Amsterdam. He called upon the Amsterdam Classis of the Reformed Church to use its influence to have the Jews expelled from the American colony. "These people have no other God than the Mammon of unrighteousness," warned Megapolensis, "and no other aim than to get possession of Christian property, and to overcome all other merchants by drawing all trade toward themselves." Surely, Megapolensis pleaded, these "godless rascals" should be expelled.

Expressing some sympathy for Stuyvesant's anti-Jewish prejudice, the Amsterdam Chamber nevertheless announced in early 1655 that Jews could travel, trade, and live in New Netherland, provided they cared for their own poor. Over the next few years, while not directly defying the company's directive, Stuyvesant and other civil officials delayed, obstructed, and otherwise made life more difficult for the Jews of New Amsterdam. In March, 1655, for example, Abraham de Lucena was arrested for selling goods on Sunday. In July, de Lucena and others petitioned to purchase land for a Jewish cemetery but were denied. Indeed, Jews were not allowed to purchase land in New Amsterdam. They also were exempted from the city militia, on grounds that other colonists would not serve with them, but were required to pay a heavy tax each month in lieu of service.

The Jews of New Amsterdam resented and resisted such treatment. In November, when Asser Levy and Jacob Barsimon, two young Jews with little money, protested the tax and asked to do service with the militia instead, the town council dismissed their protest and noted that the petitioners could choose to go elsewhere. The same message was conveyed by the heavy rates imposed upon Jews in the general levy to raise funds for rebuilding the city's defense wall. Most discouraging were the restrictions placed on Jews who wished to trade to Albany and Delaware Bay.

In 1656, the Amsterdam Chamber chastised Stuyvesant and insisted that Jews in New Netherland were to have the same rights and privileges as Jews in old Amsterdam. They could trade wholesale, rent and buy property, and enjoy the protection of the law as other Dutch citizens did. However, their religious freedom did not extend to public worship, and they were not allowed to sell retail, work as mechanics, or live and work outside a designated area of town. Despite the opposition of the Burgomasters and Schepens, Stuyvesant, ever the faithful servant of the Dutch West India Company, insisted that Asser Levy be admitted to the burgher right, which allowed him to run a business, vote in town elections, and even hold office. Jews in the city of New Amsterdam were not ghettoized, and they could work as mechanics and tradesmen as well as shopkeepers and merchants. Asser Levy became the first Jewish landowner and was one of two Jews licensed as butchers in 1660.

SIGNIFICANCE

Prejudice remained among the Dutch of New Netherland, but social and economic acceptance came to the Jewish community in New Amsterdam. They were allowed their separate burial ground, and their right to observe the Sabbath on Saturday was respected. They never established a synagogue and may not have had enough people to maintain a congregation, but regular religious services apparently were held. Asser Levy owned a Torah, and others had prayer books and shawls. Most of the Jews in New Amsterdam were Sephardim, descended from Portuguese Jews, although a few were Ashkenazi Jews from Germany, France, and Eastern Europe. Their numbers remained quite small, never more than a handful of families, and there seems to have been a good deal of migration in and out of the colony. However, the Jews of New Amsterdam were pioneers who prepared the way for the more extensive Jewish community that would emerge in early New York.

—*Ronald W. Howard*

FURTHER READING

Faber, Eli. *A Time for Planting: The First Migration, 1654-1820*. Vol. 1 in *The Jewish People in America*. Baltimore: Johns Hopkins University Press, 1992. A history of the Jewish migration to America from 1654 through 1820, focusing on Jews from Amsterdam, Lisbon, and London who settled in the United States.

Gurock, Jeffrey S., ed. *The Colonial and National Periods, 1654-1820*. Vol. 1 in *American Jewish History*. New York: Routledge, 1998. Collection of articles, including two essays by Leo Hershkowitz about Asser Levy and the early New York Jews, and the subsequent development of the New York Jewish community.

Hershkowitz, Leo. "Judaism." In *The Encyclopedia of the North American Colonies*, edited by Jacob Ernest Cook. Vol. 3. New York: Charles Scribner's Sons, 1993. Brief but incisive summary of colonial Judaism.

Kessler, Henry H., and Eugene Rachlis. *Peter Stuyvesant and His New York*. New York: Random House, 1959. Gives insight into the anti-Semitism of Dutch Calvinism and the cooperative efforts of Stuyvesant and the Dutch Reformed preachers against the Jews.

Marcus, Jacob R. *The Colonial American Jew, 1492-1776*. 3 vols. Detroit, Mich.: Wayne State University Press, 1970. Presents a detailed survey of the Jewish experience in early America, relating connections between the various Jewish communities.

Oppenheim, Samuel. *The Early History of the Jews in New York, 1654-1664*. New York: American Jewish Historical Society, 1909. Basic source for details on early Jewish settlers and their trials, tribulations, and successes.

Rink, Oliver A. *Holland on the Hudson: An Economic and Social History of Dutch New York*. Ithaca, N.Y.: Cornell University Press, 1986. An account that relates the Jewish migration to larger economic and social developments in New Netherland.

Smith, George L. *Religion and Trade in New Netherland: Dutch Origins and American Development*. Ithaca, N.Y.: Cornell University Press, 1973. An analysis of religious toleration that emerged in the northern Netherlands and its transference to New Netherland.

SEE ALSO: July, 1625-Aug., 1664: Founding of New Amsterdam; May 6, 1626: Algonquians "Sell" Manhattan Island; 1654: Portugal Retakes Control of Brazil; Mar. 22, 1664-July 21, 1667: British Conquest of New Netherland.

RELATED ARTICLE in *Great Lives from History: The Seventeenth Century, 1601-1700:* Peter Stuyvesant.

1655-1663
GRIMALDI DISCOVERS DIFFRACTION

Francesco Maria Grimaldi showed that light passing through a small opening cannot be prevented from slightly spreading on the farther side. He termed this phenomenon "diffraction" and postulated that it was caused by light having a fluid nature analogous to a flowing stream of water.

LOCALE: Bologna, Papal States (now in Italy)
CATEGORIES: Physics; mathematics; science and technology

KEY FIGURES

Francesco Maria Grimaldi (1618-1663), Italian mathematician
Sir Isaac Newton (1642-1727), English mathematician, greatly influenced by Grimaldi's work
Christiaan Huygens (1629-1695), Dutch scientist and mathematician, whose work on wave theory was confirmed by the ideas of Grimaldi

SUMMARY OF EVENT

In about 1655, while serving as a mathematics instructor at the Jesuit University of Santa Lucia in Bologna, Francesco Maria Grimaldi began an elaborate set of optical experiments that occupied him for the remainder of his life. These experiments clearly demonstrated that light propagating through air does not simply travel in straight lines, but tends to bend slightly around objects. This new phenomenon Grimaldi termed "diffraction" (from the Latin, "a breaking up") because it indicated that light has a fluid nature allowing it to flow around objects like a stream of water divides around a slender obstacle in its path.

Prior to Grimaldi's experiments scientists assumed that light always propagates rectilinearly if it remains in the same medium, which gave credence to the prevailing view that light consists of small, rapidly moving particles. It was known since antiquity that when light enters a different medium, for example, from air to water, it is bent, or refracted. Diffraction is a bending of light around objects or through openings in the same medium. Diffraction is exhibited by all types of waves—water, sound, and light—but had not been observed previously for light because the extremely small wavelengths render the effects difficult to perceive. Grimaldi's experiments on diffraction were of two different types: One type examined the shadows produced by opaque objects of different shapes, the other type examined light passing through circular apertures.

For the shadow experiments, Grimaldi allowed bright sunlight to enter a darkened room through a tiny hole (1/60 of an inch in diameter). This created a cone of light that Grimaldi projected on a white screen set obliquely to form an elliptical image of the sun. Between the hole and the screen he inserted a narrow opaque rod to create a shadow. Examining this shadow carefully, Grimaldi observed that its size was somewhat smaller than the linear projection of light rays predicted and, even more surprising, that the shadow's border was bounded by narrow fringes of color. He described these diffraction bands in some detail; there are usually three and they increase in intensity and width nearer to the shadow. The closest band consists of a central white region flanked by a narrow violet band near the shadow and a slender red band away from the shadow. Grimaldi cautioned that these color bands must be observed carefully to avoid mistaking the series for alternating stripes of light and dark.

Next, he examined the effect of varying the shape of the opaque object by replacing the rod with a step-shaped object with two rectangular corners. He meticulously recorded how the bands curved around the outer corner and continued to follow the shadow's edge. He also described that when the two series of bands from each edge of the inner corner approach they intersect perpendicularly to create regions of brighter color separated by darker areas.

Grimaldi also employed several L-shaped objects of different width to study the color bands produced. His diagrams show two sets of continuous tracks, parallel to the borders, which connect by bending around in a semicircle at the end of the L. He noted that the bands appear only in pairs, the number increasing with the width of the obstacle and its distance form the screen. He also observed that at the corners of the L, an additional series of shorter and brighter colors emerged. He diagramed these as five feather-shaped fringes radiating from the corner and crossing the paired tracks of light perpendicularly. Grimaldi compared this to the wash behind a moving ship.

Grimaldi's aperture experiment allowed the cone of light to pass through a second hole, about 1/10 inch in diameter, before being projected on a wall. The distances between the holes and between the wall and the second hole were equal at about 12 feet. Grimaldi observed that the circle of light cast on the opposite wall was slightly larger than predicted by rectilinear propagation theory, and the border displayed the same red and blue bands. He also mentioned that these diffraction effects are quite small and only observable if extremely small apertures are used.

Grimaldi also discovered that when sunlight entered a room through two small adjacent apertures, the region illuminated by the two beams was darker than when illuminated by either aperture separately. Although he did not understand that he was observing the now well-known principle of "interference of light waves," he regarded it as conclusive proof that light was not a material, particulate substance.

Grimaldi's carefully executed experiments convinced him that light had a liquid nature, a column of pulsating fluid that could produce color fringes when the luminous flow was agitated. The colors were inherent in the white light itself and not created by some outside agent. Although the diffraction effect so carefully measured and documented by Grimaldi is an unequivocal indicator that light consists of periodic waves, this notion seems not to have occurred to him.

Grimaldi detailed his experiments on diffraction, along with many other optical topics, in his comprehensive treatise *Physico-mathesis de lumine, coloribus, et iride* (1665; English translation, 1963).

SIGNIFICANCE

Encouraged by Francesco Maria Grimaldi's work, Christiaan Huygens pursued the development of a wave theory of light. He envisioned waves propagating through an invisible all-pervasive medium and established a principle demonstrating how wave fronts progressed through this medium. Using his principle, he derived the well-known laws of reflection and refraction. A consequence of the wave theory is that when light passes obliquely from a less-dense to a more-dense medium, the speed of the wave must decrease to explain the observation that the light refracts to a smaller angle.

Isaac Newton, who was also greatly influenced by Grimaldi's work, favored a particle theory of light in which refraction is explained by the particles increasing their speed when entering a denser medium. He objected to a wave theory because the predicted bending of light around corners was not observed. Grimaldi's diffraction results were explained as being due to refraction; he proposed that the density of a medium decreased near an obstacle, thus causing light to bend. Newton had observed wave interference for water waves and used it to explain anomalous tidal effects, but he did not apply this to optics. Such was the nature of Newton's fame that no one refuted him.

The issue was finally resolved in favor of the wave theory by English scientist Thomas Young (1773-1829), when, in 1802, he published experimental results documenting light interference and proving that Newton's experiments were easily explained by the wave theory. The final nail in the coffin lid of the particle theory was the experimental measurement of the speed of light underwater, accomplished in 1850 by the French physicist Leon Foucault (1819-1868). His precise measurements proved that the speed of light under water was considerably less than its speed in air, as predicted by the wave theory.

—*George R. Plitnik*

FURTHER READING

McGrath, F. A. *Grimaldi's Fluid Theory of Light*. Unpublished master's thesis. University College, London, 1969. A complete and effectual discussion of Grimaldi's life and career in science, with emphasis on his optical research.

Pedrotti, L., and F. Pedrotti. *Optics and Vision*. Upper Saddle River, N.J.: Prentice Hall, 1998. This text presents optical principles, including an entire chapter devoted to diffraction, in an easy-to-read manner with a minimum of mathematics. The introductory chapter offers a short but complete history of the sciences of vision and of light.

Waldman, G. *Introduction to Light*. Englewood Cliffs, N.J.: Prentice Hall, 1983. This book covers the nature and history of light and clearly explains optical phenomena such as diffraction.

SEE ALSO: 1673: Huygens Explains the Pendulum; Dec. 7, 1676: Rømer Calculates the Speed of Light.

RELATED ARTICLES in *Great Lives from History: The Seventeenth Century, 1601-1700:* Galileo; Francesco Maria Grimaldi; Christiaan Huygens; Sir Isaac Newton.

March 12-14, 1655
Penruddock's Uprising

The Royalist uprising led by Colonel John Penruddock and Sir Joseph Wagstaffe against the government of Lord Protector Oliver Cromwell sought to proclaim Charles II as king and restore monarchy in England. The Royalists briefly held Salisbury, England, before moving westward, where they were defeated by government forces; Penruddock and fourteen others were subsequently executed. This episode led directly to the creation of the twelve military districts in England controlled by the major-generals.

Locale: Wiltshire, England
Category: Wars, uprisings, and civil unrest

Key Figures

John Penruddock (1619-1655), leader of the failed uprising
John Desborough (1608-1680), major-general appointed by Cromwell to end the uprising
Charles II (1630-1685), disenfranchised son of the executed king Charles I and later king of England, r. 1660-1685
Oliver Cromwell (1599-1658), lord protector of England, 1653-1658
Sir Joseph Wagstaffe (fl. 1642-1662), exiled Royalist who returned to England to assist in Penruddock's Uprising
John Thurloe (1616-1668), secretary of state whose spy network uncovered many Royalist plots
First Earl of Rochester (Henry Wilmot; 1612-1658), Royalist sent from Europe by Charles to lead an uprising in northern England

Summary of Event

Penruddock's Uprising was planned to be one of a series of regional uprisings designed to overthrow the government of Oliver Cromwell (the Protectorate) and restore Charles II to the throne of England. A group of Royalist nobles known as the Sealed Knot plotted and maintained contact with Charles and the exiled Royalists in Europe. Originally, foreign assistance from Scotland and Europe was sought, but Penruddock's Uprising and the other actions planned to occur simultaneously on a national scale were to be perpetrated by English Royalists alone. Because of international developments, Charles could offer English Royalists no French or Spanish troops to support their efforts.

The defeat of young Charles at Worcester (1651) and his subsequent flight into continental exile had not been accepted by Royalists as a final defeat, and they had continued plotting. Although plagued by jealousies and divisions within their ranks, slow communication due to fear of discovery, and penetration of the Sealed Knot by Cromwell's spymaster, Secretary of State John Thurloe, the Royalists had set February 6, 1655, as the date for a series of uprisings throughout northern England (Yorkshire, Cheshire, and Lincolnshire), Wales and the vicinity (Liverpool and Shrewsbury), and southern and western England (Wiltshire, Hampshire, and Cornwall).

In December, 1654, because of information gathered by Thurloe, the Protectorate recalled troops to reinforce London, and in January-February, 1655, a number of Royalists who had been gathering weapons were arrested. Some plotters believed it best to abandon the enterprise, while other bolder men, referred to by historians as the "Action Party," sought merely to postpone it one week until February 13, 1655. The latter faction managed to procure Charles's assent; however, the messenger carrying this news did not reach England until February 14, 1655, and he was then held in Dover Castle until February 22, 1655. On February 12, 1655, the Protectorate banned horse races (which were often a convenient cover for Royalist gatherings), seized all horses within the vicinity of London, collected all caches of gunpowder, and stepped up patrols around London significantly. February 13, 1655, came and went with no Royalist uprisings.

Despite government vigilance, some Royalist plotters of the Action Party pressed ahead and rescheduled the uprisings for Thursday, March 8, 1655. Charles sent a close associate, Henry Wilmot, first earl of Rochester, along with Sir Joseph Wagstaffe to coordinate the uprisings; Charles also moved from Cologne to Middleburg, on the coast of Flanders, to be ready to sail to England should the uprisings be successful. On March 8, 1655, the Royalists managed only feeble efforts—the government had arrested a number of conspirators, some had fled, and others did nothing. A proposed attack on York to be led by Rochester aroused only one hundred Royalists, who quickly dispersed after gathering. Rochester eventually escaped to Europe. Planned attacks on Newcastle, Chester, Shrewsbury, and Nottinghamshire and along the Welsh border were prevented by the mere presence of freshly arrived government troops or timely arrests of Royalist leaders.

Thus, the only Royalist group to rise up was the one that coalesced in Wiltshire, near Salisbury, early on Monday morning, March 12, 1655. Led by Colonel John Penruddock and Sir Joseph Wagstaffe, about two hundred men took control of the marketplace and opened the jail to gain reinforcements and confiscated horses. They took the sheriff, Colonel John Dove, hostage, and the now four hundred rebels rode off to nearby towns to proclaim Charles II king and to enlist additional recruits. On Tuesday morning, March 13, 1655, the Royalists set Dove free, and it became apparent that hoped-for Royalist support from Dorset had not materialized.

News of the rising had reached Cromwell on Monday night, March 12, 1655, and he ordered Major-General John Desborough to put it down. Major-General William Boteler, in Bristol, had received news of the rising and marched toward Salisbury and Shaftesbury, where he awaited Desborough's forces. Penruddock, Wagstaffe, and their men moved further west with a government cavalry unit from Exeter in hot pursuit. The Parliamentary cavalry caught them at the village of South Molton in Devonshire on Wednesday, March 14, 1655, and after a street battle of several hours, the Royalists either fled or were captured. Penruddock surrendered, but Wagstaffe escaped and eventually made his way overseas.

Desborough sent a letter to Thurloe noting that 139 men were jailed in Exeter and that some lower ranking Royalists had not even been jailed. The breakdown of prisoners according to social status revealed forty-three gentlemen and officers, eight yeomen, nineteen husbandmen, ten servants, two innkeepers, and fifty-seven small craftsmen. Cromwell allowed trial by jury and only about one third were tried. Of the thirty-nine men condemned to death, only fourteen or fifteen were executed, including Penruddock; a number of others, perhaps as many as seventy, were transported to Barbados as punishment.

SIGNIFICANCE

Reasons adduced for the uprising's failure include the strength of the Protectorate's troops, the government's intelligence on Royalist activities, division among the Royalists, continual postponements of the uprising, lack of finances, lack of support from the great Royalist nobles, failure to mobilize the full Royalist strength, inability to engender widespread popular support by tapping into broader political, financial, social, and religious grievances, which many had against the regime, and not seeking to ally with other disaffected groups, such as radical Levellers and the Fifth Monarchy Men. It has been noted by historians that many Royalists knew of the uprisings planned for 1655 and kept the secret; however, only a few would engage in active plotting and fewer still would actively participate in the actions they had plotted. Such was the respect for and fear of the government's power and the reluctance to risk lives and fortunes.

The immediate result of the uprising was the division of England into twelve military districts, or associations, each headed by a major-general. A decimation tax of 10 percent was assessed on Royalist property. The rule of the major-generals was to provide greater security for the government and introduce godly Puritan reforms. Desborough was appointed major-general of the west.

Such a heavy-handed military government was extremely unpopular and never worked effectively with local leaders, and the decimation tax was a severe burden for the Royalists. This situation caused a very strong animosity toward standing armies, which became an important feature of English politics for many years afterward. When a taxation measure needed to continue the system of major-generals was defeated in Parliament in January, 1657, the system of major-generals slowly came undone. The attempt to introduce godly Puritan reform was not successful and helped create the view of Puritans as killjoys and people who meddled in people's private lives.

—*Mark C. Herman*

FURTHER READING

Button, Andrea. "Penruddock's Rising, 1655." *Southern History* 19 (1997). An article updating earlier treatments of the episode.

Durston, Christopher. *Cromwell's Major-Generals: Godly Government During the English Revolution.* New York: Manchester University Press, 2001. Delineates the formation of the policy to create the military districts governed by major-generals that resulted from Penruddock's Uprising.

Gardiner, S. R. *1653-1655.* Vol. 3 in *History of the Commonwealth and Protectorate.* London: Longmans, Green, 1903. Reprint. Gloucestershire, England: Windrush Press, 1989. Chapters 38 and 39 give a detailed account of Royalist plotting against Cromwell's government and of Penruddock's Uprising.

Hardacre, Paul. *The Royalists in the Puritan Revolution.* The Hague, the Netherlands: Nijhoff, 1955. One of the first comprehensive studies of Royalist attitudes and activities, this work places Royalist plotting and Penruddock's Uprising within a broader context as it investigates the Royalists in England and in exile.

Underdown, David. *Royalist Conspiracy in England, 1649-1660*. New Haven, Conn.: Yale University Press, 1960. Reprint. Hamden, Conn.: Archon Books, 1971. Underdown places the uprising within the context of Royalist attempts to restore monarchy. Chapter 7 offers a detailed description of the 1655 uprisings.

Woolrych, Austin H. *Penruddock's Rising 1655*. London: The Historical Association, 1955. This short pamphlet offers an excellent treatment of the subject.

See also: 1642-1651: English Civil Wars; July 2, 1644: Battle of Marston Moor; Dec. 6, 1648-May 19, 1649: Establishment of the English Commonwealth; Dec. 16, 1653-Sept. 3, 1658: Cromwell Rules England as Lord Protector; May, 1659-May, 1660: Restoration of Charles II.

Related articles in *Great Lives from History: The Seventeenth Century, 1601-1700:* Charles I; Charles II (of England); Oliver Cromwell.

May 10, 1655
English Capture of Jamaica

Control of Jamaica established an English presence in the Caribbean from which English privateers and pirates could attack Spanish shipping and colonies; additionally, the English developed a plantation system based on African slave labor. Formal control was ceded fifteen years after the initial attack via the Treaty of Madrid, July 8, 1670.

Locale: Jamaica in the Caribbean Sea
Categories: Wars, uprisings, and civil unrest; expansion and land acquisition; diplomacy and international relations

Key Figures

Oliver Cromwell (1599-1658), lord protector of England, 1653-1658
Sir William Penn (1621-1670), English "General at Sea" and one of the co-commanders of the expedition
Robert Venables (1612?-1687), general in command of the troops and co-commander with Penn

Summary of Event

The attack on and conquest of Jamaica were part of the Western Design, developed by England's lord protector Oliver Cromwell, to attack Spanish colonies in the Caribbean (or West Indies). This plan bore similarities to English policy under Queen Elizabeth I (r. 1558-1603). Cromwell's motivations were a combination of religious views, military concerns, and economics. Influenced by Puritan, providentialist concepts, Cromwell viewed Catholic Spain as an implacable adversary of the Protestants in general and England in particular, and it was imperative from both a religious and a military perspective to weaken or permanently cripple Spain by cutting off Spain's revenue, especially American silver and gold, from the Caribbean. Financial motivations for the plan included seizing the Spanish treasure fleet, establishing a base of operations for commerce with the Caribbean and the Americas, and possibly expanding onto the American mainland. Capturing the Spanish treasure fleet would provide immediate benefits to Cromwell's government, since the expedition would "pay for itself" and help alleviate financial problems.

The Spanish opposition to the English attempt to plant a colony at Providence Island and Spanish cruelty toward Native Americans convinced Cromwell that peaceful relations between England and Spain were not possible. Opposition to the Western Design was raised in England by those who felt the plan was too ambitious, while others advocated attacking mainland South America near the Orinoco River. Many New England colonists feared the dangers of tropical heat and disease. Planters on Barbados worried that such an attack would ruin England's reputation with Native Americans and slaves and hurt commerce.

The proposal was discussed in the Council of State in June, 1654, and in August, 1654, England demanded freedom of religion and the official right for free trade for English in Spanish territories, although there was already much "unofficial" trade. On August 18, 1654, instructions were issued to the co-commanders, General at Sea Sir William Penn and General Robert Venables. Cromwell had received assurances from the French government that the Huguenots, the French Protestants, would not be harassed, and news of a French victory over Spanish forces in the Spanish Netherlands (Flanders) had reached London; this seemed to indicate that attacking Spain was the correct policy. Poor planning plagued the expedition, however: The troops were mainly men who had been impressed into service by the press gang, the supplies and provisions were inadequate, and the divided command caused serious problems.

In December, 1654, about forty ships with three thousand troops sailed from Portsmouth, England, and when they reached Barbados, an additional five thousand raw recruits were added, in February, 1655. The ships' crews were placed on reduced rations, and Penn and Venables were squabbling. The fleet's instructions designated the main target to be either Hispaniola or Puerto Rico, with Cuba as a secondary objective. In mid-April, 1655, the fleet attempted to land on Hispaniola, but the rocky coastline posed a problem. They eventually landed about 30 miles (48 kilometers) from Santo Domingo, the island's major settlement. Sickness and a tough march to the settlement were major factors in the English defeat on April 17, 1655; after being routed again on April 25, 1655, the English withdrew. They had lost four thousand men.

The expedition then sailed to Jamaica, hoping to find something to show for its efforts. Spanish fisherman alerted authorities to the approaching English fleet, which anchored at what is now Kingston Harbor. The Spanish, recognizing that they had no way to defend against such superior forces, evacuated with their possessions. Penn led an assault with the ship *Martin* to probe the defenses of the harbor's fortress, and then the *Martin* was beached near the fortress and English troops landed without resistance on May 10, 1655. However, they lost an important advantage when they did not pursue the fleeing Spanish troops to the settlement of Santiago de la Vega.

In the following days, the English gained control of key settlements, but disease, lack of provisions, and extremely poor morale caused the English to fare poorly against the Spanish and Maroons, former slaves, who waged guerrilla warfare against them. Lack of a supporting fleet helped account for the significant toll among the English troops—about half of them were dead by December, 1655. Already, on June 25, 1655, Penn and his portion of the fleet had sailed back to England, and Venables and his ships returned shortly after that. Since neither commander had received orders to return, they were technically guilty of desertion.

Penn and Venables were jailed for their unauthorized return, and Cromwell was livid over the failure of the expedition to achieve its primary objectives. Especially galling was Penn's failure to attack the Spanish treasure fleet, which had arrived in Havana, Cuba, three weeks after he had left. Penn had received word of its arrival while at sea, but he decided against returning to the Caribbean to engage it. Venables wrote an account of the voyage in which he laid blame for the failure on poor organization, the officers, and the quality of the men, but his strongest accusation was against Penn for landing so far from Santo Domingo. Historians agree that the biggest factor in the expedition's failure was the divided command and animosity between Penn and Venables. Other factors that contributed to the expedition's failure were lack of accurate information about Spanish possessions in the Caribbean and logistical problems of operating at such a great distance from England.

SIGNIFICANCE

Spanish reaction was initially relatively mild—an embargo was placed on English trade, and English merchants and goods in Spanish ports were seized. Privateers from the Spanish Netherlands were launched against English shipping, and Spain formally declared war on England in March, 1656. The English decided against any additional large-scale expeditions and focused attention on attempting to hold on to Jamaica, encouraging English colonists to settle there, and seeking to capture the Spanish treasure fleets. Spanish guerrilla activity largely ceased after April, 1660, when Jamaica's last Spanish governor, Don Christoval Arnaldo y Ysassi, left Jamaica for Cuba, and the Maroon guerrilla leader Juan de Bolas came to terms with the English. Formal control of Jamaica was granted to England by Spain in the Treaty of Madrid, July 8, 1670.

The failure of the Western Design was Oliver Cromwell's greatest disaster, causing him to rethink whether the operation had God's blessing. Tremendous money went into the planning and provisioning of the expedition, and serious financial consequences resulted from the expedition's inability to capture the treasure fleet in order to "pay for itself." The immediate consequence was that, contrary to Cromwell's assumptions, the assault led to war with Spain in Europe. Cromwell had hoped that attacks in the New World would be tolerated without wider consequences in the Old World. Although conditions on Jamaica were extremely rough and difficult and the English government lamented the fact that few settlers migrated to Jamaica, the colony gradually stabilized and increased the English presence in the Caribbean, becoming an important part of the growing British Empire.

—*Mark C. Herman*

FURTHER READING

Baumber, Michael. *General-At-Sea: Robert Blake and the Seventeenth-Century Revolution in Naval Warfare*. London: John Murray, 1989. Part 4 is valuable for understanding the naval war between England and Spain that resulted from the Western Design and the English capture of Jamaica.

Capp, Bernard. *Cromwell's Navy: The Fleet and the English Revolution, 1648-1660.* Oxford, England: Clarendon Press, 1989. Places the Western Design and the capture of Jamaica within the broader context of Cromwell's use of the navy for military and foreign policy purposes.

Gardiner, S. R. *1655-1656.* Vol. 4 in *History of the Commonwealth and Protectorate.* London: Longmans, Green, 1903. Reprint. Gloucestershire, England: Windrush Press, 1989. Although over a century old, this classic work's treatment of the attack in chapters 45 and 48 is still extremely valuable.

Kupperman, Karen Ordahl. "Errand to the Indies: Puritan Colonization from Providence Island Through the Western Design." *William and Mary Quarterly,* 3d ser. 45 (1988): 70-99. This article focuses on the religious motivations behind English Puritan attempts to establish a "godly" settlement in the Caribbean area.

Pincus, Steven C. *Protestantism and Patriotism: Ideologies and the Making of English Foreign Policy, 1650-1668.* New York: Cambridge University Press, 1996. This work analyzes the impact that religious views and public opinion had on the formation and execution of English foreign policy.

Venning, Timothy. *Cromwellian Foreign Policy.* New York: St. Martin's Press, 1995. Chapter 5, "The Western Design," analyzes why Cromwell exercised less caution in the attack on the Spanish in the Caribbean compared with his handling of international relations with France.

See also: 17th cent.: Rise of the Gunpowder Empires; May 14, 1625-1640: English Discover and Colonize Barbados; 1630-1660's: Dutch Wars in Brazil; 1642-1684: Beaver Wars; Dec. 16, 1653-Sept. 3, 1658: Cromwell Rules England as Lord Protector; 1654: Portugal Retakes Control of Brazil; Mar. 22, 1664-July 21, 1667: British Conquest of New Netherland.

Related articles in *Great Lives from History: The Seventeenth Century, 1601-1700:* Oliver Cromwell; Philip IV.

July 10, 1655-June 21, 1661
First Northern War

The First Northern War opened with the invasion of northern Poland by King Charles X of Sweden after Polish king John II refused an alliance with Sweden against the encroaching Muscovites and Cossacks. At war's end, Sweden reached its greatest extent as an imperial nation.

Locale: Poland, Livonia, Denmark, and Sweden
Category: Wars, uprisings, and civil unrest

Key Figures

Charles X Gustav (1622-1660), king of Sweden, r. 1654-1660
Frederick William, the Great Elector (1620-1688), elector of Brandenburg, r. 1640-1688
John II Casimir Vasa (1609-1672), king of Poland, r. 1648-1668
Frederick III (1609-1670), king of Denmark and Norway, r. 1648-1670
Alexis (1629-1676), Russian czar, r. 1645-1676

Summary of Event

Charles X, the field commander of Sweden's armies in the last phases of the Thirty Years' War, ascended to the throne of Sweden upon the abdication of Queen Christina on June 6, 1654. In January of that same year, the war of the Polish-Lithuanian Commonwealth against a Cossack uprising entered a new chapter when Cossack leader Bohdan Khmelnytsky signed an alliance with the Russian czar Alexis.

That summer, 100,000 Muscovites and Cossacks drove deep into Lithuanian territory, taking Smolensk. Charles, who was anxious both to protect Swedish territory in Livonia and to build up Swedish military strength, approached Poland's John II Casimir Vasa with the offer of an alliance. Charles required Polish coastal territories and John's renunciation of his dynastic claim to Sweden's throne in return for his aid. When John refused his terms, Charles decided to attack northern Poland and carve out his own territory.

On July 10, 1655, 50,000 men and 72 cannon moved into Poland from Pomerania, while a Swedish army crossed into Lithuania from Livonia. Aside from well-defended Gdansk, Polish resistance collapsed. Charles himself led an expedition of 50,000 men from Sweden in August. Lithuanian nobleman Janusz Radziwill signed a treaty with Sweden in August, which was to align Lithuania with Sweden, and a second treaty on October 20, in which Charles assumed the title grand duke of Lithuania. Warsaw fell on September 8 and Kraków on October 19, and John fled west. In January, 1656, Sweden settled Brandenburg-Prussia's claims to East Prussian cities, ceding them as Swedish fiefs in the Treaty of Königsberg.

Swedish maltreatment of the Poles quickly kindled resentment and resistance, as did Radziwill's arrangements with Charles. By the spring of 1656, John was possessed of a considerable—and growing—army. Sweden's successes also alarmed Russia, Denmark, and Brandenburg, who formed a rough axis against Sweden. In March, Charles marched on Lwów but was forced back, narrowly escaping a trap in which he lost his artillery and baggage. Charles bought off Frederick William, the Great Elector, in the Treaty of Marienburg (Malbork) of June 25, ceding him rights to captured Baltic Polish towns in return for 8,000 troops. John retook Warsaw on June 29 but lost it a month later in the wake of the Battle of Warsaw, which saw 18,000 Swedes and Brandenburgers defeat 40,000 Poles (July). Both sides utilized a preponderance of cavalry, reflecting the influence of the steppe tradition and demonstrating Charles's adaptability as a military leader.

To the north, Alexis attacked Swedish Livonia with an army of 35,000 men in the summer, but the offensive was broken on well-defended Riga, a setback that took Russia out of the war with the signing of a three-year armistice. Renewed Polish pressure forced the Swedes and Brandenburgers back into Prussia in the fall of 1656. Poland signed an armistice with Russia in October and received aid from Austria through the Treaty of Vienna on December 1. Charles had ceded all his rights and claims in Prussia to Frederick William for more troops and enlisted the support of Transylvanian prince György Rákóczi, whom he promised the Polish throne.

In early 1657, the Swedes and Brandenburgers drove far into central Polish territory. This prompted the Danes to move against Swedish-held east central Norway and Bremen. Though meeting powerful resistance in Poland, Charles pulled out 13,000 troops and marched them against Denmark. All but abandoned by his erstwhile ally, Frederick William joined with the Poles and Austrians in the Treaty of Wehlau (Znamensk) in September, 1657, effectively ending the Polish phase of the war. Charles's army invaded Denmark, but was then stymied by a lack of naval power that would have allowed needed island hopping. The dead of winter, however, allowed a bold march over frozen waterways. The startled Danes then sued for peace and signed the humiliating Treaty of Roskilde (1658). Frederick III surrendered Scania, Halland, Blekinge, a number of strategic islands, and Trondheim in central Norway; all told, Denmark lost about half of its territory.

Lacking other viable options, Charles mounted another attack on Denmark in August, 1658, perhaps seeking to destroy the country entirely. In this second Danish war, the Swedes marched to Copenhagen and besieged the city. Dutch naval aid broke the Swedish blockade and supplied the city, while an allied army led by Brandenburg attacked Holstein and moved north, trapping the Swedes around Copenhagen. An all-out assault on Copenhagen in February, 1659, failed, and Charles was defeated at Nyborg on the Island of Fyn in November, as he was seeking to retreat westward.

Farther east, Frederick William's troops occupied Swedish Pomerania. Undaunted, Charles was planning an assault on Norway when he met his untimely death in Göteborg on February 13, 1660. Negotiations for peace proceeded rapidly.

Three treaties ended the wars that were set off by Charles. The Treaty of Oliva (May 3, 1660), signed by Sweden, Poland, Brandenburg-Prussia, and Austria, overshadowed by the French, guaranteed to Sweden territories on the southern Baltic except Kurland. John gave up his claims to the Swedish throne and relinquished Livonia to Sweden, while all parties recognized Frederick William's control of East Prussia. With the Treaty of Copenhagen (June, 1660), Sweden and Denmark affirmed most of Charles's gains, though he lost Trondheim and Bornholm. Russia and Sweden ended hostilities by signing the Treaty of Kardis on June 21, 1661.

SIGNIFICANCE

With the war, Sweden reached its greatest extent as an imperial nation. The victorious allies hemmed in the country but did not defeat it. By leaving his four-year-old son as his heir (Charles XI), Charles ensured several decades of peace. It would be another four decades before Sweden again set out on such an aggressive campaign. In fact, Sweden drifted into France's camp as a counterweight to rapidly developing Brandenburg-Prussia.

For his part, Frederick William proved the wisdom of a flexible attitude to alliances, and he won East Prussia in the bargain. The war saw Brandenburg's army increase from 1,800 to 22,000 troops, and its generals learned much from their Swedish allies. This proved to be the birth of the Prussian military state, with enormous consequences for European history. Frederick William's growing absolutism was mirrored by that of Frederick III, who gained broad and unfettered powers to modernize and defend a humbled Denmark largely at the expense of the nobility.

Poland emerged badly battered and still at war with Russia. Along with John's claim to Sweden's throne, Poland lost its orientation to the Baltic. Much, however, remained unchanged. European diplomats still believed that military victories had to be recognized and rewarded, but they tempered their generosity with a growing conviction that naked aggression, like the aggression of Charles X, had to be discouraged.

—*Joseph P. Byrne*

Further Reading

Frost, Robert I. *After the Deluge: Poland-Lithuania and the Second Northern War, 1655-1660.* New York: Cambridge University Press, 1993. A detailed chronological narrative and analysis of the political and military aspects of the Polish phase of the war.

_______. *The Northern Wars, 1558-1721.* New York: Longman, 2000. Discusses the Northern Wars in the broad context of the early national struggles for dominance in the Baltic region, integrating political, diplomatic, and military matters.

Kirby, David. *Northern Europe in the Early Modern Period: The Baltic World, 1492-1772.* London: Longman, 1990. Examines Sweden's role as a major political power, and the country's eventual decline. Discusses the evolving political and social systems of the Baltic states.

Lockhart, Paul D. *Sweden in the Seventeenth Century.* New York: Palgrave, 2004. Lockhart briefly discusses, in detail, the war as an outgrowth of the reign and ambitions of Charles X.

Nordstrom, Byron. *The History of Sweden.* Westport, Conn.: Greenwood Press, 2002. The place to begin for the reader who wants a broad overview of the country's history.

Oakley, Stewart P. *War and Peace in the Baltic, 1560-1790.* New York: Routledge, 1992. This work provides a brief but useful overview of the war from an international perspective.

See also: Summer, 1672-Fall, 1676: Ottoman-Polish Wars; 1677-1681: Ottoman-Muscovite Wars.

Related articles in *Great Lives from History: The Seventeenth Century, 1601-1700:* Alexis; Charles X Gustav; Christina; Frederick William, the Great Elector; Gustavus II Adolphus; John III Sobieski; Leopold I; Axel Oxenstierna; Lennart Torstenson.

1656
Popularization of Chocolate

The introduction of cocoa as a commodity in seventeenth century London quickly gave rise to a "chocolate culture" in Europe. The new luxury item, imported from the New World, provided the fundamental economic underpinnings by which imperialism would eventually grow, especially in Africa.

Locale: London, England
Categories: Trade and commerce; economics; agriculture

Key Figures

Anne of Austria (1601-1666), queen of France, r. 1615-1643, and queen regent, r. 1643-1651, who introduced chocolate to the French court

Christopher Columbus (1451-1506), Genoese explorer credited with first bringing chocolate to Europe

Hernán Cortés (c. 1485-1547), Spanish conquistador who popularized chocolate in Spain

Summary of Event

As a beverage, chocolate has been drunk for thousands of years. However, Europeans never realized chocolate existed until Christopher Columbus returned from his fourth voyage to the New World in 1502 with the dark brown beans that were promptly set aside in favor of silver and gold. Little did those at the Spanish court realize that these beans were used as native currency or that they were destined to become one of the world's largest agricultural crops. Their consumption would create enormous wealth for individuals and for governments alike.

Cacao is the name of the plant that produces cocoa beans, and chocolate, referred to by the early Mexicans as the "food of the gods," is an end product of the cacao bean. Solid in form, it was diluted with hot water to make a drink known as *xocolatl*, which was served to the Aztec emperor Montezuma, who was rumored to have drunk fifty cups daily. The drink was consumed as a hot liquid, its harsh bitter taste softened with sugar and vanilla. The Spanish explorer and conquistador Hernán Cortés, who conquered the Aztecs in 1521, saw great possibilities in the cultivation of cocoa: When Cortés returned to Spain in 1528, he loaded his galleons with cocoa beans. Spain kept the source of chocolate a secret for almost a century. In fact, in 1579, when English pirates boarded a Spanish galleon in search of gold and mistook cocoa beans for sheep's droppings, they burned the ship and its incredibly valuable cargo.

Because of Spain's trade monopoly with the New World, chocolate remained exclusively Spanish until theseventeenth century, when Anne of Austria married Louis XIII in 1615 and introduced the culture of coffee to the French court. It was met with skepticism, however, and came to be accepted only after medical approval. The French practice of chocolate drinking reached England by the mid-seventeenth century. In 1650, the practice was introduced at the university town of Oxford, and in 1656, "The Coffee Mill and Tobacco Roll," the first shop to serve chocolate, was opened in London by a Frenchman. In 1659, an advertisement for chocolate—one of the first advertisements for a commercial product in Britain—appeared in an English newspaper.

Chocolate was associated with the rich, as a status drink, for the next two hundred years. A sixteenth century Spanish historian by the name of Oviedo wrote: "None but the rich and noble could afford to drink *xocolatl* as it was literally drinking money." Sold in blocks, it could be grated or scraped into a cup or saucepan before adding hot milk or water. Although these solid cakes were sold for home use, in England the chocolate drink was consumed primarily in chocolate houses, which during the seventeenth century grew to be as prominent as coffeehouses. Just as they did in coffee houses, the wealthy met in chocolate houses to smoke tobacco, discuss political events and literature, and conduct business. In 1693, Italian immigrant Frances White opened White's Chocolate House, London's most famous, and possibly most notorious, chocolate house, on St. James Street. The famous diarist Samuel Pepys, in one of his entries, refers to "Mr. Bland's," where he was in the habit of taking his "morning draft of chocollatte."

While coffeehouses in England took on a puritanical character, chocolate houses came to be associated with aristocrats, politicians of questionable repute, the literati, and gamblers. Also, since chocolate was associated with Catholic Spain, the British—by this time heavily Anglican and Protestant following the Puritan interregnum of Oliver Cromwell—considered chocolate to be a decadent drink. For a while, chocolate was considered an aphrodisiac and was believed to enhance fertility in women. Therefore—as it had done with coffee, tea, and tobacco before it—Parliament began to regulate the consumption of chocolate by imposing enormous taxes. Nevertheless, the drinking of chocolate grew in popularity, especially among the well-to-do.

A man from the Middle East drinks coffee with a Chinese man who drinks tea and a South American Indian who drinks chocolate. All three beverages became fashionable in Europe during the seventeenth century. (Hulton|Archive by Getty Images)

European aristocrats were fond of chocolate in the morning, served on small tables in the bedroom and oftentimes in bed. While caffeinated coffee and tea provided an early-morning physiological jolt to middle-class workers, chocolate, which contains less caffeine, ensured the rich a leisurely entrance into an unhurried day. Porcelain pots, called chocolate pots, and special cups were designed specifically for the popular new drink. The aristocratic practice of drinking morning chocolate with one's friends soon became a popular theme for seventeenth century artists.

After its introduction into England, chocolate mixed with hot milk was often served after dinner as a form of dessert. Eventually, however, the popularity of chocolate as a daily drink in England was usurped by coffee. Interestingly, it seems coffee as a beverage of choice permeated the Protestant countries—England, the Netherlands, and France—whereas chocolate remained popular in Catholic southern Europe, especially in Spain and Italy. Its rich nutritional value ensured chocolate's continued favor in the Catholic south, since chocolate could "safely" be served as a food substitute to penitents during periods of physically uncomfortable fasts.

SIGNIFICANCE

The rapid spread of chocolate consumption helped prompt the spread of imperialism throughout Europe during the colonial age. In the seventeenth century, the Dutch broke Spain's monopoly on cocoa beans when they captured Curaçao and brought cocoa beans from the New World to the Netherlands, where the drink rapidly grew in popularity. The French trade in chocolate spread similarly after France conquered Cuba and Haiti in the later half of the seventeenth century and began growing cocoa in New World plantations.

Although initially chocolate was used solely by the rich, the conquest of Jamaica by the British in the middle of the seventeenth century assured direct access to cacao production and enabled the trade to spread and grow in popularity in Great Britain. Cocoa was used as money in this era: One hundred seeds could be used to purchase a slave.

In this era, too, the Quakers, a pacifist religious sect, advocated the use of chocolate as an alternative to alcohol among the general British population. Members of Quaker families named Cadbury, Fry, and Rowntree held a monopoly on chocolate making in Britain. They emigrated to colonial America, primarily to Pennsylvania, where the Hershey's Chocolate Company is still located.

Eventually, cocoa production changed as Europeans began to colonize Africa. Production decreased in the Caribbean and South America as a new cocoa industry took effect in Africa. In the twenty-first century, African nations are among the world's leading producers of chocolate. Thus, the European craving for chocolate played a major role in imperial acquisition and colonial expansion.

—*M. Casey Diana*

FURTHER READING

Coe, Sophie D. *The True History of Chocolate*. London: Thames & Hudson, 1996. Written by archaeologists, this book examines botany, archaeology, sociology, and economics to provide a complete and precise history of chocolate.

Lopez, Ruth. *Chocolate: The Nature of Indulgence*. New York: Harry N. Abrams, 2002. Well-illustrated guide to the Chicago's Field Museum exhibition on chocolate. Features the historical origins of chocolate, the trade, and conjectures about its future. Discusses chocolate's role in slavery, war, and medicine.

Morton, Marcia, and Frederic Morton. *Chocolate: An Illustrated History*. New York: Crown, 1986. Traces the history of chocolate from pre-Columbian Mexico to recent times. The book's myriad illustrations make the story of chocolate come alive.

Schivelbusch, Wolfgang. *Tastes of Paradise: A Social History of Spices, Stimulants, and Intoxicants*. Translated by David Jacobson. New York: Pantheon Books, 1992. Although this book deals with coffee, tea, and alcohol, it contains a highly informative and very readable section on the history of chocolate and its cultural and economic impact.

SEE ALSO: 17th cent.: Europe Endorses Slavery; 1612: Introduction of Tobacco Farming in North America; Beginning c. 1615: Coffee Culture Flourishes; Aug. 20, 1619: Africans Arrive in Virginia; 1654: Portugal Retakes Control of Brazil; May 10, 1655: English Capture of Jamaica.

RELATED ARTICLES in *Great Lives from History: The Seventeenth Century, 1601-1700:* Anne of Austria; Samuel Pepys.

1656-1662
PERSECUTION OF IRANIAN JEWS

ʿAbbās II issued a series of decrees that required Persian Jews to wear special identifying headgear or badges. The decree also required Jews in Persia to convert to Islam or face possible death. The continued persecution of Jews led also to the establishment of "ghettos," or Jewish quarters within the region.

LOCALE: Iran
CATEGORIES: Cultural and intellectual history; religion and theology; wars, uprisings, and civil unrest

KEY FIGURES

ʿAbbās the Great (1571-1629), Ṣafavid shah, r. 1587-1629
ʿAbbās II (1633-1666), great-grandson of ʿAbbās the Great, Ṣafavid shah, r. 1642-1666
Bābāʿī ibn Luṭf (d. c. 1662), author and an eyewitness to the persecution of Jews
Muhammad Beg (d. c. 1674), Ṣafavid grand vizier, 1642-c. 1674

SUMMARY OF EVENT

Little is known about the history of Jews during the middle period of the Ṣafavid Dynasty in Persia (1501-1736), except accounts written by Muslims. The single notable exception is the contemporary Jewish account written by Bābāʿī ibn Luṭf, the *Kitāb-i anusī* (c. 1662; partial translation, 1987), a "book of a forced convert" that examines the persecution of Persian Jews in the period between 1617 to 1662.

It is not clear when the Jews became established in Persia, but anecdotal evidence has suggested their arrival dated from the period of the Assyrian deportations in the eighth century B.C.E. It is known that significant migration into the area of Persia had been established by the time of Cyrus the Great (538 B.C.E.). The legend of Mordecai and Esther, likely more folk tale than actuality, suggests that religious toleration was a way of life in the Persian Empire during the period of the kings (fifth century B.C.E.). Jewish merchants were successful in a variety of fields, such as trade, gold- and silversmithing, and weaving. Following the establishment of Islam as the state religion (seventh and eighth centuries C.E.), Jews were well established throughout the region, and were professionals in banking and were skilled in handicrafts. While the precise number of Jews in Persia during this period is questionable, a twelfth century census suggests a population in the range of 200,000 persons.

The conquest of Persia by Muslim Arabs began with the defeat of the ruling Sāsānid Dynasty in the Battle at Nahāvand in 642, and Islam replaced Zorastrianism as the state religion. Non-Muslims were called *dhimmis*, or second-class citizens.

Religious tolerance of Jews fluctuated with the fortunes of the state during the ensuing centuries. To some extent, Persia represented a Jewish backwater in the Diaspora. There exists little evidence for any significant contributions to the greater Jewish philosophy or leadership during this period. In general, Jewish authority and leadership was located in Baghdad.

The ʿAbbāsid Dynasty of Persia was overthrown in 1258 with the invasion from the north by Hülegü (c. 1217-1265), brother of Kublai Khan and grandson of Ghengis Khan. The Il-Khan Dynasty, lasting from 1258 to 1353 (its power ended in 1335), was relatively open in its acceptance of diverse religions. Subsequent dynasties, however, were not as tolerant.

In 1500, Ismāʿīl I (1487-1524), the son of a murdered Ṣafavid leader, became head of an army of tribesmen that practiced Shīʿite Islam. The order had its origins in the late thirteenth century under the leadership of Persian mystic Ṣafī od-Dīn (1252/1253-1334), patronymic ancestor to the Ṣafavid Dynasty and spiritual leader of the Ṣafavid Sufi Order, including Shīʿite Turkoman tribesmen from Armenia. In the course of two years, Ismāʿīl conquered much of Azerbaijan and Armenia, and he was crowned shah (king) of Persia in 1501.

During the Ṣafavid period, Shiism became the established state religion, and once again minorities, such as the Jews, were subject to persecution. The most important ruler in this period was Shah ʿAbbās the Great. In a series of military conquests over the Turks and Tatars, ʿAbbās expanded the Persian Empire over much of what is now Iraq and Iran. ʿAbbās also was known for the efficient administration of his kingdom as well as his tolerance of other religions.

In 1642, ʿAbbās II, the ten-year-old great-grandson of ʿAbbās the Great, was crowned shah. Persecution of the Jews was resumed during ʿAbbās II's reign. In these early years, a series of ministers retained much of the power for the throne. Muhammad Beg, grand vizier to the shah, appears to have been behind much of the persecution. Hebrew books were banned and destroyed while

Persian Jews were required to wear special headgear or badges as well as pay a special tax to distinguish them from the Muslim population.

In 1656, a royal decree was issued that required Jews to undergo a forced conversion. Numbers vary, but an estimated 20,000 to 100,000 Jews underwent such conversions. Such "new Muslims" received a monetary reward and were relieved of tax and headgear requirements. Many of these "converted" Jews practiced Islam only to appease their neighbors and ensure their own safety, and secretly maintained Jewish customs. Five years later, in 1661, a second edict reversed the first edict, allowing Jews to once again practice their religion openly.

The reason for the reverse may have been, in part, an economic one. Religious tolerance, not only of Jews but also of Christian and other minorities, was an important factor in maintaining trade relations with much of Europe. In addition, Jewish merchants were significant components of the economic activity within the empire.

Even though there is little documentation for this time in Persian Jewish history, Bābā'ī ibn Luṭf's *Kitāb-i anusī* is one helpful source. Luṭf lived with his family in the city of Kāshān during these years, and he describes in some detail the ordeals suffered by the Jewish population; he most likely wrote after the second decree.

The underlying reasons for the beginnings and extent of the persecutions are obscure. In the *Kitāb-i anusī*, Luṭf suggests that the event that triggered the persecutions was the theft by Jewish jewelers of a valuable dagger belonging to the shah. The historical accuracy of such a motive is questionable and may very well represent a story simply repeated by Luṭf. It is much more likely that a complex series of events sparked the persecutions. The years were marked by religious zealotry on the part of Beg. Though politically and militarily the period was relatively quiet, government mismanagement appeared to be widespread. Continuing economic unrest within the kingdom turned the population against Jews, who historically have been the scapegoats in many countries and in many time periods. To maintain a large standing army, taxes were imposed on the Muslim population. The payment of a "bonus" to Jews who underwent conversion exacerbated the problem. Ironically, persecution by government decree was marked by an absence of fanaticism, perhaps reflecting the long period of connections and relations between Jews and the larger Muslim population.

SIGNIFICANCE

The imposition of anti-Jewish decrees confirmed that despite hundreds of years of peaceful coexistence in a Muslim country, Jewish citizens were only as safe as the current ruling house would allow. In the years following 1662, Jewish authority became even more decentralized and representatives became active within individual provinces.

"Ghettos," though the term itself was not used at this time, were established within the larger cities as so-called Jewish quarters produced their own synagogues and ritual sites. The tax board, found in the capital of Eşfahān prior to the period of the decrees, was maintained but no longer controlled all Jewish communities.

Unlike the situation within the Ottoman Empire, no rabbi oversaw Jewish affairs in Persia. Prior to the accession of the ʿAbbāsid family, the *gaon* (Jewish spiritual leader and scholar) of Baghdad would appoint the chief rabbi of Eşfahān, while representatives of the Persian Jewish community were in frequent contact with outside authorities. In the period described by Luṭf, only a *nasi*, a religious authority—but not a rabbi—oversaw affairs. His primary affair with respect to the state was the collection of taxes.

Upon the death of Shah ʿAbbās II, Jewish persecution was resumed under a series of successors, continuing through the end of the Ṣafavid Dynasty. Arguably, only the accession of Nāder Shāh (r. 1736-1747) saved the Jews from annihilation.

—*Richard Adler*

FURTHER READING

Abisaab, Rula. *Converting Persia: Shia Islam and the Safavid Empire*. New York: I. B. Tauris, 2004. A discussion of socioeconomic policies and the development of Shīʿite Islam as the dominant religious power.

Floor, Willem. *Safavid Government Institutions*. Costa Mesa, Calif.: Mazda Publishers, 2001. An account of government and other state institutions covering the period from 1502-1736 in Iran, including the reign of Shah ʿAbbās II.

Jackson, Peter, and Lawrence Lockhart, eds. *The Timurid and Safavid Periods*. Vol. 6 in *The Cambridge History of Iran*. New York: Cambridge University Press, 1986. In-depth description of social and religious history, covering the period from 1335 to the 1730's.

Moreen, Vera Basch. *Iranian Jewry's Hour of Peril and Heroism: A Study of Bābāʿī ibn Luṭf's Chronicle, 1617-1662*. New York: American Academy for Jewish Research, 1987. Moreen examines Bābāʿī's descriptions of forced conversions and analyzes the contemporary life of Persian Jewry. Includes selected translations into English of Bābāʿī's chronicle.

Sykes, Sir Percy. *A History of Persia*. Vol. 2. New York: Barnes & Noble Books. 1969. A reprint of a two-volume set that covers the history of the region. Volume 2 explores the period from the beginning of Islam through World War I.

SEE ALSO: 1602-1639: Ottoman-Ṣafavid Wars; 1623-1640: Murad IV Rules the Ottoman Empire; 1642-1666: Reign of Shah ʿAbbās II; Jan., 1665: Shabbetai Tzevi's Messianic Movement Begins; June 30, 1680: Spanish Inquisition Holds a Grandiose *Auto-da-fé*.

RELATED ARTICLES in *Great Lives from History: The Seventeenth Century, 1601-1700:* ʿAbbās the Great; Manasseh ben Israel; Shabbetai Tzevi.

1656-1667
CONSTRUCTION OF THE PIAZZA SAN PIETRO

The Piazza San Pietro, built during the era of the Counter-Reformation, was designed by architect Gian Lorenzo Bernini as a symbol of the supremacy of the Catholic Church over Christendom.

LOCALE: Rome, Papal States (now in Italy)
CATEGORIES: Architecture; religion and theology

KEY FIGURES

Gian Lorenzo Bernini (1598-1680), appointed official architect of the Piazza San Pietro in 1629
Alexander VII (Fabio Chigi; 1599-1667), Roman Catholic pope, 1655-1667
Carlo Maderno (1556-1629), architect who built the facade of St. Peter's Basilica
Paul V (Camillo Borghese; 1552-1621), Roman Catholic pope, 1605-1621
Scipione Borghese (1576-1633), a cardinal and Bernini's patron and protector
Urban VIII (Maffeo Vincenzo Barberini; 1568-1644), Roman Catholic pope, 1623-1644

SUMMARY OF EVENT

The Piazza San Pietro was built to contain the crowds that stood in front of St. Peter's Basilica for pontifical blessings and addresses during high holy days. Designed by Gian Lorenzo Bernini, the piazza became a symbol of the reach of the Catholic Church, befitting the era of the Counter-Reformation when Catholics were calling Protestants to return to the faith.

The construction of the Piazza San Pietro was part of a larger program to complete the new basilica of St. Peter's, which was initiated by Pope Julius II (1503-1513) in the early years of the sixteenth century. The early Christian basilica that stood on the site since the fourth century became dilapidated, and Julius decided to replace it with a new, more imposing structure. Many have argued that Julius's decision is partly to blame for the emergence of Protestantism, as the large expenditures on this and other papal projects, along with the sale of indulgences under his reign and that of Pope Leo X (1512-1521), are what provoked Martin Luther to nail his Ninety-five Theses to the door of All Saints Church in Wittenberg in 1517.

Between 1606 and 1612, after a long and complex construction history that spanned most of the sixteenth century and included the participation of some of the most notable architects of the Renaissance—such as Donato Bramante and Michelangelo—Carlo Maderno provided a nave and façade for the new basilica. As the official architect of St. Peter's, the task fell on him to convert the mother church of the Catholic faith from a central to a longitudinal plan church that would place all focus on the altar and the rituals performed there during Mass. This decision was made to comply with dictates enacted by the Council of Trent (1545-1563), convoked to devise strategies to fight the spread of Protestantism.

Since the tomb of Saint Peter is directly below the altar, the longitudinal plan also would place focus on the saint who was charged by Christ to establish the Catholic Church and become its first pope. As the Protestants discredited papal authority, focus on Saint Peter's tomb would symbolically denote the Papacy's God-given right to rule over Christendom. Maderno extended the basilica by adding a three-bay nave and then the façade. His intention was to also include a tower at either end, but underground springs prevented their completion. Only the bases for the towers were built, granting the façade a disproportionate relation between its length and height.

In 1655, Alexander VII gave Bernini the commission to build the piazza in front of St. Peter's. By the time of

The Piazza San Pietro, leading to St. Peter's Basilica in Vatican City, Rome. (Hulton|Archive by Getty Images)

his appointment, Bernini had already enjoyed a long relationship with the Papacy. Through his father, the sculptor Pietro Bernini, Gian Lorenzo as a child was brought to the attention of Pope Paul V and his nephew, Cardinal Scipione Borghese. The Borghese immediately recognized that Bernini was a prodigy, and by age seventeen the boy was receiving important sculpture commissions from these two men. Through them, Bernini also cultivated a friendship with Cardinal Maffeo Vincenzo Barberini. Six years after Barberini ascended the papal throne as Urban VIII, he appointed the sculptor the official architect of St. Peter's (1629).

In 1637, Bernini proposed the completion of Maderno's towers, which the pope enthusiastically approved. The first tower was almost complete when it cracked and, as a result, the project was abandoned, which caused Bernini public humiliation. In 1655, Alexander VII ascended the throne and charged Bernini with the design of the piazza, which gave the artist the opportunity to redeem himself.

In building the piazza, Bernini had to fulfill certain requisites. He was to include in his design the obelisk raised in 1586 in front of St. Peter's by the architect Domenico Fontana. He also was asked to devise a plan that would allow the pope to be seen by all who came to the piazza during his public appearances from either the benediction loggia on the basilica's facade or his private apartments on the top floor of the papal palace to the right of the basilica. Bernini complied with both requirements. He was skilled in the art of manipulating visual perception as he had designed a number of elaborate sets for theatrical productions. He took the opportunity to correct the problems of proportion in Maderno's facade by applying his skills in perception to his design.

Bernini's design consisted of a trapezoid followed by an oval enclosed by a classic colonnade at either side. By tapering the colonnades inward where the trapezoid meets the oval, Bernini was able to visually narrow Maderno's design. His inspiration came from Michelangelo's Piazza del Campidoglio on the Capitoline Hill, which also uses a trapezoid and oval, juxtaposed one over the other. In invoking the Capitoline Hill where the Roman senate once stood, Bernini's piazza connected the glory of the ancient Rome of the emperors to that of the new Rome of the popes and indicated the Church's triumph over paganism.

Bernini's colonnades seem like arms that jut out from the basilica to embrace those who stand within their confines. Bernini himself referred to these colonnades as the all-embracing arms of the Church. They were meant to symbolically extend an invitation to those who had abandoned Catholicism in favor of Protestantism to return to the Catholic faith. The arms also implied the Church's willingness to forgive those who had strayed. Also, Bernini's colonnades are capped by a balustrade and above it stand sculpted saints who either interact with the viewer or with each other. When crowds congregate in the piazza to hear and see the pope and receive his blessing, the sculpted saints seem to be commenting on the event, granting it a celebratory tone.

The Piazza San Pietro is now accessed from the Via della Conciliazione, a wide boulevard designed in 1936 under Benito Mussolini's regime and completed in 1950. In the seventeenth century, however, St. Peter's was approached through narrow, winding streets. Bernini's plan included a never-built third arm to be positioned between the two existing colonnades. His intention was to provide an element of surprise. As the faithful made their way to the piazza navigating the tight network of streets and houses and passed through one of the narrow entrances at either side of the third arm, they would suddenly be awed by the vast, open space in front of them. As the structure stands today, the contrast between the forest of columns within the arms and the open areas of the piazza offer a similar dramatic effect. Bernini sought to stimulate not only the visitors' visual but also their auditory perception. The sound of gushing water from fountains at either side of the obelisk adds a festive air to the piazza.

The Piazza San Pietro is part of the whole experience of visiting St. Peter's. Pilgrims are greeted by the colonnades and invited into the basilica. Once inside, visitors are provided with a clear, unobstructed view of the altar and the tomb of Saint Peter, the first pope, marked by Bernini's baldachin, a bronze canopy of gigantic proportions that, together with the dome, represents the Holy Trinity. Through the canopy, one sees the *Cathedra Petri* (chair of Peter), a monumental reliquary, also executed by Bernini, containing the throne of Saint Peter. Latin and Greek doctors of the Church support the throne, which is inscribed with the words *Pasce oves meas* (look after my flock). The message is clear: The pope is the heir to Saint Peter, who was charged by Christ/God to establish the one and only Church that provides humanity with salvation.

SIGNIFICANCE

Bernini's Piazza San Pietro is one of the greatest examples of architecture from the era of the Counter-Reformation. It is emblematic of the political and religious anxieties the Catholic Church was then experiencing as a result of the Protestant threat. The Church utilized all possible means to regain its political hegemony over the Christian world, including art and architecture. By utilizing symbolic, visual, and sensory elements and adding a festive mood, Bernini created an environment that celebrated the triumph of the Church over its enemies and proclaimed the supreme authority of the Papacy over Christendom.

—*Lilian H. Zirpolo*

FURTHER READING

Hibbard, Howard. *Bernini*. New York: Penguin Books, 1990. A survey of Bernini's activities as sculptor and architect, with a section on the Piazza San Pietro.

Kitao, Timothy. *Circle and Oval in the Square of Saint Peter's: Bernini's Art of Planning*. New York: New York University Press, 1974. A comprehensive study of Bernini's design for the Piazza San Pietro.

Marder, Tod A. *Bernini and the Art of Architecture*. New York: Abbeville Press, 1998. This work includes a chapter on the Piazza San Pietro and the Rome of Alexander VII.

Morrissey, Jake. *The Genius in the Design: Bernini, Borromini, and the Rivalry That Transformed Rome*. New York: Morrow, 2005. Outlines the relationship and conflict between Bernini and Francesco Borromini, the two most significant Italian Baroque architects.

Varriano, John. *Italian Baroque and Rococo Architecture*. New York: Oxford University Press, 1986. This book provides a chapter on Bernini's architectural projects, including a detailed account of the construction of the Piazza San Pietro.

Zanella, Andrea, ed. *Bernini: All His Works From All the World*. Rome: Palombi, 1993. A catalogue raisonné of Bernini's oeuvre.

SEE ALSO: c. 1601-1620: Emergence of Baroque Art; 1609-1617: Construction of the Blue Mosque; 1675-1708: Wren Supervises the Rebuilding of St. Paul's Cathedral.

RELATED ARTICLES in *Great Lives from History: The Seventeenth Century, 1601-1700:* Alexander VII; Gian Lorenzo Bernini; Francesco Borromini; Guarino Guarini; Louis Le Vau; Paul V; Urban VIII; Sir Christopher Wren.

1656-1676
Ottoman Empire's Brief Recovery

After a period of decline within the Ottoman Empire, two grand viziers of the Köprülü family initiated imperial revival. The revival would not last, however, as failed battles and conquests by the empire took their toll, uniting Christendom against the Turks and marking the beginning of the decline of a major world empire.

Locale: Ottoman Empire (now Turkey) and the Balkans

Categories: Government and politics; wars, uprisings, and civil unrest

Key Figures

Mehmed IV Avci (1642-1693), Ottoman sultan, r. 1648-1687

Hatice Turhan Sultan (1627-1683), mother of Mehmed IV Avci and Queen Mother

Köprülü Mehmed Paşa (d. 1661), Ottoman grand vizier, 1656-1661

Köprülü Fazıl Ahmed Paşa (1635-1676), Ottoman grand vizier, 1661-1676

György II Rákóczi (1621-1660), prince of Transylvania, r. 1648-1660

Michael Apafi (1632-1690), prince of Transylvania, r. 1661-1690

Summary of Event

The reign of Süleyman the Magnificent (1520-1566) marked the culmination of the Ottoman Empire as a great power. During the four succeeding reigns (to 1617), the momentum was sustained, but thereafter the empire began to decline, a decline that was only temporarily reversed during the reign of Murad IV (1623-1640). Under Murad's ineffectual successors, there was further deterioration in the once-imposing imperial structure.

Mehmed IV Avci was just six years old at the time of his accession, meaning that real power lay with the Queen Mother, Hatice Turhan Sultan (also known as Khadija Turhan Hadice), who wielded unlimited control. The young sultan was encouraged to indulge his passion for hunting. Soon, the empire began to fall apart. In particular, its protracted war with Venice over Crete, the empire's last significant colonial possession, was going badly. In June of 1656, the Venetians defeated the Ottoman fleet at the Dardanelles and occupied the nearby islands of Lemnos and Tenedos. Desperate remedies were needed. On September 15, 1656, at a meeting of the divan (council of state), the current grand vizier was dismissed and an octogenarian of comparative obscurity, Köprülü Mehmed Paşa, replaced him. Members of the Köprülü family were to retain the vizierate in almost unbroken succession until 1710. The first two Köprülü grand viziers (the second was Mehmed Paşa's son, Fazıl Ahmed Paşa) undertook vigorous reforms and military initiatives that temporarily restored the empire to much of its former prestige.

A product of the Ottoman slave-bureaucracy, Mehmed Paşa was born in Rojnik, near Berat, Albania. Trained in the sultan's palace, he graduated to a succession of governorships in Anatolia and Rumelia. By the standards of the times, his was not an exceptional career, but he had vast knowledge into how the empire worked and was a shrewd judge of individuals. He also knew the precariousness of high office in Constantinople and made his acceptance of the vizierate conditional: First, the sultan was to issue no commands on the basis of any written communications that did not originate with him; second, no high official was to act independently of him; third, he would brook no interference in the making of appointments; and fourth, the sultan was to ignore any calumnies made about him. With his conditions agreed to, he set about a thorough overhaul of the administration, placing his protégés in key positions and ruthlessly weeding out the corrupt or incompetent. Many heads rolled.

Mehmed Paşa, essentially conservative, thought up reforms aimed at ensuring a return to the glories of Süleyman's time. First, however, internal order had to be restored. Parts of Anatolia and Syria had seen rampant disorder for half a century, as brigand bands collaborated with corrupt local governors. By February of 1659, the rebel pashas (leaders) had been rounded up and executed, with the head of the foremost pasha displayed in Constantinople as a warning. Also, the war with Venice demanded immediate attention. The war fleet that had been lost at the Dardanelles was rebuilt, and it recaptured Tenebos in August and Lesbos in November of 1657, enabling a strong fight for Crete.

In the Balkans, though, the Ottoman position remained weak. From the time of the close of the Fifteen Years' War between the Ottomans and the Holy Roman Empire in 1606 (Treaty of Zsitvatorok), the vassal princes of Transylvania—Gabriel Bethlen, György I Rákóczi, and György II Rákóczi—had functioned as virtually independent rulers, setting a bad example to the voievods (princes) of Walachia and Moldavia. In 1657, without the sultan's permission, Rákóczi led an army into Poland, hoping to acquire the Polish throne. The Poles offered a spirited resistance, Rákóczi's forces withdrew, and the Crimean Tatars, loyal vassals of the sultan, fell upon the retreating army and forced its surrender. In October, 1657, Mehmed Paşa took the field, ordering the Transylvanian diet at Gyulafehérvár (now Alba Iulia, Romania), the capital, to depose Rákóczi and choose a new prince. Rákóczi defied this order, the principality was laid waste, and Gyulafehérvár burned to the ground. The newly appointed prince agreed to pay an annual tribute of 40,000 gold pieces as well as reparations, and Mehmed Paşa returned to Constantinople.

Civil war in Transylvania led to the death of Rákóczi, at Nagyvárad (now Oradea, Romania) in 1660. Mehmed Paşa sent into Transylvania a new army, which captured the great fortress of Várad (August). Transylvania was now restored to vassal status. A compliant prince, Michael Apafi, would rule Transylvania for the next three decades.

Mehmed Paşa died in 1661, after a short but strenuous administration. At his request, he was succeeded as grand vizier by his twenty-six-year-old son, Fazıl Ahmed Paşa, who provided continuity with his father's administration. Scholar and soldier, Ahmed Paşa was extremely able, having held several provincial governorships before returning to Constantinople to act as his father's deputy during the latter's final illness. While he continued his father's reforms, improving the quality and discipline of the army and using the powers of the central government to protect the non-Muslim, tax-paying peasantry (*reaya*), his military actions raised the empire's prestige to a level not seen for a century. Moreover, the harshness and abrasiveness of his father was replaced by a certain suavity that placated opposition. War with the Habsburg Dynasty during 1663-1664 started because of Austrian incursions across the Transylvanian frontier. Ahmed Paşa led his forces into Hungary, but he was defeated at Szentgotthárd (Saint Gotthard) in August, 1664. Christendom was jubilant, but the Ottoman army extracted itself virtually intact, enabling Ahmed Paşa to negotiate highly favorable terms with the Austrians.

By the Treaty of Vasvár (August 10, 1664), Austria withdrew its troops from Transylvania and acknowledged Apafi as prince. The Ottomans retained possession of Hungary and Transylvania, and Holy Roman Emperor Leopold I agreed to pay reparations. Ottoman forces were free to complete the conquest of Crete. The struggle with Venice had dragged on since 1645, and Candia (now Iráklion, island of Crete) had sustained a twenty-eight-month siege. The garrison finally surrendered in September, 1669, and the conquest of the island was complete.

Ahmed Paşa then turned his attention to the "triangle" northwest of the Black Sea, where Ottoman interests clashed with those of Poland and Muscovy. The Black Sea littoral had been firmly restored to Ottoman control by the earlier pacification of Transylvania, which had forced into line Walachia and Moldavia. Beyond Moldavia, between the lower Prut River and the lower Dniester River, was the Ottoman province of Bessarabia, east of which lay the Tatar khanate of the Crimea, an Ottoman vassal since 1475. The entire region to the north became chronically unstable since the Dnieper Cossack chieftain Bohdan Khmelnytsky (1595-1657) had led the great revolt against Poland in 1648-1654, inadvertently luring Muscovy into the resulting power vacuum.

Ahmed Paşa saw the danger to Ottoman interests inherent in the situation, and determined to occupy Podolia, which was then Polish territory located between the upper Dniester and Bug Rivers northeast of Bessarabia. Sultan Mehmed IV Avci took to the battlefield. Ottoman forces overran much of Podolia between June and December, 1672, capturing the great fortress of Kamieniec Podolski on August 27, 1672. Polish resistance collapsed, and in the Treaty of Buczacz (October, 1672), Polish negotiators ceded all Podolia, together with an annual tribute of 22,000 gold ducats. With Crete, therefore, Podolia became the last Ottoman territorial acquisition.

SIGNIFICANCE

The administration of the first two Köprülü grand viziers achieved a tangible renewal of the Ottoman Empire, but the empire could not be saved in the long run. The two fought corruption and cronyism (other than their own), they inflicted severe pain on evildoers at all levels of government, and they achieved substantial military success. In a word, they did what the Ottomans had always done best: fought and conquered. Unfortunately, that very success may have hastened its own decline.

Ahmed Paşa was succeeded as grand vizier by his brother-in-law, Merzifonlu Kara Mustafa Paşa, in 1676. Swayed by the very success of his predecessors, Kara Mustafa recklessly launched what has been called the last jihad (holy war), the failed Siege of Vienna in 1683, which led to his execution in Belgrade on the sultan's orders and to the unleashing of what has been called the last crusade. The armies of the Holy League (1684-1699) swept back the Ottoman forces to the Danube River, and at the disastrous Treaty of Karlowitz (1699), which had been negotiated by another Köprülü, Grand Vizier Amcazade Hüseyin Paşa (1697-1702), the Ottomans were forced to relinquish Hungary and Transylvania to the Habsburgs, Podolia to the Poles, and the Morea to Venice. Karlowitz marked the end of an epoch. Henceforth, the Ottoman posture would be defensive rather than offensive.

—*Gavin R. G. Hambly*

FURTHER READING

Dankoff, Robert. *The Intimate Life of an Ottoman Statesman*. Albany: State University of New York Press, 1991. This text examines the Köprülü age, as witnessed by Evliya Çelebi (1611-c. 1684), the celebrated Ottoman man of letters.

Goodwin, Godfrey. *The Janissaries*. London: Saqi Books, 1994. Goodwin provides an excellent account of the Ottoman war machine.

Greene, Molly. *A Shared World: Christians and Muslims in the Early Modern Mediterranean*. Princeton, N.J.: Princeton University Press, 2000. Greene explores the Crete of the time of the Ottoman conquest and after.

Kinross, Lord. *The Ottoman Centuries: The Rise and Fall of the Turkish Empires*. New York: Morrow Quill, 1977. Kinross provides an engaging, leisurely narrative.

Makkai, Laszlo, and Zoltan Szasz. *History of Transylvania*. Vol. 2. Toronto, Ont.: Hungarian Research Institute of Canada, 2002. A detailed account of the Ottoman presence in Transylvania.

Murphey, Rhoads. *Ottoman Warfare, 1500-1700*. New Brunswick, N.J.: Rutgers University Press, 1999. A useful work that examines seventeenth century Ottoman military campaigning.

Shaw, Stanford J. *History of the Ottoman Empire and Modern Turkey*. Vol. 1 in *Empire of the Gazis: The Rise and Decline of the Ottoman Empire, 1280-1808*. New York: Cambridge University Press, 1996. A standard scholarly history, with integrated treatment of the Candian war and Ottoman governmental developments.

Sugar, Peter F. *Southeastern Europe Under Ottoman Rule, 1354-1804*. Seattle: University of Washington Press, 1977. An authoritative account of Ottoman involvement in the Balkans.

SEE ALSO: 1623-1640: Murad IV Rules the Ottoman Empire; Aug. 22, 1645-Sept., 1669: Turks Conquer Crete; Summer, 1672-Fall, 1676: Ottoman-Polish Wars; 1677-1681: Ottoman-Muscovite Wars; July 14-Sept. 12, 1683: Defeat of the Ottomans at Vienna; 1697-1702: Köprülü Reforms of Hüseyin Paşa; Jan. 26, 1699: Treaty of Karlowitz.

RELATED ARTICLES in *Great Lives from History: The Seventeenth Century, 1601-1700:* Merzifonlu Kara Mustafa Paşa; Bohdan Khmelnytsky; Kösem Sultan; Leopold I; Murad IV.

February, 1656
HUYGENS IDENTIFIES SATURN'S RINGS

After developing an improved technique to grind lenses to precise shapes, Huygens constructed an improved 50-power telescope that helped him identify the unusual elongation of Saturn as a ring or disk surrounding the planet. Huygens also discovered Titan, Saturn's largest moon, and showed that the Orion nebula was composed of many stars.

LOCALE: The Hague, United Provinces (now in the Netherlands)

CATEGORIES: Astronomy; physics; mathematics; science and technology

KEY FIGURES

Christiaan Huygens (1629-1695), Dutch astronomer who identified Saturn's rings

Galileo (1564-1642), Italian astronomer who first observed Saturn's rings but thought they were large moons on both sides of the planet

Gian Domenico Cassini (1625-1712), Italian astronomer who believed Saturn's rings were a multitude of small particles in orbit around the planet

SUMMARY OF EVENT

In 1610, Galileo was the first to observe Saturn with a telescope. He recorded that Saturn had an odd appearance, with projections that appeared to be "handles" at both sides. Galileo, however, did not understand his observations. He thought the handles could be two large moons, one on each side of the planet, so he described Saturn as a group of three, nearly touching objects that do not move relative to one another. Two years later, in 1612, Galileo became even more puzzled when he observed that Saturn's "handles" had disappeared.

Although Saturn's ring system was first observed by Galileo, Dutch physicist and mathematician Christiaan Huygens is credited with their discovery because he was the first person to identify the observed elongation of Saturn as the presence of a disk or ring surrounding the planet.

Huygens had studied law and mathematics at the University of Leiden from 1645 until 1647, and he published a series of papers on mathematics, but actually he had trained to be a diplomat. In 1649, Huygens was a member of a diplomatic team that was sent to Denmark, but he was not offered a permanent position in diplomacy. In 1650, Huygens returned home and lived on an allowance from his father.

Both Huygens as well as his brother Constantine were interested in astronomy, but they found that the telescopes then available were too short to resolve features on the planets. The brothers gained an interest in lens grinding and telescope construction to improve the quality of their observations, and, around 1654, they developed a new and better way of grinding lenses for telescopes. Their techniques significantly reduced chromatic aberration, an effect that causes simple lenses to focus different colors of light at different points of the telescope lens. They also introduced the use of optical stops, masks along the tube of a telescope that intercept light reflected from the walls of the tube, keeping reflected light from reaching the lens and blurring the image.

Using one of his own lenses, Christiaan Huygens built a self-designed 50-power refracting telescope. With this new telescope, in 1655, he discovered Titan, the first and largest moon of Saturn. Later that year, he visited Paris and informed the astronomers there, including Ismaël Boulliau (1605-1694), of his discovery. By this time, Boulliau was a well-recognized astronomer who had published his *Astronomia philolaica* (1645), in which he adopted Johannes Kepler's idea that planets moved in elliptical orbits around the Sun.

Huygens's discovery of Titan was near the time of the "ring plane crossing" phenomenon, that is, when Saturn's rings are viewed edge-on from Earth, making them difficult to see. Thus, Huygens was unable to see the rings when he discovered Titan. In February of 1656, the true shape of the Saturn's rings was apparent to Huygens. He recognized that the bulge, which Galileo thought were two moons, actually was a thin, flat disk or ring, which did not touch the planet and was inclined to the ecliptic plane.

Huygens reported his conclusions in a message to Boulliau, in order to establish the priority of his discovery. However, Huygens did not make a public announcement of his results until 1658, in a letter to the scientific academy in Paris.

Huygens's description of Saturn's rings was not immediately accepted. At least three other astronomers offered different explanations for Saturn's bulge after Huygens's discovery. Gilles Personne de Roberval (1602-1675) proposed that Saturn emitted vapors, like a volcano, from its equatorial region. When the concentration of vapors was high enough, they would become visible as a belt around the planet. Johannes Hevelius, an astronomer from Gdansk, proposed that Saturn was not a sphere, but rather an ellipsoidal, and the bulge was simply part of the planet. Giovanni Battista Odierna (1597-1660) suggested that Saturn had two large dark areas at its equator, which appeared to observers as "handles."

Christiaan Huygens. (Library of Congress)

Even with the excellent view of Saturn that Huygens had through his improved telescope, it was not until 1659 that he correctly inferred the geometry of Saturn's rings, because he had to wait until he had observed them over a significant part of their cycle. In his *Systema Saturnium, sive de causis mirandorum Saturni phænomenôn, et comite ejus planeta novo* (1659; the system of Saturn, or on the matter of Saturn's remarkable appearance, and its satellite, the new planet; better known as *Systema Saturnium*), Huygens explained the phases and changes in the shape of the ring based on the expected view of a rigid disk surrounding the planet and inclined relative to Earth's orbital path around the Sun. Huygens noted that all earlier observations of Saturn suffered from inadequate resolution. He argued against the models proposed by Roberval, Hevelius, and Hodierna, and offered his idea of a disk surrounding Saturn at its equator but tilted at an angle of about 20 degrees to the plane of Saturn's orbit. He explained that this tilt is what causes the appearance of Saturn's ring to vary as Saturn moves around the Sun.

Although Boulliau generally accepted Huygens's idea of a ring, he believed the ring should still be seen from Earth even when edge-on. Many other astronomers were not convinced. In 1660, Eustachio Divini (1610-1685), an Italian instrument (and telescope) maker, published his "Brevis annotatio in *Systema Saturnium* Christiani Eugenii" (brief comment on Christian Huygens's *Systema Saturnium*), which attacked not only Huygens's ring theory but also the validity of his observations. This book suggested Saturn had four moons, two dark ones near the planet and two bright ones farther out. The handles appeared when the bright moons were in front of the dark ones, partially blocking them from Earth.

Huygens quickly replied with his "Brevis assertio *Systematis Saturnii* sui" (1660; brief defense of *Systema Saturnium*), pointing out that the work of other astronomers contained incorrect observations, which could only be explained by their use of inferior telescopes. Hevelius accepted the ring theory after reading "Brevis assertio *Systematis Saturnii* sui." By 1665, the matter was finally settled, when telescope quality had improved to the point that most astronomers were able to replicate Huygens's observations.

The question that faced the astronomers next was how such a disk could be stable. Huygens thought the ring was a solid structure, but Gian Domenico Cassini proposed that the ring consisted of a large number of small particles, all orbiting around Saturn. Cassini, who conducted extensive observations of Saturn using telescopes at the new Paris Observatory, noted that there was a dark gap separating the ring into two separate rings. This showed that Saturn's rings could not be a single, rigid disk, as proposed by Huygens.

In was not until 1858 that James Clerk Maxwell (1831-1879), a Scottish physicist, was able to perform a detailed mathematical analysis that showed how a ring composed of many tiny particles could be stable. By the end of the nineteenth century, astronomers were able to measure the speed of the particles at the inner and outer edges of the ring. This measurement was inconsistent with a solid rotating disk, and it agreed with the orbital speeds calculated from Kepler's laws of motion.

Huygens also used his improved telescope to view other astronomical objects. In 1656, he observed the Orion nebula and was able to show that it consisted of a large group of individual stars. He also discovered several other nebulae and double stars.

Significance

Huygens's greatest contribution to astronomy was the improvement of techniques for making telescopes. This work significantly improved their resolution, making it possible for him and future astronomers to resolve details that had been hidden from earlier astronomers. The improved telescope allowed Huygens to discover Titan, Saturn's largest moon, and Saturn's ring system. The rings around Saturn remained a unique planetary feature until 1977, when fainter rings were discovered around Uranus, and shortly after, around the two other gas giant planets, Jupiter and Neptune.

Even more important than these observations, however, was Huygens's insight that the Saturnian system was a miniature solar system, with Titan orbiting Saturn the way Earth orbits the Sun, as Nicolaus Copernicus and Kepler had proposed. Thus, Huygens's observations supported the Copernican idea of a Sun-centered (heliocentric) rather than an Earth-centered (geocentric) solar system. His work was done at a time when a great debate on the issue of a heliocentric versus geocentric system was raging among the best minds in astronomy in Europe.

Because of his great contribution to the understanding of Saturn, the National Aeronautics and Space Administration (NASA) named its Titan space probe the Huygens probe.

—*George J. Flynn*

Further Reading

Alexander, Arthur F. O'Donel. *The Planet Saturn: A History of Observation, Theory, and Discovery*. 1962.

Reprint. New York: Dover, 1980. A classic work on the scientific history of Saturn. Includes an index.

Andriesse, Cornelis D. *Christian Huygens*. Paris: Albin Michel, 2000. An excellent account of the life and achievements of Huygens.

Bell, A. E. *Christian Huygens and the Development of Science in the Seventeenth Century*. London: Edward Arnold, 1947. An excellent account of Huygens's contributions to astronomy and mathematics.

Brashear, Ronald. "Christiaan Huygens and His *Systema Saturnium*." http://www.sil.si.edu/DigitalCollections/HST/Huygens/huygens.htm. Accessed February, 2005. Brashear, the curator of Science and Technology Rare Books in the Special Collections Department of the Smithsonian Institution Libraries, provides an introduction to Huygens's major work on Saturn. The site also includes a digital version of the work in its original Latin.

Moore, Patrick. *Eyes on the University: The Story of the Telescope*. New York: Springer-Verlag, 1997. Written to commemorate the fortieth anniversary of the British television series "The Sky at Night," this illustrated account of the telescope's history is intended for general readers and amateur astronomers.

North, John. *The Norton History of Astronomy and Cosmology*. New York: Norton, 1995. North, a professor in the history of the exact sciences, discusses the telescope as part of the evolution of astronomy. Includes an index and a thirty-four-page bibliographical essay.

Struik, Dirk J. *The Land of Stevin and Huygens: A Sketch of Science and Technology in the Dutch Republic During the Golden Century*. Boston: Kluwer, 1981. A short, illustrated work that centers on Huygens as the major claim to fame of the Netherlands for the seventeenth century scientific revolution.

Yoder, Joella G. *Unrolling Time: Huygens and the Mathematization of Nature*. New York: Cambridge University Press, 2004. A 252-page account of the interrelationship between mathematics and physics in the work of the Dutch mathematician, physicist, and astronomer.

SEE ALSO: Sept., 1608: Invention of the Telescope; 1610: Galileo Confirms the Heliocentric Model of the Solar System; 1632: Galileo Publishes *Dialogue Concerning the Two Chief World Systems, Ptolemaic and Copernican*; 1665: Cassini Discovers Jupiter's Great Red Spot; 1673: Huygens Explains the Pendulum.

RELATED ARTICLES in *Great Lives from History: The Seventeenth Century, 1601-1700:* Gian Domenico Cassini; Galileo; Johannes and Elisabetha Hevelius; Christiaan Huygens; Johannes Kepler.

1657
WORK BEGINS ON JAPAN'S NATIONAL HISTORY

Tokugawa Mitsukuni, lord of Mito, initiated a project for a monumental national history, the Dai Nihon shi, *modeled on traditional Chinese dynastic histories. Mitsukuni selected the Chinese scholar Zhu Shunsui as the chief editor. Mitsukuni's perseverance established the* Dai Nihon shi *as the main history of Japan until modern times.*

LOCALE: Japan

CATEGORIES: Historiography; literature; government and politics

KEY FIGURES

Tokugawa Mitsukuni (1628-1701), lord of Mito, who set up and supported the *Dai Nihon shi* project

Zhu Shunsui (1600-1682), Chinese scholar recruited by Tokugawa Mitsukuni as an early *Dai Nihon shi* editor

Tokugawa Tsunayoshi (1646-1709), Japanese shogun, r. 1680-1709, and patron of Mitsukuni's rivals

Asaka Tanpaku (1656-1737), *Dai Nihon shi* editor who established a tradition of critical analysis

Fujita Yūkoku (1774-1826), *Dai Nihon shi* historian who advocated antishogunal activism

SUMMARY OF EVENT

Tokugawa Mitsukuni's father, the first daimyo, or lord, of Mito, was the son of the first Tokugawa shogun, Tokugawa Ieyasu, and the brother of the second Tokugawa shogun, Tokugawa Hidetada. As the second Mito daimyo, Mitsukuni was frequently in attendance at the shogun's court in Edo. Daimyos from most domains, or *hans*, were required to demonstrate their allegiance to the shogunate by alternating residence in Edo at the shogun's court with periods back in their own feudal territories, under the system generally referred to as *sankin kōtai*, "alternating service." Being closely connected with the immediate shogunal family, with his *han* relatively close to Edo, Mitsukuni was exempted from *sankin kōtai* obligations. His family had a permanent Mito domain estate of their own within the shogun's Edo Castle complex, and Mitsukuni was on close personal terms with all the shoguns who reigned during his lifetime.

Until late adolescence, Mitsukuni had little interest in his studies. This changed when his teachers introduced him to the *Shiji* (first century B.C.E.; *Records of the Grand Historian of China*, 1960) by the Han Chinese historian Sima Qian. The idealism and devotion to principle in this work moved him deeply and made him a lifelong student of history. This Chinese history covered events from earliest recorded times almost up to the author's own era. It was made up of comprehensive sequential biographies, critiques of historical figures by Sima Qian, topical essays, and explanatory tables. It was quite unlike other chronological diary-style histories. Mitsukuni adopted the ideals and analytical methods he learned from the *Shiji* and developed a lifelong respect for this Chinese history.

The noted Edo Neo-Confucian scholar Hayashi Razan, however, had a great respect for Sima Guang's *Zizhi tongjian* (late eleventh century; comprehensive mirror for governance, partial translation 1996) a Chinese history arranged mainly on chronological lines. Hayashi began a comprehensive history of Japan along the same lines in 1644, under the patronage of the shogunate. It was to be close to three hundred volumes in length, like the *Zizhi tongjian*, and titled the *Honchō tsūgan* (Japanese comprehensive mirror). Hayashi worked on it for a dozen years, but the great Meireki Fire, which incinerated much of Edo in January, 1657, destroyed much of his manuscript and notes. Hayashi Razan died soon afterward, but his son Hayashi Gahō received fresh patronage from the shogunate to resume the effort, and the Hayashi family's *Honchō tsūgan* was completed in 1670, 310 volumes in length. The next shogun, Tokugawa Tsunayoshi, continued to support Hayashi Gahō's historical and philosophical research.

The 1657 Meireki Fire also destroyed part of the Edo Castle complex, so the official Mito residence was moved from there to Komagome, in northern Edo. Perhaps in part because it seemed at the time that the Hayashi Japanese history project had ended, Mitsukuni decided to set up his own Japanese history project, using the *Shiji* format of sequential essays, rather than Hayashi's more strictly chronological format. Mitsukuni hired a staff of scholars to begin this project in Komagome. In 1661, after Mitsukuni officially succeeded to the position of Mito daimyo, the Mito Edo residence moved to new permanent quarters in Koishikawa, and the history project staff subsequently moved there as well.

In 1665, Mitsukuni invited an established scholar from China, Zhu Shunsui, to help supervise the history project. The text was written in a Japanese adaptation of classical Chinese, so Zhu was helpful as an editor, assuring stylistic authenticity as well as basic fidelity of the history to the Chinese *Shiji* model. Zhu, who had arrived in Japan in 1659, trained a generation of Mito historians in careful scholarship and the practical application of Confucian thought to the analysis of historical and contemporary issues.

Mitsukuni's Japanese history project, which came to be known as the *Dai Nihon shi* (history of great Japan), followed the *kiden* format of annals and biographies in the *Shiji*. The *hongi*, basic annals, were accounts of the lives of one hundred mythical and actual emperors, from the legendary primordial ruler Jimmu Tennō through Emperor Go-Komatsu, whose reign ended in 1412. The *retsuden*, eminent biographies, were records of the lives of court ministers, shogunate notables and officials, and other prominent historical figures. The remaining two categories were *shi*, treatises on religious rites, court ceremonies, administrative procedures, various fields of learning, and the like; and *hyō*, tables illustrating civil and military government organization, ranks and offices, and so on. During Mitsukuni's time, attention was given to the first two categories. The project took almost 250 years to complete—by 1906, there were 397 volumes in all, made up of 73 basic annal volumes, 170 biographical volumes, 126 volumes of treatises, and 28 volumes of tables.

Asaka Tanpaku, trained by Zhu Shunsui, became head of the *Dai Nihon shi* project in 1693, continuing in charge on and off for most of the next forty years. Following the lead of Sima Qian, he wrote critical analyses of historical figures in accord with Confucian standards. These critiques were later deleted on the grounds that they were "too frank." The unconventional Confucian scholar Rai Sanyō, however, later edited them as an independent book, the *Dai Nihon shi sansō* (nineteenth century; collected appraisals from the *Dai Nihon shi*).

By the mid-eighteenth century, a school of Mito history had developed, emphasizing the national importance of the imperial institution. This ideology became an important factor in the development of the imperial restoration movement. This sort of use of the writing of history as a medium for criticism brought serious sanctions from the shogunal authorities. Fujita Yūkoku, a *Dai Nihon shi* historian who became the head of all Mito official scholarship in 1807, developed a critique of the power of the shogun, and advocated local autonomy of daimyos under the national authority of the emperor. Yūkoku's son Tōko and the young Mito lord Tokugawa Nariaki both became advocates of national reform and the restoration of imperial power. They suffered periods of persecution and imprisonment for their views, resulting in Nariaki's death in confinement in 1860. Yūkoku's student and successor as Mito chief historian, Aizawa Yasushi, was also confined by the shogunate for a time.

SIGNIFICANCE

With the fall of the shogunate and the Meiji Restoration in 1868, the Mito School of History, originally founded by Mitsukuni and further developed by Fujita Yūkoku, was vindicated by events. Its views became the basis for a new official nationalism, leading to material progress but also to militarism and in turn to totalitarianism and war. In postwar Japan, the careful research reflected in the *Dai Nihon shi* continued to be emulated, but the nationalistic views of the Mito School were largely rejected.

The task of compiling the *Dai Nihon shi* was not officially completed until 1906. When the history was finally completed, the facility originally founded by Mitsukuni was converted into a historical research institute and library in Mito, still used by scholars today.

There was no other national history project or facility of the same scale in Japan until 1869, when the Meiji government established official organizations for the collection of materials and the compilation of national history. These merged over time into the present National Historiographical Institute at Tokyo University, which serves as a central data collection and research facility and helps maintain a high level of national historiographical standards. This continues the tradition of careful scholarship first established by Mitsukuni in 1657, while remaining independent from the Mito nationalism that developed later.

—*Michael McCaskey*

FURTHER READING

Boot, Willem Jan. *The Adoption and Adaptation of Neo-Confucianism in Japan: The Role of Fujiwara Seika and Hayashi Razan*. Leiden, the Netherlands: Lectura, 1982. The development of the Neo-Confucian climate of opinion preceding Tokugawa Mitsukuni.

Brownlee, John S. *Japanese Historians and the National Myths, 1600-1945: The Age of the Gods and Emperor Jinmu*. Vancouver: University of British Columbia Press, 1997. A history of the authors and processes involved in writing Japan's major works of national history, with a chapter on the *Dai Nihon shi*.

Koschmann, J. Victor. *The Mito Ideology: Discourse, Reform, and Insurrection in Late Tokugawa Japan, 1790-1864*. Berkeley: University of California Press, 1987. Analysis of the more militant Mito thought that developed from Tokugawa Mitsukuni's earlier approach.

Najita, Tetsuo. *Tokugawa Political Writings*. Cambridge, England: Cambridge University Press, 1998. A Tokugawa political and historiographical sourcebook, focused on the late seventeenth and early eighteenth centuries.

Webb, Herschel F. *The Thought and Work of the Early Mito School*. New York: Columbia University Microform Dissertation, 1958. A specialized study of the philosophy of Tokugawa Mitsukuni and the creation of the *Dai Nihon shi*.

SEE ALSO: 1603: Tokugawa Shogunate Begins; Beginning 1607: Neo-Confucianism Becomes Japan's Official Philosophy; Jan. 18-20, 1657: Meireki Fire Ravages Edo; 1680-1709: Reign of Tsunayoshi as Shogun.

RELATED ARTICLES in *Great Lives from History: The Seventeenth Century, 1601-1700:* Tokugawa Ieyasu; Tokugawa Tsunayoshi.

January 18-20, 1657
Meireki Fire Ravages Edo

A huge conflagration killed more than 100,000 people, burned part of Edo Castle, and destroyed more than 350 shrines and temples. In the fire's aftermath, greater official attention was paid to urban planning, fire prevention, and firefighting techniques.

Locale: Edo (now Tokyo, Japan)
Categories: Natural disasters; architecture

Key Figures

Abe Tadaaki (1602-1675), a prominent adviser to the shogun
Asai Ryōi (1612-1691), a contemporary chronicler of the fire
Kanazawa Kiyozaemon (fl. c. 1650), an Edo surveyor and mapmaker
Matsudaira Nobutsuna (1596-1662), a senior councillor to the shogun, 1633-1662
Tokugawa Ietsuna (1641-1680), shogun of Japan, r. 1651-1680

Summary of Event

Edo was established in 1457, when the warlord Ōta Dōkan first constructed a castle in what is now the Chiyoda Ward of Tokyo. As with other major castles in Japan, a community of merchants and artisans grew around the structure, developing randomly into a *jōkamachi*, or castle town. After Edo Castle was taken over by Tokugawa Ieyasu, who made it the administrative center of his shogunate in 1603, it was partly rebuilt, but much of its old structure was retained.

The surrounding city of Edo expanded greatly, but there remained districts of densely clustered wooden buildings and narrow meandering roads. Wide avenues and bridges were kept to a minimum because the authorities wished to avoid direct routes that could be used by attacking forces in the event of a rebellion. Narrow lanes could easily become traps for people attempting to flee, causing them to be trampled to death or killed in another way. Ferry services were used instead of bridges, making it difficult for large numbers of people to seek safety by crossing rivers. Under these conditions, it is remarkable that a major fire catastrophe did not occur for another half century.

The fire that destroyed much of the city of Edo between January 18 and 20, 1657, killed an estimated 100,000 people or more. The fire is known in Japanese history as the *Meireki no taika*, the great Meireki era fire. It is also known as the *Furisode kaji*, the long-sleeved kimono fire. The fire was popularly believed to have started at the Honmyō Temple, in the Hongō District in the northern part of the city, after a long-sleeved kimono of a deceased person was ignited during a memorial service and carried away by the wind, setting fire to nearby residences.

Another tradition held that the fire started accidentally in the nearby home of Abe Tadaaki, a powerful feudal lord and adviser to the young shogun Tokugawa Ietsuna. In this version of the story, supported by extant records in the Honmyō Temple, shogunate authorities, to avoid any connection of Abe with this enormous disaster, pressured the clergy to publicly accept blame. By law, a householder whose own home alone burned by accident was blameless, but if the fire destroyed other homes, that person was liable and could be punished severely. If a big fire spread from a temple, however, its clergy would receive only a sentence of self-imposed penitence for a specified time.

According to the *Musashi abumi* (1661; Edo circuit), an account by the contemporary writer Asai Ryōi, the fire was preceded by more than eighty continuous days without rain. The flames spread rapidly through blocks of clustered and dry wooden dwellings and were fanned by a strong northwest wind. When it seemed that the fire seemed to have burned itself out in one area, it blazed up in a new one, giving the impression that separate fires were starting, so some records suggest that there were three massive independent fires.

After breaking out in Hongō early in the afternoon of January 18, the fire spread across the city by the morning of the next day. It moved southeast to the Nihonbashi area, was carried by the wind across the Sumida River, and engulfed the Fukagawa and Honjō areas at the southeastern end of Edo. The fire also spread northwest from Hongō to the Koishikawa area, and southwest to Kōjimachi. From there the flames moved east, destroying part of Edo Castle. The fire died down in the early morning hours of January 20, having largely burned itself out. It left nothing but huge stretches of empty blackened ground in its wake.

In addition to destroying part of Edo Castle, the conflagration incinerated the residences of approximately 160 great feudal lords, close to 800 mansions of prominent Tokugawa retainers, approximately 350 temples and shrines, 60 bridges, and more than 400 blocks of densely clustered shops and homes in areas where commoners lived. More than 60 percent of Edo was left in ruins, and more people were killed than in any other fire in the city prior to the twentieth century.

Soon after the fires ended, the shogunate began to distribute ten thousand packets of silver to commoners and aristocrats alike to assist them in rebuilding, and distributed massive quantities of food to the townspeople. This prompt and unexpectedly generous relief forestalled any major public recriminations against the shogunate, concerning either negligence in fire prevention or failure to attempt to extinguish the fire at an early stage. Tens of thousands of unidentifiable bodies, many of which had been trapped in firestorms by the lack of bridges, were transported by the authorities to the other side of the Sumida River and put in mass graves. The shogunate also established a permanent Buddhist temple at the site, the Ekō-in, in memory of the victims.

The great fire prompted a concern with fire prevention, especially because the fire destroyed part of Edo Castle and threatened the shogun and his administration personally. Instead of allowing people to begin rebuilding in their original locations, the shogunate developed a plan to enlarge the city, create open spaces and fire breaks, widen roads, construct more bridges, and relocate much of the urban population in new areas. The large amounts spent by the shogunate on relief and reconstruction made it easier to relocate large numbers of people without creating civil unrest. The relief and reconstruction effort marked the beginning of rational, systematic urban planning in Japan.

Both the relief and reconstruction efforts were carried out under the overall leadership of Matsudaira Nobutsuna, a *rōjū*, or senior councillor to the shogun. Matsudaira commissioned a comprehensive land survey to plan the reconstruction, a survey that was carried out under the supervision of Hōjō Masafusa, a lower-level aristocratic official. The actual surveying work was done by Kanazawa Kiyozaemon, who had studied under a teacher well versed in Western surveying methods, resulting in the first modern survey and map of the rebuilt city of Edo.

SIGNIFICANCE

Many of the shopping and residential districts for the ordinary merchants and artisans were moved across the Sumida River, well past the location of the Ekō-in. Most of the area designated for commoners was relocated well away from Edo Castle. This new area for commoners was linked to the inner city by the construction of the Ryōgoku Bridge across the river. Many mansions of leading Tokugawa relatives of the shogun who previously lived within the Edo Castle grounds, as well as the residences of many major feudal lords and retainers, were moved to the areas where the commoners had formerly lived.

Originating as an extension of the castle and segmented by unbridged river crossings for defensive purposes, Edo was rebuilt after the Meireki fire as a true city, with many bridges and linking roads. Open spaces were created within the castle grounds, and many temples and shrines, including the Honmyō Temple, were moved from the city to distant locations. Decentralization developed new settlements well beyond the outer castle moat, greatly enlarging the city.

With disaster mitigation in mind, officials widened city streets and built embankments to serve as fire breaks. Rebuilding after the Meireki fire was guided by the first official instance of urban planning in Japanese history. The basic layout of the city remained the same from this time on, and rebuilding after subsequent disasters over the following three centuries generally followed guidelines developed by Matsudaira and his staff after the great fire.

—*Michael McCaskey*

FURTHER READING

Jinnai, Hidenobu, and Kimiko Nishimura. *Tokyo: A Spatial Anthropology*. Berkeley: University of California Press, 1995. An archaeological study of Edo and Tokyo, tracing the marked changes of many urban disasters through the years.

Naito, Akira, and Kazuo Hozumi. *Edo, the City That Became Tokyo: An Illustrated History*. Tokyo: Kodansha International, 2003. A survey of the history of Tokyo, with attention to premodern culture, urban disasters, and urban planning.

Nishiyama, Matsunosuke, and Gerald Groener. *Edo Culture: Daily Life and Diversions in Urban Japan, 1600-1868*. Honolulu: University of Hawaii Press, 1997. An English adaptation of work by a leading Japanese historian of Edo life and culture.

Seidensticker, Edward. *Low City, High City: Tokyo from Edo to the Earthquake*. Cambridge, Mass.: Harvard University Press, 1991. An anecdotal account by an authority on Tokyo, with emphasis on the premodern period.

Sorenson, Andre. *The Making of Urban Japan: Cities and Planning from Edo to the Twenty-First Century.*

London: Nissan Institute/Routledge Japanese Studies, 2002. The first comprehensive study in English of the history of Japanese urban planning.

Yonemoto, Marcia. *Mapping Early Modern Japan: Space, Place, and Culture in the Tokugawa Period, 1603-1868.* Berkeley: University of California Press, 2003. An ethnogeographical study of Tokugawa Japan.

See also: June 29, 1613: Burning of the Globe Theatre; Sept. 2, 1633: Great Fire of Constantinople and Murad's Reforms; 1651-1680: Ietsuna Shogunate; Sept. 2-5, 1666: Great Fire of London; 1675-1708: Wren Supervises the Rebuilding of St. Paul's Cathedral.

Related article in *Great Lives from History: The Seventeenth Century, 1601-1700:* Tokugawa Ieyasu.

Beginning 1658
First Newspaper Ads Appear

With the spread of literacy in the seventeenth century, a nonelite class of wealthy merchants and tradespeople with some discretionary income and the ability to read print began to emerge in England. Printers began to realize the potential for lengthier, routinely published news sheets and the audience they held, and print ads began to appear in these news sheets, marketing commodities to the new—and newly literate—middle class.

Locale: London, England

Categories: Communications; trade and commerce; economics; cultural and intellectual history

Key Figures

Marchamont Nedham (1620-1678), editor of *Mercurius Politicus*, the dominant newsbook in England, 1650-1660

Henry Muddiman (1629-1692), publisher of the *Oxford* (later *London*) *Gazette*

Sir Roger L'Estrange (1616-1704), recipient of the first monopoly for periodicals under the 1662 Licensing Act, appointed to be surveyor of the press

Summary of Event

Early English newspaper advertising grew out of three simultaneously evolving cultural forces. First, literacy began to spread in the seventeenth century. No longer was it a skill restricted to society's elite, such as the nobility. Instead, others, such as merchants, began to emphasize reading and writing. Printing, although controlled by the Stationers' Guild, was considered a skilled, prestigious trade. Furthermore, it required literacy of its practitioners. Therefore, while the overall rate of literacy remained low from a modern perspective, most people from the middle classes knew someone who could read. Also, there developed ways for the illiterate to participate in the audience for printed materials. Coffeehouses, for example, carried reading material such as pamphlets or early newspapers. Patrons would frequently read these materials aloud, thus bringing illiterate coffeehouse patrons into the audience for printed words.

Second, printed materials themselves evolved in ways designed to appeal increasingly to a distinctively seventeenth century audience. The near-constant political upheaval in England during the period of the Civil Wars, Interregnum of Oliver Cromwell, and the restoration of the Stuart monarchy under Charles II, made many anxious to know what was happening in the country. Printers and would-be correspondents catered to this desire with a variety of materials, including pamphlets, newsletters, corantos, newsbooks, and ultimately newspapers.

While these various forms overlapped, each had specific, distinguishing characteristics. News pamphlets were published occasionally, usually in response to specific events. They tended to be brief, sensationalized, or moralistic and focused on that one news event. Newsletters were actual letters, written by one person and sent to a list of subscribers. They would contain a range of foreign and domestic news depending on the audience. Often, they would include corantos.

Corantos began in Belgium, the Netherlands, and elsewhere on the Continent but gradually became available in England. They contained foreign news. At this time, English news was restricted from domestic circulation, so foreign corantos often provided the only way for curious English subjects to learn of events in their own country. For a period, some were printed in England, but most ended by the early 1630's as English society and printing laws shifted. Corantos were published at rough intervals and did contain foreign news, and they demonstrated how news materials could be disseminated from

London through the provinces, following the patterns of the book trade.

The newsbooks of the 1640's established a new genre. They were eight-page periodicals with a strong domestic focus. Newsbooks were easily available through the publisher, and they were easily identified by their consistent titles, such as *Mercurius Britannicus*. They were published regularly—every Monday, for example. While most published on Mondays and captured the news, especially Parliamentary, of the previous week, some publishers published on different days. In doing so, these publishers were able to set themselves apart by having slightly different news from that appearing in the regular Monday newsbooks. The staff of the newsbook—publisher and editors—were generally salaried; for example, Marchamont Nedham edited *Mercurius Politicus*. Thus newsbooks were the immediate precursors of newspapers.

The newspaper incorporated the successful features of each of its precursors. Newspapers retained the occasional sensational or moral news item, a characteristic of the pamphlet. Learning from corantos, they included foreign news. Like newsbooks, they contained mostly domestic news. Newspapers were published periodically, generally on schedules synchronous with the postal routes leaving London, so that the newspapers could be delivered to the provinces in a timely manner. Newspapers were also available in coffeehouses, where people were accustomed to reading material out loud. Thus, newspapers made themselves into the most relevant, reliable, and accessible source of news.

Third, economic developments in England meant that more people, such as members of the middle and upper-middle classes, had some level of discretionary funds, which could be used for occasional luxuries, such as coffee or tea. Therefore, instead of simply targeting their goods to the elite, merchants wished to find new ways to attract the attention of these new potential buyers. Previously, merchants had relied on a product's reputation, customer word of mouth, people in the street calling out about the new product, or handbills distributed in the street. The printed news offered new opportunities.

These opportunities were quietly explored, at first. In the mid-1620's, for example, a newsbook carried a notice of publication, announcing a book to be published by newsbook's own printers. It was not until 1648, though, that a newsbook carried regular advertisements. Even then, an advertisement was considered to be the same as a notice, such as a court notice. Over the next decade, however, the term "advertisement" came to have the narrower meaning represented by the 1658 *Mercurius Politicus* announcement of tea, with specific endorsements by physicians, for sale at a specific place.

Advertising, unless inserted by a member of the publication's staff, was always paid. However, even though paid advertisements could supplement a newspaper publisher's revenue, most periodicals limited the number they accepted. For example, in 1653, the *Perfect Diurnall* accepted about five or six advertisements per issue, but the *Oxford Gazette* in 1665 refused to accept any, because it felt they had no place in the periodical. The types of advertisements run were generally for commodities—new books in print, coffee, tea, medicines, and so forth.

Advertising prices were set by the printer. The rate depended upon how often the ad would run, where on the page it would be, and what kind of illustrations or embellishments would be used. Eventually, many newspapers developed the practice of separating out advertisements, usually by a heading or a horizontal rule, to distinguish news from ads.

Despite the growing demand for news, few newspapers survived the Interregnum. As a whole, most published a few issues—perhaps one, perhaps a dozen. The best published a few hundred. Then, the Licensing Act of 1662 limited the number of periodicals, granting monopolies on periodical publication to certain court favorites such as Roger L'Estrange and Henry Muddiman. Not until the final lapse of the act in 1695 were periodicals and their advertisers again able to print the kinds of news and advertisements they had printed in the 1650's.

Significance

Despite the political turmoil of the Interregnum and the Restoration, an increasing number of the middle and upper-middle classes were literate and engaged in work from which they earned more than subsistence wages. In two generations or less, these people became the core of the rapidly expanding middle class in eighteenth century Britain. The development of newspaper advertising represented both an effect and a cause of this nascent English middle class. It was an effect of the economic forces creating a new group of people with disposable income. It was a cause in the sense that advertising was one of the first forms of discourse that attempted to treat this class as an audience. It was therefore one of the first forms of discourse to impart or impose a unified, class identity upon the disparate individuals composing the middle class.

This early advertising recognized the emerging middle class as a group able to make purchases beyond what they needed for subsistence. In doing so, advertising helped develop the consumer culture of the eighteenth century, the culture that led to pianos in the parlors of farmhouses and to visits to Wedgwood's warehouses to inspect the china.

—*Clare Callaghan*

FURTHER READING

Cranfield, G. A. *The Press and Society: From Caxton to Northcliffe*. New York: Longman, 1978. Reviews the first centuries of printing, specifically the development of "the press," in England.

Handover, P. A. *Printing in London from 1476 to Modern Times*. Cambridge, Mass.: Harvard University Press, 1960. Examines developments in printing from the early modern period forward.

Harris, Michael. "Timely Notices: The Uses of Advertising and Its Relationship to News During the Late Seventeenth Century." In *News, Newspapers, and Society in Early Modern Britain*, edited by Joad Raymond. Portland, Oreg.: Frank Cass, 1999. Essay collection focuses on particular stages or features of newspapers and their audiences.

Raymond, Joad. *The Invention of the Newspaper: English Newsbooks, 1641-1649*. Oxford, England: Clarendon Press, 1996. Investigates the roots of the English newspaper. Comprehensive examination of the English newsbook.

Sommerville, C. John. *The News Revolution in England: Cultural Dynamics of Daily Information*. New York: Oxford University Press, 1996. Examines the development of the reading audiences of newspapers.

Sutherland, James. *The Restoration Newspaper and Its Development*. New York: Cambridge University Press, 1986. Investigates newspapers published between 1660 and 1720.

Walker, R. B. "Advertising in London Newspapers, 1650-1750." *Business History* 15 (1973): 112-130. Comprehensively analyzes advertising in London newspapers.

SEE ALSO: 1642-1651: English Civil Wars; Dec. 6, 1648-May 19, 1649: Establishment of the English Commonwealth; Dec. 16, 1653-Sept. 3, 1658: Cromwell Rules England as Lord Protector; May, 1659-May, 1660: Restoration of Charles II; 1662-May 3, 1695: England's Licensing Acts; May 3, 1695: End of Press Censorship in England.

RELATED ARTICLES in *Great Lives from History: The Seventeenth Century, 1601-1700:* Charles I; Charles II (of England); Oliver Cromwell.

1658-1707
REIGN OF AURANGZEB

Aurangzeb was a brilliant administrator, tireless warrior, and a cunning diplomat who imposed nominal Mughal power over most of India. His achievements were undermined by his incessant wars, punishing taxations, and a religious policy that replaced traditional Mughal toleration with a puritanical Sunni Islam that offended India's Hindu majority. The revolts and impoverishment his autocracy produced would throw the Mughal Dynasty into irreversible decline.

LOCALE: India

CATEGORIES: Government and politics; wars, uprisings, and civil unrest; religion and theology

KEY FIGURES

Aurangzeb (1618-1707), Mughal emperor of India, r. 1658-1707

Shah Jahan (1592-1666), Mughal emperor of India, r. 1628-1658

Śivājī (1627-1680), leader of Hindu resistance to Aurangzeb

SUMMARY OF EVENT

Emperor Aurangzeb came to power in 1658 after overthrowing his father, the emperor Shah Jahan, and defeating his rival brothers in a prolonged civil war. When he ascended the throne, the Mughal Dynasty held direct control over most of northern India, covering the lands of the Indus, the Ganges, and Bengal. In many of these areas, however, actual power required cooperation with local princely authorities, Hindu as well as Muslim.

To the south in the central Deccan lands and coastal regions, independent rulers of states such as Golconda, Bijapur, and the Marāthās shared with the Mughals in the wealth of India's vigorous commerce but resisted occupation if threatened.

Officially, the Mughals supported the Sunni Islamic faith and promoted the spread of Sunnism throughout its domains. In reality, the guiding principles of the regime constituted what could be called Indiaism, a judicious mix of traditional Islamic religious tolerance, Hindu pluralism, opulent patronage of Indian culture, and promotion of commercial expansion. Such policies represented a dramatic departure from the historic approaches of Muslim rulers. Traditionally, non-Muslims were disarmed, prohibited from military service, subject to special taxes, forbidden to command Muslims, and stigmatized by mandates to wear and exhibit special clothing and to behave in a deferential manner. Under the Mughals, however, high-caste Hindu princes, warriors, priests, and other members of the elite were exempt from these discriminations. The majority of Mughal subjects remained Hindus. In addition, Mughal religious pluralism had allowed non-Sunni Muslim groups such as Shia and Nizari Muslims to move around India. Interaction and dialogue between Hindus and Muslims gave rise to syncretistic movements that mixed beliefs and practices of both, producing new faiths, such as Sikhism, to compete with Sunni Islam.

Aurangzeb. (Library of Congress)

Aurangzeb represented a minority view within the Mughal household, which regarded Indiaism as failed politics and religious apostasy. As a provincial governor and military commander, the prince had come to trust his Muslim subjects over the Hindu. His father's wastrel (foolish) spending appalled him, especially the construction of the famous Taj Mahal. The constant civil wars that accompanied seemingly every succession suggested to Aurangzeb that the state needed more efficient, more centralized control over its lands. The new emperor believed also that God had called him to power to make the Mughal Dynasty a more truly Islamic state, to impose the strictures of Islamic law upon non-Muslims, to end fiscal waste and cultural extravagance, and to carry Islam deeper into the subcontinent.

Taking the title *alamgir* (world conqueror), Aurangzeb began his reign in 1658 by purging his court of luxury, slashing expenditures for all but the state and army, and sending inspectors throughout his domain to compel Muslims to observe the prayers, fasts, and laws of Sunni Islam. He invested heavily in the recruitment and training of Sunni lawyers, judges, censors, and clergy. Troops were dispatched to Kashmir and Mewar to enforce the loyalty of dissident Muslim princes. Gradual enforcement of sectarian discriminations began immediately.

Over the next twenty years, the emperor steadily increased the exactions. Non-Muslims paid higher duties, customs, and taxes than did Muslims. Pretexts were raised to confiscate lands and houses of worship. Revolts, such as that in 1669 in the Punjab, met savage repression. In 1679, the state imposed the poll-tax on all Hindus, exempting only the Rājput princely caste. Shia Muslims faced persecution as did the Sikhs. (In 1675, the ninth Sikh guru was executed for heresy.) The efficiency of Aurangzeb's new taxation system, collected by military supervisors called *mansabdars*, compounded popular resentments of Muslim and Hindu alike because of their greed.

During these decades, Aurangzeb's major foreign opposition came from the Shia sultans of the central plains and from Śivājī, Hindu leader of the Marāthā peoples of the western coastal mountains. Using both guerrilla and conventional tactics, Śivājī often eluded the Mughals, raiding border cities, inspiring revolts, and creating short-lived anti-Mughal alliances. His example led many of the Rājputs in the empire to revolt beginning in

The Mughal Empire in the 17th Century

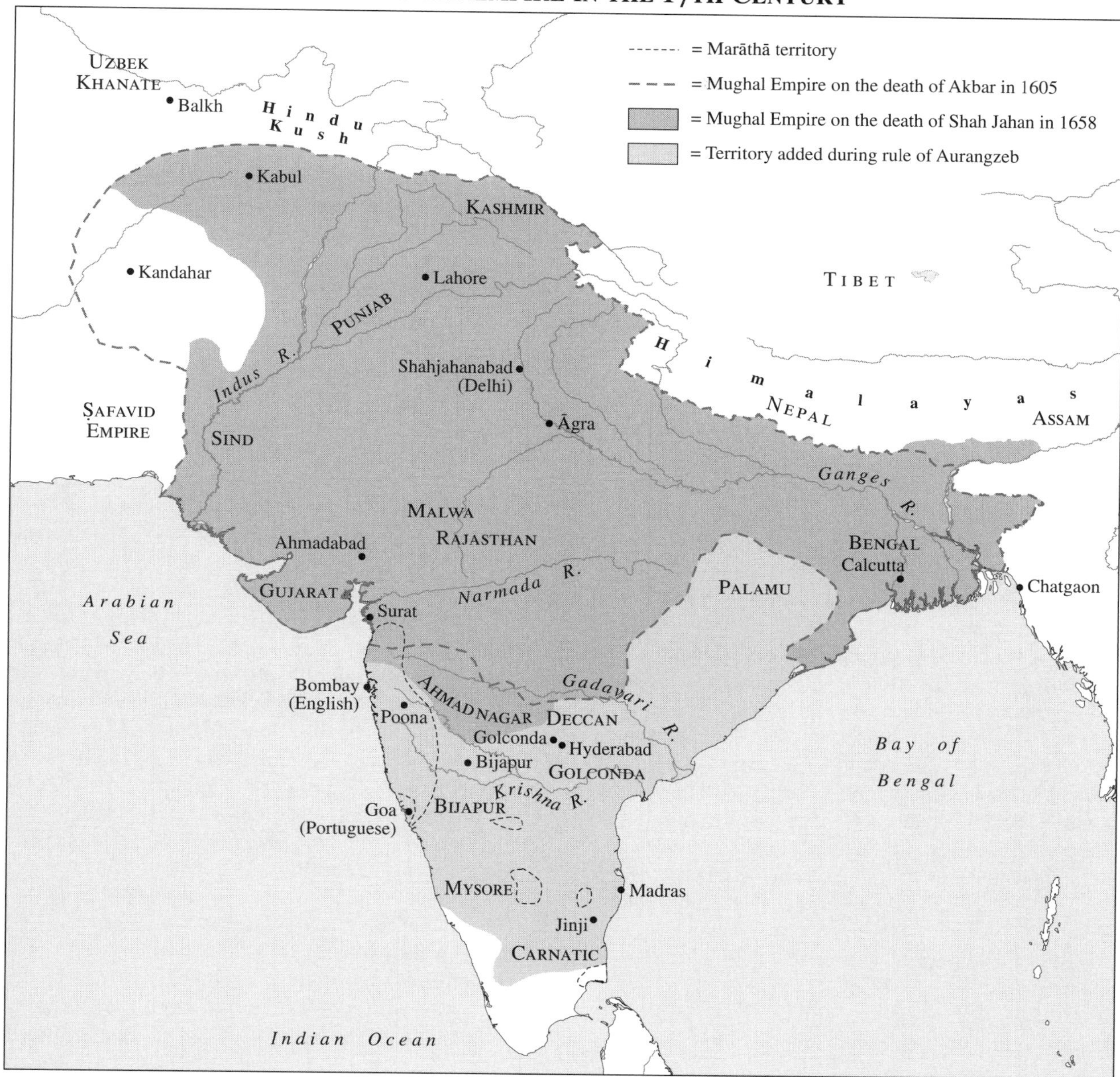

1679, a revolt that led Aurangzeb's own son, Akbar, to attempt a coup against his father under the banners of Indiaism.

Aurangzeb responded with overwhelming force. Driving Akbar south into the arms of the Marāthās, he gained enough time to marshal his domestic supporters for a new war of pacification. From 1681 to 1689, Mughal armies pounded into submission the Shia sultanates of Bijapur and Golconda. The annexation of these states increased the ranks of Muslim fighters and the rolls of non-Muslim taxpayers—although, again, Hindu nobles still received preferential treatment. Works of art were destroyed and musicians and dancers banished. Śivājī's death in 1680 also weakened the Marāthā state, and, by 1689, the Mughals had occupied most of the Marāthā land on the western and eastern coasts of India.

Nearly all of central India now came under Aurangzeb's banners.

Occupation, however, did not bring pacification. In the west, Marāthā chieftains raised armies in the mountains and routinely swept downs on towns, garrisons, and estates. In the east, the House of Śivājī established itself in the fortress town of Jinji. The Mughals besieged the town for eight years before it finally fell in 1698. (Even then, the Marāthā prince escaped the Mughals.) Many fortresses changed hands seasonally, the sieges were long, and there was pointless loss of life. Droughts, plagues, and famines combined with war to wreck local economies and prolong the misery of ordinary Indians. At the same time, European merchants in some Indian ports had made themselves virtually autonomous. The Dutch in Pulicat, the French at Pondicherry, and the English in Bombay, Calcutta, and Madras increasingly manipulated local economies, recruited mercenaries, sold arms and expertise to dissidents, and infuriated Aurangzeb with their rivalry and meddling.

The fall of Jinji energized the elderly emperor, and he resolved to reduce the chains of fortresses that sheltered the Marāthā forces and their leaders. His first campaigns in 1699-1701 captured several key Marāthā strongholds. At one battle in Ahmadnagar, Mughal forces bloodied the Marāthās. More fortresses fell and more chieftains capitulated. However, the cost of these victories proved exhausting. Aurangzeb's court and army numbered in the tens of thousands, supported further by thousands of retainers, horses, camels, and elephants. The occupation of fortresses did not end the guerrilla assaults or the relentless plundering of supplies, trains, and rear areas by smaller, swifter Marāthā bands. Meanwhile, the shifting of Mughal forces to the eastern Deccan only encouraged Marāthā chiefs in the west to attack the reduced towns and garrisons.

By 1705, Aurangzeb was almost ninety, exhausted, demoralized, and embittered. With three middle-age sons and numerous grandsons, the odds of a civil war at his death were daunting. Despite his victories and the new lands he had won, the emperor withdrew to the north to prepare for the succession. Failure crowned his last years, as Marāthā and other rebels continued to bedevil a shrinking Mughal army. Provincial governors in Bengal and other territories plotted secession openly. The imperial economy was in shambles, burdened by military debts and foreign trade slipping into the hands of Europeans. In his will, the emperor required a three-way division of the empire among his leading sons, men for whom he showed little respect. Aurangzeb died March 3, 1707. Within months, the civil war he sought to prevent broke out between his sons. The Mughal Empire began a relentless decline from which it would never recover.

SIGNIFICANCE

Ruling India for almost fifty years, Aurangzeb clearly was the last of the great Mughal emperors. In his ambition to abandon Mughal Indiaism for a more traditional Islamic government, he helped deepen the roots of Islam on the subcontinent. Extremely gifted as an administrator and a military commander, he enlarged both the state structure and the imperial army. At his death, Mughal rule extended over more territory than it had ever—or would ever—occupy.

Nonetheless, after Aurangzeb's death, the power of the Mughals declined rapidly. Instability plagued the dynasty regularly. Many provinces broke away or became semiautonomous. There were many wars, famines, and quarreling small states. British and French imperialism was relentless, laying the groundwork for the conquests of the next century.

Aurangzeb is an extremely controversial figure among historians of India. Hindu writers depict him often as a narrow-minded bigot who ruined his empire trying to impose unworkable Islamic discriminations on the non-Muslim majority he ruled. Muslim scholars tend to emphasize the need for a more centralized government in the face of internal turbulence and encroaching European imperialism. Beyond the religious context of his rule, historians continue to debate the impact of his policies on seventeenth century India.

—Weston F. Cook, Jr.

FURTHER READING

Gascoigne, Bamber. *A Brief History of the Great Moghuls*. New York: Carroll & Graf, 2002. A well-written, general history of the Mughals, first published in 1971, chronicling the empire from its founder, Bābur, through Aurangzeb. Profusely illustrated, the work presents a balanced view of Aurangzeb's reign.

Hallissey, Robert C. *The Rajput Rebellion Against Aurangzeb: A Study of the Mughal Empire in Seventeenth Century India*. Columbia: University of Missouri Press, 1977. Examines the Rājput rebellion against Aurangzeb in light of the internal dynamics of the Rājput state and the religious differences between Hindus and Muslims. Reveals the complexity of the Mughal-Rājput relationship.

Keay, John. *India: A History*. New York: Grove Press, 2000. Keay is especially adept at making the convoluted politics and wars of the era understandable for general readers.

Richards, John F. *The Mughal Empire*. New Cambridge History of India 5, part 1. New York: Cambridge University Press, 1993. Still the best single text in English on the history of the Mughal Empire.

Wolpert, Stanley. *A New History of India*. 6th ed. New York: Oxford University Press, 2000. A good overview from a classic college-level text. Includes a solid bibliography.

SEE ALSO: 1605-1627: Mughal Court Culture Flourishes; 1606-1674: Europeans Settle in India; 1632-c. 1650: Shah Jahan Builds the Taj Mahal; 1639-1640: British East India Company Establishes Fort Saint George; c. 1666-1676: Founding of the Marāthā Kingdom; 1679-1709: Rājput Rebellion; Mar. 30, 1699: Singh Founds the Khalsa Brotherhood.

RELATED ARTICLES in *Great Lives from History: The Seventeenth Century, 1601-1700:* ʿAbbās the Great; Aurangzeb; Jahāngīr; Kösem Sultan; Murad IV; Shah Jahan.

August, 1658-August 24, 1660
EXPLORATIONS OF RADISSON AND CHOUART DES GROSEILLIERS

Chouart des Groseilliers and Radisson explored and mapped the region around the shores of Lake Superior, and they developed an understanding of the financial potential of fur trading, setting in motion the events that would lead to the creation of the Hudson's Bay Company.

LOCALE: New France (now in Eastern Canada and the northeastern and midwestern United States)

CATEGORIES: Exploration and discovery; economics; trade and commerce

KEY FIGURES

Médard Chouart des Groseilliers (1625-1698), French explorer and colonial Canadian fur trader

Pierre Esprit Radisson (c. 1636-1710), French explorer and colonial Canadian fur trader and cartographer

Pierre de Voyer d'Argenson (1626-1710), fifth governor-general of New France, 1657-1661

SUMMARY OF EVENT

In 1651, Pierre Esprit Radisson moved from France with his family to New France. Shortly thereafter, he was captured by some Mohawk warriors and adopted by an Iroquois woman. Over the next two years, Radisson learned the Iroquois language and customs. Médard Chouart des Groseilliers arrived in New France in 1641 and married Radisson's half sister, Marguerite Hayet, in 1653. Chouart des Groseilliers was one of the first Frenchman in New France to realize what great riches could be garnered from trade in furs, particularly beaver pelts, around the Great Lakes region. Recognizing the insights that Radisson had gathered about Native Americans and the fur trading business, Chouart des Groseilliers hired him as a partner in 1658 to help him explore and trade furs around the region of Lake Superior (referred to as Grans Lac by Samuel de Champlain and the Western Sea by some Native Americans).

Around the end of August, 1658, Chouart des Groseilliers and Radisson organized a group of Frenchmen and some Native Americans to travel to Lake Superior. Radisson kept a journal to document the company's trip. Although it contains a number of discrepancies and great exaggerations, his journal provides a wealth of information about their travels and experiences. Without obtaining a fur-trading license and permission from the general-governor of New France, Pierre de Voyer d'Argenson, the group departed in the nighttime from Montreal, traveled up the Ottawa River, on to Lake Nipissing, down the French River to Georgia Bay, then to Sault de Sainte Marie (present-day Sault Sainte Marie, Michigan). Chouart des Groseilliers was already very familiar with the area between Montreal and Sault de Sainte Marie, having traded for furs with Native Americans and explored around Lake Huron and Lake Michigan in 1654. Arriving at Sault de Sainte Marie in early fall, the Radisson-Chouart des Groseilliers company rested there for several days and feasted on the fine food that they gathered and hunted in the area.

By early November, 1658, the group of explorers had traveled along the southern shore of Lake Superior to Chequagemon Bay (bordering the northeastern tip of present-day Wisconsin), where they built a small fort and trading post and stayed for nearly two weeks. In late November, they traveled south, passing near Lake

Pierre Esprit Radisson greeting Native Americans during his exploration of New France with Médard Chouart des Groseilliers. (The Granger Collection)

Chippewa in present-day northwestern Wisconsin. In that area, they encountered a snowstorm that made it impossible for them to go any farther and prevented them from hunting for food. They made snowshoes to get around, resorted to eating some of their dogs, and spent time with the native Menominees, who treated the explorers as though they were gods. After weathering the storms and once winter conditions were favorable, Chouart des Groseilliers and Radisson led their company westward in early 1659 to the area around present-day Mora, Minnesota, where they celebrated by feasting, dancing, and playing games. They are noted as the first Europeans to set foot in Minnesota.

For about seven weeks, Chouart des Groseilliers and Radisson explored the southern and central parts of Minnesota and then returned north to Chequagemon Bay. From there, they explored and mapped the headwaters of the Mississippi River, mapped the Pigeon and Gooseberry Rivers in northern Minnesota, traded furs with the native Sioux, and explored the western and northwestern shores of Lake Superior. They were probably the first Frenchmen to see the Mississippi River. The Gooseberry River was most likely named after Chouart des Groseilliers, "gooseberry" being the English translation of Groseilliers. Radisson and Chouart des Groseilliers recognized the great wealth that could come from fur trading around western Lake Superior and northern Minnesota. They sought a route that would connect the region to what Native Americans referred to as the Northern Sea or Salt Sea (Hudson Bay). By establishing fur trading posts along Hudson Bay, the French would be able to avoid attacks from the Iroquois to the south, minimize trading competition with the Dutch south of the Saint Lawrence River, and control the fur trade in the Great Lakes region.

While exploring the western and northern shores of Lake Superior during 1659, Radisson and Chouart des Groseilliers became the first Europeans to travel on Lake Superior. After crossing the northern part of Lake Superior in birch bark canoes, they led their company northward, exploring parts of southern Ontario, Canada. Although they did not reach Hudson Bay on this trip, they passed by James Bay, at the southern end of Hudson Bay.

On their way back to Quebec in early 1660, they encountered a band of Cree and Assiniboine Indians, traveled with them for a large portion of their remaining journey, and learned a great deal from them about the furs and minerals available around Lake Superior, as well as the location of Hudson Bay. While traveling to Quebec, they left about one-fourth of their total cache of furs at trading posts in Montreal and Trois Rivières. On August 24, 1660, Chouart des Groseilliers and Radisson arrived in Quebec with the remainder of their valuable furs. During their explorations around Lake Superior, they had successfully traded cheap implements, such as hatchets, knives, and kettles, to Native Americans for furs that could be sold by the French in Europe for great profits.

Upon their arrival in Quebec, Radisson and Chouart des Groseilliers were initially greeted with much cheering and cannon salutes from Fort Saint Louis and from the three ships waiting in the harbor for cargo to return to Europe. Within a short time, however, Governor-General Voyer d'Argenson had them arrested and imprisoned for trading furs west of Montreal without his permission and without a license. Their load of furs was confiscated without any compensation to them. The monetary gain from the furs saved France from a financial disaster. On numerous occasions, Chouart des Groseilliers and Radisson tried to convince Voyer d'Argenson to allow either themselves or other Frenchmen to explore and establish trading posts along Hudson Bay but to no avail. Voyer d'Argenson's decision proved disastrous to France when Chouart des Groseilliers and Radisson finally joined the British, which led to the establishment of the Hudson's Bay Company and the dominance of Great Britain in North America.

Significance

Chouart des Groseilliers and Radisson were the first Europeans to explore the western and northern shores of Lake Superior, the first Europeans to enter Minnesota, the first Frenchmen to see the Mississippi River, and the first Europeans to travel on Lake Superior. They explored and mapped portions of northern Michigan, northern and central Wisconsin, southern and northeast-

Explorations of Radisson and Chouart des Groseilliers, 1658-1660

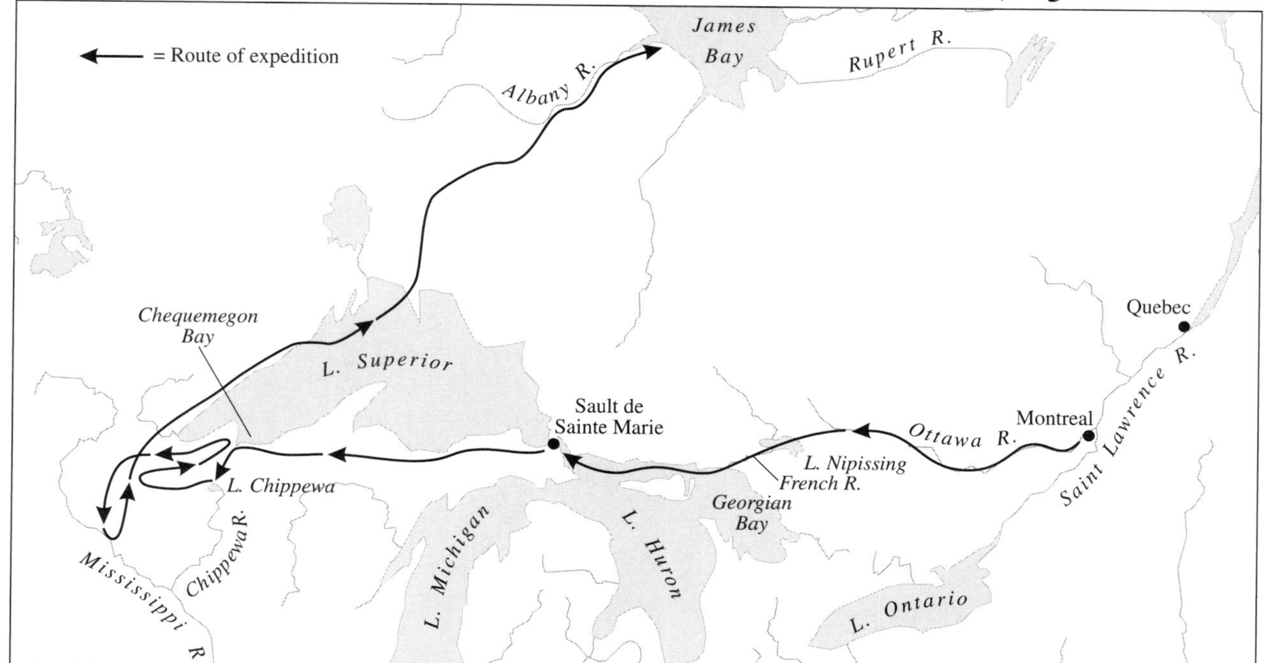

ern Minnesota, the headwaters of the Mississippi River, southern Ontario, and the shores around Lake Superior. They identified the economic potential of the fur trading business around Lake Superior, learned about Hudson Bay from Native Americans, and realized that trading posts established along Hudson Bay would be the key factor in controlling the lucrative fur trade of the Great Lakes region.

When the French declined the offer of Chouart des Groseilliers and Radisson to explore and develop the Hudson Bay area as a conduit for fur trading, the explorers switched their allegiance to the British. Their initiative led to the establishment of The Governor and Company of Adventurers of England Trading into the Hudson's Bay (Hudson's Bay Company) in 1670. The historical evolution of North America was changed forever. The economic benefits accrued through this organization played a key role in establishing Great Britain as the dominant force in North America. At its peak, in fact, the Hudson's Bay Company owned about 10 percent of all the surface land in the world.

—*Alvin K. Benson*

FURTHER READING

Fournier, Martin. *Pierre-Esprit Radisson: Merchant, Adventurer, 1636-1710*. Sillery, Que.: Septentrion, 2002. Portrays some of the legendary adventures and feats of Radisson, as well as Chouart des Groseilliers, in New France.

Laut, Agnes C. *The Pathfinders of the West*. New York: Macmillan, 1904. Reprint. New York: Freeport, 1969. A history of the men who discovered the great Northwest: Radisson, Chouart des Groseilliers, Louis de la Vèrendrye, Samuel Hearne, Alexander MacKenzie, Meriwether Lewis, and William Clark.

Lopez, Barry. *Arctic Dreams*. London: Vintage, 2001. Reviews the history of the explorers in the far north, including the fur trading activities of Radisson and Chouart des Groseilliers in the subarctic hinterlands.

Strong, Paul. *Wild Moose Country*. Minnetonka, Minn.: Cowles Creative, 1998. Recounts some of the exploits of Radisson and Chouart des Groseilliers around Lake Superior, noting that they claimed to have killed more than six hundred moose in Minnesota.

Whitfield, Peter. *New Found Lands: Maps in the History of Exploration*. New York: Routledge, 1998. Focuses on the maps made and used by explorers in the new world for exploration and economic ventures, including those of Radisson and Chouart des Groseilliers around Lake Superior.

SEE ALSO: Mar. 15, 1603-Dec. 25, 1635: Champlain's Voyages; Spring, 1604: First European Settlement in North America; Beginning June, 1610: Hudson Explores Hudson Bay; Apr. 27, 1627: Company of New France Is Chartered; 1642-1684: Beaver Wars; May, 1642: Founding of Montreal; May 2, 1670: Hudson's Bay Company Is Chartered.

RELATED ARTICLES in *Great Lives from History: The Seventeenth Century, 1601-1700:* Samuel de Champlain; Henry Hudson; Pierre Esprit Radisson.

1659
EXPANSION OF THE ALAWIS

The Alawis rose to power in Morocco out of the chaos following the fall of the Saʿdi Dynasty in 1659. Morocco was reunified not under the guise of religion, which had been used by the previous dynasties that had risen to prominence as the champions of Islam against Christian aggression. Instead, the Alawis had a political agenda: regional dominance.

LOCALE: Morocco, North Africa

CATEGORIES: Government and politics; wars, uprisings, and civil unrest

KEY FIGURES

al-Rashīd (1631-1672), sultan of Morocco, r. 1664-1672

Ismāʿīl (1645/1646-1727), sultan of Morocco, r. 1672-1727

SUMMARY OF EVENT

The Alawis, *shurafa* from Morocco's desert fringe, were originally from the oasis of Tafilalt, in southeast Morocco. A sharif (singular form of *shurufa*) was a person who claimed descent from the Prophet Muḥammad. By tradition, the founder of the Alawis (the term comes from the name Ali, Muḥammad's son-in-law) was said to have migrated from the town of Yanbo in Arabia in the early thirteenth century. For four centuries the Alawis lived in relative obscurity, enjoying prestige for their scholarship and piety among the people of the Tafilalt, but with no pretensions of playing a national or even regional political role.

The decline and fall of the Saʿdi Dynasty and the resulting civil wars brought chaos to Morocco by the mid-seventeenth century. The Tafilalt became an unowned land over which rival armies contended. The Alawis attempted to organize resistance but did so with little success until family leadership passed to Mawlay (my Lord) Muḥammad. In 1641, Mawlay Muḥammad liberated the Tafilalt, then sent his army to invade areas to the west and north. These ventures were mostly unsuccessful.

In 1659, the last sultan to rule under the Saʿdi Dynasty was assassinated, leaving Morocco without an official royal house. In the same year, Mawlay Muḥammad's brother, al-Rashīd, revolted and fled north. Al-Rashīd ended up in the mountains east of Fés, where, according to reports, he killed and plundered a wealthy Jewish merchant (sometimes identified as the ruler of a small state). Al-Rashīd used this money to build an army and was proclaimed by several tribes as sultan. When word of al-Rashīd's good fortune reached Mawlay Muḥammad, he decided it was time to put an end to the exploits of his rebellious brother.

On August 2, 1664, the armies of the opposing brothers met on the plain of Angad. One of the first shots fired struck Mawlay Muḥammad in the throat and killed him. His troops then joined al-Rashīd, which gave him a sizeable force, which swept across northern Morocco between 1666 and 1668, conquering various foes, including tribal groups, maraboutic states (those controlled by Muslim religious leaders), a state established by a pirate chief, and the city of Fés. He then turned south, massacring the tribal group that had assumed control over Marrakech and destroying still other maraboutic states.

Morocco was reunified by a holy family, although the Alawis did not use religion to justify their expansion, as had previous dynasties—the Almoravids, Almohads, and Saʿdis, who had risen to prominence as the champions of Islam against Christian aggression. The goal of the Alawis was unabashedly political: regional dominance leading to national unity under their dynasty. The victories of Mawlay Muḥammad and Mawlay al-Rashīd reestablished the *shurafa* principle: Only a descendant of the Prophet Muḥammad had sufficient *baraka* (blessedness) to govern the faithful of Morocco; only a sharif could qualify to be sultan.

Mawlay al-Rashīd died in a freak accident during a visit to Marrakech in 1672, when his horse ran into a tree. He was succeeded by his twenty-six-year-old half brother, Mawlay Ismāʿīl, who kept the throne for fifty-five years. Ismāʿīl has been seen by his detractors as cruel and bloody, a king who kept his own people in line through a policy of terror and despoliation. However, to his admirers, he was a quite different person—noble, just, intelligent, and hardworking—the person who laid the basis for the modern Moroccan nation and considered the father of his country.

Ismāʿīl began his reign by fighting a new round of civil wars, this time against his relatives, a nephew and a brother. His nephew was killed, but not until October of 1685, and the rebellions were finally crushed in March of 1687, when the ancient city of Taroudannt in the Anti-Atlas Mountains fell and its entire population put to the sword. During these wars Ismāʿīl had to besiege Marrakech twice and Fés once, which did not endear him to either of the traditional capitals, so he anointed a new capital, the city of Meknès, 40 miles west of Fés at the gateway to the Middle Atlas Mountains. Under Ismāʿīl, the centuries-old city became a splendid place with an imperial quarter surrounded by a 60-mile wall. Built with slave labor, the palace, which was actually a series of palaces, was often compared in size and elegance to the Versailles Palace, the home of the French monarchs near Paris, which had been built around the same time.

To enforce his power, Ismāʿīl built a black slave army, the *abid*. He imported as many slaves as he could, and the trans-Saharan slave trade boomed as never before. He also sent his own large-scale raiding parties into the western Sahara and lower Senegal Valley to search for black captives. However, the largest source proved to be blacks already living in Morocco. Ismāʿīl created a massive operation designed to appropriate and confiscate black slaves from all over the country. When this proved insufficient, he reduced all black men into bondage, including many who had been manumitted (freed) or who were otherwise free. Nor was his interest confined to men; black women were also taken to serve as soldiers' wives. Couples were expected to produce children to perpetuate the *abid*. The slave soldiers constituted a privileged estate divorced from the local population with no ties except to themselves and their masters. Being totally dependent on the sultan, they were completely loyal to him. They were his "special people," whom he bound to himself by a sacred oath sworn on a holy book.

Using the *abid*, Ismāʿīl renewed Moroccan attempts to expel Europeans from enclaves they had carved out along the coast of the Atlantic Ocean. In 1681, his forces took Mamura from the Spanish and three years later a siege of Tangiers forced the English to evacuate. The most important victory came in 1689, when the Moroccans took the seaport Al-Araish (Larache), meaning "desperate fighting" in Spanish. This port had been a source of contention since 1489. The Moroccan *reconquista* closed out in 1691 with the capture of nearby Arzila.

SIGNIFICANCE

Mawlay Ismāʿīl, who died in 1727, was said to have left a dazzling legacy, a most important criterion set by his contemporaries for measuring the success of a reign in Morocco—the amount of wealth amassed. His kitchen utensils as well as the bolts on his palace doors were reportedly made of pure gold. If Ismāʿīl had a great reign, however, his successors did their best to rip the country apart on behalf of their own interests.

Ismāʿīl's legion of sons kept Morocco in chaos during the ensuing three decades in a series of civil wars and palace coups. As the best-organized force in Morocco, the *abid* became the real power, elevating and deposing sultans according to which candidate offered them the most favors. The country was finally reunited in 1757 under a capable and judicious sultan known as Muḥammad III.

Somehow, the people of Morocco were not as disgusted with the Alawis as they had been with their predecessors, the Saʿdis. Throughout the chaos, the Alawi Dynasty was recognized as the legitimate ruling house of Morocco. Under Muḥammad III, the *abid* eventually took up peaceful occupations and blended into the ranks of Moroccan society. By the end of Muḥammad's reign in 1790, Morocco was set on a course that would guide it until the coming of the French.

The idea that only a sharif, a direct descendant of the Prophet Muḥammad, was pure enough to rule over Morocco has persisted into the twenty-first century, and the Alawis still sit on that nation's throne.

—Richard L. Smith

FURTHER READING

Bourqia, Rahma, and Susan Gilson Miller, eds. *In the Shadow of the Sultan: Culture, Power, and Politics in Morocco*. Cambridge, Mass.: Harvard University Press, 1999. A collection that examines the relationship between power, legitimacy, and religion in the Moroccan monarchy, with insightful comments on the early Alawis.

El Fasi, M. "Morocco." In *General History of Africa*, edited by B. A. Ogot. Berkeley: University of California Press, 1992. An excellent synopsis of the events that led to the rise of the Alawis.

Meyers, Allan R. "Slave Soldiers and State Politics in Early Alawi Morocco, 1668-1727." *International Journal of African Historical Studies* 16 (1983): 39-48. This articles explores the rise of the *abid*, its structure, and its effectiveness under Ismāʿīl.

Munson, Henry, Jr. *Religion and Power in Morocco*. New Haven, Conn.: Yale University Press, 1993. Munson focuses on a controversy involving Ismāʿīl and a marabout named al-Yusi. Also examines larger issues dealing with early Alawi power and sharifian rule in Morocco.

Valensi, Lucette. *On the Eve of Colonialism: North Africa Before the French Conquest*. Translated by Kenneth Perkins. New York: Africana, 1977. Valensi provides a strong narrative history of the early Alawi Dynasty.

Webb, James L. A., Jr. *Desert Frontier: Ecological and Economic Change Along the Western Sahel, 1600-1850*. Madison: University of Wisconsin Press, 1995. Webb explores Moroccan policy toward its southern neighbors under the early Alawis.

SEE ALSO: 17th cent.: Songhai Empire Dissolves; Sept., 1605: Egyptians Rebel Against the Ottomans; 1612: Rise of the Arma in Timbuktu; 1660-1677: A Jihad Is Called in Senegambia.

May, 1659-May, 1660
RESTORATION OF CHARLES II

The restoration of the Stuart monarchy under King Charles II marked the end of an eighteen-year Interregnum, the revival of traditional Royalist institutions in England, and the failure of the republican experiment of the Commonwealth.

LOCALE: England and the Netherlands
CATEGORY: Government and politics

KEY FIGURES

Charles II (1630-1685), king of England, r. 1660-1685
Edward Hyde (1609-1674), confidant and loyal supporter of Charles II in exile and first earl of Clarendon, 1661-1674
George Monck (1608-1670), British general and governor of Scotland
Sir John Grenville (1628-1701), agent of General Monck

SUMMARY OF EVENT

The death of Oliver Cromwell in September, 1658, and the succession of his son Richard—"Tumbledown Dick"—to the position of lord protector left England without effective leadership, either political or military. Richard Cromwell had little to recommend him as a statesman, and he did not have the confidence of the military commanders since, unlike his father, he was not a soldier. Although the army was torn by internal dissensions, it was able to maintain sufficient cohesion to prevent either Richard or his Parliament from being effective. The leaders of the army soon forced Richard to dissolve Parliament and retire from the post of lord protector.

Because it was imperative to have some kind of civilian government, the leading army officers decided, in May of 1659, to reestablish the Rump Parliament, that segment of the Long Parliament that had survived Pride's Purge in 1648. Once restored, however, the civilian members of the Rump were far from showing gratitude to the army for having reinstated them. Immediately, they began to engage in obstructionist tactics that were designed to lessen the influence of the army upon the lives of the English people. John Lambert and Charles Fleetwood endeavored in vain to reestablish full military control of the government, but the army itself was being drastically weakened by internal dissension among officers, as well as among the rank and file.

By contrast, the army in Scotland was commanded by its military governor, General George Monck, who had been remarkably successful in creating a strong unit based on mutual respect and trust between officers and men. This spirit had produced a fierce loyalty among men of all ranks to their commander. Monck himself remained an enigma, and no one knew for certain where he stood on the matter of the restoration of the Stuart monarchy. He did not aspire to become a military dictator in the

PARLIAMENT RESTORES THE STUART MONARCHY

On May 8, 1660, both houses of the English parliament passed the following proclamation, officially recognizing Charles II as king of England and bringing the Interregnum to an end.

Although it can no way be doubted but that his Majesty's right and title to his crowns and kingdoms is and was every way completed by the death of his royal father of glorious memory, without the ceremony or solemnity of a proclamation, yet since proclamations in such cases have been always used, to the end that good subjects might upon this occasion testify to their duty and respects, and since armed violence and other the calamities of these many years last past have hitherto deprived us of any such opportunity wherein we might express our loyalty and allegiance to his Majesty, we, therefore, the Lords and Commons now assembled in Parliament, together with the lord mayor, aldermen and commons of the city of London and other freemen of this kingdom now present, do, according to our duty and allegiance, heartily, joyfully and unanimously acknowledge and proclaim that immediately upon the decease of our late Sovereign Lord King Charles the imperial crown of the realm of England, and of all the kingdoms, dominions and rights belonging to the same, did by inheritance, birthright and lawful and undoubted succession descend and come to his most excellent Majesty Charles the Second, as being lineally, justly and lawfully next heir of the blood royal of this realm, and that by the goodness and providence of almighty God he is of England, Scotland, France and Ireland the most potent, mighty and undoubted King, Defender of the Faith, &c. And thereunto we most humbly and faithfully do submit and oblige ourselves, our heirs and posterities for ever.

Source: From http://personal.pitnet.net/primarysources/restoration.html. Accessed April 27, 2005.

style of Oliver Cromwell, but he was determined to bring order to English affairs. Monck was convinced that strong measures were needed if some kind of constitutional government were to be restored in England before the unstable political and military situation produced another civil war.

In January, 1660, Monck returned with his army to England and swiftly marched to London, surprising both his enemies and potential rivals. He made every effort to cooperate with the Rump Parliament, but he gradually began to use his influence within the army to reseat all the surviving members of the Long Parliament, including those who had been elected but had been unseated through Pride's Purge. Monck arranged a meeting between the Rump and the other members. As a result of this meeting, the Long Parliament was restored. After this decisive move, it was generally assumed that the next step would be the dissolution of this Parliament followed by elections for a Convention Parliament that would prepare the government and the nation for the recall of Charles II, the eldest surviving son of the executed Charles I, then living in exile in the Netherlands at the court of his brother-in-law, William II of Orange.

From January until May of 1660, Monck remained cautious despite strong pressure from members of his own family to declare his allegiance to Charles II. After the dissolution of the Long Parliament, Monck had a conference with Sir John Grenville, who was actively working for the restoration of the monarchy. Grenville acknowledged that he was striving to effect the restoration of Charles II, and the general made a profession of joining the king's cause. Caution was still necessary, since no one knew with certainty what the results of the elections for the Convention Parliament would be, and thus Grenville committed Monck's message to King Charles to memory and then destroyed the notes before crossing the English Channel.

Grenville joined the king at Breda, in the Netherlands, and together they waited for news of the coming election. When Parliament had duly assembled, it indicated its willingness to recall Charles II. Grenville was ready immediately to deliver to Parliament the king's statement, known as the Declaration of Breda. This pronouncement had been drafted with the able assistance of Edward

Crowds in London welcome Charles II upon his return from exile in France. (Francis R. Niglutsch)

Hyde, later created earl of Clarendon, who had been in regular attendance on Charles II throughout his exile. In the declaration, every effort was made to show that the king intended to work with Parliament, and it was declared that he would give his assent to whatever Parliament would decide in those controversial matters concerning the pay of soldiers, settlement of Royalist property claims, and religious toleration.

Once most of the outstanding matters had been agreeably settled, Parliament proclaimed Charles II king and set into motion the necessary preparations to bring him home from Breda. Charles landed at Dover and then proceeded to London, which he entered on May 29, 1660. The restoration of the Stuart monarchy had been achieved without bloodshed or social upheaval.

In large part, this venture had proved successful because of the extraordinary man who entered his capital on his thirtieth birthday that May morning. Against the advice of many of his counselors, Charles had accepted the crown of Scotland in January, 1651, only to discover that he was to be used and then betrayed by some of the leaders of the Presbyterian faction. Defeated by Oliver Cromwell at the Battle of Worcester on September 3, 1651, Charles II spent the next six weeks as a fugitive in his own realm. Protected by ordinary citizens, he eventually escaped to France.

SIGNIFICANCE

Once restored in 1660, Charles rewarded the men and women who had risked everything to save him, and he did not forget the rare opportunity he had to discover the true nature of the English people. No ruler of England since Alfred the Great had had such an opportunity to share the lives of ordinary citizens, and the experience transformed Charles II. Throughout the quarter of a century that he governed England, even the critics of their sovereign had to admit that Charles II had "the common touch" and that he certainly was not cursed with the haughtiness that characterized his father, Charles I, his brother, James II, and his cousin, Louis XIV.

Blessed with the political acumen of his grandfathers, James I of England and Henry IV of France, Charles II was anxious to restore order and public confidence in the Crown as soon as possible. Always the pragmatist, he chose to forgive most of those who had participated in the execution of his father and the destruction of Royalist institutions in England. This forbearance ensured him of the loyalty of many old Cromwellians and the devotion of most of his subjects for the rest of his reign. The men who effected his Restoration were richly rewarded and honored by their king as long as they lived. Among the first to enjoy the royal bounty was George Monck, who was elevated to the peerage as first duke of Albemarle.

—*Harold L. Stansell and Clifton W. Potter, Jr.*

FURTHER READING

Fraser, Lady Antonia. *Royal Charles: Charles II and the Restoration*. New York: Alfred A. Knopf, 1979. Particularly valuable for the period before the restoration. Fraser may be an apologist for Charles, but her book is entertaining, thoroughly researched, and well written.

Hause, Earl Malcolm. *Tumbledown Dick: The Fall of the House of Cromwell*. New York: Exposition Press, 1972. This is a detailed study of the reasons for the collapse of the Cromwellian system of government. The footnotes and bibliography are combined, making them difficult to use.

Hutton, Ronald. *Charles II: King of England, Scotland, and Ireland*. New York: Oxford University Press, 1989. A thoroughly researched and well-written account, this work is a perfect counter to Lady Antonia Fraser's biography because Hutton is less admiring of his subject.

_______. *The Restoration: A Political and Religious History of England and Wales, 1658-1667*. New York: Oxford University Press, 1985. A particularly useful work. Hutton offers the serious student an analysis of the politics and people of the era.

Keeble, N. H. *The Restoration: England in the 1660's*. Malden, Mass.: Blackwell, 2002. The restoration is often described as a time of stability after the turmoil of the Civil Wars. However, Keeble argues that for people living in the 1660's, the restoration initially was a time of insecurity, with no sense of finality or assurance that Great Britain had entered a new age.

Miller, John. *The Restoration and the England of Charles II*. 2d ed. London: Longman, 1997. Examines the legacy of the Civil Wars, focusing on how the wars affected the reign of Charles II. Discusses the end of the Interregnum and the parliamentary settlements that restored Charles to power.

Morrah, Patrick. *1660: The Year of Restoration*. Boston: Beacon Press, 1960. The events of 1660, both major and minor, are chronicled in detail, creating a complete picture of the restoration of Charles II. The bibliography and detailed references are particularly valuable.

SEE ALSO: Mar., 1629-1640: "Personal Rule" of Charles I; Nov. 3, 1640-May 15, 1641: Beginning of

England's Long Parliament; 1642-1651: English Civil Wars; Aug. 17-Sept. 25, 1643: Solemn League and Covenant; Dec. 6, 1648-May 19, 1649: Establishment of the English Commonwealth; Dec. 16, 1653-Sept. 3, 1658: Cromwell Rules England as Lord Protector.

Related articles in *Great Lives from History: The Seventeenth Century, 1601-1700:* Charles I; Charles II (of England); First Earl of Clarendon; Oliver Cromwell; James I; James II; John Lambert; Louis XIV; George Monck.

November 7, 1659
Treaty of the Pyrenees

The Treaty of the Pyrenees ended hostilities between France and Spain that began in 1635 in the midst of the Thirty Years' War. The two countries were reconciled by the marriage of King Louis XIV to the Spanish infanta Marie-Thérèse. Louis received several Spanish territories and agreed to reconcile himself to the duke of Lorraine and the prince of Condé, both of whom had fought for Spain.

Locale: Isle of Pheasants, Bidassoa River, on the border of France and Spain

Categories: Diplomacy and international relations; wars, uprisings, and civil unrest

Key Figures

Louis XIV (1638-1715), king of France, r. 1643-1715

Philip IV (1605-1665), king of Spain, r. 1621-1665

Jules Mazarin (1602-1661), chief minister of France, 1643-1661

Luis de Haro (1598-1661), chief minister of Spain, 1643-1661

Marie-Thérèse (1638-1683), queen consort of France, r. 1660-1683

The Great Condé (Louis II de Bourbon; 1621-1686), military leader and French rebel

Summary of Event

Bourbon France and Habsburg Spain became belligerents in 1635 in the midst of the Thirty Years' War. Spain's Philip IV aided his Austrian Habsburg relatives, while France, under the guidance of Cardinal de Richelieu and Jules Mazarin, chief ministers, worked to keep Habsburg power in check.

Mutual animosity was fueled when the Spanish supported the French uprising known as the Wars of the Fronde (1648-1653), and the French Huguenot, the Great Condé, one of the Fronde's leaders, fought successfully for Spain from the Spanish Netherlands.

France, for its part, had supported the Catalan Revolt (1640), a serious threat to the Spanish crown. French goals were largely met in the Peace of Westphalia (1648), but Philip kept Spain out of the congress, making a separate peace with the Dutch in January, 1648 (Treaty of Münster). By the mid-1650's, France was exhausted by the continued warfare with Spain and suggested a peace plan.

Among other stipulations, Louis XIV would marry the Spanish infanta Marie-Thérèse, long an aspiration of Mazarin and Louis's mother. Philip IV, who sought an Austrian marriage for his daughter, refused the overture, and the war continued. The tide turned in France's favor when Mazarin engaged the services of Cromwell's English troops in March, 1657, and orchestrated the anti-Habsburg League of the Rhine (August, 1658). Within a year French and English forces under Marshal Turenne beat the Spanish army of Flanders at the Battle of the Dunes (June 14, 1658) and quickly occupied numerous Spanish territories in the Netherlands and threatened Brussels. Spain was actively seeking peace, and negotiations began on August 13.

Both French chief minister Mazarin and Spanish chief minister Luis de Haro had served their respective kings for nearly two decades, but Mazarin proved the abler negotiator. Indeed, France held the stronger position, but Mazarin's personal acumen combined with his strong desire to leave a major foreign policy coup behind him made him irresistible. In the course of their twenty-five meetings it became clear that Mazarin had three major goals: to assert clearly the victory of the French at Spain's expense, to add strategic territory at Spain's expense, and to marry young Louis to Marie-Thérèse. Spain in fact led with the marriage proposal as a way of opening the negotiations. Philip's situation had changed with the birth of an heir, and there was little likelihood that the Marie-Thérèse or her son—and therefore a Bourbon—would inherit the Spanish throne. The negotiators decided that the Marie-Thérèse would renounce her dynastic claim upon marrying Louis. Philip sealed the re-

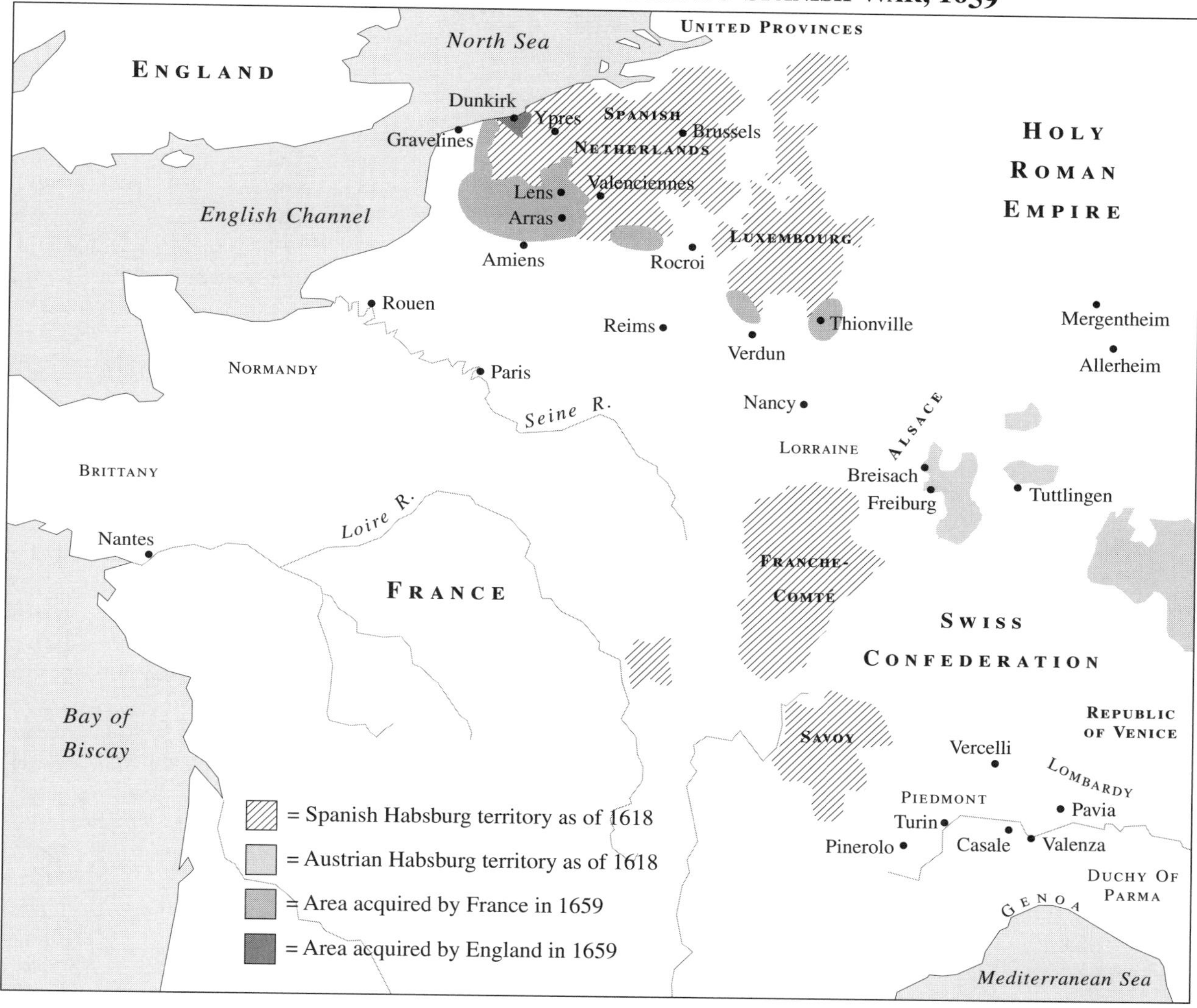

nunciation with a promised payment of 500,000 ecus, an utterly unrealistic sum given Spain's financial straits.

France relinquished any right to interfere in Spanish internal affairs as well as claims to Catalonia. In return, Spain promised to not interfere in French internal affairs and to cede the following territories: From the Pyrenees region, the French gained Roussillon and part of Cerdagne, and from the Spanish Netherlands, they gained Gravelines, Bourbourg, St. Venant, and Bergues in Flanders. The French also gained the cities of Thionville and Damvillers in Hainault, a part of Luxembourg, and Artois. France also returned a number of occupied cities to the Spanish. Louis thus gained the Pyrenees as a southern border and a considerable buffer against the Dutch to the north.

Philip treated the fate of the Great Condé as a matter of personal honor, and some of his territorial cessions were made specifically for the prince's rehabilitation and return to French public life. Condé had fought well for France, engineering several victories—including Rocroi—before turning against the young king in the Fronde. Though imprisoned for his role, Condé was released in 1651 by Mazarin, who had been under pressure from important nobles. The prince then joined the Spanish forces in the Netherlands, leading the army that was defeated at the Dunes in 1658. Louis issued the sealed letters patent

French minister Jules Mazarin signed a peace treaty with Spain, which ended decades of conflict between the two countries and marked the ascent of France as a European power and the descent of Spain and the Habsburgs. Mazarin attempted but failed to secure the Spanish Netherlands for France, however, and he died in 1661 knowing that, despite the 1659 treaty, hostilities between France and Spain would continue for many years. (Francis R. Niglutsch)

that constituted his pardon in January, 1660. Philip also had been served by the duke of Lorraine, who also was reconciled to Louis, though at a cost of part of his territory (Bar, Clermont en Argonne, Stenay, Moyenvic, Dun, and Jametz ceded to Louis) and right of passage for his troops through all of it. The final treaty consisted of seventy-four articles and covered seventy-nine folio pages. The two state ministers signed the final document on November 7, 1659, and all that was left was for the two sovereigns to do likewise.

Neither Philip nor Louis would deign to leave their national soil, but a unique solution was found by staging the signing ceremonies on the Isle of Pheasants in the midst of the Bidassoa River, an island claimed by neither country. Louis's royal architect, Louis Le Vau, designed and built the pavilion, which was placed on the very center of the island. The French half was decorated in blue and gold in the French style, while Spanish red and yellow dominated the other half. On June 6, 1660, the two monarchs met to sign the treaty. The royal guards of each lined their respective riverbanks, and the pavilion filled with distinguished bureaucrats, diplomats, and nobles, each vying with all others for splendor. As this was Louis's first trip to southern France, he took his time as he traveled to and from the ceremony, stopping at Saint-Jean-de-Luz on June 9 to marry his new bride.

Significance

The Treaty of the Pyrenees marked not only the end a quarter century of Spanish-French hostilities but also the rise to dominance of Bourbon France in Europe and the sunset of Spain and the Habsburgs.

Spain retained a large and powerful empire in the Netherlands, Italy, and the Iberian Peninsula, but its ability to project power and enforce its will was slipping away rapidly. The Habsburg encirclement of France was far stronger on paper than in reality, and Louis knew it. The position of the Spanish Netherlands was less secure than ever, a situation exacerbated by Spain's inability to pay even the first installment of the huge indemnity.

Mazarin's failure to secure the entire Spanish territoryresulted in decades of horrific conflict. For Louis, royal rights—including patrimony—were divinely bestowed and might not be renounced or otherwise alienated. He set aside his wife's renunciation upon Philip's death in 1665, an act that led to the War of Devolution (1667-1668) and the French-Dutch War (1672-1678). Louis again asserted Bourbon rights to Spanish inheritance in 1701, after the death of the weak and childless King Charles II. It took the Wars of the Spanish Succession (1701-1714) to place his grandson on the throne as Philip V.

Additionally, Pope Alexander VII was livid when he learned of the treaty: That two major Catholic powers would make peace without reference to the supreme pontiff was both an insult and a sign of declining papal prestige and influence.

—*Joseph P. Byrne*

Further Reading

Black, Jeremy. *European Warfare, 1494-1660*. New York: Routledge, 2002. Chapter 7 gives a brief overview of the Franco-Spanish conflict from 1635 to 1659.

Stradling, R. A. *Philip IV and the Government of Spain, 1621-1665*. Cambridge, England: Cambridge University Press, 1988. A positive treatise on Philip's reign, which emphasizes the king's independence after the dismissal of his court favorite, the count-duke of Olivares.

Sturdy, David J. *Richelieu and Mazarin: A Study in Statesmanship*. New York: Palgrave, 2003. Places the war and peacemaking with Spain within a broad study of Mazarin's career in diplomacy.

Treasure, Geoffrey. *Mazarin: The Crisis of Absolutism in France*. New York: Routledge, 1995. Chapter 29, "Peace with Spain," examines the hostilities and the treaty from the French point of view.

Williams, Lynn. *Letters from the Pyrenees: Don Luis Méndez de Haro's Correspondence to Philip IV of Spain*. Exeter, England: University of Exeter Press, 2000. This work includes both original letters in translation and summaries of these key documents.

See also: July 5, 1601-Apr., 1604: Siege of Oostende; Mar. 31, 1621-Sept. 17, 1665: Reign of Philip IV; May, 1640-Jan. 23, 1641: Revolt of the Catalans; July, 1643-Oct. 24, 1648: Peace of Westphalia; June, 1648: Wars of the Fronde Begin; 1661: Absolute Monarchy Emerges in France; May 24, 1667-May 2, 1668: War of Devolution; Apr. 6, 1672-Aug. 10, 1678: French-Dutch War; Aug. 10, 1678-Sept. 26, 1679: Treaties of Nijmegen; 1689-1697: Wars of the League of Augsburg.

Related articles in *Great Lives from History: The Seventeenth Century, 1601-1700:* The Great Condé; Louis XIV; Marie-Thérèse; Jules Mazarin; Count-Duke of Olivares; Philip IV; Cardinal de Richelieu; Viscount de Turenne.

1660's-1700
First Microscopic Observations

Observations through the microscope opened the doors to a previously invisible and unknown world, confirming the existence of microorganisms and producing the first descriptions of cells in plants and animals.

Locale: England, Italy, and the Netherlands
Categories: Science and technology; inventions; health and medicine; biology

Key Figures

Antoni van Leeuwenhoek (1632-1723), Dutch microscope maker
Marcello Malpighi (1628-1694), Italian physician and scientist
Nehemiah Grew (1641-1712), English botanist
Jan Swammerdam (1637-1680), Dutch biologist
Robert Hooke (1635-1703), English scientist

Summary of Event

No true cell theory existed in the seventeenth century. That red blood cells were homologous with cells in solid animal tissue was an unknown fact, and no one had inferred that the concept of the "cell" included plant and animal cells, single-cell organisms (such as the protozoa), and sex cells. Moreover, no one understood the functions of the cell, that is, no one knew how cells functioned until the invention of the microscope.

The first compound microscopes, built in the first half of the seventeenth century, were in widespread use by the 1620's. Microscopes had two or three convex lenses with an average magnification of up to 50 times normal, with the best at 100 times normal. Though single lens magnifying devices such as spectacles and flea-glass lenses existed earlier, it was not until later in the seventeenth century that lens grinders began making single lens microscopes.

Antoni van Leeuwenhoek perfected the single lens microscope with its tiny bead lens and its best magnification of more than 250 times normal in the late 1660's. While the much weaker compound microscopes were easier to use, they were subject to chromic aberrations, a problem not solved until the nineteenth century. The stronger single-lens microscope was much more difficult to use, however, as it had an extremely short focal length often requiring the lens to be placed on the object. Robert Hooke and Nehemiah Grew, and perhaps Marcello Malpighi, used compound microscopes. Jan Swammerdam constructed single lens microscopes also, some with lenses as tiny as 1 to 2 millimeters in diameter.

Hooke's *Micrographia: Or, Some Physiological Descriptions of Minute Bodies Made by Magnifying Glasses* (1665; better known as *Micrographia*), considered to be the first publication to describe cells, marked an advance over earlier microscopic work. Hooke dissected and described not only common things such as glass beads and the edges of a razors (revealing imperfections) but also natural forms such as snowflakes, molds, nettle, hair, and the head of a fly (revealing perfections).

Also, Hooke called "pores" and "cells" those structure he observed in everything from stones to living bodies such as wood, plants, and bones, theorizing that in living bodies, pores conveyed juices. The pores and cells resembled little boxes separated by "diaphragms." He believed that these cells explained some of the properties of cork, such as its lightness and buoyancy, but the pores of plants such as the carrot, fern, and reed revealed a different arrangement. Hooke also observed pores in a feather shaft. Using the terms "caverns," "bubbles," or "cells" to designate the feather-shaft pores, he described what looked more like a froth of tiny bubbles than pores separated by a diaphragm. In plants, the cells were filled with juices, though Hooke could not detect a "passage" to account for the phenomenon of "sweating." He had hoped to find analogous phenomena in animal vessels.

Grew, author of many papers and several books on plants, studied the anatomy of plant roots, leaves, reproductive parts and products, and their chemical composition, attempting to explain plant nutrition by the circulation of fluids and air. Distinguishing with the naked eye the parenchyma and ligneous tissues, he discovered that a plant's woody tissues consisted of numerous tiny "vessels" or fibers as well as separate "bubbles" or "bladders" (that is, cells composed of the parenchymatous part).

In *Anatome plantarum* (1675, 1679; plant anatomy), Malpighi illustrated the cellular arrangement of herbaceous plants such as portulaca, wheat, chicory, and hemp as well as bark and trees such as the willow and poplar. The word Malpighi used to describe this arrangement was "utriculus" (small bag), for, like Hooke, he believed the individual cell contained fluid. Malpighi is considered, along with Grew, the cofounder of the study of plant anatomy.

Cells within the solid organs of animals were more difficult to detect (lacking the plant's cell wall), but animal blood would help in the discovery of the animal cell. The first reference to red blood cells appeared in 1665, with Malpighi's observation of reddish "globules" of fat in the blood vessels of the hedgehog. (The use of the word "fat" illustrates an uncertainty, for microscopists confused fat and blood cells for some time.) Jan Swammerdam also observed red blood cells, which appeared to him also as reddish particles in a clear fluid. The date of Swammerdam's observation is not certain because his works were undated and were published posthumously by the Dutch physician Hermann Boerhaave as *Bybel der naturre* (1737-1738; *Book of Nature: Or, The History of Insects*, 1758).

Leeuwenhoek made the first definitive description of red blood cells, or "globules," in 1674, but he used the word "globule" also for particles in milk (fat particles). In a letter to Hooke dated March 3, 1682, Leeuwenhoek observed that the particles in mammalian (including human) blood shared the red color when in a group of three of four cells, and shared the same flat oval shape.

Marcello Malpighi. (National Library of Medicine)

Leeuwenhoek's next discovery, in 1688, in effect replicated a discovery made by Malpighi in 1661: the existence of capillaries. The two had thus solved a problem concerning the circulation of the blood, which had been proposed by William Harvey. Harvey, however, was been unable to see the "communication" between the veins and arteries that his theory demanded. In 1688 also, Leeuwenhoek observed red blood cells coursing through the capillaries in the tail of a tadpole. In the frog's gills, the vessels were so thin than only a single corpuscle at a time could flow through them.

Leeuwenhoek also discovered other kinds of cells, including the spermatozoan, animalcules, and bacteria. He discovered animalcules (protozoa such as ciliates and flagellates) in rainwater in 1674 and in a pepper infusion in 1676. Also in 1676, he described an animalcule, which, based on that description as well as his estimate of its size, must have been a free-living bacterium. He observed many other animalcules, including intestinal protozoa and bacteria in human plaque. In 1677, he observed spermatozoa in the semen of a man with gonorrhea.

Significance

Scientific interest in microscopy and cell theory began to wane around 1680, though Leeuwenhoek continued to publish in the field until his death in 1723. Cell theory developed in the nineteenth century, however, initiated by the work of Matthias Schleiden (1804-1881) in botany and Theodor Schwann (1810-1882) in physiology.

Seventeenth century microscopy, specifically, is noteworthy for applying the Baconian ideal of empirical science. In the preface to *Micrographia*, Hooke asserted that it was time for plain observations by scientists to replace "brain and fancy," and Swammerdam rejected book knowledge in favor of direct observation. The microscope certainly expanded the horizon of observation.

Microscopy also illustrates how mechanical philosophy was applied to subjects beyond physics. For example, Swammerdam advocated a theory of preformationism, that is, that animals were not generated but instead grew from their inception. In addition, Malpighi, Hooke, and Grew attempted to place their findings within contemporaries philosophies of nature.

—*Kristen L. Zacharias*

Further Reading

Cobb, Matthew. "Reading and Writing 'The Book of Nature': Jan Swammerdam, 1637-1680." *Endeavour* 24 (2000): 122-128. This article, by a noted Swammerdam scholar, describes the biologist's work.

Dobell, C. *Antony van Leeuwenhoek and His "Little Animals."* London: Bale and Danielsson, 1932. This work contains translations from Leeuwenhoek's observations of protozoa and bacteria as well as a description of his life. Includes illustrations.

Ford, Brian J. *Single Lens: The Story of the Simple Microscope*. New York: Harper, Row, 1985. Ford details the development and use of the microscope from its invention to the nineteenth century. Includes good illustrations.

Fournier, Marian. *The Fabric of Life: Microscopy in the Seventeenth Century*. Baltimore: Johns Hopkins University Press, 1996. Examines the work of Leeuwenhoek and four other scientists to explain the reasons for the microscope's appearance and eventual eclipse in the seventeenth century.

Harris, Henry. *The Birth of the Cell*. New Haven, Conn.: Yale University Press, 1999. A short history of the discovery of the cell, covering the seventeenth to the early twentieth century.

Hooke, Robert. *Micrographia: Or, Some Physiological Descriptions of Minute Bodies Made by Magnifying Glasses with Observations and Inquiries Thereupon*. 1665. Reprint. New York: Dover, 1961. Contains the original observation on cork and many other objects. This work is characteristic of the new philosophy of observation.

Huerta, Robert D. *Giants of Delft: Johannes Vermeer and the Natural Philosophers, the Parallel Search for Knowledge During the Age of Discovery*. Lewisburg, Pa.: Bucknell University Press, 2003. Although this book focuses on artist Jan Vermeer's perception of the world, it describes how that perception was influenced by the microscope and other discoveries in the science of optics. Several chapters describe how seventeenth century scientists created a "more optical" way of viewing the world.

Piccolino, Marco. "Marcello Malpighi and the Difficult Birth of Modern Life Sciences." *Endeavour* 23, no. 4 (1999). Focuses on Malpighi's contributions to science, including his pioneering work in microscopic medical anatomy, the composition of the human body, and the pathology of diseases.

Ruestow, Edward G. *The Microscope in the Dutch Republic: The Shaping of Discovery*. New York: Cambridge University Press, 1996. Ruestow focuses on the work of Swammerdam and Leeuwenhoek, and includes a chapter on the development of the microscope.

Wilson, Catherine. *The Invisible World: Early Modern Philosophy and the Invention of the Microscope*. Princeton, N.J.: Princeton University Press, 1995. Wilson discusses theoretical issues that influenced early microscopy, including the preformation-epigenesis dispute and the theory of contagion developed in response to the discovery of infusoria. She examines also the larger philosophical issues of the day, such as the nature of generation.

See also: 17th cent.: Advances in Medicine; Sept., 1608: Invention of the Telescope; 1672-1684: Leeuwenhoek Discovers Microscopic Life.

Related articles in *Great Lives from History: The Seventeenth Century, 1601-1700:* Galileo; William Harvey; Jan Baptista van Helmont; Robert Hooke; Christiaan Huygens; Antoni van Leeuwenhoek; Hans Lippershey; Marcello Malpighi; Jan Swammerdam; Jan Vermeer.

1660-1677
A Jihad Is Called in Senegambia

Muslim preacher Nāṣir-al Dīn waged a jihad against his desert overlords and then against the part-Muslim rulers of African kingdoms south of the Senegal River. The jihad set a pattern for popular uprisings against lax Muslim rulers and established a precedent for future Islamic reform movements across much of West Africa.

Locale: Southern Mauritania, northern Senegal
Categories: Wars, uprisings, and civil unrest; religion and theology; government and politics; economics

Key Figures

Nāṣir al-Dīn (d. 1674), Muslim preacher and jihad leader
N'diaye Sal (fl. seventeenth century), a leading Wolof marabout of Kayor, and supporter of Nāṣir al-Dīn
Detye Maram N'galgu (d. 1683), *damel*, or king, of Kayor, r. 1681-1683, who resisted the jihad
Fara Kumba (d. 1673), *brak*, or king, of Walo, who was deposed and killed by Nāṣir al-Dīn's followers

Summary of Event

Senegambia, long a focus of economic and social development in West Africa, became an early center of Islam and of trans-Saharan trade. By the seventeenth century, Senegambia also became a center of trade—including the slave trade—with Europe. Three major ethnic groups dominated the region: nomadic Moors north of the Senegal River and agricultural Wolof and cattle-herding/farming Tukulor south of the river. All three societies were stratified, consisting of warrior-nobles, free farmers or herders, artisans, and slaves.

Largely or partially Muslim, these societies also included clerical, or maraboutic, communities, which included specialists in Islamic education, preaching, and commerce; the marabouts were ranked between the nobles and the freemen. Because of their control of literacy, the marabouts also served as bureaucrats and scribes. The jihad of Nāṣir al-Dīn represented an attempt by the marabouts to seize power from the traditional elites, creating in the process a theocratic state.

Nāṣir al-Dīn was a scholar and a teacher of one of the maraboutic, or Zawiya, clans of the Moors. Following a classic Islamic reform pattern, he sought to build a Muslim theocracy that would transcend ethnic and class divisions and would resemble the ideal community of the Prophet. To accomplish this, Nāṣir al-Dīn established a *jama'a* (community) among the Mauritanian Zawiya clans, free of tribal and blood allegiances. He called his community and its followers Toubenan, from the Arabic root *tabwa* (initiation). The Toubenan were united by adherence to sharia (Islamic law) and by loyalty to Nāṣir al-Dīn, who took the title of imam. Though at first most of the Toubenan were Zawiya Moors, Nāṣir al-Dīn also promoted his reform agenda south of the river, accepting Wolof and Tukulor initiates, including N'diaye Sal, a leading marabout of the Wolof kingdom of Kayor.

Nāṣir al-Dīn began the preaching phase of his movement in the 1660's. First he sent his agents throughout southern Mauritania to spread the word, asking people to support his calls for reform. Having established a secure desert base, he expanded his propaganda campaign to the sedentary kingdoms south of the Senegal. He sent his *talibes* (students) to preach to the nominally Muslim *deniyanke satigi* (king) of Futa Toro, asking him to pray more regularly, to limit himself to four wives, and to embrace the Toubenan. After seeing his envoys rebuffed four times, politely at first and finally in chains, the leader of the Toubenan came to preach in Futa Toro. Nāṣir al-Dīn argued that the *deniyanke satigi* was an unfit ruler because he exploited and enslaved his (Muslim) people, failed to defend Muslims from attack, and because he was a "lax Muslim." Going from town to town and raising a mass following, Nāṣir al-Dīn succeeded in driving the *satigi* into exile and installing an emir (governor) in 1673, thus establishing a foothold south of the Senegal.

That same year, the marabouts of the Toubenan followed up their successes in Futa Toro by carrying their preaching campaign to the Wolof kingdoms of the Lower Senegal—the Kayor and Walo—where they were welcomed by local clerics, including N'diaye Sal of Kayor. The *damel* (king) of Kayor, Detye Maram N'galgu, tried to resist Toubenan pressure for Islamic reform, but N'diaye Sal killed him and replaced him with his brother Mafaali Gey, who converted to Islam and declared his allegiance to Nāṣir al-Dīn. However, N'diaye Sal killed Mafaali Gey for violating sharia, and then declared himself viceroy within the framework of the Toubenan theocracy. The *brak* of Walo, Fara Kumba, also resisted, but he, too, was defeated and killed by the Toubenan, and a puppet *brak* was installed. Nāṣir al-Dīn thus laid the groundwork for the military phase of his jihad through systematic propaganda campaigns—supported by dynastic intrigue—that resulted in the overthrow of the Senegambian kings.

The military phase of the jihad began in earnest in the mid-1670's. Nāṣir al-Dīn moved north into the desert to confront his old patrons, the Moorish noble clans, or Hassani, demanding that they pay him the *zakat* (Islamic tax) owed him as imam. He regarded the Hassani as fair game for jihad because they also were lax Muslims, and were "cutters of the road," that is, they interfered with trade. The Zawiya clerics fought and won three battles with the Hassani, but the third battle, in 1674, cost the life of Nāṣir al-Dīn. Most of the Zawiya, despite their grief, remained loyal to the movement and carried on under a succession of five imams until 1677. The Hassani overcame the Toubenan in the desert, and dynastic resurgence reversed them in Walo and Kayor, as a new *brak* and a new *damel*, who were not clients of Nāṣir al-Dīn, seized power. The remaining Toubenan clerics congregated in Futa Toro, where the returning *deniyanke satigi* ultimately defeated them.

Economically, Nāṣir al-Dīn's jihad can be considered a form of resistance by traditional merchants who plied the old desert side trade in grain and slaves north to Mauritania. With the support of Zawiya marabouts, the merchants tried to reorient trade to the new east-west axis. This east-west trade, supplied by European merchants, attracted slaves and grain to the French port of St. Louis at the mouth of the Senegal River in exchange for European trade goods. This trade then fed into the growing transatlantic slave trade. Tukulor and Wolof rulers south of the Senegal were seizing their own subjects, many of them Muslim, and selling them to French traders in exchange for tempting trade goods, including firearms. Nāṣir al-Dīn was able to add revolutionary luster to his jihad by undermining the legitimacy of rulers who pillaged and sold their own subjects.

Politically, the movement of the Toubenan into sedentary areas was an attempt to seize power by the local maraboutic class under the leadership of Nāṣir al-Dīn. The political ascendancy of the marabouts was feasible because they had the ideology (monotheism and sharia) and the infrastructure (teachers, jurists, scribes) necessary to sustain a viable state. Nāṣir al-Dīn's rule was rigorous and ascetic. He demanded initiation (*tabwa*) into the Toubenan and conformity to Islamic law, and he forbade the pillage and enslavement of one's own (Muslim) subjects. He also introduced classic Islamic taxation, including *zakat*, which he collected under his authority as imam and used to support his community

SIGNIFICANCE

The defeat of the Toubenan resulted in a permanent reimposition of Hassani dominance over the Zawiya clans, as well as the restoration of the Wolof and Tukulor kings. Nonetheless, Nāṣir al-Dīn's jihad continued to have an important political and ideological impact in West African history. Lines of reform tradition stretch from the Toubenan to the later Senegambian jihads of the eighteenth century. Nāṣir al-Dīn established the Muslim-style imamate as the standard form of government for all of them. He preached reform, returning to the ideal Muslim community of early Islamic times, and he also established the tradition of jihad as a means of prosecuting a reformist agenda. Though he failed to overcome the Hassani, he did temporarily establish Islamic rule over much of the Lower Senegal.

Many Tukulor clerics of Futa Toro who supported Nāṣir al-Dīn fled to other parts of Senegambia when the *deniyanke satigi* returned to power in 1677, carrying the institution of the imamate and jihad and reform traditions with them. Nāṣir al-Dīn's jihad was, therefore, the first in a series of Islamic reform movements leading up to the great West African jihad states of the nineteenth century. Some scholars argue that the jihad of Nāṣir al-Dīn laid the political, social, and religious foundations upon which much of modern West Africa was built.

—*Stephen Harmon*

FURTHER READING

Barry, Boubacar. *Senegambia and the Atlantic Slave Trade*. New York: Cambridge University Press, 1998. Barry examines the economic impact of Nāṣir al-Dīn's movement, especially as it relates to the transatlantic and trans-Saharan slave trades.

Clark, Andrew Francis, and Lucie Colvin Phillips. *Historical Dictionary of Senegal*. Lanham, Md.: Scarecrow Press, 1995. A good reference to Senegal's history.

Curtin, Philip. "Jihad in West Africa: Early Phases and Interrelations in Mauritania and Senegal." *Journal of African History* 12 (1971): 11-24. Curtin gives a brief account of the movement and its role in developing the jihad pattern in West African Islam.

Harmon, Stephen. "Islamic Reform and Community in Senegambia: c. 1660-1800." *Afrika Zamani* (1997): 55-85. Harmon examines the jihad, with a focus on its Islamic dimensions, and places it in the broader context of West African Islamic history.

Norris, H. T. "Znaga Islam During the Seventeenth and Eighteenth Centuries" *Bulletin of the School of Oriental and African Studies* 32 (1969): 496-526. Norris discusses the evolution of Islam and Islamic reform in Mauritanian society during the time of Nāṣir al-Dīn.

Northrup, Daniel, ed. *The Atlantic Slave Trade*. Boston: Houghton Mifflin, 2002. A collection of documents touching on the various issues relating mainly to trade's underlying economic factors.

Stewart, Charles. *Islam and Social Order in Mauritania*. New York: Oxford University Press, 1973. Stewart explains the clan and class structures of Moorish society and the role played in those structures by the Zawiya, or maraboutic clans.

SEE ALSO: Sept., 1605: Egyptians Rebel Against the Ottomans; 1617-1693: European Powers Vie for Control of Gorée; 1619-c. 1700: The Middle Passage to American Slavery; Oct., 1625-1637: Dutch and Portuguese Struggle for the Guinea Coast; 1640: Foundation of the Darfur Sultanate; 1659: Expansion of the Alawis.

RELATED ARTICLE in *Great Lives from History: The Seventeenth Century, 1601-1700:* Njinga.

1660-1692
BOYLE'S LAW AND THE BIRTH OF MODERN CHEMISTRY

Often called the "father of modern chemistry," Robert Boyle discovered the inverse relationship between the pressure and volume of a gas. He devised influential definitions of a chemical element, compound, and reaction. He also used his corpuscular philosophy, an atomic theory of matter, to explain his experimental results.

LOCALE: England
CATEGORIES: Science and technology; physics; philosophy

KEY FIGURES

Robert Boyle (1627-1691), Irish chemist and physicist
Robert Hooke (1635-1703), English physicist
René Descartes (1596-1650), French philosopher, physicist, and mathematician
Pierre Gassendi (1592-1655), French priest and atomist
Otto von Guericke (1602-1686), German physicist who invented the air pump
Edmé Mariotte (1620-1684), French priest and physicist
John Mayow (1641-1679), English physiologist
Richard Lower (1631-1691), English physician

SUMMARY OF EVENT

For chemistry to become a modern science, old ideas had to be abandoned and new ideas introduced. During the seventeenth century the scientist most responsible for the transformation of alchemy into chemistry was Robert Boyle. Unlike many natural philosophers of the Scientific Revolution, who viewed chemistry as either a pseudoscience or a practical craft, Boyle treated chemistry as worthy of a rigorous experimental approach.

Born into the aristocracy in Ireland, Boyle had been a child prodigy who developed his intellectual skills at Eton and, with a tutor, on a tour throughout Europe. He studied the new scientific ideas of such natural philosophers as Galileo, Pierre Gassendi, and René Descartes. After his return to England in the mid-1640's, he devoted more and more of his time to scientific studies. He became a member of a group of science enthusiasts called the Invisible College, which was the forerunner of the Royal Society, an important institution in Boyle's later career.

While at Oxford in the late 1650's, Boyle learned of Otto von Guericke's demonstration in Magdeburg, Germany, of the tremendous pressure of the atmosphere. Guericke used his invention, an air pump, to suck the air out of two metal hemispheres fitted together along a circumferential flange. Several teams of horses were unable to disjoin them, but as soon as air was reintroduced into the joined hemispheres, they readily fell apart. With the help of a talented assistant, Robert Hooke, Boyle constructed an air pump that was much more effective than the one used in Germany. Indeed, so effective was this pump at evacuating experimental vessels that *vacuum Boylianum* ("Boylean vacuum") became a standard scientific designation.

For two years Boyle used his air pump to perform a variety of experiments. He demonstrated that a feather and a lump of lead fell at the same velocity in a vacuum, that a clock's ticking was silent in a vacuum, and that electrical and magnetic attraction and repulsion remained undiminished in a vacuum. Birds and mice did not long survive in a vacuum, and a candle flame sputtered out when deprived of air. Boyle published an account of his research in his first scientific book, *New Experiments Physico-Mechanicall, Touching the Spring of the Air and Its Effects* (1660).

Because of Boyle's belief that he had created a vacuum, a controversial notion at the time, his book provoked criticisms from Aristotelians and Cartesians who believed that voided spaces were impossible in a universe completely filled with matter. In response to a particular critic, the Jesuit Franciscus Linus, Boyle devised his most famous experiment, an account of which he published in the second edition of his book in 1662. Using a seventeen-foot-long J-shaped glass tube sealed at the short end, Boyle trapped air in the sealed end by pouring mercury into the long open tube. He discovered that, when he doubled the weight of the mercury in the long tube, the volume of the trapped air was halved. This discovery of the inverse relationship between a gas's pressure and volume came to be called Boyle's Law in English-speaking countries. It was called Mariotte's Law in continental European countries, because, in 1676, Edmé Mariotte, independently of Boyle, discovered this inverse relationship with the important provision that the temperature during measurements had to be kept constant.

Robert Boyle. (Library of Congress)

As a corpuscularian philosopher, Boyle tried to explain the results of his experiments mechanically, but his corpuscles were not the same as Gassendi's or Descartes's. Boyle's corpuscles had size, shape, and mobility, though he was cautious in using these theoretical entities to account for experimental phenomena. For example, in the case of the compressibility of air, he proposed that air corpuscles might be like tiny coiled springs, but since air was also involved in chemical processes such as combustion, Boyle believed that air was a peculiar substance, an elastic fluid teaming with foreign materials.

Boyle's theoretical ideas made their appearance when he published *The Sceptical Chymist* (1661, rev. 1679). This work, often called his masterpiece, was written as a dialogue among spokespeople holding different views about the nature of chemistry. However, it was clearly an attack on the ancient Aristotelian notion that all matter is composed of four elements, earth, water, air, and fire, and a repudiation of the Renaissance view that all chemical phenomena can be explained through the three principles of salt, mercury, and sulfur.

Unwilling to rely on previous authorities, the "sceptical" Boyle emphasized that chemical ideas had to be grounded in observations and experiments. For him, no

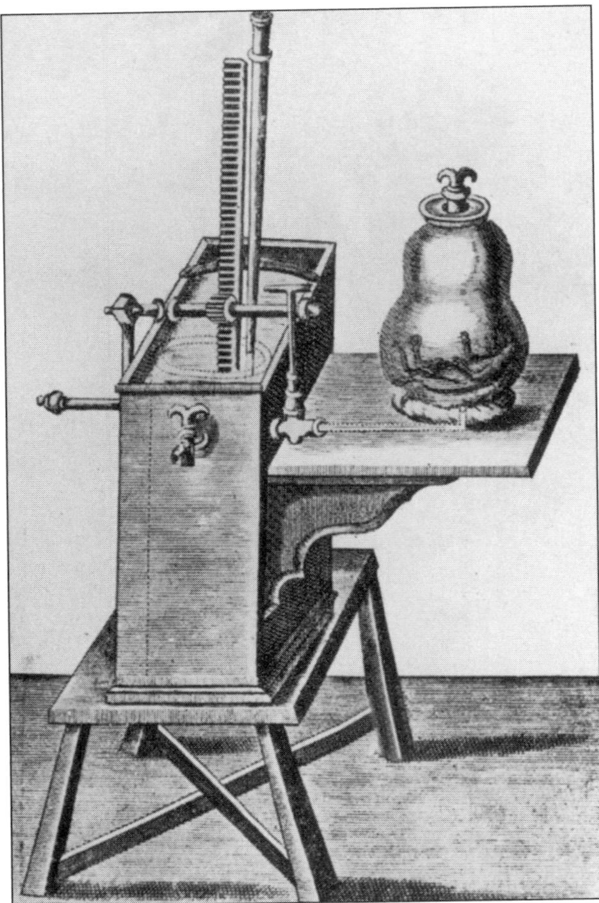

One of Boyle's experiments demonstrated that air is necessary to support animal life. Air was pumped out of a vessel containing birds, who died from suffocation. (Hulton|Archive by Getty Images)

reason existed for limiting the elements to three or four, since an element was basically a substance that could not be broken down into simpler substances. These elemental substances, which are capable of combinations in various compounds, were behind all material things and their changes. Though Boyle's "operational definition" of elements became influential, however, he found it difficult in practice to determine whether particular substances were simple or complex.

Not only did Boyle contribute to physical and theoretical chemistry, he also helped found qualitative and quantitative analysis. For example, he developed identification tests to make sure he was using pure materials. Gold was pure if it had the correct specific gravity and dissolved in aqua regia (a mixture of hydrochloric and nitric acids) but not in aqua fortis (nitric acid alone). He also used precipitates, solubility, and the colors of substances in flames as analytical tools. He was especially fascinated with color indicators as a way to distinguish acidic, alkaline, or neutral substances. He discovered that a blue plant material, "syrup of violets," turned red in acids, green in alkalis, and remained unchanged in neutral solutions.

Throughout the history of chemistry, researchers used fire to study chemical changes. Boyle knew that combustion stopped in the absence of air, but he also knew that gunpowder burned under water (he thought that the saltpeter in gunpowder acted as an air substitute). Like other researchers, Boyle also observed that, when metals were heated in air, they formed a powdery substance (a "calx") that was heavier than the original metal. He explained the weight increase as due to the addition of "igneous corpuscles," but a contemporary, John Mayow, was closer to the truth when he speculated that a substance common to air and saltpeter (now known to be oxygen) might be the cause of combustion.

Like other experimenters, Boyle discovered a connection between combustion and respiration, since he observed that a burning candle and a breathing mouse both reduced the volume of air. Mayow believed that the blood in the lungs absorbed the "combustive principle" from the air and distributed it throughout the body. Another contemporary of Boyle, Richard Lower, discovered that air could change dark venous blood to bright red arterial blood. Besides blood, Boyle was also interested in urine, from which he prepared phosphorus, whose luminosity in air intrigued him (he initiated the practice of storing phosphorus under water). Although Boyle failed to find the true role that air played in respiration and in the combustion of phosphorus, his emphasis on methodical experimentation served as an exemplar for those eighteenth century scientists who would eventually make these discoveries.

SIGNIFICANCE

Victorian writers bestowed on Boyle the epithet "father of modern chemistry" because of his realization that chemistry was worthy of study for its own sake and not just because of its usefulness to medicine and metallurgy. He also showed those natural philosophers who denigrated chemistry as an occult science that chemists, through rigorous experiments, could make important discoveries every bit as objective as those of physicists. On the other hand, some twentieth century scholars have questioned Boyle's traditional role as modern chemistry's founder. They emphasize that what Boyle meant by an element is not what modern chemists mean by it. For example, Boyle did not think that metals were elements, but the periodic table contains many metals that are genuine elements. Furthermore, Boyle did not really abandon alchemy, since he believed in its central doctrine, transmutation. He was so convinced that lead could be transformed into gold that he campaigned against an old royal decree forbidding transmutation research.

Despite the caveats of modern scholars, more chemical discoveries and theoretical ideas found in Boyle's voluminous writings have become part of modern chemistry than the work of any of his contemporaries. The air pump he invented has been called "the Scientific Revolution's greatest fact-making machine," and Boyle's experimental studies became models of the most productive way to do science. As an advocate of the experimental philosophy, he was one of the most influential members of the Royal Society, though he declined its presidency over a personal scruple about taking oaths. Though praised by physicists, Boyle saw himself above all as a chemist, and in his development of new techniques and control experiments, he had a great influence on the modern scientific research laboratory.

For his contemporaries, Boyle was the preeminent mechanical philosopher in England. He trained some important scientists, including Robert Hooke, Denis Papin (the inventor of a forerunner of the pressure cooker), and Johann Joachim Becher, an influential German chemist. During his lifetime, Boyle was also honored for his writings on natural theology. Deeply religious, he considered himself a "priest of Nature," and in his will he left substantial funds to found the Boyle Lectures for the Defense of Christianity Against Its Enemies. These lectures, which have been given for over three centuries, symbolize the lasting significance of Boyle not only to scientists but also to all human beings trying to reconcile their search for meaning in life with the worldview created by modern science.

—*Robert J. Paradowski*

FURTHER READING

Brock, William H. *The Chemical Tree: A History of Chemistry*. New York: Norton, 2000. This reissue of a book originally published in England as *The Fontana History of Chemistry* contains an analysis of Boyle's role in the origin of modern chemistry in chapter 3, "The Sceptical Chymist." A forty-page bibliographical essay and an index.

Hall, Marie Boas. *Robert Boyle and Seventeenth-Century Chemistry*. New York: Krause, 1968. This American edition of a work published by Cambridge University Press in 1958 uses Boyle's experimental work and theoretical ideas to investigate the nature of seventeenth century chemistry and the part it played in the ongoing Scientific Revolution. Bibliography and index.

Hunter, Michael, ed. *Robert Boyle Reconsidered*. New York: Cambridge University Press, 1994. This collection of studies includes analyses of Boyle's experimental methods, his philosophical viewpoint, and his relationship to alchemy. Also includes a survey of Boylean historiography.

Maddison, R. E. W. *The Life of the Honourable Robert Boyle, F.R.S.* New York: Barnes and Noble Books, 1969. This narrative of Boyle's life makes use of more accurate texts than earlier biographies, situates Boyle in his historical context, and shows how he sought to reconcile chemistry and the mechanical philosophy. Index.

Shapin, Steven, and Simon Schaffer. *Leviathan and the Air Pump: Hobbes, Boyle, and the Experimental Life*. Princeton, N.J.: Princeton University Press, 1985. The authors interpret Boyle's work in the context of seventeenth century society and through the controversy between Hobbes and Boyle over the causal structure of nature. Extensive references to primary and secondary sources and an index.

Strathern, Paul. *Mendeleyev's Dream: The Quest for the Elements*. New York: Berkeley Books, 2000. This popular thematic history of chemistry analyzes Boyle's work in chapter 7, "A Born-again Science." An annotated "further reading" section and an index.

SEE ALSO: 1601-1672: Rise of Scientific Societies; 1610: Galileo Confirms the Heliocentric Model of the Solar System; 1617-1628: Harvey Discovers the Circulation of the Blood; 1632: Galileo Publishes *Dialogue Concerning the Two Chief World Systems, Ptolemaic and Copernican*; 1643: Torricelli Measures Atmospheric Pressure; 1660's-1700: First Microscopic Observations; July 25, 1698: Savery Patents the First Successful Steam Engine.

RELATED ARTICLES in *Great Lives from History: The Seventeenth Century, 1601-1700:* Robert Boyle; René Descartes; Galileo; Pierre Gassendi; Otto von Guericke; Robert Hooke; Richard Lower; Evangelista Torricelli.

September 13, 1660-July 27, 1663
British Navigation Acts

England passed a set of laws designed to force the American colonies to trade only with the British Empire. The acts succeeded in enriching Britain, but they created tension between the home country and its colonies.

Locale: British Empire, including the American colonies
Categories: Trade and commerce; laws, acts, and legal history; diplomacy and international relations

Key Figures

Charles II (1630-1685), king of England, r. 1660-1685
John Shaw (fl. 1660's), English financier who brought the Navigation Act of 1660 before Parliament
Sir George Downing (1623-1684), member of Parliament and commissioner of customs

Summary of Event

During the Elizabethan era, England, hitherto an agricultural country, began to emerge as a great nation ready to compete with the other European nations for wealth and power. The doctrine of mercantilism that the Crown adopted decreed that a nation must attain a favorable balance of trade—that is, it must export more than it imported—in order to accumulate bullion for financing war efforts and maintaining national security. Because the navy was thought to be essential to the strength of the nation and because commercial maritime activity enhanced naval power, attention in the seventeenth century centered upon the promotion of English shipping. Success demanded the overthrow of the Dutch monopoly in the carrying trade.

All the great commercial rivals of the seventeenth century accepted the tenets that colonies existed for the benefit of the mother country and that the colonies' trade should be restricted to the mother country. As England's knowledge of its colonies and of the new products to be reaped from them increased, so did its expectation of the colonies' potential contribution to its grand scheme. England lacked definite laws relating to commercial policy, however, until 1650, when a combination of private corporate interests and the national interest motivated Parliament to enact legislation designed to attain the national goals.

Thus, in an attempt to break Dutch control of commerce, Parliament in 1650 forbade foreign ships from trading with the colonies without a license. The following year, Parliament enacted a law stating, in part, that only British-owned ships, of which the master and majority of the crew were also British, could import goods from Asia, Africa, and America into Great Britain, Ireland, or the colonies; only British ships or ships of the country of origin could import European goods into Great Britain, Ireland, or the colonies; and foreign goods could be imported into England only from the place of production. The act also prohibited British merchant ships from sailing from country to country to take on produce for import; more seriously, it provoked a two-year war with the Dutch. The entire period from 1651 to 1660 was marked by a great commercial struggle among the powers of western and northern Europe. Furthermore, the last years before the Restoration in Great Britain were fraught with uncertainty and financial difficulties.

When Charles II came to the throne in 1660, he acted upon the urging of the merchants to promote British commerce. He established two councils, one for trade and one for plantations, consisting of lords, merchants, planters, and sea captains. Through the Crown's instructions to these councils, commercial policies gradually were defined. At the same time, Parliament gave the policies statutory authority. The first of these measures was the Navigation Act of 1660, sponsored by John Shaw, a prominent financier, and Sir George Downing, later commissioner of customs.

Enacted by the Convention Parliament on September 13, 1660, and confirmed by the first regular Restoration Parliament on July 27, 1661, the act was similar to that of 1651 in many respects. Certain defects and ambiguities in the earlier act had hindered enforcement, and certain revisions were necessary. The act of 1660 provided that only British-built or British-owned ships of which the masters and three-quarters of the crew were British could import or export goods or commodities, regardless of origin, to and from the British colonies. It further restricted shipment of certain enumerated articles produced in the colonies (sugar, tobacco, cotton, indigo, ginger, speckle wood, and dyewoods) to Great Britain or its colonies and required ships sailing from the colonies to give bond that they would unload their cargoes in the realm. The enumeration clause was intended to increase England's customs revenues, to ensure its access to raw materials, and to advance domestic industries by creating employment in the trades that employed the enumerated products.

In practice, the 1660 regulations created many problems, and shippers took advantage of loopholes and ambiguities to evade the law. Probably to facilitate enforcement, Parliament passed the Act of Frauds in 1662. It restricted the privileges of the act of 1660 to ships built in England, except for ships bought before 1662.

Great Britain still had to clarify the dependent relationship of its colonies to the mother country. If the government were to recover from virtual bankruptcy incurred by the Puritans and royal debts, it could not allow the colonies to buy European products at cheaper prices, and it had to gain customs revenues from the colonial merchants. To make Great Britain the sole exporting center for colonial imports and thus constitute it as a "staple," Parliament, on July 27, 1663, passed the Act for the Encouragement of Trade. Henceforth, European goods could be imported to the colonies only from England and in English-built ships. The only exceptions to the rule were salt for the New England and Newfoundland fisheries, wine from Madeira and the Azores, and provisions, servants, and horses from Ireland and Scotland.

Significance

Because of the complexity of the Navigation Acts, administrative discretion was important in determining how they should be interpreted and enforced. In the colonies, enforcement lay with the governors, who were required to send to England reports of all vessels trading within their jurisdiction and copies of the bonds required of all ships' masters. Both colonial and English sea captains, however, found ways of continuing direct trade with Europe, and smuggling was common. In the period immediately following passage of the Navigation Acts, the colonists protested the restriction of their markets. As English markets became glutted with colonial goods, the returns that the colonists could expect decreased. The Puritans of the Massachusetts Bay Colony objected to the acts on the basis that, since they were not represented in Parliament, they were not subject to the laws passed by Parliament. Gradually, however, most colonists adjusted to compliance, and the insurrections that occurred in the years following cannot be attributed in any large sense to the Navigation Acts in isolation.

As far as England was concerned, the legislation did achieve its purpose. Colonial trade with England and British overseas shipping increased more rapidly than before. There were sufficient causes for the American Revolution apart from the Navigation Acts, and the habits of trade that the acts established lasted beyond the eighteenth century, by which time Great Britain had become the world's greatest commercial and maritime power.

—*Warren M. Billings*

Further Reading

Andrews, Charles, M. *England's Commercial and Colonial Policy*. Vol. 4 in *The Colonial Period of American History*. New Haven, Conn.: Yale University Press, 1964. Argues that the Navigation Acts were expressions of Great Britain's goal to develop a great commercial and colonial empire.

Armitage, David, and Michael J. Braddick, eds. *The British Atlantic World, 1500-1800*. New York: Palgrave Macmillan, 2002. Collection of essays about Great Britain and its colonies in America and the Caribbean. Chapter 3, an essay about the economy of Great Britain and its colonies, contains information about the Navigation Acts.

Brenner, Robert. *Merchants and Revolution: Commercial Change, Political Conflict, and London's Overseas Traders, 1550-1653*. Princeton, N.J.: Princeton University Press, 1993. Provocative revisionism on mercantilism, colonialism, the English merchant class, the role of politics, and the place of London in the commercial and maritime structure of the British Empire.

Clark, Sir George. *The Later Stuarts, 1660-1714*. Vol. 10 in *The Oxford History of England*. Oxford, England: Clarendon Press, 1955. A standard history of late seventeenth century England. Depicts the Restoration period, 1660-1685, as characterized by an elaborate and rigid system of trade regulation and protectionism, policies that originated under the Commonwealth.

Davies, Godfrey. *The Early Stuarts, 1603-1660*. Vol. 9 in *The Oxford History of England*. Oxford, England: Clarendon Press, 1959. Stresses the link between the powerful Dutch commercial empire and the aspiring English determined to compete with and surpass the Dutch.

Dickerson, Oliver M. *The Navigation Acts and the American Revolution*. Philadelphia: University of Pennsylvania Press, 1951. Analyzes the impact of the Navigation Acts in the seventeenth and eighteenth centuries, the role of mercantilism, and the origins of the American Revolution.

Harper, Lawrence A. *The English Navigation Laws*. New York: Octagon Books, 1964. The definitive work on the series of Navigation Acts of the 1650's and 1660's. Argues that the English acts were an experiment in social engineering and an early manifestation of the economic system of mercantilism.

McCusker, John, and Russell Menard. *The Economy of British America, 1607-1789*. Chapel Hill: University of North Carolina Press, 1985. Comprehensive assessment of the pre-revolutionary economy of Great Britain's American colonies. Includes information on the Navigation Acts.

Ormrod, David. *The Rise of Commercial Empires: England and the Netherlands in the Age of Mercantilism, 1650-1770*. New York: Cambridge University Press, 2003. Examines the competition between England and the Netherlands in the North Sea economy to describe how England's increasingly coherent polices of mercantilism undermined Dutch trade in the region.

SEE ALSO: May, 1630-1643: Great Puritan Migration; 1642-1684: Beaver Wars; Dec. 6, 1648-May 19, 1649: Establishment of the English Commonwealth; Oct., 1651-May, 1652: Navigation Act Leads to Anglo-Dutch Wars; May, 1659-May, 1660: Restoration of Charles II; Mar. 22, 1664-July 21, 1667: British Conquest of New Netherland; Mar. 4, 1665-July 31, 1667: Second Anglo-Dutch War.

RELATED ARTICLES in *Great Lives from History: The Seventeenth Century, 1601-1700:* Charles II (of England); First Earl of Clarendon; George Monck.

1661
ABSOLUTE MONARCHY EMERGES IN FRANCE

Taking control of affairs of state in 1661, King Louis XIV, along with his controller general Jean-Baptiste Colbert, accelerated the expansion of the monarchy's power and prestige to an unprecedented degree. More than any other ruler of the seventeenth century, Louis XIV would eventually embody the idea of absolutism in royal authority.

LOCALE: France
CATEGORIES: Government and politics; organizations and institutions

KEY FIGURES

Louis XIV (1638-1715), king of France, r. 1643-1715
Anne of Austria (1601-1666), queen of France, r. 1615-1643, queen regent, r. 1643-1651, and mother of Louis XIV
Jean-Baptiste Colbert (1619-1683), controller general, 1665-1683
Jules Mazarin (1602-1661), cardinal and chief minister, 1643-1661
Marquis de Louvois (1639-1691), war minister, who succeeded Colbert
Jacques-Bénigne Bossuet (1627-1704), tutor of Louis XIV and a French bishop
Louis XIII (1601-1643), king of France, r. 1610-1643

SUMMARY OF EVENT

The term "absolute monarch" refers to a king who possesses almost unlimited legislative, executive, and judicial powers, unchecked by countervailing forces such as regional leaders or by representative assemblies, courts, or religious institutions. In seventeenth century Europe, there were many defenders of autocracy—including Cardin Le Bret, Sir Robert Filmer, Bishop Jacques-Bénigne Bossuet, King James I, Cardinal de Richelieu, and King Louis XIV—who accepted the "divine right of kings" theory.

While condemning arbitrary and tyrannical government, they tended to assume that kings, if properly educated, would promote the general welfare of the population. Only a minority of political thinkers, including François Hotman (1524-1590), a French legal scholar and teacher, and English philosopher John Locke (1632-1704), defended an alternative doctrine of constitutionalism, advocating some separation of political powers into political institutions limited by legal documents, traditional customs, or both.

The absolute monarchy of Louis XIV was the result of a long and gradual development. In the Middle Ages, the king's powers had been severely limited by the prerogatives of the nobility, the Catholic Church, and local political institutions. In contrast to England, however, the French representative assembly of elite groups, called the Estates-General, was ineffective, primarily because of its failure to obtain any veto over spending or taxation. The courts of France, called the *parlements*, could delay the registration of royal edicts, but they could not veto the edicts. During the sixteenth century, anarchy and vio-

King Louis XIV consulting with his ministers. (Francis R. Niglutsch)

lence of the religious wars conditioned the French to assume that a powerful monarch was necessary for peace and prosperity.

After the end of the Religious Wars in 1598, King Henry IV largely restored the powers that the king had earlier possessed, and the status quo continued into the first two decades of Louis XIII's reign. In 1614, for instance, the Estates-General failed to acquire institutional authority. From 1624 to 1642, Cardinal de Richelieu, as the king's chief minister, significantly expanded the centralized powers of the Crown. He eliminated the military strongholds of the regional nobility and the Protestant Huguenots. After 1635, he established royal agents, called intendants, in the provinces as permanent residents to supervise the police force under French marshals. In 1641, after many confrontations with the *parlements*, he checked their powers to delay royal edicts.

As Louis XIV became king at the age of four, his chief minister, Cardinal Jules Mazarin, entered into a bitter struggle against the disgruntled nobles and the Parlement of Paris. During the civil war known as the Wars of the Fronde (1648-1653), the central government became impotent as the young king was dragged about the country to escape the rebels. After Mazarin finally quelled the revolts, he reestablished the intendants and reasserted the powers of the royal government, although he was unable to dominate the *parlements*.

Mazarin, who, it was rumored, was married to Anne of Austria, Louis XIV's mother, personally supervised Louis's training, which included religious indoctrination, military skills, and values appropriate to an absolute monarch. Louis was a strong personality. He developed an inveterate hatred for anyone who might seek to limit his prerogatives. Mazarin encouraged him to take an active role in the government. Entering the Parlement of Paris unannounced in 1655, Louis denounced the judges for interfering with the registration of his edicts.

In 1661, as Mazarin's health declined, Louis began meeting with high officials to discuss affairs of state. On the day after the cardinal died, he astonished his principal ministers by announcing that henceforth he would take personal charge of the government, which was a radical break from his father's practices. He ordered the chancellor and secretaries of state to not give any orders or sign any documents except by his command. When the president of the Assembly of the Clergy asked to whom he should address for busi-

Louis XIV. (R. S. Peale and J. A. Hill)

ness, Louis replied, "To me, monsieur the archbishop, to me."

For the next fifty-four years, Louis tried to control all aspects of his government, from the administrative system to the etiquette at court. Although he perhaps never said "*L'état, c'est moi*" (I am the state), he claimed a divine right to rule and identified himself with the state's operations in the *Mémoirs* he wrote for his son. He exercised great discretion in making decisions with a small group of trusted ministers, especially Jean-Baptiste Colbert, a financial genius who worked to create an economic system later called "mercantilism," which sought self-sufficiency with regulations of commerce, the awarding of monopolies to large companies, and massive constructions of roads, canals, and ports. The minister of war, the marquis de Louvois, expanded the peacetime army to 100,000 soldiers and made it more professional by limiting the purchase of officers' commissions.

Among his efforts to rein in the nobility, Louis lured them to establish residence at his court, where he encouraged a complex web of intrigue and competition for his attention. He frequently utilized his authority to issue lettres de cachet, which were officially sealed orders to arrest individuals without any explanation or judicial oversight. Although his conscience usually kept him from abusing this power, there were very few legal restraints on his right to punish enemies, as illustrated by the notorious example of the unknown "man in the iron mask." Louis's power struggle with the *parlements* continued until 1673, when he denied their right to make remonstrances against his edicts. Following his death, however, the Parlement of Paris nullified his will and reasserted the prerogative of approving or disapproving royal edicts before they became law.

Like most rulers of the century, Louis assumed that religious unity was necessary for peace and prosperity. In 1685, he revoked the Edict of Nantes, which had guaranteed the religious liberty of Huguenots. The revocation produced a wave of persecutions, driving thousands of refugees into the arms of France's enemies. Since so many of the Huguenots were competent entrepreneurs and skilled artisans, the revocation did considerable harm to the nation's economy. Also, his refusal to allow Huguenots to settle in Canada limited the colony's growth and development.

Louis always consulted with advisers, but he personally made the final decisions about war and peace. In 1667, he invaded the Spanish Netherlands, claiming that they were the rightful inheritance of his wife. Although he expanded the size of France in his first war, his success produced the enmity of the other European states. In two later wars, especially the Wars of the Spanish Succession, Louis would lose nearly all the territory he had earlier gained.

Significance

Although Louis XIV in theory asserted the prerogatives of an absolutist monarch, in practice his powers were only "absolute" in a relative sense. He was never able to ignore public opinion, the threat of rebellion, and myriad customary privileges that had long been recognized as part of France's unwritten constitution. Still, Louis could increase taxes without the interference of a representative assembly. He could simply order the arrest of his critics. From 1673 until his death, the courts presented no significant obstacles to whatever edicts he chose to issue.

With his dedication to bringing glory to France, he built the magnificent palace of Versailles and was the generous patron of numerous artists and writers. However, the costs of these cultural achievements, combined with the expensive wars that he initiated, left the country bankrupt and weakened. His religious intolerance also harmed the economy. Following his death, his legacy would encourage many observers to conclude that absolutism should be replaced by a constitutional system with strict limits on the powers of the Crown.

—*Thomas Tandy Lewis*

FURTHER READING

Beck, William. *Louis the Fourteenth and Absolutism.* New York: Bedford/St. Martin Press, 1999. A good introduction to Louis, followed by important historical documents.

Bercé, Yves-Marie. *The Birth of Absolutism: A History of France, 1598-1661.* Translated by Richard Rex. New York: St. Martin's Press, 1996. This work argues that absolutism, rather than being a legacy of the Middle Ages, was a modern creation developing from the wars and disorders of the century before 1661.

Bernier, Oliver. *Louis XIV: A Royal Life.* New York: Doubleday, 1987. An entertaining biography that refutes many traditional criticisms of Louis's reign.

Bonney, Richard. *Limits of Absolutism in Ancient Régime France.* Portland, Oreg.: Ashgate, 1995. A collection of scholarly essays by an outstanding historian of the field, emphasizing that absolutism existed only in theory, not in fact.

Lossky, Andrew. *Louis XIV and the French Monarchy.* New Brunswick, N.J.: Rutgers University Press, 1994. A comprehensive and well-written political biography.

Mettam, Roger. *Power and Faction in Louis XIV's France.* London: Basil Blackwell, 1988. Emphasizing the role of powerful families and other factions, this scholarly book argues that absolute monarchy was an aspiration rather than a reality.

Miller, John, ed. *Absolutism in Seventeenth-Century Europe.* New York: St. Martin's Press, 1990. A collection of relatively brief discussions about the practice of absolutism in major countries during the century, showing that customs and factions put major limits on political power.

Strayer, Brian. *Lettres de Cachet and Social Control in the Ancient Regime, 1659-1789.* New York: Peter Lang, 1992. A fascinating examination of an institutional practice that was symbolic of the criminal justice system under an absolutist regime.

Treasure, Geoffrey. *Mazarin: The Crisis of Absolutism in France.* New York: Routledge, 1995. A comprehensive political biography of Cardinal Mazarin.

SEE ALSO: 1610-1643: Reign of Louis XIII; Nov. 10, 1630: The Day of Dupes; June, 1648: Wars of the Fronde Begin; 1661-1672: Colbert Develops Mercantilism; May 24, 1667-May 2, 1668: War of Devolution; Apr. 6, 1672-Aug. 10, 1678: French-Dutch War; 1673: Renovation of the Louvre; 1682: French Court Moves to Versailles; 1685: Louis XIV Revokes the Edict of Nantes; 1689-1694: Famine and Inflation in France.

RELATED ARTICLES in *Great Lives from History: The Seventeenth Century, 1601-1700:* Anne of Austria; Jacques-Bénigne Bossuet; Jean-Baptiste Colbert; James I; Louis XIII; Louis XIV; Marquis de Louvois; Marie-Thérèse; Jules Mazarin; Cardinal de Richelieu.

1661-1665
CLARENDON CODE

The English parliament passed a series of penal measures against religious dissent that came somewhat unjustly to be associated with Lord Chancellor Edward Hyde, earl of Clarendon, King Charles II's chief minister. The code secured the supremacy of the Church of England, but it caused significant resentment among the populace, contributing to Clarendon's eventual downfall and to the ultimate demise of the Stuart Dynasty in the Glorious Revolution.

LOCALE: London, England

CATEGORIES: Government and politics; religion and theology

KEY FIGURES

Charles II (1630-1685), king of England, r. 1660-1685

First Earl of Clarendon (Edward Hyde; 1609-1674), lord chancellor of England, 1658-1667

Robert Sanderson (1587-1663), bishop of Lincoln

Thomas Venner (d. 1661), a leader of the radical group called the Fifth Monarchy Men

SUMMARY OF EVENT

After the English Civil Wars and the Interregnum period, the agreement under which the Stuart monarchy was restored and Charles II was crowned king of England was predicated on Charles's Declaration of Breda in April, 1660, prior to his return to England from France. That declaration pledged "liberty of tender consciences" for all English subjects. Despite that pledge, however, the Convention Parliament (April 25-December 29, 1660), which invited Charles I's son back from exile in France, failed to settle the question of religion in a manner acceptable to most English Protestants, including Presbyterians and Puritans. Numerous Englishmen wished to make the church comprehensive, and the king himself appeared to support such an idea. Indeed during the Parliamentary recess in September, 1660, Charles and his chancellor of the exchequer, the earl of Clarendon, sincerely attempted to reconcile the conflicting wishes of the Anglicans and Presbyterians.

At a joint conference of the two groups on October 25 at Worcester House (Clarendon's lodging in London), the king issued a declaration proposing a comprehensive church settlement. Quite sensibly, he recognized the help of the Presbyterians and the Catholics toward his restoration to the English throne and thus wanted an inclusive church to the extent possible. Clarendon, too, realized the dangers of alienating the non-Anglicans, especially when the army (still under Puritan influence) was not yet demobilized. Charles, however, had little idea of what sort of church the English political class would like to have. The nation had experienced a form of religious toleration in the 1650's but remained impervious to its merits. They still looked upon the papists as well as the Independent Puritans with suspicion and contempt. Quite naturally, then, the Restoration coincided with a spontaneous revival of the Church of England represented by the Anglicans or conservative Protestants.

Though successful in settling administrative, political, and financial problems and issues somewhat satisfactorily, the Convention Parliament failed to pass any measures for toleration or comprehension and was dissolved on December 29, 1660, to be succeeded by a formal election in March and April of 1661 that returned a new Parliament on May 8, 1661. With a sizable Anglican and Royalist majority, the new Parliament became known as the Cavalier Parliament (1661-1678). Precisely because they were Royalists, however, its members could not share the king's inclination toward inclusiveness and toleration, because they believed that such an attitude would embolden the king-killing, class-leveling, high-taxing sectarians and congregationalists.

Only a few months prior to the election of the Cavalier Parliament, in January, 1661, the Fifth Monarchy Men, members of a millenarian sect led by Thomas Venner, had proclaimed the reign of King Jesus in the center of London. Non-Anglicans still hoped for a tolerant church, and in fact the Anglican and Presbyterian representatives discussed the issue of comprehension at a conference, assembled by an order of the king issued on October 25, 1660. The conference took place at Savoy Palace in the Strand, home of Robert Sanderson, bishop of Lincoln, from April 15 to July 24, 1661, but by then church inclusiveness was a lost cause. Thus, between 1661 and 1665, the Cavalier Parliament sought to exclude all radical sects from public life by passing a series of anti-Puritan penal legislation, known collectively, albeit somewhat misleadingly, as the Clarendon Code.

Although the Clarendon Code was named after the staunchly Anglican lord chancellor, he was no persecutor of Puritans and he neither sponsored nor approved the laws to which his name became attached. More appropriately, the code could be labeled Cavalier. It consisted of four penal laws: the Corporation Act, the Act of Uniformity, the Conventicle Act, and the Five Mile Act. The Corporation Act of 1661 required municipal officers, on pain of eviction, to renounce the Solemn League and Covenant and to receive Anglican Communion. The Act of Uniformity of May, 1662, was the central plank of the code. It required all ministers, professors, and schoolmasters to swear oaths repudiating the Covenant and the taking up of arms against the king, while agreeing to use the Book of Common Prayer for all church services.

Both King Charles and Lord Chancellor Clarendon sought to provide some comfort to the Presbyterians, the loyal Nonconformists, who were devoted both to monarchy and to a national church. In the House of Lords, Clarendon, supported by a number of peers and several bishops, including Gilbert Shelton, the archbishop, and George Morley, bishop of Winchester, had proposed an amendment to the Bill of Uniformity that the Commons had sent up and that enjoined use of the new prayer book. The amendment empowered the king to relieve clergy from observation of the specific clauses that the Presbyterians found repugnant. However, the Lords as a body remained impervious to the idea of toleration, and the proposal was defeated. In spite of a great effort to persuade the Commons to agree to the proposal by the king's consent to the Quaker Act of 1662 (making it illegal to refuse to plead in a court of law and thus attacking the Quaker aversion to swearing oaths), the Clarendon amendment was voted down by the lower house. The upshot was that the Restoration church settlement resulted in the loss of livings for about 15 percent of the clergy in England and Wales by 1663.

All hopes for toleration and comprehension were dashed to the ground following an aborted uprising against the government in Yorkshire in October, 1663. This incident prompted Parliament to pass the Conventicle Act in 1664. This act imposed fines and even exile for three-time offenders for attending Nonconformist meetings (conventicles), that is, assemblies not held in accordance with the Book of Common Prayer and attended by five or more adults who were not members of the household in which the service was conducted. Finally, in 1665, Parliament passed the Five Mile Act forbidding all preachers and teachers who did not take the necessary oaths and declarations from coming within five miles of any town or city as well as all evicted and ejected clergy from traveling within five miles of the parish where they had been incumbents.

SIGNIFICANCE

The so-called Clarendon Code wrought a profound change in English religious life that was to endure for two and a half centuries. It ensured a fundamental nexus between Anglicanism and social, spiritual, and political conservatism. With its passage, all public office holders in England had to conform to the Church of England. Puritans as well as Catholics came to be officially defined as second-class citizens, and the former were often dubbed Nonconformists or Dissenters.

The Church of England, led by its bishops and served by its priests, reemerged as the Anglican establishment with the monarch as its Supreme Head, essentially the same institutional structure that Henry VIII (r. 1509-1547) had created and Elizabeth I (r. 1558-1603) had consolidated. However, there was a novelty highlighted by the code. Although the king continued to be the ecclesiastical supreme head, his disciplinary prerogatives had by now transferred to Parliament, which wielded the authority to enforce religious uniformity. The church ceased to be the mouthpiece of God and assumed the task of saving society from disorder rather than people's souls from hellfire. It thus emerged as an important partner of the monarchy to forge an ordered society free from the fanatical quest for a New Jerusalem espoused by their godly predecessor of the Interregnum.

—*Narasingha P. Sil*

FURTHER READING

Bucholz, Robert, and Newton Key. *Early Modern England, 1485-1714: A Narrative History*. Malden, Mass.: Blackwell, 2004. Chapter 9 contains an analysis of Restoration society, politics, and church.

Coward, Barry. *The Stuart Age: England, 1603-1714*. 1980. 2d ed. Harlow, England: Longman Group, 1994. A standard text by a distinguished specialist.

Fraser, Antonia. *King Charles II*. London: Weidenfeld and Nicolson, 1979. A most readable and reliable historical biography.

Green, Ian. *The Re-establishment of the Church of England, 1660-1663*. New York: Oxford University Press, 1978. Superbly researched and written analysis.

Harris, Tim, Paul Seaward, and Mark Goldie, eds. *The Politics of Religion in Restoration England*. Oxford, England: Basil Blackwell, 1990. A collection of revisionist specialist articles.

Kenyon, J. P. *The Stuart Constitution: Documents and Commentary*. Reprint. Cambridge, England: Cambridge University Press, 1969. A standard collection of documents and commentary by a distinguished scholar.

Seaward, Paul. *The Cavalier Parliament and the Reconstruction of the Old Regime, 1661-1667*. New York: Cambridge University Press, 1989. A lucid and illuminating analysis of the religious settlement by the Cavalier Parliament.

Whiteman, Anne. "The Re-establishment of the Church of England, 1660-63." *Transactions of the Royal Historical Society*, 5th ser. 5 (1955). Very helpful and insightful article. To be read in conjunction with the book by Green previously mentioned.

SEE ALSO: Nov. 5, 1605: Gunpowder Plot; 1611: Publication of the King James Bible; Mar.-June, 1639: First Bishops' War; Oct. 23, 1641-1642: Ulster Insurrection; 1642-1651: English Civil Wars; Aug. 17-Sept. 25, 1643: Solemn League and Covenant; Spring, 1645-1660: Puritan New Model Army; Dec. 6, 1648-May 19, 1649: Establishment of the English Commonwealth; 1652-1689: Fox Organizes the Quakers; Dec. 16, 1653-Sept. 3, 1658: Cromwell Rules England as Lord Protector; May, 1659-May, 1660: Restoration of Charles II; May 19, 1662: England's Act of Uniformity; Dec. 19, 1667: Impeachment of Clarendon; 1673-1678: Test Acts; Aug. 13, 1678-July 1, 1681: The Popish Plot; Aug., 1682-Nov., 1683: Rye House Plot; Apr. 4, 1687, and Apr. 27, 1688: Declaration of Liberty of Conscience; Nov., 1688-Feb., 1689: The Glorious Revolution; May 24, 1689: Toleration Act.

RELATED ARTICLES in *Great Lives from History: The Seventeenth Century, 1601-1700:* Charles I; Charles II (of England); First Earl of Clarendon; Oliver Cromwell; James II; Mary II; William III.

1661-1672
Colbert Develops Mercantilism

The seventeenth century witnessed the emergence of economic theory as a key factor in government policy: Mercantilism, the belief that prosperity resulted from a balance of trade that drew gold and silver into a nation's coffers, was spearheaded by France under Jean-Baptiste Colbert. He achieved some degree of solvency in French state finances during the reign of Louis XIV by addressing the corruption, inefficiency, and inequities of public revenue policies through a number of mercantilist reforms.

Locale: France
Categories: Economics; trade and commerce; government and politics

Key Figures

Jean-Baptiste Colbert (1619-1683), French controller general under King Louis XIV, 1665-1683
Louis XIV (1638-1715), king of France, r. 1643-1715
Marquis de Louvois (1639-1691), Louis XIV's war minister

Summary of Event

In the mid-seventeenth century, France was industrially and economically fragmented, had been laboring under a long-standing corrupt feudalistic system of state finance that was woefully inefficient, and had experienced twenty-five years of foreign and civil wars. Furthermore, the nation had no coherent plan to improve revenue from international trade. As a result, France had little wealth or power compared with European rivals such as England and Holland. Jean-Baptiste Colbert, who became French controller general in 1665, was determined to improve the fortunes of his country and king through an aggressive program of mercantilist reforms.

In 1661, King Louis XIV wished to publicly assume the positions of chief minister and superintendent of finance himself, but he effectively gave the real power of both offices to Colbert. The new controller general believed that France could be economically revitalized through policies based on mercantilism, an economic doctrine that emphasized the belief that national wealth was created by a favorable balance of trade that brought gold and silver (universal currency) into the country at the expense of trading rivals.

Colbert's mercantilist program, known as "Colbertisme" (Colbertism) began with the reorganization of the system of generating national revenue, which was based on taxation. The main royal tax, called the taille, was a direct tax on land and property. Nobles, the clergy, and all government officials were exempted from the taille, leaving the vast majority of the tax burden to be paid by the poorest commoners. Not only did the wealthiest citizens who owned two-thirds of the land pay no direct taxes, but the peasants were also taxed multiple times locally by these same aristocrats and clergymen. In the absence of any organized system of royal tax collection, the Crown used "tax farmers" as collectors. Tax farmers paid the royal treasury in advance and then assessed and collected taxes to recover their investment and pay their commissions. The arbitrary assessments, multiple taxations and excessive interest charged by collectors, with no real system of accounting, produced a corrupt, inefficient system that was absolutely regressive.

In 1662, Louis XIV decreed that all treasury officials would answer to his controller general. Colbert established an accounting system for the royal treasury and the concept of a "national budget." He reduced the number of local treasurers and tax farmers, and those remaining were required to submit documented accounts to Colbert. The controller general's power grew quickly, and he expanded his financial reforms. Between 1664 and 1666, he became the royal treasurer, reduced the commission of tax farmers from 25 percent to 4 percent, bought back and abolished numerous functionless salaried government offices that had been purchased earlier, and established the Chamber of Justice to audit treasurers. Colbert also succeeded in reducing the amount of revenue from the taille and increasing revenue from indirect taxes on commodities such as salt and wine, from which none were exempt. In addition, he lowered the interest rates on state loans and confiscated the excessive profits of wealthy long-time speculators for the state treasury.

The effectiveness of these reforms required the creation of a centralized nationwide jurisprudence system. In 1667, Colbert succeeded in establishing France's first uniform codified rules of judicial procedure. The uniform administration of justice usurped the traditional power of each province's high court to make and enforce its own laws, and established the civil rights of citizens within the monarchy.

Colbert realized that he could never balance the budget through tax reforms alone; that would require major changes in French industry and commerce. He sought to improve the quality and quantity of goods by establishing factories in each region that specialized in a particular product, employed all available workers, were bound by stringent quality control regulations, and were financed by private capital and royal subsidies. High quality luxury goods were produced to stop the flow of French money to the countries that had traditionally produced them. Skilled immigrant workers were brought to France to oversee the manufacture of numerous commodities, including mirrors, silk, fine textiles, and ships. Laws were passed to forbid immigrant workers from returning home and to prohibit skilled French workers from emigrating. Although Colbert did succeed in increasing foreign demand for French products, there was widespread resentment over the rules and practices of the Industrial Inspection Service. These measures served the dual purposes of increasing production for export and reducing unemployment and poverty.

Colbert began early in his career to build the French navy as an integral part of his overall plan to improve international commerce. Protective tariffs on foreign goods were central to Colbertism, but they could not be levied while France was dependent on foreign shippers. Because France possessed only thirty small ships in 1661, Colbert created a maritime budget in 1662 and significantly increased the number of oceangoing vessels, founded naval training schools, established pay and pension plans for seamen, required judges to sentence criminals to be oarsmen in galleys, and improved harbors and ports. French shipbuilders were subsidized, and French seamen convicted of serving on foreign ships faced capital punishment.

Jean-Baptiste Colbert. (Library of Congress)

Improvements in French industry coupled with the growth of the navy and merchant marine formed the basis of Colbert's policy of "progressive protectionism." In 1662, he actually reduced a modest customs tax, but, as France quickly became more competitive, it was reinstated in 1663, higher import tariffs were imposed on each specific category of goods in 1664, and those tariffs had been doubled, at minimum, by 1667.

Colbert also sought to create a more-favorable balance of trade for France by founding colonial settlements and monopolistic trading companies. The objectives of colonization were to obtain raw materials directly without going through rival nations, and to create exclusive markets for the sale of manufactured products. In this regard, other European powers had a significant head start over France. Colbert established colonial outposts in places such as Madagascar, India, the Caribbean, and Canada, but with limited success because of the indigenous populations' resentment of the one-sided economic regulations, designed to benefit France. He created trading companies and gave them exclusive rights to compete with France's rivals in various regions of the world. The disappointing performance of companies like the East Indies, West Indies, and North Sea Companies was also due, in large part, to the inflexibility of overbearing mercantilist regulations.

Colbert insisted that the glory of France also should be enhanced by artistic and intellectual advancement. He established and funded the Academies of Inscriptions, Painting and Sculpture, Architecture, and Sciences. He patronized artists and scholars, directed the creation of a French dictionary to standardize the language, and greatly increased France's artistic and literary treasures.

The first several years of Colbert's tenure as controller general, from 1665 to 1672, was a period of relative peace, state solvency, and cultural development. During this time, Colbertism

COLBERT ON MERCANTILISM

French financial officer and administrator Jean-Baptiste Colbert developed a form of mercantilism in which the state was to support manufacturing and commerce through economic regulation. Excerpted here is a letter Colbert sent to local residents and town officials of Marseilles, urging them to help the economy through increased manufacturing and trade, which would be partly subsidized by the state.

Considering how advantageous it would be to this realm to reestablish its foreign and domestic commerce, . . . we have resolved to establish a council particularly devoted to commerce, to be held every fortnight in our presence, in which all the interest of merchants and the means conducive to the revival of commerce shall be considered and determined upon, as well as all that which concerns manufactures.

We also inform you that we are setting apart, in the expenses of our state, a million livres [former French monetary unit] each year for the encouragement of manufactures and the increase of navigation, to say nothing of the considerable sums which we cause to be raised to supply the companies of the East and West Indies;

That we are working constantly to abolish all the tolls which are collected on the navigable rivers;

That there has already been expended more than a million livres for the repair of the public highways, to which we shall also devote our constant attention;

That we will assist by money from our royal treasury all those who wish to reestablish old manufactures or to undertake new ones;

That we are giving order to all our ambassadors or residents at the courts of the princes, our allies, to make, in our name, all proper efforts to cause justice to be rendered in all cases involving our merchants, and to assure for them entire commercial freedom.

Source: Jean-Baptiste Colbert, letter to the residents and town officials of Marseilles (1664), excerpted in *The Great Documents of Western Civilization*, edited by Milton Viorst (New York: Bantam Matrix, 1967), pp. 135-136.

increased state revenues dramatically, making France's economy the strongest in the world except for that of England. However, by 1672, the minister of war, the marquis de Louvois, had gained considerable influence with the king as Colbert fell from favor. Louvois undermined Colbert's policies, and he initiated an extended period of aggressive warfare, beginning with the French-Dutch War in 1672, that began France's march toward national bankruptcy and, eventually, the French Revolution.

SIGNIFICANCE

In spite of his declining status and influence after 1672, Colbert's industrial, trade, maritime, colonial, and cultural policies continued to affect France for the rest of his career and after his death. His reorganization of French industry to produce quality goods for export firmly established the competitiveness of numerous products. The trade links that survived the breakup of Colbert's trading companies remained a significant source of revenue for many years. The increase of French overseas possessions in the eighteenth and nineteenth centuries was based on Colbert's ideas on colonization. Colbert's maritime policies, including codified ordinances, uniform training, and improved harbors, have been reflected in the organization of the French navy until the present. His support of the arts, letters, and sciences made Paris the cultural center that it became and remains today.

Colbert's policies have had a continuing impact on political and economic theories and policies. His groundwork in creating more equitable laws and judicial practices had far-reaching implications for future governments, becoming a model for both the republic following the French Revolution and for the Napoleonic Code. It also is reflected in the concept of civil liberties in all democracies. French Physiocrats, in repudiating Colbert's program, were instrumental in the development of laissez-faire free market economic theories that directed economic policies around the globe for generations, and vestiges of Colbertism can be seen into the twenty-first century whenever powerful lobbies seek to obtain favorable trade agreements or protective tariffs for industries.

—*Jack Carter*

FURTHER READING

Ames, Glenn Joseph. *Colbert, Mercantilism, and the French Quest for Asian Trade*. DeKalb: Northern Illinois University Press, 1996. Includes a detailed account of Colbert's attempts to initiate mercantilist reforms.

Clark, Henry C. "Commerce, the Virtues, and the Public Sphere in Early-Seventeenth-Century France." *French Historical Studies* 21 (1998): 415-440. An analysis of the long-held traditions of generating public revenue that brought France to the brink of bankruptcy and set the stage for Colbertism.

Cole, Charles Woolsey. *Colbert and a Century of French Mercantilism.* 2 vols. Hamden, Conn.: Archon Books, 1964. More than one thousand pages present a comprehensive examination of Colbert's impact on public policy under Louis XIV and the effects on France's politics and economy.

Dent, Julian. *Crisis in Finance: Crown, Financiers, and Society in Seventeenth-Century France.* New York: St. Martin's Press, 1973. A solid exposition of the financial workings of the seventeenth century French monarchy, starkly exposing the weaknesses of the financial administration Colbert set out to reform. Detailed and scholarly, this work offers a strong portrait of the political and social world of the financiers.

Emmer, P. C., and F. S. Gaastra. *The Organization of Interoceanic Trade in European Expansion, 1450-1800.* Aldershot, England: Variorum, 1996. Examines the comparative mercantile, naval, and political strategies of various European powers for world trade, particularly in the Far East.

Levi, Anthony. *Louis XIV.* New York: Carroll & Graf, 2004. This biography contains a great deal of information on Colbert's administration and his relationship with Louis XIV.

See also: Mar. 20, 1602: Dutch East India Company Is Founded; 1606-1674: Europeans Settle in India; 1609: Bank of Amsterdam Invents Checks; 1661: Absolute Monarchy Emerges in France; Mar. 18, 1662: Public Transportation Begins; 1689-1694: Famine and Inflation in France.

Related articles in *Great Lives from History: The Seventeenth Century, 1601-1700:* Jean-Baptiste Colbert; Louis XIV; Marquis de Louvois; Jules Mazarin; Cardinal de Richelieu.

February 17, 1661-December 20, 1722
Height of Qing Dynasty

The reign of Kangxi, the second longest in Chinese history, was a remarkable period of prolonged political stability and prosperity. Kangxi completed the Manchu conquest of China and effectively consolidated the nation's borders. He also commissioned numerous scholarly endeavors, initiated large-scale public works projects, opened ports to foreign trade, and reduced taxes. During his reign, the arts flourished again and the Jesuits reached their peak of influence.

Locale: China

Categories: Government and politics; cultural and intellectual history

Key Figures

Kangxi (K'ang-hsi; 1654-1722), emperor of China, r. 1661-1722

Galdan (1645-1697), Western Mongol chief

Wu Sangui (Wu San-kuei; 1612-1678), Ming Dynasty general

Summary of Event

Kangxi ascended the imperial throne of China when he was seven years old. He was the third son of the first Qing emperor, Shunzhi (Shun-chih; r. 1644-1661). Since Kangxi was too young to rule at first, four joint regents were appointed. One of them, Oboi (d. 1669), seized power. In 1669, however, Kangxi, with the help of his powerful uncle, Songgotu (d. 1703?), and Grand Empress Dowager Xiao Zhuang, arrested Oboi and assumed power.

At the time Kangxi became emperor, the Qing Dynasty was in trouble. Although the Manchus had entered Beijing unopposed in 1644, the conquest and stabilization of the entire country proved to be a difficult. While the northern part of the country had by this time been effectively pacified, much of the south and southeastern regions remained a major problem. Most of this area was under the direct control of Wu Sangui, a former Ming general, and two other former Ming commanders that had also allied themselves with the Manchus and fought on their behalf. These regions were like independent princedoms, as they had been given as rewards by the Qing government in return for the help these defectors had given provided in consolidating the Qing regime.

In 1673, a young but determined Kangxi decided, against the strong advice of his senior advisers, to order Wu Sangui and the two ex-commanders to leave their fiefs and move to Manchuria. This decision sparked a bloody civil war, known as the Rebellion of the Three

Qing China c. 1697

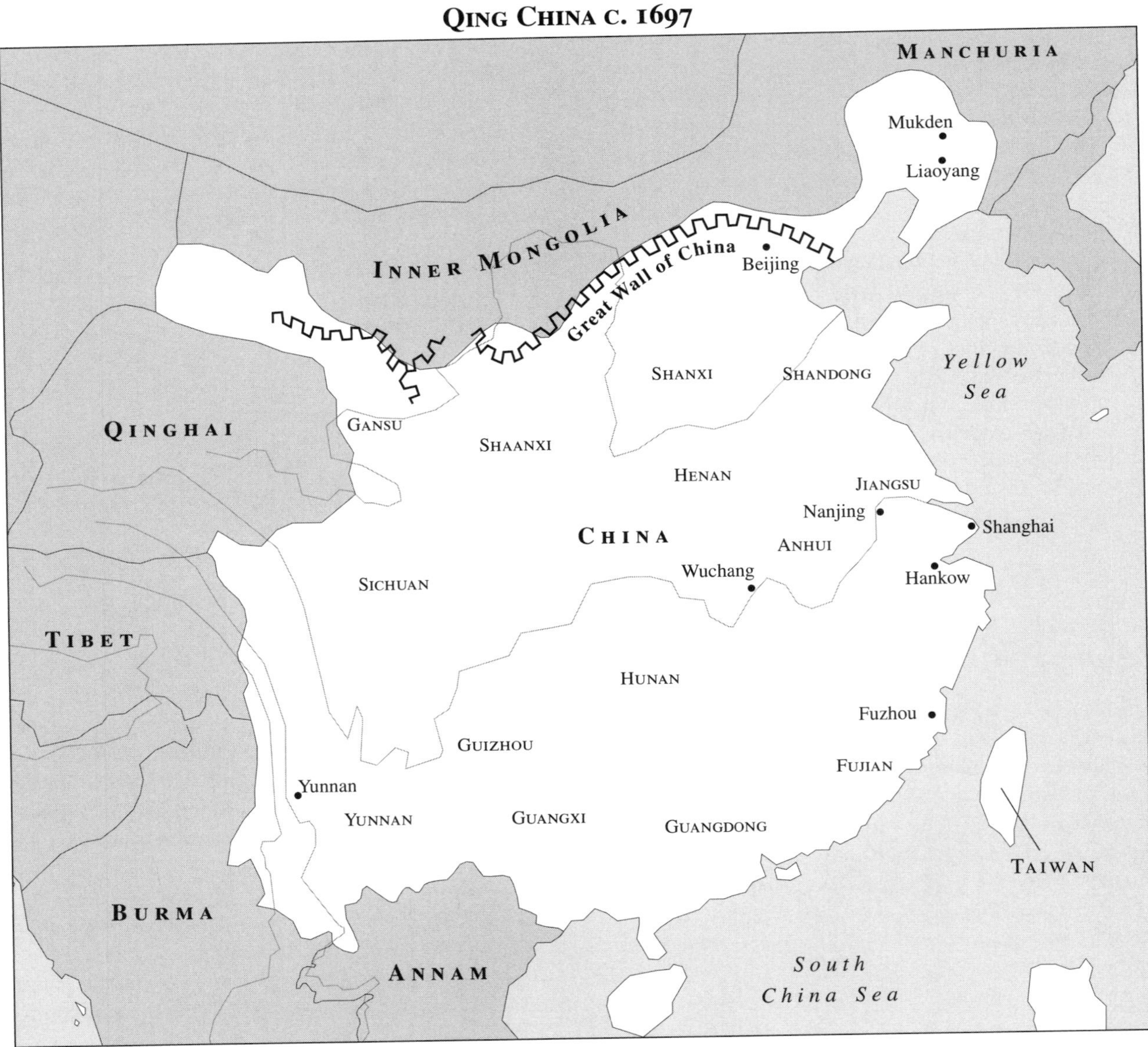

Feudatories, which lasted for eight years. In 1681, the rebellion on the mainland was at last crushed, and the entire Wu family was executed. Two years later, in 1683, a Qing fleet conquered Taiwan. These military successes unified China and stabilized the Qing Dynasty.

Kangxi next turned his attention to several longstanding and pressing troubles on China's borders. The first related to the Russian advance from the north. In the 1600's, the Russians had steadily expanded across Siberia and settled outposts along the Amur River. Kangxi considered this area part of China, and in 1685 he sent an army to attack the main Russian base, Fort Albaniz. The Russians then left, and in 1689, the Treaty of Nerchinsk was signed between the two countries, the first treaty that China signed with a European nation. The treaty regularized relations and border trade between China and Russia and resolved frontier disputes.

The next border problem Kangxi had to deal with involved the Mongols. In 1675, the Western Mongols (known as Khalkas and Tatars) rebelled in the North. Kangxi quickly put the revolt down and proclaimed himself ruler of all Mongols. Three years later, Galdan, a strong Eleuth (Western Mongol) chief, invaded what is today known as Outer Mongolia, hoping to create an independent Mongol territory, free from Chinese influence. The Eastern Mongols asked the Chinese for help, and Kangxi personally lead troops in three campaigns in 1696-1697, winning a major victory. Galdan in 1697 committed suicide and Outer Mongolia became part of the Qing empire. Later in Kangxi's reign, in 1717, Galdan's descendants took over Tibet. Kangxi responded in 1720, sending an expedition that drove the Mongols out, and Tibet became a Chinese protectorate. By his skillful handling of all these crises, Kangxi was able to consolidate and expand China's western and northern borders.

Another noted feature of Kangxi's reign was the adroit way in which he gained the support of the Chinese ruling class. He believed that since the Manchu were alien rulers and their numbers were small, the most effective way in which they could retain control of the massive and populous Chinese empire was through cooperation with the scholar official class and the maintenance of Chinese social institutions and practices. He therefore worked very hard to establish and keep good relations with the native gentry (although a number of famous scholars scorned this attempt). He accomplished this by first leaving the Ming governmental establishment largely intact, although national power during his reign did become more centralized. He retained the Confucian civil servant tradition and examination system.

Kangxi adopted a Chinese approach to governance and cultural issues. He promoted Confucius: In 1684, he paid a visit to Qufu, Confucius's hometown, to show his respect, and during his reign, he had Neo-Confucian texts collected and printed. Another way Kangxi obtained the allegiance of the Chinese gentry was by commissioning compilations of scholarly works, projects in which many Chinese scholars were employed. These included a comprehensive dictionary of Chinese characters, a history of the Ming Dynasty, and the massive scholarly work, *Gujin tushu jicheng* (1726; Wade-Giles, *Ku-chin t'u shu chi-ch'eng*; synthesis of books and illustrations of ancient and modern times). This work consisted of ten thousand chapters and made up seventeen hundred volumes. There was, however, a darker purpose to these projects. In the process of collecting the material to be included, the Qing government destroyed works that they deemed to be objectionable or critical of the dynasty. The works' authors and sometimes their entire families were executed. There is no doubt, however, that Kangxi did have a deep interest in Chinese culture. He could write good poetry and literary prose in Chinese, and during his reign, art, porcelain, fine printing, and lacquer manufacture flourished.

Despite his embrace of Chinese culture, Kangxi knew that the preservation of traditional Manchu values was necessary if the Manchu wanted to keep their authority. Consequently, a sharp distinction was drawn during his reign between Manchus and Han Chinese in governmental posts, jobs, the military, and social life. Soon after Kangxi became emperor, Manchuria was closed to Chinese immigration in order to preserve Manchu characteristics. All the top metropolitan administrative posts and some provisional positions required that a Chinese official always be balanced by a Manchu, Mongol, or Chinese bannerman. Manchus were barred from having any position save for those in the state military or civil service. Manchus were not allowed to intermarry with Chinese people, and Manchu women could not bind their feet. Hereditary banner units provided military security in key areas in the country, and Chinese bondservants (slaves) were used instead of eunuchs for private tasks and administrating the imperial household.

During Kangxi's reign, the Catholic mission thrived. In 1683, there were around 200,000 converts in the country. While these missionary activities were formally outlawed by the government, this law was often overlooked. The Jesuits were highly favored by Kangxi, and many worked at the imperial court as astronomers, interpreters, artisans, and political advisers. Late in his life, Kangxi would turn against the missionaries over what he thought was an unlawful interference in Chinese matters of state by the pope: He ultimately issued an order banning missionaries from living in China without special permission.

Economically, Kangxi's reign was a time of large-scale public and water control projects. The Huang He (Yellow River) was dredged to prevent flooding, and the Grand Canal, which transported food and goods from the south to the north, was extensively repaired. Taxes were reduced several times and ports were opened to foreign trade. Internal peace helped foster economic growth and lead to an increase in agricultural production, yet present during Kangxi's time were the beginning of trends that would create major problems for later Qing rulers. These included a steady increase in the population, a keen competition for a limited number of government jobs that would ultimately lead to a large class of unsuccessful aspirants, and the inherently conservative ideology of the imperial court system. When Kangxi died in 1722, his fourth son, the Yongzheng emperor (Yung-cheng; r. 1722-1735), succeeded him.

SIGNIFICANCE

Considered one of the golden periods of Chinese history, Kangxi's sixty-one-year reign is remarkable for its prolonged peace and prosperity. Through his wise leadership, Kangxi established Manchu control over all China and secured the northern and eastern borders, thereby producing for China a rare period of extended peace that lasted for more than a century. Politically, Kangxi won the allegiance of China's ruling class, and culturally he adapted to the Chinese system of governance, while at the same time carefully preserving his Manchu identity. He accomplished this without making most Chinese feel that their cultural traditions were threatened. He also made six famous tours of the nation to learn about local conditions, rather than staying isolated in Beijing.

For all of these reasons, Kangxi's reign greatly solidified the Qing Dynasty. Economically, during his rule, several ports were opened to foreign trade, taxes were cut several times, agricultural production increased, and large-scale public works projects were initiated. Culturally, the arts began to thrive again, especially porcelain, lacquer, and fine printing. The Jesuits reached the height of their influence in the imperial court and within China as a whole. In retrospect, however, one may also detect as present during his rule the beginnings of trends that would haunt later Qing emperors: These include a fast rise in population and the increasingly conservative ideology of the imperial court.

—*Ronald Gray*

FURTHER READING

Fairbank, John K., and Merle Goldman. *China: A New History*. Enlarged ed. Cambridge, Mass.: Harvard University Press, 1998. A good general overview of the Qing Dynasty.

Rawaski, Eveyln. *The Last Emperors: A Social History of Qing Imperial Institutions*. Berkeley: University of California Press, 2001. An informative account covering, in part, how the Qing emperors attempted to keep their Manchu identity.

Spence, Jonathan. *Emperor of China: Self-Portrait of K'ang-Hsi*. New York: Vintage Books, 1974. A revealing collection in English of Kangxi's writings.

SEE ALSO: 1616-1643: Rise of the Manchus; 1631-1645: Li Zicheng's Revolt; Apr. 25, 1644: End of the Ming Dynasty; June 6, 1644: Manchus Take Beijing; 1645-1683: Zheng Pirates Raid the Chinese Coast; 1670: Promulgation of the Sacred Edict; Dec., 1673-1681: Rebellion of the Three Feudatories; Aug. 29, 1689: Treaty of Nerchinsk Draws Russian-Chinese Border; 1699: British Establish Trading Post in Canton.

RELATED ARTICLES in *Great Lives from History: The Seventeenth Century, 1601-1700:* Abahai; Dorgon; Kangxi; Shunzhi.

March, 1661-1705
VIRGINIA SLAVE CODES

The first laws recognizing and institutionalizing slavery in Virginia were passed by the General Assembly. Based on the laws regulating white indentured servitude, the laws created vast differences between the status of black and white forced laborers, instituting a de jure, rather than merely de facto, system of racial segregation.

LOCALE: Virginia
CATEGORIES: Laws, acts, and legal history; social issues and reform

SUMMARY OF EVENT

In March, 1661, the Virginia General Assembly declared that "all children borne in this country shalbe held bond or free only according to the condition of the mother." Enacted to alleviate confusion about the status of children with English fathers and African mothers, this law was the first in a series of laws recognizing perpetual slavery in Virginia and equating "freedom" with "white" and "enslaved" with "black." This law is especially indicative of the hardening of race relations in mid-seventeenth century Virginia society, as status in the patriarchal society of England traditionally was inherited from the father. By reversing this legal concept, perpetuation of enslavement for blacks was ensured for their children, whether of black or white ancestry.

Despite the extent to which the 1661 law narrowed the options for defining Africans' status, this act did not in itself establish slavery as permanent and inescapable. Africans had two available windows through which they could obtain freedom—conversion to Christianity and manumission (formal emancipation). In 1655, mulatto Elizabeth Key had brought a successful suit for her freedom, using as her main argument the fact that she had been baptized.

In 1667, a slave named Fernando failed in a similar suit when he contended that he ought to be freed because he was a Christian and had lived in England for several years. Not only did the court deny Fernando's appeal, but also that same year the General Assembly took another step toward more clearly defining blacks' status, by declaring "that the conferring of baptisme doth not alter the condition of the person as to his bondage or freedome." Planters felt that if baptism led to freedom, they would be without any assurance that they could retain their slave property. The 1667 law built on the earlier one to define who would be a slave and was clarified in 1670 and again in 1682, when the Assembly declared that any non-Christian brought into the colony, either by land or by sea, would be a slave for life, even if he or she later converted.

In 1691, colonial leaders provided a negative incentive to masters wishing to free their slaves by declaring that anyone who set free any "negro or mulatto" would be required to pay the costs of transporting the freedmen out of the colony within six months. Although manumissions still occurred and some free blacks managed to remain in the colony, the primary status for African Americans in Virginia was that of chattel.

Although who was to be a slave in Virginia had now been defined, it had yet to be determined precisely what being a slave meant on a daily basis for Africans and their descendants. Between 1661 and 1705, nearly twenty separate laws were passed limiting, defining, and prescribing the rights, status, and treatment of blacks. In general, these laws were designed to protect planters' slave property and to protect the order and stability of white society from an "alien and savage race."

The greater the proportion of black slaves in the overall Virginia population, the more restrictive and oppressive the laws became. Whereas Africans were only 2 percent of the total population of Virginia in 1648, they were 15 percent in 1708. In certain coastal counties, such as York, the demographic picture was even more threatening. In 1663, blacks already made up 14 percent of York's population; by 1701, they counted for 31 percent of the county's inhabitants. In large part, the slave codes were motivated by the growth of the black population and whites' fears of slave uprisings.

The piecemeal establishment of slavery in these separate laws culminated in 1705 in a comprehensive slave code in Virginia. This code reenacted and strengthened a number of earlier slave laws, added further restrictions and harsher punishments, and permanently drew the color line that placed blacks at the bottom of Virginia society. Whites were prohibited from trading with, having sexual relations with, or marrying blacks. Blacks were forbidden to own Christian servants "except of their own complexion," leave their home plantation without a pass, own a gun or other weapon, or resist whites in any way.

In Virginia society, in which private property was a basic legal tenet, a slave's property was not protected: "[B]e it enacted . . . that all horses, cattle or hoggs marked of any negro . . . shall be forfeited to the use of the poore of the parish . . . seizable by the church warden thereof." Neither was slave life or limb protected by the codes. It was legal both to kill slaves accidentally while punishing them and to dismember slaves guilty of running away as a means of dissuading other slaves from also trying to escape. Slaves were not allowed to assemble for prayer, for entertainment, or to bury their dead. They could not testify against white people in court and were not given the right of trial by jury. The only protection mandated in the slave code was that masters must provide adequate food, clothing, and shelter for their slaves, and that they "not give immoderate correction," the latter provision being essentially meaningless, given that accidentally killing slaves while "correcting" them was officially sanctioned.

Many of these enactments lacked any means of enforcement, including the sole protection, and remained as almost dead letters in the statutes. Many of the harsher penalties for slave crimes—for example, the death penalty and maiming—were not carried out nearly as frequently as the laws suggest, because doing so would harm or destroy the master's property. Laws prohibiting slaves from trading or hiring themselves out were disregarded almost routinely. The disadvantage for slaves of this lack of enforcement was that laws prohibiting cruel treatment or defining acceptable levels of correction often were ignored as well. Where abuse was noticeably blatant, action against white offenders was taken only reluctantly, and punishments were insignificant and rare. Generally, laws in the economic and political interest of the white planter elite were enforced and respected; laws that restrained planters' pursuits were not.

SIGNIFICANCE

To a large extent, the laws regulating and defining slavery in Virginia grew out of the early to mid-seventeenth century laws regulating indentured servitude. Servants had also been prohibited from having sexual relations with or marrying their masters; indentured women who became pregnant through such liaisons were fined, made to serve extra time, and had their children bound out to labor. Like slaves, servants were punished for attempting to run away or for resisting their masters. Servants also were treated harshly and exploited by ruthless masters eager to get every penny's worth of effort from their laborers.

Unlike African slaves, however, white indentured servants had legal rights and were protected by the laws and courts of the colony. This distinction is crucial in understanding the significance of the slave laws, which codified, not a difference between those forced to labor and those who were free, but rather a difference between a race inherently unworthy of being free and one whose members might be temporarily bound to service. White servants ultimately served out their time, became freemen and full citizens, acquired land and servants of their own, and became respected members of the community, regardless of their earlier status. Indentured servants had rights and opportunities, but African and African American slaves, by the turn of the eighteenth century, virtually had neither.

—Laura A. Croghan

Further Reading

Boskin, Joseph. *Into Slavery: Racial Decisions in the Virginia Colony*. Philadelphia: J. B. Lippincott, 1976. Provides a brief account of the evolution of perpetual slavery and a representative selection of relevant primary documents.

Catterall, Helen T., ed. *Judicial Cases Concerning American Slavery and the Negro*. 5 vols. New York: Octagon Books, 1968. Comprehensive examination of court records related to American slavery and the experiences of African Americans in slavery.

Higginbotham, A. Leon, Jr. *In the Matter of Color: Race and the American Legal Process, the Colonial Period*. New York: Oxford University Press, 1978. Recounts the events culminating in the legal recognition of slavery in all the British mainland colonies.

Jordan, Winthrop D. *White over Black: American Attitudes Toward the Negro, 1550-1812*. New York: W. W. Norton, 1968. Examines the attitudes of British colonists toward Africans, especially concerning their religions and color. Characterizes the establishment of slavery as an "unthinking decision."

Morgan, Edmund S. *American Slavery, American Freedom: The Ordeal of Colonial Virginia*. Reprint. New York: W. W. Norton, 2003. Detailed examination of how slavery developed in seventeenth and eighteenth century Virginia.

Parent, Anthony S., Jr. *Foul Means: The Formation of a Slave Society in Virginia, 1660-1740*. Chapel Hill: University of North Carolina Press, 2003. Refutes previous historians' views that racial slavery created a Golden Age in Virginia. Instead, Parent maintains the institution of racial slavery was a calculated move by the emerging planter class to consolidate its power, with invidious consequences for Virginia and American society.

Schwartz, Philip J. *Twice Condemned: Slaves and the Criminal Laws of Virginia, 1705-1865*. Baton Rouge: Louisiana State University Press, 1988. Uses criminal trial records to examine slave resistance and whites' efforts to control threatening slave behavior. Interprets the seventeenth century as a time of adjustment or negotiation.

Shaw, Robert B. *A Legal History of Slavery in the United States*. Potsdam, N.Y.: Northern Press, 1991. Illustrates the history of slavery in terms of its legislative and judicial background, from settlement through emancipation. Early chapters discuss the evolution of early slave codes.

Wood, Betty. *The Origins of American Slavery: The English Colonies*. New York: Hill and Wang, 1997. Explains the religious and economic rationale for the use of slave labor in English colonies. Chapter 4 focuses on slaves who worked the tobacco crops in the Chesapeake colonies.

See also: 17th cent.: Europe Endorses Slavery; May 14, 1607: Jamestown Is Founded; 1617-1693: European Powers Vie for Control of Gorée; Beginning c. 1619: Indentured Servitude Becomes Institutionalized in America; 1619-c. 1700: The Middle Passage to American Slavery; July 30-Aug. 4, 1619: First General Assembly of Virginia; Aug. 20, 1619: Africans Arrive in Virginia; Nov., 1641: Massachusetts Recognizes Slavery; Beginning 1671: American Indian Slave Trade.

Related articles in *Great Lives from History: The Seventeenth Century, 1601-1700:* Aphra Behn; John Smith.

June 23, 1661
PORTUGAL CEDES BOMBAY TO THE ENGLISH

The British crown acquired the island and port of Bombay from Portugal as part of a large dowry. In 1668, the Crown granted the island to the British East India Company, leading to Bombay's expansion into a great commercial metropolis.

LOCALE: Bombay Island, west-central India (now Bombay, India)

CATEGORIES: Trade and commerce; expansion and land acquisition; government and politics; colonization

KEY FIGURES

Gerald Aungier (d. 1677), governor and commander in chief of Bombay, 1669-1677

Charles II (1630-1685), king of England, r. 1660-1685

Catherine of Braganza (1638-1705), queen consort of England, r. 1662-1685, and regent of Portugal, r. 1704-1705

SUMMARY OF EVENT

Estado da India, the name given to Portugal's Asian empire, grew rapidly in the decades following explorer Vasco da Gama's landing at Calicut in 1498, an empire that would extend from East Africa to the China seas. From its capital at Goa, forts and factories (from the Portuguese word *feitoria*, meaning a fortified trading station for European merchants in Asia) were established up and down the west coast of India to trade spices and, increasingly, textiles. Estado da India brought immense wealth to the Portuguese crown, but its Achilles' heel was an acute and perpetual labor shortage.

Portugal's ruling dynasty, the House of Aviz, ended in 1580 with the death of King Henry, leading King Philip II of Spain to annex Portugal to his vast territorial possessions. Portugal remained part of the Spanish Empire until 1640, when a successful revolt led to the establishment of a new Portuguese dynasty, the House of Braganza. Spain, however, did not recognize Portugal's independence until 1668, with the signing of the Treaty of Lisbon. Portugal's second "new" ruler, Afonso VI (r. 1656-1683), seeking international recognition, sought to marry his sister Catherine of Braganza to English king Charles II, who had been restored to his throne in 1660. There were real advantages in resuscitating the Anglo-Portuguese alliance (which dated back to 1386). Plagued by Dutch dominance in the Indian Ocean, Portugal viewed England as a counterweight to the colonial and commercial ambitions of the Netherlands.

The diplomatic preliminaries involved hard bargaining. Charles was a spendthrift and habitually penniless, while Portugal was no longer the wealthy kingdom it had once been. With difficulty, the Portuguese raised an enormous dowry of 2 million crowns, which Charles soon frittered away, but Portugal also threw in some land: Tangier, on the coast of Morocco, and the island of Bombay. The marriage treaty was signed on June 23, 1661. Catherine landed at Portsmouth on May 13, 1662, and was privately married eight days later. It was an unhappy marriage on account of Charles's flagrant infidelities, and it produced no heir, indirectly paving the way for the Glorious Revolution of 1688, when William III succeeded James II as king of England.

By the terms of the 1661 treaty, Portugal ceded "the Port and Island of Bombay in the East Indies with all its rights, profits, territories and apportenances whatever thereunto belonging," a vague definition that the English took to include, in addition, the island of Salsette, to which Bombay was attached, as far as Bassein, the islands of Elephanta and Karanja, and several other locations. On April 2, 1662, King Afonso sent a letter to Goa for the viceroy of Estado da India, Antonio de Mello Castro, ordering him to hand over Bombay immediately to the English. In fact, the viceroy was still en route for Goa, which he reached in September, 1662, only to be greeted by the royal command.

Horrified, Castro wrote back, protesting the order in the strongest possible terms. He refused to cede the island for the following reasons: First, the clause in the Anglo-Portuguese treaty was conditional upon the signing of a heretofore unsigned Dutch-Portuguese treaty. Second, Bombay harbor was the finest in India, superior even to Lisbon itself. Third, to hand over the island would endanger the faith of the Catholic converts already established there. Fourth, if Portugal abandoned this magnificent harbor, its trade on the west coast would inexorably gravitate into English hands.

This defiant letter of December 28, 1662, was carried overland by a young Jesuit, Manuel Godinho (1630-1712), author of one of the classics of seventeenth century travel. Godinho shared the viceroy's feelings about Bombay, declaring that, in the long run, its cession would benefit the Dutch only. He duly reached Lisbon and delivered the viceregal missive, but King Afonso was adamant: In another letter to Castro, dated February 8, 1664, he unequivocally ordered the island to be handed over.

Meanwhile, Castro had been using delaying tactics. King Charles's representative, Sir Abraham Shipman, had arrived in India, but Castro had, predictably, challenged his credentials. Shipman's sudden death encouraged the viceroy to prevaricate further, and on November 3, 1664, he addressed the supreme council at Goa, expressing his opinion that Shipman's commission had died with him. However, prior to his death, Shipman apparently had designated that his assistant Humphrey Cooke take over, and the supreme council, perhaps not wanting to further provoke their king's wrath, sent two commissioners to Bombay to complete the transfer (February 18, 1665). Outraged, Castro shot off two more protests to Lisbon, predicting the worst, and resigned in 1667.

It had taken nearly four years for the Portuguese authorities in India to relinquish Bombay. At this time, ultimate authority for the East India Company's factories in India was with the president in Surat, the great Mughal port north of Bombay. The current president, Sir George Oxenden (1620-1669), had ably led the defense of the English factory there when the Marāthā king, Śivājī, had sacked the city in 1664. In fact, Surat's great days as the major west coast emporium were drawing to a close because of the Marāthā-Mughal conflict in the hinterland, so that the emergence of Bombay proved well timed.

Meanwhile, King Charles's new colony was proving a financial drain, so in 1668, he leased it to the British East India Company for an annual rent of ten pounds and a large loan, and he thought himself well rid of it on such terms. At first, Oxenden in Surat served also as governor and commander in chief for Bombay, but he died in 1669 and was succeeded by Gerald Aungier. A man of great energy and foresight, Aungier was one of the unsung heroes of the British Empire in India. The experience of a second Marāthā raid on Surat in 1670 probably persuaded him that the future lay in Bombay, a virtual island and easily defensible at a time when the mainland was exposed to continuous Mughal-Marāthā depredations. He urged the company's court of directors in London to fortify the new settlement and to transfer the company's operations at Surat to Bombay.

Aungier sought to make the island impregnable. He provided harbor facilities, stabilized the currency, and set up courts of justice (according to contemporaries, somewhat arbitrary and idiosyncratic in their workings). He even created a general assembly of landowners to assess local taxation. From the outset, Aungier insisted upon complete religious toleration, in contrast to the Portuguese in Goa and the rigid enforcement of Islam by the Mughal emperor, Aurangzeb. This, as well as relative security from Marāthā plundering and Mughal exactions, soon led Indian merchants to settle on the island, notably the industrious Parsee community, which laid the foundations of Bombay's future prosperity.

Aungier also established a militia and, anticipating piracy at sea, a gunboat squadron that would evolve into the formidable Bombay Marine, a fighting navy. He was, however, well aware of the difficulty of maintaining Bombay's neutrality between the warring Mughals and Marāthās, and so he sought to establish friendly relations with Śivājī. By 1677, the year of Aungier's death, English trade at Bombay equaled that of Surat, and by 1687 had superseded it.

In 1674, physician and traveler John Fryer visited Bombay, which, he reckoned, had grown from around ten thousand inhabitants in 1665 to some sixty thousand. He describes here a flourishing pioneer settlement, with "English, Portugueze, Topazes [Indo-Portuguese Christians], Hindoos [Hindus], Moors [Muslims], Cooly Christians [low-caste laborers], most fishermen." As for the governor, Fryer writes, "he has a Council here also, and a guard when he walks or rides abroad, accompanied by a party of horse. . . . He has his chaplains, physician, surgeons, and domesticks; his linguist, and mint-master: At meals he has his trumpets usher in his courses, and soft music at the table." Fryer continues, "He [the governor] goes sometimes in the coach, . . . sometimes on horseback, other times in palenkeens. . . . Always having a Sumrero [sunshade] of state carried over him." Fryer also noted how fatal was the climate to the English, who drank to excess, "for all this gallantry, I reckon they walk but in charnel-houses."

Significance

Aungier's time came to be regarded by later generations as a Golden Age for Bombay. Before the century was out, the settlement suffered major catastrophes—the 1683-1884 revolt of naval commander Richard Keigwin (d. 1690) against the company and the war of the deputy governor of Bombay, Sir John Child (d. 1690), with the Mughals between 1688 and 1690, resulting in the siege of the town by the Mughal admiral and a humiliating capitulation to Aurangzeb; Child was later dismissed. Compared to Fort Saint George (at Madras) and to Calcutta, Bombay would long languish in obscurity, and it was not until the late eighteenth century, partly as a result of the Marāthā Wars (1775-1818) between the British and the Marāthās, that it was set upon its course to become one of the great cities of the British Empire.

—*Gavin R. G. Hambly*

FURTHER READING

Correia-Afonso, John. *Intrepid Itinerant: Manuel Godinho and His Journey from India to Portugal in 1663*. Bombay: Oxford University Press, 1990. The author examines Godinho's involvement in the negotiations that preceded the cession of Bombay.

Foster, William. "The East India Company, 1600-1740." In *The Cambridge History of India*, vol. 5. Cambridge, England: Cambridge University Press, 1929. A detailed narrative of the company's early history.

Spear, Percival. *The Nabobs*. Oxford, England: Oxford University Press, 1968. An excellent account of the early social history of the British in India.

Wheeler, James Talboys, ed. *Early Records of British India*. London: Trubner, 1878. Reprint. Madras: Asian Educational Services, 1994. Wheeler provides useful documentation of British India, including seventeenth century sources.

Woodruff, Philip. *The Men Who Ruled India*. 2 vols. London: Jonathan Cape, 1953. A vivid narrative of early British contacts with India.

SEE ALSO: 17th cent.: The Pepper Trade; 1606-1674: Europeans Settle in India; 1639-1640: British East India Company Establishes Fort Saint George; c. 1666-1676: Founding of the Marāthā Kingdom; Feb. 13, 1668: Spain Recognizes Portugal's Independence.

RELATED ARTICLES in *Great Lives from History: The Seventeenth Century, 1601-1700:* Aurangzeb; Catherine of Braganza; Charles II (of England); Śivājī.

1662
HALF-WAY COVENANT

The Half-Way Covenant expanded the pool of those eligible for Puritan baptism to include those infants whose parents had been baptized but were not yet full members of their church. The covenant encouraged increased membership in Puritan churches at a time when non-Puritan immigrants were decreasing the relative majority of strict Calvinists among the New World colonists.

LOCALE: Boston, Massachusetts Bay Colony (now in Massachusetts)

CATEGORY: Religion and theology

KEY FIGURES

Richard Mather (1596-1669), minister and principal leader in devising the Half-Way Covenant

Charles Chauncy (1592-1672), president of Harvard College and leading opponent of the covenant

Increase Mather (1639-1723), son of Richard, who initially opposed the Half-Way Covenant

John Woodbridge, Jr. (1613-1696), minister who led his congregation beyond the Half-Way Covenant and opened membership to all

SUMMARY OF EVENT

One of the most compelling questions about the Puritan Commonwealth established in Massachusetts during the seventeenth century concerns the reasons for its decline. Historians have found it difficult to determine not only why the rule of the "Saints" came to an end but also the precise time when the deterioration began. Some have contended that the system of church and state established under the leadership of such men as John Winthrop and John Cotton was so well constructed that it remained almost unchanged for many years. Others believe that Puritan ideals began to falter from the beginning and that too much stress has been placed on the pervasiveness of a group of attitudes defined as the "Puritan mind." Some historians argue that church membership declined because rigid Puritan beliefs could not survive when confronted with harsh life on the frontier. Others, however, credit the decline to natural causes: The years between generations were not always sufficient for parents to become full church members before their children were born.

Among the controversial issues that have enlivened the debate over Puritan decline is the so-called Half-Way Covenant of 1662. The most important provision of this document, endorsed by a Massachusetts General Court-sponsored synod of more than eighty ministers and laity meeting in Boston, was that children whose parents had not been admitted to full membership in a Puritan church might nevertheless be eligible for baptism. This created a new class of church membership, because those who had been baptized but had not yet testified were only partial members—they could pass church privileges on to their children but could not participate in Holy Communion or vote on church issues.

The question of membership was one that long had plagued the churches of New England. On the one hand, Puritans believed that no one should be admitted to full communion in the church who had not demonstrated sufficiently a personal experience by which he or she had become convinced that God had elected him or her to salvation. However, if one believed that prospective church members must await a message from God, what part was the church itself to play in recruiting new adherents? This problem became increasingly acute as the proportion of Puritans in New England declined in relation to the growing population of the area. It began to seem, as Jonathon Mitchel wrote, that the churches had been set up "onely that a *few old Christians* may keep one another warm while they live, and then carry away the Church into the cold grave with them when they dye."

The Half-Way Covenant did not concern the admission of new members from outside the church but attempted rather to deal with the problems raised by the children and grandchildren of the elect. Because the Puritans believed in infant baptism, they always had permitted full church members to have their children brought under the care of the congregation, although each had to await the conversion experience before being admitted to full membership. It was expected that a significant number of these young people ultimately would experience conversion, but until that time, they were not permitted to take Communion or vote on church business. This arrangement did not provide for the third generation, however, which included the children of those who had been baptized but had not become full church members.

During the early days of the Puritan Commonwealth, the churches did not have to concern themselves about the grandchildren of the elect because there were none. When they did begin to appear, there was no difficulty about those whose parents had been received into full communion with a church. The problem arose with those members of the third generation whose parents had not yet achieved full membership: Were such infants to be baptized or not? No one could say for certain that the parents of these children would not experience a conversion at some later time, because the Puritans did not believe that God necessarily informed the "Saints" of their election at any certain age. Moreover, if these infants were to be denied baptism, would it not then become necessary to expel their parents from the privileged position they had held in a church since childhood?

The answer that the Half-Way Covenant provided to this question may have confirmed a practice that was already developing in New England. The covenant stated that, in cases where children were born to parents who had not yet attained full church membership, the congregation should indeed baptize the new infants. Such persons could not, however, become full members of a church unless they subsequently experienced conversion. Both they and their parents enjoyed a kind of "half-way" membership that enabled the Puritans to maintain their rigid standards for full communion in a church and yet to provide for the possible conversion of new members. Infants baptized into a church obviously were more likely to achieve full membership than those who were excluded from the fold.

Significance

The Half-Way Covenant provided the Puritan Commonwealth with one of its most prolonged controversies. Although the Synod of 1662 had strongly endorsed the covenant, it was opposed by a small and determined group of ministers and temporarily rejected by a significant number of congregations. Most of its opponents charged that, despite claims to the contrary, the covenant would open up a church to persons who were not among God's elect. Richard Mather, one of those most responsible for the decision of the synod, found his congregation at Dorchester skeptical about the covenant, and his sons, Increase Mather and Eleazar Mather, were among its most vocal opponents.

Another influential leader of the opposition was Charles Chauncy, who, as president of Harvard College, was among the most respected scholars in the province. Nevertheless, despite such pockets of resistance as that evidenced by the refusal of Boston's Second Church to accept the covenant until 1693, the Puritan churches in New England gradually came to accept the idea of "half-way" membership. John Woodbridge, Jr., a minister in Killingworth, Connecticut, took the new covenant a step further and opened membership in his church to anyone. Not until the great religious revivals of the 1730's swept through the colonies did the covenant again come under serious attack, and by then, the Puritan Commonwealth as such had ceased to exist.

—David L. Ammerman and Geralyn Strecker

Further Reading

Bremer, Francis J. *Shaping New Englands: Puritan Clergymen in Seventeenth-Century England and New England.* New York: Twayne, 1994. This survey of Puritan history discusses the strong connection between church and state and the role the Half-Way Covenant had in trying to maintain that bond.

Burg, Barry R. *Richard Mather*. Boston: Twayne, 1982. This biography of the leading proponent of the Half-Way Covenant explains the major religious and political factors leading to membership reform.

Gordis, Lisa M. *Opening Scripture: Bible Reading and Interpretive Authority in Puritan New England*. Chicago: University of Chicago Press, 2003. Maintains that Puritan ministers did not expect to impose their views upon their congregations, but believed interpretive consensus would emerge from reading the Bible. Describes how the Half-Way Covenant was an example of how church leaders negotiated a consensus over conflicting interpretations.

Middlekauff, Robert. *The Mathers: Three Generations of Puritan Intellectuals, 1596-1728*. New York: Oxford University Press, 1971. Traces the Mather family's central role in the Half-Way Covenant controversy through Richard's support of the new doctrine and Increase's initial objection, then later support.

Miller, Perry. *From Colony to Province*. Vol. 2 in *The New England Mind*. New York: Macmillan, 1939. Reprint. Cambridge, Mass.: Harvard University Press, 1953. Argues that New England Puritanism retained its pristine quality for only one generation and that the Half-Way Covenant clearly reveals the decline of Puritan self-assurance.

Morgan, Edmund S. *Visible Saints: The History of the Puritan Idea*. New York: New York University Press, 1963. Argues that the Half-Way Covenant was not a symptom of decline but rather evidence of the Puritans' determination to maintain rigid standards of membership.

Pope, Robert G. *The Half-Way Covenant: Church Membership in Puritan New England*. Princeton, N.J.: Princeton University Press, 1969. Detailed discussion of the Half-Way Covenant by a scholar who accepts, in general, that the covenant was a sign of decline within the church.

SEE ALSO: Dec. 26, 1620: Pilgrims Arrive in North America; May, 1630-1643: Great Puritan Migration; June, 1636: Rhode Island Is Founded; Oct. 23, 1641-1642: Ulster Insurrection; Sept. 8, 1643: Confederation of the United Colonies of New England; Apr. 21, 1649: Maryland Act of Toleration; Mar. 4, 1681: "Holy Experiment" Establishes Pennsylvania.

RELATED ARTICLES in *Great Lives from History: The Seventeenth Century, 1601-1700:* John Cotton; John Winthrop.

1662-May 3, 1695
ENGLAND'S LICENSING ACTS

The Licensing Act of 1662 restored the licensing system that had been disrupted by the English Civil Wars and the Protectorate, allowing for censorship administered largely through the Stationers' Company, until Parliamentary opponents of restraints upon publication forced the licensing system to lapse in 1695.

LOCALE: England
CATEGORIES: Laws, acts, and legal history; government and politics; social issues and reform

KEY FIGURES

Sir Roger L'Estrange (1616-1704), English printer and surveyor of the press
John Locke (1632-1704), English philosopher
Charles II (1630-1685), king of England, r. 1660-1685
John Twyn (d. 1664), English printer
John Milton (1608-1674), English poet

SUMMARY OF EVENT

Systematic licensing of printed matter in England can be traced to the reign of Henry VIII (r. 1509-1547). Privileges were issued to printers as early as 1518, and a 1538 royal decree stipulated that all printed works must obtain approval from the Privy Council. However, the practical matters of censorship were left largely to the private sector. In 1557, Mary I (r. 1553-1558) granted a monopoly on publishing to the Stationers' Company, a London-based guild of booksellers. The Stationers' followed the rulings of the Court of Star Chamber, which began issuing decrees concerning printing in 1566. By 1637, Star Chamber decrees had been organized into a system of licensing in which relevant authorities approved printed matter and the Stationers' Company registered all material.

By 1662, however, the Restoration Parliament felt compelled to repair a licensing system that had been disrupted by the political instability created by the English

Civil Wars (1642-1651) and Oliver Cromwell's Protectorate government (1652-1659). In 1641, the Court of Star Chamber had been abolished by Puritan factions in Parliament, annulling the Stationers' Company's monopoly and thereby creating an explosion of printing. After political pleading by the Stationers' Company, a licensing act was passed in 1643, setting off furious debates about censorship, as in John Milton's defense of authorial freedom in the pamphlet *Areopagitica* (1644). A printing act of 1649 had recuperated some of the Stationers' Company's powers, but printing acts passed by Cromwell's parliamentary allies in the 1650's took away many of the company's arbitration powers.

After the restoration of the Stuart monarchy under Charles II, the new Parliament sought to restore the licensing system as it had been decreed in 1637. In 1662, Parliament passed the Licensing Act, the censorious intent of which is evident from its full title: "An act for preventing the frequent Abuses in printing seditious treasonable and unlicensed Bookes and Pamphlets and for regulating of Printing and Printing Presses." The 1662 legislation brought back into force the various printing restrictions that had been collected in the 1637 Star Chamber Decree and those in the 1649 Printing Act.

The Licensing Act restored the system whereby all publications had to be registered by the Stationers' Company and also brought back the 1637 limits upon the number of printers that could operate in England. Twenty master printers (plus the Cambridge and Oxford presses) and four letter founders were permitted. The Licensing Act also required that printed works obtain permission from authorities in categorized areas. For example, works on religion would require licensing from a recognized ecclesiastical leader such as the archbishop of Canterbury, while legal works would require licensing from the Office of the Chief Justice.

The year 1662 also saw the rise to power of Sir Roger L'Estrange, a Royalist aristocrat and pamphleteer who had gained the favor of Charles II in 1659 by publishing his arguments for the return of the monarchy. L'Estrange published *Considerations and Proposals in Order to the Regulation of the Press* (1662), which advocated that the royal prerogative be aggressively used in censoring the press. In 1663, L'Estrange replaced John Birkenhead as surveyor of the press, a position that empowered him to seize unlicensed printed matter. L'Estrange was also granted a monopoly on the printing of newspapers, and his two publications, the *Intelligencer* and the *News*, were the only journalistic works in England until 1665, when plague sowed enough confusion to allow for the publication of the *Oxford Gazette*.

L'Estrange proved to be a zealous enforcer of the licensing laws, being responsible for much censorship of material before publication. L'Estrange was also responsible for numerous search-and-seizure operations all across Britain. The most notorious case prosecuted by L'Estrange involved his search of the printing press of John Twyn, located in the Cloth Fair neighborhood of London. L'Estrange seized a copy of a pamphlet entitled "A Treatise of the Execution of Justice" that came from Twyn's press. In 1664, Twyn was prosecuted by L'Estrange for sedition and executed.

For the next two decades, the licensing system remained virtually unchallenged, with few significant revisions in renewals of licensing legislation. The 1662 Licensing Act was renewed by Parliament in 1664 and again in 1665, in a form that would expire in 1679. In 1684, Charles II granted a new charter to the Stationers' Company, seeking to ensure that this critical enforcement element of the licensing system remain stable. In 1685, a new Licensing Act was passed, set to expire in 1692.

With the Glorious Revolution of 1688 and the consequent rise in the political power of Parliament, however, the licensing system, which was closely linked to royal authority and administration, began to be openly challenged. During the early 1690's, the licensing system became an issue of intense debate within Parliament. Amid much debate, the Licensing Act was renewed twice, though a group of eleven members of the House of Lords issued a letter of protest, arguing that learning should not be restricted by licensers interested only in business.

Opposition to licensing was also becoming fierce in the House of Commons. The philosopher John Locke, opposed to renewal of the Licensing Act, was actively conferring with "the College," an informal group of members of Parliament that included Edward Clarke and John Freke. Locke's opposition to the licensing system, revealed in his 1693 memorandum to Clarke, was based both on his general objection to censorship (echoing Milton's 1644 *Areopagitica*) and on his opinion that the Stationers' Company's monopoly made the progress of learning subject to licensers whose only concern was business.

In an attempt to salvage licensing, a bill was put forward that aimed to take away the monopoly power of the Stationers' Company, while retaining its censorship powers. However, on May 3, 1695, the Licensing Act finally lapsed, after the House of Commons declined to renew it.

Significance

While in effect, the Licensing Acts of the seventeenth century maintained a system in which the Stationers' Company dominated publishing through its legal monopolies, while also administering broad powers of censorship. The Licensing Act of 1662 and related legislative bills helped stabilize the licensing system that had been disrupted by the Puritan Revolution and the government of Oliver Cromwell.

The furious debate over licensing that ultimately resulted in the end of the licensing system led to further debate about how to control the press. In the years following 1695, the Stationers' Company sought to revive licensing by pooling resources with Puritans demanding strict censorship. The abuses of the licensing system, as seen in the tenure of Sir Roger L'Estrange, ensured that the Stationers' Company would have to change strategies, leading to its eventual abandonment of calls to revive the licensing system.

In 1707, there was a failed attempt to introduce legislation that still included licensing provisions. In 1710, however, the Statute of Anne, which would introduce the modern system of copyright, passed through Parliament. The Statute of Anne would ensure that two of Locke's suggestions would be borne out—that no one should hold a patent on works by ancient authors and that the term of privilege to publish current authors should be of a limited duration rather than perpetual.

—*Randy P. Schiff*

Further Reading

Dutton, Richard. *Licensing, Censorship, and Authorship in Early Modern England*. New York: Palgrave-Macmillan, 2001. Focuses on the relation of the licensing system to theatrical works. Offers analysis of the practical dynamics of the regulation of printed matter in the period preceding the 1662 legislation.

Halasz, Alexandra. *The Marketplace of Print: Pamphlets and the Public Sphere in Early Modern England*. New York: Cambridge University Press, 1997. Offers in-depth analysis of the relation of print to early modern capitalist culture. Traces the histories of a number of pamphlets in order to recover the socioeconomic contexts in which they circulated.

Myers, Robin, and Michael Harris, eds. *The Stationers' Company and the Book Trade, 1550-1990*. New Castle, Del.: Oak Knoll Press, 1997. Collection of articles focused on practical aspects of the business of publishing in Great Britain. Includes articles on licensing and on censorship.

Rose, Mark. *Authors and Owners: The Invention of Copyright*. Cambridge, Mass.: Harvard University Press, 1993. Explores notions of authorship and propriety through analysis of the development of modern copyright. Offers thorough analysis of the licensing system which the Statute of Anne displaced.

See also: Nov. 3, 1640-May 15, 1641: Beginning of England's Long Parliament; 1642-1651: English Civil Wars; Dec. 16, 1653-Sept. 3, 1658: Cromwell Rules England as Lord Protector; May, 1659-May, 1660: Restoration of Charles II; Nov., 1688-Feb., 1689: The Glorious Revolution; 1690: Locke Publishes *Two Treatises of Government*.

Related articles in *Great Lives from History: The Seventeenth Century, 1601-1700:* Charles II (of England); Oliver Cromwell; John Locke; John Milton.

March 18, 1662
Public Transportation Begins

Coaches-for-hire appeared on Europe's city streets before 1630, expanding the range of conveyances for goods and people across cities. Inverting this dynamic, though, was the horse-drawn Paris omnibus system, which followed fixed routes and schedules, had set fares, and was carefully monitored by route supervisors. The basic structure of this early omnibus system remains into the twenty-first century, around the world.

Locale: Paris, France

Categories: Transportation; science and technology; trade and commerce; cultural and intellectual history

Key Figures

Blaise Pascal (1623-1662), French mathematician, physicist, and philosopher, who has been credited with designing the omnibus service

Louis XIV (1638-1715), king of France, r. 1643-1715

Duc de Roannez (Artus Gouffier; 1627-1696), governor of Poitou and cosigner of petition to Louis XIV to create service

Summary of Event

Prior to the seventeenth century in Paris, most people moved throughout the city on foot or horseback. Goods were moved in similar fashion. In the seventeenth century, however, coach-riding, a convenient way to move around the city and to mark one's prestigious social status, came to be more common. Aristocrats rode in their coaches and the financially successful, eager to follow the aristocrats, began purchasing coaches as well. In addition, social customs associated with the carriage developed: For example, the Cours de la Reine was a fashionable set of avenues near the Tuilieries, where carriages could be driven and shown and carriage passengers could see and be seen.

Carriages, horses, and maintenance were expensive, however. One carriage could cost several hundred livre per year to own and maintain, and the horse to pull the carriage could cost a few hundred livre. However, even though most people could not afford their own carriages, they still wanted the convenience of private transportation around Paris.

This led to the first carriage-for-hire businesses, including cabs with seating for two or four people, also known as fiacres. Businessman Nicholas Sauvage began the first fiacre business sometime before 1630. The fiacres were very popular with visitors and businesspeople, and remained available as long as horse-drawn cabs were on the streets. Since Sauvage did not have an exclusive privilege for operating this type of carriage-for-hire business, competitors soon arrived. As the business developed, two types of coaches could be hired: the fiacres, which could be hailed from a sidewalk, and the *carrosses sous remise*, which were hired only from the coach owner's station.

People interested in operating urban transportation businesses obtained exclusive permission from the king. This involved petitioning the king and paying a fee of thousands of livre to the royal treasury. People obtained exclusive rights to operate different kinds of vehicles on different kinds of routes. For example, a lady-in-waiting to the king's mother had the right to operate coaches between Paris and Versailles. Another company had the exclusive right to hire out a calèche, an open, four-passenger, one-horse coach.

On January 19, 1662, King Louis XIV granted a group of entrepreneurs the exclusive right to operate a public urban transportation system that followed fixed routes, had low fares, and traveled on a schedule. Blaise Pascal, who is credited with designing the service, was not one of the original petitioners to the king, though his sister Gilberte Pascal and Pascal's lifelong friend, the Duc de Roannez, were petitioners. Pascal did receive income from the venture, however.

The *carrosse à cinq sols*, called so because five sols was the fare for a single ride, began service on March 18, 1662, at 7 A.M. Its first route connected the rue Saint Antoine with the Palais du Luxembourg. On that March morning, three or four coaches were ready to depart in each direction at staggered intervals. Later in 1662, four more lines opened. Of the five lines, four were designed to intersect and thus allow passenger transfers. The fifth line, also known as the Tour de Paris, circled the city; unlike the other lines, though, it had zoned fares, much like modern subway or tram systems.

Each of the four intersecting lines had company offices at the start and end of each respective route to allow a company official, the *commis*, to oversee the day's work. The Tour de Paris route, however, had these offices along its entire route. Although the routes extended from the Louvre and Palais Royal on the west to the Palais du Luxembourg in the east, the fashionable Marais district benefited most from the omnibus service. In addition, some routes passed through the merchant and artisan centers on the Right Bank. Thus, the routes met the interests of those involved in politics, commerce, and, generally, aristocratic life.

At the company office, the *commis* monitored the arrivals and departures of the vehicles. He would also receive receipts and reports and handle clients. The coaches, which typically operated from six or seven in the morning to eight or nine at night, were sent out by the *commis* in fifteen minute intervals throughout the day. The service operated year round, except for Easter, Pentecost, All Saint's Day, and Christmas.

Each coach, designed to carry eight people, was driven by a coachman, who also collected fares, and was accompanied by a footman, who rode on the back of the carriage. The footman assisted passengers in and out of the vehicle and also counted them, providing independent reports to the *commis* as a check on the driver. Both the coachman and footman wore a simple livery, and the coaches were also marked with the city's coat of arms. Each coach had its own team of four horses: one pair for the morning work and a second pair for the afternoon. Subcontractors operated and maintained the coaches and took care of the horses.

When Louis granted the original privilege for the service, he made no restrictions on passengers the omnibuses could carry. However, when the Parlement of Paris, the Paris law court, registered the king's letter, there was inserted a provision about passengers. Liveried servants, unskilled or manual laborers, and soldiers were prohibited from riding. Women, however, were apparently not restricted, either by law or by custom. Gilberte Pascal, who was one of the petitioners to the king, commented in correspondence that several women rode during the first day of service.

The omnibuses were popular, at least among the well-to-do; even the king is said to have ridden it at least once. There are several recorded instances where members of the general public threw stones at and otherwise mocked the drivers. In one incident about a month after the service started, a driver was wounded severely, leading to the passing of laws prohibiting such violence towards the *carrosses*. The public continued to follow the coaches with stones and insults, and, ultimately, a police presence along the routes was required to restore civic order.

In 1667, the omnibus service ceased. It is thought that the firm went out of business because ridership dropped, chiefly because of petty thieves and robbers and the like riding the service. Also, Pascal died on August 19, 1662, which left the service without its original visionary.

SIGNIFICANCE

The omnibus was the first modern public transportation system. Ultimately, the 1662 service succeeded because it modeled the key features of a successful bus service: routes, a schedule, and standard fares. Indeed, the original petition even modeled the democratic ridership of later coach services. These features can be traced through later public transportation developments.

The brilliance of its design is more evident because so many public transportation systems still duplicate those original features.

Clearly, as a service that did not last more than about five years, the omnibus was not an initial success. It seems the omnibus should have survived because it appears to have been a logical extension of the thriving carriage-for-hire businesses already operating in Paris and other cities. This 1662 service, however, provided a specific transit—easy access between the chief commercial, legal, and aristocratic/royal districts and around the city—to a specific clientele, the social elite. Also, the service itself was legally an aristocratic one.

When omnibuses once again figured in Paris transportation, they were praised for being democratic vehicles. In 1828, when the next omnibus service began, observers noted the range of people who rode it, from peers to servants to clerks. Expansive routes throughout the city also helped increase ridership; in six months during its first year of operation, the chief omnibus service carried 2.5 million people.

—*Clare Callaghan*

FURTHER READING

Benard, Leon. *The Emerging City: Paris in the Age of Louis XIV*. Durham, N.C.: Duke University Press, 1970. This work dissects seventeenth century Paris, from the milieu of theater to police to transit and more.

Lister, Martin. *A Journey to Paris in the Year 1698*. Edited by Raymond Phineas Stearns. Facsimile Reprints in the History of Science 4. Urbana: University of Illinois Press, 1967. Although this travel account is set after the end of the Pascal omnibus, the patterns of carriages, riverboats, and chairs for hire are evident in this account by a British physician.

Lundwall, Eric. *Les Carrosses à cinq sols: Pascal entrepreneur*. Preface by Jean Mesnard. Paris: Science Infuse, 2000. This work explores the coach system as envisioned by Pascal, especially in the context of the history of entrepreneurship. Includes a bibliography and an index.

Mesnard, Jean. *Pascal et les Roannez*. Bruges, Belgium: Desclée De Brouwer, 1965. This account of Pascal and the family of his childhood friend, Louis François du Bouchet, later Duc de Roannez, covers the development of the omnibus in volume 2.

Papayanis, Nicholas. *Horse-Drawn Cabs and Omnibuses in Paris: The Idea of Circulation and the Business of Public Transit*. Baton Rouge: Louisiana State University Press, 1996. This analysis of Parisian transit traces it from Pascal's omnibus through the twentieth century Paris Metro.

SEE ALSO: 1661-1672: Colbert Develops Mercantilism.

RELATED ARTICLES in *Great Lives from History: The Seventeenth Century, 1601-1700:* Blaise Pascal; Louis XIV.

May 19, 1662
ENGLAND'S ACT OF UNIFORMITY

The Act of Uniformity required all clergymen, college fellows, and schoolmasters to accept the revised Book of Common Prayer. By August, 1662, more than one thousand ministers had refused to conform to the Act of Uniformity and were thus ejected from the Church of England.

LOCALE: England

CATEGORIES: Government and politics; laws, acts, and legal history; religion and theology; social issues and reform

KEY FIGURES

Charles II (1630-1685), king of England, r. 1660-1685

First Earl of Clarendon (Edward Hyde; 1609-1674), lord chancellor of England, 1658-1667

Richard Baxter (1615-1691), English author and Presbyterian minister

SUMMARY OF EVENT

During the English Interregnum, which began after Charles I was beheaded on January 30, 1649, English Puritans experienced religious liberty, first under the Commonwealth and then under the Protectorate of Oliver Cromwell. However, after the death of Cromwell in 1658 and the consequent political instability, it became apparent that a monarchical government would return. In a letter known as the Declaration of Breda written from Holland, dated April 4, 1660, Charles II, two months prior to returning to English soil, promised to administer justice and offer mercy to his subjects.

The Breda declaration, drafted with the assistance of the king's lord chancellor in exile, Edward Hyde, who would be created earl of Clarendon in 1661, expressed Charles II's desire that in his kingdom "all notes of discord, separation and difference of parties be utterly abolished" in hopes of a "perfect union." Most important to his Puritan citizenry was the promise in the Declaration of Breda that none would be punished because of diverse views regarding religion. Simultaneously, however, Charles II pledged support for legislation that Parliament deemed necessary regarding religious uniformity, thereby inviting the Cavalier Parliament to take political action.

The forthcoming Restoration of the monarchy signaled a return of government by bishops, or episcopacy, in the Church. The Presbyterians, whose political representatives had played critical roles in restoring Charles II to the throne, sought a religious settlement that would include them within the national church. Prominent Presbyterian leaders, such as Edmund Calamy and Richard Baxter, met with Charles II and Anglican divines, proposing limited church government and requesting involvement in revising the liturgy. As a result of their efforts, the Savoy Conference was held from April 15 through July 25, 1661, to revise the Prayer Book. However, the list of amendments provided at the Savoy Conference by the Presbyterian delegates was rejected by Anglican authorities. The debate regarding revision issues ensued in pamphlets produced on both sides. When the revised Book of Common Prayer was presented to the Cavalier Parliament for acceptance, only a few of the Presbyterian suggestions had been implemented; the revised text was approved by only six votes.

After first convening in May, 1661, the Cavalier Parliament sought to restore the supremacy of the Church of England and commenced work on legislation restricting religious freedom and pressing for conformity. On May 19, 1662, Charles II ratified the Act of Uniformity, a bill produced by Parliament and narrowly passed by a vote of

186-180. This law, the foundational statute of the so-called Clarendon Code, required that all preachers of religion accept the revised Book of Common Prayer and the practices of the Church of England.

Because of "the great and scandalous neglect of ministers" regarding the liturgy, the objective of the Act of Uniformity was to bring peace by a "universal agreement in the public worship of Almighty God." Unlike its predecessor, enacted in 1559 under the rule of Queen Elizabeth I, the 1662 Act of Uniformity demanded not only that every minister in England use the newly revised Book of Common Prayer but also that he publicly "declare his unfeigned assent and consent" to the text.

The act set the date of Saint Bartholomew's Day, August 24, 1662, as the deadline for every appointed minister to read the morning and evening prayers before his congregation and publicly to recite the prescribed oath contained in the bill's text. Any minister who refused to obey would be excommunicated, "void as if he was naturally dead," and deprived of his benefices and all "spiritual promotions." Additionally, this law required that lecturers and chaplains at universities pronounce an oath professing conformity to the practices of the Church of England and vowing not to take up arms against the king. The Act of Uniformity also required that every parish purchase a printed copy of the Book of Common Prayer. Those charged with disobeying this bill were either fined or imprisoned.

Significance

On August 24, 1662, more than one thousand ministers refused to obey the Act of Uniformity and consequently were ejected from the Church of England. In addition to these ministers, more than seven hundred had left since 1660. By August, 1662, the prisons in London were filled to capacity with Nonconformists from various sects, including Quakers, Baptists, and Independents.

Although presumably intended to unite British subjects, the Act of Uniformity in fact polarized religion in England and created an enduring tradition of Nonconformity. Those who chose to worship outside of the Anglican Church were called Dissenters, and numbered among them were persons such as Baxter, Calamy, Lucy Hutchinson, John Bunyan, and John Milton. During this period of persecution, Dissenting authors produced numerous pamphlets, sermons, and other literary works, the most famous of which was Milton's epic poem *Paradise Lost* (1667, 1674). Bunyan, who suffered imprisonment from 1660-1672 for illegal preaching, wrote *The Pilgrim's Progress from This World to That Which Is to Come* (Part 1, 1678; commonly known as *The Pilgrim's Progress*) while in jail.

Although Nonconformists comprised a minority of less than 6 percent of England's population, Parliament was concerned about minor uprisings and political unrest among Dissenters. As a result, the Five Mile Act, approved on March 24, 1665, declared that those ministers ejected from the Church by the Act of Uniformity were banned from residing or entering within a five mile radius of those cities and towns where they previously had preached and ministered. Those not complying with this law were fined £40 or imprisoned for six months without bail. Nevertheless, many Nonconformist preachers persisted in preaching, and secret meetings (or conventicles) were held, often in individual homes. This era of Puritan suffering, which began with the Act of Uniformity, ended with the Toleration Act of 1689 after the Glorious Revolution and the ascension of William III and Mary II to the throne of England.

—*Christopher E. Garrett*

Further Reading

Achinstein, Sharon. *Literature and Dissent in Milton's England*. New York: Cambridge University Press, 2003. Challenges traditional assumptions about the culture and literature of the Restoration and offers a thorough introduction to the Dissenting tradition.

Browning, Andrew, ed. *English Historical Documents, 1660-1714*. London: Eyre & Spottiswoode, 1966. Contains the significant texts of the Restoration period, including the Act of Uniformity and the Five Mile Act.

Cragg, Gerald R. *Puritanism in the Period of the Great Persecution, 1660-1688*. Cambridge, England: Cambridge University Press, 1957. Provides valuable insights on the historical context of the origins of Nonconformity.

Green, I. M. *The Re-Establishment of the Church of England, 1660-1663*. New York: Oxford University Press, 1978. Chapter 10 focuses on Clarendon and his role in shaping and influencing political policy, especially those acts of Parliament that compose the so-called Clarendon Code.

Hutton, Ronald. *The Restoration: A Political and Religious History of England and Wales, 1658-1667*. Oxford, England: Clarendon Press, 1985. Provides a narrative history of England from Cromwell's death to Clarendon's demise. Argues that Restoration legislation from 1660-1662 can be categorized as two settlements.

Keeble, N. H. *The Restoration: England in the 1660's*. Oxford, England: Blackwell, 2002. Combines a chronological and topical approach to studying the Restoration and offers a variety of viewpoints from contemporary Nonconformists.

Lacey, Douglas R. *Dissent and Parliamentary Politics in England, 1661-1689*. New Brunswick, N.J.: Rutgers University Press, 1969. Focuses on the political activity of moderate Nonconformists. Chapter 4 examines the impact of parliamentary acts on the Dissenters.

Matthews, A. G., ed. *Calamy Revised: Being a Revision of Edmund Calamy's "Account of the Ministers and Others Ejected and Silenced," 1660-1662*. Oxford, England: Clarendon Press, 1934. This critical edition provides an informative introduction and a useful glossary of terms. Calamy's text identifies many of the Nonconformists ejected.

Plum, Harry Grant. *Restoration Puritanism: A Study in the Growth of English Liberty*. Port Washington, N.Y.: Kennikat Press, 1972. This study offers an enlightening perspective on the Puritan experience in England during the mid-seventeenth century.

See also: 1642-1651: English Civil Wars; Aug. 17-Sept. 25, 1643: Solemn League and Covenant; Dec. 6, 1648-May 19, 1649: Establishment of the English Commonwealth; Dec. 16, 1653-Sept. 3, 1658: Cromwell Rules England as Lord Protector; May, 1659-May, 1660: Restoration of Charles II; 1661-1665: Clarendon Code; 1667: Milton Publishes *Paradise Lost*; Dec. 19, 1667: Impeachment of Clarendon; 1673-1678: Test Acts; Feb. 18, 1678: Bunyan's *The Pilgrim's Progress* Appears; Apr. 4, 1687, and Apr. 27, 1688: Declaration of Liberty of Conscience; Nov., 1688-Feb., 1689: The Glorious Revolution; May 24, 1689: Toleration Act.

Related articles in *Great Lives from History: The Seventeenth Century, 1601-1700:* Richard Baxter; John Bunyan; Charles I; Charles II (of England); First Earl of Clarendon; Oliver Cromwell; Mary II; John Milton; William III.

March 24, 1663-July 25, 1729
Settlement of the Carolinas

The Carolinas became the seat of the South in British North America, central to the tobacco and sugar plantation culture that the colonists developed and to the slave trade necessary to support that culture.

Locale: Eastern Carolinas
Categories: Expansion and land acquisition; colonization

Key Figures

Sir William Berkeley (1606-1677), governor of Virginia, 1641-1649, 1660-1677, and an original Carolina proprietor
John Colleton (fl. 1663), wealthy Barbadian planter who took the initiative in acquiring the proprietary charter for the Carolinas
John Culpeper (1644-1691/1694), leader of a rebellion against Albemarle's proprietary government
William Drummond (d. 1677), first governor of Albemarle County, 1664-1667, which became North Carolina
Edward Hyde (c. 1650-1712), first governor of North Carolina independent of South Carolina, 1711-1712
John Locke (1632-1704), English political philosopher, who helped to prepare the Fundamental Constitutions
Philip Ludwell (c. 1637-after 1710), first governor of both Carolinas
First Earl of Shaftesbury (Anthony Ashley Cooper; 1621-1683), proprietor and architect of the Carolina proprietary system
Sir John Yeamans (1611-1674), leader of South Carolina's Goose Creek faction

Summary of Event

The origins of English settlement of the Carolinas can be traced to 1629, when Charles I of England granted all land between 31° and 36° north latitude to Sir Robert Heath, who called the area "New Carolana." Heath planned to open the territory to French Protestants, or Huguenots, who were under siege in the latest of French religious conflicts. Agents of the Carolina settlers attempted to obtain supplies in Virginia to the north but were largely unsuccessful, and no settlements were established. Heath shortly thereafter gave up on the enterprise, and nothing further was attempted during Charles I's reign.

The introduction of large-scale sugar production during the early 1660's to Barbados, in the West Indies, among the wealthiest of the English colonies, had forced many small English planters to consider emigration from the island. When Sir John Colleton, a wealthy Barbadian, returned to England and gained a seat on the Council for Foreign Plantations, he conceived the idea of establishing a proprietary colony and recruiting Barbadians to settle it. For fellow proprietors, Colleton turned to powerful Englishmen who had already been associated with colonial expansion, the first earl of Shaftesbury, Sir William Berkeley, John Lord Berkeley, George Monck, the first earl of Clarendon, the earl of Craven, and Sir George Carteret. On March 24, 1663, King Charles II granted to the proprietors a charter similar to that granted by his father, redefined as all land between 29° and 36°30″ north latitude and extending west to the "South Seas"; they called the area Carolina after King Charles.

Required only to pay a nominal annual sum to the king, the proprietors possessed vast powers. They were empowered to fill offices, erect a government, establish courts, collect customs and taxes, grant land, confer titles, and determine military matters. They were obliged to guarantee the rights of Englishmen to their settlers, however, and could enact laws only with the consent of the freemen. The proprietors in England also constituted a Palatine Court, which, in addition to appointing the governor of the colonies, was empowered to disallow laws and hear appeals from the colony.

Having devised plans for the creation of three counties and having begun negotiations with two groups of prospective settlers in Barbados and New England, the proprietors drafted the "Declaration and Proposals to All That Will Plant in Carolina," which outlined a headright system of land distribution and a framework for participatory government. Sir William Berkeley received authorization to appoint a governor and council for Albemarle County (later North Carolina), and in October, 1664, he named William Drummond of Virginia as its governor. A few months later, Sir John Yeamans was commissioned governor of Clarendon County. As a further inducement to settlement, in January, 1665, the proprietors drew up the Concessions and Agreements, which provided for a unicameral legislature that included representatives of the freemen and ensured religious toleration. However, friction between new arrivals and original settlers in combination with hostility from Native American tribes and the news of better land to the south, led to the abandonment of Clarendon County in 1667.

Settlement of Carolina during this period was focused primarily on the estuaries of the southern regions rather than the large bays and dangerous banks of the north. Settlers in the region were a varied lot, consisting of a mixture of English Dissenters, French Huguenots, and Presbyterian Scots. The largest contingent, however, consisted of emigrants from Barbados; by 1671, they constituted half the population in the region.

As a system of laws, the Concessions and Agreements had proven unsatisfactory, so in 1669, the earl of Shaftesbury collaborated with his protégé, John Locke, to write the Fundamental Constitutions of Carolina. Essentially, the program called for development of a landed aristocracy for the region, in the form of 12,000-acre (4,850-hectare) baronies. Two-thirds of the land would be held by a colonial nobility. Although a "parliament" consisting of the nobility and popular representatives would sit in the colony, the proprietors in England, functioning as a Palatine Court, could veto the legislature's decisions. Some of these provisions were implemented, but the proprietors never succeeded in winning approval of the system as a whole. Few baronies were ever surveyed, and no manorial system was ever established. Reflecting the exigencies of a governing body in England removed from the day-to-day running of a colony, the actual government consisted of a governor and council appointed by the proprietors and representatives elected by the freemen. Until a Supreme Court was established in 1700, the governor and council would constitute the colony's highest court.

Despite the abandonment of the Clarendon region, Carolina's proprietors continued to develop plans for settlement of the region. Shaftesbury was able to convince the proprietors that a larger investment was essential for success. Drawing upon earlier experience and the expertise and resources of investors from Barbados, it was decided to attempt to establish a settlement at Port Royal. More than one hundred settlers, led by Joseph West, left England in August, 1669. However, after landing at Port Royal, already an important anchorage, they were persuaded by the local tribes to travel to another estuary some sixty miles up the coast. There, in April, 1670, they established Charles Town (modern Charleston).

Because the settlers were predominantly tradesmen ignorant of farming methods, many went into debt and deserted the colony. Recruitment efforts proved successful, however, and a rapid influx of settlers from Barbados and elsewhere continued to populate the colony. Many of these men moved inland, searching out the best land along the estuaries. They quickly learned the ways of agriculture. Disparate ethnic enclaves began to form, such as French Huguenots settled along the Santee and a Scottish settlement at the anchorage of Port Royal. Despite religious contention, prosperity within the colony increased. In 1674, Dr. Henry Woodward was commissioned Indian agent to establish trade with local Native American tribes; the colonists developed a thriving trade in furs and naval stores with England and in meat, lumber, and Indian slaves—a practice frowned upon by the proprietors—with the West Indies.

A large proportion of the colonists having emigrated from Barbados, this particularly significant group soon gained control of the government. Known as the "Goose Creek men," from the site of their settlement just outside of Charles Town, this faction was to determine the colony's politics for the next fifty years. Despite success in the areas of trade and farming, conflict between the proprietors and settlers over debts, land distribution, and the slave trade nearly brought an end to the colony in the 1670's. Attracted by the proprietors' promise of toleration, many Dissenters also came, only to encounter the resentment of the conservative Anglican Barbadians, who resisted the proprietors' efforts at reform; both pro- and anti-proprietary factions were formed.

During the 1670's, dissension culminated in what became known as Culpeper's Rebellion. In 1677, Thomas Miller, governor and leader of the proprietary faction, attempted to combine his position with the duties of customs collector. In December, an anti-proprietary faction established a revolutionary government and imprisoned Miller. Miller escaped to England and pleaded his case before the Privy Council; John Culpeper, a leader of the dissident group, represented the rebels. The council decided that Miller had indeed exceeded his authority. Culpeper was tried for treason but through the influence of Shaftesbury was acquitted.

When Governor James Colleton declared martial law in February, 1690, in an attempt to halt the abuses of the Native American trade and collect the quitrents, the Goose Creek men ousted him and replaced him with Seth Sothel. In 1691, Sothel was suspended by the Palatine Court and charged with treason, though Sothel's death in 1694 ended the controversy. Meanwhile, Philip Ludwell was appointed governor by the proprietors (1691), and the popular freemen's branch of the legislature was allowed to meet separately and to exercise parliamentary privileges.

Unlike the turmoil of earlier decades, the 1690's would be a decade of relative peace and prosperity. Ludwell and his successors were to reside in Charles Town, while Albemarle County, governed by Ludwell's deputy, was to retain a separate legislature. Trade with Native American tribes prospered. Perhaps even more important, during this period it became apparent that a new crop, rice, was perfectly suited for the swampy lowlands of Carolina. Rice quickly became a staple export. Critical to the development of rice farming was the large influx of African slaves into the region, bringing with them knowledge of rice cultivation. By the beginning of the eighteenth century, the black population equaled that of the white: There were approximately four thousand of each race.

The region of Albemarle, known as North Carolina after 1691, was repeatedly torn by religious strife in the first decade of the new century. Huguenots from Virginia had settled the area south of Albemarle Sound; German Palatines and Swiss had settled in the region of what would be founded as New Bern (1710). Although toleration had prevailed in the earlier years and many Dissenters held positions of power, Anglicans were determined to establish the Church of England in the colony. With the passage of the Vestry Act of 1704, Assembly members were required to take an oath of loyalty to the Church of England. The act aroused such intense opposition that deputy governor Thomas Cary was removed for attempting to enforce the law. In 1712, North Carolina was established as a separate colony; the proprietors appointed Edward Hyde deputy governor, the first governor of North Carolina to be independent of the royal governor of Carolina. The new legislature nullified the laws of the previous administrations.

SIGNIFICANCE

The Carolinas were thus a crucible for many of the controversies shaping the evolution of both the colonists' home countries and the other English colonies. Religious strife, disagreements over the proper form of colonial government and over the role of government as such, and interrelations between Europeans, Native Americas, and African slaves, all came to a head in the Carolina colonies.

The crisis in North Carolina was exacerbated by the war with the Tuscaroras, the worst Indian war in the colony's history. In September, 1711, the Tuscaroras, seeking revenge for encroachment by the settlers on their land, enslavement of their people, and unfair trading practices, attacked New Bern and other settlements from the Neuse to the Pamlico Rivers. Before the raids were over, hundreds of settlers had been massacred and their farms destroyed. Two expeditions, led by Colonel Jack

Barnwell and Colonel James More in 1712 and 1713 and aided by men from South Carolina, finally defeated the Tuscaroras. Although the war had placed the colony in dire financial straits, it drew the people together, and they entered a new period of peace.

The choice of rice as a staple crop had its greatest impact in the south. Unlike the tobacco crop, grown in the region of the Chesapeake to the north, rice growing required special water facilities to maintain an annual flooding of the fields. However, once the facilities were established, the rice crop could be grown in the same fields year after year. It was unnecessary to plant new fields or to continue shifting the settlements themselves. Thus, the settlements, once established, could maintain a semblance of stability, except for the frequent internal rivalries. Consequently, settlement followed the river systems as extensions from the city of Charles Town. By 1708, the population of the district (and in essence the entire colony) consisted of four thousand whites, forty-one hundred African Americans, and fourteen hundred Native Americans; most of the African Americans and Native Americans in the settlements were slaves.

Factional rivalries were revived at the beginning of the eighteenth century. The selection of an Anglican governor for Carolina in 1700 aroused the opposition of the Dissenters to the establishment of the Church of England in the colony; indeed, in 1704, the parish vestries had become the seats of power. The popular division over religion was superseded by a division over the issue of paper currency in 1712. As early as 1703, the colony had emitted its first bills of credit to pay for an expedition against the Spanish in Florida. Other emissions followed. The planters and tradesmen who did business solely within the colony favored the use of paper money, but the Charles Town merchants who had to pay their English creditors in specie bitterly opposed its use.

The proprietors had never moved decisively to control the long-standing abuses of trade with Native American tribes. As a result, in 1715, the Yamasee War, the longest and costliest war with Native Americans in South Carolina's history, erupted. During the conflict, people were driven from their homes to seek refuge in Charles Town. To end the abuses of trade, the Commons House of Assembly created a monopoly of the Native American trade under its own direction.

In 1718, the proprietors launched a strong attack upon some of the colony's most popular laws, disallowing measures providing for bills of credit and import duties, removing the monopoly on trade, and weakening the power of the legislature; consequently, antiproprietary sentiment crystallized in favor of royal government. All that lacked for rebellion was a catalyst.

The catalyst came in November, 1719, in the form of the rumor of an imminent invasion of the colony by the Spanish. When the assembly convened in December, it declared itself a convention and petitioned the Board of Trade to be made a royal colony. Because the region represented a major line of defense against both the French and the Spanish, King George I accepted the removal of the proprietary government, and South Carolina became a royal colony in 1719. The "royalizing" process also had its counterpart in North Carolina. The Crown bought out the proprietors on July 25, 1729, and North Carolina also became a royal colony.

—*Richard Adler*

Further Reading

Andrews, Charles M. *The Colonial Period of American History*. 4 vols. New Haven, Conn.: Yale University Press, 1934-1937. Includes a detailed discussion on the government of the Carolinas.

Canny, Nicholas, and Alaine Low, eds. *The Origins of Empire: British Overseas Enterprise at the Close of the Seventeenth Century*. Vol. 1 in *The Oxford History of the British Empire*, edited by William Roger Lewis. New York: Oxford University Press, 1998. Collection of essays by noted historians exploring numerous aspects of England's worldwide colonial expansion. Explains the founding and governance of individual American colonies, and several essays focus on English colonies in New England, Carolinas, the mid-Atlantic, and the Chesapeake.

Craven, Wesley F. *The Southern Colonies in the Seventeenth Century, 1607-1689*. Baton Rouge: Louisiana University Press, 1949. Places the settlement of the Carolinas in the context of English expansion in America. Written by noted author on colonial America.

McCusker, John, and Russell Menard. *The Economy of British America, 1607-1789*. Chapel Hill: University of North Carolina Press, 1985. A detailed description of the economic factors behind the development of North and South Carolina.

Meriwether, Robert L. *The Expansion of South Carolina, 1729-1765*. 1940. Reprint. Philadelphia: Porcupine Press, 1974. A concise history of the later years of Carolina's development.

Roper, H. L. *Conceiving Carolina: Proprietors, Planters, and Plots*. New York: Palgrave Macmillan, 2004. A history of South Carolina's proprietary government and the complex relationships between British and

Irish settlers, Huguenot refugees, Yamassee warriors, and African slaves.

Salley, Alexander S., Jr., ed. *Narratives of Early Carolina, 1650-1708*. New York: Barnes & Noble Books, 1946. Presents original accounts, including descriptions of the early explorations and life in the settlements.

See also: May 14, 1607: Jamestown Is Founded; 1612: Introduction of Tobacco Farming in North America; 1619-c. 1700: The Middle Passage to American Slavery; May 14, 1625-1640: English Discover and Colonize Barbados; Sept. 13, 1660-July 27, 1663: British Navigation Acts; Apr., 1670: Charles Town Is Founded.

Related articles in *Great Lives from History: The Seventeenth Century, 1601-1700:* Charles I; Charles II (of England); First Earl of Clarendon; John Locke; George Monck; First Earl of Shaftesbury.

1664
Molière Writes *Tartuffe*

The comedy Tartuffe *sparked public uproar and provoked outrage among the clergy, who called for its banishment and for Molière's punishment for writing a work critical of the Catholic Church. The play, which highlighted extreme religious hypocrisy during an era characterized by religious piety, was considered heretical by the pious but was loved by secular audiences. Molière was perhaps the first to show how daily life and manners could be reflected through comedy.*

Locale: Versailles and Paris, France
Categories: Theater; cultural and intellectual history; literature

Key Figures

Molière (1622-1673), French playwright
Louis XIV (1638-1715), king of France, r. 1643-1715
Jules Mazarin (1602-1661), chief minister of France, 1643-1661, and patron of Molière's early work
Cardinal de Richelieu (Armand-Jean du Plessis; 1585-1642), chief minister of France, 1624-1642, and founder of the Académie Française in 1635

Summary of Event

Jean-Baptiste Poquelin, better known as Molière, stands at the helm of French comedy. Born in Paris in January, 1622, and the son of an upholsterer, he was educated at the Jesuit College of Clermont, whose students were drawn from the middle class as well as the aristocracy. For some time he studied law, which he soon abandoned for the stage, joining a troupe named Illustre Théâtre, which failed after two years. His life was spent acting, directing, managing, producing, and writing plays in Paris and the French provinces. The satire in his comedies made him many enemies, and he was the object of slanderous attacks. His marriage was unhappy, which increased the bitterness that the public hostility brought into his life.

Tartuffe: Ou, L'Imposteur (1664; *Tartuffe*, 1732), about a pious hypocrite, is considered Molière's masterpiece. It is the most frequently performed of all his plays by the French acting company La Comédie Française. The first version of Molière's *Tartuffe* was performed in three acts at the royal court of Versailles in 1664, before the young king Louis XIV. Louis granted Molière and his troupe annual subsidies, creating the King's Troupe. News of its contents aroused scandal and outrage among Church leaders. The archbishop of Paris ordered the play denounced from every parish pulpit in Paris. Consequently, Molière reworked *Tartuffe* during the next five years, and the play was finally authorized in 1669. It was a rousing success, having a run of more than thirty performances, which was a record at the time.

During the second half of the sixteenth century, religious wars waged between a Catholic majority and a Protestant minority in France. The power of the monarchy had diminished the status and privileges of the nobility, many of whom used the religious wars in an attempt to win back what they had lost. Between 1630 and 1660, French chief ministers Cardinal de Richelieu and Jules Mazarin reestablished and extended the king's power. A failed civil uprising that began in 1648 and ended in 1653 was the last attempt to reverse this process. From 1661 to 1715, through his long reign, King Louis XIV ruled without a chief minister. Catholicism regained renewed vitality. Movements such as Gallicanism and Jansenism reflected fresh energy and piety. Other attempts to renew faith occurred in Calvinism by the Protestants and a re-

Molière discusses a performance with his troupe of players. (Francis R. Niglutsch)

vival of ancient Greek and Roman Stoicism among the educated. The most frequently named targets for Molière's satire in *Tartuffe* are the Jesuits, the Jansenists, and the Compagnie du Saint-Sacrement. According to critics, a weak case is made for the Jansenists and a stronger case has been made for the Compagnie du Saint-Sacrement, a group of powerful zealots who worked together to defend what they saw as the interests of the Church, installing their members in important positions in order to promote their own policies through existing institutions. The strongest case has been made for the Jesuits, distinguished and powerful, who viewed themselves as promoting the authority of the Church and the pope.

Tartuffe traces what Molière considered the Jesuit "invasion" of France, and that invasion's influence on French religion and culture. Politically, the play is significant in that even though it was supported by the king, it took five years and two revisions to receive permission to be performed openly and freely. The play sparked another attack in this atmosphere of renewed faith because it infuriated the deeply religious. The play centers on a rich man, Orgon, who takes a self-proclaimed religious holy man, Tartuffe, into his home, offers him his daughter's hand in marriage, and gives him property until Tartuffe's treachery is finally discovered. It is thought that Molière's Tartuffe-the-schemer was constructed to reflect Jesuit policy. Through Tartuffe's weaknesses of the flesh, Molière's satire encompasses the entire field of Jesuit moralist teachings. Tartuffe's gross behavior is said to illustrate humorously the activities of the rascal while appearing innocent in the eyes of the moralist.

Molière demonstrates that Orgon had been a good man before he was blinded and corrupted by Tartuffe's hypocrisy as well as his own beliefs; he had been a loyal Frenchman surrounded by a loyal family. When transferred from the context of the family to the wider context of the state through the use of satire, the play actually stands for Molière's belief that many who were lured by the appeal and outward trappings of religion not only dangerous but also instruments of injustice. The family's failure to counter Tartuffe's moves reflects what Molière and several of his contemporaries, such as Blaise Pascal, viewed as the helplessness of honest people attempting to oppose the advance of the Jesuits.

Critics have attacked Molière because his characters do not develop. Instead, they spring to life as recognizable and universal types in human nature, but they do not learn from experience. It must be realized that Molière's plays are about ideas embodied in funny and believable people who theatergoers can recognize as embodiments of themselves. The genius of Molière was in his exposing social hypocrisy and folly through satire. The art of comedy enhances some imperfections and weaknesses. By calling his comedies "public mirrors," Molière responded to the desire by the theatergoing public to see itself depicted on stage by creating characters with whom the viewer could identify. Faced with censorship and possible censure from those who identified themselves in his characters, his art became one of creating portrayals through techniques such as gesture, disguise, indirection, irony, ventriloquism, and public humiliation. Critics have concluded that these techniques make satire a dramatic art and not a moral commentary.

SIGNIFICANCE

Tartuffe was an attack on the hypocrite caricaturing religious practices as well as using religion for political and material ends. Many interpreted Molière's masterpiece as a condemnation of all religious practice. The controversy surrounding the play made clear how difficult it was to produce a work that was critical of the Church and its leaders, even if that criticism was accomplished through humor.

Molière was so despised by Church authorities that he was denied a Christian burial, even with King Louis XIV's intervention.

—*Marcia J. Weiss*

FURTHER READING

Bermel, Albert. *Molière's Theatrical Bounty: A New View of the Plays*. Carbondale: Southern Illinois University Press, 1990. A comprehensive review of Molière's plays in English from the standpoint of their theatrical possibilities, dramatic structures, settings, and roles, as well as their interactions.

Bloom, Harold, ed. *Molière*. Philadelphia: Chelsea House, 2003. A research and study guide containing biographical and bibliographical data. Also outlines major life events and literary accomplishments, and provides critical analysis of significant themes in Molière's works.

_______. *Molière: Modern Critical Views*. Philadelphia: Chelsea House, 2002. A collection of essays and comprehensive studies dealing with various aspects of Molière scholarship.

Brereton, Geoffrey. *French Comic Drama from the Sixteenth to the Eighteenth Century*. London: Methuen, 1977. A survey of French literature in the genre of comic drama.

Fowlie, Wallace. *French Literature: Its History and Its Meaning*. Englewood Cliffs, N.J.: Prentice-Hall, 1973. A concise history of French literature in its historical and literary context.

McCarthy, Gerry. *The Theatres of Molière*. New York: Routledge, 2002. Explores the practice and method of Molière's playwriting and acting.

Norman, Larry F. *The Public Mirror: Molière and the Social Commerce of Depiction*. Chicago: University of Chicago Press, 1999. A scholarly study of the works of Molière, with emphasis on the manner in which the works mirror society.

Polsky, Zachary. *The Comic Machine, the Narrative Machine, and the Political Machine in the Works of Molière*. Lewiston, N.Y.: E. Mellen Press, 2000. Examines the general nature of comedy and the specific nature of seventeenth century French comedy to understand how these ideas apply to six of Molière's plays.

Scott, Virginia. *Molière: A Theatrical Life*. New York: Cambridge University Press, 2000. In the first significant English biography written in many years, Scott recounts the incidents of Molière's life and describes his plays within the wider context of French seventeenth century theater.

SEE ALSO: c. 1601-1613: Shakespeare Produces His Later Plays; 1638-1669: Spread of Jansenism; Sept. 2, 1642: Closing of the Theaters.

RELATED ARTICLES in *Great Lives from History: The Seventeenth Century, 1601-1700:* Pierre Corneille; Louis XIV; Jules Mazarin; Molière; Jean Racine; Cardinal de Richelieu.

1664
Willis Identifies the Basal Ganglia

Thomas Willis published his masterpiece, Cerebri anatome, *which included groundbreaking descriptions, illustrations, and analyses of several important brain structures, especially at the base of the brain. Willis thereby became the central figure in the rapidly advancing brain studies of the seventeenth century.*

Locale: Oxford and London, England
Categories: Health and medicine; biology; science and technology

Key Figures

Thomas Willis (1621-1675), English physician, anatomist, physiologist, and chemist
Richard Lower (1631-1691), English physician, anatomist, and physiologist
Sir Thomas Millington (1628-1704), English physician and physiologist
Sir Christopher Wren (1632-1723), English architect, physiologist, and illustrator
Raymond Vieussens (1635-1715), French physician and surgeon
Nicolaus Steno (1638-1686), Danish physician, anatomist, and Roman Catholic priest
René Descartes (1596-1650), French philosopher, mathematician, and physiologist
Gerardus Leonardus Blasius (1626?-1692), Dutch physician and anatomist
Johann Jacob Wepfer (1620-1695), Swiss physician and anatomist

Summary of Event

When Thomas Willis published *Cerebri anatome* (1664; *The Anatomy of the Brain*, 1681), he effectively founded the modern neurosciences, particularly neurology and neuroanatomy. With only a few minor exceptions, knowledge of the brain and its functions had not changed much from Galen in the second century until early in the seventeenth century, and most of that "knowledge" was wrong. Scientists did not even agree that the brain was the organ of thought, and many assigned that role to the heart. The credit for the quantum leap forward represented by *Cerebri anatome* does not belong to Willis alone, however: Even though his is the only name that appears on the title page, *Cerebri anatome* was actually a collaborative effort of four University of Oxford colleagues, Richard Lower as dissector, Willis and Thomas Millington as physiologists, and Christopher Wren as illustrator.

Cerebri anatome is best known for its presentation of findings about the cerebral arterial circle, the pentagonal confluence of the two posterior cerebral arteries arising from the basilar artery, the two posterior communicating arteries, the two middle cerebral arteries, the two internal carotid arteries, the two anterior cerebral arteries, and the anterior communicating artery. Many anatomists, notably Johann Jacob Wepfer in *Observationes anatomicae* (1658), described the cerebral arterial circle before Willis, but they did not understand its purpose. It is commonly known as the "circle of Willis," because he discovered that its physiological function is to protect the brain from ischemia, or loss of blood supply.

The circle of Willis works through anastomosis, a process in which several arteries are so closely connected that they share their contents. If any of the three feeder arteries, the basilar or either of the two internal carotids, are blocked or cut, then the others instantly redistribute the blood so that the flow to the brain is not interrupted through the pairs of posterior, middle, and anterior cerebral arteries. This prevents brain damage from local anemia.

Before the eighteenth century, the only significant advocates of brain function localization were Willis, René Descartes, and Nicolaus Steno. Willis verified that the cerebellum controlled the vital functions and believed that the cerebrum was the organ of thought. Descartes performed experiments on the locus of sight and argued that the pineal gland was the seat of the soul and hence of thought. Most of Willis's analyses of Lower's brain dissections were aimed at discovering localized functions or assigning specific physiological tasks to specific parts or areas of the brain. Above all, he was looking for the seat of Aristotle's *sensus communis* (common sense), which was supposed to mediate among the data gathered by the five physical senses. Galen had believed that the ventricles were the organs of thought and that the ventricular fluid was the means by which the brain transmitted information. Willis abandoned that notion and correctly identified the cortex as the thinking part of the brain, but he incorrectly decided that the common sense was located in the corpus striatum (striped body).

The corpus striatum is the main component of the basal ganglia, which consist of all the interconnected gray matter and nerve structures that lie in two divisions deep in the center of the brain, beneath the cortex and on either side of the thalamus. Besides the physiology of the cerebral arterial circle, Willis's most important contribution to neuroscience was his work on the basal ganglia. "Ganglia" is the plural of "ganglion," which is any group or knot of nerve cells. Because of their core location, Willis believed that the basal ganglia served both the motor and the sensory functions. This guess was essentially correct, but scientists would be unable to verify it or to sort out the subtleties of the situation until the twentieth century.

Although Willis was convinced that each part of the brain had a specific function, he could not prove it. Steno agreed with Willis about cerebral localization in principle but attacked some of Willis's physiological conclusions on the grounds that Willis showed insufficient anatomical evidence for them. Steno strongly disagreed with Willis that the basal ganglia housed the common sense. He urged scientists to limit their speculation about localized brain function until they understood brain anatomy better.

Besides Willis, the most important brain researchers of the seventeenth century were Gerardus Leonardus Blasius, Descartes, Steno, and Raymond Vieussens. Together, by the end of the seventeenth century, they had discovered or described most of the gross or macroscopic anatomical structures of the brain. Blasius discovered the arachnoid, the middle of the three membranes that enclose the brain. In the dura mater, the outer of these three membranes, Willis discovered fibers crossing the superior sagittal sinus, a long duct or groove along the midline of the cranium running from the front, across the top, to the back of the brain. These fibers are now called "Willis's cords."

Thomas Willis. (Library of Congress)

Among seventeenth century books on neuroanatomy, only *Cerebri anatome* is more important than Vieussens's major work, *Neurographia universalis* (1684; general neurography). Vieussens provided the earliest precise descriptions and illustrations of many small structures in the brain, and three are named for him: "Vieussens's centrum," or centrum ovale, the white oval core of each brain hemisphere; "Vieussens's valve," a sheet of thin white tissue; and "Vieussens's ventricle," a fluid-filled space.

Much seventeenth century brain research, including Willis's, was prompted by the mind/body problem formulated by Descartes in *Discours de la Méthode* (1637; *Discourse on Method*, 1649) and *Meditationes de prima philosophie* (1641; *Meditations on First Philosophy*, 1680). Cartesian dualism claims that the self definitely exists as a thinking thing, but that the precise nature of the connection of this mind or soul with the physical world, including its own body, is difficult to ascertain. These early neurologists were seeking religious and philosophical knowledge of the soul as much as biomedical knowledge of the brain. Willis was a very religious man, and made every effort to connect his physiological and anatomical work with his conception of the brain as "the chapel of the deity" so that the Church of England could use his science in its theological disputes with other churches.

Significance

Cerebri anatome was the most important book on brain anatomy and physiology until German anatomist and physician Samuel Thomas Soemmering improved Willis's description of the cranial nerves in 1778 and Scottish anatomist and physician Alexander Monro, Secundus, published *Observations on the Structure and Functions of the Nervous System* (1783). The fact that *Cerebri anatome* remained the dominant influence in neurology and neuroanatomy for more than one hundred years is testimony not only to the precision of Lower's dissections and Willis's observations, the depth of their intelligence, and the thoroughness of their investigations, but also to the production values of the book itself. It is a beautifully executed volume, with Wren's illustrations standing out as true works of art.

The neuroanatomical and neurophysiological discoveries of Willis and his contemporaries created the modern science of the nervous system and laid the groundwork for disciplines as diverse as neurosurgery and psychiatry.

—*Eric v.d. Luft*

FURTHER READING

Brazier, Mary Agnes Burniston. *A History of Neurophysiology in the Seventeenth and Eighteenth Centuries: From Concept to Experiment*. New York: Raven Press, 1984. The standard scholarly work in this field.

Clarke, Edwin, and Kenneth Dewhurst. *An Illustrated History of Brain Function*. Berkeley: University of California Press, 1974. Beautifully produced, accessible, and authoritative.

Coulter, Harris L. *The Origins of Modern Western Medicine: J.B. van Helmont to Claude Bernard*. Vol. 2 in *Divided Legacy: A History of the Schism in Medical Thought*. Berkeley, Calif.: North Atlantic Books, 2000. The second chapter, "Seventeenth-Century Rationalism," explores the rivalry between iatrochemisty and iatromechanics.

Finger, Stanley. *Origins of Neuroscience: A History of Explorations into Brain Function*. New York: Oxford University Press, 1994. An illustrated chronological survey of the persons and concepts that have shaped neuroscience.

Frank, Robert Gregg. *Harvey and the Oxford Physiologists: A Study of Scientific Ideas*. Berkeley: University of California Press, 1980. This standard scholarly work sets Willis's research on blood, fermentation, the brain, muscles, respiration, and physiological chemistry in its historical and interpersonal context.

Meyer, Alfred. *Historical Aspects of Cerebral Anatomy*. London: Oxford University Press, 1971. Written by a neuropathologist and organized by specific regions of the brain, this book is perhaps too technical for a general readership. Willis is among the most often mentioned names.

Rocca, Julius. *Galen on the Brain: Anatomical Knowledge and Physiological Speculation in the Second Century A.D.* New York: E. J. Brill, 2003. Excellent background information on the state of neurology and neuroanatomy before Willis.

Zimmer, Carl. *Soul Made Flesh: The Discovery of the Brain and How It Changed the World*. New York: Free Press, 2004. The central character in this well-told drama is Willis, the turning point is the seventeenth century, and the main locale is Oxford. Accordingly, the subtitle of the British edition (London: Heinemann, 2004) is *Thomas Willis, The English Civil War, and the Mapping of the Mind*.

SEE ALSO: 17th cent.: Advances in Medicine; 1601-1672: Rise of Scientific Societies; 1612: Sanctorius Invents the Clinical Thermometer; 1617-1628: Harvey Discovers the Circulation of the Blood; 1660's-1700: First Microscopic Observations; c. 1670: First Widespread Smallpox Inoculations; 1672-1684: Leeuwenhoek Discovers Microscopic Life; 1676: Sydenham Advocates Clinical Observation; 1693: Ray Argues for Animal Consciousness.

RELATED ARTICLES in *Great Lives from History: The Seventeenth Century, 1601-1700:* René Descartes; Nicolaus Steno; Thomas Willis; Sir Christopher Wren.

March 22, 1664-July 21, 1667
BRITISH CONQUEST OF NEW NETHERLAND

Mercantile and territorial ambitions led to the dominance of the British in colonial North America, eliminating the Dutch as commercial rivals on the continent. The British conquest of New Netherland led to an English colonial presence stretching from what is now Canada to what is now the state of Florida.

LOCALE: New Netherland (now New York City area)
CATEGORIES: Wars, uprisings, and civil unrest; economics; trade and commerce; colonization; expansion and land acquisition

KEY FIGURES

James, Duke of York and Albany (1633-1701), proprietor of New York after 1664, king of England as James II, r. 1685-1688
Richard Nicolls (1624-1672), James's deputy and first governor of New York
Peter Stuyvesant (c. 1610-1672), director-general of New Netherland, 1647-1664

SUMMARY OF EVENT

The restoration of the Stuart monarchy to the British throne in 1660 ushered in an era of colonial expansion in the Americas. This expansion was driven by a rigorous mercantilism that called forth efforts to make colonial administration more unified. New Netherland's existence as an alien wedge between Great Britain's New England and Chesapeake colonies threatened not only English territorial and mercantile ambitions but also plans for strengthening imperial government. Playing an important role in all of this, James, King Charles II's brother and heir to the throne, was at the center of a group of merchants and noblemen who were deeply concerned by the Dutch in North America and exercised considerable influence over the king.

Charles II, James, and their supporters viewed land grants in America as a device for recouping their lost fortunes, and the region occupied by the Dutch enticed such land-grabbers. Furthermore, the Crown's attempt to unify colonial administration was frustrated by the situation of New Netherland, for its strategic geographic location impeded communications between the Chesapeake and New England colonies and made more difficult the task of defending those colonies from the French. The stubborn independence demonstrated by Puritan New England particularly disturbed the Restoration government. Following upon the earlier policy of Oliver Cromwell and the Commonwealth government, King Charles and Parliament continued to enact trade regulations against their commercial rivals, the Dutch. However, New Netherland's existence rendered enforcement of the Navigation Act ineffective.

England's mainland colonies used New Netherland as a means of circumventing the British navigation system, and the Dutch colony became a breeding ground for smugglers. Despite laws to the contrary, Dutch merchants did a thriving business in tobacco from Virginia and Maryland, and Boston regularly had Dutch ships carrying goods to and from Boston's harbor. In fact, officials in the British colonies would not enforce the trade acts against the Dutch, and it was argued that if New Netherland were in England's hands, it might well generate ten thousand pounds annually in uncollected customs revenues. The prospect of acquiring an American colony that could make him money appealed mightily to debt-ridden James.

The Crown eventually concluded that the only effective remedy for these difficulties lay in wresting control of New Netherland from the Dutch. As early as 1663, the Council for Foreign Plantations—an advisory board of merchants and privy councillors, several of whom were close advisers to James—investigated the matter of Dutch power and examined the possibility of a military operation against New Netherland. Information from English residents on the eastern end of Long Island suggested that such a military undertaking would meet with little resistance from the Dutch garrison at New Amsterdam. Plans were even made to enlist the New England militia against the Dutch.

Based upon the council's recommendations, Charles moved swiftly. March 22, 1664, he gave brother James a proprietary grant of all the land between Delaware Bay and the Connecticut River, which included the Dutch colony. Parliament approved the grant, and in April, the king nominated Colonel Richard Nicolls as lieutenant governor of the proprietary, put him in charge of a small military force, and sent him to America. Nicolls was charged with more than seizing New Netherland: He headed a special commission whose members were instructed not only to take over lands claimed by the Dutch but also to settle boundary disputes among the New England colonies and make sure that the New England governments understood they were expected to enforce the navigation acts. With the duke of York in firm control of the colony next door, it was generally thought by the Council for Foreign Plantations that New Englanders would be more likely to fall into line behind imperial policy.

Nicolls and his squadron of four ships carrying three hundred soldiers arrived off New Amsterdam in August, 1664. The lieutenant governor immediately demanded the surrender of the colony, offering liberal terms as bait. Among the terms were guarantees to the inhabitants of all the rights of Englishmen, trading privileges, freedom of conscience, the continuance of Dutch customs and inheritance laws, and up to eighteen months for the settlers to decide whether to leave. At first, Director-General Peter Stuyvesant, who had led New Netherland for the Dutch West India Company since 1647, refused to surrender and began to make preparations for the defense of his colony. However, the peg-legged Stuyvesant, having angered his people with his high-handed rule, received little support from the residents, who felt they would be no worse off under the British. Moreover, the English villages on Long Island were in full-scale revolt, and the British had spread rumors that if Stuyvesant did not surrender, New Amsterdam would be brought under siege, burned, and sacked. Bowing to the inevitable, Stuyvesant surrendered the town and its garrison of 150 soldiers on August 26, 1664. New Amsterdam was immediately renamed New York, in honor of James, duke of York.

Nicolls sent British forces both north and south to secure the surrender of the rest of New Netherland. Sir George Cartwright went up the Hudson River and obtained the surrender of Fort Orange without a fight. Cartwright renamed the town Albany, after James's other dukedom. The inhabitants there were pleased that the British were willing to allow them to have a monopoly on the fur trade. Nicolls also instructed Cartwright to negotiate a treaty with the Iroquois, whose friendship the English needed if the French and their American Indian allies were to be bested. This first British-Iroquois treaty was signed on September 26, 1664.

Contrary to his expressed orders, Sir Robert Carr, who had been sent with British soldiers to the South River (Delaware Bay), provoked a fight and stormed the small fort there, killing and wounding several and plundering the settlement of New Amstel. Outraged by Carr's violence on the Delaware, Governor Nicolls wanted erstwhile New Netherlanders to remain in New York, understanding full well that the province's most valuable resource was its settlers. In fact, most of New Netherland's estimated population of nine thousand did remain, including Stuyvesant. Against the advice of Nicolls, however, James gave away choice lands and settlements in what became New Jersey, thereby inhibiting the demographic and economic progress of his own colony.

SIGNIFICANCE

On July 21, 1667, the Treaty of Breda, which ended the Second Anglo-Dutch War, confirmed the British conquest. Except for a brief loss of control during the Third Anglo-Dutch War (1672-1674), the British retained a firm grip upon the former Dutch colony that they called New York. The acquisition of New York was part of a more extensive effort to centralize government that led, in the 1680's, to the creation of the Dominion of New England, which included New York, New Jersey, and the New England colonies.

Great Britain's conquest of New Netherland plugged the breach between the British colonies, thus forming a continuous English presence from Canada to Florida. It eliminated the Dutch as commercial rivals on the continent, gained an alliance with the Iroquois, and ultimately brought the British and the French into confrontation for continental supremacy.

—*Warren M. Billings and Ronald W. Howard*

FURTHER READING

Andrews, Charles M. *England's Commercial and Colonial Policy*. Vol. 4 in *The Colonial Period of American History*. New Haven, Conn.: Yale University Press, 1964. Discusses Anglo-Dutch rivalry and relates the conquest of New Netherland to overall British efforts to create a self-contained colonial empire.

Canny, Nicholas, and Alaine Low, eds. *The Origins of Empire: British Overseas Enterprise at the Close of the Seventeenth Century*. Vol. 1 in *The Oxford History of the British Empire*, edited by William Roger Lewis. New York: Oxford University Press, 1998. A collection of essays by noted historians exploring numerous aspects of Britain's worldwide colonial expansion. Explains the founding and governance of individual American colonies, with several essays focusing on British colonies in New England, the Carolinas, the mid-Atlantic, and the Chesapeake Bay area.

Kammen, Michael. *Colonial New York: A History*. New York: Charles Scribner's Sons, 1975. Chapters 3 and 4 examine the reasons for the British conquest, the Articles of Capitulation, and adjustments under Governor Nicolls.

Kessler, Henry H., and Eugene Rachlis. *Peter Stuyvesant and His New York*. New York: Random House, 1959.

Chapters 14 and 15 consider the British conquest from the perspective of Stuyvesant and the Dutch in New Netherland.

Merwick, Donna. *Possessing Albany, 1630-1710: The Dutch and English Experiences*. New York: Cambridge University Press, 1990. A provocative work, less concerned with the British conquest than with the cultural differences that emerged between the Dutch and English in New York, particularly Albany.

Rink, Oliver A. *Holland on the Hudson: An Economic and Social History of Dutch New York*. Ithaca, N.Y.: Cornell University Press, 1986. Chapter 8 relates the stresses and strains that weakened the Dutch West India Company's hold on New Netherland.

Ritchie, Robert C. *The Duke's Province: A Study of New York Politics and Society, 1664-1691*. Chapel Hill: University of North Carolina Press, 1977. Chapter 1 deals extensively with reasons for the British conquest.

Shorto, Russell. *The Island at the Center of the World: The Epic Story of Dutch Manhattan and the Forgotten Colony That Shaped America*. New York: Doubleday, 2004. Shorto argues that the social and political practices of New Amsterdam's inhabitants powerfully influenced the development of American democracy.

See also: Spring, 1604: First European Settlement in North America; Dec. 26, 1620: Pilgrims Arrive in North America; May 6, 1626: Algonquians "Sell" Manhattan Island; June, 1636: Rhode Island Is Founded; Apr. 21, 1649: Maryland Act of Toleration; Oct., 1651-May, 1652: Navigation Act Leads to Anglo-Dutch Wars; Summer, 1654-1656: First Jewish Settlers in North America; 1689-1697: Wars of the League of Augsburg.

Related articles in *Great Lives from History: The Seventeenth Century, 1601-1700:* James II; Peter Minuit; Peter Stuyvesant.

July 13, 1664
Trappist Order Is Founded

At a time when monastic life was becoming lax, an abbot set out to reform monastic practice at the La Trappe monastery. Following a strict regimen, the abbot's reform became known as the Trappist movement, which survived the French Revolution and grew to be an important monastic reform movement. The order exists into the twenty-first century.

Locale: La Trappe, Normandy, France
Categories: Religion and theology; organizations and institutions

Key Figures

Arman-Jean le Bouthillier de Rancé (1626-1700), religious reformer and Trappist movement founder
Claude Vaussin (d. 1670), abbot general of the Cistercians, 1645-1670
Alexander VII (Fabio Chigi; 1599-1667), Roman Catholic pope, 1655-1667

Summary of Event

The history of the monastic movement in Europe is filled with highs and lows. When the strict Benedictine Order (founded in 529) grew weak, the reforming monk, Saint Robert of Molesme (c. 1029-1111), founded a new monastery at Cîteaux in southern France in 1098. His followers were known as Cistercians, after the monastery's Latin name. For several centuries, this movement flourished, expanding to hundreds of sites and producing bishops and theologians of the Church, such as Saint Bernard of Clairvaux (1090-1153). By the early seventeenth century, the monastic movement was again in decline. Monks became lax in their practices. Many monasteries were directed by wealthy noblemen who, according to a system called commendation, were allowed to profit from the revenue of the abbeys.

One such figure was Arman-Jean le Bouthillier de Rancé, who had inherited, at the age of twelve, five rundown monasteries in the Normandy region of France, among them the Cistercian monastery of La Trappe, which was established in 1140. Born on January 9, 1626, de Rancé was the son of the secretary to Marie de Médicis, the powerful widow of King Henry IV. His godfather was the famous Cardinal de Richelieu, adviser to French kings. He was trained as a scholar and became a priest in 1651, teaching at the Sorbonne. He preached from time to time in Paris, but was known to frequent salons as much as churches.

However, the year 1657 marked a turning point for de Rancé, when he was faced with the death of a dear friend. He retreated to his castle at Véretz near Tours, where he began a life of meditation and prayer. Eventually, he decided to give away four of his monasteries, keeping only La Trappe, where he would reside. Still, he had no intention of becoming a monk. He despised them, thinking that they wasted away their lives. On April 17, 1663, however, while reading Psalm 124 during noontime prayers, he felt the call to become a monk. After a year as a novitiate at the monastery of Perseigne, he said his monastic vows on July 13, 1664, at the age of thirty-eight, becoming a genuine abbot of La Trappe. For the next thirty-six years, he would bring about monastic reform, known as the Trappist movement.

From the beginning, de Rancé was determined to revive the ancient rule of Saint Benedict at La Trappe, with strict observance of silence, seclusion, abstinence from eating meat, penance, and hard manual labor. Within the Cistercian Order, there had been extensive debate over these rules. The majority, including the abbot general of Cîteaux, Claude Vaussin, argued that a more moderate approach was necessary to attract new monks. This approach was known as the common observance, which was in contrast to the strict observance promoted at La Trappe. De Rancé was not alone. In 1598, the abbot of Charmoye had reintroduced the practice of abstinence from meat. In 1615, Abbot Denis Largentier led the monastery at Clairvaux to follow strict practices. By the time de Rancé began his reform at La Trappe, there were sixty monasteries following the strict order. However, these sixty were still in the minority, and pressure from Cîteaux was organized against Largentier.

The conflict became highly politicized, and it involved both the Papacy and the monarchy. In 1634, a new charter gave adherents of the strict observance control over the mother house at Cîteaux. When Pope Urban VIII annulled this decision, King Louis XIII, convinced that this was unfair interference in French affairs, appointed his own adviser Cardinal de Richelieu as protector of all French monasteries. Twenty-six members of the strict observance were assigned to Cîteaux in charge of administration, while opponents were expelled. Only after the death of Richelieu in 1642 was the situation reversed. The election of the all-important position of abbot general of Cîteaux was contested with every political intrigue, including the inclusion and exclusion of monks as electors, a veto by King Louis XIV, and the papal appointment of an investigative commission. The eventual election of Vaussin in 1645 was thus considered a mandate to minimize the influence of the strict observance group. Vaussin took control of the important College of Bernard in Paris and instituted a unified policy for all Cistercians.

This was the situation in which de Rancé found himself in 1664. When Pope Alexander VII summoned representatives of both sides to Rome, de Rancé was called upon to represent the strict observance against Vaussin's common observance. After a few years of negotiation, Alexander issued in 1666 a bull, *In Suprema*, which allowed two separate observances, common and strict, within the one Cistercian Order.

Administratively, strict observance would be under the authority of Vaussin, even though he supported common observance. De Rancé took this as a defeat of his position, but he returned, determined to establish the La Trappe monastery as the model for reform.

De Rancé described the reformed regiment in his principal written work *Le Traité de la sainteté et des devoirs de la vie monastique* (1683; treatise of the holiness and duties of monastic life), which explains deep sacramental life, personal prayer, and fraternal dedication in terms of love for God and love for the monastic brothers. Charity makes possible life under such harsh circumstances. The Trappist day began very early, at 2 A.M., and ended by 8 P.M. Four hours of the day were dedicated to manual labor and several more hours to formal liturgical prayer, known as the Divine Office. The rest of the day was dedicated to contemplative prayer. In contrast to his finer style of upbringing, de Rancé stressed simplicity: Sleeping arrangements were in dormitories with pallets placed on plank boards, and silence was the norm.

The austere life and denial of meat led many monks in the seventeenth century into a kind of competition to see whose austerity was more meritorious. In fact, de Rancé had the reputation of chastising other orders of monks for their laxity. In return, he was criticized for neglecting study as part of monastic life. However, members of other monasteries began to abandon their comparatively easy life in order to embrace the stricter code of La Trappe. The numbers of Trappists grew, not only from the conversions of savory characters but also from the ranks of noblemen, princes, and army officers. Others, including King James II of England and the popular preacher Jacques Bossuet, visited La Trappe for spiritual retreat.

By the time of de Rancé's death on October 27, 1700, La Trappe became one of the most impressive monasteries in France, along with a well-established network of monasteries of the strict order.

SIGNIFICANCE

The impact of the reforms of Arman-Jean le Bouthillier de Rancé can be seen a century after his death at the time of the French Revolution, when most monasteries were closed in France. Under the leadership of Augustin de Lestrange, monks from La Trappe relocated to other countries in Europe and to the United States. Instead of dying out, the movement continued to flourish. Women, too, were first admitted around this time.

After twenty-five years of absence from France, at the fall of Napoleon in 1815, some monks returned to La Trappe to reestablish the monastery. Within a few years, the number of Trappist houses in France equaled those of the common observance that were directed from Cîteaux. In 1888, Pope Leo XIII recognized the Trappists as an autonomous order, giving it the official name "Cistercians of the Strict Observance" (O.C.S.O.).

In the early twenty-first century, there are one hundred houses of Trappist monks and sixty-nine houses of nuns around the world, with seventeen in Africa, thirteen in Central and South America, and twenty-three in Asia and the Pacific. Trappist monks number twenty-five hundred, and there are eighteen hundred Trappist nuns. The best known Trappists of modern times are Thomas Keating and Thomas Merton.

—*Fred Strickert*

FURTHER READING

Kinder, Terryl N., and Michael Downey. *Cistercian Europe: Architecture of Contemplation*. Grand Rapids, Mich.: William B. Eerdmans, 2002. A leading expert on medieval architecture takes the reader on a tour of Cistercian monasteries, explaining the daily life of the monks who lived there.

Krailsheimer, A. J. *Armand-Jean de Rancé, Abbot of La Trappe: His Influence in the Cloister and the World*. Oxford, England: Clarendon Press, 1974. A scholarly study focusing on the work of the Trappist reformer.

Merton, Thomas. *The Waters of Siloe*. New York: Harcourt, Brace, 1949. Merton, a well-known twentieth century Trappist monk, examines the roots of the Cistercian Order, the seventeenth century reforms at La Trappe, and the order's development.

Nouwen, Henri J. M. *The Genesee Diary: Report from a Trappist Monastery*. Garden City, N.Y.: Doubleday, 1980. The well-known spiritual mentor's journal of his seven months in a Trappist monastery in upstate New York.

Rancé, Arman-Jean le Bouthillier de. *The Letters of Armand-Jean de Rancé, Abbot and Reformer of La Trappe*. Presented by A. J. Krailsheimer. Kalamazoo, Mich.: Cistercian Publications, 1984. From the Cistercian Studies series, this collection includes 365 translated letters, a bibliography, and indexes.

Tobin, Stephen. *The Cistercians: Monks and Monasteries of Europe*. New York: Overlook Press, 1996. A photo documentary that highlights the history of the Cistercian monastic order.

SEE ALSO: Apr. 27, 1627: Company of New France Is Chartered.

RELATED ARTICLES in *Great Lives from History: The Seventeenth Century, 1601-1700:* Alexander VII; Louis XIII; Louis XIV; Marie de Médicis; Cardinal de Richelieu; Urban VIII.

1665

Cassini Discovers Jupiter's Great Red Spot

Cassini, using an improved telescope, observed a large feature, now called the Great Red Spot, in the southern hemisphere of Jupiter. He used the motion of this feature around the planet to measure the rotational rate of Jupiter to a high degree of accuracy.

Locale: Bologna (now in Italy)
Categories: Astronomy; science and technology

Key Figures

Gian Domenico Cassini (1625-1712), Italian astronomer who is credited with discovering the Great Red Spot

Robert Hooke (1635-1703), English physicist who first observed a feature in Jupiter's southern hemisphere that may have been the Great Red Spot

Giuseppe Campani (1635-1715), Italian lens grinder and telescope maker who built the long focal-length telescope used by Cassini

Summary of Event

The Great Red Spot on Jupiter has puzzled astronomers ever since it was first seen in 1665. The development of the telescope and improvements in the resolution of telescopes made it possible to see the Spot by the middle of the seventeenth century. The size and the color of the Spot have varied significantly since it was first observed.

The English physicist Robert Hooke first reported seeing a large oval-shaped feature in the southern hemisphere of Jupiter in 1664. The oval seen by Hooke is believed to have been the Spot, although Hooke did not mention its color. Credit for the discovery of the Spot is generally given to the Italian astronomer Gian Domenico Cassini, who observed it in 1665. At that time, Cassini was a professor of mathematics and astronomy at the University of Bologna, Italy. Cassini had seen spots on Jupiter beginning in 1664, but he quickly realized that these spots were actually the shadows of Jupiter's largest moons (which Galileo had observed at the beginning of the century). Then Cassini observed an "exceptional" spot," which he called the "big permanent spot."

Cassini's many astronomical discoveries were possible because he was able to observe the sky with new, powerful telescopes made by Giuseppe Campani of Rome. Campani, and his brother, Matteo Campani-Alimensis, were experts in grinding and polishing lenses, especially lenses having a very long focal length and only small curvature. Because of their small curvature, these lenses did not suffer from the same optical problems that lenses with sharper curvatures exhibited; thus they provided clearer views of objects in the sky. Campani's telescopes employed these long-focal length lenses to greatly magnify images, allowing a planet's details to be seen. Cassini used the telescope built by Campani to study the planets Jupiter, Saturn, Mars, and Venus. Beginning in 1664, Cassini made many important discoveries, which were possible only because of the great magnification and image clarity of Campani's new telescope.

Jupiter's Spot has been continuously present since the time it was discovered by Cassini, and additional spots have been observed as the quality of telescopes improved. The Spot is located in Jupiter's southern hemisphere, about 22 degrees south of the planet's equator.

Gian Domenico Cassini. (Library of Congress)

It is a gas planet, composed mainly of hydrogen and helium. Thus, the Spot is not actually a spot on the surface of Jupiter, but, rather, a storm high in Jupiter's atmosphere. What appears to be Jupiter's surface, when viewed from Earth, is actually a layer of clouds. There are many colored bands and spots visible in these high clouds near the top of Jupiter's atmosphere, with the Spot being the largest and most easily visible of these features.

The Spot is believed to be a giant, hurricane-like storm, caused by interactions between high and low temperatures and pressures, as are hurricanes on Earth. The top of the clouds in the Spot extend about 5 miles higher than nearby clouds, and they are cooler. On Earth, hurricanes are much smaller in size then the Spot, and they last for only a few days. In addition, hurricanes on Earth are "cyclonic," that is, they are low-pressure systems. The Spot is "anticyclonic," that is, it is a high-pressure system. On Earth, hurricanes weaken considerably when they pass over land, so some scientists speculate that the Spot persists because it does not pass over "land." Other scientists suggest that Jupiter's internal heat source continues to provide energy to this giant storm, allowing it to persist for centuries.

The Spot varies in both size and color from year to year. It is an oval measuring about 17,000 miles long and 9,000 miles wide, so large that it could contain three Earths. The Spot rotates counterclockwise, with a period of 6 days. Similar structures have been seen in the atmospheres of Saturn and Neptune.

Once Cassini recognized that the Spot traveled around the planet as Jupiter rotated, he knew he could measure how long it took for the Spot to travel completely around the planet and thus determine the planet's period of rotation on its axis. The value he obtained for Jupiter's rotation period was 9 hours and 56 minutes, results he published in 1665. Cassini's value is within a few minutes of the best value obtainable with modern instruments.

Cassini continued to observe Jupiter throughout his career. In about 1690, he was the first person to report that Jupiter's atmosphere displayed "differential rotation," the motion of some features around the planet at slightly different rates than others. Cassini may also have seen the effects of a comet impacting Jupiter. Between December 5 and December 23, 1690, Cassini observed a feature that appeared in the planet's atmosphere. That feature is similar to features observed in 1994, when more than twenty fragments of the comet Shoemaker-Levy 9 hit the planet. Japanese astronomers Isshi Tabe and Junichi Watanabe have interpreted Cassini's drawings to indicate that he observed the effects of a similar comet impact in 1690.

Significance

It was not until 1878 that Jupiter's Great Red Spot was named. It had changed into a very intense red color, a change noticed by many observers around the world. The colors in Jupiter's clouds are still not completely understood, however. Scientists believe the reddish color results from chemical compounds containing sulfur and phosphorus, but the reason why the colors keep changing is not understood.

The Spot has persisted for more than three hundred years, providing evidence for how long storms can last in the atmosphere of Jupiter. The survival of a single storm for this long has forced planetary scientists to develop new ideas about how storms develop, evolve, and survive, since their persistence on gas giant planets clearly is much different from storms on rocky planets.

Cassini's discovery of the Spot allowed him to develop techniques to obtain precise measurements of the rotation rates of Jupiter, Saturn, and Mars by observing the time it takes for a feature to move completely around the planet. These techniques are still employed by contemporary astronomers to measure rotation rates of planets, moons, and asteroids. In recognition of Cassini's studies of gas giant planets, the National Aeronautics and Space Administration (NASA) named its Saturn orbiter the Cassini spacecraft, which was launched in October, 1997.

—*George J. Flynn*

Further Reading

Asimov, Isaac. *Jupiter, the Largest Planet*. New York: Ace, 1980. A 247-page, well-illustrated account of Jupiter, from the earliest discoveries of its distance, size, and satellites to recent discoveries regarding its atmosphere, composition, and the Spot.

Beatty, J. K. "A Comet Crash in 1690?" *Sky and Telescope* 93 (April, 1997): 111. Summarizes a new Japanese interpretation of Cassini's 1690 sketches of Jupiter, suggesting he saw the results of a comet impact.

Débarbat, S., and C. Wilson. "The Galilean Satellites of Jupiter from Galileo to Cassini, Rømer, and Bradley." In *Planetary Astronomy from the Renaissance to the Rise of Astrophysics*. Part A, edited by René Taton and Curtis Wilson. New York: Cambridge University Press, 1989. An excellent account of Cassini's contributions to the measurement of the positions and eclipses of the moons of Jupiter.

Rogers, J. H. *The Giant Planet Jupiter*. New York: Cambridge University Press, 1995. A comprehensive account of the discoveries about Jupiter and its satellites, written for a general audience. Begins with a review of the telescopic observations and continues through the modern era of results from spacecrafts.

Schorn, Ronald A. *Planetary Astronomy: From Ancient Times to the Third Millennium*. College Station: Texas A&M University Press, 1999. Includes sections describing Cassini's numerous contributions to the observations of the planets, particularly Jupiter and Saturn.

See also: Sept., 1608: Invention of the Telescope; 1609-1619: Kepler's Laws of Planetary Motion; 1610: Galileo Confirms the Heliocentric Model of the Solar System; 1632: Galileo Publishes *Dialogue Concerning the Two Chief World Systems, Ptolemaic and Copernican*; Feb., 1656: Huygens Identifies Saturn's Rings; 1673: Huygens Explains the Pendulum.

Related articles in *Great Lives from History: The Seventeenth Century, 1601-1700:* Gian Domenico Cassini; Galileo; Robert Hooke; Christiaan Huygens; Johannes Kepler.

1665-1681
Construction of the Languedoc Canal

The Languedoc Canal provided a practical link between the Atlantic and Mediterranean coasts of France and enhanced the economic development of the Languedoc region. The canal was the greatest European engineering project undertaken since the fall of the Roman Empire.

Locale: Languedoc, southern France
Categories: Engineering; architecture; economics; trade and commerce; transportation

Key Figures

Pierre-Paul de Riquet de Bonrepos (1604-1680), French businessman and salt-tax collector responsible for building the canal
Jean-Baptiste Colbert (1619-1683), controller general under King Louis XIV, 1665-1683
François Andreossy (1633-1688), French engineer who worked on the canal
Pierre Campmas (fl. seventeenth century), *fontainier*, or water manager, of Revel, France
Louis XIV (1638-1715), king of France, r. 1643-1715

Summary of Event

In early 1681, French workmen dug the final stretches of the Languedoc Canal, and in mid-May of that year a procession of two boats and twenty-three barges set out from the French city of Toulouse on the Garonne River, across southern France, to the port of Sète on the Mediterranean Sea. It was now possible to transport goods by water directly between the Atlantic and Mediterranean coasts of France.

Also known as the Canal du Midi (Midi Canal) or the Canal Royale des Deux Mers (Canal of the Two Seas), the Languedoc Canal was a dream long before it became a reality. French king Francis I had envisioned linking the two coasts by digging a canal between two partially navigable rivers, the Garonne and the Aude, and had sought the advice of renowned Italian artist and inventor Leonardo da Vinci in 1516. Subsequently, King Henry IV undertook construction of the shorter Briare Canal in northern France (finished in 1642), but it was only under the later reign of King Louis XIV that the Languedoc Canal actually came into being.

The prime mover behind the new canal was businessman and tax collector Pierre-Paul de Riquet de Bonrepos, who had been intrigued with the possibility of linking the Atlantic and the Mediterranean since his childhood. Consulting with Pierre Campmas, who oversaw the water supply of the town and district of Revel, and François Andreossy, a professional engineer trained in Paris, Riquet chose what appeared to be the most practical route for such a link. Riquet then approached French controller general Jean-Baptiste Colbert in 1662 with an outline of his scheme.

Subsequently a royal commission was appointed, and Riquet was required in 1665 to dig a small test canal to confirm the practicality of channeling water to the route's high point. Colbert was then able to secure royal financing in 1666, to which Riquet initially added a very substantial amount of his own fortune.

In the past, shallow or otherwise unnavigable rivers had sometimes been fitted with "flash locks." In this system, the water level behind a dam was allowed to rise, at which time narrow gates were opened. Boats or barges then swept through if they were headed downstream or were pulled through with ropes if headed upstream—methods that were dangerous or slow, depending on the vessel's direction. For his canal, Riquet utilized "pound" locks, which enclosed a body of water only slightly larger than a typical boat between two gates. This system, which may have been introduced to France by Leonardo da Vinci on his 1516 visit and which was utilized in the Briare Canal, allowed the water level to be adjusted quickly, safely, and efficiently.

The Languedoc Canal eventually stretched 150 miles (241 kilometers) between Toulouse and Sète and involved 101 locks. It rose 207 feet (64 meters) from Toulouse to its summit, only to fall 620 feet (189 meters) by the time it reached the Mediterranean coast. Riquet's engineers and workmen built three aqueducts to carry the canal over rivers and 139 bridges to allow road traffic to cross the canal. A special channel was cut through the lagoon of the Étang de Thau to carry the canal to its eastern terminus, the new port of Sète, the construction of which had begun in 1666. Trees were planted along the canal's towpaths to shade the animals and men destined to pull the canal's vessels.

Throughout the project, Riquet faced difficulties that at the time appeared insurmountable to most of his contemporaries. His canal was to be a "watershed" or "summit level" canal, meaning that it would cross the high point between two large drainage systems. Thus, one of the most formidable obstacles to its success involved assuring a constant supply of water. Riquet solved the problem by constructing what would be the largest dam of its time, the Saint-Ferreol, on the Laudot River in the Montagne Noire (Black Mountain) massif. This immense dam created a reservoir capable of feeding the canal for most, if not quite all, of the year.

Faced with an unstable ridge near his hometown of Béziers, Riquet set his men to work digging the 540-foot (165-meter) Malpas Tunnel, creating the first canal tunnel in history—a feat said to have taken only six days! At Fonserannes, again near Béziers, Riquet designed a steep, eight-step "staircase" of locks, allowing a vessel to pass vertically through almost 64.5 feet (about 19.5 meters) within the brief horizontal span of 919 feet (280 meters).

Besides being a visionary and an indefatigable worker, Riquet was a generous master. When construction was at its peak, he employed some 12,000 workers, many of them women, and is said to have paid them the equivalent of a months' salary for a six-day workweek, which they received in spite of sickness or bad weather. Toward the end of the project, Riquet lost the backing of the French government and was forced to sell most of his property to finance the remainder of the canal. When he died on October 1, 1680, less than two miles (three kilometers) remained to be dug. The job was completed under the supervision of his son Mathias, and the canal was opened with great ceremony on May 15 the following year.

Significance

The Languedoc Canal had been the greatest European engineering project undertaken since the fall of the Roman Empire more than a millennium before. Built soon after the completion of the Briare Canal, it incorporated the technological lessons learned from the earlier project and involved several advances of its own. Linking the Garonne River (and thus the Atlantic coast) with the Mediterranean Sea, the new canal saved French merchants the time, danger, and expense of sailing around their problematic neighbor Spain, which levied a duty on all goods transported through the Strait of Gibraltar. Vessels on the canal carried not only wine, oil, leather, and textiles but also passengers—more than 100,000 per year by the mid-nineteenth century.

Pierre-Paul de Riquet de Bonrepos had anticipated that the canal would enrich the inhabitants of the towns through which it passed, and had accordingly insisted that such towns help defray the enormous costs of the project. Yet it was only in 1724 that the canal managed to pay for itself, after which all profits passed on to Riquet's descendants. During the second half of the nineteenth century, however, the canal began to suffer from competition with railroads and went into decline, a situation that its acquisition by the French government in 1898 did little to halt.

On December 7, 1996, UNESCO (the United Nations Educational, Scientific and Cultural Organization) declared the Languedoc Canal a World Heritage Site. Many later engineering projects of its scale have been purely utilitarian in design, but the Languedoc Canal winds gracefully through the southern French countryside, its locks, aqueducts, and bridges designed to please the eye as well as meet the practicalities of commerce. No cargo has passed through the canal since 1979, but boats and barges carry an ever-increasing number of tourists and sightseers every year.

—*Grove Koger*

Further Reading

Bordry, François. "A Canal in Southern France." *UNESCO Courier* 50 (September, 1997): 37-38. An overview published soon after the canal became a

UNESCO World Heritage Site. Illustrated with color photographs.

Geiger, Reed G. *Planning the French Canals: Bureaucracy, Politics, and Enterprise Under the Restoration.* Newark: University of Delaware Press, 1994. Geiger's second chapter, "The French Canals to 1815: An Ambiguous Tradition," surveys the early development of canals in the country. Includes notes, maps, bibliography.

Hadfield, Charles. *World Canals: Inland Navigation Past and Present.* New York: Facts on File, 1986. Extensive, well-organized historical survey with several pages devoted to the Languedoc Canal. Includes numerous maps and black-and-white illustrations.

Mukerji, Chandra. "Cartography, Entrepreneurialism, and Power in the Reign of Louis XIV: The Case of the Canal du Midi." In *Merchants and Marvels: Commerce, Science, and Art in Early Modern Europe*, edited by Pamela H. Smith and Paula Findlen. New York: Routledge, 2002. This work treats the canal as an entrepreneurial project and as an experiment in visual representation.

Payne, Robert. *The Canal Builders: The Story of Canal Engineers Through the Ages.* New York: Macmillan, 1959. A survey placing the Languedoc Canal in historical context. Includes black-and-white illustrations and a select bibliography.

Rolt, L. T. C. *From Sea to Sea: The Canal du Midi.* London: Allen Lane, 1973. The standard account in English, detailed but very readable. Supplemented by maps, illustrations, appendices (including a complete listing of locks), and a short bibliography.

Smyth, Andrew. "The Canal du Midi." *History Today* 53, no. 8 (August, 2003): 5-6. An overview of the project by the author of a guidebook to travel on the canal. Illustrated with color photographs.

See also: 1661: Absolute Monarchy Emerges in France; 1661-1672: Colbert Develops Mercantilism; Mar. 18, 1662: Public Transportation Begins.

Related articles in *Great Lives from History: The Seventeenth Century, 1601-1700:* Jean-Baptiste Colbert; Louis XIV.

January, 1665
Shabbetai Tzevi's Messianic Movement Begins

At the celebration of Pentecost in Gaza, a young rabbi announced his vision of the arrival of the Messiah. Jews throughout the Ottoman Empire and in Europe joined the mystic Shabbetai Tzevi and his movement, which emphasized inner union with the divine, a symbolic approach to Jewish law, and women's equality.

Locale: Gaza, Palestine
Category: Religion and theology

Key Figures

Shabbetai Tzevi (1626-1676), Jewish mystic who claimed to be the Messiah

Nathan Ghazzati (1644-1680), rabbi of Gaza who claimed to have a vision of Tzevi as the Messiah

Summary of Event

The mid-seventeenth century was an apt time for messianic movements. Mystics such as Isaac ben Solomon Luria had encouraged the study and interpretation of Kabbalah as the primary catalyst for the coming of the Messiah and a world of *tiqqun*, or harmony. One date for the coming, 1648, was taken from the Zohar, but that year brought the beginning of a decade of severe Chmielnicki massacres of Jews in Poland and the Ukraine (1648-1649). Because the Messiah was to come after a great disaster, the massacres heightened expectation. However, the year of the Messiah's coming had to be revised to 1666.

At Pentecost prayers in Gaza in the Holy Land in early 1665, a previously unknown rabbi by the name of Nathan Ghazzati announced that the Messiah had appeared to him in a vision. Nathan would wait until summer of the following year, after one year of repentance and a renewal of faith, to reveal the name of the Messiah: Shabbetai Tzevi, a Jewish mystic from İzmir, Asia Minor (now in Turkey). The rule of the Ottoman Empire would be transferred to Tzevi, not through violence but through prayer and the singing of hymns. Jews, including the lost ten tribes of Israel, would return to the Holy Land where the resurrection of the dead would take place.

Previous Jewish messianic movements had focused on the requirement of the observance of law and in miraculous signs. Nathan had written that the focus would be on a deep and genuine faith prepared by repentance and meditation and that followers should not expect external signs. Tzevi was identified by Nathan as having been born in 1626 and thus nearing the biblically significant age of forty.

Nathan's words were considered credible because of his reputation as a scholar and a dynamic preacher. Even more significant is that Nathan had experienced his initial vision—a light lasting twenty-four hours and a voice identifying Tzevi by name—in January, 1665, *before* he made the acquaintance of Tzevi. In March, Tzevi arrived in Gaza with two other delegates from the Jewish community in Cairo to inquire about rumors that the Messiah had arrived. Nathan responded by falling on his face in obeisance, but Tzevi only laughed in surprise. In the next months, the two became well acquainted and certain about the revelations. Tzevi soon came to believe he was the Messiah, and the Shebbetian movement began.

It was not long until legendary stories were circulating about Tzevi. What is clear is that he came from a family of merchants in İzmir in Asia Minor, had studied the Torah, and was ordained at the age of eighteen. Yet at the age of twenty-five, he had been expelled from his hometown by the local rabbinate and had wandered throughout the eastern Mediterranean area until he found his way to Jerusalem. While there his ascetic lifestyle and devotion to study had impressed the Jewish community, who sent him on a fund-raising trip to Egypt.

Less certain is the date of his birth in 1626, thought to be the same day that commemorates the destruction of the Jerusalem temple. Through the years, scholars had predicted that the Messiah would be born on this particular day. Likewise, there was controversy about Tzevi's marriage in Cairo in March of 1664 to a young woman named Sarah. The marriage was most unusual for the ascetic character of Tzevi, because Sarah had the reputation of a prostitute in Mantua, Italy. She and her brother likely were survivors of the 1648 massacre in Poland, and they fled to Amsterdam as orphans. Sarah, just a young girl, announced that she was destined to someday marry the Messiah. Detractors said that the marriage between Tzevi and Sarah had been staged, but followers saw it as a sign that Tzevi was indeed the Messiah.

The excitement over Nathan's prophesy spread so quickly that there were communities of followers throughout the Ottoman Empire and as far away as northwestern Europe. There was a spontaneous outbreak of prophesizing, as men and women uttered aloud revelations. Part of the prophesizing was influenced by the preaching of Nathan, which focused on faith and repentance, and part was due to the charismatic example set by Tzevi, who often worked himself into a trance and sang with a sweet, melodious voice.

From his earlier days in İzmir, Tzevi learned about freedom from Jewish law. Women were invited to read the Torah in public. Traditional fasts were abolished and replaced with days of celebration. Nonkosher foods found their way on banquet menus. His most offensive action, however, was to utter the divine name in worship, something considered blasphemous. So the response against him was divided. Rabbinic groups in Jerusalem condemned him.

Tzevi returned to İzmir with fanfare. He dressed in royal robes and began delegating future ruling roles to followers. He sent out decrees and letters, signing his name as Annointed of the God of Jacob and AMIRAH, an anagram for "our lord and king, his majesty be exalted." He adopted the symbol of a holy serpent, the let-

An engraving of Jewish mystic Shabbetai Tzevi blessing his followers. (The Granger Collection)

ters of which in Hebrew had the numerical equivalent of the word "messiah."

Until this time, the Ottoman government had been disinterested in Tzevi's actions. However, in January of 1666, while sailing to Istanbul, Tzevi was arrested by the Turks and then imprisoned for nine months in Gallipoli. His followers assumed that this would lead to a direct confrontation with the sultan, after which the Messiah would begin his rule. Instead, at their meeting in September, Tzevi publicly announced that he had converted to Islam rather than succumb to execution, and he took the name Kapici Bashi.

In some ways Tzevi's conversion marked the end of the Shabbetian messianic movement. Many followers deserted him, but others joined him in apostatizing. However, Nathan and others declared that Tzevi's action marked a stage only, in which the true nature of the Messiah remained hidden while he descended to the depths of evil. Followers were urged to focus on repentance and not on the mysterious character of the Messiah. For the next ten years, Tzevi remained duplicitous. For the Ottomans, he made a public show of Muslim prayers and reading the Qur'ān. Yet, among his friends, he continued to read the Torah, to recite the Jewish prayers, and to keep the feasts, such as Passover. However, his support gradually waned until his death on September 17, 1676, in Dulcigno, Albania (now Ulcinj, Montenegro), where he had been exiled.

Significance

The Shabbetian messianic movement is often described in terms of either the tragedy of its leader or of the misguided gullibility of its followers. The movement clearly shows that there had been longing for a faith and for hope in an era of extreme suffering.

The tragic end to Shabbetian messianism was so great that it often has been considered the last major messianic movement in Judaism. Yet, in some minor forms, it did continue long after Shabbetai Tzevi's apostasy and death. In Turkey, a Shabbetian Donmeh sect of Judaism existed until the twentieth century. Its followers practiced Islam "on the outside." In Poland, the Frankist movement converted to Catholicism while its followers remained Jewish at heart. The leader of this group was Jacob Frank (c. 1726-1791), who considered himself the new Shabbetai Tzevi.

Many of the characteristics of the Shabbetian movement influenced modern Judaism. One example is that the Shabbetian focus on the experiential character of Judaism resurfaced in the eastern European Hasidic movement of the eighteenth century. Another example is Reform Judaism adopting the Shabbetian movement's assimilating character, its focus on the equality of women, and a symbolic approach to Jewish law.

—Fred Strickert

Further Reading

Freely, John. *The Lost Messiah: In Search of the Mystical Rabbi Sabbatai Sevi*. Woodstock, N.Y.: Overlook Press, 2003. This is a popular account based primarily on the work of Gershom Scholem. The author, a travel writer, makes the story interesting through his own acquaintance with the cities where Shabbetai flourished.

Liebes, Yehuda. *Studies in Jewish Myth and Jewish Messianism*. Translated by Batya Stein. Albany: State University of New York Press, 1993. A study, originally in Hebrew, that includes an examination of Tzevi's movement. Chapters include "Sabbatean Messianism" and "Sabbetai Zevi's Religious Faith."

Schaefer, Peter, and Mark R. Cohen, eds. *Toward the Millennium: Messianic Expectations from the Bible to Waco*. Leiden, the Netherlands: E. J. Brill, 1998. A collection of sixteen scholarly essays, including several concerning Shabbetai specifically. The works come from a symposium on messianic movements.

Scholem, Gershom. *Sabbatai Sevi: The Mystical Messiah*. New York: Littman, 1997. Originally written in Hebrew in 1957 and published in English in 1976, this volume remains the standard resource on this topic. The author takes a scholarly approach, evaluating every contemporary letter, document, and liturgical book written in response to Tzevi and the movement.

See also: 1656-1662: Persecution of Iranian Jews.

Related articles in *Great Lives from History: The Seventeenth Century, 1601-1700:* Manasseh ben Israel; Shabbetai Tzevi; António Vieira.

March 4, 1665-July 31, 1667
Second Anglo-Dutch War

Commercial and colonial rivalries between the Dutch and the English led to the second of three naval wars fought between the two countries. Most of the engagements occurred in the English Channel and North Sea between Europe's two strongest maritime powers. Aggressive actions from France hastened peace negotiations, which produced a compromise, the Treaty of Breda.

Locale: English Channel, North Sea, coast of Western Africa, and Caribbean Sea

Categories: Wars, uprisings, and civil unrest; trade and commerce; government and politics; expansion and land acquisition

Key Figures

Michiel Adriaanszoon de Ruyter (1607-1676), Dutch admiral

Johan de Witt (1625-1672), grand pensionary of the United Provinces and policymaker

Sir George Downing (1623-1684), English ambassador to the Dutch Republic

Sir Robert Holmes (1622-1692), English naval commander

James, Duke of York and Albany (1633-1701), brother of Charles II, heir to the throne, lord high admiral, and king of England as James II, r. 1685-1688

George Monck (1608-1670), first duke of Albemarle, English naval commander

Prince Rupert (1619-1682), Bohemian-born English naval commander

Summary of Event

Although the First Anglo-Dutch War ended in 1654, by the 1660's issues flowing from that conflict had never been completely resolved. Political maneuvering within England and the Dutch Republic and the fact that both countries were aggressively seeking commercial advantages in the Americas, Africa, Asia, and northern Europe led to the outbreak of hostilities.

In October, 1663, an English fleet commanded by Sir Robert Holmes captured a series of Dutch trading posts along Guinea's Gold Coast (West Africa). The grand pensionary of the Dutch Republic, Johan de Witt, secretly ordered Dutch commander Michiel Adriaanszoon de Ruyter to recapture the posts, which he did in 1664. De Ruyter later harassed English ships in the Caribbean and off the coast of Newfoundland before returning to the North Sea. An English fleet captured the Dutch colony of New Amsterdam in North America, without firing a shot, on September 7, 1664. To honor James, duke of York and duke of Albany, the colony was renamed New York. In December, 1664, an English fleet attacked a Dutch merchant fleet returning from Smyrna to the Dutch Republic. All of these actions occurred before the English formally declared war on March 4, 1665.

Scholars of naval history note that the English navy totaled about 160 ships with 5,000 guns and 25,000 sailors, and the Dutch had 135 ships and only slightly fewer guns and sailors. In 1664, English merchants presented evidence to a committee in the House of Commons that the Dutch had hurt their trade. The chief complaint was that the Dutch had refused to hand over Pulo Run in the Banda Islands in the East Indies. These merchants with support from young English courtiers and the very anti-Dutch English ambassador to the Dutch Republic, Sir George Downing, were pushing for war. English claims to sovereignty of the seas in the English Channel and their demands that Dutch ships salute the English flag were issues left over from the First Anglo-Dutch War.

The first move after the declaration of war was the duke of York's patrolling off Texel in the Netherlands with a fleet of 100 ships in late April, 1665, as a show of force, but he could not maintain this presence and retreated to the mouth of the Thames River. De Witt had strengthened the Dutch navy since the end of the First Anglo-Dutch War in terms of numbers of ships, and better provisioning and equipping, so when the two fleets met for the first clash of the war at Lowestoft off the English coast on June 3, 1665, the English encountered more than 100 Dutch ships, the largest Dutch fleet ever assembled. In a bloody fight, the English defeated the Dutch, who lost 17 ships (including their flag ship) and some 5,000 men, whereas the English lost one ship and 700 men. The duke of York failed to follow up this tremendous advantage, so the Dutch were able to withdraw and regroup.

English fleets missed de Ruyter's fleet returning from North America and another Dutch merchant fleet from Asia. The war widened when the English attacked Dutch merchant vessels in Bergen in Danish territory and the Danes fired upon the English from their fortress. The English declared war on Denmark in August, 1665. England's troubles were compounded by the outbreak of bubonic plague in 1665 and the entry of the French into the war on the side of the Dutch in 1666.

The next great naval battle, the Four Days' Battle, occurred in the English Channel off Dover between June 1 and June 4, 1666, resulting in a Dutch victory. De Ruyter commanded 84 ships and 9 fireships; English commander George Monck had 54 ships. This bloody battle exhibited substantial broadside firing, the boarding of ships, and use of fireships, causing the loss of 15 to 20 English ships and thousands of Englishmen. Dutch losses and casualties amounted to about half those of the English. Prince Rupert and his fleet of 22 English ships arrived two days after this enormous battle. His ships had been sorely missed by the English.

The Two Days' Battle, or St. James Day Fight, of July 25-26, 1666, was an English victory for Monck over de Ruyter, and Holmes ravaged 150 Dutch ships along the Dutch coast. He also sacked the Dutch town of West-erschelling on the island of Terschelling in an action called Holmes's Bonfire. However, in late 1666, the English began to suffer a notable shortfall in revenue, partly because of the plague, the Great Fire of London (September), and the disruption of trade because of the war. As a consequence, the English government did not have enough money to equip and maintain the fleet, which curtailed naval activity and led to the worst English disaster of the war—the Dutch attacks on the Thames and Medway Rivers in June of 1667.

Ironically, these raids took place while peace negotiations at Breda were underway. The majority of the English fleet was in port at Portsmouth and Harwich, and along the Medway and Thames Rivers. English informants from the Netherlands warned the English government that the Dutch were preparing a major expedition that might attempt a landing in England. The English government ignored the warning, believing that the

The fleets of Dutch admiral Michiel Adriaanszoon de Ruyter and English commander George Monck, fighting in the English Channel, 1666. (Hulton|Archive by Getty Images)

Bohemian-born Prince Rupert fought for the English as a naval commander. (Library of Congress)

Dutch would not want to jeopardize the peace negotiations and also because Louis XIV, king of France, had launched an attack on the Spanish Netherlands, starting the War of Devolution (1667-1668).

De Witt's bold plan was successful because he recruited disaffected English sailors with knowledge of the Thames and Medway Rivers. The objectives were to destroy the English ships on the Medway and at the dockyards at Chatham. Although the commanders and officers were reluctant to undertake such a bold strike because of the treacherous Medway River and its chain barrier to protect it, the Dutch succeeded in an amazing attack from June 11 to 14, 1667, in which they towed away the English flagship *Royal Charles* and burned or sunk the *Royal James*, *Loyal London*, *Royal Oak*, and several other ships. In the meantime, Dutch raiders had attacked the Isle of Sheppey and destroyed the fortress of Sheerness. This humiliating defeat for the English allowed the Dutch to equalize the number of warships had by each navy. The Dutch now dominated the English Channel and the North Sea, which caused the English to push for a swift conclusion to the peace negotiations.

SIGNIFICANCE

The Treaty of Breda, July 31, 1667, ended the conflict. The Dutch kept Pulo Run, which they had turned over to England in April, 1665, but had recaptured shortly thereafter. Surinam, captured from England in 1667, remained in Dutch possession and New York (New Amsterdam) was retained by the English. The procedures for search of cargoes were defined, and the Dutch were to strike their colors for English warships in the English Channel and North Sea. A major gain for the Dutch was a modification of England's Navigation Act (1660) which allowed the Dutch to transport to England in Dutch ships merchandise from the Dutch Republic, Spanish Netherlands, and German territories.

Along the Guinea coast, the English retained Cape Coast Castle, which enabled them to continue a profitable trade in slaves and ivory. Both sides benefited and both sides made concessions. In January, 1668, England, the Dutch Republic, and Sweden signed the Triple Alliance against French aggression, but in 1670, France and England signed the secret Treaty of Dover to prepare for a joint war against the Dutch, resulting in the Third Anglo-Dutch War (1672-1674) and the French-Dutch War (1672-1678).

—*Mark C. Herman*

FURTHER READING

Boxer, C. R. *The Anglo-Dutch Wars of the Seventeenth Century*. London: Her Majesty's Stationery Office, 1974. This short work, which is profusely illustrated, provides a concise summary of the wars.

Bruijn, Jaap R. *The Dutch Navy of the Seventeenth and Eighteenth Centuries*. Columbia: University of South Carolina Press, 1993. This detailed work summarizes the conflicts in which the Dutch fought but also analyzes policy, tactics, administrative structure, and the development of the officer corps, and describes the crews and ships.

Hainsworth, Roger, and Christie Churches. *The Anglo-Dutch Naval Wars, 1652-1674*. Phoenix Mill, England: Sutton, 1998. This work describes the wars and places them within the context of the wars of the seventeenth century. It has many illustrations and maps that enhance the reader's understanding of the battles.

Jones, J. R. *The Anglo-Dutch Wars of the Seventeenth Century*. New York: Longman, 1996. This analytical work argues that economic factors were not the primary motivations for English involvement in the Second Anglo-Dutch War.

SEE ALSO: July 5, 1601-Apr., 1604: Siege of Oostende; Oct., 1625-1637: Dutch and Portuguese Struggle for the Guinea Coast; Mid-17th cent.: Emergence of the Guinea Coast States; Oct., 1651-May, 1652: Navigation Act Leads to Anglo-Dutch Wars; Mar. 22, 1664-July 21, 1667: British Conquest of New Netherland; May 24, 1667-May 2, 1668: War of Devolution; Jan. 23, 1668: Triple Alliance Forms; Apr. 6, 1672-Aug. 10, 1678: French-Dutch War; Aug. 10, 1678-Sept. 26, 1679: Treaties of Nijmegen; 1689-1697: Wars of the League of Augsburg; Sept. 20, 1697: Treaty of Ryswick.

RELATED ARTICLES in *Great Lives from History: The Seventeenth Century, 1601-1700:* Charles II (of England); James II; George Monck; Samuel Pepys; Prince Rupert; Michiel Adriaanszoon de Ruyter; Peter Stuyvesant.

Spring, 1665-Fall, 1666
GREAT PLAGUE IN LONDON

London suffered northwestern Europe's last major outbreak of bubonic plague, ending the second pandemic that began with the Black Death of 1347-1352. Despite the deaths of seventy thousand or more people, the city rapidly recovered, in large part because of the localized nature of the epidemic.

LOCALE: London, England
CATEGORIES: Health and medicine; natural disasters

KEY FIGURES

Charles II (1630-1685), king of England, r. 1660-1685
Samuel Pepys (1633-1703), English royal administrator and diarist
Thomas Sydenham (1624-1689), English physician
Daniel Defoe (1660-1731), English novelist

SUMMARY OF EVENT

England had suffered outbreaks of plague every ten or fifteen years since the Black Death of 1347-1352. Though societal means of dealing with the pestilence, such as quarantines and boards of health, had developed since the fourteenth century, medical knowledge of the disease and its causes and vectors had not advanced. English society had learned to accept and even expect the plague, though especially heavy attacks could kill thousands and disrupt normal life for months. The year 1603 saw the greatest seventeenth century visitation, and 3,597 Londoners died in an outbreak in 1647. Between 1629 and 1636, the city lost an annual average of 1,500 people to plague, and the later 1640's saw an average of 1,072 plague deaths annually.

In the decade and a half leading up to 1665, however, plague deaths averaged only 14 per year in London, which housed nearly half a million people. Bills of Mortality—weekly publications that listed London deaths by cause—had been introduced in the 1520's and had long served as barometers that might predict heavy outbreaks. For the year 1664, they listed a mere five Londoners dead of the plague, at a time when nearby Amsterdam in the Netherlands was being ravaged by an epidemic. In 1663-1664, some thirty-five thousand Amsterdamers succumbed to the disease, but an embargo on Dutch shipping and an extremely cold winter in 1664-1665—the Thames River was frozen solid for two consecutive months—seemed to promise a safe new year in England.

Though virtually plague-free in the early 1660's, Britons did suffer from malaria and other diseases that struck during the unusually warm summers. Despite the frigid winter, the spring of 1665 was also unseasonably warm, raising fears of plague brought from the Netherlands. The quarantine period for inbound ships was raised to forty days and mandated for twenty-eight port towns all around the island. The *Intelligencer*, a London newspaper, printed the plague reports from the weekly Bills of Mortality in order to stem these fears. Before May 1, the periodical reported only three deaths attributable to plague, and it reported only forty-three in May itself.

Despite the tiny rise, many remained unconvinced by the data, since its collection was dependent on very unreliable people who could easily err in their diagnosis or be bribed. Since May, 1665, families with plague would by law be shut in until all members died or showed no more signs of the disease, Londoners had good reason to avoid being labeled as potential plague carriers. By mid-June, the number of reported plague dead rose to 112 per week. Both royal and civic authorities avoided formal acknowledgment of plague, since an official announcement would invite sudden flight from the city, disruption in local tax gathering and trade with other countries and regions, and interference with the preparations for war with the Dutch.

In June, reported plague deaths rose to 590, though all were limited to only five large suburban parishes. The gentry now began to abandon the city, and the royal family, including Charles II, left for Hampton Court. In Marylebone, a pest-house was constructed to house the diseased poor, and on June 21, local officials began to seal off the area most affected from the rest of the city in hopes of containing the epidemic. Officials shut down theaters on June 5, the Inns of Court in mid-month, and all London schools in July.

Despite these precautions, July saw the plague spread across all 130 of London's parishes, taking a total of 5,667 lives. Samuel Pepys, an administrator for the Royal Navy, sent his family away but, like other heads of households, remained in the city to continue working. He discussed the effects of the plague in his famous diary, remarking that the city seemed nearly deserted by late July. The four weeks of August saw reported plague death totals of 2,817; 3,880; 4,237; and 6,102. September saw these weekly numbers rise to 6,988; 6,544; and 7,165; and then fall again to 5,533, for a monthly total of 26,230.

Officials combated the epidemic by keeping bonfires in the streets stoked to dry out the supposedly pestilential damp air; houses where plague had visited were fumigated with gunpowder smoke, brimstone, or incense, and a multitude of cats, dogs, and birds that were suspected of somehow carrying the disease were destroyed. Thieves sacked abandoned homes, burial rites were curtailed, and bodies were dumped in mass graves. Individuals sought to avoid the disease by fleeing—a tactic of the well-to-do, including physicians like Thomas Sydenham—or by medicating themselves with tobacco, secret cures, and patent medicines developed during earlier plagues and wearing toad amulets. Preachers—those who remained—harangued their congregations for angering a God who was now justly punishing them. Quakers and other religious dissidents were treated as scapegoats by Anglicans and Puritans alike.

Monthly death tolls dropped from October through December to 1,050; 652; and 987, respectively, and Lon-

An artist's rendering of the plague shows the dead being carted away in the background while the dying huddle on the street in the foreground. (Hulton|Archive by Getty Images)

don was repopulated in December and January. The year 1666 saw around 1,800 plague burials, bringing the total plague death toll in London to 68,596, about 70 percent of the total of 97,300 deaths from all causes in London for the period, according to the Bills of Mortality. Skeptics at the time distrusted the bills and claimed the figure to be much higher: The earl of Clarendon thought 160,000 plague deaths more likely. Historians who trust the bills claim 70,000 to 75,000 deaths, for a total loss of 15 percent of the city's population, compared to perhaps 50 percent loss in the late 1340's. Skeptical historians place the death toll rather higher, around 100,000, in the light of the insufficiencies of the bills.

SIGNIFICANCE

The Great Plague of 1665-1666 marked the last major outbreak of the disease in England. The economic recession and population loss were rapidly reversed, and London's total recovery was only suppressed by the Second Anglo-Dutch War and the Great Fire of 1666. Migration from across England reinforced the depleted population, which returned to its pre-plague level in 1668.

Culturally, the plague inspired novelist Daniel Defoe's *Journal of the Plague Year* (1722), which blends his own childhood recollections with the historical record and fictional material. After fleeing London, poet John Dryden wrote several major works, including *Annus Mirabilis* (1667), and absentee London physician Sydenham penned his treatise on pestilential fevers in the plague's wake. It was while shunning plague-struck Cambridge in 1665 that Sir Isaac Newton made many of his key scientific discoveries, including formulating his theory of gravitation.

Plague also spread to other parts of England, as Pepys notes fearfully in his diary and as the example of the village of Eyam still commemorates. Plague struck Eyam in August, 1665, and the villagers imposed quarantine on themselves. By late 1666, 257 of perhaps 350 villagers had succumbed, with few if any surviving by flight. By the 1660's, plague had all but disappeared from many regions in Europe, though it would strike again mercilessly in the Mediterranean region, as at Lyon (1672 with some 60,000 victims) and Marseilles (1720-1722, killing perhaps 80,000).

—*Joseph P. Byrne*

FURTHER READING

Backscheider, Paula R., ed. *A Journal of the Plague Year, Daniel Defoe*. New York: Norton, 1992. Contains text of Defoe's novel and numerous short articles about the work.

Bell, Walter George. *The Great Plague in London in 1665*. New York: AMS Press, 1976. Long the definitive study of the event and still important for its valuable narrative material.

Boghurst, William. *Loimographia: An Account of the Great Plague of London in the Year 1665*. New York: AMS Press, 1976. A valuable contemporary account reprinted for modern readers.

Champion, J. A. I. *London's Dreaded Visitation: The Social Geography of the Great Plague in 1665*. London: Centre for Metropolitan History, 1995. Impact of population location on patterns of plague effects.

Hodges, Nathaniel. *Loimologia: Or, An Historical Account of the Plague in London in 1665*. New York: AMS Press, 1994. Valuable contemporary account.

Latham, Robert, and Williams Matthews, eds. *The Diary of Samuel Pepys*. 11 vols. Berkeley: University of California Press, 2000. See especially volumes 6 and 7 on Pepys's observations on the plague and its effects.

Moote, A. Lloyd, and Dorothy C. Moote. *The Great Plague: The Story of London's Most Deadly Year*. Baltimore: Johns Hopkins University Press, 2004. Written by a historian and a microbiologist, this study of London in the plague year details the ways in which the upper and lower segments of society were rendered interdependent by the epidemic.

Porter, Stephen. *The Great Plague*. Stroud, Gloucestershire, England: Sutton, 1999. Well illustrated modern narrative treatment that covers all of England.

Shrewsbury, J. F. *History of Bubonic Plague in the British Isles*. New York: Cambridge University Press, 1970. Places the 1665 plague in the context of earlier epidemics.

Slack, Paul. *Impact of Plague in Tudor and Stuart England*. London: Routledge, Kegan & Paul, 1985. Important analytical overview of effects of early modern plagues on England.

SEE ALSO: 17th cent.: Advances in Medicine; Mar. 4, 1665-July 31, 1667: Second Anglo-Dutch War; Sept. 2-5, 1666: Great Fire of London; 1676: Sydenham Advocates Clinical Observation.

RELATED ARTICLES in *Great Lives from History: The Seventeenth Century, 1601-1700:* Charles II (of England); First Earl of Clarendon; Samuel Pepys; Thomas Sydenham.

October 29, 1665
Battle of Mbwila

Hostilities between the Kingdom of Kongo and the Portuguese colony of Angola erupted into war. At the Battle of Mbwila, King Antonio I of Kongo and Kongolese noblemen were killed, leading to the decline of the kingdom.

Locale: Angola
Category: Wars, uprisings, and civil unrest

Key Figures

Antonio I (d. 1665), *manikongo*, or king, of Kongo, r. 1661-1665
Diogo Cão (fl. 1480-1486), Portuguese explorer, who led the first Portuguese expedition into central Africa
Nzinga Nkuwu (John I; d. 1506), *manikongo* of Kongo, r. c. 1480-1506
Afonso I (Nzinga Mbemba; d. 1543), *manikongo* of Kongo, r. 1506-1543
Alvaro I (d. 1587), *manikongo* of Kongo, r. 1567-1587
Alvaro II (d. 1614), *manikongo* of Kongo, r. 1587-1614
Alvaro III (d. 1622), *manikongo* of Kongo, r. 1615-1622
Garcia II (d. 1661), *manikongo* of Kongo, r. 1642-1661
Salvador Correia de Sá e Benevides (1594-1688), Portuguese commander on the Angolan coast and governor of Angola

Summary of Event

The Battle of Mbwila was an epic culmination of the intrusion of the Portuguese colony of Angola into the rivalries that characterized the relations between Kongo and its neighbors in central Africa. The Portuguese were not the only ones whose dealings interfered with the hegemonic designs of the Kongolese in central Africa. There were others—Loango, Ndongo, and Imbangala, and other Europeans, such as the Dutch, who were equally meddlesome in Kongo's affairs—but it was the Portuguese, however, who were arguably the most obsessive in their determination to impose their will on Kongo, creating conditions that led to the Battle of Mbwila.

Looking at the arrival of the Portuguese in central Africa, one would not have imagined that they would unleash events that would lead to the decline of Kongo. When the Portuguese arrived in central Africa in the fifteenth century, they found that Kongo was one of the most powerful states there. The kingdom was stable, and it was ruled by the *manikongo*, or king. Captain Diogo Cão, the leader of the first Portuguese expedition into central Africa, was so impressed with the power and prestige of Kongo when he arrived there in 1483 that he immediately sent "gifts and messages" to the *manikongo* of Kongo, Nzinga Nkuwu. This event laid the foundation for more contacts between the Portuguese and the Kongo kingdom.

By 1491, Portuguese presence in Kongo had increased significantly, as mercenaries, traders, and missionaries operated in the kingdom. Seeking to exploit their presence, the *manikongo* Nzinga Nkuwu converted to Christianity and took the name John. Through a strategic alliance with the Portuguese, Kongo expanded its tentacles and occupied many territories in the region. The expansion of Kongolese power moved in tandem with increasing Portuguese presence in the region, enhancing Portuguese status just as much as it was consolidating Kongolese power. By the beginning of the sixteenth century, the Portuguese ceased being merely instruments of Kongolese imperialism; they became rivals at the very time when the slave trade was becoming a major aspect of European mercantilism and a source of friction among various nation-states.

During the sixteenth century, Portuguese missionaries, traders, and technicians who came to the kingdom engaged in, to the chagrin of Kongo, activities that were inimical to the interests of Kongo. Portuguese interference in Kongolese internal politics became common. When King Afonso I (Nzinga Mbemba) died in 1543, the Portuguese and other interested parties tried to consolidate their positions in the kingdom by placing their own candidate on the throne, leading to violent power struggles. Several kings came and went in rapid succession, and instability was endemic.

In 1567, Alvaro I came to power. Within a short time, Alvaro formally placed Kongo under the control of the Portuguese, in exhange for their military assistance against the Imbangala (the Jagas), who had in 1568 invaded Kongo and forced King Alvaro and his supporters to flee for their lives to an island in the middle of the Congo River. The Imbangala invasion thus consolidated the Portuguese presence in Kongo. However, although the formalization of this relationship provided the Kongolese with a formidable ally against its hostile neighbors, it unpalatably reminded them of the extent to which they had lost power and had become dependent on others for their own protection.

In 1576, the Portuguese moved to consolidate their presence along the coast of central Africa by establishing a new colony around the mouth of the Kwana River and naming it Angola. The Portuguese used this base to interfere in the affairs of Kongo, and many conflicts ensued between the Portuguese and Kongo. Quarrels over land, especially on the lower Bengo and Dande Rivers, were common. Confrontations occurred over things such as mining rights. When King Alvaro sent a Portuguese subject who had attempted to assassinate him to Luanda for punishment, the would-be assassin was given rewards and set free.

Still, the kings of Kongo, including Alvaro I, did not lose hope of regaining their traditional power and reining in the Portuguese, especially at their base in Angola. When Alvaro I died in 1587, he was replaced by Alvaro II, who tried to expand his power while controlling the activities of the Portuguese and their allies. Diplomatic overtures were made to the Vatican, and maneuvers for technical and commercial assistance were made among other European nations. When Alvaro III came to power in 1615, his reign was similarly consumed by Kongolese relations with Portuguese Angola, and a brief war was fought between the two nations in 1622.

The war of 1622 marked the end of uneasy peace between Kongo and the Portuguese in Angola. It signaled the collapse of measures taken earlier by Kongo rulers Alvaro II and Alvaro III to control Angola, and it foreshadowed a deterioration of relations that would be dramatized by the outbreak of the Battle of Mbwila in 1665. The war of 1622, moreover, exacerbated political and commercial fissures that had been brought under control by Alvaro II. During the next nineteen years, Kongo was ruled by six kings in quick succession. Various factions competed for power, often with deepening involvement of the Portuguese with ulterior motives. By the end of the first half of the seventeenth century, Kongo teetered precariously on the precipice of destruction, and no king remained in power long enough to provide the kingdom with stability and protection against the depredatory activities of the Portuguese, especially those based in Angola.

Kongo experienced a temporary respite from these problems when the Dutch invaded and occupied Angola in 1641. Garcia II, who came to power in Kongo the year following the Dutch invasion, took the opportunity to reassert Kongolese hegemony. Although Dutch interests in the region often conflicted with those of the Kongolese—especially as the Dutch were also involved in the slave trade—they created room for Garcia to try to maneuver Kongo out of the clutches of the Portuguese. Adeptly blending international and local diplomacy and Christian and traditional religious practices, Garcia consolidated power and emerged as one of the greatest kings of Kongo. Centralized power reemerged. Garcia's exploits earned him the nickname *kimpanku*, the sorcerer. His reign, from 1642 to 1661, brought stability, and for a time it seemed as if conflicts that had wracked Kongo had been curbed. In retrospect, Garcia's reign marked the last phase of effective Kongo unity.

By 1648, the Portuguese had defeated the Dutch and were back at their base in Angola, determined to teach Kongo a lesson for supporting the Dutch. Garcia tried to forestall war with diplomacy, but his maneuvers did not succeed, as tensions rose between the Portuguese and Kongo. Salvador Correia de Sá e Benevides, the governor of Angola and a military commander, rejected Garcia's diplomatic overtures and demanded that Mbwila, Dande Valley, and Luanda Island be transferred to Angola as payment for damages incurred during the Dutch occupation. He demanded tax exemption for all Portuguese goods and the right to control gold and copper mines in the whole of Kongo. He demanded the right to oversee all Kongo's international relations, especially those with Europe. Although Garcia accepted most of these terms after much hesitation, he refused to cede his mines. He refused to budge even as the Portuguese and their allies continued to threaten him. During the next decade, these disputes between the Portuguese and the Kongolese simmered. By the time Garcia died in 1661, the relations between the Portuguese and the Konglese were so bad that it was only a matter of time before war would erupt.

When Antonio I replaced Garcia as the new king, he inherited the provocative Portuguese demands on Kongo. Looking to provoke Kongo further, the Portuguese in Angola started to extend their territory into the Dembos, an area Kongo considers its own. Sometime in the mid-1660's, a Portuguese force clashed with the Kongolese over the leadership of Mbwila, with Antonio supporting the ruler and the Portuguese supporting the ruler's opponent. Mobilizing men from every province, Antonio decided to retaliate and avenge the humiliation his kingdom had suffered since the Portuguese had arrived in the region two centuries before. By October, 1665, the armies were ready to confront each other. According to some sources, the Kongolese army consisted of 70,000 soldiers reinforced by about 200 musketeers.

Other sources suggest the army numbered more than "100,000 soldiers . . . about 800 shield-bearers, and 190 musketeers." The Portuguese deployed around 6,000 to 7,000 bowmen and 466 musketeers. Crucially, King Antonio himself was in command of the Kongolese troops.

Fighting started on October 29, 1665, with the Kongolese on the attack. All seemed to be going well for the Kongolese when disaster struck. At a critical moment in the battle, the Portuguese musketeers launched a fusillade of shots, and Antonio was fatally wounded. The death of Antonio in the battlefield threw the Kongolese army into a panic. Demoralized, the soldiers retreated in disarray. More than five thousand Kongolese soldiers were killed, including a number of Antonio's sons and nephews, four of the seven governors of Kongolese seven provinces, and many members of the nobility.

SIGNIFICANCE

After the death of Antonio I, Kongo was never again stable. In retrospect, Garcia's reign between 1641 and 1661 was the last time Kongo remained a united state. With the death of Antonio, many factions emerged and competed for power. Civil wars became common once again, especially during succession to the throne, and famine and epidemics exacerbated the misery. Kongo was beset by many problems. Virtually every king who came to the throne after Antonio I did so by military means.

During the latter half of the seventeenth, and throughout the eighteenth centuries, various factions fighting for power split the kingdom into various separate regions. In 1709, after numerous wars, Pedro IV came to the throne, but his ascension did not stop the decline of the Kongolese state. His successors continued to witness a steady deterioration of the power of Kongo during the eighteenth century. By the end of the eighteenth century, the power and influence of Kongo had virtually disappeared. Although many factors, such as the lack of proper instruments for managing succession, contributed to the decline of the Kongo kingdom, one cannot ignore the impact of the Portuguese in the region, the slave trade, and the interference of the Portuguese colonies of São Tome and Angola.

—*Meshak Owino*

FURTHER READING

Birmingham, David. "Central Africa from Cameroon to the Zambezi." In *The Cambridge History of Africa*, edited by J. D. Fage and Roland Oliver. Vol. 4. New York: Cambridge University Press, 1975. A discussion of the region.

Broadhead, Susan H. *Historical Dictionary of Angola*. Metuchen, N.J.: Scarecrow Press, 1992. A compendium of useful information, including descriptions of proper names, a chronology, historic maps, a table comparing colonial and modern names, and a bibliography of primary and secondary sources.

Duffy, James. *Portuguese Africa*. Cambridge, Mass.: Harvard University Press, 1959. A study of Portugal's territories on the African continent.

Hair, P. E. H. "Discovery and Discoveries: The Portuguese in Guinea, 1444-1650." *Bulletin of Hispanic Studies* 69 (1992): 11-28. A broad look at the Portuguese in West Africa, including Angola, with helpful historiographical information.

Thornton, John K. *The Kingdom of Kongo: Civil War and Transition, 1641-1718*. Madison: University of Wisconsin Press, 1983. Thornton examines the Kongo Kingdom from the perspective of its internal battles, beginning in 1641.

_______. *Warfare in Atlantic Africa, 1500-1800*. London: University College of London Press, 1999. A more wide-ranging history of wars and warmaking along the West African coast.

Vansina, J., and T. Obenga. "The Kongo Kingdom and Its Neighbors." In *General History of Africa*, edited by B. A. Ogot. Vol. 5. Berkeley: University of California Press, 1992. A modern study of the Kongo Kingdom and the surrounding region.

SEE ALSO: 1617-1693: European Powers Vie for Control of Gorée; c. 1625: Formation of the Kuba Kingdom; Oct., 1625-1637: Dutch and Portuguese Struggle for the Guinea Coast; 1630-1660's: Dutch Wars in Brazil; Aug. 26, 1641-Sept., 1648: Conquest of Luanda; 1644-1671: Ndongo Wars; 1654: Portugal Retakes Control of Brazil; Late 17th cent.: Rise of Buganda.

RELATED ARTICLES in *Great Lives from History: The Seventeenth Century, 1601-1700:* John IV; Njinga.

c. 1666
STRADIVARI MAKES HIS FIRST VIOLIN

Building on a tradition established by several generations of fine violin makers, Antonio Stradivari brought the craft to such a high level that his instruments are regarded by many as the best in the world.

LOCALE: Cremona, Italy
CATEGORIES: Music; art; cultural and intellectual history

KEY FIGURES

Antonio Stradivari (1644?-1737), master violin maker
Andrea Amati (c. 1510-c. 1578), founder of the Amati school of violin making
Arcangelo Corelli (1653-1713), Italian composer and violinist whose compositions and performances helped popularize the violin throughout Europe
Nicolò Amati (1596-1684), a likely teacher of Stradivari and Andrea Guarneri
Andrea Guarneri (c. 1626-1698), violin maker, who apprenticed with Stradivari under Nicolò Amati

SUMMARY OF EVENT

The town of Cremona, on the Po River in the Lombardy region of Italy, has been known since the Middle Ages as a center of culture. During the Renaissance, when bowed string instruments appeared in many forms, the family of violins began to take shape. Andrea Amati, a master violin maker in Cremona, is credited with helping to define the proportions and design of these new instruments, which he began labeling in the 1560's. He shared this craft with his son and established a shop that was well respected and continued for several generations.

This was the tradition that Stradivari would have learned when he became an apprentice in the Amati shop, most likely in the late 1650's. By this time, Amati's grandson Nicolò Amati had inherited the master's business. Both Stradivari and Andrea Guarneri (destined to become a famous maker in his own right) were pupils of Nicolò.

By the middle of the seventeenth century, instruments of the violin family had emerged in Europe as the most popular variety of bowed stringed instruments. Italian musicians such as Arcangelo Corelli wrote and performed extensively for the new instrument, and international demand for fine violins increased during this period. The viola da gamba and other bowed instruments that had been prominent during the Renaissance remained in use, however, and the Cremonese violin makers continued to make them, as well as guitars.

Stradivari's parents, Alessandro Stradivari and Anna Moroni, were married in Cremona in 1622, but it is likely that they left during the years of famine (1628-1629) and plague (1630). The town of Cremona was ravaged by famine and plague, and its population was reduced by half, but its tradition of instrument building, led by the Amati family, managed to survive. According to practices of the time, Stradivari would typically have entered his apprenticeship when he was about twelve years old. In most cases it would take about three years for an apprentice to start making his own instruments, and still longer for him to start putting his own name on the labels. The first violin bearing Stradivari's name dates from 1666. The label on this instrument mentions that he was Amati's pupil. As was common at that time, the label's inscription was in Latin, and his name was Latinized as Stradivarius.

Although not many of Stradivari's violins made before 1680 survive, his earliest violins have shapes that are somewhat less rounded and more angular than those of Amati, but in most respects, Stradivari followed the patterns he had learned, and he sometimes embellished the instruments with delicate inlays.

He must have developed enough confidence in his own abilities to be able to support a family, because in 1667, he married Francesca Feraboschi. After he and his family moved to the Piazza San Domenico in Cremona in 1680, he began producing many more violins and cellos under his own name and established his shop in his home, where he would remain for the rest of his career. His reputation began to grow, too. In 1682, a set of instruments was ordered and eventually presented to James II, who became the king of England in 1695.

After 1684, when his teacher Nicolò Amati died, Stradivari came to be regarded by many as the world's leading violin maker. He made many subtle changes and adjustments in construction and constantly experimented with his work. He is said to have developed the ability to carve spontaneously, sometimes without a template, so that his decisions were made on the spot, through intuition as well as conscious planning.

Hoping to understand the physical reasons for the beautiful sound and durability of the Stradivari violins, violas, and cellos, many have studied the physics and biochemistry of his instruments. The instruments' glue, ground coating, and varnish have all been studied, as

Violin maker Antonio Stradivari in his workshop. (Library of Congress)

well as how the wood was prepared and the significance of shape and thickness. Research has revealed that during this period, the violin makers of Cremona and Venice used a ground layer (between the wood and the regular varnish) with a high mineral content, especially silicon and aluminum. The varnish itself was applied in very thin layers, to maintain the resonance of the instrument while protecting the wood.

The thickness of the wood in the bodies of Stradivari's instruments generally increases toward the center, but rather than applying a strict formula without variation, he appeared to have made constant adjustments to thickness based on the unique qualities of each piece of wood.

SIGNIFICANCE

Although Stradivari's sons Francesco and Omobono were trained in violin making, they did not make violins under their own names, and they died soon after their father, who passed away after more than half a century of work. After Stradivari's death, his fellow apprentice's grandson, Bartolomeo Giuseppe Guarneri (1698-1744), continued to make fine violins, but he was the last famous carrier of the Amati violin tradition, a tradition that had lasted for more than two centuries.

Stradivari's fine instruments have been imitated so thoroughly that authenticity sometimes becomes an issue in terms of assessing value. Also, some of the violins made toward the end of his life were probably made by apprentices under his supervision, just as Stradivari himself had first worked under Amati.

Some instrument builders became obsessed with discovering the "secret" of Stradivari's success and so sought to isolate various components of his craftsmanship, but the essential design of the instrument has changed very little since his time.

In addition to furnishing a prototype for subsequent centuries of instrument makers, Stradivari's creations have directly impacted generations of musicians, as many of the instruments have remained in active use through the centuries since Stradivari's death. Great musicians would rise to fame, spend most of their careers playing on the Stradivari masterpieces, and then lovingly pass them on to the next generation. Most of the instruments, especially the violins, were eventually given colorful names that referred to famous owners and musicians.

More than six hundred of his instruments still exist, and many of them are still played in concert by well-known musicians, not just for novelty but also for sound. The instruments were made so well that they surpass most contemporary instruments in quality, in spite of technological innovation.

—*John Myers*

Further Reading

Chiesa, Carlo, and Duane Rosengard. *The Stradivari Legacy*. London: Peter Biddulph, 1998. Chiesa and Rosengard examine Stradivari's last will and testament, which they had rediscovered in the course of their research. The work includes contextual analysis, full commentary, and complete text (with English translation) of all four versions of the will, with related documents. Includes color photographs of six Stradivari instruments.

Cho, Charles. "Secrets of the Stradivarius: An Interview with Joseph Nagyvary." *Scientific American* (June, 2002). Nagyvary summarizes more than twenty-five years of his applied scientific research into the biochemistry and physics of the Stradivari violins.

Hill, W. Henry, Arthur F. Hill, and Alfred E. Hill. *Antonio Stradivari: His Life and Work, 1644-1737*. New York: Dover, 1963. An unabridged reprint of the monumental work by the Hill brothers, first published in 1902. Includes new supplementary indexes and an introduction by Sydney Beck. An extremely detailed study of various parts of the instruments as well as biographical data. Photos of instruments, illustrations.

Kolneder, Walter, and Reinhard Pauly. *The Amadeus Book of the Violin*. Portland, Oreg.: Amadeus Press, 1998. An updated version of the work first published in 1972. This substantial volume includes complete coverage of materials and construction, the history of the instrument, and anecdotes. An excellent overview places Stradivari's work in a larger context.

See also: c. 1601: Emergence of Baroque Music.

Related articles in *Great Lives from History: The Seventeenth Century, 1601-1700:* Arcangelo Corelli; James II.

c. 1666-1676
Founding of the Marāthā Kingdom

Hindu Marāthā warrior and later king, Śivājī, using guerrilla tactics and supported by bands of Marāthān horsemen, captured a hill fortress in India's Western Ghats at the expense of neighboring Muslim states. Forced to surrender to Mughal emperor Aurangzeb, Śivājī escaped and returned to his land Mahārāshtra to resume his campaigns. The Marāthān Kingdom survived into the eighteenth century.

Locale: India

Categories: Government and politics; wars, uprisings, and civil unrest; expansion and land acquisition

Key Figures

Śivājī (1627-1680), founder and *chatrapati*, or king, of the Marāthā Kingdom, r. 1674-1680

Śahājī (1594-1664), father of Śivājī

Jījī Baī (fl. seventeenth century), mother of Śivājī

Sambhājī (1657-1689), Śivājī's son and heir, r. 1680-1689

Aurangzeb (1618-1707), Mughal emperor of India, r. 1658-1707

Afẓal Khān (d. 1659), Muslim general of the Bijapur sultanate

Summary of Event

The history of India is, in part, the story of the religions of India and their relationships and conflicts. The birthplace of Hinduism and Buddhism, as well as Jainism and Sikhism, it was a foreign import, Islam, that threatened to remake all of India into the Islamic image. Muslims entered India in force in the 900's and 1000's. By the sixteenth century, the most successful of the Muslim kingdoms was the Mughal Empire.

By the Mughal era, Buddhism had largely died out in India, although it became the religion for most of the populations of East Asia and Southeast Asia. In the Punjab of northwest India, the younger religion of the Sikhs had established a foothold, but the greatest threat to Mughal political and territorial unity came from the Hindus, by far the largest religious group in India. However, religious differences were not the only issues that divided India. Political ambitions, cultural differences, economic problems, and military aspirations combined with issues of religion and ethnicity to make India's history often appear to be the history of little more than conflict.

The Mughals, including the leadership, were Muslims, but most of the emperors were relatively tolerant of their Hindu and other non-Muslim subjects. The notable exception was Emperor Aurangzeb, who adopted the name Alamgir, or world conqueror. His religious intolerance made him the most hated of all Mughal rulers by non-Muslim Indians. It was during his long reign that the Hindu Marāthās emerged to challenge Mughal supremacy.

Mahārāshtra (the Great Country), was in the northern part of India's Western Ghats along the coast between Goa and Bombay. The Marāthās were Hindus, but they could not be subdued by the Mughal Sunnis or the Shī'ites of the sultanates of the Deccan peninsula because of the rugged mountainous environment of the Western Ghats. At times, Hindus served the various Islamic rulers, notably as warriors. Śahājī was a Hindu landholder under the Muslim sultanates of Ahmadnagar and Bijapur, who later served the Mughals under Aurangzeb's father Shah Jahan. Śahājī switched his allegiance back to the sultan of Ahmadnagar. Using guerrilla tactics suited to the Deccan terrain, Śahājī resisted for several years, but in 1636 he was forced to surrender to a combined Mughal-Bijapur alliance and was banished to the city of Pune (Poona), which eventually became the capital of Mahārāshtra.

It was Śahājī's son, Śivājī, who became the legendary leader of the Marāthās and the first king. Born in 1627 to Śahājī's first wife, Jījī Baī, Śivājī was raised by his mother, who was a devout Hindu. Deeply imbued with the traditions of Hinduism, to Śivājī, Islam was a foreign import to be rooted out from Mahārāshtra. How broadly Śivājī perceived his rightful territories is impossible to know, but at a minimum it included the northern region of the Western Ghats. He never differentiated between the Shī'ite sultanates of the Deccan and the Sunni Mughals, and like the Indian nationalists of the late nineteenth and twentieth centuries for which he became an inspiration in their campaign against Great Britain, Śivājī demanded *svaraj*, or self-rule and independence. Whether Śivājī's motivations were exclusively religious is doubtful. During his career, he made use of Muslim warriors as well as Hindus, and considerations of power and resources were as important as the Hindu-Muslim rivalry.

At about the age of twenty (around 1647), and while his father was still a hostage of the Bijapur sultanate, Śivājī gathered Marāthā supporters, most of whom were well acquainted with the mountainous terrain of the region, and began raiding caravans traveling through the area. Seizing a number of mountain tops, he built formidable fortresses, such as that of Sinhagarh (the fortress of the lion), a place with such a stark cliff face that it was said Śivājī was successful only by using a giant lizard to assist him in reaching its heights and overpowering the Muslim garrison. He has aptly been called one of the fathers of guerrilla warfare.

After a decade of costly raids, in 1659, the Bijapur sultan dispatched Afẓal Khān to root out and destroy Śivājī. Afẓal Khān isolated Śivājī at Pratapgarh (fortress of valor), forcing him to sue for peace. In a famous episode, Śivājī demanded that he discuss his surrender directly with the Bijapur general. They met just outside the fortress walls, and although they were supposed to be unarmed, both had weapons. Śivājī was barely five foot tall and Afẓal Khān a foot taller. Śivājī wore a loose-fitting robe that concealed his hands and the two weapons he held, a dagger in one hand and razor-edged "tiger" claws in the other. Afẓal Khān collapsed and died when "embraced" by Śivājī, and the Marāthān troops quickly overcame the Bijapur forces.

The more formidable Mughal army was soon sent to the Deccan, and once again Śivājī faced potential defeat. In a daring raid in 1663, Marāthā raiders secretly entered the Mughal-occupied city of Pune, nearly succeeding in assassinating the Mughal general. The following year, Śivājī led a successful expedition to Surat in Gujarat, north of Mahārāshtra, where he looted the city. In response, Aurangzeb, the Mughal emperor, dispatched a large army of fifteen thousand soldiers under Rājput raja Jai Singh to bring the Hindu warlord to heel. Jai Singh cornered Śivājī at Purandhar in 1665, forcing him to surrender twenty of his twenty-five fortresses and to agree to serve under the Mughals. When he attended Aurangzeb's court, he was placed under arrest. However, he escaped, supposedly carried out in a food or laundry basket, and returned to his home territories. By 1670, he had recaptured most of his fortresses and again raided Surat and sites in the Mughal Deccan and captured Pune.

The culmination of Śivājī's campaign for *svaraj* occurred in 1674. That year, in the traditional Hindu coronation ceremony, Śivājī was crowned *chatrapati*, or lord of the universe. Hindu kings were to belong to the *ksatriya* caste, and a long genealogy, perhaps bogus, was necessarily established. Five thousand supporters swore allegiance to Śivājī, who was acclaimed as the reincarnation of the god Lord Śiva, and eleven thousand Hindu Brahman priests chanted mantras from the Vedas, the sacred writings of Hinduism. In subsequent years, Śivājī seized territories in the far southeast around Madras. Aurangzeb, occupied at the time in Afghanistan, was unable to prevent it, and he did not return to the Deccan until after Śivājī's death from fever in 1680 in Rājgarh.

SIGNIFICANCE

The coronation of Śivājī did not end the quest for Marāthān *svaraj*. During the reign of Śivājī's son, Sambhājī, Aurangzeb campaigned extensively in the Deccan. Replicating his father's guerrilla tactics, Sambhājī long-eluded the Mughals, but, in 1689, he was captured and tortured to death. Raja Ram, his younger brother, continued the conflict until his death in 1700, and Raja Ram's widow, Tara Baī, kept alive the flame of Marāthā independence. Aurangzeb died in 1707 without taking full control of Mahārāshtra.

By the 1730's, with the decline of the Mughals, the Marāthās became the greatest single power in fragmented India. However, Mahārāshtra was more of a confederacy than a centralized kingdom. By the mid-eighteenth century, the British East India Company, the ultimate outsider, was inexorably taking control of the Indian subcontinent, and in the following century, India would become Britain's "jewel in the crown." Among Hindus, however, Śivājī had not been forgotten. In the 1890's, radical Hindu nationalists justified terrorism and assassination of British officials in the name of Śivājī, and by the late twentieth century, Śivājī became an iconic figure among India's Hindus, particularly among religious extremists who desired a Hindu-only India.

—*Eugene Larson*

FURTHER READING

Bhave, Y. G. *From the Death of Shivaji to the Death of Aurangzeb: The Critical Years*. New Delhi, India: Northern Book Center, 2000. An exploration of Mughal rule and Hindu resistance from the time of Śivājī's death until Aurangzeb's death.

Gascoigne, Bamber. *A Brief History of the Great Moghuls*. New York: Carroll & Graf, 2002. This well-written, general history of the Mughals, originally published in 1971, chronicles the rise and fall of the empire from its founder, Bābur, through Aurangzeb. Profusely illustrated, it presents a compelling portrait of Śivājī's struggles against Aurangzeb.

Gordon, Stewart. *The Marathas, 1600-1818*. Vol. 4 in *The New Cambridge History of India*, edited by Gordon Johnson, C. A. Bayly, and John F. Richards. New York: Cambridge University Press, 1993. A comprehensive history of the Marāthās and their kingdom, including a chapter on Śivājī and the Marāthā polity.

Keay, John. *India: A History*. New York: Atlantic Monthly Press, 2000. This well-written history of India discusses the exploits of Śivājī and his influence on modern Indian politics.

Laine, James W. *Shivaji: Hindu King in Islamic India*. New York: Oxford University Press, 2003. A controversial work in which Laine traces the origins and development of Śivājī's legend to offer a complex and unconventional view of Hindu-Muslim relationships in India.

Pearson, M. N. "Shivaji and the Decline of the Mughal Empire." *Journal of Asian Studies* 35 (February, 1976): 221-236. Focuses on the relationship between Śivājī and Aurangzeb, and on the decline of Mughal power created by, among other things, Aurangzeb's expeditions into the Deccan.

Sardesai, G. S. *New History of the Marathas*. 3 vols. Bombay, India: Phoenix, 1953. This classic work is considered to be the best history of the Marāthās.

Wolpert, Stanley. *A New History of India*. 7th ed. New York: Oxford University Press, 2004. This frequently updated general history of India provides a broad historical context for understanding Śivājī's role during the Mughal period.

SEE ALSO: 1605-1627: Mughal Court Culture Flourishes; 1606-1674: Europeans Settle in India; 1632-c. 1650: Shah Jahan Builds the Taj Mahal; 1639-1640: British East India Company Establishes Fort Saint George; 1658-1707: Reign of Aurangzeb; June 23, 1661: Portugal Cedes Bombay to the English; 1679-1709: Rājput Rebellion; Mar. 30, 1699: Singh Founds the Khalsa Brotherhood.

RELATED ARTICLES in *Great Lives from History: The Seventeenth Century, 1601-1700*: ʿAbbās the Great; Aurangzeb; Jahāngīr; Kösem Sultan; Murad IV; Shah Jahan; Śivājī.

September 2-5, 1666
GREAT FIRE OF LONDON

The Great Fire of London devastated the city, but it also destroyed the vermin that had caused recurrent plague there for centuries. The fire gave the restored King Charles II an opportunity to demonstrate his compassionate leadership.

LOCALE: London, England
CATEGORIES: Natural disasters; architecture

KEY FIGURES

Thomas Farrinor (fl. 1666), the king's baker of Pudding Lane
James, Duke of York and Albany (1633-1701), brother of Charles II and king of England as James II, r. 1685-1688
Charles II (1630-1685), king of England, r. 1660-1685
Sir Christopher Wren (1632-1723), founding member of the Royal Society, architect, and builder
Thomas Bludworth (fl. 1666), lord mayor of London
Samuel Pepys (1633-1703), secretary to the British Admiralty Office and diarist

SUMMARY OF EVENT

The Great Fire of London began insignificantly enough on the evening of Saturday, September 1, 1666. Thomas Farrinor, the king's baker, went to bed at 10:00 P.M., leaving some kindling too near the smoldering coals of his oven in Pudding Lane, near Thames Street in the city of London. By 1:00 A.M. on September 2, he was awakened by a servant and found his house filled with smoke.

Farrinor escaped with his wife and daughter through an attic window along a gutter to an adjoining house. His maid died, trapped in the blaze. Soon thereafter, Lord Mayor Thomas Bludworth was called, but he considered the fire to be of little importance and returned to bed. Samuel Pepys, secretary of the British Admiralty and a noted diarist, was roused by servants in his home in Seething Lane, but he also returned to bed with limited concern, unaware that a strong east wind was blowing dangerous sparks onto the roofs of adjacent houses and nearby warehouses, many of which held tallow, oil, spirits, and other highly flammable goods.

By morning, some three hundred houses and the north end of London Bridge were reported to be on fire. Later in the day, the steelyard was blazing out of control. With many of London's buildings built of pitch-covered timber, firefighters using buckets of water, hand pumps, and long-handled fire-hooks to pull down burning timbers found their efforts of little use as the fire intensified and began to grow. Because the mayor and others were afraid of being held responsible for compensation, they refused to order the demolition of buildings in the path of the spreading fire, which probably would have contained it.

On Monday, September 3, more than 0.5 miles (0.8 kilometers) of riverfront buildings, from London Bridge to Cannon Street, were destroyed. This destruction was soon followed by the whole of Lombard Street and the Royal Exchange. Merchants refused to allow the demolition of Billingsgate Fish Market. It burned later that day, and the fire spread to the western edges of the city at Baynard's castle. Pepys went to the royal palace in Whitehall to warn King Charles, who ordered that houses be pulled down and sent his brother, James, duke of York and Albany, to oversee demolition after the lord mayor continued to be unable to enlist and organize the firefighting efforts of London citizens.

Tuesday, September 4, was the worst day. By then, all of the waterfront buildings from west of the Tower of London past the Three Cranes were destroyed, and the fire began to spread northward up the small hill toward Cheapside and the heart of the city of London. In the evening, Saint Paul's Cathedral was destroyed, along with all of Cheapside and the Guildhall. Continued high winds spread the fire to the north and west of Newgate, burning the Inner Temple. As the fire fanned westward in a giant arc, propelled by the wind and poorly built houses and shops, fire containment units were established to halt its spread. They were effective but were helped greatly by the diminution of the wind, which allowed the firefighters to halt, control, and eventually dowse the flames.

On Wednesday, September 5, with nearly five-sixths of the city burned, subsiding winds and the effective demolition of buildings had the fire under control by midnight. On Thursday, September 6, two hundred soldiers were brought in to prevent further fires from sparks and smoldering embers. Each unit, headed by a representative from the government or nobility, had five justices of the peace, the parish constable, thirty soldiers, and one hundred citizens. King Charles rode from point to point on horseback, at first to inspect the damage but then to calm those fleeing or encourage those fighting the fire, frequently offering money rewards for valiant efforts.

The duke of York was placed in control of the city and in charge of guards intent on keeping the peace and preventing looting and other disorder. The king also talked to refugees camped out in Moorfields and defused rumors that arsonist plots by Papists or foreign powers had started the fire. Seamen were enlisted from the dockyards and began the systematic demolition of whole streets with gunpowder. This, with a fortunate diminution of the strong winds, brought about the end of the fire.

Only eight people died in the fire or its aftermath, largely because of chaotic but successful voluntary evacuation. The loss of property, however, was catastrophic. During the four days of the fire, 13,200 houses burned and 100,000 people were made homeless. Four hundred streets, alleys, and courtyards were ruined with great masses of rubble and collapsed buildings. Five-sixths of the city of London—some 400 acres (162 hectares)—was wiped out. Almost the entire medieval city was destroyed, including the huge gothic Saint Paul's Cathedral, the medieval Guildhall, Tudor Royal Exchange, 44 of the 51 halls of the city livery companies, and 84 of London's 109 parish churches.

This engraving, taken from Chamberlain's History of London *(1770), shows the giant flames of the Great Fire leaping higher than buildings.* (Hulton|Archive by Getty Images)

SIGNIFICANCE

Despite the horrific destruction to property, there were several positive outcomes of London's Great Fire. First, the substantial London population of rats was eliminated. They had been the major contributors to the spread of the plague in 1665, only the latest episode in a recurring and deadly epidemic.

The diary accounts of prominent Londoners, such as Samuel Pepys and John Evelyn, contributed to the art of English prose; minor writers, such as Thomas Vincent, and major ones such as, John Dryden, memorialized the Great Fire and its significance. In addition, the nearly complete destruction of the old and dilapidated medieval and Tudor London provided unprecedented and unique opportunities for the comprehensive rebuilding of the city. This rebuilding process brought attention to the genius of Sir Christopher Wren, whose architectural designs dominated the London cityscape for the next 250 years and provided major contributions to the monumental architecture of the world's urban centers.

Coming in the first decade of the restored monarchy, after the Commonwealth and Interregnum, the demonstrated and compassionate leadership of King Charles II and his brother, the duke of York, helped to stabilize the immediate catastrophe and encourage long-term confidence in the monarchy and royal government. The ineptness of the lord mayor contributed to the impressiveness of the royal leadership, but the king and the duke showed practical and activist understanding in following the advice of Samuel Pepys and other advisers to halt the fire by demolishing decrepit buildings in its path. More important, they showed wise and compassionate understanding in encouraging the firefighters and calming the fears of the refugees about arsonists and foreign invaders, who were rumored to have started the fire as part of a feared invasion by the French or the Dutch, then enemies of the English.

—*Xavier Baron*

FURTHER READING

Aubin, Robert Arnold. *London in Flames, London in Glory: Poems on the Fire and Rebuilding of London, 1666-1709*. New Brunswick, N.J.: Rutgers University Press, 1943. This is the most comprehensive of the dozens of broadsides and other published poetic responses to the fire.

Barker, Felix, and Peter Jackson. "The Great Fire." In *London: Two Thousand Years of a City and Its People*. London: Cassell, 1974. Standard history of London, brilliantly and copiously illustrated. It is invaluable for establishing the historical context before and after the fire.

Baron, Xavier, ed. *London, 1066-1914: Literary Sources and Documents*. East Sussex, England: Helm Information, 1996. Includes lengthy excerpts from all of the major written accounts of the Great Fire in poetry and prose, including the work of John Dryden, John Evelyn, Samuel Pepys, Thomas Wright, and Thomas Vincent.

Bell, Walter G. *The Great Fire of London*. London: Bodley Head, 1920. Although at times somewhat pedestrian, the book's wealth of detail makes it the foundation for all later research.

Hanson, Neil. *The Great Fire of London: In That Apocalyptic Year, 1666*. Hoboken, N.J.: John Wiley & Sons, 2002. Popular narrative, lively and well-written, based upon first-hand accounts. Offers several theories about the origin of the blaze.

Milne, Gustav. *The Great Fire of London*. London: Historical, 1986. Written by a member of the Museum of London's archaeological department, the book is thorough and factual. It includes excerpts from personal and official accounts of the fire, and more than one hundred photographs and illustrations.

Tinniswood, Adrian. *By Permission of Heaven: The Story of the Great Fire of London*. London: Jonathan Cape, 2003. Tinniswood, an architectural historian, examines the political, legal, and cultural significance of the fire, and describes how London was rebuilt to become a stronger, safer, and more habitable city.

SEE ALSO: 1642-1651: English Civil Wars; Dec. 6, 1648-May 19, 1649: Establishment of the English Commonwealth; Dec. 16, 1653-Sept. 3, 1658: Cromwell Rules England as Lord Protector; May, 1659-May, 1660: Restoration of Charles II; Mar. 4, 1665-July 31, 1667: Second Anglo-Dutch War; Spring, 1665-Fall, 1666: Great Plague in London.

RELATED ARTICLES in *Great Lives from History: The Seventeenth Century, 1601-1700:* Charles II (of England); John Dryden; John Evelyn; James II; Samuel Pepys; Sir Christopher Wren.

1667
CONSECRATION OF THE FIRST CATHEDRAL IN MEXICO

In 1667, the Metropolitan Cathedral in Mexico City was officially dedicated, following nearly a century's worth of building and design. From that point, the cathedral became the architectural and ceremonial focal point of the city's Catholic and Spanish heritage.

Locale: Mexico City, New Spain (now Mexico)
Categories: Architecture; organizations and institutions; religion and theology

KEY FIGURES

Pedro Moya de Contreras (c. 1530-1591), archbishop of Mexico
Antonio Sebastian de Toledo (fl. 1664-1673), marqués de Mancera, viceroy of Mexico City, r. 1664-1673
Manuel Tolsá (1757-1816), Spanish architect
Rodrigo Pacheco y Osorio (d. 1650), marqués de Cerralvo and viceroy of Mexico City, r. 1624-1634
Juan Gómez de Trasmonte (fl. mid-seventeenth century), architect
Carlos de Sigüenza y Góngora (1645-1700), historian
Rodrigo Diaz de Aguilera (fl. mid-seventeenth century), architect
Melchor Pérez de Soto (1601-1655?), architect and astrologer

SUMMARY OF EVENT

In 1667, the Metropolitan Cathedral in Mexico City (sometimes referred to as the Cathedral of Mexico or the Cathedral of the Ascension of Mary) was officially dedicated by the city's civic and religious leaders. A grand example of Spanish architecture during the colonial period, the cathedral had been originally established in 1563, near the site of former Aztec pyramids. Over the next hundred years, steady work was performed on the building and a regular stream of architects contributed to the cathedral's evolving design. In 1572, Archbishop Pedro Moya de Contreras laid the first stone, and in 1667 the building was formally dedicated by Antonio Sebastian de Toledo, the marqués de Mancera. Although work continued on the cathedral up through the nineteenth century, the present-day building is easily recognizable from its presentation in 1667.

The first church in Mexico City had been built around 1524, shortly after the Spanish conquest and nearly coincident with the appointment of Fray Juan de Zumárraga to the bishopric of Mexico. Forty years later, a new cathedral was established just north of the older church. The erection of the new cathedral was part of the first of two great "waves" of building in Mexico City that took place during the colonial period. Different designs had been proposed for the new cathedral, and the resulting plan followed closely the styles that were then typical of late sixteenth century Spanish architecture. It was during this period that the cathedral's walls and vaults were begun.

The second great wave of work on the cathedral took place from 1630 through the 1660's. In 1629, Mexico City had been besieged by massive rainstorms, which caused flooding that left the city submerged for nearly five years. During this time, some of the city's leaders had proposed abandoning the flooded city and establishing a new capital on the shore of Lake Texcoco. However, Rodrigo Pacheco y Osorio, the marqués de Cerralvo, the viceroy of Mexico City, ardently resisted the proposed plan to move the capital, and he eventually prevailed. Over the next several years, he oversaw an extensive effort to rebuild the city's civic and religious buildings. The result of this large-scale renovation was a steady influx of architects and builders who implemented much of the city's Baroque architecture, most notably seen in the cathedral itself.

As the centerpiece of the city's rebuilding project, the cathedral drew a number of prominent architects, from both New and Old Spain. The most famous of these was the architect Juan Gómez de Trasmonte, who worked on the cathedral from 1640 to 1661. Some of his work on the cathedral was completed in 1681 by Rodrigo Diaz de Aguilera, while the construction of the cathedral's temple was overseen by Melchor Pérez de Soto, a Spaniard who had been driven out of his country by the Inquisition, apparently because of his demonstrated interest in astrology. Work on the cathedral during this period had largely followed the plans that had been established at the beginning of the seventeenth century, although Trasmonte had at one point proposed a radical plan for expanding the girth of the pillars. Although his plan was rejected, the contribution of so many architects ensured a wide variety of styles and ornamentation.

By common assent, the cathedral that was dedicated in 1667 represented a remarkable synthesis of European architectural styles. For example, the numerous vaults added to the cathedral during this period are clearly Gothic or neo-Gothic, while the temple's altars are clearly Baroque in appearance. The three most prominent styles incorporated into the building are classical, neoclassical, and Baroque, the last of which was the predominant "new" architectural style in colonial Mexico. In this respect, the cathedral reflected the developing architectural styles of the home country, Spain, even as it helped to produce a flourishing of Baroque architecture in the colonial city itself. Even at its dedication, the cathedral was commended for its relatively seamless incorporation of multiple styles, such as the mixture of neoclassical and Baroque elements in its huge facade—which, unlike the walls and vault, had been constructed in the seventeenth century, at the height of Baroque vogue.

Almost immediately after its dedication, the cathedral assumed prime importance in the symbolic and mythological character of the city. The dedication itself can be seen as a politically charged event, and it has been argued that the newly appointed viceroy staged the ceremony partly to confirm his civic authority. Shortly after the cathedral's dedication, the well-known Baroque historian Carlos de Sigüenza y Góngora devoted an entire volume to the history of the Mexico City cathedral, although the work itself has not survived. The development of the cathedral's architecture continued long after its dedication, and in 1813 the architect Manuel Tolsá added a balustrade and changed the cathedral's cupola in order to emphasize the building's synthetic appearance.

SIGNIFICANCE

The dedication of the Metropolitan Cathedral in the seventeenth century was the ceremonious acknowledgment of two important trends in colonial Mexico, one architectural and the other sociopolitical. Architecturally, the cathedral embodied the dramatic influence of European styles, especially the Baroque, in colonial Latin America. In many ways the Baroque style became more entrenched in Mexico than in many parts of Europe, where it was sometimes considered gaudy or eclectic. The cathedral both embodied the presence of the Baroque in colonial Mexico and encouraged the spread of this architectural style throughout the rest of the city over the next two centuries.

At the same time, the inauguration and dedication of the cathedral helped to solidify the city's role as the capital of colonial Mexico, a position that had been somewhat precarious since the disastrous flood of 1629.

Moreover, the Catholic Church had been both an intrusive and a controversial presence in the social and political life of Mexicans since its introduction to the New World in the sixteenth century, stretching its arms into areas ranging from the establishment of governing clergy to the codification of marriage laws. Thus, the cathedral's dedication in 1667 reaffirmed, in both symbolic and practical terms, the continuation of the Church's influence in daily life.

—*Joseph M. Ortiz*

FURTHER READING

Baird, Joseph A. *The Churches of Mexico, 1530-1810*. Berkeley: University of California Press, 1962. A concise history of the major churches and cathedrals in Mexico, with attention paid to historical context, major architects, and architectural details. Several photographs, biographies of architects, a glossary, and a bibliography.

Leonard, Irving A. *Baroque Times in Old Mexico: Seventeenth-Century Persons, Places, and Practices*. Ann Arbor: University of Michigan Press, 1959. A lucid account of the social and cultural life of colonial Mexico, with much attention paid to religious and cultural institutions in Mexico City during the period. Bibliography.

Schwaller, John F., ed. *The Church in Colonial Latin America*. Wilmington, Del.: Scholarly Resources, 2000. A collection of essays on the role of the Catholic Church in seventeenth century Mexico, dealing with the Church's influence on political and social institutions (such as marriage), as well as the ritualization of religious practices and ceremonies in specific locations, such as the church in Mexico City. Suggested readings, bibliography.

Weismann, Elizabeth Wilder, and Judith Hancock Sandoval. *Art and Time in Mexico from the Conquest to the Revolution*. New York: Harper & Row, 1995. A well-illustrated book on colonial architecture in Mexico, with a chapter devoted to the cathedrals that were built in the sixteenth and seventeenth centuries. Several photographs, bibliography.

SEE ALSO: 1604-1680: Rise of Criollo Identity in Mexico; 1648: Cult of the Virgin of Guadalupe.

RELATED ARTICLE in *Great Lives from History: The Seventeenth Century, 1601-1700:* Sor Juana Inés de la Cruz.

1667
MILTON PUBLISHES *PARADISE LOST*

John Milton published Paradise Lost, *arguably the greatest epic poem in English. The poem justified the ways of God philosophically, and it enriched the body of Christian literature with detailed descriptions of the Fall, Heaven, and Hell. It has since been adopted by poets and readers as a key text in the struggle for human liberty.*

LOCALE: England
CATEGORY: Literature

KEY FIGURE

John Milton (1608-1674), English poet and pamphleteer

SUMMARY OF EVENT

John Milton's epic poem *Paradise Lost* (1667, 1674) was published in ten books in its first edition and in twelve books in its second edition. The poem's composition may have begun as early as the 1650's and was based on an outline conceived sometime near 1640. Milton initially conceived of his work as a sacred drama modeled on Greek classical tragedy, and his final version contains long speeches reminiscent of soliloquies in Elizabethan plays.

Paradise Lost was the product of Milton's long career of dissent. He disliked the ritualism of the Church of England, giving up his plan to become a minister and resolving to be a poet. In 1639, he supported the attempts of Presbyterians to reform the Church of England and published several pamphlets on the reformation of England and its church. He gradually broke away from the Presbyterians and took a more radical stand, writing that subjects had the right to depose and execute an unworthy king. He was a defender of Oliver Cromwell, whose Puritan followers beheaded Charles I in 1649 and had Cromwell declared lord protector of England in 1653. A member of Cromwell's government, Milton went into hiding after the restoration of King Charles II in 1660. Emerging when a general amnesty was declared, Milton lived quietly in the years during which he produced his

Milton dictates Paradise Lost *to his daughter*. (R. S. Peale and J. A. Hill)

most important poem—often considered the greatest epic in modern literature.

Milton based his masterpiece on the Bible and on the subsequent commentary by the Catholic Church fathers and by Protestant theologians. Also important was his reading of classical writers, especially Homer and Virgil, who established the epic form that Milton emulated. Other sources include Edmund Spenser's *The Faerie Queene* (1590, 1596), Ludovico Ariosto's *Orlando furioso* (1516, 1521, 1532; English translation, 1591), and Torquato Tasso's *Gerusalemme liberata* (1581; *Jerusalem Delivered*, 1600). Indeed, part of the distinction of *Paradise Lost* is its simultaneous embodiment of both seventeenth century European and classical learning.

The poem centers on Satan's rebellion against God. Out of this transgression of divine law, the universe was created and the Garden of Eden spoiled. The genesis of human nature was to be found in this prelapsarian world (world before the Fall), and Milton's great object was to elaborate the idea of the *felix culpa*, or fortunate Fall, a doctrine in which the Fall from Eden was part of God's great plan, because it was necessary to realize the potential both of humanity and of the larger Creation. Milton saw human beings as challenged by the Fall to transcend their corruption and the burden of mortality that Original Sin had imposed upon them.

Paradise Lost is not only a religious poem, however. The contest between Satan and God and their battle for humankind's soul reflect Milton's own concerns about the nature of power, of government, and of social relationships. His poem was created in the aftermath of the English Civil Wars and the restoration of the monarchy. In Milton's mind, religion and politics were inseparable. In both the political and religious realms, he felt pressed to argue for the concept of just authority.

As a republican who opposed the monarchy and believed in representative government, Milton created characters who reason and debate rather than simply purvey received wisdom. Ideas in *Paradise Lost* are conceived through the exchange of free minds and are not justified by the concept of authority alone. Indeed, this spirited language of dissent prompts some readers to view the poem as an allegory of events in mid-seventeenth century England.

SATAN'S FIRST GLIMPSE OF ADAM AND EVE

Milton's Paradise Lost *skillfully depicts both the awe and the hatred felt by Satan for humankind, emphasizing that the envy that motivates his seduction of Eve is rooted in his recognition of the grandeur and dignity of one of God's greatest creations. Reproduced below is the initial description of Adam and Eve, seen for the first time through the eyes of the fallen angel.*

Two of far nobler shape erect and tall,
Godlike erect, with native Honor clad
in naked Majesty seem'd, for in thir looks Divine
The image of thir glorious Maker shone,
Truth, Wisdom, Sanctitude severe and pure,
Severe, but in true filial freedom plac't;
Whence true autority in men; though both
Not equal, as thir sex not equal seem'd;
For contemplation hee and valor form'd,
For softness shee and sweet attractive Grace,
Hee for God only, Shee for God in him:
His fair large Front and Eye sublime declar'd
Absolute rule; and Hyacinthine Locks
Round from his parted forelock manly hung
Clust'ring, but not beneath his shoulders broad:
Shee as a veil down to the slender waist
Her unadorned golden tresses wore
Dishevell'd, but in wanton ringlets wav'd
As the Vine curls her tendrils, which impli'd
Subjection, but requir'd with gentle sway,
And by her yielded, by him best receiv'd,
Yielded with coy submission, modest pride,
And sweet reluctant amorous delay.

Source: From *Paradise Lost*, by John Milton. In *John Milton: Complete Poems amd Major Prose*, edited by Merritt Y. Hughes (Indianapolis: Odyssey Press, 1957), book 4, lines 288-311.

Reason, free will, and predestination—as well as God's decision to send his only Son to redeem humankind—are debated by Adam, the angel Raphael, and Christ. In spite of Raphael's careful explanations, Adam and Eve yield to Satan's temptation, and the last third of the poem concerns their repentance and quest to establish "a Paradise within," as they are banished from their perfect garden. This event is what Milton terms fortunate, for out of the pain and sorrow of this lapse, human beings struggle with good and evil, enlarging their souls even as they continue to battle their sinful natures.

SIGNIFICANCE

Paradise Lost has been treated as the repository of English tradition, a great poem that stands on the merits of its brilliant blank verse, the extraordinary characterization of Satan, and the high quality of its drama and intellectual disputation. Satan is revealed as a great field general, mustering his troops, defying God's central authority, establishing his own kingdom in Hell, and seducing humankind to his manic and ambitious project. Endowing this supernatural figure with a very human personality made evil a compelling, intimate reality that readers of all generations have found fascinating, if troubling.

Seventeenth and eighteenth century readers admired the sheer genius of Milton's architectonic poem, the way he structured his arguments and boldly retold biblical passages as narrative, bringing key episodes to the climaxes associated with classical drama, yet later critics such as Joseph Addison and Samuel Johnson viewed Milton's achievement warily, becoming somewhat disturbed by the force of Satan's subversive arguments, which coursed through the poem in a way that threatened to overturn its pious purpose. Romantic readers fastened on precisely this insurgent quality, fascinated with Satan as the questing Romantic hero, opposed to the status quo and boldly pursuing a new world of his own making. For poets such as William Blake, William Wordsworth, Percy Bysshe Shelley, and John Keats, *Paradise Lost* became a touchstone, exemplifying the individual's quest for distinction and his or her right to challenge the status quo. Unlike their predecessors, the Romantics did not shy away from the suspicion that Satan, not God, was the center of the poem. This emphasis tended to overlook Satan's self-destructive and antisocial aspects, however.

Twentieth century commentators expressed widely differing views as to the nature and the quality of the poem. One group found it excessively abstract, for all its drama and moments of narrative drive. Another group defended the work's integrity and the unity of Milton's poetic and political themes, restoring a reading of the poem close to Milton's own. A still later generation of critics explored Milton's belief in patriarchal authority, challenging his creation from feminist and Marxist standpoints. Psychoanalytic critics have examined the poem's characters, finding that Milton employs an extraordinarily sophisticated psychology that repays repeated readings.

In many respects, *Paradise Lost* remains what it was on its first day of publication, a contentious and capacious work that invites contrary interpretations and fierce debates. The poem's great stature derives from its dialectic structure and story line. It is, in sum, an engine of argument, an intense series of exchanges about the nature of the universe, the existence of God, the quality of human nature, and the power of poetry to embody a universal vision.

Paradise Lost has been called an "open text," whose meaning accrues with each generation's interpretations. Although Milton's own politics and personality clearly infuse his work, his employment of language and issues of identity rivals Shakespeare's poetry as a constantly moving vehicle of expression that continues to generate alternative readings.

—*Carl Rollyson*

FURTHER READING

Bloom, Harold, ed. *John Milton: Modern Critical Views*. New York: Chelsea House, 1986. Contains several essays on *Paradise Lost* with extensive index entries, chronology, and bibliography. Bloom's introduction is an excellent introduction to the poem and its background.

Danielson, Dennis, ed. *The Cambridge Companion to Milton*. New York: Cambridge University Press, 1989. Essays on Milton's epic style, use of language, theology, his treatment of Satan, and his treatment of women. Illustrations and index.

Davies, Stevie. *Milton: New Readings*. New York: St. Martin's Press, 1991. A detailed discussion of the process of reading *Paradise Lost*. Includes notes, chronology, and bibliography.

Hill, Christopher. *Milton and the English Revolution*. New York: Viking Press, 1977. A classic study, especially fine on the development of Milton's politics, his interpretation of Christian doctrine, and his use of history, myth, and allegory in *Paradise Lost*. Extensive notes and bibliography.

Lewalski, Barbara Kiefer. *The Life of John Milton: A Critical Biography*. Malden, Mass.: Blackwell, 2002. Recounts Milton's life and career, focusing on how he developed his ideas and art. Lewalski demonstrates how Milton invented himself as a new kind of author with radical politics, reformist poetry, and a prophetic voice. Detailed notes, bibliography, and index.

Miller, David M. *John Milton: Poetry*. Boston: Twayne, 1978. Highly recommended as an introduction to Milton's life, times, and major poems. Includes chronology, notes, and selected bibliography.

Milton, John. *Complete Poems and Major Prose*. Edited by Merritt Y. Hughes. New York: Macmillan, 1957. The best and most comprehensive one-volume edition of Milton's work, with very detailed notes.

SEE ALSO: c. 1601-1613: Shakespeare Produces His Later Plays; 1642-1651: English Civil Wars; Dec. 6, 1648-May 19, 1649: Establishment of the English Commonwealth; Dec. 16, 1653-Sept. 3, 1658: Cromwell Rules England as Lord Protector; May, 1659-May, 1660: Restoration of Charles II.

RELATED ARTICLES in *Great Lives from History: The Seventeenth Century, 1601-1700:* Charles I; Charles II (of England); Oliver Cromwell; John Milton.

1667
PUFENDORF ADVOCATES A UNIFIED GERMANY

Samuel von Pufendorf argued that the Holy Roman Empire and its territorial states were inherently unstable because of the absence of a unified sovereignty—even the Holy Roman Emperor had limited actual power. Pufendorf called for replacing this instability with a strong German state specifically—an absolute monarchy.

LOCALE: Holy Roman Empire of the German Nation (now in Germany)
CATEGORIES: Government and politics; philosophy

KEY FIGURES

Samuel von Pufendorf (1632-1694), German political and legal philosopher and historian
Karl Ludwig (1617-1680), elector of the Palatinate, r. 1648-1680

SUMMARY OF EVENT

The complex political entity called the Holy Roman Empire of the German Nation was a unique arrangement that evolved from the Middle Ages as a result of wars, treaties, intrigue, and numerous compromises. Before the Thirty Years' War, the empire encompassed the present-day countries of Germany, the Netherlands, Switzerland, Belgium, the Czech Republic, Austria, parts of France, and northern Italy. The empire was composed of a large number of estates of varying sizes that were mostly governed by kings, princes, or bishops. The empire's titular head, the Holy Roman Emperor, was elected by seven electors, who were rulers of major territories within the empire. The sharing of powers between the emperor and the territorial rulers led to frequent, bitter disagreements, culminating in the destructive Thirty Years' War, which lasted from 1618 to 1648.

The Peace of Westphalia (1648) made a number of important changes in the constitutional structures of the empire. Switzerland and the Netherlands became fully independent nation-states. Elsewhere, the institutional powers of the emperor and the imperial court were diminished, while the territories acquired additional powers, such as the right to enter into treaties. As a result, the territorial governments would develop more and more into sovereign states, thus preventing German-speaking people from forming a single nation-state similar to the models of England and France. The further division of the empire into Catholic and Protestant territories, moreover, meant an end to the medieval notion of the "unity" of Western Christendom under the leadership of the pope and the Holy Roman Emperor.

Before the Thirty Years' War, most German legal scholars—almost all of them employees of the state—had attempted to defend the imperial government by arguing that it corresponded to the categories of government that were found in Aristotle's political philosophy. In order to fit the empire into Aristotelian categories, these legal scholars had emphasized the preponderance of either the monarchical or the aristocratic elements of the constitution. As a result of the suffering and destruction of the war, however, it was probably inevitable that many German intellectuals would find such an approach less than persuasive and conclude that the Holy Roman Empire was in need of structural change. Samuel von Pufendorf was one of the major political philosophers in Germany to emphasize this critical perspective.

During his youth, Pufendorf's personal experiences in the war encouraged him to seek political structures conducive to peace and order. While a student at the University of Leipzig and Jena, he studied Aristotle and other classical writers, and he was influenced even more by the writings of Hugo Grotius and Thomas Hobbes. Like many intellectuals of the century, Pufendorf was greatly impressed with scientific advances, and he came to believe that it was possible to use scientific methods in developing a scientific theory of structural change. Through his philosophical friends, he attracted the interest of the tolerant Calvinist ruler of the Palatinate, Elector Karl Ludwig, to whom he dedicated his first book, on jurisprudence, *Elementorum jurisprudentiae universalis* (1660; English translation, 1929), which attempted to reconcile the theories of Grotius and Hobbes. Also in 1660, the elector appointed Pufendorf to a seat of international law at the University of Heidelberg.

It was at Heidelberg that Pufendorf wrote and published his strong critique of the empire, *De statu imperii Germanici* (1667; *The Present State of Germany*, 1690). Because of the controversial nature of the book, he concealed his identity with the pseudonym Severinus de Monzambano. Arguing that the empire had a unique form of government that did not fit into the traditional categories, even if interpreted loosely, he characterized the empire as "an irregular state-body, much like a monster." He was especially troubled by the lack of an undivided sovereignty in either the emperor or in territorial rulers. He disliked the fact that territorial rulers and estates shared much of the sovereignty over subjects of the empire. In his view, this "irregular constitution of government" was the principle reason that Germany was unable to preserve internal order or defend against external threats.

Pufendorf recommended that Germany should became an absolutist monarchy, as in France under King Louis XIV. If accomplishing this were impossible, he suggested that the second-best option was the breakup of the empire into fully independent and sovereign states. He recognized, however, that it would take many years for either of these changes to take place.

Meanwhile, in order to maintain peace and stability under the status quo, Pufendorf insisted that it was essential to safeguard the legal rights of all members of the empire. Although his constitutional theories were highly abstract, he tried to examine the ways in which constitutional structures actually operated in practice—a perspective usually missing in other political philosophers of the time.

Although he shared many of Hobbes's views about the need for a unified sovereignty, he believed that rulers had an obligation to defend the well-being of their subjects. Anticipating several ideas of John Locke, Pufendorf defined the purpose of the state in terms of natural law and asserted that individuals possessed natural rights and liberties. A pious Lutheran, he believed that principles of natural law were established by God, the divine lawgiver. Unlike Locke, he located the full sovereignty of the state in the ruler and failed to recognize that enforcement of individual rights required parliamentary or judicial institutions. Pufendorf insisted on the rights of subjects, but he greatly minimized the strong tendency of absolutist regimes to violate these rights.

Samuel von Pufendorf. (Library of Congress)

Apparently, Pufendorf's authorship of *De statu imperii Germanici* was widely known, and it provoked a considerable amount of unpleasant controversy. In 1667, when Charles XI of Sweden offered him a full professorship in law at the University of Lund, he quickly accepted, and he would live in Sweden for the next eighteen years. Pufendorf indicated no sense of regret about living in a non-German speaking country, for he followed the supranational Humanist tradition of seeking an appreciative patron wherever he might be located. Even when advocating German unification, Pufendorf appeared to lack a sense of German patriotism.

In his later writings, Pufendorf formulated a complex variant of "enlightened absolutism," sometimes called "natural-law absolutism," which insisted on the absolutist leader's duty to respect natural rights and liberties. His most esteemed work, *De jure naturae et gentium* (1672; *Of the Law of Nature and Nations*, 1703), is an encyclopedic study of law, which includes the theory that human sociality is based on a sense of natural justice implanted in the hearts of all humanity by God. A condensed version for the general reading public was published as *De officio hominis et civis juxta legem naturalem* (1673; *The Whole Duty of Man According to the Law of Nature*, 1691).

His next work was a 33-volume history of Sweden, which is not often read but is praised for its factual precision. His two-volume study of comparative history, *Einleitung zu der Historie des vornehmsten Reiche und Staaten* (1682; *An Introduction to the History of the Principal Kingdoms and States of Europe*, 1697), further clarified his arguments in favor of a unified sovereignty for Germany. Soon thereafter, when reacting to Louis XIV's policy of religious intolerance, he wrote a book advocating a separation between religion and the state.

SIGNIFICANCE

The developments of the next two centuries would confirm much of Pufendorf's position on the structural weakness of the Holy Roman Empire of the German Nation. Unable to evolve into a viable nation-state, the empire continued to deteriorate until it was finally dissolved by Napoleon in 1806. Pufendorf, however, underestimated the ability of the territorial units of the empire—such as Brandenburg-Prussia, Bavaria, and Baden—to develop into powerful states. Reflecting the experiences of his age, it is not surprising that Pufendorf greatly underestimated the adaptability of federalism and failed to see its advantages for large heterogeneous populations.

Pufendorf's political writings anticipated many of the ideas and values of the Enlightenment of the next century. He is recognized as one of the earliest German proponents of enlightened absolutism, which relied on the conscience of leaders to protect individual rights and liberties. Some historians, including John Gagliardo, argue that Pufendorf was the first major theorist of German public law to analyze the Holy Roman Empire from a historical and descriptive approach. Previous theorists had been so preoccupied with the categories of classical Aristotelian politics that they had tended to ignore the realities of the imperial government in practice.

—*Thomas Tandy Lewis*

FURTHER READING

Carr, Craig. *Political Writings of Samuel Pufendorf.* New York: Oxford University Press, 1994. The editor's introduction to this collection provides a useful summary of Pufendorf's mature views on natural law, sovereignty, and absolutism.

Dufour, Alfred. "Pufendorf." In *The Cambridge History of Political Thought, 1450-1700*, edited by Jimmy H. Burns and Mark Goldie. New York: Cambridge University Press, 1991. A good analysis of Pufendorf's theories about government and natural law.

Gaglilardo, John. *Reich and Nation: The Holy Roman Empire as Idea and Reality, 1763-1806.* Bloomington: Indiana University Press, 1980. A useful account of the constitutional history of the empire, emphasizing Pufendorf's historical approach, which looked at how the empire operated in practice.

Haakonssen, Knud, ed. *Grotius, Pufendorf, and Modern Natural Law.* Brookfield, Vt.: Ashgate, 1999. This work discusses various aspects of Pufendorf's philosophy, including his ideas on the modern state and human rights, and an analysis of his place in the history of ethics.

Hunter, Ian. *Rival Enlightenments: Civil and Metaphysical Philosophy in Early Modern Germany.* New York: Cambridge University Press, 2001. Asserts that Pufendorf's civil philosophy was fundamentally different from the metaphysical approaches of philosophers Gottfried Wilhelm Leibniz and Immanuel Kant.

Krieger, Leonard. *The German Idea of Freedom: History of a Political Tradition.* Boston: Beacon Press, 1957. Krieger argues that Pufendorf was a proponent of a limited form of absolutism, which he calls "natural-law absolutism."

Schneewind, Jerome. *The Invention of Autonomy: A History of Modern Moral Philosophy.* New York: Cambridge University Press, 1997. A scholarly survey that views Pufendorf as a pivotal moral philosopher on the way to Kant's theory of autonomy.

SEE ALSO: 1618-1648: Thirty Years' War; 1630-1648: Destruction of Bavaria; 1640-1688: Reign of Frederick William, the Great Elector; July, 1643-Oct. 24, 1648: Peace of Westphalia; 1661: Absolute Monarchy Emerges in France.

RELATED ARTICLES in *Great Lives from History: The Seventeenth Century, 1601-1700:* Frederick William, the Great Elector; Leopold I; Samuel von Pufendorf; Friedrich Hermann Schomberg.

April, 1667-June, 1671

Razin Leads Peasant Uprising in Russia

Don Cossack leader Stenka Razin led one of the largest and most brutal peasant and Cossack rebellions against serfdom in Russian history. The rebellions ended with the brutal—and spectacular—deaths of Razin and countless followers. Razin remains a part of Russian and Ukrainian folklore.

Locale: Russia and Ukraine
Categories: Wars, uprisings, and civil unrest; social issues and reform

Key Figures

Stenka Razin (c. 1630-1671), a leader of the Don Cossacks
Alexis (1629-1676), czar of Russia, r. 1645-1676

Summary of Event

The Stenka Razin rebellion, an important peasant and Cossack uprising, became one of the legendary events (along with the later Pugachev uprising in 1773-1774) of popular resistance to serfdom. The Cossacks, whose name comes from the Turkic term meaning free warriors, appeared primarily in the sixteenth century as frontier warriors fighting the Tatars in southern Russia (now called the Ukraine, or the borderland). Living as free men and warriors, the Cossacks settled along the Dnieper, Don, and Volga Rivers and attracted slaves and peasants fleeing serfdom.

The Dnieper Cossacks, or Zaporozhe Host (Beyond the Cataracts Host), established a fortified camp (*sich*) on Khortitsa Island and chose its leaders (*hetman*) in an assembly (*rada*). The Don Cossacks were also concentrated on an island fortress—Cherkassk, and chose a leader, the *ataman*, during an assembly (*krug*). The Cossacks generally disliked agriculture because they associated it with serfdom.

The Cossacks had an uneasy relationship with both the Polish and Russian governments. While they valued their independence, many Cossacks entered into Polish or Russian service. Dnieper Cossacks who served the Polish government were called "registered Cossacks." The Russian government relied upon the Don Cossacks for military support against the Crimean Tatars and paid the Cossacks an annual subsidy (*zhalovanie*) in coin and kind. As thousands of Russian peasants and slaves fled to the Don (between 1645 and 1670, the population rose to twenty-five thousand), the Don Cossacks split into two major groups. The older community, which was located "downstream" and controlled the best fishing and hunting areas, dominated the assemblies. Its members received Muscovite subsidies and grain. The newer refugees, known as the "upstream" or "naked ones," could not enter the assemblies and were denied the best fisheries and hunting territories. The "naked ones" were a volatile group and quickly joined Razin, but the split between "upstream" and "downstream" Cossacks would prove fatal to Razin's rebellion, as the older, more traditional Cossacks remained loyal to Moscow.

The spread of Russian serfdom was a major cause of Razin's rebellion. During the Time of Troubles (1598-1613), an earlier Cossack rebellion led by Ivan Bolotnikov (1606-1607) almost toppled the government. Serfdom was fully legalized in the 1649 law code (Ulozhenie). The Thirteen Years' War (1654-1667) between Russia and Poland devastated Ukraine. By 1667, perhaps as much as one-fifth of the Ukrainian population had perished from war, famine, and plague. The debasement of Russian coinage caused the 1662 Copper Riot and resulted in the torture and exile of hundreds from Moscow. Many peasants refused to pay their taxes and would run off to the borderlands. At the same time, the 1666 Church Council irrevocably split the church into one of Orthodoxy and one of dissident Old Believers. Czar Alexis was confronted with the Razin rebellion when the government was recovering from war and trying to bring order to the church.

Razin was from an old established Cossack family near Cherkassk. As a "downstream" Cossack he participated in a delegation to Moscow to discuss the annual subsidy. Like many other Cossacks, he traveled to the Solovetsky monastery in the White Sea to pray at the shrines of Saints Savva and Zosima. It is not clear why Razin rebelled and championed the poorer "upstream" Cossacks, but rebellion ran in his family. His brother and uncle led rebel brigades, and his mother was executed during the uprising. There is also a tale about the Russian execution of another brother, which may explain a motive of vengeance. Razin was noted for his drinking and violent temper, but he also was charismatic, courageous, and appeared possessed of magical qualities.

As he robbed merchants on the lower Volga, Razin, somewhat in "Robin Hood" fashion, is said to have promised freedom and safety to those who joined him. What may have begun as simple pirating soon mushroomed into open rebellion. Russian troops sent against him either were defeated or defected. From the spring of 1668 to the summer of 1669, Razin continued to raid the area around the Caspian Sea and even defeated—although with high casualties—a Persian fleet. Razin acquired an aura of invincibility. Passing safely through Astrakhan and Tsaritsyn (now Volgograd) on the lower Volga River, he reached the Don with a growing reputation. In a year of grain shortages and diminished subsidies, Razin's followers rapidly grew. Impressed perhaps by the weaknesses of the Russian government in Astrakhan and Tsaritsyn, Razin was joined by hundreds of Dnieper Cossacks and raised the banner of rebellion, perhaps hoping to gain control of the lower Volga. He always expressed his loyalty to Czar Alexis but he called for the removal of treasonous nobles (boyars), the restoration of the subsidy, and freedom for slaves and serfs.

The Cossacks took Tsaritsyn, brutally killing its defenders. For several weeks, they plundered noble and merchant homes. Rather than march north, Razin turned south toward Astrakhan. Many of the town garrison troops (*streltsy*) suffered from inadequate and infrequent pay. They often proved untrustworthy and opened their towns to the Cossacks. In 1669, Razin and some ten thousand followers approached Astrakhan, a center of salt production and Moscow's major trade entry point to Persia. The defending *streltsy* were unreliable, and the city fell to Razin. He governed through Cossack assemblies, looted churches and homes, and tortured and murdered government and military officials.

In the summer of 1670, Razin proceeded up the Volga and took Saratov and Samara (Kuybyshev) without a struggle as poor townsfolk and *streltsy*, greeting him with the traditional welcome of bread and salt, opened the gates. Russian administration was replaced by Cossack assemblies, officials were executed, prisoners were released from jails, and tax records were destroyed. Proclamations (so-called seditious letters) written by lower clergy, who lent a religious fervor to the rebellion, called for the deaths of the "bloodsuckers" of the peasantry; thousands responded, burning manor homes. Landlords, who fled to the towns, were killed by Cossacks or townsmen. Some Finnish tribesmen, fearing further loss of their autonomy and resenting forced Christianization and the confiscation of their lands, joined the rebellion.

Yet Turkic tribes—often rivals to the Cossacks—held back or participated with token numbers. The bulk of Razin's followers consisted of Cossacks, peasants, poor townsfolk, vagrants, convicts, and *streltsy*. Women played an important role as well, sometimes leading rebel troops. Razin was seen as a deliverer, a messiah—one who was the true "father" of his people. Using these beliefs, he put forward a claimant to the throne—the dead son of Alexis, Czarevich Alexis Alekseevich, now "miraculously" still alive and in Razin's camp. He also had an imposter posing for the ousted Patriarch Nikon, whom Razin cast as an opponent of the boyars. This strategy may have alienated Razin from many Old Believers, who opposed Nikon's church reforms.

Significance

By September, 1670, Razin's followers numbered some twenty thousand, but they were undisciplined and given to looting and acts of vengeance. The government called upon seasoned and well-equipped troops to return from the war in Poland. While Razin besieged Simbirsk, other Cossack detachments took a number of towns and spread the revolt throughout the middle Volga. Simbirsk was defended by loyal troops, however, and was strengthened by reinforcements and superior artillery and cavalry. Razin was wounded in the head and leg and almost killed. Hundreds of Cossacks were captured and then hanged, shot, or quartered. Simbirsk (Ulianovsk) was the turning point in the rebellion. Pitched battles continued into the winter of 1670-1671, but the Cossack army dwindled as tens of thousands suffered brutal repressions. The methods of government executions defy description: impalement, quartering, disemboweling, beheading, tearing by flesh hooks. Hanging was the simplest of deaths. Bodies and amputated limbs hung on hooks. Whole villages were burned and decimated.

Razin eventually made his way back to his fortress, Kagalnik Island, on the Don. In April, 1671, the "downstream" Cossacks captured the fortress and turned Razin and his brother over to the Russians. Razin was brought to Moscow, personally questioned by the czar, and tortured. Razin's limbs were pulled out of joint, his body burned with a hot iron, and he was beaten with a knout (a flogging whip). On June 16, 1671, in Red Square, he was quartered, his head and limbs were mounted on stakes, and his body was thrown to dogs. His mother and uncle were also executed, while his brother was killed years later after Czar Alexis's death.

Legends and songs of Razin's rebellion became part of a traditional folklore of Russian and Cossack peasant resistance, and there are many landmarks in his name along the Volga. Also, a stirring symphonic poem, *Stenka Razin* (1885), by Russian composer Aleksandr

Konstantinovich Glazunov (1865-1936), is a musical memorial to his turbulent life.

—*Lawrence N. Langer*

Further Reading

Avrich, Paul. *Russian Rebels, 1600-1800*. New York: W. W. Norton, 1972. The best analysis available in English of Razin and of other Cossack rebellions.

Gordon, Linda. *Cossack Rebellions: Social Turmoil in Sixteenth-Century Ukraine*. Albany: State University of New York Press, 1983. A history of Cossack rebellions and their social consequences.

Longworth, Philip. *Alexis: Tsar of All the Russias*. London: Franklin Watts, 1981. A basic history of the reign of Alexis.

_______. *The Cossacks*. New York: Holt, Rinehart, and Winston, 1970. A good, well-documented historical introduction to the Cossacks.

O'Brien, C. B. *Muscovy and the Ukraine: From the Pereiaslavl Agreement to the Truce of Andrusovo, 1654-1667*. University of California Publications in History 74. Berkeley: University of California Press, 1963. A study of war and diplomacy in Ukraine prior to the Razin rebellion.

Ure, John. *The Cossacks: An Illustrated History*. Woodstock, N.Y.: Overlook Press, 2002. This illustrated text includes information about Razin's rebellion.

Vernadsky, George. *The Tsardom of Moscow, 1547-1682*. New Haven, Conn.: Yale University Press, 1969. Volume 5 of Vernadsky's *A History of Russia*. A standard history by a Russian-born, American historian, supplemented with maps, an extensive bibliography, and a glossary of Russian terms.

See also: Jan. 29, 1649: Codification of Russian Serfdom; July 10, 1655-June 21, 1661: First Northern War; 1672-c. 1691: Self-Immolation of the Old Believers; Summer, 1672-Fall, 1676: Ottoman-Polish Wars; 1677-1681: Ottoman-Muscovite Wars.

Related articles in *Great Lives from History: The Seventeenth Century, 1601-1700:* Alexis; Nikon; Stenka Razin; Michael Romanov; Sophia.

May 24, 1667-May 2, 1668
War of Devolution

Determined to expand France's boundaries north and east, King Louis XIV used an ancient legal inheritance statute as a pretext for attacking the Spanish Netherlands and Franche-Comté. Though successful militarily, the French saw their full ambitions stymied by the Triple Alliance of 1668 and had to surrender most of their gains in the Treaty of Aix-la-Chapelle.

Locale: Spanish Netherlands (now Belgium); Franche-Comté province (now in France)

Categories: Wars, uprisings, and civil unrest; diplomacy and international relations; expansion and land acquisition

Key Figures

Louis XIV (1638-1715), king of France, r. 1643-1715

Marie-Thérèse (1638-1683), queen consort of France, r. 1660-1683, and daughter of King Philip IV of Spain

François-Michel Le Tellier (1639-1691), marquis de Louvois, French minister of war

Hugues de Lionne (1611-1671), French foreign minister

Sir William Temple (1628-1699), English diplomat

Johan de Witt (1625-1672), grand pensionary of the United Provinces, 1653-1672

Charles II (1630-1685), king of England, r. 1660-1685

Leopold I (1640-1705), Holy Roman Emperor, r. 1658-1705

Viscount de Turenne (Henri de La Tour d'Auvergne; 1611-1675), marshal general of France

The Great Condé (Louis II de Bourbon; 1621-1686), cousin to Louis XIV, marshal of France

Summary of Event

King Louis XIV likely was never really in love with his wife, Marie-Thérèse, daughter of King Philip IV of Spain. The marriage had been arranged during his minority by Queen Mother Anne of Austria and Chief Minister Jules Mazarin for diplomatic and political reasons, and King Louis (who really was in love with Marie Mancini, Mazarin's niece) considered it to be little more than part of his dynastic duty. However, upon Philip IV's death in 1665, the French saw the opportunity to exploit his marriage to Marie-Thérèse to expand France's boundaries.

The legal concept of "devolution" became the crux of Louis XIV's claims to territories administered under the Spanish crown. Lawyers for the French court argued that the inheritance laws of Brabant, and some of the other provinces of the Spanish Netherlands (modern Belgium) and Franche-Comté specified that any children of a first marriage (including daughters) took precedence over children of any subsequent marriage (even over males). The French advocates submitted to the Spanish Council of Regency that the successor to Philip IV, the child-king Charles II, was the child of Philip's second marriage, to his cousin Mariana de Austria. On the other hand, the infanta (heir) Marie-Thérèse was the eldest daughter of Philip IV through his first marriage to Isabella (Elizabeth) of France; and therefore, even though Charles II was entitled to rule Spain under the inheritance laws of that country, Spanish possessions in the Netherlands should rightfully fall to Marie-Thérèse (and, in effect, to Louis XIV) under the statutes of devolution. When the regents rejected the idea, Louis XIV began making plans for war against Spain.

France believed it was necessary to neutralize England, which had a long history of interest and involvement in the Spanish Netherlands. The Stuart king, Charles II, was secretly given a subsidy by Louis, in return for a pledge of noninvolvement, good for one year. The new war minister, François-Michel Le Tellier, had been organizing and equipping a massive army, which Louis deployed along the northern border with the Spanish Netherlands, and placed it under the command of his most accomplished marshal, Henri de La Tour d'Auvergne, Turenne. On May 24, 1667, Turenne, with King Louis riding alongside, crossed the border and encountered little effective resistance. Overrunning the provinces of Flanders and Hainault, French forces saw major fighting only at the city of Lille, which was besieged by Turenne from September 16 to September 26 1667, when it was finally taken by storm.

The phenomenal success of the French army, however, began to alarm Johan de Witt, grand pensionary for the Netherlands. Notwithstanding that the Dutch were at that time engaged in war with England and that Louis XIV had been providing them material assistance, the sudden collapse of Spain in the southern Netherlands meant that there was a genuine potential that the buffer between France and Holland would disappear and that de Witt's country would have the powerful Bourbon state as its neighbor. To prevent this, de Witt heightened efforts to end the Anglo-Dutch conflict.

England's king Charles II was himself under pressure from Parliament to take measures to limit growing French influence in the Low Countries, and his secret deal with Louis XIV was soon to expire. Taking the politically pragmatic approach, Charles sent Sir William Temple to negotiate with de Witt for an end to the conflict between the Dutch and the English (the Second Anglo-Dutch War), resulting in the Treaty of Breda on July 31, 1667. (The treaty, ironically, also was fostered by Louis's top diplomat, Hugues de Lionne.) Temple was also tasked with determining a course of action with regard to French successes against the Spanish. On January 23, 1668, the Dutch pensionary had forged the Triple (Grand) Alliance between the United Provinces, England, and Sweden, which had entered into the agreement in return for secretly receiving Dutch subsidies. All was carried under such tight confidentiality that Louis XIV was totally unaware of the extent to which opposition was building against his schemes. At this stage, too, the allied countries limited themselves to rather mild statements urging cessation of hostilities and a negotiated settlement.

In early 1668, King Louis decided to expand hostilities to Spanish Franche-Comté, entrusting this attack to his next leading marshal, Louis II, the Great Condé. Condé's army entered the province in February, 1668, and Spanish resistance there proved even more futile: In two weeks, the French were in total control. At this juncture, however, the states of the Triple Alliance assumed a less moderate posture and implied that they might intervene militarily on the Spanish side if the war continued. Taken aback, Louis deeply resented this turn of events but, since Holy Roman Emperor Leopold I had secretly given him assurances that the Spanish Empire would be divided between them after the death of Charles II, the French king agreed to come to the peace table.

Deliberations were carried forward during March and April, with de Lionne and Temple assuming prominent roles, and resulted in the signing of the Treaty of Aix-la-Chapelle on May 2, 1668. Under the terms of the agreement, the French army withdrew from Franche-Comté (fortifications there were demolished and the province was effectively demilitarized), and gave back certain towns and territories in Flanders and Hainault, notably Cambrai and Saint-Omer. The French were allowed to keep and garrison Lille, Oudenarde, Tournai, and nine other cities along their northern frontier.

Significance

Though Louis XIV put Europe on notice that France was willing and able to use its overwhelming military might as a foreign policy instrument, he received his first major international setback. The Triple Alliance of 1668 was a harbinger of the coalitions that would be forged during the course of the next forty-five years as a counterbalance to Louis's territorial ambitions. In the short term, Louis was so indignant at what he perceived as ingratitude and treachery on the part of the Dutch government that he set about to diplomatically isolate the United Provinces in order to set up a massive military campaign there. The end result was the outbreak of the French-Dutch War of 1672-1678.

—*Raymond Pierre Hylton*

FURTHER READING

Doyle, William. *Old Regime France, 1648-1788*. New York: Oxford University Press, 2001. This is a helpful volume that places the war into its overall context. The work is one of the few sources that sets forth the significance of Leopold I's secret proposal.

Goubert, Pierre. *Louis XIV and Twenty Million Frenchmen*. New York: Vintage Books, 1972. Goubert gives a good though somewhat limited outline of the events leading up to the conflict. He concentrates, however, on the overall, long-term effects.

Lossky, Andrew. *Louis XIV and the French Monarchy*. New Brunswick, N.J.: Princeton University Press, 1994. Lossky explains in detail the legal concept of devolution and its implications for French policy.

Lynn, John A. *The Wars of Louis XIV*. New York: Longman, 1999. In spite of the diplomatic setback, the War of Devolution is considered by the author to be one of Louis XIV's more successful endeavors.

Wolf, John B. *Toward a European Balance of Power, 1620-1715*. Chicago: Rand McNally, 1970. Wolf gives a fine, detailed account of the conflict, though he differs with some historians in seeing Sir William Temple as the actual instigator of the Triple Alliance.

SEE ALSO: July 5, 1601-Apr., 1604: Siege of Oostende; Nov. 7, 1659: Treaty of the Pyrenees; 1661: Absolute Monarchy Emerges in France; Mar. 4, 1665-July 31, 1667: Second Anglo-Dutch War; Jan. 23, 1668: Triple Alliance Forms; Feb. 13, 1668: Spain Recognizes Portugal's Independence; Apr. 6, 1672-Aug. 10, 1678: French-Dutch War; Aug. 10, 1678-Sept. 26, 1679: Treaties of Nijmegen; 1689-1697: Wars of the League of Augsburg; Oct. 11, 1698, and Mar. 25, 1700: First and Second Treaties of Partition.

RELATED ARTICLES in *Great Lives from History: The Seventeenth Century, 1601-1700:* Charles II (of England); Charles II (of Spain); Jean-Baptiste Colbert; The Great Condé; Leopold I; Louis XIV; The Mancini Sisters; Marie-Thérèse; Philip IV; Viscount de Turenne; William III.

December 19, 1667
IMPEACHMENT OF CLARENDON

The removal of Clarendon as Charles II's chief adviser left the government of England to a dissolute king intent on attaining absolute power and a set of self-serving, corrupt courtiers, thus setting the stage for the Glorious Revolution of 1688.

LOCALE: England
CATEGORY: Government and politics

KEY FIGURES

First Earl of Clarendon (Edward Hyde; 1609-1674), chief adviser to Charles II and lord chancellor of England, 1658-1667

Charles II (1630-1685), king of England, r. 1660-1685

James, Duke of York and Albany (1633-1701), brother of Charles II and king of England as James II, r. 1685-1688

George Villiers (1628-1687), second duke of Buckingham

Barbara Palmer (née Villiers; 1640-1709), countess of Castlemaine, countess of Southampton, duchess of Cleveland, and a mistress of Charles II

Henry Bennet (1618-1685), first baron Arlington, 1665-1672, Clarendon's successor, and first earl of Arlington, 1672-1685

SUMMARY OF EVENT

The impeachment of Edward Hyde, first earl of Clarendon and England's lord chancellor, was the first step in a concerted action to remove him from power. For some time, powerful enemies at court and in Parliament had been plotting against Clarendon, while King Charles II had grown increasingly annoyed by the chancellor's criticisms of his personal conduct. After the disastrous ending of the Second Anglo-Dutch War in 1667, Charles dismissed Clarendon as lord chancellor, thus leaving the way open for Parliament to proceed with his impeachment.

Impeachment of Clarendon

Edward Hyde had long been one of the advisers of King Charles I. A member of both the Short and Long Parliaments, he was a moderate by nature. Though he was a loyal monarchist, he was also a constitutionalist, and although he was a loyal Anglican, as a statesman he believed that it was wiser to tolerate other faiths than to persecute them. Early on in the constitutional crisis of the 1640's, he had urged the king to consider the demands of Parliament instead of taking high-handed action against that body, but his advice was ignored until it was too late.

In 1645, with England torn by civil war, the king asked Hyde to take young Prince Charles, the heir to the throne, to safety in the west of England. Over the next six years, Hyde and Charles saw each other intermittently, but after his father was beheaded and he was recognized as Charles II, the young king summoned Hyde to Paris, where he become the king's chief adviser, working tirelessly toward a restoration of the Stuart monarchy. Toward that end, he managed to keep Charles from renouncing his Anglican faith and converting to Catholicism, and he encouraged the easy-going king in his antipathy toward religious persecution. Hyde also tried to keep in check Charles's infatuation with the idea of becoming an absolute monarch on the model of the glittering King Louis XIV of France, whom Charles had observed so closely during his impressionable years.

When Charles II returned to England in May, 1660, Hyde was with the new king. Hyde was already lord chancellor, having been appointed two years earlier. However, within the next eleven months, he became chancellor of Oxford, was raised to the peerage as Baron Hyde of Hindon, and was created Viscount Cornbury and earl of Clarendon. For the next seven years, Clarendon, as he was now called, dominated the administration. Unfortunately, in some cases his advice was not heeded. For example, though he pressed for religious toleration, the new Parliament, which was made up of Anglicans, took revenge on the Dissenters with a set of measures that became known as the Clarendon Code, despite the fact that Clarendon himself had opposed such action.

Clarendon tried to dissuade his daughter Anne Hyde from marrying James, duke of York and Albany; however, after they did marry and produced offspring, it was rumored that this was all part of a Machiavellian plan and that Clarendon had deliberately arranged the marriage of Charles to a barren princess so that his own grandchildren would inherit the throne. In fact, the stoutly Anglican Clarendon would have preferred to have Charles marry a Protestant instead of the Catholic Catherine of Braganza.

Edward Hyde, first earl of Clarendon. (R. S. Peale and J. A. Hill)

When Charles found himself in financial difficulties, Clarendon helped to negotiate the sale of Dunkirk to France, but he did not himself profit from the transaction. Nevertheless, the public blamed Clarendon for what they saw as England's humiliation, and in 1665, when Clarendon built a lavish new house in Piccadilly, they called it Dunkirke-house, because, according to the diarist Samuel Pepys, they believed that it was being constructed with bribe-money from the sale of Dunkirk. Others referred to it as Holland-house, having heard that Clarendon had been bribed by the Dutch to stop his nation from attacking them. Clarendon had, indeed, argued against the war, only to be overruled by the duke of York, who had dreams of personal glory and hopes of substantial profits. However, when the Dutch sailed up the Medway to Chatham, set fire to the docks and to three warships, and then towed away the king's flagship, the *Royal Charles*, the British public held Clarendon personally responsible and vandalized his new house.

Meanwhile, Clarendon's enemies at court were working to turn Charles against him. Among them were Charles's beloved sister, Henrietta Maria, who had long blamed Clarendon for blocking an Anglo-French alliance; his mistress Barbara Palmer, the countess of Castlemaine, of whom Clarendon disapproved; and a group of five courtiers led by the mercurial George Villiers, second duke of Buckingham, and including also Henry Bennet, first baron Arlington, who would become Clarendon's replacement as Charles's chief minister. This group was known as the Cabal, since the initials of their names could be arranged to spell that word.

When Clarendon had been threatened with impeachment in 1663, Charles had protected him. Now, however, Charles was tired of being lectured about his behavior. Moreover, he knew that Clarendon's unpopularity both with Parliament and with the public made him an ideal scapegoat. On August 30, 1667, Charles sent a warrant to Clarendon, demanding that he surrender the Great Seal of his office. On November 11, the House of Commons voted to impeach him, though without specific charges, but the House of Lords rejected the motion. While the two branches of Parliament squabbled, Clarendon fled to France. From Calais, he sent a letter to the Lords reiterating his innocence of all charges and making it clear that he left England only to prevent further dissension. On December 18, however, the House of Commons voted to banish Clarendon and to make any communication with him an act of treason; the Lords passed the bill on December 19.

Significance

From the time of the Restoration until his fall, Clarendon was, next to the king, the most powerful man in England. His aims were noble. He wanted Charles to rule over a constitutional monarchy, in which Parliament, the king, and a group of honest public servants would work together for the public good. When Clarendon was overruled, events generally demonstrated that he had been right. However, he was almost always blamed for the very actions he had advised against. With Clarendon gone, his nation entered into a period marked by disorder, disharmony, corruption, and blatant contempt for the constitution, which could well have led to another civil war but instead ended in the bloodless Glorious Revolution.

Ironically, Clarendon's most lasting achievement may well have been not as a statesman but as a historian. During the final seven years of his life, he wrote his memoirs and finished the monumental *The History of the Rebellion and Civil Wars in England* (wr. 1647-c. 1671, pb. 1702-1704), which he had begun two decades before. Clarendon's works continue to be regarded as essential sourcebooks for students of the seventeenth century, valuable not only for their factual content but also for the author's insightful comments about those around him and the times in which they lived.

—*Rosemary M. Canfield Reisman*

Further Reading

Coote, Stephen. *Royal Survivor: The Life of Charles II.* New York: Palgrave, 2001. Clarendon's impeachment is attributed primarily to a cynical, wily king's determination to assert his power. Illustrations, bibliography, and index.

Keeble, N. H. *The Restoration: England in the 1660's.* Malden, Mass.: Blackwell, 2002. In the chapter entitled "Royal Servants: Clarendon and the Cavalier Parliament," the author shows how Clarendon unknowingly played into the hands of his enemies.

Kishlansky, Mark. *A Monarchy Transformed: Britain, 1603-1714.* London: Penguin, 1996. Contends that changes in the concept of the monarchy under the Stuarts made Clarendon's downfall inevitable. Maps, bibliography, and index.

Lee, Maurice, Jr. *The Cabal.* Urbana: University of Illinois Press, 1965. The first chapter of this book explains how Clarendon misunderstood the political climate and the people whose support he needed.

Miller, George. *Edward Hyde, Earl of Clarendon.* Boston: Twayne, 1983. Although this volume in Twayne's English authors series deals primarily with Clarendon's writing, it begins with a useful chapter on Clarendon's life. Chronology, notes, bibliography, and index.

Scott, Jonathan. *England's Troubles: Seventeenth-Century English Political Instability in European Context.* New York: Cambridge University Press, 2000. The author details what he calls the "first phase of the restoration," which was guided by Clarendon.

See also: Nov. 3, 1640-May 15, 1641: Beginning of England's Long Parliament; 1642-1651: English Civil Wars; May, 1659-May, 1660: Restoration of Charles II; 1661-1665: Clarendon Code; Mar. 4, 1665-July 31, 1667: Second Anglo-Dutch War; Nov., 1688-Feb., 1689: The Glorious Revolution.

Related articles in *Great Lives from History: The Seventeenth Century, 1601-1700:* Catherine of Braganza; Charles I; Charles II (of England); First Earl of Clarendon; James II; Louis XIV; Samuel Pepys.

January 23, 1668
Triple Alliance Forms

England, Sweden, and the United Provinces of the Netherlands established an alliance to curb the expansionist policies of French king Louis XIV. The alliance formed specifically to prevent the French from annexing Spanish territory in the Low Countries and the Rhine Valley.

Locale: England, Sweden, the Netherlands, France, Belgium, and Spain

Categories: Diplomacy and international relations; wars, uprisings, and civil unrest; expansion and land acquisition

Key Figures

Charles II (1630-1685), king of England, r. 1660-1685
Charles XI (1655-1697), king of Sweden, r. 1660-1697
Henrietta Anne (1644-1670), duchess of Orléans
Magnus Gabriel De la Gardie (1622-1686), regent of Sweden, r. 1660-1672
Johan de Witt (1625-1672), Dutch diplomat
Christoph Delphicus von Dohna (1628-1668), Dutch-born Swedish diplomat and field marshal
Louis XIV (1638-1715), king of France, r. 1643-1715
Marie-Thérèse (1638-1683), queen consort of France, r. 1660-1683
Philip IV (1605-1665), king of Spain, r. 1621-1665
William of Orange (1650-1702), stadtholder of the Netherlands, r. 1672-1702, and king of England as William III, r. 1689-1702
Sir William Temple (1628-1699), English-Irish diplomat and author

Summary of Event

Taking advantage of the weakness of central Europe after the Thirty Years' War, French king Louis XIV sought to extend the borders of France into the Rhine valley, the Alps, and the Pyrenees; to stalemate the Habsburg Dynasty in Austria, Spain, the Low Countries, and the Holy Roman Empire; and to restore Roman Catholicism to England. As his religious fervor was often indistinguishable from his political and territorial ambition, he set his sights particularly on Protestant lands.

The Low Countries consisted of the United Provinces of the Netherlands (roughly equivalent to the Netherlands of today) and the Spanish Netherlands, roughly equivalent to today's Belgium. The United Provinces, also called the Dutch Republic, was created by the Peace of Westphalia in 1648, and it struggled to maintain its independence and identity as a Protestant enclave. The region was attractive economically to would-be conquerors because of its position at the mouth of the Rhine River, a major trade route. The river, controlled predominantly by the Catholics, was a buffer between France and the Dutch Republic.

Louis's wife, Marie-Thérèse, was born María Teresa, the daughter of King Philip IV of Spain and his first wife Elizabeth (Isabella). His male heir (the future King Charles II) was by his second wife Mariana de Austria. By the Treaty of the Pyrenees in 1659, which ended twenty-four years of war between France and Spain, and as part of the conditions under which Philip would allow her to marry Louis, Marie-Thérèse renounced all claims to succeed her father in any of his domains. Upon the death of Philip in 1665, Louis alleged that Spain had never paid him the full dowry of 500,000 crowns, so therefore the marriage terms in the Treaty of the Pyrenees were null and void. He invoked an archaic Brabantian law, the *jus devolutionis*, which declared that children of first wives inherit the throne before the children of subsequent wives. On this basis, Louis asserted that the Spanish Netherlands properly belonged to France. When Spain refused to accept this rational, Louis declared war.

French armies invaded the Spanish Netherlands on May 24, 1667, thus starting the War of Devolution. With more than fifty thousand troops against Spanish garrisons totaling only about eight thousand, France easily overran city after city. By the end of the year most of the strategic places in the Spanish Netherlands were in French hands. Early in the new year France began invading Franche-Comté and other Spanish territories along the Rhine. Naturally alarmed, the Dutch Republic appealed to England and Sweden for help.

The Dutch and English had been fighting each other during the Second Anglo-Dutch War from 1665 to 1667. The Treaty of Breda among the Dutch Republic, England, France, and Denmark, which ended that war on July 31, 1667, moderately favored the English, yet the treaty gained significant prestige at home for its Dutch architect, Johan de Witt. The two recent combatants quickly found common ground in their anxiety about what Louis might do to the map of Europe. De Witt and English envoy Sir William Temple concluded an anti-French alliance called the Triple, or Grand, Alliance, on January 23, 1668, amid expectations that Sweden would soon join. In the 1660's, Sweden was the major power in the Baltic region and its support was greatly coveted by any nation making war in northern Europe. Swedish king Charles XI, ruling through his regent Magnus Gabriel De la Gardie, dispatched Christoph Delphicus von Dohna to negotiate with de Witt and Temple. Dohna and Temple concluded their part of the negotiations in early February of 1668 for the treaty that created the Triple Alliance against France.

The crux of the treaty was that the English, Dutch, and Swedes would protect the Dutch Republic by defending the Spanish Netherlands against any French incursion. Sweden entered the alliance on condition that Spain would pay all Swedish troops involved in any ensuing war with France. Spanish diplomats were not involved in the negotiations, and Temple exceeded his authority in agreeing to this condition, but he had sufficient leverage to guarantee it, given that Spain was so keen to check French aggression. Spain agreed in May, 1668, at Temple's insistence, to pay Sweden 480,000 crowns for its part in the alliance, but it took Spain two years to pay.

Louis, apparently wishing to avoid a major war against three Great Powers until all his possible diplomatic schemes had been tried, immediately offered to make peace. He reasoned correctly that the Triple Alliance was fragile and that he would soon have ample opportunity to pursue his quest for land west of the Rhine. The Triple Alliance gained mostly favorable terms against Louis in the Treaty of Aix-la-Chapelle, signed on May 2, 1668. France returned the Burgundian region of Franche-Comté to Spain but kept about half of what it had conquered in the Netherlands.

Marie-Thérèse of France had to give up her claim to the throne of Spain—her country of birth—to marry French king Louis XIV, because her father, King Philip IV of Spain, had feared Louis's territorial ambitions. A military alliance of the Dutch Republic, England, and Sweden formed after France invaded the Spanish Netherlands with the intention of seizing the region it believed it was entitled to by Louis's marriage to Marie-Thérèse. (Library of Congress)

Significance

The Triple Alliance's ascendancy over Louis was short-lived because his clever diplomacy quickly undermined it. Using Henrietta Anne, sister of King Charles II of England and sister-in-law of Louis, as an intermediary, the two kings concluded the secret Treaty of Dover on June 1, 1670. Charles promised to abandon the Triple Alliance, convert to Catholicism, try to convert England, announce his conversion as soon as politically safe, and support France's policies in Europe. Louis promised to pay the English king in both troops and money for these concessions. Neither king followed through on these agreements, but, in 1672, when Louis launched another war against the Dutch, Charles dutifully sided with France. An angry Dutch mob murdered de Witt on August 20, 1672, blaming him for both the French invasion and the loss of English support.

William of Orange, nephew of Charles II, was elevated to stadtholder on July 2, 1672, and soon turned the tide of war in favor of the Dutch. After significant military and naval victories against the French, the English, and their allies, William made separate peace with England in the Treaty of Westminster, signed on February 19, 1674, with terms strongly favoring the Dutch. The end to the Third Anglo-Dutch War did little to check Louis, whose pride had been wounded at Aix-la-Chapelle. By the end of his own war against the Dutch (1672-

1678), the Dutch Republic was secure, but France had gained or regained most of the territory it had coveted in 1667.

—*Eric v.d. Luft*

Further Reading

Dunlop, Ian. *Louis XIV*. New York: St. Martin's Press, 2000. A comprehensive biography of King Louis.

Ekberg, Carl J. *The Failure of Louis XIV's Dutch War*. Chapel Hill: University of North Carolina Press, 1979. An analysis of the causes and consequences of the 1672-1678 French war against the Dutch.

Faber, Richard. *The Brave Courtier, Sir William Temple*. London: Faber and Faber, 1983. The standard biography of Temple.

Haley, Kenneth Harold Dobson. *An English Diplomat in the Low Countries: Sir William Temple and John De Witt, 1665-1672*. Oxford, England: Clarendon Press, 1986. The standard work on the diplomacy of the War of Devolution and its aftermath.

Lindenov, Christoffer. *The First Triple Alliance*. Translated by Waldemar Christian Westergaard. Copenhagen, Denmark: Rosenkilde and Bagger, 1947. Transcriptions of documents and other primary sources pertaining to the 1668 alliance.

Lynn, John A. *The French Wars, 1667-1714: The Sun King at War*. Oxford, England: Osprey, 2002. Concentrates on the military aspect of these conflicts.

Price, J. Leslie. *The Dutch Republic in the Seventeenth Century*. New York: St. Martin's, 1998. An account of how the Protestant Netherlands survived wars with Spain, France, and England to become one of the major European economic powers of its time.

Rowen, Herbert Harvey. *John de Witt, Grand Pensionary of Holland, 1625-1672*. Princeton, N.J.: Princeton University Press, 1978. The standard biography on de Witt.

_______. *John de Witt, Statesman of the "True Freedom."* New York: Cambridge University Press, 1986. An insightful study of the Dutch diplomat's tragic attempts to stave off French invasions.

Sonnino, Paul. *Louis XIV and the Origins of the Dutch War*. New York: Cambridge University Press, 2002. A carefully researched narrative of the intrigues that culminated in war between the alliance of France, England, and Sweden and the alliance of the Netherlands, Spain, and the Holy Roman Empire.

Zanger, Abby E. *Scenes from the Marriage of Louis XIV: Nuptial Fictions and the Making of Absolutist Power*. Stanford, Calif.: Stanford University Press, 1997. Examines the causes of the War of Devolution.

See also: July 5, 1601-Apr., 1604: Siege of Oostende; July, 1643-Oct. 24, 1648: Peace of Westphalia; Nov. 7, 1659: Treaty of the Pyrenees; 1661: Absolute Monarchy Emerges in France; Mar. 4, 1665-July 31, 1667: Second Anglo-Dutch War; Apr. 6, 1672-Aug. 10, 1678: French-Dutch War; Aug. 10, 1678-Sept. 26, 1679: Treaties of Nijmegen; 1689-1697: Wars of the League of Augsburg; Sept. 20, 1697: Treaty of Ryswick; Oct. 11, 1698, and Mar. 25, 1700: First and Second Treaties of Partition.

Related articles in *Great Lives from History: The Seventeenth Century, 1601-1700:* Charles II (of England); Charles II (of Spain); Louis XIV; Marie-Thérèse; Philip IV; William III.

February 13, 1668
Spain Recognizes Portugal's Independence

The Portuguese monarchy passed to Spanish Habsburg rule in 1580 after the death of the Aviz Dynasty's last ruler, Henry. In 1640, Portugal reasserted its independence under a new dynasty, the Braganza, but Spain did not recognize Portuguese independence until 1668, with the Treaty of Lisbon.

Locale: Iberian Peninsula
Categories: Government and politics; wars, uprisings, and civil unrest

Key Figures

John IV (1604-1656), king of Portugal, r. 1640-1656
John of Austria (1629-1679), Spanish military leader
Friedrich Hermann Schomberg (1615/1616-1690), German-born leader of Portuguese military forces

Summary of Event

A sovereign country for more than eight centuries, Portugal lost its independence for a period of sixty years, from 1580 to 1640. The last member of the Aviz Dynasty died without an heir in 1580. The most powerful monarch in Europe was the neighbor of Portugal, Philip II, king of Spain and heir of the powerful Habsburg Dynasty. He laid claim to and obtained the Portuguese throne, ruling in that country as Philip I of Portugal.

Initially, the Spanish monarch was accepted by the Portuguese. He was the center of a constellation of kingdoms and territories in the Iberian Peninsula, Austria, portions of Italy and the Netherlands, the Americas, Africa, and Asia. His realm was centered in Castile, the kingdom that was the core of the Spanish Empire and ruled by the Habsburg Dynasty, which had originated and was based in Austria.

The acceptance in Portugal of the Spanish monarch occurred for several factors. Philip agreed to leave the administration of Portugal in the hands of Portuguese nobles, ecclesiastics, and bureaucrats. As the king of Portugal, he would be advised concerning Portuguese affairs by a council, comprised exclusively of Portuguese members. Significant economic and cultural advantages complemented this political autonomy and stability.

Portugal and its colonies obtained access to the vast wealth and markets of the Spanish Empire in the Americas. Portuguese shippers and merchants were no longer limited to the Portuguese colony of Brazil but could trade throughout South and Central America and the Caribbean. The Portuguese led in the trade of African slaves to these regions. Moreover, there was vast Spanish wealth to pay for Portuguese goods because of the growing exploitation of silver from mines in Upper Peru (Bolivia).

The economic, political, and military power of Spain elevated its language and culture to central importance in Europe. Portuguese writers and artists could circulate their ideas and works in Europe through their proximity and relationship with Spain.

Not everyone in Portugal accepted the loss of the country's sovereignty. The situation was more favorable to the ruling classes than to others. There were incidents of isolated popular rebellion. An illegitimate offspring in the Aviz Dynasty claimed to be the rightful king of Portugal and led a short-lived rebellion. However, this movement died out.

Initially, to the Portuguese ruling class, therefore, the loss of national sovereignty had more advantages than disadvantages. However, changing circumstances in Spain and its empire gradually altered that balance; and the disadvantages mounted. Philip died in 1598, succeeded by his son Philip III (Philip II in Portugal). The new king inherited not only the throne but also an accumulation of debt and royal bankruptcies consequent to his father's war and military engagements throughout the world. The mineral wealth of Spain from the Americas was in decline, and European competitors, especially the French, Dutch, and English, preyed upon that wealth. As resources declined, however, Philip III had no perception of the need or inclination to restrict the expenditures of his government. This economic situation worsened throughout his reign. When he died in 1621, his son Philip IV (Philip III in Portugal) inherited a vastly debilitated and desperate Spanish monarch and empire. Portugal, intimately a part of this realm, grievously suffered the consequences.

One of the great enemies of Catholic Spain was the Protestant Netherlands, which had long challenged Habsburg rule over its region. Steadily throwing off this foreign control, the Dutch became a rising maritime power. As such they preyed upon the Portuguese empire, the weakened subordinate of Spain. Throughout the early seventeenth century, Portugal lost control of its colonies in Brazil, Africa, and Asia to Dutch aggression.

The Portuguese empire increasingly came under attack because of its association with Spain. Within the Spanish empire, Portuguese merchants, traders, and merchants increasingly met opposition to their successful inroads.

Not only did the Portuguese increasingly lose territorial and economic advantages because of their forced association with Spain, they also began to suffer fiscally and politically. As the revenues of the Spanish Empire declined, the Spanish government attempted to increase its income by raising taxes and duties. Uprisings against these measures erupted in various parts of the Habsburg realm. To quell them, Spain demanded greater levies of soldiers and arms from other parts of its domains. To ensure that Portugal conformed to the new Spanish measures, Spanish administrators came increasingly to replace Portuguese administrators in the government of Portugal.

Under the circumstances of mounting territorial, economic, financial, political, and military losses, the Portuguese ruling class resolved to reassert Portugal's independence. The task of leading this secession fell to one of the principal aristocrats, John, the duke of Braganza, a leading landowner with the strongest claim to the Portuguese throne. (The duke became king of Portugal as John IV in 1640.)

The initial declaration of Portuguese independence could not be immediately countered by Spain. Catalonia was also in revolt, and this threat was aggravated by Catalonia's establishing an alliance with France, the most powerful threat to Spain in Europe. Only after 1656, with the death of John and devastating wartime losses by Spain to France, did the Spanish government try to amend its loss of Portugal by reconquering the country.

This task was given to the Spanish military leader, John of Austria, an illegitimate son of Philip IV. In 1663, his forces penetrated southern Portugal and occupied the city of Évora. They then tried to advance farther west into the country but were overextended. In trying to return to Évora, the Portuguese pursued and defeated the Spanish in the Battle of Ameixal that summer. This defeat repeated itself three years later at the Battle of Montes Claros. John of Austria met the Portuguese forces under the leadership of the skilled German general Friedrich Hermann Schomberg, who was supported by the governments of two of Spain's principal enemies in Europe: England and France. Realizing with the defeat at Montes Claros that it could not reconquer Portugal, Spain recognized the country's independence by the Treaty of Lisbon on February 13, 1668.

Significance

With support from Spain's European rivals, Portugal obtained Spanish recognition of its independence in 1668, more than a generation after declaring it in 1640. This Portuguese victory, however, had come at great cost. After numerous worldwide conflicts with the rising Dutch maritime empire, the Portuguese confronted the loss of most of their rich colonies in Asia. Portugal had been able to regain the northeast portion of Brazil, which the Dutch had occupied, and its slave-producing colonies in western Africa. However, just as Portugal had only been able to regain its independence through foreign (European) aid, it also was able to regain Brazil and its African colonies only through Brazilian (foreign) support. From the middle of the seventeenth century on, Brazil steadily became the sustaining force of the Portuguese economy. Indeed, after 1645, the heir to the Brazilian throne bore the title of prince of Brazil.

Spain's loss of Portugal was part of the larger disintegration of Spanish and Habsburg power in Europe through the last half of the century. The heir of Philip IV, and stepbrother of John of Austria, was Charles II. A physically and mentally disabled monarch, he left no heirs. When he died in 1700, the Habsburg Dynasty in Spain ended, as had the Aviz in 1580. The successor to Charles II came from the archenemy of Spain, the Bourbon Dynasty, beginning there with Philip IV, grandson of French king Louis XIV.

—Edward A. Riedinger

Further Reading

Darby, Graham. *Spain in the Seventeenth Century*. London: Longman, 1994. Examines the economic, political, and military conditions of the reign of Philip IV in relation to the Spanish administration of Portugal and other areas of the Habsburg realm.

Elliot, John Huxtable. *Imperial Spain, 1469-1715*. New York: St. Martin's Press, 1964. Analyzes economic conditions and sociopolitical developments in the rise and fall of the Spanish Empire.

Marques, Antonio de Oliveira. *History of Portugal*. New York: Columbia University Press, 1976. Volume one examines conditions that ended the Aviz Dynasty in Portugal and brought about the rise of the Braganza Dynasty.

Russell-Wood, A. J. R. *The Portuguese Empire, 1415-1808: A World on the Move*. Baltimore: Johns Hopkins University Press, 1998. Includes analysis of the functioning of the Portuguese Empire under the period of Spanish rule from 1580 to 1640.

Wheeler, Douglas L. *Historical Dictionary of Portugal.* Lanham, Md.: Scarecrow Press, 2002. Includes entries for the principal figures and events for the period of Spanish rule in Portugal and the movement for Portuguese independence.

See also: 17th cent.: Rise of the Gunpowder Empires; Mar. 31, 1621-Sept. 17, 1665: Reign of Philip IV; 1630-1660's: Dutch Wars in Brazil; May, 1640-Jan. 23, 1641: Revolt of the Catalans; May 24, 1667-May 2, 1668: War of Devolution; Feb., 1669-Jan., 1677: John of Austria's Revolts.

Related articles in *Great Lives from History: The Seventeenth Century, 1601-1700:* Catherine of Braganza; Charles II (of Spain); John of Austria; John IV; Count-Duke of Olivares; Philip III; Philip IV; Cardinal de Richelieu; Friedrich Hermann Schomberg.

1669
Steno Presents His Theories of Fossils and Dynamic Geology

By establishing that physical Earth indeed has a history, with geologic strata deposited by sedimentation and mountains and valleys formed by the collapse of plains, Steno explained the nature of marine fossils found far from the sea. His work may be considered the first modern form of paleontology and the first presentation of a geology of changes over time.

Locale: Florence, Italy
Categories: Science and technology; geology

Key Figures

Nicolaus Steno (1638-1686), Danish anatomist and naturalist
Ferdinand II de' Medici (1610-1670), grand duke of Tuscany, r. 1621-1670
Thomas Bartholin (1616-1680), Danish physician, naturalist, anatomist, and physiologist
Erasmus Bartholin (1625-1695), Danish mathematician and physician
Henry Oldenburg (1619-1677), English first secretary of the Royal Society of London
Francesco Redi (1626-1697), Italian physician to Ferdinand II

Summary of Event

Though the Greeks had observed the presence of petrified seashells inland and correctly concluded that the sea had once covered the land and deposited the shells, fossils posed several difficulties for the seventeenth century mind. First, no clear idea existed to explain fossils as the remains of once-living beings. The concept of "fossil" included anything buried in the earth or lying on its surface, and comprised a continuum from things clearly inorganic—such as gemstones—to things clearly resembling living organisms.

Interpreting fossils as organic did not follow for several reasons. Some of these fossils had formed crystals and hence seemed to be inorganic. Another conclusion held that the resemblance of such fossils to organisms was fortuitous: They were "sports" (jokes) of nature. Moreover, that many organic fossils were of extinct, unknown species further obscured their nature. A second issue involved how to explain the formation of fossils. According to the Aristotelian view, fossils grew from seeds in the Earth; the neo-Platonic idea held that a molding force created the fossils in a web of affinities that united all parts of the universe. Neither view required the notion that the fossils resembling life forms were organic. A final difficulty arose from the location of the fossils, especially seashell forms located on mountains far from the sea. The biblical flood provided a reasonable explanation.

Whereas several authors of the sixteenth and early seventeenth centuries, including Leonardo da Vinci, argued that fossils were of organic origin, an understanding of the nature of fossils ultimately rested upon a theory of geological change. In the seventeenth century, Nicolaus Steno provided the first such theory.

Born Niels Stensen, Steno received training at the University of Copenhagen from Thomas Bartholin, perhaps the most famous anatomist of the day, and from his younger brother Erasmus, a mathematician, physician, and Cartesian scholar. Steno received additional training in Amsterdam, at the University of Leiden, and in Paris. Having gained a reputation for his anatomical studies, Steno arrived in Florence in March, 1666, where Ferdinand II de' Medici, the grand duke of Tuscany, received him and appointed him to a post that provided a living.

He was also elected to the Accademia del Cimento (Academy of Experiments), founded in 1657 by Leopold de' Medici, brother of the grand duke. The academy's members included Francesco Redi, a physician who performed experiments to discredit spontaneous generation.

With the help of Ferdinand, Steno published in 1667 a work on the action of muscular contraction, to which he attached his findings from the dissection of the head of a shark caught in October of 1666. His examination of its teeth convinced Steno of the organic origin of fossilized shark teeth known as "tongue stones," which he had observed in rocks during sojourns with Ferdinand. To support his theory, Steno had to argue convincingly that tongue stones had been produced in the sea and that they could not have grown in or on the Earth. One of his arguments rested on the observation that some of them had eroded and thus were quite old. He then presented an explanation that the fossils had formed in soil that was not firm and was covered with water. The soils containing the fossils thus were sediments, an image suggested perhaps by Steno's early experience with chemical precipitates. Despite these arguments, Steno asserted that he drew no conclusions concerning the origins of the fossils.

Two years later, Steno published *De solido intra solidum naturaliter contento dissertationis prodromus* (1669; *The Prodromus to a Dissertation Concerning Solids Naturally Contained Within Solids*, 1671; better known as *Prodromus*), a work significant for its presentation of principles governing geologic history. A major goal was to explain how a solid—including a fossil or a crystal—could have formed within rocks. In the first part of this work, Steno argued definitively that fossilized animal and plant parts were formed in exactly the same way as the parts of living animals. He explained that the hard organic parts impressed their form on soft sediments. Furthermore, Steno noted that because fossil shells as well as fossil plants and the fossil remains of other animals resembled living species, it follows that fossils were organic. To account for the hardness of fossils, Steno suggested that the original matter had lost volatile particles or had taken on particles from its surroundings. Thus, he explained the nature and origin of the fossils.

In response to the problem of location, especially of marine fossils far from the oceans, Steno devised an explanation of the formation of geologic strata (rock layers). One of his principles stated that strata formed successively, with the lower stratum solidifying before the formation of the next stratum—the so-called principle of superposition. The original strata, laid down horizontally, could be lifted up or slipped down by the subsequent actions of fires and waters. Steno applied these principles to an explanation of Tuscan geology: the region's geology formed first by the deposition of layers and then by the undermining of those layers by subterranean water or heat, which carved out caverns that then collapsed. The resulting valley filled with water, causing further sedimentation and collapsing layers.

According to Steno's theory then, shells could be deposited during the first stage and wind up on mountains in a later stage. Throughout this work, however, Steno was careful to point out that his ideas did not contradict Scripture, and he incorporated the biblical flood into his scientific thought. These efforts succeeded, for the book easily gained the approval of the censors, one of whom was his friend Francesco Redi.

Significance

Steno's work garnered a positive reception in England, where it also generated much debate. The secretary of the Royal Society of London, Henry Oldenburg, translated *Prodromus* into English, and *Philosophical Transactions* published reviews of Steno's work. One difficulty with Steno's work is the "young" age of the fossils studied, for the Tuscan fossils were only 5 million years old, while the English fossils were 300 million years old. For example, Martin Lister noted that while the fossils of Tuscany did indeed resemble living specimens, those found in the quarries of England, such as the ammonites (extinct mollusks), bore no resemblance to any known species and therefore could not be rightly considered the remains of organisms. To some, then, Steno's theories raised the issue of extinction, a phenomenon incompatible with belief in creation by an all-good, all powerful God. The general acceptance of extinction would come more than a century later, as *Prodromus* was reprinted several times in the eighteenth century.

Steno's work may be considered the first modern work on paleontology as well as the first presentation of a "dynamic" geology, or a geology of changes over time. During the eighteenth century, his theory of fossils prevailed and scholars accepted his geological principles. Another important aspect of his work involved his use of the scientific method. Like Galileo, he sought efficient causes for the phenomena he studied, that is, only immediate physical causes and not supernatural ones, and he affirmed the importance of personal observation. In his explanation of the development of fossils and gemstones, he relied on chemical and mechanical processes.

—*Kristen L. Zacharias*

Further Reading

Cutler, Alan. *The Seashell on the Mountaintop: A Story of Science, Sainthood, and the Humble Genius Who Discovered a New History of the Earth.* New York: Dutton, 2003. A very readable account of the life of Steno, which focuses on his geological theories.

Dryburgh, Peter. "Nicholas Steno and the Foundations of Geology." *Edinburgh Geologist* 41 (Autumn, 2003): 3-11. A brief account of Steno's life and scientific contributions.

Kardel, Troels. *Steno: Life, Science, Philosophy.* Copenhagen, Denmark: Danish National Library of Science and Medicine, 1994. A scholarly assessment of Steno's scientific work, focusing mainly on his anatomical studies, with some attention to his geological work and philosophy of science. Includes English translations of two anatomical works by Steno.

Rudwick, Martin J. S. *The Meaning of Fossils: Episodes in the History of Paleontology.* Chicago: University of Chicago Press, 1985. A classic treatment of fossils and paleontology from the sixteenth to the nineteenth century. Chapter 2 discusses Steno.

Steno, Nicolaus. *The Prodromus of Nicolaus Steno's Dissertation Concerning a Solid Body Enclosed by Process of Nature Within a Solid.* Translated by John G. Winter. 1916. Reprint. New York: Hafner, 1968. A translation of the work in which Steno detailed his theory of geologic formations and presented his ideas on minerals, fossils, and other formations on Earth.

See also: 1601-1672: Rise of Scientific Societies; 1637: Descartes Publishes His *Discourse on Method*.

Related articles in *Great Lives from History: The Seventeenth Century, 1601-1700:* Thomas Burnet; René Descartes; Galileo; John Ray; Nicolaus Steno.

February, 1669-January, 1677
John of Austria's Revolts

As the leader of two armed insurrections, John of Austria was successful in forcing out Spain's queen regent and her advisers and gaining the office of first minister, but during his two years as Spain's first minister he was unable to enact most of the reforms he had promised or to reverse Spain's decline.

Locale: Madrid, Zaragoza (Saragossa), Spain
Categories: Wars, uprisings, and civil unrest; government and politics; diplomacy and international relations

Key Figures

John of Austria (1629-1679), illegitimate son of King Philip IV of Spain
Philip IV (1605-1665), king of Spain, r. 1621-1665
Charles II (1661-1700), king of Spain, r. 1665-1700
Mariana de Austria (1634-1696), queen of Spain, r. 1649-1665, and queen regent, r. 1665-1675, second wife of Philip IV and the mother of Charles II
Johann Eberhard Nithard (1607-1681), an Austrian Jesuit, confessor and court favorite to Queen Mariana, Inquisitor General, and first minister
Fernando de Valenzuela (1630-1692), an adventurer who was selected first minister by Mariana

Summary of Event

As the son of the actress Maria Calderon, who was King Philip IV's favorite mistress, John of Austria (Don Juan José) was given privileges that were not accorded to any of his father's other illegitimate children. Not only was he given a substantial income and a princely education, but in 1642, before going off to battle, Philip even issued a proclamation declaring John his son, thus making him the only one of the king's illegitimate children ever to be officially acknowledged.

At age eighteen, John began to establish his reputation as a courageous military leader, though not always an effective one, and also as a peacemaker, as evidenced by his popularity in Catalonia after he had put down a decade-long uprising. Even after being defeated by the Portuguese in 1663, he remained Spain's outstanding general and obviously a far more capable leader than the heir to the throne would ever be, for Philip's only surviving legitimate son, Charles, who was the product of the king's marriage to his niece Mariana de Austria, was both physically and mentally disabled.

With his father aging and Charles so feeble, John saw his opportunity. His ambition was to be named *infante*, or prince, and be made first minister. However, Queen Mariana had been working hard to turn Philip against John. When he arrived to see his dying father, Philip had him sent away. Moreover, the king did not include him in the council he set up to advise Mariana, who would be regent until Charles reached his majority. With Philip's death in 1665, there began a bitter struggle between the many grandees who supported John and Mariana's favorites. Among these was Johann Eberhard Nithard, an Austrian Jesuit, who came to court with Mariana at her marriage to serve as her confessor. When Mariana made Nithard the Inquisitor General and thus an ex officio member of the council, the prince's party decided to take action.

They began with a plot to seize Nithard. However, this scheme was discovered in October, 1668, and only a timely warning from a friend on the council saved John from being arrested. He fled to Aragon and Catalonia, where he began planning a coup with his aristocratic friends. Meanwhile, he circulated rumors among the common people about reforms he would make if he were in power. In February, 1669, John marched toward Madrid with some four hundred supporters on horses. Before Queen Mariana, he proclaimed that he would not disband his forces until she dismissed and exiled Nithard. Reluctantly, she complied, but John's supporters were not organized enough to obtain for John the post of first minister. He had to settle for an appointment as vicar general of Aragon and return to Zaragoza.

Mariana replaced Nithard with Fernando de Valenzuela, an uneducated adventurer of obscure birth who had married one of the queen's maids of honor and was rumored to have become the queen's lover. The fact that he was nicknamed "the palace ghost" because of his access to the queen demonstrated that, though he held no official position, Valenzuela was the most powerful person at court.

There were many at court who secretly sympathized with John, however, among them Charles's tutor. Although Charles was intellectually limited, he did have the Habsburg pride, and as he grew older, it was easy to develop in him a sense of his rights as a monarch. When he turned age fourteen in November, 1675, thus attaining his majority, Charles was persuaded to assert his independence by summoning John to court. However, Charles could not withstand his strong-willed mother for long. John was sent back to Zaragoza, and after being banished for a few months, Valenzuela was recalled to court in April, 1676, made a marquis, and appointed first minister.

Almost without exception, the aristocrats were finally united, not only in opposition to Mariana and Valenzuela but also in their support of John. On December 15, 1676, twenty-four of the most prominent grandees in Spain issued a manifesto, demanding that Charles send away the Queen Mother, imprison Valenzuela, and install John as his primary adviser. Galvanized into action, Charles managed to slip out of the Alcázar, and from the safety of his retreat at Buenretiro he issued a command for the banishment of Valenzuela, sent an order for his mother to remove herself to Toledo, and wrote to his half brother, asking for his help. John needed no urging. On New Year's Day, 1677, he set forth from Zaragoza for Madrid, gathering forces on the way. By the time he reached Madrid, his army numbered fifteen thousand. There was no resistance. Valenzuela was found hiding at El Escorial and was arrested, stripped by the king of his property and titles, and sent to the Philippines to work in the mines. He never returned to Spain, but died in Mexico in 1692. Mariana was banished to Toledo, though she would return to court two years later. John became first minister and the virtual ruler of Spain.

John soon set about to implement the reforms he had promised. He demanded reports from his regional administrators, which eventually resulted in reducing taxation; he created an effective committee to deal with trade; and he enacted monetary reforms, thus halting inflation. He also strengthened ties with France by arranging a marriage between the king and Marie-Louise d'Orléans, French king Louis XIV's niece, which brought Charles great happiness. Because of his physical disabilities, though, there would be no children. Unfortunately, John remained in power just two-and-a-half years. He died on September 17, 1679.

SIGNIFICANCE

The reigns of the last two Habsburgs are generally described as a period when Spanish power and prestige reached its nadir, and certainly there was no period in history when the government in Madrid was weaker, more corrupt, and less effective. However, John's career had broader implications for the future than many have realized. He was the first leader to unite in a common cause traditionally antagonistic groups such as the Aragonians and the Castilians, the aristocracy and the populace, and even the various factions among the grandees themselves; thus he has been called the first popular leader in Spanish history. Interestingly, John was also the first to succeed in staging a coup.

Moreover, it is significant that his rise to power was based not merely on general opposition to an unpopular regime but also on the promise of sweeping reforms. It is true that because of famine and disease in Spain and military disasters abroad, in addition to the palace intrigues fomented by the queen, many of these reforms could not be effected during his brief tenure. However, by rejecting the limitations imposed by his birth and successfully rebelling against those in power, John moved his people toward a more open-minded attitude toward intellectual and social change. Thus, his revolt can be seen as a turning-point in Spanish history, the beginning of a period of reform and renewal.

—*Rosemary M. Canfield Reisman*

Further Reading

Bowen, Marjorie. *Sundry Great Gentlemen: Some Essays in Historical Biography*. Freeport, N.Y.: Books for Libraries Press, 1968. Bowen provides a detailed and insightful study of Charles II.

Kamen, Henry. *Empire: How Spain Became a World Power, 1492-1763*. New York: HarperCollins, 2003. Kamen argues that Spain rose to power not by conquest but through its collaboration with other countries. Includes maps, illustrations, and an index.

_______. *Spain, 1469-1714: A Society of Conflict*. London: Longman, 1983. A good history of Spain that includes an excellent discussion of the revolt and its aftermath. Glossary, appendices.

Livermore, H. V. *A History of Spain*. New York: Minerva Press, 1968. The chapter "The Later Habsburgs" is a good starting point for a study of the period.

Lynch, John. *The Hispanic World in Crisis and Change, 1598-1700*. Malden, Mass.: Blackwell, 1992. Lynch argues that John was not a reformer but a dictator motivated by his ambition, whose death enabled Spain to return to a real government.

Stradling, R. A. *Philip IV and the Government of Spain, 1621-1665*. New York: Cambridge University Press, 2002. First published in 1928, this work remains the definitive study of Philip's reign.

See also: Mar. 31, 1621-Sept. 17, 1665: Reign of Philip IV; May, 1640-Jan. 23, 1641: Revolt of the Catalans; Feb. 13, 1668: Spain Recognizes Portugal's Independence; Oct. 11, 1698, and Mar. 25, 1700: First and Second Treaties of Partition.

Related articles in *Great Lives from History: The Seventeenth Century, 1601-1700:* Charles II (of Spain); John of Austria; Louis XIV; Philip IV.

c. 1670

First Widespread Smallpox Inoculations

Techniques of inoculation, or "variolation," against smallpox, which had long been practiced in China, were further developed and widely used there in the seventeenth century. The spread of these techniques throughout the world, especially to the Turkish Ottoman Empire, eventually took them to Great Britain in the early eighteenth century and resulted in the first modern vaccination techniques.

Locale: China, Eastern Europe, Ottoman Empire, and Africa

Categories: Health and medicine; biology; science and technology

Key Figures

Li Shizhen (Li Shih-chen; 1518-1593), Chinese scientist and writer

You Chang (Yu Ch'ang; fl. mid-seventeenth century), Chinese medical writer

Mehmed IV Avci (1642-1693), sultan of the Ottoman Empire, r. 1648-1687

Summary of Event

The origins of the types of smallpox inoculations that found widespread application in seventeenth century China can be traced to the tenth century, when Song Dynasty Prime Minister Wang Dan's oldest son died of smallpox, and he called on medical experts, scholars, scientists, and sorcerers to find a way to protect his remaining family members. In response, a Daoist hermit who practiced alchemy reportedly revealed the secret of smallpox inoculation, which some sources claim may have been in existence since the sixth century in China. However, the procedure was not commonly performed for more than five hundred years. A 1596 book on botany and medicine by Li Shizhen contains the earliest known published description of the procedure.

Seventeenth century Chinese writers reported that general knowledge and the common application of smallpox inoculation did not occur until the period 1567-1572. You Chang's *Wen yuan ge shou chao ben* (1643; miscellaneous ideas in medicine; reprinted as *Yu yi cao*, 1971; tales of herbs) gave a detailed description of the procedure, which basically consisted of introducing dried smallpox scabs into the body through inhalation or on a cotton plug that was inserted in the nose. By the seventeenth century, the potential danger of "variolation," which stemmed from introducing the live smallpox virus, rather than dead or weakened versions, had been significantly reduced by refining the procedure—an impressive feat, given that these refinements had to be achieved at a time when viruses had not yet been discovered.

Despite their ignorance of viruses per se, Chinese medical authorities understood that the smallpox scabs used for inoculations had to be weakened, or attenuated, in order to avoid transmitting the full-blown disease, and guidelines for safe variolation were established. They knew the difference between *Variola major*, the most deadly form of the disease, and *Variola minor*, the less virulent type. Scabs were to come from *Variola minor*, and no unattenuated scabs were to be used. Scabs from patients who had themselves been inoculated and developed a mild infection were preferred. The procedure was made even safer by using scabs produced through several generations of inoculations, that is, scabs from a patient who had been variolated with scabs from an earlier variolation, and so forth, for a number of generations.

Methods for artificially weakening the virus even further were also developed. Scabs were aged for a month or so in a sealed bottle, which reduced their potency. If supplies of new scabs were limited, older scabs were combined with the newer ones to produce an attenuated powder. It is now known that these attenuation procedures killed 80 percent of the viruses used for inoculations. They greatly reduced the chance of transmitting smallpox while still generating sufficient antibodies to protect against the disease. The inoculations also strengthened the immune system by stimulating the body's production of a substance called interferon. The end result was a relatively safe and effective method of creating a lifetime immunity to a long-dreaded disease. The Chinese also developed an oral vaccine in the 1600's, with some claimed success. Healthy people who took pills that were made from the fleas found on cows reportedly were protected from smallpox, to some extent.

Variolation migrated from China to the Middle East and was actively promoted by traders who claimed that it had protected them and, in some cases, their human cargo. The Middle Eastern version of the procedure involved recovering fluid from the pustules of someone with a mild case of smallpox and introducing it into a superficial puncture or scratches, usually on the patient's arm. Caravans from the Circassian region (the Republics of Adygea, Karachay-Cherkessia, and Kabardino-Balkaria, located in the Caucasus) introduced variolation to the Ottoman Empire in 1670. Sultan Mehmed IV Avci preferred the reputedly beautiful women of the Caucasus for his harem in the court of the Sublime Porte in Istanbul and had many imported. These women, who were inoculated as children in parts of their bodies where the scars could not be seen, disseminated information on variolation to the court. The practice became relatively widespread when it was found that between 1-3 percent of inoculated patients died, compared to 30 percent or more of the people who contracted smallpox naturally.

Variolation for smallpox also found its way to Africa in the seventeenth century. Crude inoculation practices may have existed in Africa for hundreds of years prior to the 1600's, but there is evidence that variolation procedures similar to those in the Ottoman Empire were used in seventeenth century Africa. The most common African procedure was only a slight variation on the Middle Eastern version: Fluid from smallpox pustules was deposited into a shallow cut, usually on the patient's leg or arm, rather than into a puncture or scratches.

The practice of variolation migrated from Africa to colonial America through the slave trade. Onesimus, a slave who was a servant to the Reverend Cotton Mather of Boston, Massachusetts, had been variolated in Africa as a child in the seventeenth century. In 1706, he explained the procedure to his master, and Mather became a strong advocate of its use. Initially, however, he found only one doctor who was willing to inoculate a small number of patients, and the procedure remained very controversial for decades, severely limiting its application in the American colonies.

SIGNIFICANCE

Crude smallpox variolation techniques had been practiced in various parts of the world for hundreds of years prior to the seventeenth century. However, the refinement of inoculation technology in late sixteenth century China made the procedure safer and more effective, leading to its widespread use throughout the seventeenth century, which saved millions of lives in China and in the other regions to which it was exported.

The introduction of this procedure to England in the following century began a series of events that dramatically altered the course of history. Lady Mary Wortley Montague, who lived in Turkey between 1716 and 1718, learned about variolation there and had her five-year-old son inoculated. Upon returning to England, she had her four-year-old daughter variolated before the most prominent physicians in the country. The procedure soon became widespread when trials showed that most who were inoculated did not become ill when exposed to smallpox.

This "Turkish method" of inoculation did pose some risk, because it used material from smallpox sufferers (the term "variolation" comes from "variola," the technical term for smallpox). In 1796, British physician Edward Jenner discovered that inoculation with fluid from the sores of people with cowpox, which was related to smallpox but was not lethal, would provide immunity from smallpox. This procedure was called "vaccination," from *vacca*, which means cow. Like the seventeenth century Chinese, Jenner used the fluid from the sores of patients who had been vaccinated earlier to ensure quality control, and the end result was similar: the development of immunity and the production of interferon. By the mid-nineteenth century, the British government had outlawed variolation and made vaccination mandatory in order to control smallpox. Jenner's breakthrough is credited not only with the global eradication of smallpox by 1980 but also with the creation of the science of immunology, which has produced numerous vaccines against crippling and lethal diseases and holds promise for the control of others.

—*Jack Carter*

Further Reading

Barquet, Nicolau, and Pere Domingo. "Smallpox: The Triumph over the Most Terrible of Ministers of Death." *Annals of Internal Medicine* 127 (1997): 635-742. A comprehensive history of the global spread of smallpox, the resulting epidemics, and early Chinese inoculation practices that eventually led to modern vaccination techniques.

Baxby, Derrick. "The End of Smallpox." *History Today* 49, no. 3 (March, 1999): 14-16. Explains how high seventeenth century smallpox mortality rates in England and inoculation techniques from the East gave rise to vaccinations, which were made compulsory.

Plotkin, Susan L., and Stanley A. Plotkin. "A Short History of Vaccination." In *Vaccines*, edited by Stanley A. Plotkin and Walter A. Orenstein. 4th ed. Philadelphia: Saunders, 2004. Includes discussions of various types of smallpox inoculation techniques in seventeenth century China, their migration to England via the Ottoman Empire, and the modern vaccination techniques that resulted.

Vetter, Richard, and Donna Hoel. "Vaccines and the Power of Immunity." *Postgraduate Medicine* 101 (1997): 154-159. A concise history of smallpox inoculation techniques, their spread to colonial America and Great Britain, and the resulting development of the contemporary science of immunology.

See also: 17th cent.: Advances in Medicine; 17th cent.: Birth Control in Western Europe; 1617-1628: Harvey Discovers the Circulation of the Blood; 1617-c. 1700: Smallpox Epidemics Kill Native Americans; 1660's-1700: First Microscopic Observations; 1664: Willis Identifies the Basal Ganglia; 1672-1684: Leeuwenhoek Discovers Microscopic Life; 1676: Sydenham Advocates Clinical Observation.

Related articles in *Great Lives from History: The Seventeenth Century, 1601-1700:* The Bernoulli Family; Chen Shu; Anne Conway; Saint Isaac Jogues; Kangxi; Mary II; Katherine Philips; Shunzhi; Squanto; Kateri Tekakwitha.

1670
Popularization of the Grand Tour

The publication of Richard Lassels's The Voyage of Italy *marks the first use of the term "Grand Tour" to describe the education that young Englishmen, and sometimes Englishwomen, could gain through a tour of Europe.*

Locale: France, Switzerland, Italy, Austria, Germany, the Low Countries (Belgium and the Netherlands)
Categories: Cultural and intellectual history; education; literature

Key Figures

Richard Lassels (c. 1603-1668), priest and traveling tutor
Simon Wilson (fl. seventeenth century), friend of Lassels who prepared *The Voyage of Italy* for publication
Richard Lumley (1650-1721), English aristocrat to whom Lassels bequeathed his manuscript of *The Voyage of Italy*
Thomas Whetenhall (fl. seventeenth century), friend and traveling companion of Lassels
Catherine Whetenhall (d. 1650), Thomas Whetenhall's wife and traveling companion
David Murray (fl. seventeenth century), Scottish aristocrat who asked Lassels to guide him on a tour

Summary of Event

Some aspects of what would come to be known as the Grand Tour had been features of upper-class English life since the sixteenth century, but the inclusion of Italy in the tour became common only in the 1630's and 1640's. The phrase itself appeared in print in the first important guidebook in English, *The Voyage of Italy* (1670), by Catholic priest Richard Lassels. Lassels had traveled widely and was typical of the tutors and scholars guiding their patrons through Europe in the mid-seventeenth century.

Lassels was born about 1603, probably in the English county of Lincolnshire. This was a period of religious persecution, and the Catholic family into which Lassels was born had lost much of its wealth through fines for boycotting the services of the Church of England, which had supplanted Catholicism as the established church during the reign of English monarch Henry VIII. Lassels attended Douai College in the Spanish Netherlands and was ordained a priest in 1632. Because of his faith, he was destined to spend much of his time abroad, making a living as one of a growing number of traveling tutors. In this capacity, Lassels became familiar with most of the major European countries, including Italy, which he visited five times.

Since the Italian city of Rome was the seat of the Catholic Church, it was natural that Lassels gravitated to the southern European country. He made his first visit in 1637-1638 as an agent representing Anglo-Catholic interests and seems to have made a conscious decision to begin accumulating the knowledge of ancient and modern Italy that he would later display in his travel works. A second trip came in 1649-1650, during which Lassels accompanied his friend Thomas Whetenhall and his wife, Catherine Whetenhall. Traveling via Paris, the group visited Turin, Rome, Venice, and Padua, where Catherine Whetenhall died unexpectedly on July 6, 1650. Soon afterward, Lassels wrote *Voyage of the Lady Catherine Whetenhall from Brussels into Italy in the Holy Yeare, 1650*. Lassels would travel again to Italy in 1651-1652 and 1658.

Meanwhile, knowledge of Lassels's expertise was growing. In 1654, Scottish aristocrat David Murray asked Lassels to accompany him to Italy, but Lassels seems to have been involved as tutor with another household at the time. Upon Murray's request, he instead produced a guide based loosely on the account he had written after his trip with the Whetenhalls. Dedicated to Murray, the result was called *Description of Italy* (1654).

Lassels wrote at least two versions of his crowning work, *The Voyage of Italy* (1670), the first in 1660-1661 and the second in 1664. The first was based on Lassels's first four trips to Italy and described four possible itineraries. Prepared after a fifth, brief trip to Italy in 1663, the 1664 version allowed Lassels to expand upon his earlier manuscript and to add an additional itinerary. The extended title that Lassels gave his manuscript, here set out in its original spelling, indicates its scope: *The Voyage of Italy; or, A Compleat Journey Through Italy; With the Characters of the People, and the Description of the Cheif Townes, Churches, Monasteryes, Libraryes, Pallaces, Gardens, Tombes, Villas, Antiquities, Pictures, Statues: As Also of the Interest, Government, Riches, Strength &c of the Princes.*

Although not the first guidebook in English, it was the first to use the phrase "Grand Tour" in print: "And no man understands Livy and Caesar . . . like him who hath made exactly the *Grand Tour* of France and the *Giro* [tour or excursion] of Italy." Lassels's references to Roman historian Livy and statesman and writer Julius Caesar underscored his belief that a clearer grasp of the classical world could be gained by seeing firsthand the lands that were its setting. He did not, however, neglect the artistic achievements of the Renaissance, that period of European history marked by its rediscovery of classical Greece and Rome, or ignore Italy's current political situation. This combination of ancient and modern concerns became standard in the decades to follow, as the Grand Tour became a familiar fixture of life among the wealthy.

Lassels was to die, appropriately enough, on his way to Italy once again—in this case accompanying his patron, Richard Lumley, and a friend, Simon Wilson. He became ill in southern France and died in September, 1668, in the city of Montpellier. Lassels bequeathed a manuscript of *The Voyage of Italy* to Lumley, and it was printed in Paris under the supervision of Wilson, who edited Lassels's manuscript and inserted some of his own material.

Significance

By the end of the seventeenth century and the beginning of the eighteenth, the Grand Tour came to be accepted as an integral part of a gentleman's education. Participants usually ranged in age from eighteen to twenty and were guided by such tutors as Richard Lassels. No matter how well informed the tutor, however, the group was likely to carry one or more guidebooks, of which *The Voyage of Italy*, if not quite the first, came to be one of the most popular. It was reprinted in London and Paris and soon appeared in German and French translations.

The itinerary of the Grand Tour would normally include Paris, Switzerland, and the Italian cities of Milan, Florence, Naples, Venice, and particularly Rome. Next came Austria, Germany, and the Low Countries known today as Belgium and the Netherlands. A typical Grand Tour might last from two to four years, during which time participants were expected to polish their languages and broaden their appreciation of art, architecture, and music. They might also meet the future leaders and administrators of the countries through which they passed—contacts sure to be of value when they themselves assumed the reins of leadership. In addition, the tour offered its participants an opportunity for sexual adventure and general dissipation, a fact not lost on scandalized critics.

—Grove Koger

Further Reading

Black, Jeremy. *Italy and the Grand Tour*. New Haven, Conn.: Yale University Press, 2003. A re-creation of "ordinary" British tourists' experiences based on diaries and letters.

Burgess, Anthony, and Francis Haskell. *The Age of the Grand Tour: Containing Sketches of the Manners, Society and Customs of France, Flanders, the United Provinces, Germany, Switzerland and Italy in the Letters, Journals and Writings of the Most Celebrated Voyagers Between the Years 1720 and 1820, with Descriptions of the Most Illustrious Antiquities and Curiosities in These Countries*. New York: Crown, 1967. A lavish, oversize volume emphasizing the eighteenth century and made up largely of selections from the works of authors on the tour. Black-and-white and color illustrations, notes on authors and artists.

Chaney, Edward. *The Evolution of the Grand Tour: Anglo-Italian Cultural Relations Since the Renaissance*. Rev. ed. Portland, Oreg.: Frank Cass, 2000. Essays dealing specifically with the tour in Italy as well as with the evolving cultural interrelationship between England and Italy.

Chaney, Edward, and Richard Lassels. *The Grand Tour and the Great Rebellion: Richard Lassels and "The Voyage of Italy" in the Seventeenth Century*. Geneva: Slatkine, 1985. Chaney provides a lengthy introduction to Lassels's 1654 *Description of Italy*, reprints its text for the first time, and supplements it with a series of appendices. A scholarly work, but the only practical source for details of Lassels's life. Extensive notes, bibliography.

Hibbert, Christopher. *The Grand Tour*. New York: Putnam, 1969. A popular account. Black-and-white and color illustrations, list of sources.

Redford, Bruce. *Venice and the Grand Tour*. New Haven, Conn.: Yale University Press, 1996. Explores the artistic and intellectual impact of the Italian city on participants in the Grand Tour. Illustrations.

Stoye, John. *English Travellers Abroad, 1604-1667: Their Influence in English Society and Politics*. Rev. ed. New Haven, Conn.: Yale University Press, 1989. Discusses English travelers (including Lassels) in Italy, Spain, France, and the Low Countries. Notes, bibliography, illustrations.

Wilton-Ely, John. "'Classic Ground': Britain, Italy, and the Grand Tour." *Eighteenth-Century Life* 28 (2004): 136-165. A lengthy review article dealing with, among other works, *The Evolution of the Grand Tour* by Edward Chaney.

See also: 1624-1640's: Japan's Seclusion Policy.

Related articles in *Great Lives from History: The Seventeenth Century, 1601-1700:* Nathaniel Bacon; Nicholas Ferrar; William Penn; Sir John Suckling.

1670
Promulgation of the Sacred Edict

Qing emperor Kangxi decreed the Sacred Edict in 1670 in order to regulate the behavior of his subjects, impose social order throughout China, and provide political legitimacy for Manchu rule. The edict was publicly read on the first and fifteenth day of every month in every village and town in the country.

Locale: China
Categories: Government and politics; laws, acts, and legal history

Key Figure

Kangxi (K'ang-hsi; 1654-1722), emperor of China, r. 1661-1722

Summary of Event

In 1670, Kangxi, the sixteen-year-old Qing emperor of China, issued an edict containing sixteen moral maxims he wanted his subjects to observe in their daily lives. This document is referred to as the *Sheng yu guang xun*, or Sacred Edict. It was believed that the principles proclaimed in the Sacred Edict would set the norm for behavior, instill social order, and create unity among the different regions and ethnic groups of China. The edict was also intended to provide political legitimacy for the Manchus, whose Qing Dynasty had governed China since 1644. Although this edict was drafted for Kangxi by his Chinese advisers, he was quite familiar with orthodox Chinese political and moral philosophy, based upon the teachings of the sage Confucius, which formed the ideological basis for this decree. Kangxi was a remarkably strong-willed individual even at this young age. He became emperor at the age of seven and began making his own decisions when he was thirteen. In 1669, the year before the issuance of the Sacred Edict, he took control of the government from the regent Oboi (d. 1669).

The Sacred Edict was issued at a time when Manchu control of China was tenuous. The country had yet to be brought under complete control, and large areas of the south, known as the Three Feudatories, were held by three former Ming Dynasty generals who had helped the Manchus seize power in 1644. Because of the unstable situation and the fact that the Manchus were alien conquerors and small in number, the Manchu elite, especially Kangxi, realized that if they were to retain power and rule effectively, they had to obtain the support of the Chinese scholar official class (mandarins) who formed the backbone of the traditional ruling class.

One central long-standing political problem that the Manchus had to solve concerned local control of the population. China at this time had a population of around 120 million, while there were only 2 or 3 million Manchus, and the total number of government officials was an inconsiderable thirty to forty thousand at best. Consequently, imperial authority did not extend below the county (*xian*) level. Therefore, district magistrates, the lowest ranking civil officials, had to rely upon the support of local elites (gentry) to maintain stability and order; the relationship between the two was frequently rocky.

To deal with this difficult problem, the Manchus reached back to a technique employed by the first Ming Dynasty emperor, Hongwu. Like the Manchus, Hongwu realized (albeit grudgingly) that to rule properly, he needed the support of the Chinese ruling class. Hongwu also saw that Confucian ethics could serve as a useful ideological tool for controlling populations. In 1397, he ordered posted in all villages in China a mainstream Neo-Confucian decree called the Six Maxims (*Liu yu*), which consisted of six simple moral injunctions. Village elders were required to read the maxims publicly six times a month. The maxims stressed filial piety, keeping harmonious relations with neighbors, moral instruction, respect for elders, and the importance of working hard and not committing bad deeds.

In 1652, the new Manchu government adopted this Confucian approach and also promulgated the Six Maxims. It assumed that the best way to ensure social order was through a broad educational effort, stressing morality, rather than simply relying upon compulsion. In 1659, an Imperial Edict improved dispersal of the maxims throughout the general population. Eleven years later, this Neo-Confucian ideological campaign was widened and strengthened with Kangxi's promulgation of the Sacred Edict.

The Sacred Edict was publicly read on the first and fifteenth day of each month in every village and town in China, including the remote Pescadores Islands. All citizens were required to attend these readings. The edict consisted of sixteen moral maxims, and each maxim was written in seven Chinese characters. The original version of the edict was succinctly written in classical Chinese. Like Hongwu's six rules, Kangxi's Sacred Edict began

THE SACRED EDICT

Qing Emperor Kangxi's 1670 Sacred Edict—which consisted of sixteen moral maxims written in seven Chinese characters—regulated behavior, imposed social order throughout China, and legitimized Manchu rule. The edict was publicly read on the first and fifteenth day of every month in every village and town in the country. The maxims are excerpted here.

1. Esteem most highly filial piety and brotherly submission, in order to give due importance to the social relations.
2. Behave with generosity toward your family, in order to illustrate harmony.
3. Cultivate peace and concord in your neighborhoods, in order to prevent quarrels.
4. Recognize the importance of farming, in order to ensure a sufficiency of food.
5. Show that you prize moderation and economy, in order to prevent the lavish waste of your means.
6. Encourage schools, in order to make correct the practice of the scholar.
7. Eliminate strange doctrines, in order to exalt the correct doctrine.
8. Lecture on the laws, in order to warn the ignorant.
9. Show courtesy, in order to make manners and customs good.
10. Labor diligently at your proper callings, in order to stabilize the will of the people.
11. Instruct sons and younger brothers, in order to keep them from doing what is wrong.
12. Put a stop to false accusations, in order to preserve the honest and good.
13. Warn against sheltering deserters, in order to avoid being involved in their punishment.
14. Fully remit your taxes, in order to avoid being pressed for payment.
15. Unite in hundreds (territorial units), in order to put an end to thefts and robbery.
16. Remove anger, in order to show the importance due to the person and life.

with general principles of good behavior and finished with specific, concrete injunctions about advisable or undesirable behavior.

Unlike Hongwu's six rules, however, the Sacred Edict primarily emphasized self-cultivation instead of the observance of conventions. Self-cultivation (*hsiu shen*) referred to the Confucian belief that humankind's basic nature is good and embodies *jen* (humanity, benevolence) that can be intuited by the mind. This method required a person constantly to practice self-scrutiny (*fan-sheng*), use teachers as guides and models, and employ the mind's innate ability to distinguish between right and wrong to guide behavior.

The first three principles of the Edict, as well as the ninth, were concerned with social order. Maxims six, seven, and eleven dealt with proper learning, the avoidance of false beliefs, and the importance of elder family members being moral educators and models in their families. Since orthodox Confucianism was officially considered the only true doctrine, the seventh maxim was specifically directed against Christianity, geomancy, popular superstitions and religious sects, secret societies, witchcraft, and certain forms of Daoism and Buddhism.

Injunctions four, five, and ten referred to employment and subsistence. Rule four mentioned mulberry trees because they were grown as food for silkworms, which made clothing. The remaining maxims, twelve through sixteen and eight, emphasized strict obedience to the law and explained how the public peace was maintained. The edict revealed the influence of the idealistic Neo-Confucian school of Sung Learning, which served as the official state orthodoxy during Kangxi's reign as well as much of the rest of the Qing Dynasty. This school accentuated the importance of positive example and moral education.

Soon after the appearance of the decree, numerous detailed commentaries appeared, written in the Chinese vernacular, to ensure that all Chinese were fully able comprehend the document's message. In the early eighteenth century, Zhang Boxing (Chang Po-hsing; 1652-1725), a scholar and governor of Fukjian (Fukien), composed three versions of the edict: one illustrated with popular sayings for "people of average intelligence," one with classical allusions for the literati, and one utilizing rhymes for people in the countryside. The Sacred Edict was also expanded by two later Qing Dynasty emperors, and several supplementary edicts relating to it were issued. In 1724, Kangxi's son, Emperor Yongzheng (Yung-cheng; r. 1722-1735), who thought the edict was too short and concise, greatly enlarged the expositions in a lengthy text, the Amplified Instructions of the Sacred Edict (*Sheng-yu kuang-hsun*). Kangxi's grandson, Emperor Qian-long (Ch'ien-lung; r. 1735-1796), also issued an ancillary decree to the edict.

Significance

While the Sacred Edict was relatively effective in curtailing the rapid spread of Christianity and secret societies, helpful in solidifying Confucian values, and a useful tool for imposing ideological control on the grassroots level of Chinese society, the ritual of reading the edict later frequently degenerated into an empty ceremony. The successful implementation of the edict was dependent upon the local gentry taking the maxims seriously and assuming overall responsibility for public morals and civic conduct. Some did, but many did not.

Recently, historians have argued that the Sacred Edict was also important because it provided the basis for Chinese village compacts or community covenants (*xiang yue*). In fact, several researchers investigating village regulations in the south of China in the early 1990's were surprised to find that a large number of compacts in use were heavily influenced in wording and ideas by Kangxi's Sacred Edict. The influence of the edict also extended beyond China. The famous 1890 Japanese Imperial Rescript on Education, which had a very important effect upon the development of the Japanese educational system, was influenced by the Sacred Edict.

The 1670 promulgation of Emperor Kangxi's Sacred Edict helped provide the ideological basis for Manchu rule, which was quite unstable at the time; imposed social order at the local level of Chinese society; and popularized and reinforced core Confucian values such as filial piety, propriety, moral education, respect for scholarship, and self-cultivation, thereby providing a norm for proper conduct. It enforced a sense of unity across the fifteen hundred districts of imperial China, whose borders greatly expanded during Kangxi's reign. It also implicitly warned members of the literati to not deviate from the reigning Confucian orthodoxy in their writings.

In addition, the Sacred Edict generally lessened the spread of Christianity, secret societies, and unorthodox doctrines. It contributed to the development of village compacts, an influence that was still present in some village regulations in southwest China as late as the early 1990's. The edict was later amplified by Emperors Yongzheng and Qian-long. It also had an influence upon the composition of the Japanese Meiji emperor's celebrated 1890 Imperial Rescript on Education. The edict was still publicly read after 1900, but by this time the only people who attended the ceremony were those who were obliged to do so.

—*Ronald Gray*

Further Reading

Confucius. *The Analects of Confucius*. Translated by Simon Leys. New York: W. W. Norton, 1997. The most famous book of Confucius's teachings, which had a major influence on the writing of the Sacred Edict. This translation also contains useful essays and notes on Confucius's philosophy.

Rawski, Evelyn. *The Last Emperors: A Social History of Qing Imperial Institutions*. Berkeley: University of California Press, 2001. An interesting account of how the Qing emperors, including Kangxi, maintained their Manchu identity while adopting a Confucian model of governance.

Spence, John. "The Kang-Hsi Reign." In *The Cambridge History of China*. Vol. 9. New York: Cambridge University Press, 2002. A good overview of Kangxi's reign.

See also: 1616-1643: Rise of the Manchus; Apr. 25, 1644: End of the Ming Dynasty; June 6, 1644: Manchus Take Beijing; 1645-1683: Zheng Pirates Raid the Chinese Coast; Feb. 17, 1661-Dec. 20, 1722: Height of Qing Dynasty; Dec., 1673-1681: Rebellion of the Three Feudatories; Aug. 29, 1689: Treaty of Nerchinsk Draws Russian-Chinese Border.

Related articles in *Great Lives from History: The Seventeenth Century, 1601-1700:* Abahai; Chongzhen; Dorgon; Kangxi; Shunzhi; Tianqi.

1670-1699

Rise of the Asante Empire

The Asante Empire emerged from the union of loosely affiliated Asante states. The new union devoted its military resources to territorial expansion, which established Asante as the mightiest imperial power among the Akan states of western Africa.

Locale: Central and southern Ghana (West Africa)
Categories: Expansion and land acquisition; government and politics; trade and commerce; wars, uprisings, and civil unrest

Key Figures

Obiri Yeboa (d. 1670's), established the supremacy of the Oyoko clan and lineage
Osei Tutu (c. 1660-1717), founder and first ruler of the Asante Empire, r. 1680-1717
Okomfo Anokye (d. 1690's), chief priest of Asante

Summary of Event

West Africa was made up of many empires collectively called the "forest kingdoms." They included the Akan states, of which Asante became the most powerful. The region was rich in gold and kola nuts and served as a junction for converging trade routes. Such conditions contributed to the rise of Asante in the seventeenth century. The emerging Akan states began to explore international commerce, leading to the economic and political potential of the Akan.

The growth of the population as well as economic and political competition among the Akan was rampant. The intense competition that developed between the Akan states of Denkyira and Akwamu for control of regional resources led to their mutual demise and the emergence of the Asante power state.

The leadership of the Oyoko clan also led to Asante's emergence as a powerful state, spearheading the development of several Asante ministates. In the middle of the 1600's, the nation's evolution was constrained because it was controlled by its neighbor, Denkyira. Eventually, the Oyoko clan consolidated its control around its principal settlement, Kumasi, and overcame Denkyira domination. Asante then began to develop as a major military and commercial power in the Gold Coast region of western Africa (modern Ghana), from sea to savanna. The greatest factor in Asante's development was the initiative of the Oyoko monarchs. Under Obiri Yeboa, who was killed in battle in the 1670's, the supremacy of the Oyoko clan was acknowledged by all in the Kumasi area and the other ruling lineages that were taken into the Oyoko line. That lineage established the nuclear states of Asante-Bekwai, Juaben, Kokofu, Kumasi, Mampong, and Nsuta.

Osei Tutu built on this foundation and established the spiritual unity of Asante. He chose Kumasi as the nation's capital and instituted a constitution that acknowledged the supremacy of the Kumasi. In so doing, he took the title *asantehene*, or head of the Asante state, and became the founder and first ruler of the Asante Empire.

Earlier, Osei had been a chief of the small state of Kumasi. Between 1680 and 1690, he believed that a merger or consolidation of the small separate Asante kingdoms was essential if they were to survive against the powerful Denkyira to the south. Osei had been a hostage in the court of Denkyira, but he escaped to the powerful state of Akwamu, where he was exposed to new ideas concerning militarism and politics. He returned to Kumasi with an entourage of Akwamu, including the high priest Okomfo Anokye, who would play a crucial role in the crystallization of the Asante state. It is believed that Okomfo's magical prowess propelled the first *asantehene*, Osei, to subdue the *denkyirahene* (king of Denkyira) and destroy the power of Denkyira at the Battle of Feyiase.

Okomfo developed the military structures of Asante power. He also wrote the Asante code of legal edicts, seventy laws that underpinned the state's moral and social order. He planted a sword in Kumasi, perceived as an enduring replica of the nascent Asante union.

The kings of the member states of Asante were integrated into the new political union by various means. They became commanders of the national army and formed a council of advisers to the *asantehene*. Once his reforms were complete, Osei began to expand the state, acquiring many new territories and incorporating them into the Asante union. The Asante state would emerge between 1670 and 1680, when Osei assumed the leadership of a number of the Akan matrilineal clans in and around Kumasi. By the end of the seventeenth century, Osei had defeated Denkyira, whose empire was dissolved virtually overnight, leaving Asante unchallenged as the major power in the western forest land.

Predating the rise of Asante were the kinship-oriented Akan microstates, so Osei and his advisers crafted an innovative strategy to create wide political integration. These changes included the institution of a new all-

Asante council, the Kotoko Council, as the ruling body. Also, Osei and his advisers nurtured a new national ideology. Osei's legendary religious aide, Okomfo, is said to have magically conjured up a golden stool as a symbol of Asante unity and presented it to the *asantehene*, a symbol that would transform a temporary alliance into a permanent union.

The Asante kingdom, which had originated as a loose grouping of chiefdoms under Osei, had risen into a formidable military power. The chiefs paid tribute to Osei, tribute collected from the villages and from gold-mining profits. The chiefs also provided soldiers for the *asantehene*'s standing army. Osei's federation conquered neighboring Akan states, and by the end of the seventeenth century, the Asante kingdom controlled most of the gold fields of the forest. The *asantehene*, through taxation and trading, was able to maximize his profit from the gold business. The Asante union came to dominate almost the entire territory of what is now Ghana, and it did so until annexed at the end of the nineteenth century by the British.

Significance

Osei Tutu fostered the spiritual and political basis for unity and conducted successful wars against his neighbors. During his reign, the size of Asante nearly tripled, expanding Asante to the coast, which included it in the slave and gun trades.

By the end of Osei's rule in 1717, the Asante union became even more powerful. Osei's successor, Opoku Ware I, followed with more conquests deep into the gold-producing regions of Banda, Gyaman, and southward, dominating Akyem, Akwapim, and Akwamu. Also, he would enter Accra in 1744. Additional campaigns followed, and by the time of Opoku's death in 1750, Asante was unchallenged among the Akan states.

Asante power was used to exploit the gold and slave trade and in the process acquire firearms used to reinforce Asante's might. Few states could mount effective opposition to the kingdom. The Fante seemed at first to be successful in resisting Asante encroachment. Later, however, Asante delivered a series of defeats to the Fante, defeats that ultimately brought British intervention. After protracted conflicts between Asante and the British, Asante was defeated in the nineteenth century and incorporated into the British colony of the Gold Coast (Ghana).

—*Kwasi Sarfo*

Further Reading

Ajayi, J. F. A., and Michael Crowder, eds. *History of West Africa*. New York: Longman, 1985. A reference volume on Asante and other regional empires.

Daaku, Kwame Yeboa. *Trade and Politics on the Gold Coast, 1600-1720*. Oxford, England: Oxford University Press, 1970. Daaku discusses the commercial context for the rise of Asante.

Davidson, Basil. *African Kingdoms*. New York: Time-Life Books, 1974. A survey of Asante and companion civilizations.

Fage, J. D., and William Tordoff. *A History of Africa*. 4th ed. New York: Routledge, 2002. This updated edition examines the factors and conditions favorable to the rise of Asante.

McCaskie, T. C. "Komfo Anokye of Asante: Meaning, History, and Philosophy in an African Society." *Journal of African History* 27, no. 2 (1986). McCaskie explores the spiritual genesis of Asante.

Meyerowitz, Eva L. R. *The Early History of the Akan States of Ghana*. London: Red Candle Press, 1974. Meyerowitz explores the growth of Asante in its early years.

Rattray, R. S. *Ashanti*. 1923. Reprint. Oxford, England: Clarendon Press, 1969. A detailed study of the emergence and development of Asante.

_______. *Ashanti Law and Constitution*. Oxford, England: Clarendon Press, 1969. In this work first published in 1929, Rattray focuses on the moral and legal foundation of Asante.

See also: Beginning c. 1601: Expansion of the Oyo Kingdom; 1612: Rise of the Arma in Timbuktu; 1619-c. 1700: The Middle Passage to American Slavery; Oct., 1625-1637: Dutch and Portuguese Struggle for the Guinea Coast; 1630-1660's: Dutch Wars in Brazil; Mid-17th cent.: Emergence of the Guinea Coast States; Late 17th cent.: Decline of Benin.

Related articles in *Great Lives from History: The Seventeenth Century, 1601-1700:* Maurice of Nassau; Njinga.

April, 1670
CHARLES TOWN IS FOUNDED

The English founded the first permanent European settlement in South Carolina, eventually displacing Spanish claims. With immigrants coming from British Barbados, France, Scotland, and Ireland, and with the arrival of African slaves, Charles Town became one of the most racially and religiously diverse colonies in the New World.

LOCALE: Charles Town, South Carolina
CATEGORIES: Colonization; expansion and land acquisition

KEY FIGURES

Charles II (1630-1685), king of England, r. 1660-1685
Henry Woodward (c. 1646-c. 1686), liaison between Europeans and the Kiawah Indians

SUMMARY OF EVENT

In 1562, Huguenots (French Protestants) escaping from the Catholic-Protestant wars in France settled in Port Royal, South Carolina, under the leadership of Jean Ribaut, but this settlement quickly failed. In 1629, King Charles I of England gave a grant to Sir Robert Heath to resettle Huguenot refugees from England to South Carolina, but this plan also failed. In 1669, the Spanish were still the major European power in the Carolina area. Although the Spanish claimed Carolina, however, their closest settlement was 200 miles (320 kilometers) away in Saint Augustine, Florida.

England also made claim to Carolina, and the English challenged Spain's claim. The Stuart monarchy was restored in 1660, when Charles II became king of England, and in 1662-1663 he gave Carolina as a grant to the eight lords proprietors who had helped him regain the throne. In 1669, one of the proprietors, the earl of Shaftesbury, Anthony Ashley Cooper, took charge of the project and began to develop the area for economic reasons. Three ships, the *Carolina*, the *Port Royal*, and the *Albemarle*, left England for the seven-month voyage to America. The *Albemarle* wrecked and was replaced in Barbados by the *Three Brothers*, and the *Port Royal* wrecked and was not replaced, but in April, 1670, the *Carolina* entered what is now called Charleston harbor, followed by the *Three Brothers* on May 23. The two ships brought approximately 148 people.

The immigrants had planned to settle at Port Royal, about 60 miles (100 kilometers) from present-day Charleston, but landed by mistake a little north of Charleston. They still planned to go to Port Royal, but the cacique (chief) of the local Kiawah tribe persuaded them to settle in the Charleston area instead, partly to help protect the Kiawahs from the Spanish and Spanish-allied Native Americans, such as the Westoes. Contrary to the "wild savage" image held by the English, the Kiawahs lived in semipermanent homes in villages, practiced some diversified agriculture, and had a fairly developed political system. Henry Woodward, an Englishman, had lived with the Kiawahs for several years and had good relations with them, which in turn helped develop good relations between the Kiawahs and the settlers.

The English went five miles northwest up the Ashley River and then west a short distance up Old Towne Creek, to the first high land that afforded a view of the river, so Spanish ships could be seen before they reached the settlement. Marshlands and a short palisade also helped the defense. Because of the threat of attack by the Spanish or by Spanish-allied Native Americans, Charles Town (briefly called Albemarle Point) was developed as a fort, with people sleeping inside and working outside during the day. Later in 1670, Spaniards from Saint Augustine attempted to attack but were defeated, because Native Americans friendly to the English warned them of the planned attack. In the 1670's, there were battles with the Westoe and Stono tribes. In 1686, another attempted attack by the Spanish and their Indian allies was stopped by a hurricane.

The settlers traded with the Indians, largely for animal furs and skins, and obtained lumber, tar, and pitch from the forests. About fifteen different crops were experimented with, but corn was the main food raised. Cattle were raised, and fish and wild animals were plentiful. There were problems (for example, malaria), but fewer than in most other settlements.

Charles Town became very popular among Barbadians, who needed a place to move to escape from overcrowding and a lack of land on Barbados. In 1671, more than one hundred Barbadians (mostly of English heritage) had joined the settlement. Industrious and business-oriented, the Barbadians soon exercised a powerful economic and political influence. By 1672, there were thirty houses and about two hundred people at Charles Town. By 1680, the settlers had moved the settlement back down the Ashley River to where it joined the Cooper River to form the bay or harbor area, a few miles west of the Atlantic Ocean.

An eighteenth century view of Charles Town, South Carolina. (Library of Congress)

One of the unique features of Charles Town at its new location was that it was a planned city, following the checkerboard plan proposed for London after the Great Fire of 1666. At the time, only in Philadelphia and Charles Town were the streets laid out before the city was built. By 1680, approximately one thousand people lived in Charles Town. By 1690, with one thousand to twelve hundred residents, Charles Town was the fifth largest city among the North American colonies that would become the United States, after Boston, Philadelphia, New York, and Newport. By 1700, Charles Town still was an 80-acre (32-hectare) fortified city-state, four squares long by three squares wide, surrounded by a wall. Six bastions helped protect the city. Many farms and plantations existed outside the city, and the city had become a trading center for the farms, plantations, and native villages, with rivers and original Indian trails becoming the avenues of commerce into the city. Deerskins and beaver skins remained important, but rice had become the major economic crop by the early 1700's.

By 1717, the Spanish threat had waned, unfriendly local tribes had been defeated in the Yamasee War, and friendly local tribes had settled primarily as farmers and hunters along local river areas in South Carolina. In 1717, the wall was removed from around the city to allow growth. Pirates remained a problem until 1718.

Significance

Charles Town was unique in its early ethnic mixture. Some scholars think that one African slave was on the *Carolina* in 1670, but even if this were not the case, African slaves were brought in soon afterward. Some of the Africans were free, and many, whether slave or free, were skilled craftsmen. There was a relatively small white middle class, because the large white wealthy class stymied middle-class growth, and an even smaller white craftsman class, because of the predominance of free Africans and African slaves as expert craftsmen. Against strong opposition from the lords proprietors, some Native Americans were enslaved. Huguenot refugees from England, France, and other places began moving to the city in the mid-1680's. The Barbadians and Huguenots soon formed the largest part of the cultural and political elite of the area.

Close contact was maintained with Barbados, and these ties also helped the Barbadians and the city to prosper. Barbadian architecture, Huguenot wrought iron, and formal gardens became hallmarks of Charles Town. The proprietors encouraged Dissenters (Protestants who were not members of the Church of England) to move to Charles Town in order to limit the power of the Barbadians. Immigrants, mostly Calvinist Presbyterians, came from Scotland and Ireland, and they engaged in political conflict with the Barbadians and Huguenots. Quakers, and by 1695 Spanish and Portuguese Jews, also settled in Charles Town.

Charles Town remained unique in its tolerance of religious and ethnic diversity. It was the only major city in the colonial era that did not exclude undesirable strangers and probably was the least religious of the early major cities. In fact, Charles Town developed a well-deserved reputation as a cultured, wealthy, and pleasure-oriented city, a place of theaters, gambling, horse racing, dancing, and drinking. Much of this was possible only through exploitation of African slaves to provide most of the manual labor.

In 1970, Charles Town Landing was developed as a state park and major tourist attraction on the site of the original Charles Town settlement, celebrating the tricentennial of the 1670 settlement, which is also considered the tricentennial of South Carolina. A reconstruction of a village of the 1600's; a forest with animals found in Charles Town in 1670—such as black bears, bison, bobcats, alligators, snakes, and puma—a crop garden with tobacco, rice, indigo, cotton, sugar cane, and other crops grown in season; a reproduction of a seventeenth century trading vessel docked at the original landing area; a museum; a theater; and other re-creations showed many facets of the 1670 settlement.

—Abraham D. Lavender

Further Reading

Canny, Nicholas, and Alaine Low, eds. *The Origins of Empire: British Overseas Enterprise at the Close of the Seventeenth Century*. Vol. 1 in *The Oxford History of the British Empire*, edited by William Roger Lewis. New York: Oxford University Press, 1998. Collection of essays by noted historians exploring numerous aspects of Britain's worldwide colonial expansion. Explains the founding and governance of individual

American colonies, and several essays focus on British colonies in New England, Carolinas, the mid-Atlantic, and the Chesapeake.

Fraser, Walter J. *Charleston! Charleston! The History of a Southern City*. Columbia: University of South Carolina Press, 1989. A detailed account of Charleston's settlement and history.

Jones, Lewis P. *South Carolina: A Synoptic History for Laymen*. Rev. ed. Orangeburg, S.C.: Sandlapper, 1978. Includes several chapters on the early history of the Charleston area.

Lavender, Abraham D. *French Huguenots: From Mediterranean Catholics to White Anglo-Saxon Protestants*. New York: Peter Lang, 1990. A general history of Huguenots that includes analysis of naming patterns in Charleston, illustrating early cultural assimilation among Huguenots, English, and others.

Osborne, Anne Riggs. *The South Carolina Story*. Orangeburg, S.C.: Sandlapper, 1988. Includes a detailed discussion of Charles Town's settlement and a chapter on the pirates in the Charles Town area.

Rosen, Robert. *A Short History of Charleston*. 2d ed. Charleston, S.C.: Peninsula Press, 1992. Separate chapters are devoted chronologically to Charleston's history, including two chapters on its early history.

Wallace, David Duncan. *South Carolina: A Short History, 1520-1948*. Columbia: University of South Carolina Press, 1961. Considered to be a classic history of South Carolina. Gives detailed information on Charleston's settlement and history.

SEE ALSO: May 14, 1607: Jamestown Is Founded; Beginning c. 1619: Indentured Servitude Becomes Institutionalized in America; 1619-c. 1700: The Middle Passage to American Slavery; May 14, 1625-1640: English Discover and Colonize Barbados; Apr. 21, 1649: Maryland Act of Toleration; Summer, 1654-1656: First Jewish Settlers in North America; Mar. 24, 1663-July 25, 1729: Settlement of the Carolinas; Sept. 2-5, 1666: Great Fire of London.

RELATED ARTICLES in *Great Lives from History: The Seventeenth Century, 1601-1700:* Charles I; Charles II (of England).

May 2, 1670
HUDSON'S BAY COMPANY IS CHARTERED

Responding to the plans of Chouart des Groseilliers and Radisson, the British chartered the Hudson's Bay Company to exploit the potential fur trade of North America. The company's political and economic power ensured British dominance in Canada.

LOCALE: Hudson's Bay, Rupert's Land (now Hudson Bay, Canada)

CATEGORIES: Trade and commerce; organizations and institutions; expansion and land acquisition; colonization

KEY FIGURES

Médard Chouart des Groseilliers (1625-1698), French colonial Canadian explorer and fur trader

Pierre Esprit Radisson (c. 1636-1710), French colonial Canadian explorer, fur trader, and cartographer

Prince Rupert (1619-1682), duke of Bavaria, first governor of Rupert's Land, 1670-1682

Pierre Le Moyne d'Iberville (1661-1706), French raider of Hudson Bay who almost drove out the English

Zachariah Gillam (d. 1682), captain of the *Nonsuch*

Charles II (1630-1685), king of England, r. 1660-1685

SUMMARY OF EVENT

In 1670, England and France were deeply entrenched in the struggle for North America. Although outwardly friendly, King Louis XIV of France and King Charles II of England secretly struggled for dominance. Two French Canadian *coureurs de bois* (woodrunners) and explorers, Pierre Esprit Radisson and Médard Chouart des Groseilliers, became pawns in the battle for North America.

Radisson and Chouart des Groseilliers, his brother-in-law and partner, were alleged to be the first white explorers to enter Minnesota. They explored Lake Michigan, the Straits of Mackinac, and Green Bay. In 1659-1660, the two men traded for furs in the northern fur areas with the Illinois, Sioux, and Cree tribes. Upon their return to New France (now Quebec), leading a flotilla of sixty fur-laden canoes, they were prosecuted by the French authorities for illegal trading, and their furs were confiscated. Although they appealed to the French court in 1661, their petitions were ignored. Acting through Colonel George Cartwright, a commissioner sent to Boston by the newly restored British monarchy to help settle British colonial boundaries, the brothers-in-law entreated Charles II and his cousin, Prince Rupert, duke of

Bavaria, to fund an expedition to Hudson Bay. This area had been located sixty years earlier by Henry Hudson during his fourth voyage, in which he attempted to discover the Northwest Passage to Cathay.

Radisson and Chouart des Groseilliers arrived in England during 1665, the year of the Great Plague. The British referred to them as Mr. Radishes and Mr. Gooseberry (*groseilliers* means gooseberry bushes in French). Fascinated by the adventurers' idea that the Bay of the North could be approached by sea rather than the normal Saint Lawrence River route by canoe (information given to the explorers by the Cree), King Charles II and Prince Rupert envisioned rich fur harvests. In 1667, Sir George Carteret invested the first £20 in the new venture.

It took until June 5, 1668, to equip two decrepit but serviceable ships—the *Eaglet*, captained by William Stannard, with Radisson on board, and the *Nonsuch*, commanded by Captain Zachariah Gillam, with Chouart des Groseilliers on board—with the necessities for an exploratory journey to Hudson Bay. When they finally did set sail, the *Eaglet* was forced to return to England on August 5; the *Nonsuch* continued to Hudson Bay, where, on the east coast of James Bay, on a stream he called the Rupert River, Chouart des Groseilliers established Fort Charles, a trading station. The party wintered with the help of friendly Cree Indians, with whom Captain Gillam signed a treaty of amity and traded muskets, hatchets, steel knives, needles, and trinkets for pelts.

Chouart des Groseilliers left Hudson Bay in June, 1669, and returned to the court of Charles in October with a shipload of luxurious furs: ermine, lynx, and beaver. For the British monarchy, this shipment represented an alternative source to the Baltic fur market. At that time, Baltic furs were used by England in trade with Russia in exchange for commodities vital to the shipbuilding industry, including hemp and tar. Charles now realized that fur, rather than gold, was the real treasure of the New World.

On May 2, 1670, Charles granted a royal charter, composed on five sheepskin parchment sheets, under the Great Seal of England to his privy councillor, Prince Rupert. The charter granted the newly established "Governor and Company of Adventurers of England Trading into the Hudson's Bay" (commonly known as the Hudson's Bay Company) title to all land and a trade monopoly within the drainage basin of Hudson Bay: "all those Seas Streightes Bayes Rivers Lakes Creekes and Soundes in whatsoever Latitude they shall be that lye within the entrance of the Streightes commonly called Hudsons Streightes together with all the Landes and Territoryes." The area was to be called Rupert's Land, with the company maintaining the mineral and fishing rights and the right of exclusive trade. Traders encroaching on this expanse of land would be imprisoned and forfeit their ships and merchandise, with one-half the value going to the company, the other half to the British crown. The charter also included in its right of exclusive trade all lands accessed by the waterways of Rupert's Land.

Other founding adventurers, whose investment shares were priced at £300, included Anthony Ashley Cooper, the first earl of Shaftesbury; Robert Boyle, chemist and founding member of the Royal Society; Robert Vyner, the king's banker; Francis Millington, customs commissioner; John Fenn, paymaster of the Admiralty; Sir George Carteret, financier; John Portman, banker and goldsmith; Sir John Griffith, city magnate; James Hayes, private secretary to Prince Rupert; John Kirke, merchant; Kirke's brother-in-law, Sir Edgar Hungerford; Henry Bennet, first baron Arlington (soon to be first earl); Sir John Robinson, lieutenant of the Tower of London; and William Pretyman, merchant to India. Lady Margaret Drax, a colonial widow advised by Hayes, became the first female stockholder.

The charter granted the company complete judicial power, including the right to sue and be sued, to hold land and dispose of it, and, if necessary, to wage war. The company was to be controlled by a governor and an elected committee of seven. Charles named Prince Rupert the first governor of Rupert's Land, a position he maintained until his death in 1682. The only provision mandated upon the company was the payment of two elk and two black beavers should the British monarch, or his successors, ever decide to set foot on Rupert's Land.

SIGNIFICANCE

Charles had no idea of the expanse of Rupert's Land, which spread over nearly 40 percent of modern Canada: It included Ontario, Quebec, Manitoba, most of Saskatchewan, southern Alberta, the northern area of the Laurentian Mountains, and the region to the south past the forty-ninth parallel and west through the Red River Valley to the Rocky Mountain divide. The area covered by all streams draining into Hudson Bay encompasses 1.5 million square miles (3.9 million square kilometers).

The desire for ermine, lynx, and beaver, used for the immensely fashionable beaver pelt hats and as insignias of rank and wealth, grew. Soon, trading posts, or bay posts as they were called, lined Hudson Bay, James Bay, the Arctic Ocean, and the interior. As trade escalated, the beaver skin became the monetary unit, the "coin of the realm," with a single skin worth five pounds of sugar and ten skins worth a gun. The Hudson's Bay Company outfitted the indigenous peoples of Canada and used them to trap.

Intermittent problems with France continued. In 1697, Pierre Le Moyne d'Iberville raided Hudson Bay and almost drove the English out. In 1713, the Treaty of Utrecht sanctioned the British possession of Hudson Bay, but this new land became the site of a ruthless fur trade, which became most vicious from 1789 to 1821, after the rival North West Company arrived. During this era, John Jacob Astor made his fortune by forming the American Fur Company. The Hudson's Bay Company maintained domination over Rupert's Land until the Deed of Surrender in 1869, at which time it sold its land to the new Dominion of Canada in exchange for £300,000 and western farmland. Ultimately, the company sold all its land, preserving some mineral rights; after World War I, it cultivated interests in retail department stores, real-estate investment, and petroleum and natural gas production.

—M. Casey Diana

FURTHER READING

Fournier, Martin. *Pierre-Esprit Radisson: Merchant, Adventurer, 1636-1710*. Translated by Mary Ricard. Sillery, Que.: Sepentrion, 2002. Comprehensive treatment of Radisson's life, including his involvement with the Hudson's Bay Company. Refutes historians' claims that Radisson and Groseilliers were disloyal to their English business partners, maintaining they remained with the Hudson's Bay Company until political turmoil forced the two Frenchmen to leave England.

Newman, Peter C. *Company of Adventurers*. New York: Viking, 1985. A concise study of Hudson Bay. Includes a comprehensive bibliography and maps.

_______. *Empire of the Bay*. Toronto: Madison Press, 1989. Oversized book filled with colorful illustrations, including photographs, depicting the history of the Hudson's Bay Company. Includes a comprehensive chronology.

Nute, Grace Lee. *Caesars of the Wilderness: Médard Chouart, Sieur des Groseilliers, and Pierre Esprit Radisson, 1618-1710*. 1943. Reprint. St. Paul: Minnesota Historical Society Press, 1978. A comprehensive biography of both Chouart des Groseilliers and Radisson, covering the discovery and exploration of New France and the development of the fur trade. Extensive bibliography.

Ray, Arthur J. *The Canadian Fur Trade in the Industrial Age*. Toronto: University of Toronto Press, 1990. Covers the history and economic conditions of Hudson's Bay Company, the fur trade, and the natives of North America. Plates, illustrations, many bibliographical references.

Rich, Edwin Ernest. *Hudson's Bay Company, 1670-1870*. 2 vols. New York: Macmillan, 1961. Extensive and approachable, with illustrations of key players, a map, and a foreword by Sir Winston Churchill.

SEE ALSO: Mar. 15, 1603-Dec. 25, 1635: Champlain's Voyages; Beginning June, 1610: Hudson Explores Hudson Bay; Apr. 27, 1627: Company of New France Is Chartered; 1642-1684: Beaver Wars; 1642-1700: Westward Migration of Native Americans; May, 1642: Founding of Montreal; Aug., 1658-Aug. 24, 1660: Explorations of Radisson and Chouart des Groseilliers; Mar. 22, 1664-July 21, 1667: British Conquest of New Netherland; Beginning 1673: French Explore the Mississippi Valley; Dec., 1678-Mar. 19, 1687: La Salle's Expeditions.

RELATED ARTICLES in *Great Lives from History: The Seventeenth Century, 1601-1700:* Robert Boyle; Samuel de Champlain; Charles II (of England); Henry Hudson; Pierre Le Moyne d'Iberville; Louis XIV; Pierre Esprit Radisson; Prince Rupert; First Earl of Shaftesbury.

Beginning 1671
American Indian Slave Trade

British colonists exploited intertribal rivalries and desires of Natives Americans for European goods to gain slaves and establish dominance over Spanish claims in North America.

Locale: South Carolina

Categories: Social issues and reform; colonization; economics; trade and commerce

Key Figures

Francis Le Jau (1665-1717), French Huguenot minister who opposed Indian slavery

James Moore (1640-1706), Carolina governor who led an attack on Florida Indians in 1704

Summary of Event

The earliest known instance of Carolina Indians being captured and enslaved was in 1520, when Spanish explorers took them to provide slaves for sugar plantations in Santo Domingo. In 1663, William Hilton, an Englishman, also captured natives from the Carolina coast for Caribbean slave owners. In 1670, Charles Town was settled by the English. In 1671, after the defeat of Kusso warriors and the taking of numerous captives, English colonists initiated the Indian slave trade when Henry Woodward was commissioned to open trade in Indian slaves with Indians of rival tribes.

Carolina included what is now South Carolina and North Carolina until 1713, but between the 1670's and 1730, almost all of Carolina's American Indian trading occurred in Charles Town, which was the hub of the area that became South Carolina. Agriculture and forest industries also were part of Carolina's economy, but trading with the natives became the most lucrative aspect of the Carolina economy. Deerskins, leathers, and furs were the most important exports from this trading, but slavery also early became an important part of the trade. Although American Indian slaves existed in other areas (Virginia, for example), only South Carolina developed Indian slavery as a major part of its commerce. As a result, South Carolina enslaved more Native Americans than any other English colony.

The Carolina traders had an advantage in developing a thriving trade with Native Americans all the way to the Mississippi River for several reasons. The Carolina colony got an early start in the trade, there were no mountains blocking the westward expansion of Carolina trading, and Carolina traders could trade directly with the tribes that had goods they wanted, rather than going through other tribes as middlemen (in the northeastern United States, the Iroquois acted as middlemen between other American Indians and the Europeans).

The enslavement of Indians by Carolina traders did have some opposition. From 1680 until 1730, South Carolina was under the active or nominal leadership of eight lords proprietors, headquartered in London, who recognized the crucial financial importance of developing trade with the Indians. The lords proprietors knew that the enslavement of Native Americans ultimately would hurt their general trade with the Indians by leading to uprisings.

A few proprietors also owned stock in the Royal African Company (begun in 1672), which was bringing slaves from Africa, and they did not want competition from a full-blown trade in American Indian slaves. Some prominent local leaders also spoke against American Indian slavery. For example, Francis Le Jau, a French Huguenot minister, publicly criticized the slave trade. In 1720, sixteen prominent businessmen issued a statement against the enslavement of American Indians. As a group, Charles Town's Huguenot merchants were more opposed to native slavery, although a few did own Indian slaves. The proprietors were not opposed to slavery in principle, however, and they wavered in their opposition.

Against this limited opposition, major factors encouraged slavery. The selling of captives into slavery in order to pay volunteer soldiers was an old custom in Europe, with military commanders and pirates routinely enslaving people on ships they captured. For example, some Jews escaping the Spanish Inquisition in the 1490's were captured by pirates and sold into slavery. The idea that slavery was better than death and that the Indians would murder their captives if they did not have the option of selling them was used as a moral justification for slavery.

Although this rationale was accurate in some cases, however, it did not take into account the great increase in the phenomenon of Native Americans capturing other Native Americans as a direct result of the institution of a market for slaves—a market created by the Europeans. Prior to European contact, slavery had been practiced by some American Indians, who frequently sold captives as slaves, but not on a large scale and generally without the harsh treatment common to European slavery. In addition, the enslavement of both American Indians and Africans got strong support in Charles Town, because a large proportion of Charles Town's political and economic establishment immigrated from the Caribbean and brought a strong tradition of slavery with them to South Carolina.

The trade in American Indian slaves became an important part of the national conflicts involving Great Britain, Spain, and France for control of the Americas. Indians were drawn into these conflicts, often allying with a European power against other Indians allied with another European power. In 1680, for example, Indians allied with the British in Carolina began raids against Indians allied with the Spanish Catholic missions in Georgia and northern Florida. The British and Spanish had attempted attacks on each other, and the English feared that the natives in Georgia and Florida would ally with the Spanish to attack Carolina. At the same time, the availability of a large number of Indians, who were easy to capture because of their sedentary village life, was tempting to slave traders. For example, in 1704, under James Moore, fifty British soldiers and one thousand Indians from Carolina took large numbers of Indian slaves from the Spanish areas.

Although the Europeans actually kidnapped or captured American Indians themselves in the early years of the slave trade, mostly from coastal areas, they soon began to rely on other Indians to do the capturing as the slave trade increased and moved farther away from the coast. Encouraging Native American allies to capture other Indians and deliver them into slavery became a major part of the strategy of the slave dealers. In 1712, for example, the Tuscaroras of North Carolina killed some English and German settlers who had taken their land. The governor of North Carolina announced the availability of Indian slaves to induce South Carolina officials to send him military help. South Carolina expeditions—comprising mostly American Indians—killed more than one thousand Tuscaroras, mostly men. More than seven hundred, mostly women and children, were sold into slavery. Peaceful Indians along the route back to South Carolina also were captured and enslaved.

In 1715, the Yamasees in South Carolina revolted against the Carolina traders because of the traders' dishonest practices, such as cheating when weighing deerskins and furs. The Yamasees were defeated only because the Cherokees allied with the Carolina traders to capture Yamasees to sell as slaves, the proceeds from which sales they used to buy ammunition and clothing from the Carolinians. After that time, Carolina deliberately played one tribe against another. The exposure of Native Americans to European clothing, ammunition, rum, and other goods led to a rising desire for more European products, which further encouraged Indians to capture other Indians for exchange.

In 1699, the French settled on the Gulf coast, in proximity to the Indians of the lower Mississippi River area, who were being threatened by attack and enslavement from Carolinian slave traders and their Indian allies. This opposition from the French increased the risk and cost of capturing lower Mississippi River natives and, by 1720, largely ended the English slave trading.

SIGNIFICANCE

Indians composed one-fourth of the slaves in Carolina in 1708, numbering fourteen hundred out of fifty-five hundred slaves, but the percentage generally decreased after that, for several reasons. Native Americans were more likely than Africans to try to escape. Although Indians had to beware of other hostile Indians, they frequently were successful in their attempts, because they were in or relatively near their native homelands. For this reason, and because of the heavy demand for slave labor on the Caribbean sugar plantations, Native American slaves usually were sold to Caribbean traders. Some were also sold to New England.

In addition, Native American slaves were more susceptible to European diseases and hence had a greater death rate from sickness than did African slaves. Early writers also described American Indian slaves as being more docile than African slaves, ascribing this alleged trait to the Indians' sense of independence. For these reasons, Indian slaves usually were less desirable than, and cost much less than, African slaves. Because large numbers of Native American men were killed, a high percentage of American Indian slaves were women, partly explaining a significant mixture of African and Indian genealogies.

Although some American Indian slavery continued for several more decades, the practice basically had ended by 1730 in Carolina, with the Carolina traders turning to other trades and the English turning their American Indian slavery concerns to central America.

—Abraham D. Lavender

FURTHER READING

Crane, Verner. *The Southern Frontier, 1670-1732*. Ann Arbor: University of Michigan Press, 1929. A classic work on relations between European settlers and American Indians in the South.

Greene, Jack P., Rosemary Brana-Shute, and Randy J. Sparks, eds. *Money, Trade, and Power: The Evolution of Colonial South Carolina's Plantation Society.* Columbia: University of South Carolina Press, 2001. Collection of essays about South Carolina's economic development, including a demographic profile of Indian slavery in the colonial era.

Hatley, Tom. *The Dividing Paths: Cherokees and South Carolinians Through the Era of Revolution.* New York: Oxford University Press, 1993. Examines the culture of the South Carolina settlers and the Cherokees, focusing on the mutual history that links the two groups.

Rozema, Vicki. *Footsteps of the Cherokees: A Guide to the Eastern Homelands of the Cherokee Nations.* Winston-Salem, N.C.: John F. Blair, 1995. Devotes several pages to American Indian slavery, helping to expand the previously small amount of attention given to this topic.

Waddell, Gene. *Indians of the South Carolina Lowcountry, 1562-1751.* Reprint. Spartanburg, S.C.: Reprint Co., 1980. Describes how enslavement was one of several major factors in the extinction of South Carolina's lowcountry tribes.

Weatherford, Jack. *Native Roots: How the Indians Enriched America.* New York: Fawcett Columbine, 1991. One chapter is devoted to American Indian slaves, with a section describing the important part played by Charleston merchants in Indian slavery.

Wright, J. Leitch, Jr. "Brands and Slave Cords." In *The Only Land They Knew: The Tragic Story of the American Indians in the Old South.* New York: Free Press, 1981. Gives details on the Carolina slave trade in American Indians, with emphasis on historical details.

See also: 17th cent.: Europe Endorses Slavery; 1619-c. 1700: The Middle Passage to American Slavery; Aug. 20, 1619: Africans Arrive in Virginia; Nov., 1641: Massachusetts Recognizes Slavery; 1642-1684: Beaver Wars; Mar., 1661-1705: Virginia Slave Codes; Mar. 24, 1663-July 25, 1729: Settlement of the Carolinas; Apr., 1670: Charles Town Is Founded.

Related articles in *Great Lives from History: The Seventeenth Century, 1601-1700:* Aphra Behn; Pocahontas; Squanto.

Late December, 1671
Newton Builds His Reflecting Telescope

Newton was the first person to produce a reflecting telescope that worked as well as a refracting telescope. Presenting this telescope to the Royal Society brought Newton to the attention of the international scientific community, and he quickly used the society as a forum in which to present his new theory of light and colors.

Locale: Cambridge and London, England
Categories: Science and technology; physics; inventions

Key Figures

Sir Isaac Newton (1642-1727), English scientist, mathematician, and inventor
Isaac Barrow (1630-1677), mathematics professor at Cambridge who sponsored and encouraged Newton
Robert Hooke (1635-1703), curator of experiments for the Royal Society and often a severe critic of Newton
René Descartes (1596-1650), French philosopher and mathematician whose book on optics influenced Newton

Summary of Event

Sir Isaac Newton came from an inauspicious rural background and was largely unknown until he made his first reflecting telescope while at Cambridge University. He began showing it, with justifiable pride, in 1669. Eventually, word of the device reached members of the Royal Society of London—a society begun in 1660 as a group of scientists and others who met weekly to discuss items of interest. A member of the society, Newton's mentor and former mathematics professor Isaac Barrow, presented Newton's second telescope to the Society late in December, 1671. Delighted with the telescope, the Society requested more information. Newton obliged them and also took the opportunity to present them with his "New Theory on Light and Color" in February, 1672. Suitably impressed, they elected Newton a member of the Royal Society and thereby brought the young mathematics professor into contact with the leading scientists of the day.

The first known reflecting telescope was made by the Italian Jesuit Nicolas Zucchi in about 1616, but it was Newton who made the first reflecting telescope that rivaled refracting telescopes (which use lenses instead of mirrors). Newton had always been good at constructing things. Even as a boy, he filled his room with tools and various mechanical clocks and other devices he had made.

The key to Newton's telescope was its "speculum," or metal mirror. After experimenting with several alloys from which to construct the mirror, he settled on using copper, tin, and a little silver. Since that seemed to tarnish too quickly, when he made his next telescope, he substituted arsenic for the silver. The materials had to be carefully melted, combined, poured out to cool, ground to the proper shape, and painstakingly polished. The resulting speculum was 1.3 inches (3.3 centimeters) across. He fastened it in the bottom of a 6-inch (15.25-centimeter) pasteboard tube and mounted a much smaller flat mirror at the top of the tube. The flat mirror was tilted so that it reflected the image from the main mirror out through an eyepiece lens mounted in the side of the telescope. The telescope was focused by turning a large metal screw to move the main mirror. It magnified about 40 times, and Newton boasted that he could use it to read the Royal Society's printed journal from 100 feet (30 meters) away!

At the time, it was widely believed that white light was pure and simple and that it became colored as it was degraded by passing through glass. If a white light ray strikes the surface of a prism at an angle so that different parts of the ray travel through different amounts of glass, it was supposed that those parts of the incident ray would degrade by different amounts and therefore emerge as various colors. Newton began a series of experiments in 1664 to determine if this were so, and it was the results of these experiments that he presented to the Royal Society as his theory of light and color.

Although Newton ground and polished his own lenses, it is believed that he purchased his prisms at Cambridge's midsummer fair. To use these prisms, he darkened his room and allowed sunlight to enter only through a small hole in the window shutter. The sunbeam made a round, bright spot—an image of the Sun—on the far wall. Next, he placed a prism in the sunbeam and watched the bright spot spread into rainbow colors. Newton described its shape as an oblong with straight sides and curved top and bottom. He named this rainbow-colored oblong the "spectrum," from a Latin word for ghost; thus, the rainbow is the ghost of light. Newton was surprised to find the spectrum five times longer than it was wide. Its width was about the same as the sun's original image and was what was expected given the angular size of the sun, the size of the hole in the shutter, and the distance to the wall, but there was no simple geometric explanation for the length of the spectrum.

Newton next made a small hole in a board and placed this board behind the prism so that only light of a single color could reach the wall. Then he placed a second prism between the board and the wall. The path of the colored beam was bent by the second prism, but the color was not further changed. Since red light, for example, passed through the second prism without further changing color, the prisms clearly were not "degrading" the light. Another explanation for color change had to be found. Newton removed the board and placed the second prism near the first so that the full spectrum fell on it. As he inverted the second prism so that it was upside-down compared with the first prism, the spectrum on the wall collapsed back into the bright circular image of the sun. That is, passing the light through more glass did not "degrade" it into more colors, but converted it back into white light.

After many more experiments to prove that these results were not caused by imperfections in the prisms, the size or shape of the hole in the shutters, the fact that the Sun's rays are not quite parallel (he made the same obser-

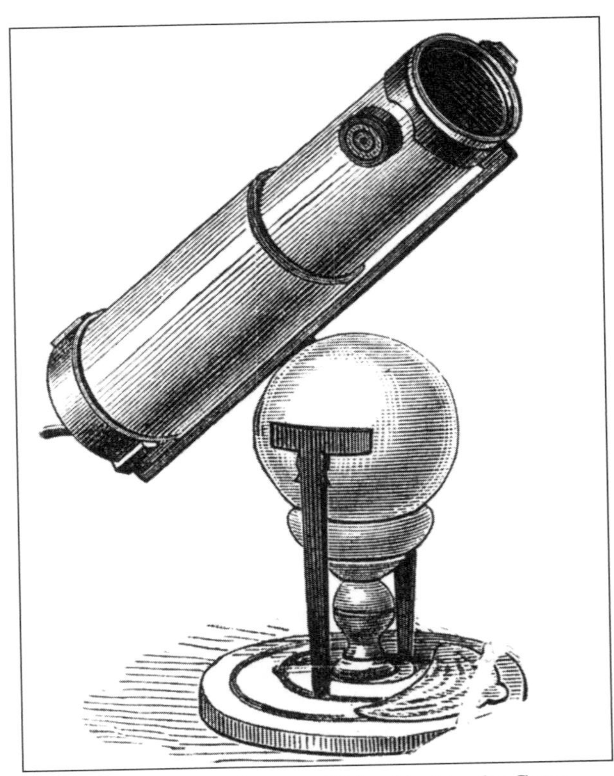

Newton's reflecting telescope. (Hulton|Archive by Getty Images)

vations using the planet Venus), or any other aspect of the experiment, Newton became convinced that white light is compound and that the rainbow colors are primary. That is, the eye's response to seeing a mixture of the rainbow colors all coming from the same spot is to see white. To emphasize this, he painted the sectors of a disk various colors, and then showed that it looked white while it was spinning rapidly.

Robert Hooke, a fellow of the Royal Society, believed that light was a wave motion in an all-pervading substance called the aether, but Newton believed that a light ray consisted of a stream of "corpuscles" (small particles). He argued that if light were a wave, an object would not cast a sharp shadow, since waves would bend around the object into the shadow region. In either case, when a ray of light passes through a prism, its path is bent, or "refracted," as it passes from air into glass, and again as it passes from glass back into air. Newton described the various colors of light as having different "refrangibilites"; that is, different capacities to be refracted.

Newton's theory of light and color did not depend upon knowing whether light consisted of particles or waves, but in his paper he unwisely included the claim that after reviewing his experiments perhaps everyone would agree that light was a particle phenomenon. To Newton's consternation, Hooke immediately claimed that Newton had proven no such thing and went on to argue about that while ignoring Newton's experimental findings. Although Newton quickly agreed that the claim had not been proven and stated that either the wave or the particle model could support his findings, Hooke would not be satisfied. Their disagreement eventually became so heated that Newton refused to publish his major work on optics until after Hooke died.

Significance

All of the large telescopes today, including the Hubble Space Telescope, are direct descendants of Newton's reflecting telescope. Without them, we would know relatively little about the universe beyond Earth's atmosphere. To put Newton's telescope in perspective, it took about fifty years for technology to advance enough consistently to make significantly better reflecting telescopes than his.

René Descartes calculated that the surface of a lens should not be spherical in shape but hyperbolic, in order to focus a point source of light into a single sharp image point. The fuzziness of an image formed by a spherically surfaced lens is called spherical aberration. Newton found that chromatic aberration, the inability of a lens to focus all of the colors simultaneously, was a thousand times worse than spherical aberration. Since chromatic aberration is inherent in the properties of light and glass, Newton switched from trying to make a perfect lens to building a reflecting telescope (which does not suffer from chromatic aberration). In actual fact, Newton suspected chromatic aberration could be overcome by combining lenses with different refracting powers, but he found the reflecting telescope more appealing.

Perhaps more important than any of Newton's devices or discoveries was the way in which he did science. Between them, Galileo (who died the year Newton was born), Christiaan Huygens (Newton's contemporary), and Newton himself made purely philosophical science unacceptable. They established as a widely accepted criterion the modern view that good science should be tied to both good experimental evidence and mathematical models.

—*Charles W. Rogers*

Further Reading

Berlinski, David. *Newton's Gift: How Sir Isaac Newton Unlocked the System of the World*. New York: Simon & Schuster, 2002. A biography that concentrates on Newton, the man, not on his science.

Westfall, Richard S. *Never at Rest: A Biography of Isaac Newton*. New York: Cambridge University Press, 1980. One of the classic biographies of Newton, complete and comprehensive.

White, Michael. *Isaac Newton: The Last Sorcerer*. Reading, Mass.: Perseus Press, 1997. A biography of Newton as both scientist and alchemist.

See also: 1601-1672: Rise of Scientific Societies; Sept., 1608: Invention of the Telescope; 1610: Galileo Confirms the Heliocentric Model of the Solar System; 1615-1696: Invention and Development of the Calculus; 1632: Galileo Publishes *Dialogue Concerning the Two Chief World Systems, Ptolemaic and Copernican*; 1637: Descartes Publishes His *Discourse on Method*; 1655-1663: Grimaldi Discovers Diffraction; Feb., 1656: Huygens Identifies Saturn's Rings; 1660's-1700: First Microscopic Observations; 1665: Cassini Discovers Jupiter's Great Red Spot; 1673: Huygens Explains the Pendulum; Summer, 1687: Newton Formulates the Theory of Universal Gravitation.

Related articles in *Great Lives from History: The Seventeenth Century, 1601-1700:* René Descartes; Galileo; Robert Hooke; Christiaan Huygens; Sir Isaac Newton.

1672-1684
Leeuwenhoek Discovers Microscopic Life

Leeuwenhoek's pioneer work in designing, building, and using microscopes and his discoveries of protozoa and bacteria laid the foundation for the modern science of microbiology.

Locale: Delft, Holland, United Provinces (now in the Netherlands)

Categories: Biology; health and medicine; science and technology; inventions

Key Figures

Antoni van Leeuwenhoek (1632-1723), Dutch biologist and microscopist

Pierre Borel (1620?-1671/1689), French physician and botanist

Regnier de Graaf (1641-1673), Dutch physician and anatomist

Nehemiah Grew (1641-1712), English physician and botanist

Robert Hooke (1635-1703), English mathematician and general scientist

Zacharias Janssen (1580-c. 1638), Dutch lens grinder and inventor of the compound microscope

Giovan Battista Hodierna (1597-1660), Italian astronomer, naturalist, and Roman Catholic priest

Henry Oldenburg (1619-1677), German-English diplomat and administrator, first secretary of the Royal Society of London, and first editor of its journal *Philosophical Transactions*

Francesco Stelluti (1577-1646/1652), Italian mathematician and naturalist who coined the term "microscope"

Jan Swammerdam (1637-1680), Dutch physician and naturalist

Summary of Event

Microscopy began in the late sixteenth century but did not become widespread and respected among scientists until the middle of the seventeenth century. The first published illustrations of microscopic specimens appeared in 1625, as drawings of parts of bees in Francesco Stelluti's *Melissographia*. Giovan Battista Hodierna invented the technique of sectioning anatomical structures for microscopic examination, and he published his studies of sectioned insect eyes in 1644.

Pierre Borel was the first to apply microscopy to medical problems. In 1653, he published his discovery of red blood cells, and in 1655, motivated by historical interest, he traced the origin of microscopy to Zacharias Janssen's invention of the compound microscope around 1590. Jan Swammerdam recorded his description of red blood cells in 1658 and published the results of his microscopic investigations of insects in 1669.

The most important event in microscopy before Antoni van Leeuwenhoek was the publication in 1665 of Robert Hooke's magnificently illustrated *Micrographia: Or, Some Physiological Descriptions of Minute Bodies Made by Magnifying Glasses* (better known as *Micrographia*), which announced Hooke's discovery and naming of the cell as the basic biological structure.

Leeuwenhoek was working as a draper, merchant, and minor government official in Delft when he began grinding lenses sometime between 1668 and 1672. By 1672 his lenses were as powerful as any that then existed. What started as a hobby soon made him famous. Inspired in part by *Micrographia*, Leeuwenhoek examined all kinds of substances and concoctions, carefully recording his observations in his diary.

In an April 28, 1673, letter to Henry Oldenburg, Regnier de Graaf brought Leeuwenhoek's work to the attention of the Royal Society of London, then the most prestigious scientific organization in the world.

Antoni van Leeuwenhoek. (Library of Congress)

Oldenburg published an excerpt from this letter in *Philosophical Transactions of the Royal Society* (May 19). As the readers reacted enthusiastically to its descriptions of molds, bees, and lice, Leeuwenhoek followed with a letter to Oldenburg about the legs and stingers of bees (August 15). Part of this letter appeared in the October 6 issue and was accompanied by illustrations. A selection of extracts from these letters was published by the society as *A Specimen of Some Observations Made by a Microscope* (1673). Thereafter, Leeuwenhoek was a popular and frequent contributor to the journal.

Excerpts from Leeuwenhoek's letters of August 15, 1673, and April 7, 1674 (pb. April 27), and from his letters of June 1 and July 6 (pb. September 21), dealt with microscopic aspects of blood, hair, milk, saliva, brain tissue, bone, and other animal components. The subject matter of his September 7, 1674, letter (pb. November 23, 1674) was similar, but the last paragraph described his examination of water from Lake Berkel. Leeuwenhoek wrote, "among all which there crawled abundance of little animals . . . some of these little creatures were above a thousand times smaller than the smallest ones, which I have hitherto seen. . . ." This was the first mention in any scientific literature of independent unicellular life and probably referred to the alga spirogyra and some species of protozoa.

Leeuwenhoek's undated letter (pb. September 26, 1675) reported his observations of the optic nerve, blood, sugar and salt crystals, and plant sap. Increasingly encouraged throughout the 1670's by Nehemiah Grew, Leeuwenhoek turned more attention toward botanical phenomena. His April 23, 1676, letter (pb. July 18) concerned mostly plant life and mentioned Grew several times, but it also recounted his finding in wine "small living Creatures, shaped like little eels."

Leeuwenhoek's most celebrated contribution to the Royal Society was his letter of October 9, 1676, "Concerning Little Animals by Him Observed in Rain- Well- Sea- and Snow- Water; as Also in Water Wherein Pepper Had Lain Infused" (pb. March 25, 1677). Here he described "animalcula or living Atoms," reported that he had first noticed them in standing rainwater in 1675, and provided clear measures of their tiny size. Most of the creatures depicted in this letter were protozoa, but at least one type was a bacterium. In stagnant pepper water that was still for several days, he saw "incredibly small" animals that he computed were each smaller than one-millionth of a grain of sand. This was the first published mention of bacteria. Leeuwenhoek's March 23, 1677, letter (pb. April 23) answered some questions and clarified some points about these various "little animals."

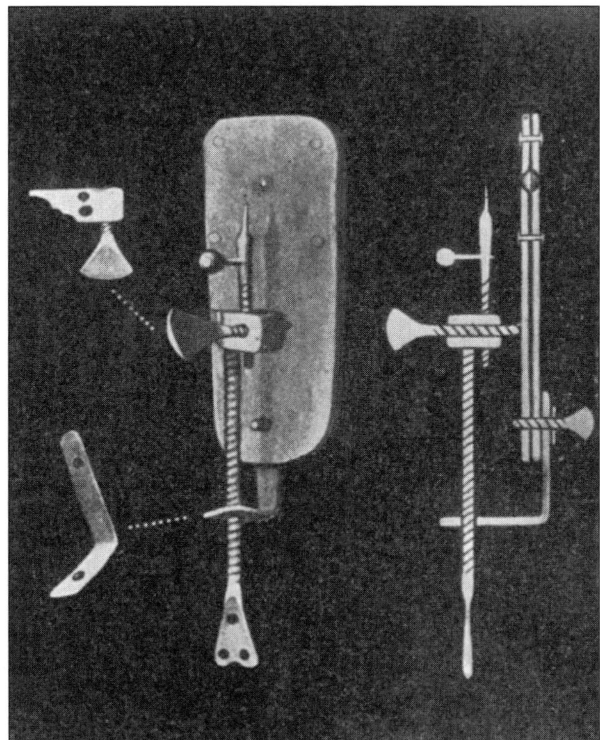

A diagram of Leeuwenhoek's microscope, in its constituent parts. (Hulton|Archive by Getty Images)

In 1677 and 1678, Hooke confirmed Leeuwenhoek's results by reproducing several of these experiments with protozoa in water infusions. While doing this, Hooke may have been the second scientist to see bacteria. He wrote privately to Leeuwenhoek in December of 1677 of having seen through the microscope what appeared to be "gygantick monsters in comparison of a lesser sort which almost filled the water." The former were certainly protozoa, and the latter were likely bacteria.

Although Leeuwenhoek probably discovered bacteria in 1676, the earliest published illustrations of these findings did not appear until his letter of September 17, 1683 (pb. May 20, 1684). This letter included the first specific descriptions and drawings of the round, rod-shaped, and spiral forms of bacteria, which later scientists named cocci, bacilli, and spirochaeta respectively.

Observing bacteria and protozoa was just a small part of Leeuwenhoek's scientific project. After 1677, the "little animals" under his lens were mostly spermatozoa. His letters published from 1683 to 1685 show more interest in salts, minerals, the anatomy of the eye, and spermatozoa than in protozoa and bacteria. He remained a hobbyist and seemed content to let others delve more deeply into his discoveries, although few did during his lifetime.

Leeuwenhoek believed that his greatest accomplishment was being elected a fellow of the Royal Society in 1680. Even though he knew no language other than Dutch, his correspondence to Oldenburg and subsequent secretaries of the Royal Society was always warmly received, and much of it was duly translated into English and quickly published.

SIGNIFICANCE

Along with Hooke, Leeuwenhoek can be considered the founder of microbiology. In his long and fruitful career, he discovered protozoa, bacteria, spermatozoa, and the crystalline lens of the eye. He gave the first accurate descriptions of red blood cells and many other basic components of life, and he invented the technique of staining microscopic specimens to better observe their features. Although the function and physiology of most of the living structures that Leeuwenhoek saw would not begin to be understood until the nineteenth century, he proved in his own time the indispensability of the microscope for science in general and underscored the importance of using the most powerful lenses available, in the best possible light, and with the keenest attention to observed detail.

—*Eric v.d. Luft*

FURTHER READING

Dobell, Clifford, ed. *Antony van Leeuwenhoek and His "Little Animals": Being Some Account of the Father of Protozoology and Bacteriology and His Multifarious Discoveries in These Disciplines*. New York: Dover, 1960. A reprint of the standard 1932 edition of a richly annotated selection of Leeuwenhoek's most important works in English, including a much fuller text of the famous October 9, 1676, letter that appeared in *Philosophical Transactions*.

Ford, Brian J. *The Leeuwenhoek Legacy*. London: Farrand, 1991. A meticulous scholarly study based on research in the archives of the Royal Society.

_______. *Single Lens: The Story of the Simple Microscope*. New York: Harper & Row, 1985. A history of the development and use of the simple microscope from the period before Leeuwenhoek's discoveries through the nineteenth century. More than half of the book is devoted to Leeuwenhoek.

Fournier, Marian. *The Fabric of Life: Microscopy in the Seventeenth Century*. Baltimore: Johns Hopkins University Press, 1996. Examines the work of Leeuwenhoek and four other scientists to explain the reasons for the microscope's appearance and eventual eclipse in the seventeenth century.

Gest, Howard. *Microbes: An Invisible Universe*. Washington, D.C.: ASM Press, 2003. A history of microbiology from the time of Leeuwenhoek to the beginning of the twenty-first century.

Hooke, Robert. *Micrographia: Or, Some Physiological Descriptions of Minute Bodies Made by Magnifying Glasses with Observations and Inquiries Thereupon*. 1665. Reprint. New York: Dover, 1961. Contains the original observation on cork and many other objects. This work is characteristic of the new philosophy of observation.

Huerta, Robert D. *Giants of Delft: Johannes Vermeer and the Natural Philosophers, the Parallel Search for Knowledge During the Age of Discovery*. Lewisburg, Pa.: Bucknell University Press, 2003. This work shows the symbiotic relationship between art and science as exemplified in the work of Leeuwenhoek and of Dutch artist Vermeer.

Leeuwenhoek, Antoni van. *The Select Works of Antony van Leeuwenhoek: Containing His Microscopical Discoveries in Many of the Works of Nature*. Translated by Samuel Hoole. New York: Arno Press, 1977. A relatively easy introduction to a complicated body of primary source material.

Mansuripur, Masud. "The van Leeuwenhoek Microscope." In *Classical Optics and Its Applications*. New York: Cambridge University Press, 2002. This chapter situates Leeuwenhoek's contribution within the wider context of the history of microscopy.

Ruestow, Edward Grant. *The Microscope in the Dutch Republic: The Shaping of Discovery*. New York: Cambridge University Press, 1996. Ruestow compares the work of Swammerdam and Leeuwenhoek and relates both scientists to their contemporary culture.

SEE ALSO: 17th cent.: Advances in Medicine; 1601-1672: Rise of Scientific Societies; 1617-1628: Harvey Discovers the Circulation of the Blood; 1660's-1700: First Microscopic Observations; c. 1670: First Widespread Smallpox Inoculations; 1676: Sydenham Advocates Clinical Observation.

RELATED ARTICLES in *Great Lives from History: The Seventeenth Century, 1601-1700:* William Harvey; Jan Baptista van Helmont; Robert Hooke; Christiaan Huygens; Antoni van Leeuwenhoek; Hans Lippershey; Marcello Malpighi; Nicolaus Steno; Jan Swammerdam; Thomas Sydenham; Jan Vermeer.

1672-c. 1691
SELF-IMMOLATION OF THE OLD BELIEVERS

Under a mandate from the Russian church and state to accept revised religious practices and rituals, thousands of conservative Russian Christians took their own lives, often by burning themselves in their churches, rather than desert their traditions.

LOCALE: Muscovy (now Russia)
CATEGORIES: Religion and theology; wars, uprisings, and civil unrest; social issues and reform

KEY FIGURES

Avvakum Petrovich (1620/1621-1682), Russian priest and leader of the Old Believers, who organized the opposition to Patriarch Nikon and his religious reforms
Nikon (1605-1681), patriarch of the Russian Orthodox Church, 1652-1658, who initiated a sweeping range of reforms
Alexis (1629-1676), Russian czar, r. 1645-1676, who first supported and then opposed Patriarch Nikon
Evrosin (fl. mid-seventeenth-early eighteenth century), monk and Old Believer who published an influential tract opposing self-immolation
Fyodor III (1661-1682), czar of Russia, r. 1676-1682
Ioakim (1620-1690), patriarch of Moscow, 1674-1690
Ivan Khovansky (d. 1682), Russian military commander and sympathizer with the Old Believers
Feodosiya Morozova (1632-1675), Russian noblewoman who became a symbol of the Old Belief
Sophia (1657-1704), queen regent of Russia, r. 1682-1689, daughter of Czar Alexis, sister of Czars Fyodor III and Ivan V, and half sister of Czar Peter the Great

SUMMARY OF EVENT

The Old Belief was a response to efforts by the Russian church and state to change traditional religious practices and rituals. By the seventeenth century, the belief that the end of the world was close at hand had spread through many parts of Russian society. An effort at union between the Greek Orthodox Church and the Roman Catholic Church, followed by the fall of the Byzantine (Greek) Empire to Turkish invaders in the mid-fifteenth century, had convinced many Russians that Russia remained alone as the only true Orthodox Christian nation. Rapid social change encouraged Russians by the late sixteenth century to believe that the end of the world, a time of struggle between good and evil, was close.

In the middle of the seventeenth century, a group of church reformers, led by Nikon, patriarch of Moscow, attempted to change Russian religious paintings, texts, and rites so that they reflected original Greek forms more closely. In particular, the reformers replaced the Russian method of crossing oneself with two fingers by a three-fingered crossing, ordered that alleluias be sung in threes rather than in the customary twos, and changed the prescribed manner for bowing in church. Those who rejected these changes as evil, foreign corruptions of the true faith became known as the Old Believers, and they were condemned by church councils in 1666 and 1667. The Old Believers organized their resistance under the guidance of Avvakum Petrovich, a priest, and of other clergy, who aided the movement as leaders.

The Russian church and government began actively persecuting the Old Believers to make them conform to the new rites. Although officials tried persuasion and propaganda, they also turned to brutal attacks on those who refused to abandon the old ways. After the council of 1667, Czar Alexis commanded that all Russians swear they would be faithful to the new rites. Under Czar Alexis's son, Czar Fyodor III, soldiers tried to force rebellious believers into following this command. The boyarina, or noblewoman, Feodosiya Morozova became one of the most famous of the persecuted. She was arrested in 1671 by troops under the leadership of Ioakim, who was then the archimandrite of the Chudov Monastery and later patriarch of Moscow. She was taken to prison and tortured for four years in an effort to get her to renounce her faith. At the end of 1675, she starved to death.

Initially, the Old Belief was concentrated mainly in monasteries; however, it soon spread to peasants. Discontentment with their oppressed position in Russian society led many peasants to see the Old Belief as a rejection of the entire political order and as a rejection of religious change. The czar's government, official church hierarchy, landowners, and new cultural influences from western Europe were perceived as evidence of an Antichrist taking over the worldly affairs of Russia, as the end of the world approached.

Old Believers dispersed into the remote areas of Russia to escape official pressures. For many, suicide became a means of rejecting the influences of the Antichrist. Apparently, the first suicides occurred in 1665 and 1666. A hermit known as Kapiton preached that the Antichrist was already ruling the world. Small groups of Kapitonists, as his followers were called, began practicing purification by fire, burning themselves to death. The year 1672 marked the beginning of large-scale self-immolation, when peasants locked themselves in churches rather than surrender to besieging authorities. The practice spread rapidly. In 1679, a priest by the name of Dometian in the region of Tiumen organized his parishioners into a self-sacrifice by burning. Rather than surrender to the czar's soldiers, seventeen hundred of Dometian's followers locked themselves in their church and burned to death after setting fire to the building.

The persecution intensified after Czar Fyodor's death. His sister, Sophia, managed to seize control of the state in the name of her brother, Ivan V, and her half brother, Peter the Great, both of whom were minors and were declared co-czars. Queen Regent Sophia relied on elite army corps, known as the *streltsy*, to take power. However, many of the *streltsy*, including their popular commander, Prince Ivan Khovansky, sympathized with the Old Believers. Sophia realized that a rejection of the reforms sponsored by her father would raise doubts about her father's virtue and, by extension, about her own right to rule. She had Khovansky arrested, flogged, and then executed after she became regent.

The persecution of the Old Believers intensified in 1682, and self-immolations increased. In that year, Patriarch Ioakim issued his spiritual decree, which condemned the Old Belief. In that same year, under Ioakim's guidance, the church completed a new council, which had begun in 1681. The council laid down a new set of measures designed to combat those who did not follow the revised rites. These measures prohibited Old Believers from gathering to worship, even in their own homes, and it required priests to report Old Believers to the government so that the government could take action. As a result, even more of the religious dissidents killed themselves. According to one estimate, about two thousand people burned themselves to death between 1676 and 1687 in one district of Iaroslavl alone. Nearly three thousand Old Believers locked themselves in the Paleostrovsky Monastery on Lake Onega and died by fire in 1687. A commonly cited figure holds that twenty thousand people had put themselves and their churches in flames by 1690.

After 1690, the mass suicides by burning became much less common, although they did not disappear completely. In part, self-immolations may have subsided because some Old Believer leaders argued against the practice. The monk Evrosin, in 1691, published an influential tract against suicide called *Otrazitel'noe pisanie o novoizobretonnom puti samoubiistvennykh smerti* (refutation of the newly invented system of suicides) to persuade people that killing themselves was not religiously sanctioned or justified.

SIGNIFICANCE

The suicides of the Old Believers illustrated the depth of the division between conservative Russian believers and the Russian church and state. For much of the history of Russia, from the seventeenth century onward, a substantial minority of the Russian population rejected the existing political, religious, and social order.

The memory and legend of the self-immolation of the Old Believers became a lasting part of Russian culture. The nineteenth century Russian composer Modest Petrovich Mussorgsky drew on the story of Prince Ivan Khovansky and his reported connections to the Old Believers for the opera *Khovanshchina* (1886). After the character of Khovansky has been executed, Old Believers gather at a hermitage in a forest outside Moscow and set their hermitage and themselves on fire, anticipating the approaching government troops.

—*Carl L. Bankston III*

FURTHER READING

Crummey, Robert O. *The Old Believers and the World of Antichrist: The Vyg Community and the Russian State, 1694-1855*. Madison: University of Wisconsin Press, 1970. One of the most influential and widely cited books in English on the Old Believers.

Kliuchevsky, V. O. *A Course in Russian History: The Seventeenth Century*. Translated by Natalie Duddington. Armonk, N.Y.: M. E. Sharpe, 1994. A translation of a classic work by one of Russia's most eminent historians. Chapter 15 examines the church schism.

Kotilaine, Jarmo, and Marshall Poe, eds. *Modernizing Muscovy: Reform and Social Change in Seventeenth Century Russia*. New York: Routledge Curzon, 2004. A collection of articles providing an encyclopedic account of politics, society, and religion in seventeenth century Russia. Includes helpful references in footnotes of each article, and an index.

Michels, Georg Bernhard. *At War with the Church: Religious Dissent in Seventeenth Century Russia*. Stanford, Calif.: Stanford University Press, 1999. A study of the religious dissenters involved in the schism of the Russian church. Attempts to reconstruct popular culture to understand the behavior and thoughts of the dissenters.

Millar, James R. *Encyclopedia of Russian History*. New York: Macmillan, 2003. A comprehensive four-volume source that includes entries on Avvakum, Alexis, and Nikon.

Robbins, Thomas. "Apocalypse, Persecution, and Self-Immolation: Mass Suicides Among the Old Believers in Late-Seventeenth-Century Russia." In *Millenialism, Persecution, and Violence: Historical Cases*, edited by Catherine Wessinger. Syracuse, N.Y.: Syracuse University Press, 2000. A good discussion of the cultural attitudes that played a part in the Old Believer suicides. Makes some comparisons with mass suicides by members of modern cults.

See also: 1632-1667: Polish-Russian Wars for the Ukraine; Jan. 29, 1649: Codification of Russian Serfdom; 1652-1667: Patriarch Nikon's Reforms; Apr., 1667-June, 1671: Razin Leads Peasant Uprising in Russia.

Related articles in *Great Lives from History: The Seventeenth Century, 1601-1700:* Alexis; Avvakum Petrovich; Nikon; Stenka Razin; Sophia.

April 6, 1672-August 10, 1678
French-Dutch War

Making claims to territory and citing economic grievances, Louis XIV invaded the Netherlands. The Dutch people soon rioted and made William of Orange hereditary monarch, while gaining the support of Spain, the Holy Roman Empire, and Brandenburg. The French retreated and eventually ended hostilities by signing the Treaty of Nijmegen in 1678.

Locale: Belgium, the Netherlands, and the Lower Rhine River area (now in Germany)

Categories: Wars, uprisings, and civil unrest; government and politics; economics; expansion and land acquisition

Key Figures

Louis XIV (1638-1715), king of France, r. 1643-1715

Johan de Witt (1625-1672), head of the States Party and grand pensionary of the United Provinces, 1653-1672

Viscount de Turenne (Henri de la Tour d'Auvergne; 1611-1675), French commander in Flanders, 1672-1675

The Great Condé (Louis II de Bourbon; 1621-1686), French military commander, 1672-1675

Michiel Adriaanszoon de Ruyter (1607-1676), Dutch admiral

Sébastien Le Prestre de Vauban (1633-1707), French siege engineer

William III (1650-1702), stadtholder of the Netherlands, r. 1672-1702, and king of England as William III, r. 1689-1702

Summary of Event

In the Treaty of Aix-la-Chapelle that ended the War of Devolution on May 2, 1668, King Louis XIV of France received several Spanish territories. The French were to withdraw from Franche-Comté and return several towns and territories in Flanders and Hainault, notably Cambrai and Saint-Omer. The French kept Lille, Oudenarde, Tournai, and nine other cities along their northern frontier. To guarantee Spain's interests if Louis should overstep these territorial gains, Sweden, Spain, and the United Provinces of the Netherlands (the Dutch Republic) formed the Triple Alliance, also called the Grand Alliance.

From 1668 to 1672, Louis had worked to isolate the Dutch, agreeing in principle with the English to attack the United Provinces. He also increased maritime pressure on the Dutch, paid the Swedes to block German aid to the Dutch in the event of hostilities, and fostered alliances with north German states. In 1671, Louis formally complained that Dutch bans on French products constituted economic retaliation, and he secretly prepared for war. Early in 1672, he added Cologne to Münster as German allies, and, on March 23, an English fleet opened the Third Anglo-Dutch War by attacking the Dutch Levant fleet near the Isle of Wight. On April 6, Louis, too, declared war on the United Provinces.

Immediately, Viscount de Turenne took 23,000 French troops down the Sambre River and headed for Maastricht, while the Great Condé led 30,000 French troops in an occupation of Lorraine, eventually meeting Turenne at Visé on the Meuse. The Dutch pulled back from their Rhineland fortresses in Cleves to protect Maastricht. On

May 18, Münster declared war on the Dutch, with Cologne following suit shortly after. Meanwhile, a French fleet under the command of the comte d'Estrée was sailing to join the English fleet under James, the duke of York (the future King James II). Dutch Admiral Michiel Adriaanszoon de Ruyter could not act quickly enough to prevent their joining forces, but he did manage to attack, divide, and badly damage the combined forces at Solebay on June 6. This Dutch victory temporarily prevented any Anglo-French naval interference in Dutch waters.

The French armies decided to bypass heavily defended Maastricht, isolating it and proceeding up the Rhine River through underdefended Cleves. Turenne mopped up the defenses on the left bank, and Condé those on the right. Münster invaded the Dutch provinces of Overijssel and Lingen, and, on June 11, the French army reunited at Emmerich near Arnhem. Outnumbered three to one and outflanked by the French, the Dutch field army retreated into the Netherlands proper, toward Utrecht, and was closely followed by the French. Though this greatly tightened the Dutch lines of communication and supply and presented a much more compact front, the Dutch government determined that it was necessary to open the sluices of the dikes and flood the polders, creating a water barrier between the French and the Dutch provinces of Holland, Zeeland, and Utrecht. This effectively halted the French advance, and so Louis symbolically departed from the army on August 1, to keep from being personally tainted by a defeat. Farther east, Cologne and Münster moved into the provinces of Groningen and Friesland, so that by early fall, nearly two-thirds of Dutch territory was in enemy hands.

The military retreat was devastating to the Dutch people. They responded by rioting in Utrecht and Arnhem immediately before the French arrived in mid-June. In Holland and Zeeland, terrified people rebelled against the States Party, led by Johan de Witt, that controlled the country. The aristocratic leaders of the party openly advocated capitulation in late June, while the middle- and

The French, seeking land it thought was rightfully theirs, attacked the province of Holland, setting off another war between France and the Dutch Republic. In this depiction, the French pillage a Dutch village in 1672. (Francis R. Niglutsch)

lower-class Dutch favored continued resistance. Riots broke out in Delft, Gouda, Rotterdam, and Scheidam on June 29, with rioters demanding that William of Orange, leader of the opposition Orangist Party, be made stadtholder, or supreme military commander. Zeeland voted for William on July 2, Holland voted for him the next day, and others followed. In captured cities, Louis granted religious freedom but insisted on installing Catholic clergy in major churches, which was clearly a slap at the Calvinist hegemony.

French plundering of the countryside led to further resentment and antigovernment rioting in Amsterdam, Delft, Haarlem, and Leiden in early September. The unseated de Witt was murdered by an angry mob in The Hague on August 20. The Holy Roman Empire, and Brandenburg's Frederick William, the Great Elector—angered by the French violation of Cleves—had pledged assistance to the Dutch in late spring. By fall, their moves against the Rhineland diverted Louis's attention from the stagnant "water line" in the Netherlands and forced Cologne's army into a defensive mode.

The French campaign that began in the spring of 1673 focused on taking Maastricht, which it did on June 30. A renewed attempt by a joint Anglo-French fleet to secure the Dutch coast for a military landing was brilliantly thwarted by de Ruyter off the Zeeland coast on June 14, and again a week later near Schoneveldt. A fourth naval defeat—at Texel on August 21—forced the English to sue for peace, marking the end of the Third Anglo-Dutch War with the signing of a peace treaty on February 19, 1674.

In late summer, 1673, Spain and the Holy Roman Empire joined the Dutch in the Hague Convention, and William III went on the offensive. Allied armies freed Naarden and attacked Cologne. Louis moved his armies back from the water line, abandoned Utrecht, and sued for peace as well. Unwilling to leave Louis in possession of so much of the Netherlands, the allies rejected his offer. In April, 1674, the allies forced Münster out of the war, and by June, Louis held only Maastricht and Grave in Dutch territory.

On May 28, the German diet declared war on France, and soon after Denmark provided support, too. William's army of 65,000 men unsuccessfully battled Condé's 45,000 French troops around Grave, while Turenne managed to parry an imperial thrust in the Rhineland led by Count Aeneas Caprara. Turenne beat the imperial forces at Sinzheim (June 16), later laying waste to much of the Palatinate and threatening Heidelberg. Granted a greatly enlarged army, Turenne defeated a much stronger imperial and Brandenburger army at Enzheim (October 4) and again in a daring midwinter attack near Colmar.

Despite England's withdrawal, French naval forces continued to harry Dutch shipping, seriously interfering with Dutch commerce, depressing their economy, and forcing them to maintain high levels of taxation. Turenne died in 1675 at Nieder Sasbach, the same year the French retreated from the Rhineland, and in 1676, William attempted a siege of Maastricht, which was unsuccessful. In 1677, the French invaded the Spanish Netherlands again, seizing Valenciennes, Cambrai, and Saint Omer in a series of classic sieges directed by Sébastien Le Prestre de Vauban. William, with an army of 30,000 allied troops, tried desperately and unsuccessfully to retake Saint Omer at the Battle of Mont Cassel (April 11). In November, William married Mary Stuart (the future Queen Mary II), which led to an Anglo-Dutch treaty of defense (January 10, 1678) and put him in line for the English throne, which he gained in 1689.

Maneuvering before the inevitable peace negotiations, Louis besieged Ghent and Ypres in the spring of 1678 and offered peace terms on April 15. In the Treaties of Nijmegen, he dealt with the Dutch (August 10), with Spain (September 17), and with the empire (February 6, 1679). Louis's gains in the Spanish Netherlands included Franche-Comté, Valencienes, Cambrai, Aire, Saint Omer, Ypres, Condé, and Bouchain.

SIGNIFICANCE

For all of Louis's expenditures, his territorial gains were minimal. However, the territories he gained were strategically important, providing him with a deeper buffer and advanced line of defense. For the Dutch, however, the war brought important political and economic changes. During the more than six-year war, many merchants took flight from Amsterdam, and with them went a great deal of portable capital from the city, which led to its weakening as Europe's financial center. The Dutch countryside was ravaged not only by the French armies but also by defensive flooding. On the positive side, de Ruyter's naval campaigns effectively ended the Anglo-Dutch naval wars and curbed English naval pretensions—for the moment.

Constitutionally, the United Provinces fell into the hands of William of Orange, who would soon become King William III of England, uniting the interests of the two states. The replacement of the ruling aristocracy with a virtual monarch would prove a significant development in the history of the Dutch state. Furthermore, the United Provinces greatly enlarged and strengthened its army and fortifications, providing a far more effective defensive posture in the face of Louis's continued hostility and desire for territorial aggrandizement.

—*Joseph P. Byrne*

Further Reading

Chartrand, René, and Francis Back. *Louis XIV's Army*. London: Osprey, 1996. A well-illustrated account of the weapons, uniforms, and tactics of Louis's military.

Childs, John. *Warfare in the Seventeenth Century*. London: Cassell, 2001. A broad discussion of warfare in the era, with specific treatments of the 1672 campaigns, the Battle of Maastricht, and Turenne's Rhineland campaigns in 1674-1675.

Israel, Jonathan. *The Dutch Republic: Its Rise, Greatness, and Fall, 1477-1806*. New York: Oxford University Press, 1998. Provides a well-developed discussion of the war's background, military phases, and effects on the Dutch state.

Lynn, John A. *The Wars of Louis XIV*. New York: Longman, 1999. Provides a detailed study of the war in its various military and diplomatic phases.

See also: July 5, 1601-Apr., 1604: Siege of Oostende; 1617-1693: European Powers Vie for Control of Gorée; 1640-1688: Reign of Frederick William, the Great Elector; 1642-1684: Beaver Wars; Nov. 7, 1659: Treaty of the Pyrenees; 1661: Absolute Monarchy Emerges in France; Mar. 4, 1665-July 31, 1667: Second Anglo-Dutch War; May 24, 1667-May 2, 1668: War of Devolution; Jan. 23, 1668: Triple Alliance Forms; Aug. 10, 1678-Sept. 26, 1679: Treaties of Nijmegen; 1689-1697: Wars of the League of Augsburg; Sept. 20, 1697: Treaty of Ryswick; Oct. 11, 1698, and Mar. 25, 1700: First and Second Treaties of Partition.

Related articles in *Great Lives from History: The Seventeenth Century, 1601-1700:* The Great Condé; Frederick William, the Great Elector; James II; Louis XIV; Mary II; Michiel Adriaanszoon de Ruyter; Viscount de Turenne; Sébastien Le Prestre de Vauban; William III.

Summer, 1672-Fall, 1676
Ottoman-Polish Wars

The Ottoman-Polish Wars, which devastated the Ukraine, were sparked by a confluence of Ukrainian/Cossack unrest and Turkish imperialism. Poland gained a Polish king, the Ukraine was freed from Polish control, and Poland benefited culturally as it blended its own artistic styles with those of the Ottomans.

Locale: Southern marches, Polish-Lithuanian Commonwealth

Categories: Wars, uprisings, and civil unrest; diplomacy and international relations

Key Figures

John III Sobieski (1629-1696), Polish commander during war with the Ottomans, and king of Poland, r. 1674-1696

Mehmed IV Avci (1642-1693), Ottoman sultan, r. 1648-1687

Michael Korybut Wisniowiecki (1640-1673), king of Poland, r. 1669-1673

Summary of Event

Hit by a deluge of rebels and invaders since 1648, the Polish-Lithuanian Commonwealth, or Rzeczypospolita, engaged yet another foe in the 1670's, fighting a series of wars with the Ottoman Empire. Although pledged to "perpetual friendship and alliance" by a treaty of 1533, Turkish victories in the Balkans and Hungary pushed the sultan's armies closer to the commonwealth, while regional politics drew both countries to war.

These wars centered in the Wild Lands, the sparsely settled frontier zone of the southern Ukraine and home of the Cossacks, a collection of adventurers, bandits, pirates, and mercenaries. Seldom unified under one leader, Cossack military factions maintained fortified outposts, such as the Zaparozhskaia Sich, located on an island in the Dnieper River.

Fearless and contemptuous of authority, Cossacks prized their independence above all else. Although a problem for their neighbors, Cossacks were most often at odds with the Ottomans or Tatars. Both Moscow and Poland-Lithuania used Cossacks as border guards, mainly to protect the Wild Lands, and beyond, against Tatar raiders. Tatars, Muslim descendants of the Mughals, maintained a predatory state based in the Crimea. Every year, *tchambouls* (large parties of Tatar horsemen), which could total up to 20,000 men, moved north looking for loot and slaves.

These raids were but one part of a complex series of rebellions and invasions, along with general chaos, that racked the Ukraine between 1648 and 1667. Cossacks aligned for and then against both the commonwealth and Moscow. Finally, the new leader of the Tatars, Khan ʿAdil Giray, forged an alliance with Petro Doroshenko's Cossack faction for a grand raid into Polish territories.

The end of the summer of 1667 saw a combined Tatar-Cossack army of nearly 30,000 men crossing the frontier. Noted for their horsemanship and raiding skills, Tatars and Cossacks were excellent light cavalry. Jan Pasek, a contemporary chronicler, said the troops were difficult to pin down and hard to kill. He also warned that the horsemen were wily opponents, for "flight is to no avail, and pursuit is irksome."

Despite their status as first-rate cavalrymen, Tatar-Cossack armies lacked artillery, and they were easily disrupted by massed musket fire. Leaders in Warsaw knew this, and because they refused to believe that Orthodox Christian Cossacks would make common cause with Muslim Tatars, they thus refused funds for building a counterforce. Poland-Lithuania's local commander, John III Sobieski, combining his personal retinue with local troops, had just 8,000 soldiers.

Moving into the Polish sector of the Wild Lands placed the invaders in Podolia (now in western Ukraine), a land of plains, hills, swamps, and sparse forests dominated by the Dniester and Southern Bug Rivers. The Dniester is navigable for its entire length, whereas the Southern Bug is interrupted by swamps and rapids. Podolia also featured Kamieniec Podolski, a powerful fortress and arms depot.

Brilliant tactics allowed Sobieski to defeat the Tatar-Cossack alliance. Using Kamieniec Podolski, strategically placed earthworks, and mobile wagon forts, he divided his army into small mutually supporting units. Each had the task of holding river crossings, smashing enemy raiders, or falling back on fortified positions when faced by superior numbers. Taking 3,000 of his best soldiers, Sobieski constructed a fortified camp at Podhajce, which allowed him to cut the invaders' main supply line. A large Tatar-Cossack force moved to besiege his position but was routed when the Poles launched a night assault in October, 1667.

John III Sobieski. (Hulton|Archive by Getty Images)

Sobieski next secured a truce, but he also asked for reinforcements. Parsimonious magnates who dominated Poland-Lithuania's parliament, or Sejm, refused to fund this request, arguing that Sobieski was capable of dealing with any contingency. Their focus was not on military affairs but rather on the election of a new monarch, because John II Casimir Vasa (Jan Kazimierz), who had reigned since 1648, had abdicated on September 16, 1668.

After considerable politicking, Michael Korybut Wisniowiecki, leader of a Ruthenian magnate family greatly disliked by the Cossacks, became king of Poland in September, 1669. A pious fool who "could speak eight languages but had nothing intelligent to say in any of them," he would only make enemies and encourage dissension within his semi-anarchic government.

Doroshenko positioned himself to benefit from this by aligning his Cossacks with the Ottomans. Thus encouraged, Sultan Mehmed IV Avci declared himself "the protector of the Cossacks," sending an Ottoman army northward while calling up his Tatar vassals. Poland-Lithuania now faced a severe challenge, as the combined enemy forces had a significant advantage in numbers and the Ottomans possessed a first-rate army.

Comprising cavalry, artillery, and elite Janissary infantry, the Ottoman army numbered 80,000 men who moved into Podolia during the hot summer of 1672. On August 29, after a siege of just seven days, Kamieniec Podolski surrendered. This powerful fortress was symbolic of the weakened state of Polish-Lithuanian armies, for despite having more than 200 cannon, it had a garrison of just 250 men, all but four incapable of serving as artillerymen.

Sobieski responded with a 150-mile razzia (plundering raid) into Tatar/Cossack-controlled Ukraine, destroying forts, arms depots, and enemy villages. In early October, he smashed smaller Tatar forces, killing, capturing, or dispersing nearly 22,000 enemy riders. Although a brilliant raid that showed Sobieski could "out-Tatar the Tatars," this did not stop Polish diplomats from accepting the Treaty of Buczacz, which recognized Podolia as an Ottoman fief administered by Doroshenko and required a yearly tribute of 22,500 gold ducats to the sultan.

Unwilling to ratify this humiliating document, the Sejm instead voted to raise a 40,000-man army for a war of revenge. Sobieski started this campaign with additional defeats of Tatar raiders at Niemirów, Komarno, and Kałusza. Dispersed by Sobieski's superior tactics, the Tatars were hunted down by enraged peasants, and in the words of Pasek, "died like dogs."

These setbacks sent Tatars reeling back to the Crimea and also deprived the Ottoman army of valuable scouts. Split into three parts, 30,000 were entrenched at Khotin, on the Dniester River. Sobieski, now reinforced with a similar-sized force, managed to sneak up and launch a surprise attack in November, 1673. Routed, the Ottomans attempted to flee over a single bridge, which quickly collapsed under the weight of the troops. The Ottoman force was annihilated, and the Poles captured 120 guns, hundreds of standards, and plenty of loot. Pasek noted that camels from the Turkish supply train were so common that "you could even get one for a servant's nag."

Sobieski followed up his victory with an offensive into Ottoman-dominated Moldavia, forcing the Turkish garrison at Jassam to abandon the town and flee south. In addition, he detached a force to regain Kamieniec Podolski. Neither action was completed before news arrived that King Michael had died on November 10, one day before Sobieski's triumph at Khotin. In the Rzeczypospolita, kings did not inherit the throne but were instead elected.

Sobieski returned to Warsaw, where his victories over Cossacks, Tatars, and Turks made him a candidate for the throne. After some debate, the hero of Khotin became the king of Poland-Lithuania on May 19, 1674. In addition, the Sejm authorized funding for a new army, which had disintegrated after its victory at Khotin, to fight the Ottomans. It was organized just in time, as a new force of more than 100,000 Turkish soldiers crossed the Dniester and advanced on Lwow.

Sobieski again used his hit-and-run tactics backed by mobile wagon forts and earthworks. On August 24, 1675, at the Battle of Lwow, he demolished a Tatar army of 20,000. Reconcentrating his forces, Sobieski drove the Ottomans back into Moldavia. The final battle of the war took place at Zurawno in the fall of 1676. Again, Sobieski employed earthworks and his wagon forts to protect his 20,000 troops from the 100,000 Turks and Tatars under İbrahim Paşa. Spirited assaults only produced heavy Ottoman losses, while Sobieski advanced his redoubts to within musket range of the Turkish main camp. At this point, İbrahim suggested negotiations, and a conclusion to the Ottoman-Polish Wars came with the Treaty of Zurawno. Poland-Lithuania surrendered part of Podolia but paid no tribute.

SIGNIFICANCE

Ottoman-Polish conflicts of the 1670's produced significant consequences. First, Sobieski's victories allowed him to trump foreign-backed candidates in the already corrupt and complicated process of electing a Polish monarch. In turn, this created an anti-Turkish king quite willing to take his army to relieve Vienna during the famous Ottoman siege of 1683.

The Ukraine, devastated by a decade of warfare that locals dubbed the *ruina* (the ruin), never effectively returned to Polish control. On a cultural note, the rich spoils from captured Ottoman camps influenced fashion and art in late seventeenth century Poland, creating a unique blend of Polish-Ottoman designs.

—John P. Dunn

FURTHER READING

Kolodziejczk, Dairiusz. *Ottoman-Polish Diplomatic Relations, Fifteenth-Eighteenth Century: An Annotated Edition of Ahdnames and Other Documents*. Leiden, the Netherlands: Brill, 2000. Primary diplomatic documents translated and with useful notes.

Ostrowski, Jan, ed. *Land of the Winged Horsemen: Art in Poland, 1572-1764*. Alexandria, Va.: Art Services International, 1999. Superb photographs of Polish armor and weapons, along with commentary on how conflict created a blending of Polish and Turkish artistic styles.

Pasek, Jan Chryzostom. *Memoirs of the Polish Baroque*. Edited and translated by Catherine Leach. Berkeley: University of California Press, 1976. Pasek's diaries form an important primary source on late seventeenth century Poland. He provides interesting details on the fights between Tatars and Turks during the 1670's.

Subtelny, Orest. *Ukraine: A History*. 3d ed. Toronto: University of Toronto Press, 2000. An authoritative history of the Ukraine.

Turk ve Islam Eserleri Muzesi. *War and Peace: Ottoman-Polish Relations in the Fifteenth-Nineteenth Centuries*. Istanbul, Turkey: 1999. An exhibition catalog with articles and photographs relating mainly to events of the 1500's and 1600's.

See also: 1638: Waning of the *Devshirme* System; Aug. 22, 1645-Sept., 1669: Turks Conquer Crete; July 10, 1655-June 21, 1661: First Northern War; 1656-1676: Ottoman Empire's Brief Recovery; Apr., 1667-June, 1671: Razin Leads Peasant Uprising in Russia; 1677-1681: Ottoman-Muscovite Wars; July 14-Sept. 12, 1683: Defeat of the Ottomans at Vienna; 1684-1699: Holy League Ends Ottoman Rule of the Danubian Basin; Beginning 1687: Decline of the Ottoman Empire; Jan. 26, 1699: Treaty of Karlowitz.

Related articles in *Great Lives from History: The Seventeenth Century, 1601-1700:* Alexis; John III Sobieski; Bohdan Khmelnytsky; Ivan Stepanovich Mazepa.

c. 1673
Buxtehude Begins His Abendmusiken Concerts

After becoming church organist in Lübeck, Dieterich Buxtehude began directing the Abendmusiken, a series of organ and vocal concerts that became famous throughout Europe. The series lasted for almost thirty-five years, during which time it caught the attention of several of the Continent's leading composers and musicians, including a young Johann Sebastian Bach.

Locale: Lübeck, Germany
Categories: Music; cultural and intellectual history

Key Figures

Dieterich Buxtehude (1637-1707), Danish-born organist and composer
Johann Sebastian Bach (1685-1750), German organist and composer
Franz Tunder (d. 1667), German organist and composer
Peter Hindrich Tesdorpf (1648-1723), German merchant

Summary of Event

Around 1673, the Danish-born composer Dieterich Buxtehude established an annual concert series in Saint Mary's Cathedral in the north German city of Lübeck. The concerts came to be known as the Abendmusiken (evening music) and regularly consisted of a large-scale production of vocal and instrumental performances. The series, held in its original format until 1810, a century after Buxtehude's death, garnered the attention of several of Europe's leading musicians and became a defining cultural institution of the city itself.

Buxtehude most likely began his musical studies under the tutelage of his father, Johannes Buxtehude, who was a church organist in Helsingør, Denmark. In addition, as a student in one of the Latin schools in Helsingør, the younger Buxtehude most likely would have studied music theory and composition. By the early seventeenth century, Denmark (particularly Copenhagen) had become a well-known center for musical study and performance, largely through the generous patronage of King Christian IV (1588-1648). A rich tradition of organ composition and performance had already been established in this region by the time Buxtehude reached adulthood, and, in 1658, he attained the position of church organist at Saint Mary's in Helsingborg. In 1660, Buxtehude returned to Helsingør to assume the organist post in that city's Saint Mary's Church.

In 1668, Buxtehude was appointed the official organist at Saint Mary's Cathedral in Lübeck, Germany, at that time one of the most prestigious music positions in Europe. Buxtehude succeeded the well-known organist Franz Tunder, who had died the previous year. Shortly after moving to Lübeck, Buxtehude became a citizen of the city and married Anna Tunder, the daughter of his professional predecessor at Saint Mary's. Although Lübeck had gone through years of economic decline, largely as a result of expenses incurred during the Thirty Years' War (1618-1648), it had remained one of the leading musical centers in Europe. Buxtehude's appointment thus gave him access to a larger and more diverse circle of musicians than he had previously known.

While Buxtehude's professional duties at Saint Mary's consisted, primarily, of composing and performing organ works for the regular church services, the musical contacts and influence he developed by way of his position there helped him establish the Abendmusiken concerts. Although his predecessor, Franz Tunder, had been in the habit of presenting concerts at the church during his own tenure, Buxtehude was responsible for establishing a regular format for the series of concerts, which occurred annually and which were organized on a greater scale than the performances that had been presented by Tunder. The earliest Abendmusiken concerts in this tradition began around 1673, only five years after Buxtehude arrived at Lübeck, and by 1690, they had become prominent fixtures in the cultural life of the city. By that time it was impossible to speak of the Abendmusiken without reference to its famous director.

Although the Abendmusiken concerts originally had been held on Thursday evenings, Buxtehude eventually settled on presenting them during the afternoon on each of the five Sundays between Saint Martin's Day (November 11) and Christmas. The concerts featured the joined forces of organ, instrumentalists, chorus, and vocal soloists, the highlight of which was a large-scale work generally known as a *dramma per musica*. This form, which Buxtehude had instituted into the Abendmusiken by 1678, is a dramatic work set to music, usually with a complete libretto for chorus and soloists and significant orchestration. Although the genre is often described as an early form of opera, the performance of a *dramma per musica* is not staged (the singers and musicians are placed on the stage as in a concert performance), and the libretto is based more on allegorical themes than on dramatic story lines. In this respect, it resembles more closely a classical oratorio. For example, one of Buxtehude's earliest presentations of the genre in Lübeck, titled "The Wedding of the Lamb," was a loosely connected set of choral pieces based on the biblical passage that describes, in largely allegorical terms, the marriage between Christ and the Church. In the musical drama, Christ and Church are each represented by soloists (who even perform a kind of love duet), and they are accompanied by a full choir (representing the heavenly angels) and several instrumentalists.

Considering that almost all serious music in the seventeenth century was funded through religious or political institutions, Buxtehude's Abendmusiken concerts were notable for their reliance on civic support. Buxtehude's financial supporters included many of the city's leading businesspeople, including the merchant Peter Hindrich Tesdorpf, who had been a strong influence in the city's commercial guilds. While the excellence of the musical performances would have been reason in themselves to support the series, it is also likely that the international reputation of the concerts only could have helped the city's economic trade, which had undergone a serious decline in the seventeenth century. At any rate, the series attracted a regular number of visitors over the years, many of whom came to experience firsthand the remarkably splendid new form of music that Buxtehude had developed. The most famous attendee of the Abendmusiken during Buxtehude's tenure was undoubtedly the young Johann Sebastian Bach, who was reported to have traveled on foot from Arnstadt, Germany (more than 200 miles away), to hear the Abendmusiken and Buxtehude's organ performances. Although Buxtehude died in 1707, his predecessors continued to present the Abendmusiken concerts until the French occupation of Lübeck in 1810.

SIGNIFICANCE

The Abendmusiken concerts instituted by Buxtehude, which, for the most part, were maintained in the same format through the early nineteenth century, significantly enhanced Lübeck's reputation as an international center of musical innovation and excellence. More important, the reputation of the Abendmusiken among European musicians had the effect of popularizing and developing Buxtehude's brand of dramatic music. At the least, the concerts demonstrated both the feasibility and appeal of amalgamating a large group of singers and musicians to perform a large-scale work. In this respect, works as diverse as Beethoven's Ninth Symphony (1824), with its massive choral finale, and German composer Carl Orff's *Carmina burana* (1937) can trace their origins in part to the performances in Lübeck.

The Abendmusiken also provided a venue for Buxtehude's organ compositions and performances, which were considerably innovative and influential in their own right. Upon Bach's return to Arnstadt after his four-month sojourn in Lübeck, his listeners detected an increased improvisatory and elaborate style in his organ performances, directly due to Buxtehude's influence and the Abendmusiken. Although most of Buxtehude's copious musical output in its original form is lost, transcriptions of his work made by Bach during his time in Lübeck have preserved some of the most notable examples of Buxtehude's works.

—*Joseph M. Ortiz*

Further Reading

Carter, Tim, and John Butt, eds. *The Cambridge History of Seventeenth-Century Music*. Chapel Hill: University of North Carolina Press, 2005. A comprehensive study of seventeenth century Western music, including Buxtehude's contributions to organ composition and the Abendmusiken. Essays address religious, political, social, and academic contexts. Includes illustrations, musical examples, and a bibliography.

Snyder, Kerala J. *Dieterich Buxtehude: Organist in Lübeck*. New York: Schirmer Books, 1987. A cogent, comprehensive study of Buxtehude's life and works, with significant analysis of the organ works and vocal music. Includes selected writings and compositions as well as several illustrations, musical examples, archival references, and a bibliography.

Webber, Geoffrey. *Northern German Church Music in the Age of Buxtehude*. Oxford, England: Clarendon Press, 1996. Webber examines the vocal and instrumental music of Buxtehude and his contemporaries within the context of the European church music tradition. Includes illustrations, musical examples, a bibliography, and maps.

Wolff, Christoph. "Dietrich Buxtehude and Seventeenth-Century Music in Retrospect." In *Church, Stage, and Studio: Music and Its Contexts in Seventeenth-Century Germany*, edited by Paul Walker. Ann Arbor, Mich.: UMI Press, 1990. Wolff focuses on Buxtehude's vocal and chamber music compositions, particularly his contribution to the oratorio. Includes musical examples and illustrations.

See also: c. 1601: Emergence of Baroque Music; Feb. 24, 1607: First Performance of Monteverdi's *La favola d'Orfeo*; c. 1666: Stradivari Makes His First Violin.

Related articles in *Great Lives from History: The Seventeenth Century, 1601-1700:* Arcangelo Corelli; Girolamo Frescobaldi; Claudio Monteverdi; Johann Pachelbel; Heinrich Schütz.

Beginning 1673
French Explore the Mississippi Valley

French explorers charted and occupied the Mississippi Valley and points west, founded Louisiana, and set the stage for conflict with the British a century later.

Locale: Mississippi River Valley
Categories: Exploration and discovery; colonization; expansion and land acquisition

Key Figures

Sieur de La Salle (René-Robert Cavelier; 1643-1687), French nobleman and explorer
Louis Jolliet (1645-1700), French explorer and trapper
Jacques Marquette (1637-1675), Jesuit priest and chronicler of Jolliet's journey
Pierre Le Moyne d'Iberville (1661-1706), founder of the first French settlement on the Gulf of Mexico
Jean-Baptiste Le Moyne (sieur de Bienville; 1680-1767), brother of Iberville and founder of Mobile and New Orleans
Jean-Baptiste Talon (c. 1625-1694), colonial intendant who licensed the first expeditions to the Great Lakes
Comte de Frontenac et Palluau (Louis de Buade; 1622-1698), sponsor of La Salle's expeditions

Summary of Event

Expanding upon Samuel de Champlain's explorations in the early 1600's, Jean Nicolet opened the Ottawa River route to Lake Huron, Lake Michigan, and Green Bay in 1634. Nicolet then traveled up the Fox River; probably crossed the portage at what is now Portage, Wisconsin, to enter the Mississippi Valley; and may have proceeded south into what is now northern Illinois. During this trip, natives of the Mascouten tribe told him of a "great water" three days' travel to the west. Although this probably was the Mississippi River, Nicolet thought it was the Pacific Ocean.

In 1671, Nicholas Perrot guided Simon François Daumont, sieur de St. Lusson, to Sault Sainte Marie. St. Lusson formally took possession of the area for France and signed trade treaties with sixteen western tribes in 1672. Perrot was the first man licensed to explore the Great Lakes by Jean-Baptiste Talon, intendant in charge of the French colonial judiciary and finances. Earlier, however, Médard Chouart des Groseilliers and Pierre Esprit Radisson had led an illegal exploratory trade mission to Chequamegon Bay on Lake Superior, from 1654 to 1660. It appears that Radisson also traveled west to Mille Lacs (Minnesota) and perhaps to the Mississippi River.

Talon also engaged Louis Jolliet to explore the Mississippi River. In 1673, Jolliet, accompanied by Jacques Marquette, a Jesuit priest, left Michilimackinac and traveled across Lake Michigan to Green Bay and up the Fox River. They then portaged the Wisconsin River, thus entering the Mississippi Valley, and descended the Wisconsin River to its mouth. They canoed down the Mississippi River as far as the mouth of the Arkansas River, where they became convinced that the Mississippi River flowed into the Gulf of Mexico, not the Gulf of California, and that it was therefore not a potential route to the Pacific Ocean. Jolliet and Marquette returned up the Mississippi River. Discovering the mouth of the Illinois River, they ascended it. From the Illinois River, they portaged to the Chicago River, leaving the Mississippi Valley and entering Lake Michigan.

In 1672, Talon had left for France, turning over the colonial government to Louis de Buade, comte de Frontenac et Palluau. Frontenac envisioned building a series of forts west of the Appalachian Mountains to exclude the English from the Mississippi Valley. He then hoped to tap the rich fur supply and ship it to France from either Quebec or a new city to be constructed near the mouth of the Mississippi River. Frontenac made René-Robert Cavelier, sieur de La Salle, who was fluent in eight American Indian languages and very effective in dealing with the tribes, his chief agent. La Salle already had explored the Ohio River to the falls at present-day Louisville in 1669-1670.

On May 12, 1678, King Louis XIV and Jean-Baptiste Colbert, the king's minister, signed letters patent giving La Salle a five-year trade monopoly in the West. In the spring of 1679, La Salle sent a party westward toward the land of the Illinois and began building his own sailing ship, the *Griffon*, which became the first to sail the lakes. On August 27, he arrived aboard his ship at Michilimackinac. Sending the *Griffon* back from Green Bay, La Salle then proceeded south to the mouth of the Miami River (now St. Joseph). During the next two years, he made three trips into the Illinois River Valley, penetrating to the Mississippi River in futile attempts to continue on down that river to the gulf. Forts were built and de-

Father Jacques Marquette preaches to Native Americans he encountered while exploring the Mississippi River Valley with Louis Jolliet. (Francis R. Niglutsch)

THE MARQUETTE/JOLLIET AND LA SALLE EXPEDITIONS, 1673-1682

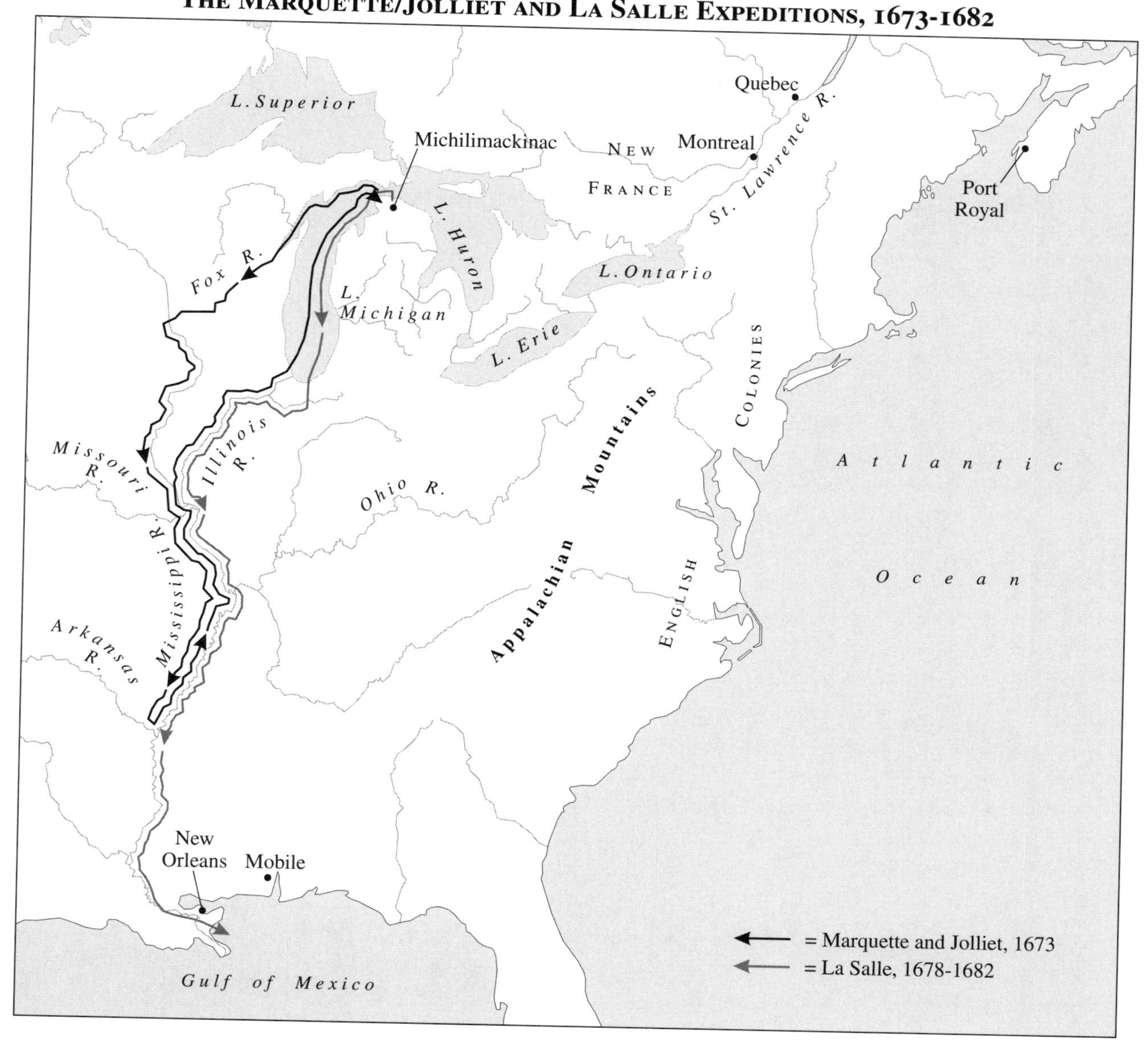

stroyed, the *Griffon* was lost, and trading parties failed. On April 9, 1682, La Salle found the mouth of the Mississippi River, claimed the whole area for France, and named it Louisiana after Louis XIV.

In 1683, La Salle again returned to France and obtained royal support to establish a fortified colony about 180 miles (290 kilometers) above the mouth of the Mississippi River. In 1684, La Salle left France with four ships, one hundred soldiers, and three hundred settlers. Failing to find the river's mouth and plagued by Spanish raiders, shipwreck, and desertion, La Salle and 180 survivors finally landed at Matagorda Bay, Texas, where he constructed a fort. After an exploratory trip to what is now West Texas, he returned to Fort St. Louis. A few days later, the expedition's only remaining ship was lost and La Salle decided that the expedition's only hope was to seek relief overland from Illinois. Starting on January 27, 1687, La Salle took seventeen men, leaving twenty-three behind to guard the fort. La Salle was murdered during a mutiny near the Brazos River, but six men struggled onward to Post aux Arkansas, near the junction of the Arkansas and Mississippi Rivers. La Salle's lieutenant, Henri de Tonty, had established the post while searching for La Salle.

Meanwhile, Daniel Greysolon, sieur de Lhut, explored the western Lake Superior region, discovering the Falls of Saint Anthony at present-day Minneapolis. Pierre Le Moyne d'Iberville rediscovered the mouth of the Mississippi River and was instrumental in founding Fort Maurepas (now Biloxi) in 1699. His brother, Jean-Baptiste Le Moyne, sieur de Bienville, established Mobile in 1702 and New Orleans in 1718.

Significance

French exploration and occupation of the Mississippi Valley led directly to the clash with Great Britain in the French and Indian War (1754-1763). This cost France its American empire and ultimately contributed to the American Revolution. Nevertheless, the French left a substantial legacy: The *coureurs de bois* (fur traders) had gathered basic information about the trans-Mississippi West that was used by American mountain men and the British Hudson's Bay Company nearly a century later. The French also made a lasting contribution to the culture of the north woods and Louisiana. Louisiana became a refuge for French colonists forced out of New France (Canada) by the English, and it became the center of Acadian, or Cajun, culture in the United States after the Louisiana Purchase.

—*William L. Richter and Ralph L. Langenheim, Jr.*

Further Reading

Balesi, Charles J. *The Time of the French in the Heart of North America, 1673-1818*. Chicago: Alliance Française Chicago, 1992. Focuses on the history of the Illinois country.

Crouse, Nellis M. *Lemoyne d'Iberville: Soldier of New France*. Ithaca, N.Y.: Cornell University Press, 1954. Biography of the man who founded the first French settlements on the Gulf coast.

Ekberg, Carl J. *French Roots in the Illinois Country: The Mississippi Frontier in Colonial Times*. Urbana: University of Illinois Press, 1998. History of French Creole settlements in Illinois, describing the agricultural practices, commerce, and other aspects of the settlers' life and culture.

Kellogg, Louise P. *The French Regime in Wisconsin and the Northwest*. Madison: State Historical Society of Wisconsin, 1925. Discusses early exploration, mining, and the fur trade in the Great Lakes and Wisconsin.

La Salle, Nicolas de. *The La Salle Expedition on the Mississippi River: A Lost Manuscript of Nicolas de La Salle, 1682*. Translated by Johanna S. Warren, edited by William C. Foster. Austin: Texas State Historical Association, 2003. Nicolas de La Salle (no relation to the explorer) was one of the men on sieur de La Salle's 1682 Mississippi River expedition. A rare copy of Nicolas's journal of that voyage was recently discovered at the Texas State Archives. This translation and analysis of the journal reveals new information about the historic exploration.

Nasatir, Abraham P. *Before Lewis and Clark: Documents Illustrating the History of the Missouri, 1785-1804*. 2 vols. St. Louis, Mo.: St. Louis Historical Documents Foundation, 1952. The author's introduction to the first volume is a fine narrative of French Missouri River exploration between 1673 and 1804.

Parkman, Francis. *The Discovery of the Great West: La Salle*. 1889. Reprint. Westport, Conn.: Greenwood Press, 1986. The first comprehensive account of La Salle's explorations, based on copies of most of the original documents in French and other archives.

Speck, Francis B. *The Jolliet-Marquette Expedition, 1673*. Glendale, Calif.: Arthur H. Clark, 1928. A definitive study of the Jolliet-Marquette expedition.

Weddle, Robert S., Mary Christine Morkovsky, and Patricia Galloway, eds. *La Salle, the Mississippi, and the Gulf*. Translated by A. L. Bell and Robert S. Weddle. College Station: Texas A&M University Press, 1987. Documents pertaining to La Salle's exploration of the Mississippi Valley and Texas.

See also: Mar. 15, 1603-Dec. 25, 1635: Champlain's Voyages; Spring, 1604: First European Settlement in North America; Apr. 27, 1627: Company of New France Is Chartered; 1642-1684: Beaver Wars; May, 1642: Founding of Montreal; Aug., 1658-Aug. 24, 1660: Explorations of Radisson and Chouart des Groseilliers; May 2, 1670: Hudson's Bay Company Is Chartered; Dec., 1678-Mar. 19, 1687: La Salle's Expeditions; May 1, 1699: French Found the Louisiana Colony.

Related articles in *Great Lives from History: The Seventeenth Century, 1601-1700:* Samuel de Champlain; Pierre Le Moyne d'Iberville; Louis Jolliet; Sieur de La Salle; Jacques Marquette; Pierre Esprit Radisson.

1673
Huygens Explains the Pendulum

Christiaan Huygens's The Pendulum Clock *explains how his accurate pendulum clock was first built in 1656, the mathematics behind its accuracy, the important properties of pendula, centrifugal force, and the acceleration of gravity.*

Locale: Paris, France
Categories: Science and technology; physics; mathematics

Key Figures

Christiaan Huygens (1629-1695), Dutch mathematician and physicist who invented the pendulum clock
Marin Mersenne (1588-1648), French philosopher, mathematician, and scientist who encouraged Huygens and challenged him to measure the acceleration of gravity
Galileo (1564-1642), Italian astronomer and physicist who was the first to study the pendulum
Sir Isaac Newton (1642-1727), English scientist and mathematician who was both a critic and a supporter of Huygens

Summary of Event

When Christiaan Huygens was only seventeen years old, he developed a proof showing that the distance a freely falling body covered increased with the square of the time it has fallen. His proud father passed this on to his friend, Marin Mersenne, one of the foremost scientists of the time. Delighted and impressed, Meresenne encouraged the young Huygens to continue his scientific studies and suggested that he work on properties of the pendulum and also on measuring the distance a freely falling body fell in the first second after being released (this is equivalent in modern terms to measuring the acceleration of gravity).

Huygens worked on these problems over the years, and he reported his results in his most important book, *Horologium oscillatorium sive de mortu pendulorum ad horologia aptato demonstrationes geometricae* (1673; *The Pendulum Clock*, 1986). To measure the acceleration of gravity, *g*, Huygens improved an experiment of Mersenne in which a ball was dropped simultaneously with the release of a pendulum of known period. At its lowest point, the pendulum struck a vertical board, making a sound. The initial height of the ball was adjusted until the sound of its striking the floor was simultaneous with that of the pendulum striking the board, thereby accurately measuring the time it took for the ball to fall. Huygens found a value equivalent to the modern value of *g* correct to within 0.1%.

During these investigations, Huygens also related the speed with which a suspended object swings to the tension in the cord holding it and to the centrifugal force. He arrived at the correct result that the centrifugal force is proportional to the square of the velocity and inversely proportional to the radius of the circular path.

One of the great technological problems of Huygens's day was how to determine the position of a ship exactly when it was far out at sea. Good star maps already existed, so that in principle, a navigator could measure how far above the horizon a few bright stars were, and then he could calculate where on Earth one had to be to have that view of the sky. Of course, the stars wheel across the sky each night, so that the navigator also needed to know at what time the measurements were made. Unfortunately, mechanical clocks were accurate only to within about 15 minutes per day, which could produce navigational errors of 250 miles that were clearly unacceptable.

Mechanical clocks driven by a spring tended to run fast or slow depending upon how tightly the spring was wound. Huygens was a keen follower of Galileo. Galileo had suggested that the steady swinging of a pendulum might be used to regulate a clock, but Huygens was the first to construct such a clock successfully. Like Isaac Newton, Huygens was gifted both in mathematics and in constructing mechanical models. He combined these talents to construct a pendulum clock in 1656. As it swung back and forth, the pendulum mechanism allowed a gear to advance only one tooth at the end of each pendulum swing, producing the characteristic "tick-tock" sound. The mechanism also gave the pendulum a slight nudge to keep it in motion. This clock was accurate to within about one minute per day.

Huygens continued to analyze and refine his clocks, finally publishing his results in *The Pendulum Clock* in 1673. He had discovered that the period of a pendulum depended upon the square root of the pendulum's length; that is, if a pendulum was twice as long as another pendulum, its period was the square root of two (1.41) times as long.

A simple pendulum consists of a light string or rod extending downward from a pivot and having a weight, called a bob, on the lower end. Huygens found that a

Dutch mathematician and astronomer Christiaan Huygens working on his pendulum clock. (Hulton|Archive by Getty Images)

lens-shaped bob had less air resistance and made the clock more accurate. If the mass of the string or rod cannot be ignored compared with the mass of the bob, and especially if mass is attached to the pendulum above the bob, the pendulum is no longer "simple." Such a pendulum, whose mass is not concentrated in a small bob, is called a "compound" or a "physical" pendulum. Huygens showed that a compound pendulum acted like a simple pendulum with its mass concentrated at a point called the "center of oscillation." This allowed Huygens to predict the effect of adding small masses above the bob to adjust the pendulum's period. Analyzing the physical pendulum also required Huygens to develop the concept of "rotational moment of inertia," the effect a mass distribution has on the ease with which it can be made to rotate about an axis.

Huygens discovered that the period of a pendulum is constant only if the amplitude of its swing is small, a condition that could not be maintained on a rocking ship at sea. He used clever mathematical analysis to show that the pendulum would be isochronous; that is, its period would remain constant regardless of the swing's amplitude if the path of the bob were a cycloid. A cycloid is the shape traced out by a point fixed on the rim of a wheel as the wheel rolls along the ground. A cycloid can be pictured as a wire that is first bent into the shape of a semicircle, and then the ends are pulled a bit farther apart, making the curve flatter.

Huygens made the bob follow a cycloidal path by suspending the pendulum between a pair of guide plates shaped like a portion of a cycloid and by using a ribbon for the upper part of the pendulum that was between the guide plates. In action, near the end of the pendulum's swing, the ribbon swung up against a guide plate and matched its contour. This shortened the pendulum's length and made the period nearly independent of the amplitude of the swing.

He made his ships' clocks in pairs so that if one stopped or needed repair, the other would keep on running. In practice, he hung them side by side from a wooden beam, and he was astounded to find that regardless of how they were started, after about thirty minutes the pendula were exactly 180 degrees out of phase. (When one pendulum was at the extreme right end of its swing, the other was at the extreme left end of its swing.) He correctly concluded that otherwise-imperceptible vibrations were traveling along the support beam from one clock to the other, a condition known as "weak coupling between the pendula." Huygens believed that this effect would help keep his clocks accurate, and, in fact, they were accurate to within about 10 seconds per day.

Significance

Christiaan Huygens's expression for centrifugal force, when combined with Johannes Kepler's third law of planetary motion (which relates the time it takes a planet to go around the sun and its distance from the sun), immediately implies that the gravitational force between the sun and the planets becomes stronger or weaker in inverse proportion to the square of the distance between the planet and the sun. This, in turn, immediately led Newton to his law of gravity.

Probably more than any other three scientists, Galileo, Huygens, and Newton diverted science into the channel in which it now flows. All three were adept with their hands; they ground lenses, built models, and made the equipment they needed for experiments. They all were excellent observers and meticulous experimenters. Their work represents an increase in both the use and sophistication of mathematics. Galileo established mathematics as essential to understanding nature, Huygens used more subtle and abstract mathematics to arrive at his results, and Newton went beyond the boundaries of geometry, algebra, and trigonometry to invent calculus. Without Huygens, Newton might not have achieved so much.

—Charles W. Rogers

FURTHER READING

Andriesse, Cornelis D. *Titan kan niet slapen: Een biografie van Christiaan Huygens*. Translated by Sally Miedema as *Titan: A Biography of Christiaan Huygens*. Utrecht, the Netherlands: University of Utrecht, 2003. A fine, recent biography. Huygens discovered Saturn's moon Titan and was a "titan" among the scientists of his day.

Bennett, Matthew, et al. "Huygens's Clocks." *Proceedings of the Royal Society of London* 458 (2002): 563-579. An excellent description of clock pairs built by Huygens for navigation at sea, and of his discovery of their natural synchronization. Only the well-prepared should brave the mathematical proofs of section 4.

Huygens, Christiaan. *Christiaan Huygens' "The Pendulum Clock: Or, Geometrical Demonstrations Concerning the Motion of Pendula as Applied to Clocks."* Translated with notes by Richard J. Blackwell, and introduced by H. J. M. Bos. Ames: Iowa State University Press, 1986. The first English translation of Huygens's major work on the pendulum clock.

Klarreich, Erica G. "Huygens's Clocks Revisited." *American Scientist* 90 (2002): 322-323. A popular-level summary of the Matthew Bennett et al. article.

Struik, Dirk J. *The Land of Stevin and Huygens: A Sketch of Science and Technology in the Dutch Republic During the Golden Century*. Boston: Kluwer, 1981. A short, illustrated work that centers on Huygens as the major claim to fame of the Netherlands for the seventeenth century scientific revolution.

Yoder, Joella G. *Unrolling Time: Huygens and the Mathematization of Nature*. New York: Cambridge University Press, 2004. A 252-page account of the interrelationship between mathematics and physics in the work of the Dutch mathematician, physicist, and astronomer. Excellent at putting concepts in their historical context.

SEE ALSO: 1609-1619: Kepler's Laws of Planetary Motion; 1615-1696: Invention and Development of the Calculus; 1632: Galileo Publishes *Dialogue Concerning the Two Chief World Systems, Ptolemaic and Copernican*; 1637: Descartes Publishes His *Discourse on Method*; 1654: Pascal and Fermat Devise the Theory of Probability; 1655-1663: Grimaldi Discovers Diffraction; Feb., 1656: Huygens Identifies Saturn's Rings; 1665: Cassini Discovers Jupiter's Great Red Spot; Dec. 7, 1676: Rømer Calculates the Speed of Light.

RELATED ARTICLES in *Great Lives from History: The Seventeenth Century, 1601-1700:* Pierre de Fermat; Galileo; Francesco Maria Grimaldi; Robert Hooke; Christiaan Huygens; Johannes Kepler; Marin Mersenne; Sir Isaac Newton; Blaise Pascal.

1673
Renovation of the Louvre

King Louis XIV introduced a competition between architects and artists to complete the construction of the Louvre palace, a project that started in the mid-sixteenth century. The palace was enhanced with classical Roman architecture to reflect the triumph and power of the French state. It stands as one of the world's largest and best-known museums, which was established in 1793.

Locale: Paris, France
Categories: Architecture; art; cultural and intellectual history; organizations and institutions

Key Figures

Henry IV (1553-1610), king of France, r. 1589-1610
Louis XIV (1638-1715), king of France, r. 1643-1715
Gian Lorenzo Bernini (1598-1680), Italian Baroque artist
Louis Le Vau (1612-1670), French architect
Claude Perrault (1613-1688), French architect, physician, and scientist
Charles Le Brun (1619-1690), French painter
Jean-Baptiste Colbert (1619-1683), French controller general

Summary of Event

The Louvre began as a camp for the Vikings during their unsuccessful siege of Paris in 885. In 1190, King Philip II chose the Louvre as the site of a crusader's castle to defend against the Normans and English along the Seine River. It consisted of a dungeon and towers within a thick wall. The fortress was transformed in the sixteenth century for King Francis I, so that he could build a Renaissance palace, and in 1564, Queen Catherine de Médicis commissioned the Tuileries Palace, a small château that was to be built in the western fields of the Palais de Louvre (Louvre palace). It never was completed.

Thirty years later, King Henry IV chose the Louvre for his place of residence and quickly started construction to expand the palace and its courtyard. In 1593, Henry began work on the Grand Galerie (which housed the royal artists beginning in 1608), and he had the Tuileries connected with the main palace in 1594.

The Thirty Years' War (1618-1648) stalled work on the palace, as France, Spain, the Holy Roman Empire, and the majority of Europe were fighting one another. The war ended in 1648, and peace between Spain and France came eleven years later with the Treaty of the Pyrenees (1659), making money available to restart construction. King Louis XIV soon requested plans from architects for the design of the east facade. He wanted the palace to represent order and to reflect classical antiquity, now known as French classicism. The Baroque schemes of architect Louis Le Vau and artist Gian Lorenzo Bernini were therefore rejected.

Nevertheless, Le Vau succeeded to the post of architect to the king in 1654. He was in charge of the completion of the south wing and was entrusted to design an east facade. He simply continued the design from the western-south facade to the eastern-south facade. However, he designed the central pavilion and east facade to be unique to French taste; thus, his proposal for the eastern facade (c. 1659) was daring. The Baroque period can be seen in an oval vestibule projecting from the facade. The wide oculus (wide eyelike opening or ornament) for pedestrians was meant to reflect the Roman pantheon and antiquity. In addition, the light entering the oculus symbolizes King Louis XIV as the Sun King. The facade of the Tuileries Palace, connected to the Louvre, was remodeled by Le Vau and his assistant, François d'Orbay. Outside Tuileries to the west, a new garden was built for Louis in 1664 by André Le Nôtre.

The French council requested that Bernini, even after his plan had been previously rejected, submit his new ideas for the Louvre. Bernini sent his designs to Paris in February, 1665. Construction overseer Jean-Baptiste Colbert first accepted Bernini's plan, but he eventually rejected it because he found it to be unsafe to natural elements and to be "not French." The council had resented southern Europe, especially Italy, since the Thirty Years' War, and wanted French contributors and French ideas. The council wanted the east facade to reflect the epitome of French nationalism, and not the work of Bernini. However, the French court, especially Louis, was eager to include Bernini in the construction of the eastern facade. The French court sent for Bernini in June of 1665, and he remained in Paris for five months. However, the production was too far along for Bernini's designs to be included. Louis promised Bernini that he would commission him to build an equestrian statue after the Louvre was completed, but the council rejected the idea.

By the spring of 1667, Louis and Colbert were desperate to complete construction. They also had a sense of na-

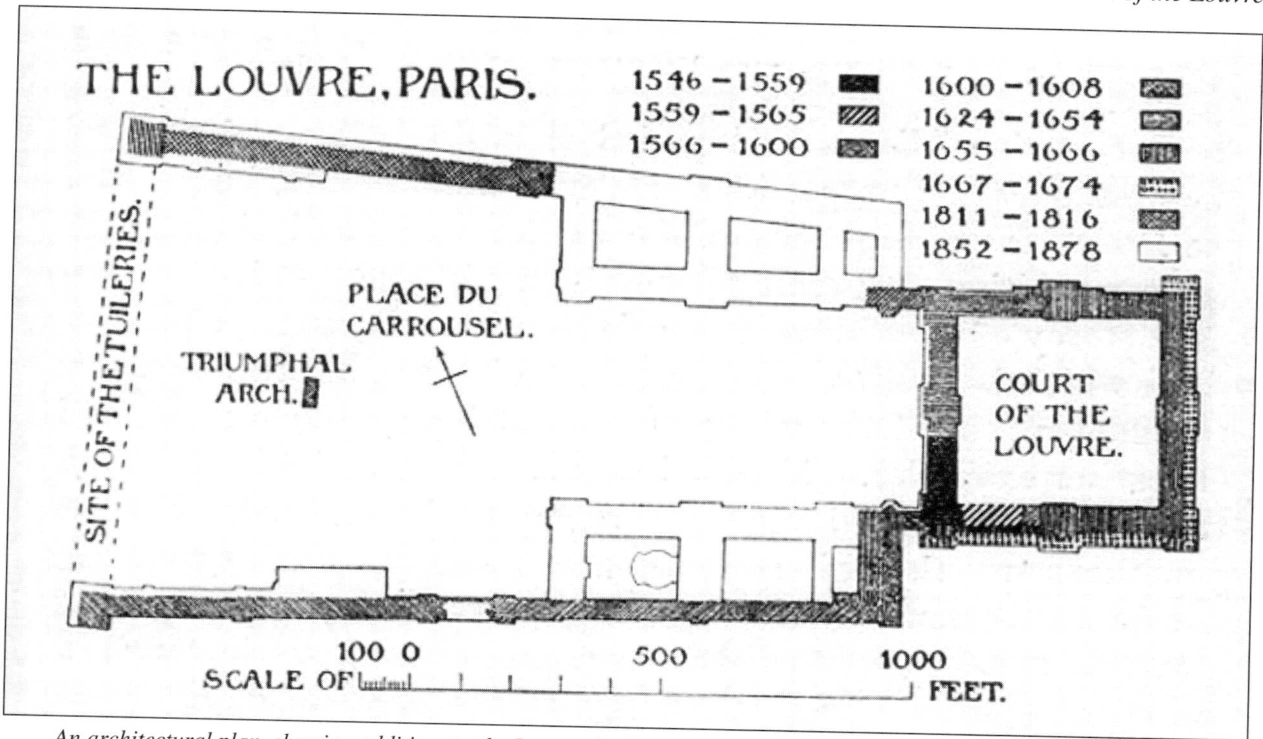

An architectural plan, showing additions to the Louvre, beginning in 1546 and continuing to 1878. (Longmans, Green)

tional pride, so they allowed only native French architects to submit their designs. Louis and Colbert wanted to entrust the design to the Petit Conseil, which included the expertise of Le Vau, Claude Perrault, and Charles Le Brun. Le Brun was responsible for transforming the portrait gallery into the Gallery of Apollo. The gallery was a long barrel-vaulted room with a lunette on each end. The main picture on the ceiling of the barrel vault was to depict Apollo on his horse-drawn chariot transforming the sky in his daily course. Night is personified as Diana and Morpheus. Twelve tondos depict the labors of each month of the calendar year. Zodiac signs are presented across the sky. Le Brun's gallery was to represent Louis as the new order.

On June 17, 1665, the first stone for the east facade was laid in a great ceremony conducted by Louis. Anne of Austria, queen-mother of Louis, died in the Louvre in 1666. In 1667, the construction of the colonnade began, as laborers and their machines, instruments, and tools worked to reflect the strength and wealth of the Crown. A medal was struck into the east facade in 1673, indicating that work was finished there. The facade reflected triumph and order through the symmetry of the colonnade and central portal. The pediments above the windows reflected classic antiquity and reinstated the triumph of the French monarchy. Before the Louvre's renovations were completed, Louis left the palace for good in 1682, just nine years after renovations began, as he and his court moved from Paris to Versailles.

SIGNIFICANCE

The Louvre is one of the largest museums in the world, housing artworks from around the globe. It fuses French and Italian classical elements and epitomizes French taste. It is also a symbol of absolute monarchy.

For many centuries the seat of French power, the Louvre still contains a few national administrative offices. The palace, opened as a public museum in 1793 during the French Revolution, is representative of French nationalism.

—*Shannon A. Powell*

FURTHER READING

Adams, Laurie Schneider. *Key Monuments of the Baroque*. Boulder, Colo.: Westview Press, 2000. A general overview of the Baroque period in Europe.

Berger, Robert W. *The Palace of the Sun: The Louvre of Louis XIV*. University Park: Pennsylvania State University Press, 1993. Berger focuses on the construction, design, and planning of the Louvre during Louis XIV's reign.

Bezombes, Dominique. *The Grand Louvre*. Paris: Moniteur, 1994. A modern description of the Louvre that provides maps of its continued construction through the years and gives a broad description of each time period.

Bresc-Bautier, Genevieve. *The Architecture of the Louvre*. Paris: Editions Assouline, 1995. A highly informative work that examines the entire history of the Louvre, from its beginning as a medieval castle to the design of "the pyramid" by architect I. M. Pei in the early 1980's.

See also: c. 1601-1620: Emergence of Baroque Art; 1618-1648: Thirty Years' War; Nov. 7, 1659: Treaty of the Pyrenees; 1661: Absolute Monarchy Emerges in France; 1682: French Court Moves to Versailles.

Related articles in *Great Lives from History: The Seventeenth Century, 1601-1700:* Anne of Austria; Gian Lorenzo Bernini; Jean-Baptiste Colbert; Charles Le Brun; André Le Nôtre; Louis Le Vau; Louis XIV; François Mansart.

1673-1678
Test Acts

The Test Act reinforced the religious and political supremacy of the Anglican Church by prohibiting Catholics and Protestant Dissenters from holding offices in the government and military.

Locale: England

Categories: Government and politics; laws, acts, and legal history; religion and theology

Key Figures

Charles II (1630-1685), king of England, r. 1660-1685

First Earl of Shaftesbury (Anthony Ashley Cooper; 1621-1683), leader of the Exclusion effort in Parliament and founder of the Whigs

James, Duke of York and Albany (1633-1701), brother of Charles II and king of England as James II, r. 1685-1688

Titus Oates (1649-1705), fabricator of the Popish Plot

Louis XIV (1638-1715), king of France, r. 1643-1715

Mary Stuart (1662-1694), daughter of James II and queen of England as Mary II, r. 1689-1694

William III of Orange (1650-1702), stadtholder of the United Provinces, r. 1672-1702, and king of England as William III, r. 1689-1702

Summary of Event

The Anglican Church, or Church of England, regained its position as the dominant religion in England upon the restoration of the Stuart monarchy in 1660 under Charles II. The new king, son of the executed Charles I, brought back to England both kingship and the religion that had dominated the country since Henry VIII.

Charles, however, was widely viewed as sympathetic toward Catholicism. His brother and presumed successor, James, duke of York (the future James II), was a Catholic. In 1670, Charles entered into a secret agreement with King Louis XIV of France that involved a promise by Charles to become a Catholic in return for a French subsidy. The bargain may have been more political and military than religious, but it did parallel actions that demonstrated an apparent predilection for Catholicism on the part of the king.

Charles issued Declarations of Indulgence in 1662 and 1672, which licensed Dissenting preachers as well as their places of worship. The king's actions also permitted Catholics to worship in private. Parliament opposed these measures, however, and passed a Test Act in 1673. This act required those who would hold civil or military offices to take Communion in the Church of England, swear allegiance to the Crown, and reject the doctrine of transubstantiation. The latter was a Catholic doctrine asserting that during Mass the Communion bread and wine are transformed into the body and blood of Christ. The doctrine of transubstantiation was seen as a defining character of Catholics, so much so that in 1676, Parliament proposed an oath for future monarchs in which the monarch affirms, "I do believe that there is not any transubstantiation in the sacrament of the Lord's Supper, or in the elements of bread and wine, at or after the consecration thereof by any person whatsoever."

These provisions of the Test Act were designed to eliminate both Protestant Dissenters and Catholics from any significant role in government or the military. Catholics believed that Communion entailed transubstantiation, and Puritans refused to take Communion at all. The act would thus consolidate the privileged position of the Church of England while securing the government against groups associated with rebellion and revolution.

The Test Act led to the resignation of the duke of York as lord high admiral of England. In 1677, the duke of York's eldest daughter, Mary, married the Protestant William III of Orange, a union that would prove crucial to the success of the Glorious Revolution of 1688.

The Test Act not only was an important event within the religious struggles among Catholics, Protestant Dissenters, and adherents of the Church of England but also was a watershed regarding the struggle between Crown and Parliament. Charles II had revived the concept of the divine right of kings—the belief that the monarch derives his or her right to rule from God. Parliament, however, while wishing no repetition of the revolutionary zeal that had led to the execution of King Charles I, nevertheless realized that the reigning king had been "made" by citizens of England, who had invited his return to England following the failed tenure of Richard Cromwell. Parliament thus intended to play a major role in the political life of the country, and passage of the Test Act was an example of Parliament's determination to wield considerable power in relation to the king.

Religious and political action soon coalesced in attempts to exclude the duke of York from the line of succession. With such a measure, Charles, who had no legitimate heirs, would be succeeded by his Catholic brother, a prospect that proved distasteful, even frightening, to many English subjects. Some feared an effort to make England a Catholic nation again.

Anti-Catholic sentiment was increased in 1678 by an alleged plot to kill the king, replace him with his Catholic brother, and, with the help of the French, return England to the Catholic fold. Titus Oates, whom history has judged to be a liar, announced this so-called Popish Plot, giving a deposition to a judge, Sir Edmund Berry Godfrey, who was later found murdered. Godfrey's murder seemed to substantiate the allegations. Contributing further to the apparent credibility of the plot were documents found in the possession of the duke of York's secretary, Edward Coleman, that established a continuing communication between the secretary and the private confessor to King Louis XIV, Père La Chaise. The plot's supposed conspirators, including Coleman and Oliver Plunkett, the Catholic archbishop of Armagh, were executed. In addition, a second Test Act was passed in 1678, excluding all Catholics except the duke of York from both Houses of Parliament, and thereby depriving Catholics of representation in the government of England.

Anti-Catholic and Parliamentarian zeal combined to foster three exclusion bills from 1679 to 1681, which proposed to replace the duke of York with James, duke of Monmouth, Charles II's eldest illegitimate son and a Protestant. Political maneuvering by the king—including moving Parliament to Oxford, where Royalist sentiment was traditionally strong, and dissolving Parliament—prevented any of the bills from becoming law. The poet John Dryden entered the political battle on the side of Charles II and the antiexclusion forces with his poems *Absalom and Achitophel, Part I* (1681) and *The Medall: A Satyre Against Sedition* (1682). The leader of the exclusionary effort, the earl of Shaftesbury, finally was arrested, charged with treason, and imprisoned in the Tower of London. Shaftesbury eventually was acquitted by a friendly London jury, but the effort to exclude the duke of York from the throne was brought to an end.

SIGNIFICANCE

Despite Charles II's efforts to promote greater religious freedom for the Dissenters, many of them supported Shaftesbury and became part of the political party that later came to be called the Whigs, in opposition to the Royalist party that would later be known as the Tories. A new alignment was occurring, with Dissenters, who often were small businessmen and shopkeepers, participating in an alliance of the city and middle-class citizens against the country and gentry, which tended to be Royalist. As these factions developed into the Whigs and the Tories, they formally institutionalized, for the first time, a two-party system within Parliament, fundamentally changing the nature of British politics.

The remaining years of Charles's reign saw the king abandon any efforts to aid the Dissenters, instead enforcing the penal statutes aimed at the Dissenters. Further widening the gulf between the king and the Dissenters was the Rye House Plot in 1683, an attempt by several Dissenters to kill both Charles and James as they returned from the Newmarket races. The king's Catholic inclinations, however, continued to thrive, as Charles, ruling without Parliamentary support, relied on French subsidies. Near the end of his life, Charles formally became a Catholic. He died on February 6, 1685, and was succeeded by his brother, James II, whose fate would be closely bound up with the religious struggles of his brother's reign.

—*Edward J. Rielly*

FURTHER READING

Ashley, Maurice. *England in the Seventeenth Century*. 3d ed. Baltimore: Penguin Books, 1967. Ashley's book, first published in 1952, remains a succinct, informative, and readable overview for those not very familiar with the century.

Condren, Conal. *The Language of Politics in Seventeenth-Century England*. New York: St. Martin's Press, 1994. As this book illustrates, political rhetoric in the century often was as important as political action, and many times they were inseparable.

Edwards, David L. *Christian England*. Vol. 2. Grand Rapids, Mich.: William B. Eerdmans, 1984. Part of a three-volume set, this volume examines the impact of, and the relationships among, Catholics, Dissenters, and Anglicans in England from the Reformation to the eighteenth century.

Greaves, Richard L. *Secrets of the Kingdom: British Radicals from the Popish Plot to the Revolution of 1688-1689*. Stanford, Calif.: Stanford University Press, 1992. The third in a series of books about British radicalism explores political and religious radicalism in the late seventeenth century.

Hill, Christopher. *The Century of Revolution: 1603-1714*. 2d ed. New York: Routledge, 1991. Written by one of the greatest historians of this period, the volume explores political, religious, economic, and intellectual currents.

Keeble, N. H. *The Literary Culture of Nonconformity in Later Seventeenth-Century England*. Athens: University of Georgia Press, 1987. Keeble's book examines the philosophy of nonconformity within the context of seventeenth century literature.

Ogg, David. *England in the Reign of Charles II*. 2d ed. Oxford, England: Clarendon Press, 1955. One of the greatest historians of the period offers what remains a classic study of the latter part of the seventeenth century.

Pollock, John. *The Popish Plot: A Study in the History of the Reign of Charles II*. Rev. ed. Cambridge, England: Cambridge University Press, 1944. This book explores the reign of Charles II by focusing on religious-political issues.

See also: 1642-1651: English Civil Wars; May, 1659-May, 1660: Restoration of Charles II; 1661-1665: Clarendon Code; May 19, 1662: England's Act of Uniformity; Aug. 13, 1678-July 1, 1681: The Popish Plot; Aug., 1682-Nov., 1683: Rye House Plot; Apr. 4, 1687, and Apr. 27, 1688: Declaration of Liberty of Conscience; 1688-1702: Reign of William and Mary; Nov., 1688-Feb., 1689: The Glorious Revolution; May 24, 1689: Toleration Act.

Related articles in *Great Lives from History: The Seventeenth Century, 1601-1700:* Charles II (of England); John Dryden; James II; Louis XIV; Mary II; Duke of Monmouth; Titus Oates; First Earl of Shaftesbury; William III.

December, 1673-1681
Rebellion of the Three Feudatories

Three former Ming generals, who had sided with the Manchus when the Mings fell, desired to retain control of the lands they had been allowed to administer under the Qing Dynasty. They rebelled against their Manchu overlords in 1673, a rebellion that was finally crushed in 1681.

Locale: Southern and southwestern China
Categories: Government and politics; wars, uprisings, and civil unrest

Key Figures

Kangxi (K'ang-hsi; 1654-1722), Qing emperor of China, r. 1661-1722
Wu Sangui (Wu San-kuei; 1612-1678), one of the Three Feudatories
Wu Shifan (d. 1681), grandson and heir of Wu Sangui
Shang Kexi (d. 1676), one of the Three Feudatories
Shang Zhixin (d. 1680), son of Shang Kexi
Geng Jimao (d. 1671), one of the Three Feudatories
Geng Jingzhong (d. 1682), son of Geng Jimao

Summary of Event

In the early seventeenth century, the Ming ("bright") Dynasty, which had ruled China from 1368, succumbed to an invasion by the non-Chinese Manchus from the north, establishing the Qing ("pure") Dynasty in 1644. The Ming collapse was largely due to internal weaknesses, and the Manchu invasion saw a number of Ming officials give support to the foreigners. The Ming general, Wu Sangui, was one of those who sided with the Manchus at the time of the Ming disintegration instead of supporting Li Zicheng, a native Chinese rebel claimant to the throne. Li was uneducated, and his followers pillaged the capital of Beijing, and although the Manchus had only a semi-civilized heritage, they had adopted a number of Chinese governing practices.

Li's defeat in 1644 and the death of another Chinese rebel opponent of the Ming, Zhang Xianzhong, in 1647 did not lead to an entirely peaceful Manchu takeover, as there were numerous other members of the Ming family who subsequently claimed the imperial throne. The last legitimate Ming claimant, the prince of Gui, fled into Burma but was turned over to Wu Sangui in 1661 and executed the following year.

In the seventeenth century, the population of China was approximately 120 million. In comparison, the Manchus numbered only a few million. Given the disparity in numbers, the Qing had little choice but to employ Chinese in both civil and military capacities. The Manchus adopted policies that would differentiate them from their Chinese subjects, including maintaining their own language and customs and expelling many native Chinese farmers from the area around Beijing, turning the land over to Manchus. In addition, male Chinese were forced to adopt the Manchu hairstyle, which required that the forehead be shaved and the hair on the back of the head be braided in a queue.

Intermarriage was effectively prevented between the two groups, inasmuch as the Manchus disapproved of the Chinese custom of female foot binding. Although there were Manchu garrisons throughout much of China, the limited Manchu population was centered in north China, near their original homelands, and around Beijing. By necessity, the Qing allowed much of southern and southwestern China to be administered by Chinese generals who had proved their loyalty to the new, foreign dynasty.

Far from Beijing, the vast area of southern China, with its varied semitropical and mountainous landscapes, was unsuited to the use of cavalry, the foremost element in the Manchu military tradition. During the last years before the seizure of the prince of Gui, three Chinese generals, Wu Sangui, Geng Jimao, and Shang Kexi, led the Qing campaigns in the south. The former had been crucial in the Manchu victory over the rebel Li Zicheng in 1644, and the latter two had sworn loyalty to the Qing as early as 1633, had been enrolled in the Manchu armies as "bannermen," and had played significant roles in the triumph over the Ming. In recognition of their accomplishments and their proven loyalty, the three were made Manchu princes and their sons were married to daughters of Qing nobles.

Most significantly, the three generals were placed in charge of several provinces in the south of China. Geng ruled Fujian (Fukien) province in the southeast from the city of Fujian on the coast, Shang controlled Guangdong (Kwangtung) and Guangxi (Kwangsi) provinces from Guangzhou (Canton), and further west, Wu Sangui governed the provinces of Huizhou (Hui-chou) and Yunan and parts of Hunan and Sichuan (Szechuan). Known as the Three Feudatories, the three Chinese generals were responsible not only for military affairs but also for civil government, including the collection of taxes. They were not merely administrators or bureaucrats for the Qing emperors in Beijing; rather, they were given extensive subsidies and established trade monopolies in salt, gold, copper, and ginseng within their territories. Thus, they reaped considerable private profits. It is estimated that the private incomes of the Three Feudatories approximated the worth of 10 million ounces of silver each year.

As in similar feudal situations elsewhere, Geng, Shang, and Wu assumed that their feudatories would be made hereditary and that they would pass their territories on to their sons. In 1671, Shang Zhixin took over military responsibilities in Guangdong as the result of the illness of his father, Shang Kexi, and Geng Jingzhong seized control of Fujian province when his father, Geng Jimao, died the same year. In 1673, Shang Kexi asked the emperor if he could retire because of his illness, with the implication that his son would replace him as the new feudatory. Geng Jingzhong and Wu Sangui had also made inquiries about making their feudatories permanent. If that was allowed to occur, it could well have resulted in the dismemberment of China between the several feudatories in the south, with Manchu rule restricted to the area north of the Yangtze River. It was thus a crucial moment for Chinese national identity and for the Qing Dynasty.

The decision rested with the Kangxi emperor. Born in 1654, he had ascended the throne in 1661 as a young boy. Discussion regarding the future of the feudatories had been ongoing for several years by this time, and ultimately Kangxi, unlike some of his advisers, believed that centralized rule necessitated that the feudatories not be allowed to become hereditary and thus possibly independent. When the emperor indicated that he would not surrender to the demands of the feudatories, Wu Sangui rebelled against the Qing in December, 1673, seizing much of Hunan province, and established a new dynasty, the Zhou, a conscious historical reference to one of China's earliest dynasties. In Fujian, Geng Jingzhong joined the rebellion in 1674 and invaded Zhejiang province to the north. The third of the original feudatories, Shang Kexi, remained loyal to the Qing, but his son, Shang Zhixin, seized power from his elderly and ill father and joined the uprising in 1676.

With their significant military and financial resources, the Three Feudatories were formidable foes for the Qing. Wu Sangui appealed to Chinese patriotism by ordering the abolishment of the Manchu queue and implying that a Ming descendant might become the first emperor of a new dynasty. Wu urged Kangxi to leave China and return to Manchuria, but in retaliation, the emperor ordered the execution of Wu's hostage son. Many native Chinese gave support to the Rebellion of the Three Feudatories, some because the Manchus were perceived as foreigners, others because they were intimidated by the military forces of the rebels. Many others undoubtedly attempted not to take sides in what was a bloody civil war.

In spite of obvious advantages, the Three Feudatories were never able to act together in opposing the Qing armies sent by Kangxi to end the rebellion. Wu Sangui declared himself emperor of the Zhou in 1678, but he died later that year. His grandson and heir, Wu Shifan, committed suicide in 1681 when besieged by Qing forces. Geng Jingzhong had abandoned the rebellion in 1676, and Shang Zhixin surrendered to the Manchus in 1677, in part because he was at odds with Wu Sangui. Even though Kangxi had supposedly restored their princely rank after their submission, Geng and Shang were subsequently executed.

SIGNIFICANCE

It was Kangxi, who reigned until 1722 and became the very model of a Chinese emperor in spite of his Manchu heritage, who made the ultimate decision to no longer tolerate the separatist ambitions of the Three Feudatories. The economic costs were too great in subsidizing the feudatories, but so was the threat to Qing rule and the unity of China. Although the rebellious provinces remained areas of concern for decades and were not entirely incorporated into China until the eighteenth century, instead of a politically divided China under the control of military warlords, Kangxi created a centralized government under civilian control, a system that lasted largely unchanged until the Revolution of 1911.

—*Eugene Larson*

FURTHER READING

Crossley, Pamela Kyle. *The Manchus*. Oxford, England: Blackwell, 1997. A modern study that surveys the establishment of the Qing and the challenge of the feudatories.

Mote, F. W. *Imperial China, 900-1800*. Cambridge, Mass.: Harvard University Press, 1999. An excellent recent work that includes an extensive discussion of the reign of Kangxi.

Spence, Jonathan D. *Emperor of China*. New York: Random House, 1974. A brilliant reconstruction of the ideas, policies, and personality of Emperor Kangxi.

_______. *The Search for Modern China*. New York: W. W. Norton, 1990. The best one-volume survey of China from the end of the Ming to the present.

SEE ALSO: 1616-1643: Rise of the Manchus; 1631-1645: Li Zicheng's Revolt; Apr. 25, 1644: End of the Ming Dynasty; June 6, 1644: Manchus Take Beijing; 1645-1683: Zheng Pirates Raid the Chinese Coast; Feb. 17, 1661-Dec. 20, 1722: Height of Qing Dynasty; 1670: Promulgation of the Sacred Edict; Aug. 29, 1689: Treaty of Nerchinsk Draws Russian-Chinese Border.

RELATED ARTICLE in *Great Lives from History: The Seventeenth Century, 1601-1700:* Kangxi.

Late 17th century
Decline of Benin

The Edo kingdom of Benin, a highly organized state located in the forests of south-central Nigeria, had expanded into Yoruba and Igbo territories and incorporated Edo-speaking peoples by the end of the sixteenth century. However, dynastic and political crises set the stage for the decline of the state, forcing it to virtually recoil into its heartland by the end of the seventeenth century.

Locale: Benin, Southern Nigeria (West Africa)
Categories: Expansion and land acquisition; government and politics; wars, uprisings, and civil unrest

Key Figures

Ehengbuda (d. 1600), *oba* of Benin, r. late 1500's to 1600
Ahenkpaye (fl. c. mid-1600's), *oba* of Benin, r. mid- to late 1600's
Akenzua I (fl. c. late 1600's), *oba*, or ruler, of Benin, r. late 1600's

Summary of Event

The kingdom of Benin had emerged as a powerful state in the forests of south-central Nigeria by the early sixteenth century. At its height by the early seventeenth century, the Benin Empire had stretched west to Lagos (now in Nigeria); established varying degrees of overlordship over the eastern Yoruba communities of Owo, Akure, and Ado-Ekiti, together with their subordinate settlements; and had established its sway eastward over the western Igbo communities. In the immediate vicinity, Benin incorporated Edo-speaking groups—the Esan, Afenmai, and Owan—in effect acknowledging that Benin was the source of their chieftaincy and cultural institutions. Benin also had expanded toward the coast, establishing contacts with European traders and controlling the offshoot Itsekiri kingdom.

A central feature of the kingdom was the monarchy, which served as the fulcrum of social, political, and economic activities in the state. Until the 1630's, the *oba* (ruler) was actively involved in leading military campaigns. He was assisted in the administration of the state by the three orders of chiefs–*uzama*, *eghaevbo n'ore* (town chiefs), and *eghaevbo n'ogbe* (palace chiefs)—who acknowledged his suzerainty. However, there were struggles between the Crown and the chiefs that led to disputes over succession and to civil wars, weakening the state in the seventeenth century. Such conflicts pitted a despotic monarchy against restive subjects (including the chiefs) who were aiming to check the excesses of the monarchy.

However, stable rule under able *obas* led to the rapid development of the kingdom. Arts and crafts, as well as regional and international trade, flourished. Guilds were established for brass-casting, a royal art, and for traders on the various routes that radiated from the capital. The guilds operated under royal patronage, and Bini traders enjoyed diplomatic immunity in the subject territories. The king also held a royal monopoly on items such as ivory and European wares. Taxes, tribute, and profit from trade constituted the economic basis of royal power.

Consequently, on one hand, royal power was bolstered, leading to greater despotism. On the other hand, the chiefs sought to wrest as much autonomy as was possible from the *oba*. Accordingly, the chiefs exploited disputed succession to extract concessions from rival claimants to the throne. The propensity for civil wars in many cases of disputed succession tended to weaken the authority of the *oba*.

Against this background of internal struggles for power and influence, the death in 1600 of Oba Ehengbuda while on an expedition in the coastal lagoons had a negative impact on the state and its institutions, especially the monarchy itself. The *oba* was no longer to command the army in person, a practice that had been introduced by Ehengbuda himself but that became tradition. Under Ehengbuda, the Iyase, head of the town chiefs, often had commanded the army, but that responsibility now passed to the Ezomo, an *uzama* chief. Henceforth, the *oba* became a secluded semidivine ruler, confined to the palace except for the few occasions in the year when official ceremonies called for him to appear in public. His life and schedule became more rigorously regimented, and the palace chiefs who controlled access to him accordingly enhanced their position at his expense.

The increasing influence of the palace chiefs upset the delicate balance of power in the kingdom. Paradoxically, these chiefs, who had been raised to counter the influence of the *uzama*, had developed as well into a growing center of power. One example of their rising power was their ability to change the mode of succession from primogeniture to one that enabled them to influence the choice of a prince who was pliable. Consequently, the palace chiefs succeeded in enthroning a series of weak *obas* for much of the seventeenth century. These were mainly old men or those who had an outside chance but whose accession was facilitated to weaken the monarchy vis-à-vis the chiefs. However, successful claimants who later attempted to assert themselves were susceptible to intrigues by the chiefs. Consequently, the monarchy suffered a discernible decline in the seventeenth century, though this was masked by the economic prosperity of Benin.

The prosperity of the state derived from the collection of tribute in foodstuffs and in slaves or livestock twice per year from proximate and distant subject provinces respectively, from tolls on commercial traffic into the city, and from the booming trade with the Europeans, especially in cloth and ivory. The *oba* and the chiefs held a monopoly on the pepper and ivory trades with the Europeans. The chiefs collected tolls and tribute, only half of which they remitted to the *oba*. However, the distribution of wealth from trade, tribute, and tolls eventually would generate conflict between the monarchy and the chiefs, including the major crisis that led to the deposition of Oba Ahenkpaye, who appeared to have attempted to recover part of the lost influence and accompanying economic perquisites of the monarchy.

Despite Benin's decline at the end of the seventeenth century, the kingdom's arts and crafts remain prized artifacts, including this bronze statue of a Benin court horn blower. (The Granger Collection)

Tradition relates that Ahenkpaye was deposed because he "usurped" the privileges of the chiefs and was perceived to be tightfisted. His fall in the closing decade of the seventeenth century was made possible by a rare unity of the three orders of chiefs. However, this unanimity did not endure in the face of the conflicting interests of the contending chiefly and royal power blocs in the kingdom. A major split between the town and palace chiefs over their respective shares of the wealth accruing from external trade led to a protracted civil war. After several years of attrition, which left the capital city in ruins, peace was restored, with Oba Akenzua reasserting royal power and effecting some fundamental reforms.

Significance

The kingdom of Benin had developed into a sizable empire in south-central Nigeria by the end of the sixteenth century. However, the death of Oba Ehengbuda in 1600 led to a fundamental change in the military and political systems of Benin. The *oba* was now forbidden to lead the army in person. The Iyase, leader of the town chiefs, and the Ezomo, an *uzama*, took over the role of head of the army while the *oba* became a secluded, semidivine potentate. The consequent increase in the influence and wealth of the chiefs steadily undermined the position of the monarchy, thus setting the stage for the manipulation of succession to the throne and political instability.

The political decline of Benin in the seventeenth century was, however, accompanied by the economic prosperity of the state, which further aggravated the conflict between the Crown and the chiefs. The devastating civil war of the last decade of the century was followed by the emergence of Oba Akenzua, who introduced reforms and restored the former glory of the state. He established primogeniture as the rule of succession to obviate interference by the chiefs and introduced the practice of installing the crown prince (*edaiken*) in the lifetime of an *oba*, a practice that subsists into the twenty-first century. One cannot understand subsequent developments, which have contemporary implications, without a knowledge of seventeenth century events in Benin.

—*Ayodeji Olukoju*

FURTHER READING

Ajayi, J. F. A., and Michael Crowder, eds. *History of West Africa*. 3d ed. Vol. 1. London: Longman, 1985. Contains two chapters on Benin history in the wider context of intergroup and interstate relations.

Akintoye, S. A. "The North-Eastern Yoruba Districts and the Benin Kingdom." *Journal of the Historical Society of Nigeria* 4, no. 4 (1969): 539-553. An authoritative study of relations between Benin and the subject peoples of northeast Yorubaland.

Bradbury, R. E. *The Benin Kingdom and the Edo-Speaking Peoples of South-Western Nigeria*. London: International African Institute, 1957. A detailed ethnography of the Benin kingdom and the Edo-speaking peoples.

________. *Benin Studies*. London: Oxford University Press, 1973. Bradbury is a leading authority on Benin history.

Egharevba, J. U. *A Short History of Benin*. 4th ed. Ibadan, Nigeria: Ibadan University Press, 1968. The fundamental text on Bini history, a collection of traditions, which deserves to be read critically.

Igbafe, P. A. "Benin in the Pre-colonial Era." *Tarikh* 5, no. 1 (1975): 1-16. A concise account of the origins and development of the Benin kingdom.

Ikime, O., ed. *Groundwork of Nigerian History*. Ibadan, Nigeria: Heinemann, 1980. Contains a good synthesis by a leading expert on Benin history.

Ryder, A. F. C. *Benin and the Europeans, 1485-1897*. London: Longman, 1969. A detailed and reliable study of relations between Benin and the Europeans from the fifteenth century to the British conquest.

SEE ALSO: 17th cent.: Songhai Empire Dissolves; Beginning c. 1601: Expansion of the Oyo Kingdom; 1612: Rise of the Arma in Timbuktu; 1619-c. 1700: The Middle Passage to American Slavery; Oct., 1625-1637: Dutch and Portuguese Struggle for the Guinea Coast; Mid-17th cent.: Emergence of the Guinea Coast States; 1670-1699: Rise of the Asante Empire.

RELATED ARTICLE in *Great Lives from History: The Seventeenth Century, 1601-1700:* Njinga.

Late 17th century
RISE OF BUGANDA

As the powerful East African kingdom of Bunyoro declined, Buganda, Bunyaro's former tributary, created a unique centralized monarchy that enabled its domination of Uganda.

LOCALE: Uganda

CATEGORIES: Government and politics; expansion and land acquisition

KEY FIGURES

Kato Kintu (fl. fourteenth century), first *kabaka*, or king, of Buganda

Mujambula (fl. seventeenth century), *katikkiro*, or prime minister, of Buganda

Tebandeke (fl. seventeenth century), *kabaka* of Buganda

Mwanda (fl. eighteenth century), *kabaka* of Buganda

SUMMARY OF EVENT

The origins of east central Africa's traditional monarchies date to the 1300's, according to oral histories. Tied to the rise of these states are the widely varying origins of modern Uganda's ethnic groups. A favorable high-altitude climate and reliable rainfall made Uganda attractive to Bantu-speaking farmers who came from West Africa around 500 B.C.E. Displacing the area's original hunter-gatherer inhabitants, they cleared dense forests northwest of Lake Victoria for banana cultivation. Depicted in legends as supernatural but probably a Bantu subgroup, the Cwezi founded clan-based chiefdoms, which coordinated work, settled disputes, and performed rituals but could govern limited areas only.

Between the fourteenth and sixteenth centuries, Nilotic-speaking Luo cattle herders migrated south from Sudan, displaced the Cwezi, and established several kingdoms, notably the BaBito kingdom of Bunyoro, south of Lake Albert, and the BaHima kingdom of Ankole, west of Lake Victoria. By 1400, Bunyoro dominated what is now Uganda and parts of Rwanda and Tanzania. Bunyoro established buffer states to protect its southern boundaries from the BaHima by the mid-1500's. The region suffered droughts, famines, political upheavals, and mass migrations from 1588 to 1621, known in some traditions as the era of Nyarubanga, that which is sent by God.

During the 1600's, Buganda and other former BaBito tributaries created strong centralized kingdoms as Bunyoro's power declined amid succession disputes. First paying tribute to the BaBito, these kingdoms broke away and faced constant war with Bunyoro, which tried vainly to bring them to submission.

Located in an area of alternating hills and swamps between Bunyoro and Lake Victoria, Buganda (the Ganda kingdom) was closely associated with Bunyoro. However, when and how the two separated is uncertain. Speaking Luganda (the Ganda language), the Baganda (the Ganda people; sing., Muganda) are Bantu, with some Nilotic ties. Their early history has been passed down in several different versions. Common to all is the triumph of a conquering hero (king) named Kato Kintu over a ruthless renegade prince, Bemba, and his unification of the five original Baganda clans. Becoming the first *kabaka*, the victorious Kato slept in his enemy's house at Naggalabi, where all subsequent *kabakas* have been crowned. Following Bemba's ouster, a conclave of clan elders was held on Nnono hill. This important meeting laid down Buganda's system of governance and the relationship between the clans and *kabaka*. Later, Kato established his court at Nnono. In the twenty-first century, the Baganda refer to issues of deep significance as being "from Nnono."

Kato cleverly allied himself by marriage with the original hereditary clan leaders. Buganda's political system empowered all clans. The *kabaka* could identify with any clan, unlike Bunyoro's *omukama* (king), who was chosen exclusively from the BaBito clan. Probably originating as first among equals, the *kabaka* became both *ssaabasajja*, chief of men, and *ssaabataka*, chief of chiefs. The former role made him his people's father and source of all authority, while the latter role gave him the final word in disputes. Although succession was patrilineal, each *kabaka* identified also with his mother's clan. By virtue of giving birth to a *kabaka*, the *namasole* (king's mother) was highly respected. She was given a palace and servants because she was not allowed to remarry, but she held no formal government role.

The unusual attachment of *kabakas* to their mothers' clans also might relate to the *kabaka*'s need for support in succession disputes. For similar reasons, the *kabaka*'s male relatives were often kept in prison. *Kabakas* married wives from all clans. Their successors were chosen from among the princes, each of whom was identified by his mother's clan. However, eldest sons were ineligible for succession. Thus, the throne was seldom seen as the property of a single clan.

Historians estimate that Buganda was established in the early to mid-fourteenth century. However, lack of written records makes it difficult to accurately establish the duration of each king's reign. Confusing Kato, the first *kabaka*, with Kintu, the first man on Earth in Baganda legend, many early scholars concluded that Kato was mythological. Apparently, when Kato established his legitimacy as *kabaka*, he took the name Kintu, knowing that the Baganda associated it with the father of all people. He also named his principal wife Nambi, after the creator god Ggulu's daughter, the original Kato's wife. Reigns before that of Mwanga I (twenty-third *kabaka*) have been estimated with much difficulty. For example, Baganda tradition speaks of a great battle between the sun and moon during the reign of the sixteenth *kabaka*, Jjuuko. Historians have correlated this with a solar eclipse in 1680. However, another eclipse occurred in 1520, but neither year seems to fit other events.

In the mid-1600's, the eighteenth *kabaka*, Tebandeke, and his *katikkiro* (prime minister), Mujambula, further centralized power by challenging spiritual mediums. Buganda's religious life was rich with spirits. Associated with their clans, spirits of all the deceased required careful attention. Dead *kabakas*' jawbones and umbilical cords were preserved in shrines that became pilgrimage centers. Accompanying spirits of the dead were natural, often feminine, spirits known as *balubaale*. *Kabakas* frequently consulted *balubaale* mediums despite evidence that they sometimes colluded with clan chiefs to oppose royal power. Angry at the rewards demanded for a service, Tebandeke destroyed all *balubaale* shrines. Later, he cured himself of madness by becoming a medium. His successor, Ndawula, son of Jjuuko, refused such a religious role. Hence, a division between religious and political authority was drawn, giving Buganda's monarchy a peculiarly secular character.

Significance

By the end of the 1600's, though ruling over territory less than one-tenth that of modern Buganda, the *kabakas* had consolidated their rule. In the early 1700's, Kabaka Mwanda accelerated Buganda's territorial expansion, largely at the expense of Bunyoro. He appointed commoners as officials to counter the influence of clan chiefs. Free of outside penetration until the nineteenth century, Buganda controlled a large territory between the

Nile and Kagera Rivers and was divided into counties, subcounties, parishes, and, finally, villages.

In the mid-1800's, Arab traders and European explorers reached Buganda. In response, Kabaka Mutesa I experimented with both Islam and Christianity, while ensuring all power remained in his hands. His son Mwanga tried in vain to destroy both foreign faiths. Visiting Buganda in 1875, Henry Morton Stanley estimated its troop strength to be 125,000. He found Buganda's capital to be a well-ordered town of about 40,000 surrounding the king's hilltop palace. Eventually, the *kabakas* collaborated with the British to defeat Bunyoro, which was armed by Arab traders after 1869. They were rewarded with much BaBito territory. Under colonial rule, Baganda chiefs were employed in Bunyoro and other non-Baganda areas. Luganda became the dominant language. Resistance to British imperialism became equally anti-Baganda.

In 1962, Uganda became independent under a federal constitution giving the *kabaka* special powers. The next year, it became a republic, with Kabaka Mutesa II as its first president. Opposed by Prime Minister Milton Obote and unable to reconcile his conflicting traditional and modern roles, he fled the country. Uganda's traditional kingdoms were abolished in 1967 but restored as constitutional monarchies in 1993. The dynasty founded by Kato and strengthened by Tebandeke and Mwanda continues into the twenty-first century.

The graves of four *kabakas* at Nabulagala, popularly known as the Kasubi Tombs, is a UNESCO (United Nations Educational, Scientific, and Cultural Organization) heritage site.

—*Randall Fegley*

FURTHER READING

Chrétien, Jean-Pierre. *The Great Lakes of Africa: Two Thousand Years of History*. Translated by Scott Straus. New York: Zone Books, 2003. An excellent history drawing on colonial archives, oral traditions, and archaeological, anthropological, and linguistic evidence.

Kiwanuka, S. *History of Buganda: From the Foundation of the Kingdom to 1900*. London: Longman, 1971. Kiwanuka provides a good, comprehensive history of Buganda.

Low, D. A. *Buganda in Modern History*. Berkeley: University of California Press, 1971. This thorough survey of Buganda's history is accompanied by Low's *The Mind of Buganda: Documents of the Modern History of an African Kingdom* (1971).

Nyakatura, John. *Anatomy of an African Kingdom: A History of Bunyoro-Kitara*. Norwell, Mass.: Anchor Press, 1973. Nyakatura traces Bunyoro's history from its earliest times to the twentieth century.

Ray, Benjamin. *Myth, Ritual, and Kingship in Buganda*. New York: Oxford University Press, 1991. Ray provides an interpretation of Buganda's kings, myths, rituals, shrines, and regalia in precolonial to postindependence times.

Reid, Richard J. *Political Power in Pre-Colonial Buganda*. Athens: Ohio State University Press, 2002. Reid explores the economic and military basis of Buganda's power.

Wrigley, Christopher. *Kingship and State: The Buganda Dynasty*. New York: Cambridge University Press, 1996. Wrigley's history surveys Buganda's royalty.

SEE ALSO: Early 17th cent.: Rise of Rwanda; 17th cent.: Emergence of Luba Governance; c. 1625: Formation of the Kuba Kingdom; Aug. 26, 1641-Sept., 1648: Conquest of Luanda; 1644-1671: Ndongo Wars; Apr., 1652: Dutch Begin to Colonize Southern Africa; Oct. 29, 1665: Battle of Mbwila; Beginning c. 1682: Decline of the Solomonid Dynasty.

RELATED ARTICLE in *Great Lives from History: The Seventeenth Century, 1601-1700:* Njinga.

Late 17th century
SULAWESI TRADERS MAKE CONTACT WITH AUSTRALIAN ABORIGINES

Mariners from the Sulawesi region of Indonesia, following trade winds in a hunt for the sea worm known as bêche-de-mer, *first made trade contact with Aborigines along the northern coast of Australia. The relationship thus shaped Aboriginal language, culture, and customs.*

LOCALE: Northern coast of Australia (now Gove Peninsula, Arnhem Land, Australia) and the southern Indonesian archipelago (now Sulawesi)
CATEGORIES: Exploration and discovery; trade and commerce

SUMMARY OF EVENT

Although Australia has been called an isolated continent and saw its first European settlers only two centuries ago, there were earlier visitors to Australia from other lands. Sometime in the late seventeenth century, traders from the Indonesian region of Sulawesi sailed to the northern coast of Australia for trade purposes. For centuries, traders from the area of southern Sulawesi later known as Macassar (now Ujung Pandang) sailed to northern Australia with the northwest winds of the monsoon season. Their objective was to collect trepang (a type of sea cucumber or sea slug also known as *bêche-de-mer*), which were prolific in the northern Australian waters, to sell in Chinese markets, where they were considered a culinary delicacy and an aphrodisiac.

The traders brought with them metal knives, cloth, tobacco, and wetland rice. Other items traded included pigments, narcotics, body adornments, songs, and stories. In addition to the sea slugs, the Australian Aborigines traded turtle shells, outrigger canoes, and sails. In some cases, Aborigines traveled to Macassar. This trade lasted until the early twentieth century, when Australia passed laws to protect the trepang industry in that country. There is no evidence to indicate that this trade relationship was anything other than harmonious.

At times, as many as two thousand Macassan traders were scattered in temporary processing camps along Australia's Cobourg Peninsula and the coast of the Gulf of Carpentaria. To a small extent, the Macassans employed Aboriginal labor to help with the drying and processing of the trepang. Interestingly, the Aborigines did not eat the trepang themselves, because it is poisonous unless prepared correctly (once dried and properly prepared, however, it is free of the poison).

The trepang were collected by spearing them, often at depths up to 40 feet (more than 12 meters). Many of the divers were Aboriginal. A dredging process was also used by harnessing two dugout canoes and scooping the trepang from the seabed. According to the Australian National Maritime Museum, the Macassans prepared the trepang by first splitting them open, boiling them in seawater, and pressing them under stones. The body was then stretched open with slivers of bamboo and preserved by sun drying and slow smoking in smokehouses. The Macassans brought with them ready-made thatch panels for camp buildings and the other necessary supplies.

Wind patterns most likely were the basis for the trade route between Sulawesi and northern Australia. The monsoon winds from the northwest began blowing in December, enabling the Macassans to sail southeast to Australia. Sometime in April or May, the return monsoon began blowing from the southeast out of the Australian desert, and the trip home could begin. A large boat called a *prahu*, leaving the Sulawesi port city of Macassar in December, could rely on a steady wind across the open Timor Sea to a landfall on the Cobourg Peninsula of northern Australia, a distance of about 1,000 miles (about 1,600 kilometers). By the eighteenth century, this trip took between ten and fifteen days. Assuming the earlier trips were just as speedy, this was not an unreasonable time.

The *prahus* were often owned by Chinese traders, and the dried trepang eventually found its way to the markets of Guangzhou (Canton), China. The sailors of Sulawesi, like all island peoples in Asia and the Pacific, were well known for their navigational skills and could read the environment and make navigational decisions based on their understanding of indicators such as wave patterns.

SIGNIFICANCE

The Sulawesi traders took advantage of the relative proximity of Australia to their home to establish a flourishing trade economy with the Aborigines of the northern Australian coast. The influence of the Sulawesians on the spiritual and material life of northern Australia can still be seen today. Some authorities argue that the Aborigines of the northern coast became better traders than their kindred in other parts of Australia because of their experience trading with the Macassans. The trepang trade bound the Aborigines to the Macassans. The exchange of goods between these two peoples served as a binding force whose effects can be seen today in the preponderance of Macassan words used by Aborigines, including Macassan place-names adopted by the Aborigines along the northern coast. Music, language, and ceremonial aspects of traditional life in Arnhem Land were shaped by the Aborigines' contact with Macassan traders.

Strangely, although it is known that many of the sailors in the region were followers of Islam, there is no indication that the religion ever sprouted among the Aborigines. Islamic maps of northern Australia, particular one drawn by Abū Isḥāk Ibrāhim ibn Muḥammad al-Fārisī al-Istakhri, date back to at least 934, and Islam had spread throughout the Indonesian archipelago by the end of the eleventh century. Whether the later Macassan sailors were followers of Islam cannot readily be established, but they evidently did not proselytize the Aborigines with whom they came in contact. Some have argued, by contrast, that the All-Mother cult of the Aborigines, which embodied a vision of Aboriginal unity, may have migrated northward with the sailors to Sulawesi and then evolved into the Earth Mother beliefs of some Southeast Asian cultures.

Another legacy of the trepang trade are the tamarind trees that grow along the northern coast of Australia. The trees are not native to Australia but were planted by the Sulawesi traders to provide a source of vitamin C to prevent scurvy. Whether this floral influence extended in the opposite direction—from Australia to Sulawesi—is a matter of conjecture.

Today, the knowledge of the Australian contact with the Macassan traders has essentially vanished from the consciousness of European Australia, but the memory still remains among legends of the tribal peoples of the north shore.

—Dale L. Flesher

FURTHER READING

Collins, G. E. P. *Makassar Sailing*. New York: Oxford University Press, 1992. Deals with the history, social life, and customs of the Sulawesi people.

Macknight, C. C. *The Early History of South Sulawesi: Some Recent Advances*. Clayton, Vic.: Centre of Southeast Asian Studies, Monash University, 1993. Provides an overview of trade by Sulawesians, primarily after 1200. The emphasis is on ceramics and funerary practices, with some mention of trade with Australia.

_______. "The Nature of Early Maritime Trade: Some Points of Analogy from the Eastern Part of the Indonesian Archipelago." *World Archaeology* 5, no. 2 (October, 1973): 198-208. An overview of trade from ancient times to the twentieth century.

Rolls, Eric C. *Sojourners: The Epic Story of China's Centuries-Old Relationship with Australia: Flowers and the Wide Sea*. St. Lucia: University of Queensland Press, 1992. Covers the ethnic relationship of Australians with other Southeast Asians. Illustrations, maps, bibliographic references, index.

Swain, Tony. *A Place for Strangers: Towards a History of Australian Aboriginal Being*. New York: Cambridge University Press, 1993. Analyzes the historical coexistence of Aborigines and other peoples, with one section focusing on the Macassan traders. The general principle of the book is that Aborigines have sought to accommodate outsiders and make a place for strangers.

SEE ALSO: 17th cent.: Age of Mercantilism in Southeast Asia; 17th cent.: The Pepper Trade; Beginning Spring, 1605: Dutch Dominate Southeast Asian Trade; Apr. 29, 1606: First European Contact with Australia; 1699: British Establish Trading Post in Canton.

RELATED ARTICLES in *Great Lives from History: The Seventeenth Century, 1601-1700:* William Dampier; Abel Janszoon Tasman.

1675-1708
WREN SUPERVISES THE REBUILDING OF ST. PAUL'S CATHEDRAL

Christopher Wren overcame financial, political, and religious obstacles to create one of the great architectural monuments in history, St. Paul's Cathedral, and introduced the Renaissance and Baroque styles into British architecture.

LOCALE: London, England
CATEGORIES: Architecture; religion and theology

KEY FIGURES

Christopher Wren (1632-1723), architect for the rebuilding of St. Paul's Cathedral
Charles II (1630-1685), king of England, r. 1660-1685

SUMMARY OF EVENT

Within days of the Great Fire of 1666 that devastated London, Christopher Wren submitted rebuilding plans to the British monarch, King Charles II. Wren's father had served as chaplain to the king's father, Charles I, at Windsor Castle, where young Christopher and Charles II, then prince, played together as children. This lifelong friendship gave Wren access to the innermost circle of Charles II and secured for Wren the coveted position of surveyor general to the Crown. Unable to finance the rebuilding of an entire city, Charles II instead commissioned Wren to rebuild more than fifty of the city's churches, among them St. Paul's Cathedral.

Wren came to his career in architecture late in life. He had originally trained in science and mathematics at Oxford, where he excelled in astronomy and anatomy. Wren later served as a professor of astronomy at Oxford, and he was a founding member (1661) and later president (1681-1683) of the Royal Society. This interest in scientific inquiry and practicality served Wren well when he eventually turned his attention to the study of architecture.

In 1663, Wren visited Rome, where he studied the classical architecture of the ancients and the Renaissance and Baroque masters, which inspired Wren to pursue a career in architecture. By 1666, the year of London's Great Fire, Wren had received only two architectural commissions, one for the Pembroke College chapel in Cambridge and the other for the Sheldonian Theater in Oxford. Thus, it was in spite of Wren's lack of experience that the king commissioned him in 1668 to rebuild the city's churches and the city's cathedral, St. Paul's, seat of the bishop of London.

From the start, Wren encountered obstacles to his plans for St. Paul's. With the entire city in ruins, the government was in a dire financial situation. The governmental officials eventually raised a portion of the rebuilding funding by levying a tax on coal, but financing problems were to face Wren throughout the building of the great cathedral. In addition, there were political challenges. Every architectural design proposal required the approval of Parliament, a body of men from various political and social camps, each one of whom had his own vision for the style and scale of London's most important church. Buildings dedicated to St. Paul had graced Ludgate Hill in central London since 604; each had been destroyed and subsequently rebuilt. Therefore, there was great governmental and public interest in the plans for the newest St. Paul's on this important site.

The St. Paul's that had stood on the site until the Great Fire of 1666 was a timber-framed, medieval Gothic style building with a tall but unstable spire over the crossing. Even before the fire, Wren had proposed replacing the spire with a classical dome. Following the fire, the medieval style cathedral was so badly damaged that Wren was asked to design an entirely new structure for the site.

Wren's first design for St. Paul's was submitted in 1669 and is now referred to as the First Model. Based on the scale of the previous St. Paul's, the plan was judged too modest for a new cathedral. In 1672, Wren submitted a second plan, the Greek Cross Design, calling for a monumental church with a huge classical dome rising over the crossing. This plan was radical in both its classical Italian Renaissance detailing and its centralized plan. The powerful and conservative Anglican clergy balked at a design so reminiscent of Catholic Italy and successfully argued that the Anglican liturgy called for a basilica plan with an elongated nave in the Gothic tradition. Wren's Greek Cross Design was abandoned.

In 1675, Wren submitted a third design, referred to as the Warrant Design, in which he addressed the concerns of the Anglican clergy by elongating the nave and the choir and adding spire-like elements to the exterior reminiscent of the earlier Gothic structure. Charles II quickly approved this design and included a provision that Wren had the freedom to change his design elements during construction. Wren took full advantage of this provision, making substantial alterations to the Warrant Design as construction progressed. Wren eliminated three bays in the nave, removed the spire and expanded the dome, and heightened the aisles. By the time the cathedral was declared complete on October 20, 1708, on the occasion of his 76th birthday, Wren had introduced a fully classical religious building into Anglican England.

Wren's completed design for St. Paul's was based on a combination of Renaissance and Baroque styles that were popular in France and Italy but specifically rejected by the Anglican clergy in England. By changing his design slowly during the building process and by hiding most of the construction under scaffolding, Wren introduced his innovative classical design elements slowly. By the time potential critics became aware of a radically new classical element, it was too late to change. Little by little, by perseverance, tenacity, and clever manipulation, Wren created the first fully classical Anglican building in England.

The facade of St. Paul's was based on the east facade of the Louvre, with two tall stories, topped by a classical balustrade and flat roof. Pediments crown the two projecting transept porticoes on the north and south sides. The elongated nave and choir run east to west for a total of 596 feet (182 meters) and are of equal length. The magnificent dome, designed after Michelangelo's dome of St. Peter's in Rome, rises 365 feet (111 meters) to the top of the cross (one foot for each day of the year) and spans 112 feet (34 meters) in diameter.

St. Paul's Cathedral. (Macmillan)

Although appearing as one monumental whole, the dome actually consists of three domes: an outer dome, an inner dome, and an inner structural cone between. The arrangement provides for three circular galleries, the internal Whispering Gallery and the external Stone and Golden Galleries. A classical lantern caps the top of the great outer dome, which appears to be held aloft by a classical colonnaded drum of Corinthian columns, reflecting the influence of Donato Bramante's Tempietto in Rome.

Stones from the old St. Paul's were used in the foundation of the new St. Paul's. During construction, one stone caught Wren's attention; it was marked in Latin "resurgam," meaning, "I shall rise again." Wren had the word, along with a phoenix, carved on the pediment above the south portal. The remainder of the cathedral was built of Portland stone, a limestone from the Isle of Portland, in Dorset. Wren himself placed the first foundation block when construction began, and he set the last stone upon the cathedral's completion.

Wren was appointed royal architect in 1669, a post he held for more than forty-five years. He was knighted Sir Christopher in 1675. During his career, Wren designed over fifty churches in London, twenty-three of which still stand, as well as many significant secular buildings and residences. Upon his death in 1723, Sir Christopher Wren was interred in the crypt he had designed within St. Paul's Cathedral, the first person to be entombed there. Wren's Latin epitaph translates as, "Reader, if you seek a monument, look around you."

Significance

Out of London's tragedy, the Great Fire of 1666, came one of the world's greatest architectural monuments, St. Paul's Cathedral. Christopher Wren's brilliant vision for this magnificent cathedral took over a decade to design and more than thirty years to bring to fruition. In his design for St. Paul's, Wren introduced classical elements into the British architectural vocabulary and brought about what architectural historians refer to as the English "Wrenaissance." His architectural style is sometimes categorized as English Baroque, but Wren's extensive use of purely classical Renaissance elements, in conjunction with carefully selected Baroque flourishes, places St. Paul's on the cusp of these two great architectural styles.

Since its completion, St. Paul's has served as the site of most of the important royal events in British history, including the funerals of Horatio Nelson, the duke of Wellington, and Winston Churchill, and the wedding of Prince Charles and Lady Diana. Surviving the ravages of war and the effects of time for three hundred years, St. Paul's stands tall against the London skyline, a symbol of the amazing intellect and tenacity of Christopher Wren and the profound faith and endurance of the British people.

—*Sonia Sorrell*

FURTHER READING

Hart, Vaughan. *St. Paul's Cathedral: Sir Christopher Wren, London, 1675-1710*. London: Phaidon, 2003. Wren's classical design incorporated principles of natural and timeless beauty. Illustrated.

Jardine, Lisa. *On a Grander Scale: The Outstanding Life and Tumultuous Times of Sir Christopher Wren*. New York: Harper Collins Perennial, 2004. Wren's life and careers within the context of the late seventeenth century.

Keene, Derek, Arthur Burns, and Andrew Saint. *St. Paul's: The Cathedral Church of London, 604-2004*. New Haven, Conn.: Yale University Press, 2004. Traces the religious, political, and social history of St. Paul's. Lavishly illustrated.

Levine, Joseph M. *Between the Ancients and the Moderns: Baroque Culture in Restoration England*. New Haven, Conn.: Yale University Press, 1999. Discussion of the tension between classicism and creativity during the late seventeenth century.

Saunders, Ann, and Sampson Lloyd. *St. Paul's: The Story of the Cathedral*. London: Collins & Brown, 2003. Concise overview of the history of the cathedral.

Smart, David H. "Christopher Wren and the Architectural Context of Anglican Liturgy." *Anglican Theological Review* 77, no. 3 (Summer, 1995): 290-307. Wren's theological bases for his church designs.

Tinniswood, Adrian. *His Invention So Fertile: A Life of Christopher Wren*. New York: Oxford University Press, 2002. Wren's life as noted scientist, mathematician, astronomer, inventor, and architect.

SEE ALSO: Sept. 2-5, 1666: Great Fire of London.

RELATED ARTICLES in *Great Lives from History: The Seventeenth Century, 1601-1700:* Charles II (of England); Sir Christopher Wren.

June 20, 1675
METACOM'S WAR BEGINS

Metacom's War was the most devastating and largest-scale Native American war of resistance against the European colonists, destroying many colonial settlements and claiming the lives of more than one-tenth of the total population of New England.

LOCALE: New England colonies

CATEGORIES: Wars, uprisings, and civil unrest; colonization; diplomacy and international relations

KEY FIGURES

Metacom (King Philip; c. 1639-1676), Wampanoag grand sachem, r. 1662-1676

Massasoit (Ousamequin; c. 1580-1661), Wampanoag grand sachem, r. before 1620-1661

Wamsutta (Alexander; d. 1661), Wampanoag grand sachem, r. 1661

Benjamin Church (1639-1718), prominent colonial soldier

SUMMARY OF EVENT

Metacom's War, also known as King Philip's War, began on June 20, 1675, when Wampanoag, or Pokanoket, warriors began looting English houses in southern Plymouth Colony (now in Massachusetts) on the edge of Wampanoag country. Serious fighting began at Swansea on June 24.

The causes of the conflict were both economic and cultural. Through a series of treaties, much land had passed from the possession of the Wampanoags into the hands of English settlers, and the remaining Wampanoag homeland, Mount Hope Peninsula on Narragansett Bay, was in danger of being completely surrounded by English settlements. This expansion of English-controlled territory had brought many Indians under English political control, with the imposition of alien social mores. English courts, for example, sometimes sentenced tribesmen to fines or whippings for violating the Sabbath by such activities as firing a gun on Sunday. There also was growing pressure on Native Americans to convert to Christianity. Tribal chiefs (called sachems in New England) and religious leaders (powwows) strongly opposed conversion, because it tended to weaken their traditional influence.

Massasoit, the paramount sachem of the Wampanoags and an ally and friend of the English since 1621, had died in 1661, and after his death, tensions rapidly mounted. Massasoit's eldest son, Wamsutta, called Alexander by the English, became sachem on his father's death. Wamsutta died in 1661, shortly after being required by English authorities to explain rumors that he was considering an uprising. Another son, Metacom or Metacomet, known to the English as King Philip, became sachem, and the next few years witnessed a series of disputes. By 1671, friendly Native Americans were warning Puritan authorities that King Philip was organizing an alliance of tribes to join with the Wampanoags in a war of extermination against the English.

While the evidence for such a conspiracy is strong, war, sparked by the trial and execution at Plymouth of three Wampanoags for murder, seems to have broken out before Metacom's alliance was perfected. In January, 1675, a Christian Wampanoag named John Sassamon, who had just warned Plymouth of Metacom's plans, was found murdered. On the testimony of an Indian who claimed to have witnessed the deed, three Wampanoags, including an important counselor of Metacom, were convicted and hanged on June 8. Metacom apparently was unable to restrain the rage of his warriors, and violence broke out before he was ready.

The war quickly spread to Connecticut and Massachusetts Bay Colony and later to Rhode Island, as other tribal groups, drawn in by Metacom's diplomacy or angered by threats from colonial authorities, went on the attack. The Wampanoags were joined by the related Sakonnet and Pocasset bands to the east of Narragansett Bay, by Nipmucks from the interior of Massachusetts, by the Narragansetts of present-day Rhode Island, and by smaller groups such as the river tribes of the Connecticut Valley.

The English colonists were supported by American Indians who often were the traditional enemies of tribes in Metacom's alliance, so Indian New England was not united in Metacom's War. The Mohegans and Pequots of southern Connecticut served with the English, as did hundreds of Christian Indians from the "praying towns" of Massachusetts Bay Colony. The Niantics of southern Rhode Island remained neutral. Metacom sought the assistance of the Mohawks of New York Colony to the west, but the Mohawks aided the English by attacking their old Wampanoag enemies.

Metacom, grand sachem of the Wampanoags. (R. S. Peale and J. A. Hill)

In the early months, the Wampanoags and their allies, well armed with trade muskets, were too skillful and aggressive for the English. They repeatedly ambushed parties of colonial militiamen and assaulted and burned outlying English towns. Unskilled in forest warfare and distrustful of friendly tribesmen, the colonists were unable to pin down the enemy. The English usually had no inkling of the town chosen for attack, so they had to spread their forces over a large territory to protect it all. The hostile sachems, on the other hand, concentrated their forces and often greatly outnumbered the defending garrison.

By using Indian allies as scouts, English militia officers learned to avoid ambush and to operate more effectively in the forest. Eventually, special colonial units that could remain in the field for weeks were used to pursue American Indian bands; disease, cold, and starvation aided the colonists in wearing the tribes down. The most effective such unit was a small, mixed force of English militia and Indian allies commanded by Captain Benjamin Church of Plymouth Colony. It was Church's company that eventually ran down Metacom and the handful of Wampanoags still with him, directed by a surrendered Wampanoag to a swamp where they had taken refuge.

Metacom was killed, shot by an Indian while trying to slip away once more, on August 12, 1676. By this time, as starving groups of Indians straggled in to surrender, the war was dragging to a close. The much larger population and economic resources of the English had won out. In spite of the warriors' initial successes, it had become clear that there was no real prospect of driving the English into the sea. To the northeast in New Hampshire and Maine, where the Abenaki peoples had risen against the English, the war continued into 1678.

Both sides used ruthless methods, often killing women, children, and the elderly. Indian attackers regularly attempted to burn colonists' houses with the inhabitants inside them and sometimes tortured prisoners. Perhaps the most strikingly ruthless act committed by the English took place in the Great Swamp Fight, December 19, 1676. A force of a thousand militiamen marched into a frozen swamp deep in the Rhode Island forest, led there by a Narragansett turncoat, and attacked perhaps one thousand Narragansetts sheltered in a log-walled fort. Forcing their way inside, the English set the fort afire. As many as six hundred Narragansetts, many of them women and children, perished in the blaze. Some eighty Englishmen were killed or later died of wounds.

Significance

Metacom's War has been called the bloodiest war, proportionally, in the nation's history, with some nine thousand of the eighty thousand people in New England killed. Of these, one-third were English and two-thirds Indian. Of New England's ninety towns, fifty-two were attacked and seventeen completely burned. The frontier of settlement was pushed back many miles. The military power and the independence of the tribal people of southern New England had been crushed forever. Hundreds of Native American captives, including Metacom's wife and small son, were sold into slavery by the colonial governments to help defray the war's cost. Other captives, considered to be important war chiefs or those responsible for particular atrocities, were tried and publicly executed.

—Bert M. Mutersbaugh

Further Reading

Bourne, Russell. *The Red King's Rebellion: Racial Politics in New England, 1675-1678*. New York: Oxford University Press, 1990. A detailed treatment of the war that is especially critical of the motives and acts of the colonists. Maps, illustrations, and index.

Drake, James David. *King Philip's War: Civil War in New England, 1675-1676*. Amherst: University of Massachusetts Press, 1999. Unlike many authors, who maintain King Philip's War was a battle between two different cultures—one Native American and the other British—Drake argues the conflict was a civil war within a more cohesive New England culture.

Josephy, Alvin M., Jr. "The Betrayal of King Philip." In *Patriot Chiefs: A Chronicle of American Indian Resistance*. Rev. ed. New York: Penguin Books, 1993. Josephy devotes a chapter of his book to Metacom's relations with the British colonists.

Leach, Douglas Edward. *Flintlock and Tomahawk: New England in King Philip's War*. New York: Norton Library Edition, 1966. This elegantly written study, long considered the standard modern account of the war, indicts English land hunger as a cause of the war. Maps, illustrations, and index.

Lepore, Jill. *The Name of War: King Philip's War and the Origins of American Identity*. New York: Alfred A. Knopf, 1998. A very readable text filled with interesting and pertinent anecdotes and little-known facts. Examines the cultural implications of the ways in which the settlers chronicled the war.

Lincoln, Charles A., ed. *Narratives of the Indian Wars, 1675-1699*. New York: Scribner's, 1913. Reprint. New York: Barnes & Noble Books, 1941. Contains a number of contemporaneous accounts of the war, including *The Soveraignty & Goodness of God . . . the Captivity and Restoration of Mrs Mary Rowlandson*, Rowlandson's account of her capture in the attack on Lancaster, Massachusetts, in 1676. Her often reprinted classic is the earliest American captivity narrative. Rowlandson reports firsthand exchanges with Metacom, who at times traveled with the mixed band that held her prisoner.

Malone, Patrick M. *The Skulking Way of War: Technology and Tactics Among the New England Indians*. Baltimore: Johns Hopkins University Press, 1991. Study of Native American military tactics and their evolution under the influence of European weapons and methods. Argues that New England's natives adopted the more ruthless methods of total war through English influence and example. Map, illustrations, and index.

Schultz, Eric B., and Michael J. Tougias. *King Philip's War: The History and Legacy of America's Forgotten*

Conflict. Woodstock, Vt.: Countryman Press, 1999. An in-depth history of the war as well as a guide to the sites of the raids, ambushes, and battles.

Slotkin, Richard, and James K. Folsom, eds. *So Dreadful a Judgment: Puritan Responses to King Philip's War, 1676-1677*. Middletown, Conn.: Wesleyan University Press, 1978. Six contemporaneous accounts, including Rowlandson's narrative and the liveliest, best contemporary description of the fighting, Thomas Church's *Entertaining Passages Relating to Philip's War* (1716), based on the recollections of his father, Captain Benjamin Church.

See also: Mar. 22, 1622-Oct., 1646: Powhatan Wars; Feb. 22-27, 1632: Zuñi Rebellion; July 20, 1636-July 28, 1637: Pequot War; 1642-1684: Beaver Wars; Aug. 10, 1680: Pueblo Revolt.

Related articles in *Great Lives from History: The Seventeenth Century, 1601-1700:* Massasoit; Metacom; Mary White Rowlandson.

1676
Sydenham Advocates Clinical Observation

Thomas Sydenham's publication in 1676 of his major work, Observationes Medicae, *was a milestone in the progress of modern clinical medicine. Both in this book and by personal example, he encouraged physicians to build their practice on direct evidence and experiment rather than on following the authority of the ancients.*

Locale: London, England

Categories: Health and medicine; science and technology; literature

Key Figures

Thomas Sydenham (1624-1689), English physician

John Locke (1632-1704), English physician and philosopher

Robert Boyle (1627-1691), Irish mathematician, physicist, and chemist

William Harvey (1578-1657), English physician and physiologist

Sir Christopher Wren (1632-1723), English architect, physiologist, and illustrator

Francis Bacon (1561-1626), English philosopher, politician, and scientist

Charles de Barbeyrac (1629-1699), French Hippocratic physician

Summary of Event

Until the time of Thomas Sydenham, the practice of clinical medicine in Europe was chiefly determined by physicians following the authority of ancient authors, primarily Hippocrates and Galen. These physicians were not blind followers, but they were led more by the content of standard texts than by the actual details of each patient's disease or injury. They learned more about medicine by reading and by being taught than by observing, experimenting, or doing. Sydenham was always distrustful of material gleaned from textbooks, believing instead that medicine could be learned only at the bedside of the patient. His mind was open to whatever he could learn directly from his patients but often closed to even the most promising clinical advances from the purely scientific approach.

Sydenham was not impressed by William Harvey's discovery of the circulation of the blood in 1628 or by any other recent advances in physiology, anatomy, or academic medicine. Despite his physiological studies with Christopher Wren at Oxford, Sydenham was not persuaded that Wren's laboratory experiments with injection would have any clinical importance. He was a supremely practical man, not given to theorizing or abstraction, and was more interested in curing diseases than in speculating about their causes. Despite this rigorous empiricism, his observations led him to develop several theories of the origins and transmissions of certain diseases. He accepted the humoral theory of Hippocrates that the healthy body is in balance with nature but realized that the authority of Hippocrates, Galen, and other ancient authors derived from their own original use of empirical methods in medicine and concluded that subsequent physicians would honor these founders of medicine more by emulating their methods than by following their words.

In 1655, Sydenham left his fellowship at All Souls College, Oxford University, moved to London, and established the medical practice in Westminster that he kept until his death. He resolved to bring to patient care the strictly empirical methods that Francis Bacon had recently brought to general scientific inquiry. Encouraged by Robert Boyle, Sydenham observed his patients very closely, taking special note of environments, atmospheric conditions, and any other factors that might influence their fevers, epidemics, or acute distress, even such apparently disjoint factors as the presence of fleas near typhus cases.

Sydenham, Boyle, and John Locke shared similar social, political, and scientific goals that enhanced their solid friendship. Locke and Sydenham collaborated on several philosophical and medical projects, and certainly the way that Sydenham conducted his medical practice was influenced by Locke's liberalism. The three friends enjoyed such a close and creative intellectual symbiosis that their biographers sometimes have difficulty sorting out who contributed what to their collaborative results. They shared the belief that medicine must constantly experiment in order to serve its primary function, to cure disease.

Sydenham's influence during his lifetime was stronger on the Continent than in Britain. Locke's Huguenot friend, Charles de Barbeyrac, shared Sydenham's commitment to Hippocratic empiricism over non-experimental methods of practicing medicine. Sydenham may have visited Montpellier around 1659 to study under Barbeyrac, but more likely, Sydenham never left England and Barbeyrac learned from Sydenham through Locke. Barbeyrac is generally thought to be the author of the controversial *Traités nouveaux de medecine* (1684; new essays in medicine), published anonymously in Lyons.

In 1676, Sydenham published *Observationes Medicae* (medical observations), a monumental revision and expansion of his *Methodus curandi febres* (1666; method of curing fevers), which had been dedicated to Boyle. Sydenham wrote the first edition while in the country to escape the London plague of 1665. A revised edition of 1668 bore the fruits of two decades of precise and detailed observations of patients. It offered the first useful distinction between measles and scarlet fever. In subsequent editions of *Observationes Medicae* and in other books, he presented clear and patient-oriented descriptions of rheumatism, smallpox, dysentery, pneumonia, malaria, edema, tuberculosis, rheumatic chorea, anemia, nervous disorders, and various fevers, as well as gout, from which he himself suffered. His investigations into the causes of diseases were aimed at learning how to treat symptoms and prevent outbreaks, rather than at just increasing the store of medical knowledge.

Sydenham's trial-and-error experiments with diverse therapies led to several significant advances, such as prescribing cinchona bark ("Peruvian bark") for malaria, opiates to ease suffering, fresh air and exercise for tuberculosis and other chronic debilitating conditions, and iron tonic for anemia. Like most physicians of his time, he used bloodletting but did not take great quantities of blood, and he relied chiefly upon vegetable *materia medica* and noninvasive methods. He invented laudanum, the solution of opium in alcohol that was the standard remedy for many ailments until the end of the nineteenth century. He claimed that opium was the most widely applicable and most effective of all remedies.

Thomas Sydenham. (Library of Congress)

Sydenham's respect for nature augmented his flexible approach to diagnosis and therapy. His clinical reputation rests largely on the fact that his patients felt better after he visited them. Even if he could not cure them, they appreciated his fatherly concern and gentle therapeutics. He believed that even though each disease must run its natural course, the physician, by enlisting nature, could reduce the patient's suffering along this course.

Significance

Modern empirical methods in clinical medicine began with Sydenham. His many followers, especially the posthumous ones, extended his positive influence on the everyday practice of medicine for at least two centuries.

Several professional medical organizations in Great Britain have been named for him, most notably the Sydenham Society, which existed from 1843 to 1857, and the New Sydenham Society, which existed from 1859 to 1907. Both published important series of medical classics.

Since Sydenham's observations and case reports often later proved to be the basis of new scientific knowledge, the science of medical statistics can be said to have begun with these investigations. His statistical methods and data, and especially his tendency to differentiate sharply and subtly between diseases, contributed to the development of epidemiology. His belief that each disease was a specific product of nature made him a precursor of nosology, the eighteenth century medical philosophy that sought to classify all diseases as if they were entities. His use of cinchona was probably his most influential therapeutic innovation. By the time Pierre Joseph Pelletier and Joseph Beinaimé isolated quinine from it in 1820 and François Magendie publicized its chemical preparation in 1822, cinchona was already one of the most successful and frequently used drugs in European and American medicine.

Sydenham might even be considered the ultimate source of the "evidence-based medicine" (EBM) movement, which has been steadily gaining favor among physicians ever since it was founded by David Sackett, Gordon Guyatt, and Archibald Cochrane at McMaster University in the early 1990's. EBM is the systematic process of using the best evidence from current medical literature to treat each particular case.

—*Eric v.d. Luft*

Further Reading

Bates, Donald George. *Thomas Sydenham: The Development of His Thought, 1666-1676*. Unpublished doctoral dissertation, Johns Hopkins University, Department of the History of Medicine, 1975. Frequently cited study of the most significant decade in Sydenham's life.

Dewhurst, Kenneth, ed. *Dr. Thomas Sydenham, 1624-1689: His Life and Original Writings*. London: Wellcome Historical Medical Library, 1966. Selected texts with biographical analysis.

French, Roger Kenneth, and Andrew Wear, eds. *The Medical Revolution of the Seventeenth Century*. New York: Cambridge University Press, 1989. Includes Andrew Cunningham's "Thomas Sydenham: Epidemics, Experiment, and the 'Good Old Cause,'" an account of how medical innovation confronts medical tradition.

Meynell, Geoffrey Guy. *Authorship and Vocabulary in Thomas Sydenham's "Methodus" and "Observationes," with an Appendix on Isolating Key Words and Phrases*. Dover, England: Winterdown Books, 1995. Brief key to Sydenham's masterpiece.

Milton, J. R. "Locke, Medicine, and the Mechanical Philosophy." *British Journal for the History of Philosophy* 9, no. 2 (June, 2001): 221-243. Examines Locke's relationship with Sydenham, Barbeyrac, and other physicians.

Newman, George. *Thomas Sydenham: Reformer of English Medicine*. London: British Periodicals, 1924. Commendatory pamphlet in honor of the three-hundredth anniversary of Sydenham's birth.

Rather, Lelland J. "Pathology at Mid-Century: A Reassessment of Thomas Willis and Thomas Sydenham." In *Medicine in Seventeenth-Century England: A Symposium Held at UCLA in Honor of C. D. O'Malley*, edited by Allen G. Debus. Berkeley: University of California Press, 1974. Argues that Sydenham was the better doctor, but Willis was the better scientist.

Walmsley, Jonathan Craig. *John Locke's Natural Philosophy (1632-1671)*. Unpublished doctoral dissertation, King's College, University of London, 1998. Concentrates on the mutual influence of Boyle, Locke, and Sydenham in the philosophy of medicine.

Walmsley, Peter. *Locke's Essay and the Rhetoric of Science*. Lewisburg, Pa.: Bucknell University Press, 2003. Shows how Boyle's and Sydenham's ideas on science and medicine influenced Locke's later work.

See also: 17th cent.: Advances in Medicine; 1601-1672: Rise of Scientific Societies; 1612: Sanctorius Invents the Clinical Thermometer; 1617-1628: Harvey Discovers the Circulation of the Blood; 1637: Descartes Publishes His *Discourse on Method*; 1660-1692: Boyle's Law and the Birth of Modern Chemistry; 1664: Willis Identifies the Basal Ganglia; c. 1670: First Widespread Smallpox Inoculations; 1672-1684: Leeuwenhoek Discovers Microscopic Life.

Related articles in *Great Lives from History: The Seventeenth Century, 1601-1700:* Robert Boyle; William Harvey; John Locke; Santorio Santorio; Thomas Sydenham; Sir Christopher Wren.

May 10-October 18, 1676
Bacon's Rebellion

Virginia planters led by Nathaniel Bacon responded to their inability to acquire new land by rising up against both Virginia's governor and local Native Americans. Though ultimately contained, the rebellion resulted in a restructuring of Virginia's government by the English crown.

Locale: Eastern Virginia
Categories: Wars, uprisings, and civil unrest; government and politics; agriculture

Key Figures

Nathaniel Bacon (1647-1676), English planter and rebel leader
Joseph Ingram (fl. 1676), commander of the rebel forces after Bacon's death
Sir William Berkeley (1606-1677), governor of Virginia, 1641-1649, 1660-1677
Robert Beverly (fl. 1676), clerk of the General Assembly and Berkeley's chief lieutenant in the suppression of the rebellion
John Berry (d. 1715) and
Francis Moryson (d. 1678?), two of the royal commissioners sent to investigate causes of the rebellion
Herbert Jeffreys (d. 1678), third royal commissioner, who succeeded Berkeley as governor

Summary of Event

Instability was an unavoidable side effect of the rapid growth of the English population in Virginia after 1640. Competition for political power and social position increased after 1660, as the earlier settlers entrenched themselves in local political offices. Land hunger was also a problem: Since the end of the second Powhatan War in 1646, the Powhatans had held the land north of the York River, which had the effect of hemming in English expansion. Land ownership was a requirement for the vote as well as the key to personal fortune. Later settlers, many of whom had come to Virginia as indentured servants, found high land prices and limited opportunities, and they began to view the land held by the Powhatans as the answer to their problem. At the same time, the return of the Susquehannocks to the northern Chesapeake meant the extension of their war with the Iroquois into the area. That European settlers should be caught in the crossfire of this war was inevitable and also helped fuel frustrations.

A prosperous economy might have counteracted unstable political and social conditions, but Virginia's economy stagnated after 1660. Chronic overproduction of an inferior quality of tobacco, aggravated by restrictive features of the Navigation Acts, drove the price of tobacco down. Expensive experimentation with methods of diversifying the economy and the need for defense measures against the Dutch and the natives resulted in high taxes. In 1674, the colonists were further taxed to send agents to London to lobby against proprietary land grants. Circumstances conspired to exacerbate the planters' miseries, and Governor Sir William Berkeley's ineffectual leadership led to a general disaffection toward the government. Berkeley's own comfortable circumstances, derived in part from a profitable monopoly in the fur trade with local tribes, seemed to prove his indifference to the planters' troubles.

The events immediately leading to the rebellion of 1676 grew out of a dispute between a planter and members of the Doeg tribe in June, 1675. After forces of Virginians pursuing the Doegs murdered numbers of friendly Susquehannocks on two separate occasions, the Indians increased the intensity of their raids throughout the fall and winter. Governor Berkeley angered the planters in the frontier settlements when he countermanded the order for a force to proceed against the marauding warriors. In keeping with Berkeley's overall American Indian policy, the Assembly committed the colony to a defensive war, and the governor ordered the erection of a chain of forts on the frontier. Berkeley's solution was no solution in the planters' view, as the forts would add to the burden of taxation and hemmed in further settlement. The settlers' worst fears about Berkeley had been confirmed.

In April, an impatient group of upcountry planters persuaded one of their number, Nathaniel Bacon, to lead a band of volunteers against the Indians. What followed on May 10 was a war of extermination, in which Native Americans of all tribes, friendly or hostile, were killed. Bacon, the son of an English gentleman and related to Berkeley through marriage, had not arrived in Virginia until 1674, but he had already been appointed to the Council of State. Governor Berkeley refused Bacon's request for a commission to raise volunteers and sent several letters warning him against becoming a mutineer. Unable to head off Bacon with his force of three hundred men, Berkeley, on May 26, 1676, declared him a rebel.

Nathaniel Bacon confronts the Virginia General Assembly. (Gay Brothers)

On the same day, the governor dissolved the Long Assembly and called for the first general elections in fifteen years, promising that the new Assembly would deal with the American Indian threat and any other grievances.

Bacon's success in killing some natives prompted the residents of Henrico County to send him to Jamestown as one of their new burgesses, but the governor ordered his capture before he could take his seat. Bacon confessed his error and received a pardon from the governor. Several days later, he slipped off to Henrico. The June Assembly met for twenty days and passed a series of acts dealing with the prosecution of the war with the natives and with various local problems, especially concerning the misuse of political power. Although Bacon has often been credited with pushing through reform legislation, he did not return to Jamestown until June 23, when the session was nearly over. Arriving with five hundred armed men, he terrorized the governor and the burgesses into granting him a commission to fight the natives.

As soon as Bacon marched toward the falls of the James River, Berkeley again proclaimed him a rebel and, together with his lieutenant, Robert Beverly, tried to raise a force against him. Failing in his attempt, Berkeley fled to the eastern shore, leaving Bacon in control of the western shore. Upon arriving in Middle Plantation, Bacon issued a manifesto, the Declaration of the People, which accused the governor of numerous offenses against the colonists and called for his surrender. While Bacon then proceeded to seek out and attack the friendly Pamunkey Indians, Berkeley returned to Jamestown and, having reached an agreement with Bacon's garrison, took possession of the capital. Several days later, Bacon arrived with six hundred troops and besieged the town. The faintheartedness of Berkeley's men forced the governor to concede the town. Bacon burned it on September 19. A little more than a month later, the rebellion fell apart at the news of Bacon's sudden death of the "bloody flux" and "lousey disease," possibly dysentery.

Significance

On January 29, the royal commissioners John Berry, Francis Moryson, and Sir Herbert Jeffreys arrived from England along with one thousand English soldiers to in-

Bacon's Declaration of Rebellion

Nathaniel Bacon's declaration of rebellion against the governor of Virginia is striking in its wording: Bacon clearly portrays the governor as a criminal and himself as the rightful representative of the interests of the people of Virginia. After listing eight major grievances against the governor and his allies, Bacon in the section reproduced below claims the authority to charge all citizens of Virginia with apprehending Governor Berkeley and to punish them if they support the government against the rebels.

And we do further demand that the said Sir William Berkeley with all the persons in this list be forthwith delivered up or surrender themselves within four days after the notice hereof, or otherwise we declare as follows.

That in whatsoever place, house, or ship, any of the said persons shall reside, be hid, or protected, we declare the owners, masters, or inhabitants of the said places to be confederates and traitors to the people and the estates of them is also of all the aforesaid persons to be confiscated. And this we, the commons of Virginia, do declare, desiring a firm union amongst ourselves that we may jointly and with one accord defend ourselves against the common enemy. And let not the faults of the guilty be the reproach of the innocent, or the faults or crimes of the oppressors divide and separate us who have suffered by their oppressions.

These are, therefore, in his Majesty's name, to command you forthwith to seize the persons above mentioned as traitors to the King and country and them to bring to Middle Plantation and there to secure them until further order, and, in case of opposition, if you want any further assistance you are forthwith to demand it in the name of the people in all the counties of Virginia.

Source: From "Declaration of Nathaniel Bacon in the Name of the People of Virginia, July 30, 1676," in *Massachusetts Historical Society Collections*, 4th ser., 9 (1871): 184-187.

vestigate the uprising and restore order. Berkeley nullified the royal pardons that they brought for the rebels and ordered the execution of twenty-three men. His extreme cruelty was criticized by the commissioners, and Jeffreys formally took over the government in April upon Berkeley's recall by the Crown. Although Bacon was dead, the disorder and protest continued under the leadership of Joseph Ingram. It would not end until 1683, with the reconfiguring of imperial government in Virginia. The rebellion had demonstrated that a nominal democracy in which land was the key to enfranchisement could not work if newcomers had no realistic hope of gaining land for themselves.

—Warren M. Billings and Kelley Graham

Further Reading

Billings, Warren M. *Sir William Berkeley and the Forging of Colonial Virginia*. Baton Rouge: Louisiana State University Press, 2004. A biography of the governor who declared Bacon a rebel and crushed Bacon's Rebellion.

Fausz, J. Frederick. "Merging and Emerging Worlds: Anglo-Indian Interest Groups and the Development of the Seventeenth-Century Chesapeake." In *Colonial Chesapeake Society*, edited by Lois Green Carr et al. Chapel Hill: University of North Carolina Press, 1988. Details the changing English view of the Native Americans in the Chesapeake from "noble savages" to important trading partners.

Horn, James. *Adapting to a New World: English Society in the Seventeenth-Century Chesapeake*. Chapel Hill: University of North Carolina Press, 1994. A scholarly but lively study of the extent to which English colonists in the Chesapeake were influenced by their homeland in their attitudes about race, authority, and other matters.

Middlekauff, Robert. *Bacon's Rebellion*. Chicago: Rand McNally, 1964. A good collection of the primary documents associated with the uprising, beginning with Berkeley's American Indian policy and concluding with the official report submitted to London.

Mouer, L. Daniel. "Digging a Rebel's Homestead." *Archaeology* 44, no. 4 (July/August, 1991): 54. Describes the causes of Bacon's Rebellion and the rebellion's implications for archaeology.

Tate, Thad W., and David L. Ammerman. *The Chesapeake in the Seventeenth Century: Essays on the Anglo-American Society*. Chapel Hill: University of North Carolina Press, 1979. An essential collection of articles addressing race relations, class structure, and the demographics of the seventeenth century Chesapeake. Includes a historiographic discussion of Bacon's Rebellion.

Washburn, Wilcomb E. *The Governor and the Rebel*. Chapel Hill: University of North Carolina Press, 1957. A classic study of the small details of the uprising; generous in its forgiveness of Governor Berkeley.

Webb, Stephen Saunders. *1676: The End of American Independence*. Cambridge, Mass.: Harvard University Press, 1985. Places the rebellion in a larger context, as a prerevolutionary condition, while providing a detailed study of the events of 1676-1677.

SEE ALSO: May 14, 1607: Jamestown Is Founded; 1612: Introduction of Tobacco Farming in North America; July 30-Aug. 4, 1619: First General Assembly of Virginia; Aug. 20, 1619: Africans Arrive in Virginia; Mar. 22, 1622-Oct., 1646: Powhatan Wars; Sept. 13, 1660-July 27, 1663: British Navigation Acts.

RELATED ARTICLES in *Great Lives from History: The Seventeenth Century, 1601-1700:* Nathaniel Bacon; John Smith.

December 7, 1676
RØMER CALCULATES THE SPEED OF LIGHT

Rømer's measurement of the speed of light was the first clear demonstration that light travels with a finite velocity. Although his value was off by about 25 percent, his method was correct in principle and demonstrated the value of using careful measurements of time with the pendulum clock developed by Christiaan Huygens, which provided a substantial improvement in accuracy to less than a second. A more-accurate value was obtained fifty years later by James Bradley using another astronomical method.

LOCALE: Paris, France

CATEGORIES: Science and technology; astronomy; mathematics; physics; cultural and intellectual history

KEY FIGURES

Ole Rømer (Olaus Roemer; 1644-1710), Danish astronomer whose study of Jupiter's moons helped determine the speed of light

Galileo (1564-1642), Italian physicist and astronomer who discovered the moons of Jupiter and made one of the first attempts to measure the speed of light

Christiaan Huygens (1629-1695), Dutch physicist and astronomer who invented the pendulum clock and assisted Rømer in calculating the speed of light

James Bradley (1693-1762), third astronomer royal in England whose measurements on the aberration of starlight led to the first accurate measurement of the speed of light

Gian Domenico Cassini (1625-1712), Italian astronomer and first director of the Paris Observatory

SUMMARY OF EVENT

Before the seventeenth century, scientists believed that the speed of light was infinite. In about 1607, Galileo attempted to measure the speed of light with the aid of an assistant on a hilltop at some distance away with a covered lamp. When the assistant saw Galileo uncover a similar lamp, he then uncovered his lamp and Galileo tried to observe the time for the light to travel to the assistant and back again. He concluded that the transmission of light was either instantaneous or extremely rapid. The first observations showing that the speed of light is finite were made by Ole Rømer in Paris in 1675.

Rømer had been born in Åarhus, the largest city in Jutland, Denmark, on September 25, 1644, and studied astronomy in Copenhagen. He assisted in determining the exact location of Tycho Brahe's observatory on the island of Hveen in 1671 and then went to Paris in 1672. He remained for nine years at the new Paris Observatory of the Académie Royale de Sciences (Royal Academy of Sciences), making careful observations of the moons of Jupiter. In 1675, he discovered an inequality in the motion of the moon Io, the closest and fastest of the four large moons of Jupiter discovered by Galileo in 1610.

Using the new pendulum clock invented in 1657 by Christiaan Huygens, a fellow foreign member of the Académie Royale de Sciences, Rømer determined that the 42.5-hour orbital period of the moon Io was a maximum of 13 seconds longer when Earth was moving away from Jupiter and 13 seconds shorter when it was approaching (42.5 hr. ± 13 sec.). He recognized that this phenomenon occurred because the light took longer to reach Earth as it moved away from Jupiter and less time as Earth moved toward Jupiter in each 42.5-hour orbit of Io.

To determine the range of variations in the orbital period, Rømer observed consecutive eclipses of Io as it passed behind Jupiter, noting the times when it emerged from each eclipse. Since these emergences of the moon from eclipses are not instantaneous events, there were some errors in his measurements. From these variations, he calculated that light would take about 22 minutes to cross Earth's orbit (compared with a modern value of about 16 minutes). On November 22, 1675, Rømer read a paper to the science academy, in which he announced that an eclipse of Jupiter's moon Io would occur about 10 minutes later than the time predicted from the average orbital period as measured in 1668 by Gian Domenico Cassini, director of the Paris Observatory and also a foreign member of the science academy.

Working with the aid of Huygens, Rømer combined the 22-minute time for light to cross Earth's orbit with the diameter of Earth's orbit as determined by Cassini in 1671, a value that was 7 percent too small. By taking the ratio of the distance to the time, he found the speed of light to be about 230 million meters per second, or about three-fourths of the modern value of nearly 300 million meters per second. Rømer published his discovery in a short paper titled "Demonstration touchant le mouvement de la lumière trouvé" (demonstration concerning the discovery of the movement of light) in the *Journal des Savants* on December 7, 1676. At the request of the Danish King, Rømer returned to Denmark in 1681 as royal mathematician and professor of astronomy at Copenhagen University.

The first accurate measurement of the speed of light was made some fifty years after Rømer's measurements by the English astronomer James Bradley in 1728, also using an astronomical method. Bradley was trying to find evidence for Earth's motion around the Sun by measuring the annual stellar parallax, the shifting angle of the stars that should result from Earth's motion in a six-month period. Rømer also had attempted to measure this parallax, but he had failed to detect any change. Although Bradley also failed to measure any parallax, he did notice a relatively large shift in angle of one second of arc in just three days and in the wrong direction to qualify as the annual parallax.

According to some accounts, Bradley's explanation of the anomalous star angles he observed occurred to him while sailing on the Thames River and noticing how a steady wind caused the wind vane on the mast to shift relative to the boat as it changed directions. He reasoned that the apparent shift in star angles resulted from the orbital motion of Earth relative to the constant speed of light. This "aberration of starlight" is similar to the apparent angle of vertically falling raindrops relative to a moving observer. The angle of stellar aberration is given approximately by the ratio of Earth's forward orbital speed to the speed of light. Careful measurements of this angle combined with the known speed of Earth allowed Bradley to obtain a value of 295 million meters per second for the speed of light, slightly too small (by less than 2 percent).

Bradley's precise measurements of stellar aberration not only improved the value for the finite speed of light but also provided the first direct evidence for the motion of Earth as suggested by the Copernican theory some 200 years earlier. Further careful measurements of star angles by Bradley revealed in 1732 the nodding motion of Earth's axis called nutation, resulting from variations in the direction of the gravitational pull of the moon. For these achievements, he was named the third astronomer royal in England. His value for the speed of light was not improved until terrestrial measurements were begun in mid-nineteenth century France, improving on the original method of Galileo by using reflected light and rapid timing by rotating wheels.

Significance

Even though Ole Rømer's value for the speed of light was about one-quarter too small, his *method* was correct and revealed that light has a finite speed. By showing that light travels nearly one million times faster than sound, Rømer provided evidence that eventually showed that light cannot consist of a mechanical propagation like sound, but is actually an electromagnetic wave as demonstrated in the nineteenth century.

James Bradley's improved method for measuring the speed of light began a quest for precision that finally revealed the true nature of light and gave the first direct evidence for the motion of the Earth. Terrestrial measurements a century after his work gave the most accurate values for the speed of light and revealed that light travels more slowly in water than in air, confirming the wave nature of light. When electromagnetic studies showed that light is propagated by electric and magnetic fields, the speed of the resulting electromagnetic waves could be calculated from electric and magnetic constants as measured in the laboratory, and the result matched the observed speed of light. In Einstein's theory of relativity, the speed of light is seen as one of the fundamental constants of the universe.

—*Joseph L. Spradley*

Further Reading

Alioto, Anthony M. *A History of Western Science*. 2d ed. Upper Saddle River, N.J.: Prentice Hall, 1993. This book includes a brief discussion of the work of Rømer and Bradley in the context of the debate between particle and wave theories of light.

Cohen, I. Bernard. *Roemer and the First Determination of the Velocity of Light*. New York: Burndy Library,

1944. This fifty-page monograph of Rømer's work on the speed of light also contains illustrations and a bibliography.

Crump, Thomas. *A Brief History of Science as Seen Through the Development of Scientific Instruments*. New York: Carroll & Graf, 2001. This book includes brief discussions of the work of Rømer, Huygens, Cassini, and Bradley.

Huygens, Christiaan. *Treatise on Light*. Vol. 34 in *Great Books of the Western World*, edited by R. M. Hutchins. Chicago: William Benton, 1952. Translation by Silvanus P. Thompson of *Traite de la lumiere* (wr. 1678, pb. 1690). Rømer's measurement of the speed of light is discussed in chapter 1 of Huygens's classic *Treatise on Light*.

See also: 1601-1672: Rise of Scientific Societies; 1609-1619: Kepler's Laws of Planetary Motion; 1610: Galileo Confirms the Heliocentric Model of the Solar System; 1623-1674: Earliest Calculators Appear; 1632: Galileo Publishes *Dialogue Concerning the Two Chief World Systems, Ptolemaic and Copernican*; 1654: Pascal and Fermat Devise the Theory of Probability; 1655-1663: Grimaldi Discovers Diffraction; Feb., 1656: Huygens Identifies Saturn's Rings; Late Dec., 1671: Newton Builds His Reflecting Telescope; 1673: Huygens Explains the Pendulum.

Related articles in *Great Lives from History: The Seventeenth Century, 1601-1700:* Gian Domenico Cassini; Galileo; Francesco Maria Grimaldi; Christiaan Huygens; Johannes Kepler; Sir Isaac Newton.

1677-1681
Ottoman-Muscovite Wars

The Ottoman Empire sought to strengthen its hold over the newly annexed province of Podolia by extending its suzerainty over the Dnieper Cossacks, who were protected by the Muscovites. Instead, the Muscovites advanced into the southern steppes and the Ottomans began their retreat from the northern coastal region of the Black Sea.

Locale: Dniester, Bug, and Dnieper Rivers (western Ukraine)

Categories: Wars, uprisings, and civil unrest; expansion and land acquisition

Key Figures

Merzifonlu Kara Mustafa Paşa (1634/1635-1683), Ottoman grand vizier, 1676-1683

Petro Doroshenko (1627-1698), hetman, or leader, of the Zaporozhian Cossacks, 1665-1676

Yurii Khmelnytsky (1641-1685), hetman of the Zaporozhian Cossacks, 1657 and 1659-1663, and Right-Bank hetman, 1677-1681 and 1685

Summary of Event

The Ottoman-Russian Wars of 1677-1681 marked the culmination of half a century of instability in the western *ukraina* (borderlands), now called the Ukraine, but the timing of the conflict was occasioned by the defeat in 1676 of Petro Doroshenko, hetman of the Zaporozhian Cossack Host and an Ottoman vassal, by his rival, Ivan Samoilovych, a Muscovite protégé.

In the first quarter of the seventeenth century, the Polish-Lithuanian Commonwealth was the dominant power in eastern Europe, with frontiers stretching from the Baltic almost to the Black Sea, including the province of Podolia between the Dniester and Bug Rivers, the ancient cities of Kiev and Pereyaslavl, and the Zaporozhian Cossacks, who were longtime Polish vassals. Facing these territories were the Ottoman client-principality of Moldavia (Boghdan), the Ottoman province of Bessarabia (Bujak), and the Tatar khanate of the Crimea (an Ottoman dependency since 1475). Conflict was a foregone conclusion over these vast, empty grasslands, with their shifting and mobile population, ethnically and cultural diverse settlers, and nondelineated frontiers.

In 1620, war broke out between the two dominant powers, Poland and the Ottoman Empire. The Polish king, Sigismund III Vasa (r. 1587-1632), to offset his failures against the Swedes and the Muscovites in the north, sent troops south to assist the Austrian Habsburgs against Gabriel Bethlen, Protestant prince of Transylvania (r. 1613-1629), and the sultan's vassal. Iskender Paşa of Ochakov (Özü), Bessarabia, then launched an invasion of the commonwealth and inflicted a decisive defeat on the Poles at Cecora on the Pruth (September, 1620). One year later, a Polish force, besieged in Khotin on the Dniester River, broke out and mauled the encircling Turks so badly that Sultan Osman II (r. 1618-1622) opened negotiations (Treaty of Cecora, October, 1621), restoring the status quo.

Throughout the great Cossack revolt against Poland, which was led by Bohdan Khmelnytsky (r. 1648-1657), the Tatars were active, although undependable, allies of the Cossacks. However, once Khmelnytsky realized that his Cossacks and the Poles were too well-matched for either one to gain a permanent advantage, he turned to the sultan and offered, in return for military assistance, to place the Zaporozhian Host under Ottoman suzerainty on terms similar to those enjoyed by the voievods (princes) of Moldavia and Walachia, the prince of Transylvania, and the Crimean khan. Khmelnytsky's plans foundered, however, on the unwillingness of the Orthodox Christian Cossacks to submit to even nominal Muslim overlordship. Even before Khmelnytsky's death in 1657, the Cossack-Tatar alliance had disintegrated, and the Left-Bank Dnieper Cossacks had placed themselves under the Muscovite czar's protection (Treaty of Pereyaslavl, January, 1654).

With Khmelnytsky dead, the entire Ukrainian borderlands sank into what Cossack historiography knows as *ruina* (the ruin). The Ukraine was now a vacuum, and the Cossacks were caught between a Polish Scylla and a Muscovite Charybdis, although these events had attracted the attention of Constantinople. The second Köprülü grand vizier, Fazıl Ahmed Paşa (1661-1676), was determined to conquer Podolia, which would thus form a glacis (buffer zone) protecting Moldavia and Bessarabia from Polish aggression. Between 1670 and 1672, his forces overran Podolia and captured its capital of Kamieniec-Podolski. By the Treaty of Buczacz (October, 1672), mediated by the Crimean khan, the Poles acquiesced in the loss of the province, which thereby became the last Ottoman territorial acquisition, and agreed to pay an annual tribute of twenty-two thousand gold ducats.

Yet the Ottoman hold over Podolia remained tenuous. Future Polish revenge could be taken for granted, while Muscovite pressure since the Treaty of Pereyaslavl was building in the northeast. Podolia was remote from Constantinople, and although there was an Ottoman presence in Bessarabia, and the Crimean khan was in striking distance of the steppes, the grand vizier turned to the Cossacks.

At this juncture, there arose a new Cossack champion, Petro Doroshenko, a thirty-eight-year-old colonel who had served under Khmelnytsky. In 1666, he was elected Right-Bank hetman, made Cossack reunification his long-term objective, instituted much-needed reforms, and created a mercenary force of twenty thousand troops to offset the divisive power of the *staryshyna*, the Cossack elite. Like Khmelnytsky, Doroshenko recognized the threat posed to Cossackdom by both Poland and Muscovy (which, in the Treaty of Andrusovo of 1667, had effectively partitioned the Ukraine between them). So Doroshenko submitted to the sultan, who appreciated him as a useful ally.

In 1667, Ottoman troops combined with Cossack units to invade Galicia and force the Polish king to recognize Doroshenko's virtual autonomy. Doroshenko was now an Ottoman vassal comparable to the voievod of Moldavia and the Crimean khan. In 1668, proclaiming himself hetman of all Ukraine, Doroshenko invaded the Left Bank, provoking hostility from Poles and Muscovites alike, while the Cossack rank and file were again, as in Khmelnytsky's time, riled by their subordination to an infidel sultan.

For a time, Doroshenko stayed the course. When Fazıl Ahmed Paşa embarked upon the invasion of Podolia (1670-1672), Doroshenko brought 12,000 Cossacks to join the Ottoman army of 100,000. However, the tide turned against the hetman when, in 1675-1676, a Muscovite army supported by Left-Bank Cossacks under their new hetman, Samoilovych, attacked the fortress of Chyhyryn, the symbol of Right-Bank Cossackdom. Doroshenko found himself fighting side by side with his Muslim overlords against his fellow Cossacks. His position became untenable: He surrendered the Left-Bank hetmanate to Samoilovych and ended his days in enforced exile near Moscow.

These events threatened to undermine the security of Ottoman Podolia, since the defection of Doroshenko meant the loss of a friendly Left-Bank Cossack enfilade (protective battle line) to the east. To make matters worse for the Ottomans, Fazıl Ahmed Paşa died in 1676. He was replaced by his foster brother and brother-in-law, Merzifonlu Kara Mustafa Paşa, an experienced soldier and administrator, who was called upon to deal with the crisis in the Ukraine. The grand vizier's solution was to return Yurii Khmelnytsky, the inept son of the famous Bohdan, who had been held as a hostage in Constantinople for the past six years, to the Ukraine. Despite Yurii's record of incompetence, there was magic in the Khmelnytsky name, and Kara Mustafa made him hetman of the Right Bank, granting him the grandiloquent title of prince of Sarmatia and Ukraine, lord of the Zaporozhian Host.

With the Ottomans at peace with the Poles, Moscow was now the principal threat to Ottoman overlordship on the steppes, and Kara Mustafa Paşa declared war. The first year of campaigning (1677) achieved little, although the contestants employed exceptionally large forces: The grand vizier's troops were said to number 200,000 (probably an exaggeration), while the Muscovite commander was said to have 70,000 troops of his own and 50,000 Left-Bank Cossacks.

In 1678, the grand vizier had a better year. In August, he took Chyhyryn, his main objective, while permitting Yurii Khmelnytsky to make an incursion onto the Left Bank, which proved disastrous. There was more desultory fighting in 1679 and 1680, and the grand vizier gave orders for the construction of forts on the Bug and the Dnieper Rivers. However, there was nothing to be gained from further campaigning. Kara Mustafa had not enhanced his reputation, and he was already turning his attention to affairs in Hungary. In January, 1681, Ottomans and Muscovites negotiated the Treaty of Baghchiseray through the auspices of the Crimean khan, Murad Giray (r. 1678-1683). There were no surprises: The Right Bank was recognized as an Ottoman dependency, and the Left Bank as Muscovite. Yurii Khmelnytsky was provided with compensatory territory in Podolia, but he mismanaged it horribly, and since the grand vizier no longer had any use for him, he was executed in Kamieniec-Podolski in 1685. He was replaced in 1687 by Ivan Stepanovich Mazepa.

SIGNIFICANCE

Wasteful in troops and treasure, and with widespread devastation, the Ottoman-Muscovite Wars of 1677-1681, although militarily quite inconsequential, were significant as the culmination of a complex series of conflicts going back half a century and as the event that triggered Muscovy's advance into the southern steppes. Although Kara Mustafa Paşa surely did not intend it, the Treaty of Baghchiseray marked the beginning of the Ottoman retreat from the northern littoral of the Black Sea.

—*Gavin R. G. Hambly*

FURTHER READING

Barker, Thomas M. *Double Eagle and Crescent*. Albany: State University of New York Press, 1967. Barker provides useful background to Kara Mustafa Paşa's career.

Kurat, A. N. "The Ottoman Empire Under Mehmed IV." In *The New Cambridge Modern History*. Vol. 5. Cambridge, England: Cambridge University Press, 1961. An excellent overview of the period.

Murphey, Rhoads. *Ottoman Warfare, 1500-1700*. New Brunswick, N.J.: Rutgers University Press, 1999. Murphey's work is very useful concerning seventeenth century Ottoman campaigning.

Shaw, Stanford J. *History of the Ottoman Empire and Modern Turkey*. 2 vols. Cambridge, England: Cambridge University Press, 1976. The definitive history of the Ottoman Empire.

Stevens, Carol Belkin. *Soldiers of the Steppe*. De Kalb: Northern Illinois University Press, 1995. Stevens's excellent work will help readers understand Muscovy's southern advance.

Subtelny, Orest. *Ukraine: A History*. 3d ed. Toronto: University of Toronto Press, 2000. The most authoritative history of the Ukraine in English.

SEE ALSO: May 19, 1622: Janissary Revolt and Osman II's Assassination; 1632-1667: Polish-Russian Wars for the Ukraine; July 10, 1655-June 21, 1661: First Northern War; 1656-1676: Ottoman Empire's Brief Recovery; Apr., 1667-June, 1671: Razin Leads Peasant Uprising in Russia; Summer, 1672-Fall, 1676: Ottoman-Polish Wars; July 14-Sept. 12, 1683: Defeat of the Ottomans at Vienna.

RELATED ARTICLES in *Great Lives from History: The Seventeenth Century, 1601-1700:* Alexis; John III Sobieski; Merzifonlu Kara Mustafa Paşa; Bohdan Khmelnytsky; Ivan Stepanovich Mazepa; Stenka Razin; Sigismund III Vasa.

February 18, 1678
BUNYAN'S *THE PILGRIM'S PROGRESS* APPEARS

John Bunyan's The Pilgrim's Progress *creatively combined traditional religious allegory, seventeenth century popular fiction, and expository dialogue to produce a classic depiction of the Reformed view of sanctification. It was a testament to the sufferings of Protestant Nonconformity under the great persecution of the Stuart Restoration government and an enduring affirmation of the liberty of the biblically faithful conscience.*

LOCALE: London, England
CATEGORIES: Literature; religion and theology

KEY FIGURES

John Bunyan (1628-1688), author of *The Pilgrim's Progress*
Nathaniel Ponder (1640-1699), publisher of *The Pilgrim's Progress*
John Gifford (d. 1655), first pastor of Bedford Church
Charles II (1630-1685), king of England, r. 1660-1685

SUMMARY OF EVENT

John Bunyan's *The Pilgrim's Progress from This World to That Which Is to Come* (Part 1, 1678; commonly known as *The Pilgrim's Progress*) gave imaginative expression to the English Puritan experience of the seventeenth century. The story's protagonist, Christian, journeys from his original home, the City of Destruction (where he had been known as Graceless), on an epic quest beset with many dangers, toils, and snares, to reach his new home in the Celestial City. Bunyan's central metaphors of wayfaring and warfare and his general method of allegory had deep roots in the Christian and medieval literary traditions. The images of a race of faith and the whole armor of God trace back to Paul's epistles.

The most popular English allegory of the late middle ages, William Langland's *The Vision of William, Concerning Piers the Plowman* (c. 1362 A Text, c. 1377 B Text, c. 1393 C Text; commonly known as *Piers Plowman*), had combined these same religious images and, much like Bunyan's work, had presented them in the form of a dream. *The Pilgrim's Progress* was distinctive, however, because it invested these traditional literary forms with the vigorous idiom of the English common people. Bunyan's work was also distinctive because it conceived pilgrimage less as a prescribed itinerary than as a spiritual progress, less as the attainment of an end than as a process of seeking truth.

Bunyan's achievement drew on a personal story of wayfaring and warfare that was emblematic of England's century of revolution. Bunyan was born at Elstow, near Bedford, in the agricultural midlands. His family origins lay in the yeomanry but, like many with a similar middling background, rural enclosure and price revolution in the sixteenth and early seventeenth centuries led his family to experience steadily declining fortunes. Thus, Bunyan, alone among the major figures in English literature, had little formal education. Like his father before him, he was compelled to eke out a living as a traveling tinker.

The increasing social and economic differentiation of seventeenth century England left its mark on *The Pilgrim's Progress:* A succession of characters—Lord Luxurious, Sir Having Greedy, the schoolmaster Mr. Gripe-

John Bunyan. (Library of Congress)

man of the town Love-gain of the country of Coveting, and the figure of the muckraker—satirize the breakdown of England's moral economy and perhaps even suggest an incipient awareness of class. At the same time, the chapbooks and emblem books that formed the intellectual universe of the provincial tradesman also left their mark on *The Pilgrim's Progress*. The foul fiend Apollyon, the hobgoblins and dragons of the Valley of the Shadow of Death, the Giant Despair, and the dungeons of Doubting Castle all had their antecedents in folktales and romances such as stories about Sir Bevis of Southampton or Richard Johnson's *The Most Famous History of the Seven Champions of Christendome* (1608).

CHRISTIAN PASSES POPE AND PAGAN

In the passage reproduced below, the protagonist of The Pilgrim's Progress, *Christian, emerges from the Valley of the Shadow of Death to find a fearsome cave at which many such spiritual travelers have lost their lives. The narrator's commentary upon the ease with which Christian bypasses this danger provides an insight into Bunyan's understanding of the contemporary status of Catholicism and Paganism in England.*

Now I saw in my dream, that at the end of this valley lay blood, bones, ashes, and mangled bodies of men, even of pilgrims that had gone this way formerly; and while I was musing what should be the reason, I espied a little before me a cave, where two giants, POPE and PAGAN, dwelt in old time; by whose power and tyranny the men whose bones, bloood, ashes, &c., lay there, were cruelly put to death. But by this place Christian went without much danger, whereat I somewhat wondered; but I have learnt since, that PAGAN has been dead many a day; and as for the other, though he be yet alive, he is, by reason of age, and also of the many shrewd brushes that he met with in his younger days, grown so crazy and stiff in his joints, that he can now do little more than sit in his cave's mouth, grinning at pilgrims as they go by, and biting his nails because he cannot come at them.

Source: From *The Pilgrim's Progress*, by John Bunyan (New York: George Routledge and Sons, 1892), p. 85.

Whatever the debt of *The Pilgrim's Progress* to popular fiction, it owed more to the religious ferment of the English Civil Wars of 1642-1651 and the Commonwealth of 1649-1660. The traditional chivalric hero was transformed into the austere Presbyterian knight of Samuel Butler's *Hudibras* (parts 1-3, 1663, 1664, 1678), Sir Samuel Luke, under whom Bunyan served in the years 1644-1647. The marvels and monsters, fearful dreams, and dreadful visions that had consumed the young Bunyan were now contained by conduct books such as Arthur Dent's *The Plaine Mans Path-Way to Heaven* (1601), which Bunyan began to read as he left the national church for the Bedford independent congregation in the years 1647-1651. Indeed, the expository dialogue typical of the Puritan homiletic tradition formed by far the greatest part of *The Pilgrim's Progress*.

This expository dialogue brought into focus for Bunyan the resolution of the spiritual crisis that he underwent between the years 1648 and 1655. With the encouragement of John Gifford, the first pastor of Bedford Church, Bunyan turned to a close reading of the Bible, especially Paul's epistles, and to a study of Martin Luther's commentary on Galatians. Most important, Bunyan discovered the comfort of the Calvinist conception of God's merciful providence and its dramatic conception of the atonement as Christ's victory over humanity's bondage to sin. Not unlike Christian in *The Pilgrim's Progress*, Bunyan had found release in the recognition that grace was sufficient.

Under the Commonwealth, Bedford Church and other independent congregations enjoyed a relatively high degree of freedom. In the years after 1655, Bunyan himself rose to prominence among England's many "mechanic preachers," and the familiar images of country life that were the staple of their sermons fill the pages of *The Pilgrim's Progress* as well. With the restoration of Charles II and the Stuart monarchy in 1660, however, old Puritans like Bunyan faced a fundamental choice. *The Pilgrim's Progress* was a plea to hold fast to a collective faith and an active evangelical Calvinism. Bunyan's text employed a veritable parade of characters, from Worldly-Wiseman and Shame through Save-all to Parson Two-tongues, Money-love, and Temporary, to satirize the allurements of latitudinarianism and an easy conformity to the reestablished Church of England. At the same time, *The Pilgrim's Progress* used the comic character Talkative to satirize the temptations of an antinomian inwardness among politically disenfranchised Nonconformists.

The Pilgrim's Progress focused not on the conversion of the individual Graceless but on the recurring struggles of sanctification that Christian and his companions Faithful and Hopeful endured. Bunyan knew these recurring struggles well. On November 12, 1660, Bunyan was arraigned under the Elizabethan Conventicle Act. For much of the next twelve years, he was confined to the

Bedford county jail. Composed during these years, *The Pilgrim's Progress* was a protest against religious repression. It held up to Restoration government and society the mirror of Vanity Fair.

In this mirror, Judge Hategood condemned Christian and Faithful under the statutes of pharaoh and the tyrants Nebuchadnezzar and Darius merely for their differences: Christian and Faithful did not dress or speak like the local traders, and they preferred truth to the wares of the marketplace. *The Pilgrim's Progress* also borrowed the baroque cruelty of Faithful's death—with its scourgings, lancings, stonings, and burning—from John Foxe's *Actes and Monuments* (1563). It did this to make a twofold point: On one hand, the episode revealed the inward corruption of apparently decent folk devoted only to outward peace and prosperity. On the other hand, it affirmed the sanctity and ultimate victory of the biblically faithful conscience.

The frontispiece to the second volume of The Pilgrim's Progress, *published in 1684.* (Hulton|Archive by Getty Images)

On February 18, 1678, the Nonconformist printer Nathaniel Ponder published the first edition of *The Pilgrim's Progress*. The delay between composition and publication owed much to renewed repression; during the first six months of 1677, Bunyan was once again in Bedford county jail. But the delay also owed something to Bunyan's careful consideration of the important Restoration debate over "plain style." To the Nonconformist who worried that literary language might obscure the pure light of Scripture, and even more to the gentleman bishop who saw true religion in the clear evidence of good works or the member of the Royal Society who saw true philosophy in replicable experiments and verifiable observations, Bunyan replied with a defense of allegory. A leap of faith required a leap of imagination and a willingness to understand the world in terms of the Word rather than words in terms of the world.

SIGNIFICANCE

John Bunyan's work in many ways resisted the intellectual developments that would lay the groundwork for the European Enlightenment in the next century. Nevertheless, *The Pilgrim's Progress* survived and indeed thrived, becoming second only to the Bible itself as the most published work in English. Not only did Bunyan's allegorical method allow *The Pilgrim's Progress* to avoid the Restoration government's continuing censorship of dissenting works, but it also augured a move from a more militant, millenarian Nonconformity, in which wayfaring was a form of warfare, to a more pastoral, tolerant Nonconformity, in which warfare was replaced by wayfaring. "Let Truth be free," Bunyan proclaimed, "to make her Salleys upon Thee, and Me."

This move from governance to guidance gave *The Pilgrim's Progress* an appeal far beyond its initial audience of Protestant Nonconformists. By the time of Bunyan's death in 1688, on the eve of the Glorious Revolution, *The Pilgrim's Progress* had already gone through twelve editions. By 1700, over thirty thousand copies of *The Pilgrim's Progress* had been printed in twenty-two editions, and by 1740, the seventy editions included Methodist, Quaker, Anglican, and even Roman Catholic versions. *The Pilgrim's Progress* had become an embodiment of the open communion Bedford Church—a meetinghouse of metaphor in which all could participate.

—*Charles R. Sullivan*

Further Reading

Cragg, Gerald R. *Puritanism in the Period of the Great Persecution, 1660-1688*. Cambridge, England: Cambridge University Press, 1957. A useful survey of the Puritan experience under the Stuart Restoration.

Greaves, Richard A. *Glimpses of Glory: John Bunyan and English Dissent*. Stanford, Calif.: Stanford University Press, 2002. Although occasionally marred by a tendency to psychologize Bunyan, this exhaustive biography presents *The Pilgrim's Progress* in terms of the metaphors of wayfaring and warfare.

Hill, Christopher. *A Tinker and a Poor Man: John Bunyan and His Church, 1628-1688*. New York: W. W. Norton & Company, 1988. The classic interpretation of John Bunyan in his social and historical context.

Sharrock, Roger. *John Bunyan*. New York: St. Martin's Press, 1968. A brief and accessible introduction by one of the twentieth century's leading students of Bunyan and *The Pilgrim's Progress*.

See also: c. 1601-1613: Shakespeare Produces His Later Plays; 1642-1651: English Civil Wars; Dec. 6, 1648-May 19, 1649: Establishment of the English Commonwealth; Dec. 16, 1653-Sept. 3, 1658: Cromwell Rules England as Lord Protector; May, 1659-May, 1660: Restoration of Charles II; 1667: Milton Publishes *Paradise Lost*.

Related articles in *Great Lives from History: The Seventeenth Century, 1601-1700:* John Bunyan; Charles II (of England).

August 10, 1678-September 26, 1679
Treaties of Nijmegen

The treaties of Nijmegen ended a series of wars involving the Dutch, the Holy Roman Emperor, Spain, Lorraine, France, England, Denmark, and Sweden. King Louis XIV of France, in a bid for territorial aggrandizement along his northern and eastern borders, launched the French-Dutch War in 1672. The treaties ended hostilities and redistributed land among the Dutch, the French, the Spanish, and the empire.

Locale: Nijmegen, the Netherlands

Categories: Wars, uprisings, and civil unrest; government and politics

Key Figures

Charles V Leopold (1643-1690), duke of Lorraine, 1675-1690, who refused restoration under the terms of the treaty

Frederick William, the Great Elector (1620-1688), elector of Brandenburg, r. 1640-1688, and opponent of France and Sweden

Leopold I (1640-1705), Holy Roman Emperor, r. 1658-1705, and opponent of Louis XIV

Louis XIV (1638-1715), king of France, r. 1643-1715, who benefited from the treaties

William III of Orange (1650-1702), stadtholder of the Netherlands, r. 1672-1702, and king of England as William III, r. 1689-1702, who opposed Louis XIV

Summary of Event

French king Louis XIV launched an attack on the Dutch in 1672 in order to support his interpretation of certain territorial clauses of the Peace of Westphalia (1648) and to create more defensible borders. The French-Dutch Wars began in 1672, when Louis's ally England attacked the Dutch at his behest, after France had helped to subsidize England's war against the Netherlands in the 1660's. This subsidy committed England to help France in 1672. The 1672 conflict widened as German states, the Holy Roman Emperor, and Spain entered the war, while Denmark and Sweden fought over territory and commercial privileges in Scandinavia. These conflicts were ended by the treaties of Nijmegen.

The French gained an early advantage in the war, which emboldened them to reject Dutch efforts to end the conflict in 1672. The Dutch had been forced to flood their own country by opening the dikes that protect the below-sea-level land. William of Orange ordered the flooding to forestall additional French gains. In 1672-1673, the war expanded to France's eastern frontier with the entry of German states and Holy Roman Emperor Leopold I.

In 1674, the Dutch and English made a separate peace at Westminster, which ended their conflict and brought increasing pressure to bear on France, which was involved in fighting in the Pyrenees along the French-Spanish border and in Sicily as Louis XIV sought to gain a foothold in southern Italy by supporting a tax revolt in Messina.

Because France's military and diplomatic position worsened, Louis XIV supported the calling of a peace conference, the Congress of Nijmegen, in January, 1676, but wrangling over the arrangements and the opposition of William of Orange delayed any serious negotiations until 1677. The participants also sought to wait on favorable military developments to strengthen their negotiating positions. Several factors contributed to the willingness of the Dutch to accept French terms, which were first presented in April, 1678. The Dutch were under an extremely heavy financial burden and the French captured Ghent on March 12, 1678; the Dutch had made an alliance with their former enemy, England, in March, 1678, and William of Orange married Mary Stuart, niece of English king Charles II (r. 1660-1685).

The first Treaty of Nijmegen between the Dutch and the French concluded on August 10, 1678, and gave the Dutch important economic advantages, as the French tariffs of 1664 and 1667 were revoked. The French returned Maastricht to the Dutch, although with the stipulation that Catholicism could be freely practiced there. Furthermore, the Dutch were to remain neutral in future conflicts. William attempted to undo the treaty by attacking the French at St. Denis on August 14, 1678, but he was defeated.

Spain could not continue fighting without the support of the Dutch, forcing Spain to reach agreement with France (September 17, 1678). This agreement was broader in territorial scope and provided France with a more defensible border with the Spanish Netherlands. France received Franche-Comté along its eastern border and a series of towns, most of which the French had captured in 1676 and 1677: Valenciennes, Cambray, the Cambrésis, Aire, Poperingen, St. Omer, Ypres, Condé, Bouchain, Maubeuge, Warneton, Cassel, and some smaller, nearby dependencies. France ceded the following towns to the Spanish Netherlands: Charleroi, Binche, Oudenarde, Ath, Courtray, Limburg, Ghent, Rodenhus, Leuze, St. Ghislain, and Waes. In addition, Puycerda in Catalonia was returned to Spain, and French troops evacuated Messina. Spanish losses were much more significant than the gains. The agreement also provided for the betrothal of Louis XIV's niece Marie-Louise d'Orléans to Spanish king Charles II (r. 1665-1700); they were married in November, 1679.

On February 6, 1679, France, the Holy Roman Emperor, and Sweden came to terms, with France gaining Freiburg on the eastern side of the Rhine River and a passage to Breisach; the emperor kept Philippsburg. Arrangements concerning Lorraine were complicated. France kept Longwy and Nancy along with certain military roads, and Charles V Leopold, duke of Lorraine, was to be restored to his duchy; however, he refused to accept the conditions and did not take possession. The emperor had to free French ally Bishop Wilhelm Egon von Fürstenberg, whom the emperor had imprisoned during the course of the war. The elector of Brandenburg, Frederick William, had to return most of Pomerania along the Baltic Sea coast to Sweden, France's ally. Louis XIV had acted on Sweden's behalf in accepting this treaty without consulting Sweden. France received territory, but Louis's pursuit of additional gains provoked the Wars of the Grand Alliance (1688-1697)—also known as the Wars of the League of Augsburg or Nine Years' War—and the Wars of the Spanish Succession (1701-1714).

Ancillary agreements were reached between the Dutch and Swedes on October 12, 1679, which, in effect, recognized the earlier treaties. On September 2, 1679, Denmark and France signed an agreement at Fontainebleau in France. The Danish-Swedish conflict was terminated by a treaty agreed to at Lund, Sweden, on September 26, 1679, that ratified territorial provisions of the other arrangements, but a series of secret articles pledged unprecedented cooperation between the two Scandinavian crowns. They were not to make alliances without apprising the other, war was to be engaged in only after informing the other party, and any joint military action would necessitate a sharing of any territorial gains. This was quite a change in the light of the bloody conflict between them (1675-1679).

Significance

Louis XIV, able to dictate most of the peace terms, received high-standing *gloire* (glory or reputation), as he became the most powerful European prince. He pursued an aggressive policy against his Protestant subjects, the Huguenots, and an equally aggressive policy that had gained territory without having to resort to war. The so-called Chambers of Reunion at Breisach, Besançon, and Metz ruled that certain territories or dependencies were possessions of the French king because of their long-standing connections to areas recently obtained by France. In this fashion, most of Alsace, including Strassburg, was annexed by September, 1681. Such aggressive actions aroused resentment but did not provoke a military response against France initially. However, Louis XIV continued such tactics until other European countries felt compelled to respond in 1686 by forming the League of Augsburg, which included the German states, the Holy Roman Emperor, Sweden, and Spain.

In May, 1689, William of Orange, who directed the formation of the League of Augsburg, brought the Netherlands and England into the league, forming the Grand (Triple) Alliance. Many of the territorial changes of the treaties of Nijmegen between France, the Dutch, Spain, the Holy Roman Emperor, and German states were revisited in the Wars of the Grand Alliance, which were ended by the Treaty of Ryswick (1697) and William's accession to the throne of England as William III, and the Wars of the Spanish Succession, which were ended by the Treaty of Utrecht (1713) and the Treaties of Rastatt and Baden (1714).

—*Mark C. Herman*

Further Reading

Bots, J. A. H., ed. *The Peace of Nijmegen*. Amsterdam: Holland Universiteits Pers, 1980. A collection of essays remembering the treaties after three hundred years. In English and French. Includes a bibliography.

Carsten, Frank, ed. *The Ascendancy of France: 1648-88*. Vol. 5 in *The New Cambridge Modern History*. Cambridge, England: Cambridge University Press, 1961. A number of chapters in this work examine Louis's war with the Dutch, the provisions of the treaties, and their aftermath. Especially relevant is chapter 9.

Lynn, John A. *Giant of the Grand Siècle: The French Army, 1610-1715*. New York: Cambridge University Press, 1997. This detailed study clearly presents the importance of the French army in Louis's pursuit of his foreign policy objectives.

_______. *The Wars of Louis XIV*. London: Blackwell, 1999. The most detailed survey to date of Louis's military actions, which provides analysis of the peace treaties that ended those conflicts.

Wolf, John B. *Louis XIV*. New York: W. W. Norton, 1968. This massive biography provides extensive treatment of the French-Dutch War and a perceptive analysis of the provisions of the treaties of Nijmegen and their impact on France.

See also: July 5, 1601-Apr., 1604: Siege of Oostende; July, 1643-Oct. 24, 1648: Peace of Westphalia; Nov. 7, 1659: Treaty of the Pyrenees; Mar. 4, 1665-July 31, 1667: Second Anglo-Dutch War; May 24, 1667-May 2, 1668: War of Devolution; Jan. 23, 1668: Triple Alliance Forms; Apr. 6, 1672-Aug. 10, 1678: French-Dutch War; 1688-1702: Reign of William and Mary; Nov., 1688-Feb., 1689: The Glorious Revolution; 1689-1697: Wars of the League of Augsburg; Sept. 20, 1697: Treaty of Ryswick; Oct. 11, 1698, and Mar. 25, 1700: First and Second Treaties of Partition.

Related articles in *Great Lives from History: The Seventeenth Century, 1601-1700:* The Great Condé; Frederick William, the Great Elector; Leopold I; Louis XIV; Marquis de Louvois; Viscount de Turenne; William III.

August 13, 1678-July 1, 1681
The Popish Plot

Titus Oates fabricated tales of a plot to overthrow the Protestant government of England and restore Catholicism as the state religion. Although fictional, rumors of the plot fueled preexisting anti-Catholic hysteria and resulted in violent purges and the passage of anti-Catholic legislation.

Locale: Primarily London and its environs, England
Categories: Government and politics; religion and theology; wars, uprisings, and civil unrest

Key Figures

Titus Oates (1649-1705), fabricator of the Popish Plot
Charles II (1630-1685), king of England, r. 1660-1685
James, Duke of York and Albany (1633-1701), unpopular Roman Catholic heir presumptive to the throne of England and later King James II, r. 1685-1688
Israel Tonge (1621-1680), Oates's mentally deranged accomplice
Sir Edmund Berry Godfrey (1621-1678), the magistrate whose mysterious death accelerated the public hysteria
First Earl of Shaftesbury (Anthony Ashley Cooper; 1621-1683), leader of the Exclusion effort in Parliament and founder of the Whigs

Summary of Event

On August 13, 1678, Christopher Kirkby, an amateur chemist, who, from time to time, helped Charles II in the royal laboratory, informed the king that his life was in danger from a Roman Catholic plot. Genuine and bogus assassination conspiracies attributed to Catholics had been a part of the fabric of English life since the reign of Queen Elizabeth I. At first, King Charles was inclined to dismiss Kirkby's fears, but he finally agreed to grant him and his informant a private audience that very evening. When he heard the evidence—forty-three articles detailing the plot—presented by Israel Tonge, Charles II was convinced that the supposed plot was a total fabrication. Tonge was obviously paranoid about Roman Catholics, and the king of England did not have the time or the inclination to listen to any more of his accusations. He left for Windsor the following day, but while he was absent, the details of the supposed plot became public.

The primary author of the Popish Plot was not Israel Tonge but Titus Oates. A liar and a cheat, accused of being a pedophile, Oates also had been expelled from a Jesuit seminary for his aggressive sexual behavior. Whether he sought revenge or merely notoriety, Oates ignored the royal dismissal of his invention and sought a more gullible ear into which he might pour his lies. Thomas Osborne, earl of Danby and later first duke of Leeds, the king's chief minister, not only listened, he believed. When Charles II returned to London, he was forced to permit Oates and Tonge to present their evidence before the Privy Council. This time, the two prevaricators named specific individuals involved in the plot and described how the murder was to be accomplished. The king caught Oates in several falsehoods; he made the two appear foolish and unworthy of another hearing. The king then departed for the races at Newmarket. The whole matter might have ended there except for two unrelated events, which would lead to the judicial murder of a number of innocent individuals.

The correspondence of Edward Coleman was seized. He had been secretary to the duke of York and was currently serving in that capacity to the duchess of York. Over the years, Coleman had written a number of letters to persons of importance in France expressing his hope that England might be led back to the Roman Catholic faith. These sentiments would lead to his conviction on a charge of treason and give credence to Oates and his story. On October 17, moreover, the body of Sir Edmund Berry Godfrey, a Westminster justice of the peace, was found in a ditch far from the place where he had last been seen five days earlier. It was Godfrey who had taken depositions from Oates and Tonge in late September. While scholars believe that Godfrey committed suicide, Oates immediately declared that the hapless justice was a victim of assassins. His funeral was turned into an anti-Catholic demonstration, and an innocent Catholic, Miles Prance, was convicted and executed for the supposed murder. He was sent to his death on the testimony of William Bedloe, a crony of Titus Oates. London now became an armed camp, as its citizens feared the worst.

At this point, Anthony Ashley Cooper, the first earl of Shaftesbury, the leader of the faction in Parliament that would come to be known as the Whigs and the moving force behind the radical Green Ribbon Club, decided to use the public hysteria to advance the cause of excluding the Roman Catholic duke of York from the royal succession. The choice of the Whigs as a successor was James Scott, first duke of Monmouth, the eldest of Charles II's illegitimate sons. The Whigs forged documents indicating that Charles had married Monmouth's mother and convinced the young duke they were genuine. He became determined to reach the throne. The king was equally determined that Exclusion would be defeated.

Before the crisis ended, a number of innocent men would be executed for treason; the last victim died on July 1, 1681. The king could not save the lives of the condemned without abrogating the laws of England and interfering with due process, and this he would not do lest he be accused of seeking to establish absolute monarchy in England. Neither could he prevent the imprisonment of the hapless Danby, who had been entrapped by the Whigs, nor could he refuse to accept his political enemies into his council. However, he could bide his time, and that he did.

The crisis over Exclusion ended in March, 1681, when Charles II dismissed the Parliament that he had summoned to meet in Oxford. The Whigs had assembled to celebrate their triumph over the royal will as well as the replacement of James, duke of York, by James, duke of Monmouth, as the heir presumptive. Instead, they found that a monarch who had been willing to wait for the perfect moment to make his move had confounded them. The legitimate succession was safe for the moment. Shaftesbury and his confederates were dismissed from the royal service, and Danby would be released from prison in 1684. Israel Tonge had died in 1680 still believing that he had saved England from a Catholic invasion. Titus Oates made his fatal mistake by accusing Queen Catherine of being directly involved in the plot to kill her husband. Charles II acted quickly, and Oates was sent to the Tower where he remained until William III ordered him released in December, 1688.

SIGNIFICANCE

Before it ran its course, the Popish Plot was the direct cause of the imprisonment and execution of a number of innocent Roman Catholics. This bogus plot was responsible for the passage of the Papists' Disabling Act in 1678, a law that excluded Roman Catholics from sitting in Parliament until 1829, when it was finally repealed. The failure of the Whig faction to exclude James, duke of York, from the succession after the Popish Plot led them to attempt the assassination of both Charles II and his brother in 1683. The discovery of this actual Rye House Plot resulted in the trial and execution of a number of prominent Whigs, the same men who had endorsed the judicial murder of the innocent victims of the Popish Plot. Perhaps the only positive result of the Popish Plot was the passage of the Habeas Corpus Act, one of the pillars of modern liberty.

—*Clifton W. Potter, Jr.*

Further Reading

Coote, Stephen. *Royal Survivor: The Life of Charles II.* New York: St. Martin's Press, 2000. A study of the political sagacity of Charles II, and how he faced and survived each successive crisis of his reign.

Fraser, Antonia. *King Charles II.* Reprint. London: Phoenix Press, 2002. The most balanced biography of the king, it places the events of the Popish Plot in their proper context.

Greaves, Richard L. *Secrets of the Kingdom: British Radicals from the Popish Plot to the Revolution of 1688-1689.* Stanford, Calif.: Stanford University Press, 1992. Links the Popish Plot to the successive attempts to alter the nature of the English government, which finally ended with the Glorious Revolution.

Harris, Tim. *London Crowds in the Reign of Charles II: Propaganda and Politics from the Restoration Until the Exclusion Crisis.* New York: Cambridge University Press, 1987. An in-depth study of the component that made the mass hysteria during the Popish Plot so effective and dangerous.

Jones, J. R. *The First Whigs: The Politics of the Exclusion Crisis, 1678-1683.* London: Oxford University Press, 1961. A thorough study of the men who used the Popish Plot to alter the legitimate succession.

Kenyon, John P. *The Popish Plot.* Reprint. London: Phoenix Press, 2000. The standard work on the subject with an excellent bibliography and notes.

Marshall, Alan. *The Strange Death of Edmund Godfrey: Plots and Politics in Restoration London.* Stroud, Gloucestershire, England: Sutton, 1999. The most scholarly and complete study of one of pivotal events in the Popish Plot.

Miller, John. *Popery and Politics in England, 1660-1688.* Cambridge, England: Cambridge University Press, 1973. Deals with the role of Roman Catholicism in the development of political parties in England during the Restoration.

Tomalin, Claire. *Samuel Pepys: The Unequalled Self.* New York: Vintage Books, 2002. Examines the career of the most famous Restoration civil servant and his involvement in the madness of the Popish Plot.

See also: May, 1659-May, 1660: Restoration of Charles II; 1661-1665: Clarendon Code; May 19, 1662: England's Act of Uniformity; Dec. 19, 1667: Impeachment of Clarendon; 1673-1678: Test Acts; 1679: Habeas Corpus Act; Aug., 1682-Nov., 1683: Rye House Plot; Nov., 1688-Feb., 1689: The Glorious Revolution; May 24, 1689: Toleration Act.

Related articles in *Great Lives from History: The Seventeenth Century, 1601-1700:* Charles II (of England); James II; First Duke of Leeds; Mary II; Titus Oates; First Earl of Shaftesbury; William III.

December, 1678-March 19, 1687
La Salle's Expeditions

La Salle led expeditions to explore the Illinois and Mississippi Rivers, built forts and started colonies, and took possession of the entire Mississippi Valley for France. Despite misfortunes, attacks by envious enemies, and the failure of his last voyage, La Salle gave France control of half of the North American continent and challenged Spanish control of the Gulf Coast.

Locale: North America
Categories: Exploration and discovery; expansion and land acquisition; colonization

Key Figures

Sieur de La Salle (René-Robert Cavelier; 1643-1687), French explorer of the Mississippi River
Henri de Tonty (1650?-1704), La Salle's lieutenant in the western expeditions
Louis Hennepin (1626-1701), French Franciscan friar and explorer
Louis XIV (1638-1715), king of France, r. 1643-1715

Summary of Event

During his first sojourn in Canada (1666-1669), the sieur de La Salle discovered the Ohio River and learned that the Mississippi River flowed south to the Gulf of Mexico. He saw the opportunity for France to control the Mississippi, monopolize the western fur trade, and challenge Spanish control of the Gulf Coast. Hence, in 1677, La Salle returned to France to seek royal support as an explorer. On May 12, 1678, King Louis XIV granted him a patent of nobility, a seigneurial grant of Fort Frontenac (Kingston, Ontario), and permission to explore the Mississippi to the Gulf of Mexico and claim the territory for France. La Salle was granted a monopoly on trade in buffalo hides and ownership of lands and islands around any forts he built. He completed his task within the five-year limit of the patent but failed on his last voyage to establish a colony at the mouth of the Mississippi.

La Salle and his lieutenant, Henri de Tonty, arrived in Canadian New France on September 15, 1678, and organized a plan of exploration. La Salle quickly learned that his patent had evoked the enmity of the Jesuits and the French fur traders and merchants, who saw in La Salle a dangerous rival for control of the Great West. These enemies conspired to prevent his success and even to kill him on several occasions, but La Salle persisted in his plan.

In December, 1678, after engaging shipbuilders and supplies for two boats, La Salle, Tonty, and Friar Louis Hennepin left Quebec. They ascended the Saint Lawrence River to Fort Frontenac. La Salle sent Tonty ahead to build a fort at Niagara Falls. La Salle followed with boats and supplies, arriving on January 22, 1679, at Cayuga Creek, above Niagara Falls. There, La Salle began building the *Griffon*, the first large sailing vessel on the Great Lakes.

On January 29, 1679, La Salle joined Tonty below the falls on the shore of Lake Erie. There he built Fort Niagara, whence they would launch their expedition to the Illinois River. Learning that the boat bringing supplies had wrecked, La Salle left Tonty in charge at the fort while he returned to Frontenac to buy new boats and supplies. Tonty completed the *Griffon* and towed it upriver to await La Salle's return. On August 7, 1679, La Salle and Tonty launched the *Griffon* on Lake Erie. Passing through the Strait of Detroit, they loaded the *Griffon* with furs then sailed across Lake Huron and down the coast of Lake Michigan to Michillimackinac (Mackinac Island), the Jesuit center and headquarters of the lawless *couriers de bois*. From there, La Salle sent the *Griffon* on to Fort Frontenac, loaded with enough furs to pay off his debts.

In September, La Salle and fourteen men embarked on Lake Michigan to return to Fort Niagara. Due to storms on the lake, they did not reach the Saint Joseph River until November 1, 1679. There, La Salle built Fort Miami and waited for Tonty, who arrived on November 21. On December 3, 1679, they ascended the Saint Joseph River toward modern South Bend, Indiana, where a five-mile portage would lead them to the Illinois River. Down the Illinois River, La Salle negotiated an alliance with the Illinois Indians, built Fort Crevecoeur, and began constructing a 40-ton (36,000-kilogram) boat for exploring the Mississippi. On March 1, 1680, La Salle left for Fort Frontenac to get supplies and equipment for the new boat, leaving Tonty and fifteen men at Fort Crevecoeur. Before leaving, La Salle sent Michel Accau, Antoine du Gay, and Friar Hennepin out to explore the Illinois River and the Upper Mississippi River, which they did. They were held captive for two months by the Dakota Sioux and barely escaped death.

La Salle's winter journey to Frontenac was delayed by snow, rain, frozen lakes and rivers, and sickness. La Salle arrived at Frontenac on May 6, 1680, having traveled 1,000 miles (1,610 kilometers) in 65 days. On the way, La Salle learned that the *Griffon* and another ship from France loaded with his goods had been wrecked at the mouth of the Saint Lawrence River. A letter from Tonty arrived on July 22, informing him that the men at Fort Crevecoeur had deserted, destroying the fort and all stores they could not carry. Another message said the deserters had recruited more men and were on their way to kill La Salle. La Salle set an ambush, killed two, and arrested the other mutineers.

His fortune gone, La Salle's future now depended upon his finding the Mississippi River. Over the next year, he formed a defense alliance with the tribes of the west against the Iroquois, rebuilt his forts, and enlarged the colony in the Illinois Valley. In October, 1681, La Salle and Tonty returned to Fort Miami and prepared to depart on the Mississippi expedition on December 21, 1681.

Finding all streams frozen, they sledded down the Illinois River and arrived at the Mississippi River on February 6, 1682. As soon as the ice cleared, they embarked again to follow the river to its mouth. On the afternoon of February 13, they reached the confluence of the muddy Missouri River coming from the West. Three days later, they passed the mouth of the Ohio River on the east. On February 24, they encamped for hunting at Third Chickasaw Bluffs before they proceeded southward.

La Salle planted the King's Arms at stops along the way and visited the towns of the Arkansas, Taensas, Natchez, and Caroas Indians. By April 7, 1682, La Salle reached the mouth of the Mississippi River in the Gulf of Mexico. On April 9, he formally claimed for France all territory drained by the Ohio and Mississippi Rivers and their tributaries. He named the territory La Louisiane (Louisiana) in honor of the French King, Louis XIV.

On the return journey, La Salle was stopped for forty days by severe illness. He sent Tonty ahead to build a fort at Starved Rock, a natural fortress, and to begin assembling the colony and Indian settlements. When he was able, La Salle joined Tonty, and they completed storehouses, dwellings, and a surrounding palisade for Fort Saint Louis. The western Indians saw La Salle as their protector against the Iroquois and gathered around the Fort—twenty thousand of them, including four thousand warriors.

On May 12, 1683, La Salle's patent expired. His patron, Count Frontenac, had been replaced by Le Febvre de La Barre, an enemy who sent false reports about La Salle to the king. King Louis XIV ordered French troops to occupy Fort Saint Louis. Tonty remained at the fort, and La Salle sailed for France. Upon his arrival in France in 1683, he sought the king's support for a voyage to the Mississippi River through the Gulf of Mexico, aimed at establishing a colony and two forts at the river's mouth to defend France's claims against the Spaniards.

La Salle's final voyage to North America proved fatal. The voyage began at La Rochelle, France, on July 24, 1684. Numerous misfortunes and an ongoing quarrel between La Salle, who wanted sole command, and the Marquis de Beaujeu, who had authority over the ships, kept the crews and colonists upset. Due to faulty maps and a dense fog, La Salle missed the mouth of the Mississippi River and landed his colonists on the Texas coast at Matagorda Bay on February 20, 1685. From

La Salle's expeditions came to a sudden end when members of his party mutinied and murdered him in what is now East Texas. (Hulton|Archive by Getty Images)

his fort in Texas, he made several attempts to locate the Mississippi River. On his last excursion, La Salle was murdered by Pierre Duhaut, a companion, on March 19, 1687, in East Texas.

Significance

Although La Salle's last expedition was a failure, his discovery of the Mississippi River gave France half a continent, territory stretching from Minnesota to the Gulf of Mexico and from the Alleghenies westward to the Rocky Mountains—the future Louisiana Purchase territory of the United States of America. His colony in Texas allowed the United States to claim Texas as part of the Louisiana Purchase (1803), until the U.S.-Spanish boundary dispute was settled by the Adams-Onis Treaty (1819).

—*Marguerite R. Plummer*

Further Reading

Abbott, John S. C. *American Pioneers and Patriots: The Adventures of the Chevalier de Salle and His Companions*. Vol. 1. New York: Dodd & Mead, 1875. Recounts LaSalle's journeys and relations with Native Americans.

Chesnel, Paul. *History of Cavalier de La Salle, 1643-1687: Explorations in the Valleys of the Ohio, Illinois, and Mississippi*. New York: Putnam, 1932. Based on La Salle's letters, reports to King Louis XIV, and other documents.

Cox, Isaac Joslin, ed. *The Journeys of René Robert Cavelier, Sieur de La Salle*. Vol. 1. Austin, Tex.: Pemberton Press, 1968. Edited reprint of the memoirs of Henri de Tonty, the Franciscan friars, and Jean Cavalier.

_______. *The Journeys of René Robert Cavelier, Sieur de La Salle*. Vol. 2. Austin, Tex.: Pemberton Press, 1968. An edited version of *Joutel's Historical Journal of Monsieur de La Salle's Last Voyage to Discover the River Mississippi*.

Parkman, Francis. *La Salle and the Discovery of the Great West*. Vol. 1 in *France and England in North America*. New York: Literary Classics of the United States, 1983. Updated version of the 1869 edition. Copious notes, maps, index, and annotated bibliography.

See also: Apr. 27, 1627: Company of New France Is Chartered; 1642-1684: Beaver Wars; May, 1642: Founding of Montreal; Aug., 1658-Aug. 24, 1660: Explorations of Radisson and Chouart des Groseilliers; Beginning 1673: French Explore the Mississippi Valley; May 1, 1699: French Found the Louisiana Colony.

Related articles in *Great Lives from History: The Seventeenth Century, 1601-1700:* Sieur de La Salle; Louis XIV.

1679
Habeas Corpus Act

A writ of habeas corpus *is a judge's order for law enforcement officials to bring prisoners before the court to determine the legality of their imprisonment. The parliamentary statute of 1679 significantly expanded the ability of prisoners to petition for* habeas corpus *relief and of judges to grant such relief. It therefore enlarged a fundamental protection in England against arbitrary or illegal arrests.*

Locale: London, England
Categories: Laws, acts, and legal history; government and politics; social issues and reform

Key Figures

Charles II (1630-1685), king of England, r. 1660-1685
First Earl of Shaftesbury (Anthony Ashley Cooper; 1621-1683), English statesman, opposition leader, and lord president of the Privy Council, 1679-1681
Francis Jenkes (1640-1686), obscure man imprisoned for disloyal speech in 1676
First Earl of Clarendon (Edward Hyde; 1609-1674), lord chancellor of England, 1658-1667
Titus Oates (1649-1705), English priest and dissembler who fabricated the Popish Plot

Summary of Event

The writ of *habeas corpus* is often called "the great writ of liberty." Literally Latin for "you have the body," this writ had its origins in the judicial decisions of the English common law system. Although not mentioned in the Magna Carta of 1215, the writ became a major component of the charter's requirement that a freeman must not be deprived of liberty contrary to "the law of the land." Use of the writ actually began in the 1230's as a way for judges to force defendants to respond to summonses. A century later, the Court of King's Bench was issuing writs of *habeas corpus cum causa* (to have the body with cause), demanding that sheriffs show cause for holding prisoners in custody. By the early seventeenth century, writs were an established way for judges to defend their prerogatives and to ascertain whether sheriffs were holding prisoners contrary to the principles of due process.

In the 1620's, *habeas corpus* became an issue in the bitter dispute between Charles I and Parliament. A number of wealthy English citizens were imprisoned by order of the king's Privy Council for refusing to loan the Crown money to raise an army. The forced loans were themselves a royal ruse to circumvent Parliament, which had the sole power to authorize new taxes—the normal source of funding for warfare. In 1627, Sir Thomas Darnel and four other prisoners applied to the Court of King's Bench for a writ of *habeas corpus*. When the five prisoners were taken before the court, their lawyers argued that they were imprisoned contrary to principles of due process. The Court, however, held that the king's order was sufficient grounds for imprisonment, because all justice flowed from the king. The holding angered members of Parliament who believed in limiting the powers of the monarchy.

When Parliament next assembled, its members included jurist Sir Edward Coke and other strong defenders of popular rights. Coke was the main member of a special commission that questioned the judges about Darnel's Case (also known as the Five Knights' Case). Dissatisfied with the judges' replies, Coke participated in the drafting of the Petition of Right, a statement of civil liberties sent to the king in 1628. Among its principles, the petition asserted that no subject was to be imprisoned without a show of cause and that a writ of *habeas corpus* must not be denied for any person detained for any reason. Although the king was forced to declare that he accepted the petition, he ignored its provisions, and the following year he dissolved Parliament, inaugurating the period of Personal Rule. A year after the Personal Rule had ended, in 1641, the Long Parliament passed a Habeas Corpus Act, which authorized the judges of the high courts to issue writs. The act of 1641, however, proved too weak to restrain executive power during the turbulence of the English Civil Wars and the Protectorate.

When the monarchy was restored in 1660, Charles II was committed to preserving and expanding royal prerogatives. Responding to the arbitrary proceedings of his lord chancellor, the first earl of Clarendon, liberal members of Parliament tried to expand English subjects' right to petition for a writ of *habeas corpus*. In 1668, a bill failed in the House of Commons, and the next year another bill failed in the House of Lords.

In 1670, Bushell's Case did much to raise public awareness about the significance of the writ. Edward Bushell and his fellow jurors were imprisoned for refusing to convict William Penn and William Mead of taking part in an unlawful assembly. When Lord Chief Justice Sir John Vaughan of the Court of Common Pleas granted Bushell's petition for a writ, he declared that the *habeas corpus* writ was the "most usual remedy" for preventing

THE HABEAS CORPUS ACT OF 1679

The Habeas Corpus Act of 1679 provided all prisoners with a right to have their situation reviewed by a judge in order to determine whether their imprisonment was legitimate. The central passage of the law is excerpted here.

[Be] it enacted by the King's most excellent majesty, by and with the advice and consent of the lords spiritual and temporal, and commons, in this present parliament assembled, and by the authority thereof. That whensoever any person or persons shall bring any habeas corpus directed unto any sheriff or sheriffs, gaoler, minister or other person whatsoever, for any person in his or their custody, and the said writ shall be served upon the said officer, or left at the gaol or prison with any of the under-officers, under-keepers or deputy of the said officers or keepers, that the said officer or officers, his or their under-officers, under-keepers or deputies, shall within three days after the service thereof as aforesaid (unless the commitment aforesaid were for treason or felony, plainly and specially expressed in the warrant of commitment) upon payment or tender of the charges of bringing the said prisoner, to be ascertained by the judge or court that awarded the same, and endorsed upon the said writ, not exceeding twelve pence per mile, and upon security given by his own bond to pay the charges of carrying back the prisoner, if he shall be remanded by the court or judge to which he shall be brought according to the true intent of this present act, and that he will not make any escape by the way, make return of such writ. . . .

Source: From the University of Virginia Religious Freedom Page. http://religiousfreedom.lib.virginia.edu/sacred/habeas_corpus_1679.html. Accessed April 27, 2005.

an illegal deprivation of liberty. Bushell's Case was doubly significant: It not only helped to establish the importance of *habeas corpus*, but it also stood as a landmark in protecting the independence of juries as determiners of guilt or innocence, rather than mere mouthpieces of judges.

In 1675, the Lords and Commons had a strong disagreement about the circumstances in which *habeas corpus* might be used. Following termination of the 1675 session, an "obscure individual" named Francis Jenkes was imprisoned because of a treasonous speech he had made at Guildhall. When his case reached the King's Bench, Lord Chief Justice Sir Richard Raynsford refused to consider a writ of *habeas corpus*, because the court was on vacation. Jenkes's friends took the case to Lord Chancellor Heneage Finch, later the first earl of Nottingham, who also reported that writs could not be issued during times of vacation. The case of Jenkes underscored the limited protection that *habeas corpus* afforded.

When Parliament met in 1677, the House of Commons passed a bill designed to make the writ of *habeas corpus* more effective. As the House of Lords began debating the bill, the High Court of Peers ordered the first earl of Shaftesbury to be imprisoned on unspecified charges of contempt. When Shaftesbury appealed to the King's Bench for a writ of *habeas corpus*, the responding judge found that the imprisonment was illegal but nevertheless ruled that the King's Bench had no authority to interfere with the proceedings of the High Court of Peers in Parliament. Shortly thereafter, a priest named Titus Oates created a frenzy of anti-Catholic fears with his fabricated stories of a Jesuit plot to assassinate the king. Shaftesbury took advantage of the so-called Popish Plot to attack the king's ministers and to promote further limitations on royal prerogatives. The plot helped him to build up an organization of followers within Parliament, later called Whigs.

The majority of the commoners in the "Whig" Parliament of 1679, elected at the height of the Popish Plot, were highly critical of executive power. The stormy session was devoted to two major issues, the writ of *habeas corpus* and the impeachment of the lord treasurer, Thomas Osborne, first earl of Danby and later first duke of Leeds. Following Danby's impeachment, the House of Commons passed a strong *habeas corpus* bill after caustic debates and several compromises. In the House of Lords, the bill was approved by a margin of a single vote, reportedly by counting the vote of an elderly peer twice. Charles II then reluctantly gave his approval.

The statute of 1679 required that a speedy judicial hearing be conducted to determine the legality of a subject's imprisonment on a criminal charge. The law specified that the lord chancellor or any of the judges of the three common-law courts might issue a writ of *habeas corpus* "at all times and in all cases." It explicitly included writs for persons that the king considered as threats to national security. It disallowed re-committal for the same offense after a person was released by a writ, and it prohibited evasion by transferring a prisoner to another jurisdiction. Very harsh penalties were provided for judges who failed to follow the requirements of the law, but there were limitations as well. The law did not prevent a judge from requiring excessive bail for release, and it did not apply to commitments ordered by the House of Commons, as was Danby's unfortunate situation. In addition, the writ could be used only in criminal cases, not for imprisonment resulting from civil suits or debt.

Significance

The famous jurist William Blackstone referred to the Habeas Corpus Act as a "second Magna Carta and stable bulwark of our liberties." Although few of its provisions were original, the act corrected important defects that had frequently allowed the Crown to disregard the writ of *habeas corpus* in the past. Thenceforth, the Crown's law-enforcement officials would find it much more difficult to deprive a person of liberty based on ill-founded charges. One indication of the act's effectiveness was the fact that James II asked Parliament for its repeal, which was refused. Since the act resulted from the conflict between the Crown and the Parliament, however, it is not surprising that it did little to prevent abuses by the legislative branch.

The protections of *habeas corpus* writs would continue to expand in subsequent years. English settlers in North America and elsewhere adopted the writs as part of their judicial systems. The United States Constitution, for example, stipulates that the right of citizens to petition for a writ of *habeas corpus* can be suspended only in times of rebellion or insurrection. The British parliament in 1814 and 1869 eliminated many of the limitations of the 1679 law.

—*Thomas Tandy Lewis*

Further Reading

Blackstone, William. *Commentaries on the Laws of England*. Vol. 3. Reprint. Oxford, England: Oxford University Press, 1970. Available in many editions, the third volume of this classic work includes a clear sum-

mary of the writ of *habeas corpus* as understood in the eighteenth century.
Coote, Stephen. *Royal Survivor: A Life of Charles II.* New York: St. Martin's Press, 1999. A succinct and clearly written biography that provides the historical context for the passage of the law.
Duker, William. *A Constitutional History of Habeas Corpus*. Westport, Conn.: Greenwood Press, 1980. The first chapter presents an excellent history of the writ, although the English terminology is confusing for people not familiar with the English legal system.
Hurd, Rollin. *A Treatise on the Right of Personal Liberty and on the Writ of Habeas Corpus*. New York: Da Capo Press, 1972. Includes a great deal of valuable material, although its organization and writing style are intimidating.
Hutton, Roland. *Charles the Second: King of England, Scotland, and Ireland*. New York: Oxford University Press, 1989. An excellent introduction to his life, with excellent analysis of the political controversies of the time.
Kutler, Luis. *World Habeas Corpus*. Dobbs Ferry, N.Y.: Oceana, 1962. A general history of the writ, with only a short summary of the passage of the 1679 law.
Sharpe, Robert J., and D. R. Zellick. *Law of Habeas Corpus*. New York: Oxford University Press, 2004. A standard work by two Canadian jurists, emphasizing modern law but providing a good summary of the historical development of the writ.
Walker, Robert. *The Constitutional and Legal Development of Habeas Corpus as the Writ of Liberty*. Stillwater: Oklahoma State University Publications, 1960. An excellent work of legal history, although like most American writers, Walker is more interested in U.S. law than in the English background.

See also: Dec. 18, 1621: The Great Protestation; May 6-June 7, 1628: Petition of Right; Mar., 1629-1640: "Personal Rule" of Charles I; Nov. 3, 1640-May 15, 1641: Beginning of England's Long Parliament; 1642-1651: English Civil Wars; Dec. 6, 1648-May 19, 1649: Establishment of the English Commonwealth; Dec. 16, 1653-Sept. 3, 1658: Cromwell Rules England as Lord Protector; May, 1659-May, 1660: Restoration of Charles II; 1662-May 3, 1695: England's Licensing Acts; Aug. 13, 1678-July 1, 1681: The Popish Plot; Apr. 4, 1687, and Apr. 27, 1688: Declaration of Liberty of Conscience; Feb. 13, 1689: Declaration of Rights; May 24, 1689: Toleration Act.

Related articles in *Great Lives from History: The Seventeenth Century, 1601-1700:* Charles I; Charles II (of England); First Earl of Clarendon; Sir Edward Coke; First Duke of Leeds; Titus Oates; William Penn; First Earl of Shaftesbury.

1679-1709
Rājput Rebellion

Mughal emperor Aurangzeb provoked a thirty-year-long rebellion among the Rājputs that ended the long-established Mughal-Rājput partnership. The failure to maintain this partnership contributed to Mughal decline, the rise of the Marāthās, and, perhaps, later European hegemony.

Locale: Rajasthan, northern India
Categories: Wars, uprisings, and civil unrest; government and politics

Key Figures

Aurangzeb (1618-1707), Mughal emperor of India, r. 1658-1707
Prince Akbar (d. 1704), Aurangzeb's son
Jaswant Singh (d. 1678), raja of Marwar, r. 1638-1678
Ajit Singh (1679-1724), Jaswant Singh's son and raja of Marwar, r. 1707-1724
Raj Singh (1629-1680), *rana* of Mewar, r. 1658-1680
Jai Singh (1653-1698), Raj Singh's son and *rana* of Mewar, r. 1680-1698

Summary of Event

Although 1526 marks Bābur's establishment of the Mughal Empire in India, its real architect was Bābur's grandson, Akbar (r. 1556-1605), who brought northern and central India under his sway. During the 1560's, he became embroiled with various Rājput chieftains in Rajasthan, southwest of Delhi. These were Hindu warrior-princes who ruled clansmen (*thakurs*) whose values and way of life resembled those of medieval European feudal society, upholding ancient traditions of chivalrous and heroic conduct.

Among the most prominent Rājput states were Mewar (Udaipur), Marwar (Jodhpur), Amber (Jaipur), Jaisalmer, Bikaner, Kotah, Bundi, and Alwar. Since the eleventh century, the Rājputs had resisted waves of Muslim invaders from what is now Afghanistan. Their martial qualities, spirit of independence, and strategic location meant that Akbar could not undertake extensive conquests throughout India without first breaking them.

Akbar was both a pragmatist and a visionary. Contemporary sources fail to explain the process, but after he had defeated some Rājput leaders and neutralized others, he inaugurated a policy of rapprochement that evolved into a Mughal-Rājput partnership. Some Rājput princes (for example, Raja Bihari Mall of Amber) voluntarily submitted and became Mughal imperial officers to whom the emperor granted *mansabs* (ranks in the imperial hierarchy with an obligation to maintain a designated number of troops). As *mansabdars* of the empire, these Hindu princes could become army commanders or provincial governors like their Muslim counterparts. Nowhere else in the history of Islam did Muslim rulers show such confidence in non-Muslim subjects. In time, some Rājput princes gave their daughters to be Akbar's wives: The daughter of Raja Bihari Mall, Jodha Bai (d. 1623), was to be the mother of Akbar's son, Jahāngīr (1605-1627). Between these elite Rājputs and the Mughal Dynasty there occurred a degree of cultural assimilation, such as happened in few other societies where Muslims and non-Muslims lived so closely. Akbar even permitted his Rājput wives to practice their religion within the imperial harem.

During the sixteenth and seventeenth centuries, due largely to this Mughal-Rājput partnership, the Mughal Empire expanded until, during the reign of Akbar's great-grandson, Aurangzeb, it embraced most of the Indian subcontinent. Akbar's son, Jahāngīr, half Rājput, followed Akbar's example, as did Jahāngīr's son Shah Jahan (r. 1628-1658), whose mother was also a Rājput princess.

When Shah Jahan fell ill in 1658, his four sons, all children of his Persian wife, Arjumand Banu Begam (later known as Mumtaz Mahal, reportedly for whom he built the Taj Mahal), embarked upon a fratricidal struggle for succession. The eventual victor, Aurangzeb, then proceeded to eliminate his rivals. Unlike his two elder brothers, Aurangzeb was a fanatical Sunni Muslim. He believed that Islam in India was in danger of being spiritually diluted by heresy and heterodoxy, and he sought to restore the pristine Islam of the time of the Prophet. The Rājput princes were bound to regard Aurangzeb's personality with distaste, and he reciprocated their dislike. Aurangzeb, it may be surmised, would have much preferred his commanders to be devout Muslims. Still, for the first twenty years of his reign, the Mughal-Rājput partnership survived, if slightly tattered.

In 1678, however, Raja Jaswant Singh of Marwar, one of Shah Jahan's best generals, died at Jamrud while fighting the Pathans. He died without heirs, and Aurangzeb, as his overlord, resolved to annex Marwar (in accordance with the practice known during the times of British India as the doctrine of lapse). At the time of his death, however, one of the raja's wives (a princess from Mewar) was pregnant, and she eventually gave birth to a son and heir, Ajit Singh, in Lahore (1679). The baby was to be brought to Delhi on Aurangzeb's orders, and, it was said, he was to be brought up in the imperial harem as a Muslim. This and the annexation of the state were utterly repugnant to the Marwar *thakurs*. One of their most daring, Durgadas, managed to kidnap mother and child and bring them back to Marwar. However, to evade Mughal pursuers, Durgadas later spirited them away to Mewar, where the *rana*, Raj Singh, angered by Aurangzeb's actions, provided sanctuary. He was outraged not only by the Mughal invasion of Marwar but also by Aurangzeb's reimposition of the *jizya*, the hated but canonical poll tax levied on non-Muslims, which Akbar had abolished. Raj Singh became the heart and soul of Rājput intransigence.

Aurangzeb, in addition to sending an army of occupation into Marwar, despatched another force against Mewar in a war of attrition extending from 1679 to 1681. In the fighting that followed, Raj Singh proved a master of guerrilla warfare in the harsh and inhospitable Aravalli hills. Given the struggle in Marwar and Aurangzeb's desire to proceed south to the Deccan, the emperor rather surprisingly entered into negotiations with Raj Singh's son, Jai Singh. Jai Singh ceded three *parganas* (administrative districts) in lieu of paying *jizya* and having the Mughal army evacuate Mewar. However, by then the damage had been done. The genie of mutual distrust that now characterized Mughal-Rājput relations could never be put back in the bottle.

Aurangzeb's dealings with the Rājputs were further exacerbated by the conduct of his third and favorite son, Prince Akbar, whom he had sent against the *rana* of Mewar. Akbar's forces had been defeated, and Aurangzeb, highly displeased, had transferred the prince to the Marwar front. Relations between father and son rapidly deteriorated, and Akbar, breaking with the emperor, threw in his lot with the Rājputs, dreaming of being placed on the imperial throne with their help. Marching with a large Rājput force to Ajmer (January 15, 1681) while the main Mughal army was in Mewar, he could have seriously threatened Aurangzeb, if he had acted vigorously. Instead, he idled his time there, allowing the wily Aurangzeb to sow seeds of suspicion between him and his new allies. The policy worked. The Rājputs abandoned him, mistrusting his motives, and the prince fled to the Deccan to seek sanctuary with the Marāthā king, Sambhājī. Aurangzeb followed him to the Deccan, where he remained for the rest of his reign. In addition to his determination to crush the Marāthās, he had a long-standing ambition to annex the Shīʿite sultanates of Bijapur and Golconda. Not long after, Prince Akbar fled to Persia, where he died in 1704.

Meanwhile, the withdrawal of the imperial presence from Rajasthan left the exasperated and disaffected Rājputs with considerable de facto independence. As noted, Aurangzeb had been forced to negotiate with Rana Jai Singh (in 1681) to enable the emperor to proceed to the Deccan, but with regard to Marwar, the struggle became a veritable thirty years' war, with resistance headed by the redoubtable Durgadas. By the time of Aurangzeb's death in 1707, Ajit Singh, mentored by Durgadas, was twenty-eight years old. Aurangzeb's successor, Bahādur Shāh, had made peace with Ajit Singh in 1709, acknowledging him as Marwar's legitimate ruler. Thereafter, Ajit Singh came to the imperial court, playing politics.

In 1714, he married a daughter to the emperor Muhammad Farrukhsiyar (r. 1713-1719) and acquired governorships of Ajmer and Gujarat. In 1721, however, he was removed from office for collaborating with the Marāthās, although he was forgiven in 1724. Shortly thereafter, he was murdered by his eldest son, Bakht Singh, supposedly for incest with Bakht Singh's wife. Despite his less than heroic personality, he remained, even through his opium-sodden last years, the central (although perhaps largely passive) player in the great drama that had led to the alienation of the Rājputs from Mughal rule. His second son, Abhai Singh, succeeded him, but whereas the father flirted ineffectively with the Marāthās, the son remained close to the imperial court. Seemingly, pro- or anti-Marāthā sentiment had little to do with religion, but was a question of political expediency.

SIGNIFICANCE

The Mughal Empire grew and flourished partly as a result of the Mughal-Rājput partnership initiated by Akbar. Through religious fanaticism, obstinacy, and mistrust, Aurangzeb effectively destroyed that partnership. Had he continued to enlist the Rājputs and their military skill, he might have solved the Mughal Empire's concerns of the northwest frontier: the Marāthās and the Deccani sultanates. Instead, he squandered military staffing and resources on the Rājput struggle.

—*Gavin R. G. Hambly*

FURTHER READING

Chandra, Satish. *Parties and Politics at the Mughal Court, 1707-1740*. 1959. Reprint. New York: Oxford University Press, 2002. An excellent resource on the Rājput involvement in later Mughal politics.

Gascoigne, Bamber. *A Brief History of the Great Moghuls*. New York: Carroll & Graf, 2002. This well-written, general history of the Mughals chronicles the rise and fall of the empire from its founder, Bābur, through Aurangzeb. Illustrated.

Hallissey, Robert C. *The Rajput Rebellion Against Aurangzeb*. Columbia: University of Missouri Press, 1977. The best available account, with an excellent bibliography.

Richards, John F. *The Mughal Empire*. New York: Cambridge University Press, 1992. A comprehensive account of the Mughal empire. Strongly recommended.

Sharma, G. N. *Mewar and the Mughal Emperors*. Agra: Agarwala, 1962. A detailed narrative of Mughal-Mewar relations.

Tod, James. *Annals and Antiquities of Rajasthan*. London: Smith, Elder, 1829-1832. Reprint. 2 vols. New Delhi, K. M. N., 1971. A superb example of nineteenth century, Anglo-Indian historiography, and still indispensable reading.

SEE ALSO: 17th cent.: Rise of the Gunpowder Empires; 1605-1627: Mughal Court Culture Flourishes; 1606-1674: Europeans Settle in India; 1632-c. 1650: Shah Jahan Builds the Taj Mahal; 1658-1707: Reign of Aurangzeb; c. 1666-1676: Founding of the Marāthā Kingdom.

RELATED ARTICLES in *Great Lives from History: The Seventeenth Century, 1601-1700:* ʿAbbās the Great; Aurangzeb; Jahāngīr; Kösem Sultan; Murad IV; Shah Jahan; Śivājī.

Beginning 1680's
Guerra dos Bárbaros

Brazilian-Portuguese frontiersmen fought indigenous populations in the northeast interior of Brazil in a series of battles called the Guerra dos Bárbaros, the war of the barbarians. The frontiersmen conquered vast stretches of arid land and transformed them into cattle ranges.

Locale: Northeast interior of Brazil
Categories: Wars, uprisings, and civil unrest; economics; agriculture; environment; expansion and land acquisition

Key Figures

Canindé (fl. late seventeenth century), an indigenous leader who signed a peace treaty with colonial Brazilian authorities, which was later ignored

Domingos Jorge Velho (1614?-1703), a mixed-race frontiersman from southern Brazil who settled in the northeastern interior, searching for fugitive slaves

Manuel Álvares de Morais Navarro (d. 1746), a Brazilian frontiersman who led a massacre of indigenous peoples at Jaguaribe River

Summary of Event

The Portuguese, who first settled Brazil in the early sixteenth century, established sugar plantations on fertile lands along the Atlantic coast. An arid hinterland that is beyond a mountain range extending along the coast dominates the Brazilian northeast and extends for thousands of miles, descending to the Amazon River basin.

Two linguistically distinct groups of indigenous peoples occupied the coast and highlands of Brazil at the time of the Portuguese conquest. Along the coast were tribes of Tupi Indians, an indigenous group whose language was part of the Tupi-Guaraní language family. They formed the vast majority of the indigenous population in eastern South America. The interior highlands were occupied primarily by the less-numerous Gê-speaking peoples. The Tupi gave the name Tapuya to the upland indigenous who did not speak the Tupi language.

To obtain fertile coastal land for sugar plantations, the Portuguese first battled the Tupi. Occupying much of the northeastern coast during the sixteenth century, the Portuguese traveled over the mountains for more land during the following century. In the southern province of São Paulo, bands of mixed-race Portuguese and indigenous peoples, known as *bandeirantes*, hunted for precious metals and stones and for indigenous people to enslave.

With few Portuguese women in Brazil, the white male colonists coupled with indigenous women or black slaves from Africa, thereby producing children who were indigenous Brazilian and Portuguese. Moving into the northeastern highlands, the Brazilian-Portuguese confronted desperate indigenous resistance, initiating a long series of wars known as the Guerra dos Bárbaros, or war of the barbarians. The movement of the Portuguese into the northeastern interior was delayed during the first half of the seventeenth century because of the Dutch invasion and occupation of coastal land. Only after the Dutch were defeated and driven out by the middle of the century could the Brazilian Portuguese concentrate on moving into the interior. In the northeastern interior, the vast reaches of arid land were useful for cattle raising only.

Corrals of several hundred head of cattle were set up in the spare river valleys of the region. As the corrals grouped into ranches, tens of thousands of cattle came to occupy and range over the interior. They competed for its sparse sustenance with the indigenous populations, for whom the area was their last source of food. Cattle were of value to the Portuguese not only for beef but also for hides, suitable for clothing as well as packing and preserving material.

By the 1680's, cattle grazers were occupying the interior of Bahia, the principal northeast province, which was south of the São Francisco River. The indigenous populations fiercely resisted these advances, slaughtering pioneer inhabitants in their isolated settlements and capturing or killing their cattle. The earlier inexperienced frontiersmen were no match against indigenous resistance, so the colonial authorities called upon the experienced *bandeirante*, indigenous fighters of the south. The authorities contracted with one of fighters' principal leaders, Domingos Jorge Velho, who had moved northeast to establish a frontier ranch.

Cattle ranchers sought to advance westward. After Bahia, they moved into the river valley terrains of Rio Grande and the provinces to its west. Ranchers and some civil authorities wanted to exterminate the indigenous, since they began to revolt with greater and greater ferocity against the advancing ranchers and their hordes of cattle. However, religious authorities emphasized that the indigenous threat could be curtailed by evangelizing the indigenous and by settling them in villages. A key issue among ranchers and colonial authorities was the concept of a "just war." Indigenous resistance to conversion and village settlement was considered sufficient reason to engage in a just war to eliminate the threat.

Some of the most intense battles of the Guerra dos Bárbaros occurred in the valley regions of the Açu River in western Rio Grande and the Jaguaribe River in the eastern part of the neighboring province of Ceará. Indigenous peoples along the Açu River valley formed a federation led by the Janduin tribe and its chief, Canindé, who destroyed cattle and settlers in the late 1680's. With other ranchers and indigenous hunters, Velho succeeded in capturing Canindé and more than two thousand of his followers by the end of the decade.

Extraordinarily, Canindé and his lieutenants journeyed to the capital, Salvador, to negotiate a treaty of surrender with the colonial authorities. By the treaty, the rebellious indigenous agreed to convert to Christianity and the authorities agreed to recognize indigenous land rights in restricted villages. However, anticipating the outcome of nearly all such treaties between indigenous populations and invading ranchers in the Americas in the centuries to come, the "reserved" indigenous lands were reduced and absorbed through the years.

A notorious massacre of indigenous peoples occurred along the Jaguaribe River in 1699, under the instigation of the Brazilian-Portuguese fighter Manuel Álvares de Morais Navarro, who had been attempting to stir up hostility between settled tribes. He also hoped to pacify the region to reduce indigenous occupation. The indigenous resisted, and then attempted to welcome him to their settlement. Nevertheless, leading a small contingent of troops, he massacred several hundred individuals, wounding and maiming several hundred more. Outraged missionaries had him prosecuted and jailed, but he ended his days as a colonial administrative authority. By 1716, northeastern Brazil was so pacified that the colonial government could remove its last contingent of *bandeirante* troops against the now vanquished "barbarian" indigenous peoples.

Significance

At the beginning of the sixteenth century, the indigenous population of northeastern Brazil amounted to several million inhabitants. Two centuries later, because of disease, massacres, and coupling within populations (interbreeding), they numbered a fraction of that number. The territory of Brazil essentially had reached the dimensions to which it extends today. A significant indigenous population would remain in the Amazon River basin, but only because of its hostile environment, which made the area safe from early colonial settlement. During the twentieth century, this territory came under government control and also suffered outside invasion.

Ultimately, treaties had little to do with preserving indigenous lands. At most, treaties delayed the reduction or absorption that is inevitable with every population. The cattle wars in colonial Brazil for the lands of the indigenous presaged events in the rest of the Americas in following centuries, particularly during the nineteenth century. Demands for grain and meat in industrial and urban regions of the world required that vast territories in southern Argentina and the western United States be opened to agriculture and ranching. The Argentine pampas and the American plains would soon witness the last of indigenous populations in their native lands as well.

—*Edward A. Riedinger*

Further Reading

Dean, Warren. *With Broadax and Firebrand: The Destruction of the Brazilian Atlantic Forest*. Berkeley: University of California Press, 1995. Dean reviews human intervention in the ecological and environmental history of colonial Brazil.

Hemming, John. *Red Gold: The Conquest of the Brazilian Indians*. Rev. ed. London: Pan, 2004. An authoritative work on the history of the indigenous peoples of Brazil during the colonial period.

Morse, Richard M. *The Bandeirantes: The Historical Role of the Brazilian Pathfinders*. New York: Knopf, 1965. A classic study of the expansion of the Brazilian frontier from the sixteenth through the eighteenth centuries.

Puntoni, Pedro. *A Guerra dos bárbaros: Povos indígenas e a colonização do sertão nordeste do Brasil, 1650-1720*. Estudos históricos, vol. 44. São Paulo, Brazil: EDUSP, 2002. An unpublished doctoral dissertation that provides updated, detailed research on the cattle range wars against the indigenous in northeast Brazil. Reviews events regionally and chronologically.

Richards, John F. *The Unending Frontier: An Environmental History of the Early Modern World*. Berkeley: University of California Press, 2003. Richards's work includes the chapter "Sugar and Cattle in Portuguese Brazil."

Weber, David J., and Jane M. Rausch, eds. *Where Cultures Meet: Frontiers in Latin American History*.

Wilmington, Del.: SR Books, 1994. Weber examines *bandeirante* pioneers and Amazon indigenous populations.

See also: Oct., 1625-1637: Dutch and Portuguese Struggle for the Guinea Coast; 1630's-1694: Slaves Resist Europeans at Palmares; 1630-1660's: Dutch Wars in Brazil; June-Aug., 1640: *Bandeirantes* Expel the Jesuits; 1654: Portugal Retakes Control of Brazil; Feb. 13, 1668: Spain Recognizes Portugal's Independence; Early 1690's: Brazilian Gold Rush.

Related articles in *Great Lives from History: The Seventeenth Century, 1601-1700:* Piet Hein; António Vieira.

1680-1709
Reign of Tsunayoshi as Shogun

The earliest years of Tsunayoshi's reign were characterized by reform-minded administrative measures, but adviser Hotta Masatoshi's death in 1684 facilitated Tsunayoshi's assumption of total power, allowing the shogun and his favorites to debase coinage and to cause his people hardship through excessive and unrealistic edicts.

Locale: Japan
Category: Government and politics

Key Figures

Tokugawa Tsunayoshi (1646-1709), Japanese shogun, r. 1680-1709
Keishō-in (1624-1705), Tsunayoshi's mother and ally of Yanagisawa
Hotta Masatoshi (1634-1684), chief supporter of Tsunayoshi, 1680-1684
Yanagisawa Yoshiyasu (1659-1714), Tsunayoshi's chamberlain, 1688-1709
Hayashi Hōkō (1644-1732), Confucian adviser to Tsunayoshi and succeeding shoguns

Summary of Event

Tokugawa Tsunayoshi was born in 1646, the fourth son of the shogun Tokugawa Iemitsu, who had already been in power for twenty-three years at that time. His mother was the daughter of an affluent Kyōto grocer, but she was subsequently adopted by the samurai Honjō Munemasa, steward of the aristocratic Nijō family in Kyōto. Having gained aristocratic status this way, she was later selected as one of Shogun Iemitsu's concubines. When Iemitsu died in 1651, ten-year-old Ietsuna, Tsunayoshi's older brother by a different mother, became shogun, and five-year-old Tsunayoshi was awarded a stipend and household of his own. He was treated well and looked after by the shogunate administration, and specialist physicians were sent to him whenever he felt ill.

After his mansion in the shogun's Edo Castle complex burned down during the Meireki Fire in 1657, Tsunayoshi stayed in a villa in the Koishikawa district of Edo and subsequently moved to a larger estate by the Sumida River. In 1661, the adolescent Tsunayoshi was made a daimyo, or domain lord, in Ueno province, with his own staff and guard troops and a castle at Tatebayashi, in present-day Gunma prefecture. He was also awarded the national title of *saishō*, or state counselor, and continued to spend most of his time at the shogun's court in Edo.

After Iemitsu's death in 1651, Tsunayoshi's mother was given the status of shogun's widow, with the honorific title of Keishō-in. She continued to influence Tsunayoshi's decisions until her death in 1705, often with benevolent goals in mind, although Tsunayoshi's implementations of Keishō-in's advice at times exceeded her intentions. She encouraged Tsunayoshi to study and follow Confucian ideals, so he promoted Confucian studies, even giving his own public lectures on Confucianism to captive audiences. The devoutly Buddhist Keishō-in urged her son to take measures as shogun to prohibit cruelty to animals in Japan, but the result was his 1685 *Shōrui-aware* edict, prohibiting the killing of all living things, including fish, forcing the Japanese people to become total vegetarians for a quarter century.

After his reform-minded adviser Hotta Masatoshi was assassinated in 1684, Tsunayoshi took real power for himself, surrounding himself with sycophantic officials. Yanagisawa Yoshiyasu, initially Tsunayoshi's personal attendant, having ingratiated himself with both Tsunayoshi and Keishō-in, gained more and more personal authority. In 1688, Yanagisawa was made both *sobayōnin*, or chamberlain, to the shogun and daimyo of Kawagoe (modern Saitama prefecture). In 1701, Yanagisawa was granted the new surname Matsudaira, making him an honorary Tokugawa relative. In the same year

Lord Asano was forced to commit suicide as the result of court intrigue by the shogun's protocol chief Kira Yoishinaka, and Asano feudal land was confiscated as an additional punishment. These arbitrary actions provoked a famous revenge attack in Edo by Asano retainers in 1702, in which Kira was killed.

Yanagisawa, an ally of Kira, was popularly regarded as Kira's protector and has been portrayed as a villain in popular dramas about the Asano incident ever since. The seizure of the Asano feudal lands by the shogunate was part of a larger pattern of confiscation of feudal lands, increasing peasant and samurai resentment. Such confiscation was designed to bring Tsunayoshi greater income and power. A year after Tsunayoshi forced the popular Asano samurai raiders to commit suicide, he promoted Yanagisawa to the position of daimyo of Kōfu (modern Yamanashi Prefecture), in 1704. This favoritism made Tsunayoshi even less popular, yet Yanagisawa remained one of his chief advisers until the end of Tsunayoshi's reign.

On the other hand, Yanagisawa was the patron of the famous Confucian scholars Ogyū Sorai and Hosoi Kōtaku, pandering to Keishō-in's promotion of Confucianism. Tsunayoshi had a great respect for learning and studied literature and art under the guidance of some of the most outstanding scholars and artists of his time. His literature and poetry mentor was Kitamura Kigin, the leading authority on Murasaki Shikibu's *Genji monogatari* (c. 1004; *The Tale of Genji*, 1925-1933) and the teacher of the haiku master Matsuo Bashō. Kigin and his son Koshun were both given lifetime posts as scholars in residence at Edo Castle by Tsunayoshi.

On the other hand, the shogun's famous painting tutor, Hanabusa Itchō, himself a follower of Bashō in poetry and of the *ukiyo-e* pioneer Hishikawa Moronobu in contemporary art, incurred Tsunayoshi's personal displeasure. He was banished to Miyakejima, a volcanic island in the ocean south of Edo. Itchō spent ten years in exile there and was allowed to return to Edo only after Tsunayoshi's death.

In the field of Confucian learning, and in matters affecting education in general, Tsunayoshi took the advice of Hayashi Hōkō, the third-generation heir of a family of leading Confucian scholars. Hayashi was nearly the same age as Tsunayoshi and had become the head of his family in 1680, the same year Tsunayoshi became shogun. In 1690, Tsunayoshi ordered the construction of a Confucian school and temple complex at Shōheizaka in the Kanda district of Edo, appointing Hayashi as its director. The school flourished as a center of classical Confucian learning and later became the first official center for the study of Western learning in Edo as well.

In 1695, Tsunayoshi was told by astrology-minded courtiers that, being born in the Year of the Dog, things would go better for him if he treated dogs well. As a result, he ordered special treatment for all dogs. It became a crime to mistreat any dog, and numerous shelters for stray dogs were also established at the expense of local taxpayers. These measures incensed a populace that had seen meat-eating effectively criminalized for a decade already. Popular resentment resulted in the epithet *inu kubō*, the "Dog Shogun," used behind his back when he was alive, which has become the epithet by which Tsunayoshi is popularly known in Japanese history.

SIGNIFICANCE

After Tokugawa Ieyasu created the Tokugawa shogunate and made himself the first shogun in 1603, his son Tokugawa Hidetada and grandson Tokugawa Iemitsu consolidated Tokugawa power. Iemitsu's son, Tokugawa Ietsuna, was only ten years old when he became shogun in 1651, so older advisers held the real power, and they remained very influential until Ietsuna died in 1680. Ietsuna's younger brother Tsunayoshi, in his mid-thirties when he became shogun, had already been a daimyo and therefore had firsthand experience wielding feudal power. At first, Tsunayoshi had to defer to his powerful adviser Hotta Masatoshi, but after Hotta's death he took full authority himself.

Tsunayoshi used his power to do some good things, such as establishing a national Confucian academy and promoting education. Some other measures, however, such as criminalization of cruelty to animals, were carried to extremes that created enormous resentment among the common people. Tsunayoshi also confiscated the estates of many feudal vassals on various pretexts, increasing shogunal territory and income but alienating many domain lords and samurai. He also surrounded himself with sycophantic courtiers who were highly unpopular, and his government spent extravagantly while debasing the coinage for its own profit.

As the result of such measures, Tsunayoshi became unpopular among the people and the aristocracy and came to be viewed as a national villain by succeeding generations. Tsunayoshi's traditional image as a tyrannical and villainous shogun contributed to long-lasting popular disdain for the shogunate itself and facilitated the ultimate overthrow of the shogunate a century and a half later.

—*Michael McCaskey*

Further Reading

Bodart-Bailey, Beatrice, ed. *Kaempfer's Japan: Tokugawa Culture Observed*. Honolulu: University of Hawaii Press, 1999. Firsthand description of Tsunayoshi's Japan by Engelbert Kaempfer (1651-1716), a German physician and natural scientist stationed at the Dutch enclave in Nagasaki from 1690 to 1692 who visited Edo.

Growden, Haydn D. *Tsunayoshi Tokugawa: The Dog Shogun*. Tokyo: Shingumi Resources, 1999. Entry-level, illustrated account of Tsunayoshi's life.

Mass, Jeffrey, and William Hauser. *The Bakufu in Japanese History*. Stanford, Calif.: Stanford University Press, 1985. An analysis of Tokugawa feudalism, regional government, and the status of samurai.

Toby, Ronald P. *State and Diplomacy in Early Modern Japan: Asia in the Development of the Tokugawa Bakufu*. Stanford, Calif.: Stanford University Press, 1991. A history of Tokugawa Japan's relations with other East Asian countries.

Totman, Conrad D. *Politics in the Tokugawa Bakufu, 1600-1843*. Cambridge, Mass.: Harvard University Press, 1967. The authoritative history in English of Tokugawa politics and government, up to the beginnings of Western penetration.

Tsukahira, Toshio George. *Federal Control in Tokugawa Japan: The Sankin Kotai System*. Cambridge, Mass.: Harvard University Press, 1966. A study of modes of control of domain lords, viewed as a sort of federalist system.

Turnbull, Stephen R. *Samurai Warlords: The Book of the Daimyō*. London: Blandford, 1989. Popular account of rule by domain lords under the Tokugawa shogunate.

See also: 1603: Tokugawa Shogunate Begins; Beginning 1607: Neo-Confucianism Becomes Japan's Official Philosophy; 1615: Promulgation of the *Buke shohatto* and *Kinchū narabini kuge shohatto*; 1624-1640's: Japan's Seclusion Policy; 1651-1652: Edo Rebellions; 1651-1680: Ietsuna Shogunate; Jan. 18-20, 1657: Meireki Fire Ravages Edo; 1688-1704: Genroku Era.

Related articles in *Great Lives from History: The Seventeenth Century, 1601-1700:* Hishikawa Moronobu; Matsuo Bashō; Tokugawa Ieyasu; Tokugawa Tsunayoshi.

June 30, 1680
Spanish Inquisition Holds a Grandiose *Auto-da-fé*

King Charles II celebrated his marriage by staging an auto-da-fé, *a judicial sentence or act of faith that became one of the most spectacular* autos-da-fé *ever conducted in Spain. More than one hundred persons were tried on charges of secretly practicing Judaism, and at least nineteen burned as heretics and fifty-four sentenced to life imprisonment. The legacy of the Spanish Inquisition includes anti-Semitism and xenophobia, a distrust, fear, or hatred of foreign influences.*

Locale: Plaza Mayor, Madrid, Spain

Categories: Religion and theology; government and politics

Key Figures

Charles II (1661-1700), king of Spain, r. 1665-1700

Mariana de Austria (1634-1696), queen of Spain, r. 1649-1665, Charles's mother, and queen regent, r. 1665-1696

Francisco Rizzi (1614-1685), court artist who made large paintings of the *auto-da-fé*

José Vicente del Olmo (1611-1696), a contemporary observer who wrote a commentary on the *auto-da-fé*

Summary of Event

Although the legal term "inquisition" technically denoted a judicial inquiry by trained judges, it has commonly been used to describe the persecution of heretics by special Church courts. The inquisition of the medieval Catholic Church was first established in the thirteenth century in an effort to stamp out heretical groups that were especially strong in southern France.

The Spanish Inquisition, which was authorized by the Papacy in 1478, differed from other tribunals in two ways. First, it was directly under the authority of the Crown. Second, in its early stages it was directed primarily at the *conversos* (Judaizers), Jews converted to Christianity who were suspected of secretly practicing Jewish rituals. Even though the Spanish Inquisition later expanded its focus to include Protestants, liberals, and alleged witches, it continued to concentrate much of its attention on the *conversos* and their descendants.

An engraved depiction of a procession leading to an auto-da-fé, *the public execution of those condemned by the Inquisition, in a Spanish town square.* (Frederick Ungar)

In Spain, the Supreme Council of the Inquisition (commonly called the Suprema), which usually had six members, was presided over by the Inquisitor General, who was nominated by the Crown and appointed by the pope. The other members of the Suprema were appointed by the king. The Inquisitor General usually was able to exercise authority over the policies and activities of the Suprema. If disagreements arose, the decision would be made by majority vote.

Surviving documents are inexact about the number of victims punished by the Spanish Inquisition. The first serious historian of the topic, Juan Antonio Llorente, who had access to many archives that no longer exist, claimed that between 1481 and 1782 the Spanish Inquisition condemned 341,450 persons to severe penalties, with 31,912 persons burned at the stake. He estimated that two-thirds of the trials took place before 1698. In contrast, many contemporary historians, including Edward Peters, estimate that fewer than four thousand death sentences were carried out during the entire three hundred years of the Spanish Inquisition.

During the seventeenth century, the largest wave of religious persecutions and *autos-da-fé* occurred during the reign of the last of the Habsburg monarchs, Charles II, who was king from 1665 to 1700. Because Charles was mentally and physically disabled, his mother, Mariana de Austria, served as regent during most of his reign. Even though Spain was declining as an economic and military power, the Inquisitor General still asserted his authority by holding several waves of ceremonies. In 1675, a young *converso*, Alonso López, was burned at the stake, and the effigies of six Portuguese *conversos* were also burned. These ceremonies marked the beginning of an aggressive search for Judaizers. Within three years, agents of the Suprema had rounded up 237 suspects. In 1679, at least five *autos-da-fé* were held in

Malloca, with a total of about 221 reconciliations, about a dozen executions, and a record confiscation of property.

In 1679, Charles married Marie-Louise d'Orléans, the niece of King Louis XIV of France. As part of the marriage celebration, the Crown and the Suprema jointly sponsored a grandiose *auto-da-fé* at Madrid's Plaza Mayor on June 30, 1680. A famous Baroque artist working for the Crown, Francisco Rizzi, depicted the festive occasion in a series of large paintings, now on display at the Prado Museum in Madrid. Another witness to the event, José Vicente del Olmo, recorded his observations in his *Relación histórica del auto general de fe* (1680; partial English translation, 1997).

The *auto-da-fé* was announced a month before it took place. On March 29, the ceremony began with a religious procession through the streets of Madrid. Leading the procession were merchants who had furnished the wood for the burnings. Next came Dominican priests, then the fifty guards of the Inquisition, followed by members of the nobility and officials of the Inquisition. Most of the Madrid churches held large masses, and friars spent most of the night singing psalms.

On June 30, approximately fifty thousand people gathered for the *auto-da-fé*, which lasted for fourteen hours. The king and his court sat on a balcony atop a scaffold that was 50 feet in height and 50 feet in length. The Suprema and the King's Council sat on similar balconies next to the king. The Inquisitor General sat at the highest balcony. Symbols of Christianity and military power were prominently displayed. During the proceedings, the 118 accused *conversos* had ropes around their necks and wore yellow sanbenitos, sleeveless coats painted with devils and flames. They also wore 3-foot-tall pasteboard caps marked with inscriptions citing their heresies. The reading of each person's sentence, one of the centerpieces of the *auto-da-fé*, lasted several hours.

The most reliable sources indicate that eighteen prisoners were condemned as relapsed Judaizers, although the exact numbers are disputed. The condemned were turned over to the secular government, and they were then transported by donkey outside the city gate to the *quemadero* (the place to be burned), where they were executed before a small crowd at midnight. Those who showed signs of repentance were strangled before they were burned, and those who did not repent were burned alive. The king himself lit the fire. Of the other prisoners, fifty-four persons who had been condemned for first-time offenses were sentenced to life imprisonment and had their property confiscated. The others were either found innocent or reconciled to the Church. None of the names of the accused appeared in the published accounts.

Following the *auto-da-fé*, the Suprema continued its aggressive search for Judaizers and other heretics. Another wave of *autos-da-fé* hit in 1691, with approximately eighty-six *conversos* prosecuted in four separate events. The only well-known victim of the Inquisition during Charles II's reign was Froilan Diaz, a Dominican priest who served two years as the king's confessor. In 1700, he was arrested on charges of casting a demonic spell on the king. Even though Diaz was found innocent at trial, the Inquisitor General, who was a personal enemy, kept him under house arrest. The next king, Philip V, ordered his release. For the next two decades, the Suprema conducted a few proceedings only, but the early 1720's would see yet another wave of *autos-da-fé*.

Significance

The *auto-da-fé* of 1680 was the most spectacular and well-publicized *auto-da-fé* of the seventeenth century, and it became famous as a result of Rizzi's paintings and del Olmo's book. In most ways, though, it was rather typical of the inquisitorial ceremonies. From 1675 to 1730, according to historian Henry Kamen, the Spanish Inquisition prosecuted more than twenty-two hundred persons for Judaizing. Of these, he estimated that 3 percent of the victims were burned at the stake and more than three-fourths spent a few years in prison. The Suprema, which conducted its last public execution in 1826, was abolished by royal decree in 1834.

Because of the Inquisition's wrath and power, few identifiable Judaizers or other alleged heretics were in Spain by the middle of the eighteenth century. The legacy of the Inquisition, nevertheless, included anti-Semitism and xenophobia that would continue well into the twentieth century. Although the Inquisition was certainly not the primary cause for the slow progress in Spain's development, it undoubtedly promoted attitudes and political structures that were not conducive to modernization or cultural advancement.

—*Thomas Tandy Lewis*

Further Reading

Alcalá, Angel, ed. *The Spanish Inquisition and the Inquisitorial Mind*. New York: Columbia University Press, 1987. A large collection of scholarly essays devoted to the causes and consequences of the Spanish Inquisition.

Baigent, Michael, and Richard Leigh. *The Inquisition*. London: Penguin, 1999. A worthwhile summary, although it provides only sketchy information about the seventeenth century.

Haliczer, Stephen, ed. *Inquisition and Society in Early Modern Europe*. London: Croom Helm, 1987. A good collection of essays that compares the inquisitions of other countries.

Kamen, Henry. *The Spanish Inquisition: A Historical Revision*. New Haven, Conn.: Yale University Press, 1997. The most scholarly and dependable account of the history of the Inquisition in English, with an excellent bibliography and a significant translated portion of del Olmo's account of the *auto-da-fé* of 1680.

Lea, Henry Charles. *A History of the Inquisition in Spain*. 4 vols. New York: AMS Press, 1966. Based on archival research, Lea's pioneering work describes how the Inquisition was organized, but it provides few numbers and little information about events of the seventeenth century.

Llorente, Juan Antonio. *A Critical History of the Inquisition in Spain*. 1823. Reprint. Williamstown, Mass.: J. Lilburn, 1967. A classic work by the former secretary-general to the Inquisition. Most modern historians think that Llorente exaggerated the number of victims.

Nada, John. *Carlos the Bewitched: The Last Spanish Habsburg, 1661-1700*. London: Jonathan Cape, 1963. A still-useful account of Charles II and his reign.

Peters, Edward. *Inquisition*. New York: Free Press, 1988. A helpful summary of the history of the Inquisition, although it does not include much information about the seventeenth century.

Stradling, R. A. *Europe and the Decline of Spain: A Study of the Spanish System*. New York: Routledge, 1981. Stradling places the Spanish Inquisition in historical context.

SEE ALSO: 1656-1662: Persecution of Iranian Jews; June 2, 1692-May, 1693: Salem Witchcraft Trials.

RELATED ARTICLE in *Great Lives from History: The Seventeenth Century, 1601-1700:* Charles II (of Spain).

August 10, 1680
PUEBLO REVOLT

The Pueblo Revolt was the most successful Native American uprising against European colonial authority. Although the Spanish retook the area twelve years later, the revolt ensured the survival of the Pueblo Indians as a distinct people.

LOCALE: Rio Grande Valley
CATEGORIES: Wars, uprisings, and civil unrest; colonization

KEY FIGURES

Popé (d. 1692), Tewa medicine man and major instigator of the revolt
Luis Tupatú (fl. 1680), Picuris Indian leader, successor to Popé, and a principal aide during the revolt
Antonio Malacate (fl. 1680), Keresan leader of the revolt
Antonio de Otermín (fl. 1680), governor of New Mexico in 1680
Alonso Garcia (fl. 1680), Otermín's lieutenant governor in 1680
Diego José de Vargas (1643-1704), New Mexico's governor in 1692
Juan de Oñate (1550-1630), founder and first Spanish governor of New Mexico

SUMMARY OF EVENT

The first permanent European colony in Pueblo territory was established by Juan de Oñate in 1598. The jewels and gold of the fabled Seven Cities of Cíbola had proven to be a myth, but the Spanish still intended to settle the land. Franciscan friars came to seek converts to Catholicism, while civilian authorities and settlers sought their fortunes in mining, trading, and ranching. The entire Spanish system was based on the use of American Indian labor. In order to secure this labor, the Spanish imposed the *encomienda* system, which gave large land grants to holders, known as *encomanderos*. The part of this program known as *repartimiento* bestowed upon the *encomanderos* the right to the labor of any nearby natives. Annual taxes also were collected from the natives in the form of produce, textiles, and other resources.

The Spanish were able to impose these measures with their guns and horses and frequent displays of force. Harsh physical punishments were meted out for even slight infractions. The Franciscans—who recognized no belief system except their own and thus felt justified in exterminating Pueblo religion—saved the most extreme measures for natives practicing their traditional beliefs. Father Salvador de Guerra, in 1655, had an "idolator" at

Oraibi whipped, doused with turpentine, and burned to death. Even missing the daily Mass could bring a public flogging.

This unrelenting assault on native beliefs and practices was the single greatest cause of the Pueblo Revolt. The people believed that harmony within the community and with the environment was maintained through their relationships with a host of spirit figures called kachinas. They communicated with the kachinas at public dances and in ceremonies conducted in their circular churches, called *kivas*. It seemed no coincidence to the natives that when priests stopped these practices, things began to go wrong.

Severe droughts, famine, Apache raids, and epidemics of European diseases reduced a population of fifty thousand in Oñate's time to seventeen thousand by the 1670's. Three thousand were lost to measles in 1640 alone. At times between 1667 and 1672, people were reduced to boiling hides and leather cart straps for food. The abuse of women and shipment of Pueblo Indians south to work as slaves in the silver mines of Mexico made it seem that the moral as well as the physical universe was collapsing. Calls were made to return to the old ways.

In 1675, forty-seven Pueblo Indians were arrested for practicing their religion. All were whipped, three were hanged, and one committed suicide. One deeply resentful survivor was a Tewa medicine man for San Juan Pueblo named Popé. Incensed by this oppression, he began planning retribution, but his task was formidable: The Spanish label "Pueblo" obscured the fact that the various Pueblo Indians were not of one tribe but rather were members of a collection of autonomous villages that cherished their independence and rarely acted in unison. Although they shared many cultural features, three major language families were represented in the Rio Grande area alone, Zuñi, Keresan, and Tanoan. The latter had three distinct dialects of its own: Tiwa, Tewa, and Towa. Hopi villages where a Uto-Aztecan language was spoken lay farther west. Because of this diversity and independence among the tribes, previous revolts had been localized affairs and were suppressed quickly.

In hiding at Taos Pueblo, fifty miles north of the Spanish capital at Santa Fe, Popé began building a multilingual coalition. He enlisted the great Picuris leader Luis Tupatú, a Tiwa speaker who was influential in the northern Rio Grande pueblos; Antonio Malacate, a Keresan spokesman from pueblos to the south; the Tewa war leader Francisco El Ollita of San Ildefonso; and many others. His role becoming more messianic, Popé claimed inspiration from spirit contacts. Gradually, a plan emerged to expel the Spanish from Pueblo territory entirely.

The time came in August of 1680. Runners were sent out bearing knotted maguey cords, each knot representing one day. The uprising was to begin the day the last knot was untied. Governor Antonio de Otermín was told by informants that the revolt would occur on August 13, but Popé had advanced the day to August 10, and the Spanish were caught completely by surprise. Just nine miles north of Santa Fe, the citizens of Tesuque killed Padre Juan Pio early that morning as he came to gather them up for Mass, and upheaval soon swept the countryside as eighty years of frustration came to a boil.

Lieutenant Governor Don Alonso Garcia led soldiers on a sweep to the south of the capital and encountered such destruction that he organized the survivors for evacuation south. They left for El Paso del Norte (now Juarez) on August 14. The next day, Governor Otermín found himself besieged in Santa Fe by five hundred Pueblo Indians who demanded that he free any slaves and leave the territory. He responded by attacking, but when the opposition increased to more than two thousand warriors and Otermín's water supply had been cut, he abandoned the capital. On August 21, Otermín led more than one thousand settlers south, meeting Garcia's group on September 13, and the whole bedraggled column reached El Paso on September 29.

Four hundred civilian settlers and twenty-one of thirty-three priests had been killed. To undo their conversions, baptized Puebloans had their heads washed in yucca suds. A new kachina entered the pantheon of Pueblo spirit figures. He was known among the Hopi as Yo-we, or "Priest-killer." In the years following the revolt, the coalition began to unravel, as drought, disease, and Apache raids continued to plague the tribes. Popé, who had become something of a tyrant himself, died in 1692. That same year, Spain reconquered the area, and the new governor, Don Diego José de Vargas, entered Santa Fe on September 13.

SIGNIFICANCE

The Pueblo Revolt did much more than dispel the stereotype that Puebloans were unassertive and peaceful farmers who could not unify. It also was much more than a twelve-year respite from colonial oppression. It catalyzed transformations in Native American cultures in many directions. Large numbers of Spanish sheep came into the hands of the Navajo, forming the core of a new herding lifestyle. Weaving skills, possibly passed along by Puebloans fleeing Spanish reprisals, soon turned the wool into some of the world's finest textiles. Previously forbidden horses, now freed by the hundreds, became widely traded. Within a century, tribes such as the Nez Perce, Cayuse, and Palouse to the northwest, Plains Cree to the north, and Sioux, Cheyenne, and others to the east became mounted. With the mobility to access the great bison herds of the Plains, the economic complex that became the popular image of the Native American evolved.

The continued importance of the Pueblo Revolt to all Native Americans was demonstrated during the tricentennial of 1980. Cultural events celebrating the "First American Revolution" were held all across the United States. The revolt was seen as a symbol of independence and religious freedom. It was also recognized that some Puebloans who chose to settle with Otermín at El Paso in 1680 subsequently had lost most of their language, arts, and customs. After three centuries, the Puebloans see their ancestors' revolt as a key reason for their survival as a distinct people.

—*Gary A. Olson*

FURTHER READING

Hackett, Charles W. *Revolt of the Pueblo Indians of New Mexico and Otermín's Attempted Reconquest, 1680-1682*. Translated by Charmion Shelby. 2 vols. Albuquerque: University of New Mexico Press, 1942. The definitive report on the subject to date.

Hait, Pam. "The Hopi Tricentennial: The Great Pueblo Revolt Revisited." *Arizona Highways* 56, no. 9 (September, 1980): 2-6. The entire issue is a beautifully illustrated exploration of Hopi culture and how its persistence is a tribute to the Pueblo Revolt.

Hill, Joseph. "The Pueblo Revolt." *New Mexico Magazine* 58 (June, 1980): 38. An overview of the subject, with nine illustrations.

Josephy, Alvin M., Jr. *The Patriot Chiefs: A Chronicle of American Indian Resistance*. Rev. ed. New York: Penguin Books, 1993. Gives an account of the precursors to the revolt but presents no consideration of the aftermath.

Knaut, Andrew L. *The Pueblo Revolt of 1680: Conquest and Resistance in Seventeenth Century New Mexico*. Norman: University of Oklahoma Press, 1995. Knaut, a history professor at Duke University, analyzes the revolt and the events leading to it.

Ortiz, Alfonso, ed. *Southwest*. Vol. 9 in *Handbook of North American Indians*, edited by William C. Sturtevant. Washington, D.C.: Smithsonian Institution, 1979. This volume of the *Handbook* contains a brief article by Joe S. Sando that describes the planning of the Pueblo Revolt.

Page, James K., Jr. "Rebellious Pueblos Outwitted Spain Three Centuries Ago." *Smithsonian* 11 (October, 1980): 221. Tells the story through Padre Pio's last day. Good observations on the revolt's modern significance.

Roberts, David. *The Pueblo Revolt: The Secret Rebellion That Drove the Spaniards Out of the Southwest*. New York: Simon & Schuster, 2004. In his history of the war Roberts examines why the revolt succeeded and what happened to the Pueblos between 1680 and 1692, when they were easily conquered by a new Spanish force.

Silverberg, Robert. *The Pueblo Revolt*. Introduction by Marc Simmons. Lincoln: University of Nebraska Press, 1994. An account based mainly on Hackett's earlier work. Introduction considers the revolt's legacy three centuries later.

Weber, David J., ed. *What Caused the Pueblo Revolt of 1680?* Boston: Bedford/St. Martin's, 1999. Collection of essays by various historians, examining the many factors leading to the revolt.

SEE ALSO: 1604-1680: Rise of Criollo Identity in Mexico; 1615: Guamán Poma Pleas for Inca Reforms; 1617-c. 1700: Smallpox Epidemics Kill Native Americans; Mar. 22, 1622-Oct., 1646: Powhatan Wars; 1630's-1694: Slaves Resist Europeans at Palmares; Feb. 22-27, 1632: Zuñi Rebellion; July 20, 1636-July 28, 1637: Pequot War; 1642-1684: Beaver Wars; 1642-1700: Westward Migration of Native Americans; Beginning 1671: American Indian Slave Trade; June 20, 1675: Metacom's War Begins; Beginning 1680's: Guerra dos Bárbaros.

RELATED ARTICLES in *Great Lives from History: The Seventeenth Century, 1601-1700:* Massasoit; Metacom; Opechancanough; Pocahontas; Powhatan; Squanto.

March 4, 1681
"Holy Experiment" Establishes Pennsylvania

William Penn established a haven for the Society of Friends, or Quakers, and their "holy experiment." Empowered to design his own government, Penn and the other colonists restructured the fundamental governmental bodies several times, striving for an effective structure and representing an experimental phase in the design of democracy in the American colonies.

Locale: Pennsylvania
Categories: Colonization; expansion and land acquisition; government and politics; religion and theology

Key Figures

William Penn (1644-1718), proprietor of the Pennsylvania Colony
William Markham (1635?-1704), Penn's cousin and personal agent in the colony
Charles II (1630-1685), king of England, r. 1660-1685

Summary of Event

On March 4, 1681, King Charles II of England granted to William Penn a charter creating the colony of Pennsylvania. Named for his father, Sir William Penn, an admiral who had aided Charles's accession, the younger Penn received the charter in payment of a debt of sixteen thousand pounds sterling that the king owed to him.

The charter made Penn proprietor of the Pennsylvania Colony. In many ways, it was similar to other proprietary charters, in that it made Penn the owner of all lands in the province, with authority to structure and run the colony. Under the charter, Penn was empowered to grant property, establish the form of government, appoint a governor, and initiate and promulgate laws with the advice and consent of the freemen in the assembly. The Pennsylvania charter was unique, however, in its restriction of proprietary prerogatives.

Three provisions of the charter ensured the enforcement of the Navigation Acts passed by Parliament prior to the establishment of the colony. Laws passed in the colony were to be submitted to the king for his confirmation or disallowance, with the king retaining the right to hear and decide appeals from the courts of the province. The Church of England was assured a place in the colony. In addition to these laws limiting the colonial government's power, however, the charter contained a promise that the king would not impose taxes "unless the same be with the consent of the proprietary, or chiefe governour, or assembly, or by act of Parliament." These provisions implemented England's new colonial policy of limiting provincial self-government and centralizing the empire as a means of securing its commercial and defensive interests.

Penn's avowed purpose in establishing a colony in America was to found a "holy experiment" based on Quaker principles. Pennsylvania was to be a holy commonwealth, similar to other religion-based colonies like Massachusetts Bay and characterized by peace, brotherly love, and religious toleration, which would serve as "an example . . . to the nations." At the same time, the colony would offer a haven to Quakers who were being persecuted in England for their Nonconformist beliefs.

One month after receiving his charter from the king, Penn began advertising the new province to prospective settlers in England, Ireland, and Wales. *Some Account of the Province of Pennsylvania* was published in April, 1682, the first of eleven such publications designed to attract colonists. Settlers began to arrive in Pennsylvania in the summer of 1682. The promise of community drew many of them: Immigrants coming to Pennsylvania would be settling among those of the same country or even of the same region.

Penn dispatched his cousin William Markham to the colony to serve as his deputy governor until the proprietor's arrival. Not until August 30, 1682, did Penn himself set sail for the colony in the ship *Welcome*, along with about one hundred colonists. Shortly before leaving England, he had obtained the Lower Counties (Delaware) from the duke of York, an intimate friend, thereby gaining ocean access for his new colony. In fact, the duke of York did not possess clear title to these lands, and Penn found himself defending his claim to the territory against Lord Baltimore. Pennsylvania's right to rule the region persisted until a charter in 1701 granted the Lower Counties the right to self-government.

Negotiations for the land that was to become Philadelphia and its surrounding area were concluded with the Lenni Lenape tribe, whom the settlers called the Delaware, in the summer of 1682. Blankets, bolts of cloth, and other goods were exchanged for the signatures of twelve Lenni Lenape sachems, or chieftains. Later purchases would be made from the native peoples of the Susquehanna River region, the Susquehannocks, and the Iroquois as the Pennsylvania colony expanded. In contrast with other Europeans' poor record of promises made and quickly broken in the New World, Penn seems to have been genuinely concerned with being fair to the Native Americans with whom he dealt.

Like other proprietors in the New World, Penn hoped to profit from the sale or rent of land in his colony, but his primary aim was a religious one. He was a member of the Society of Friends, or Quakers, organized by George Fox in the late 1640's. One of the many radical religious sects that emerged from the turbulence of the English Civil Wars, the Quakers embraced the Puritan social ethic but went beyond Puritanism to reject formal creeds and worship. The faith was founded on the belief that the Holy Spirit, which Quakers called the Inner Light, dwelled within each person.

Belief that one's Inner Light placed one in communication with God meant that Quakers, like Puritans, rejected the idea of clergy as intermediaries. Their ecclesiastical organization shows the influence of the Puritan theory of congregationalism: Each congregation, or "meeting," was completely autonomous, although a hierarchy of meetings ultimately developed, similar in structure and purpose to that of the Presbyterians. Quakers differed from Puritans in their rejection of a national church. Like other sectarians, Quakers insisted on separation of church and state and viewed the meeting as a voluntary association composed only of believers. Two important consequences of Quaker religious beliefs were egalitarianism and humanitarianism.

Before sailing to America, Penn had drawn up the "first frame of government" to serve as a constitution for the new colony. It provided for a governor appointed by the proprietor, a council of seventy-two members that was to be the source of all legislation, and an assembly of two hundred, which had the power to accept or reject bills initiated by the council. Both the council and the assembly were elective bodies. More than 150 laws were passed by the legislature implementing the "holy experiment."

In 1696, Governor William Markham issued a third frame, which further modified suffrage requirements, reduced the council to twelve members and the assembly to twenty-four, and granted the latter body the right to initiate legislation. A fourth frame, known as the Charter of Privileges, was drawn up by Penn in 1701. It created a one-house legislature by vesting legislative power in the assembly, subject to the governor's veto, and limiting the

William Penn negotiates for land with Lenni Lenape sachems. (Gay Brothers)

council to executive and judicial powers. The council was appointed by the governor instead of being elected by the freemen. This marked the end of proprietary rule in Pennsylvania, save in the appointment of a governor. The unicameral legislature that was created endured until the American Revolution.

Penn issued the Charter of Privileges in order to end almost twenty years of quarreling between council and assembly, the former asserting its superior status against the latter's demands for a greater share in the government of the colony. The assembly had considerably enlarged its power from 1692 to 1694, when the colony was under royal rule. Markham's third frame, issued after the Crown returned Pennsylvania to Penn, had extended the prerogatives of the assembly, and the Charter of Privileges' establishment of a unicameral legislature represented a further triumph for that body.

Although he had inherited wealth, one reason Penn embarked on the troublesome business of a new colony was to make his personal fortune. It is, however, difficult to say whether Pennsylvania was a success from the viewpoint of the Penn family. Penn spent much of the first twenty years of his colony's life in England, entrusting his interests to a series of governors and agents. The result was less than satisfactory, as Penn was imprisoned for debt and was forced to mortgage Pennsylvania in 1708.

SIGNIFICANCE

With the council eliminated as both a legislative and an elective body, the assembly redirected its opposition to the governor. In the early eighteenth century, two parties dominated Pennsylvania politics, the Proprietary Party, led by James Logan, which sought to centralize authority in the hands of the governor and the council, and the Popular Party, led by David Lloyd, which sought to expand the powers of the assembly.

The main political issue was the Quaker principle of pacifism, which underwent a critical test in 1756, when warfare between the Iroquois tribes and European settlers erupted on the frontier. A declaration of war against the Lenni Lenape and Shawnee Indians by the governor and the council resulted in the Quakers' decision to withdraw from the assembly rather than compromise their stand against the war. This withdrawal ended almost seventy-five years of Quaker rule over the colony of Pennsylvania. For those seventy-five years, Pennsylvania was the only government in the New World, or anywhere else, to be run by pacifists, a situation the very concept of which was alien to most Europeans given the turbulence of world in which they lived. The tradition of Quakerism is still strong in Pennsylvania, which contains many meetinghouses and Quaker schools.

—*Anne C. Loveland and Kelley Graham*

FURTHER READING

Doerflinger, Thomas. *A Vigorous Spirit of Enterprise: Merchants and Economic Development in Revolutionary Philadelphia*. Chapel Hill: University of North Carolina Press, 1986. An interesting study that challenges the older concept of a Quaker merchant aristocracy in prerevolutionary Philadelphia.

Dunn, Richard, and Mary Maples Dunn, eds. *The World of William Penn*. Philadelphia: University of Pennsylvania Press, 1986. An outstanding collection of articles reevaluating the politics and religious issues of early Pennsylvania history.

Geiter, Mary K. *William Penn*. New York: Longman, 2000. Assesses Penn's religious and political significance in America and Britain.

Nash, Gary B. *Quakers and Politics: Pennsylvania, 1681-1726*. Princeton, N.J.: Princeton University Press, 1968. Unlike earlier historians of colonial Pennsylvania, Nash approaches his subject not from a religious angle but from the viewpoint of the sociology of politics.

Penn, William. *The Papers of William Penn*, edited by Mary Maples Dunn et al. 5 vols. Philadelphia: University of Pennsylvania Press, 1981-1987. An essential collection of primary materials, with informative introductions and bibliography.

Schwartz, Sally. *"A Mixed Multitude": The Struggle for Toleration in Colonial Pennsylvania*. New York: New York University Press, 1987. Explores the development and consequences of Quaker toleration in an increasingly diverse colony.

Soderlund, Jean R., et al. *William Penn and the Founding of Pennsylvania, 1680-1684: A Documentary History*. Philadelphia: University of Pennsylvania Press, 1983. A documentary study of the political, economic, and social origins of Pennsylvania on both sides of the Atlantic.

SEE ALSO: Dec. 26, 1620: Pilgrims Arrive in North America; May, 1630-1643: Great Puritan Migration; Fall, 1632-Jan. 5, 1665: Settlement of Connecticut; June, 1636: Rhode Island Is Founded; Apr. 21, 1649: Maryland Act of Toleration; 1652-1689: Fox Organizes the Quakers.

RELATED ARTICLES in *Great Lives from History: The Seventeenth Century, 1601-1700:* Charles II (of England); William Penn.

Beginning c. 1682
DECLINE OF THE SOLOMONID DYNASTY

The Christian kingdom of Ethiopia, recovering from the trauma of a sixteenth century invasion by Muslim forces, was once again confronted by massive population movements from its periphery. Triggered by profound ecological and demographic changes in the southern part of the country, this rapid expansion of the pastoral community into the central plateau contributed to the further disorganization of the centralized state apparatus and the decline of the Solomonid Dynasty.

LOCALE: Ethiopia, Gondar
CATEGORIES: Government and politics; wars, uprisings, and civil unrest

KEY FIGURES

Za Dengel (d. 1604), emperor of Ethiopia, r. 1603-1604
Susenyos (d. 1632), emperor of Ethiopia, r. 1607-1632
Fasilides (d. 1667), emperor of Ethiopia, r. 1632-1667
John I (d. 1682), emperor of Ethiopia, r. 1667-1682
Iyasu I the Great (1662-1706), emperor of Ethiopia, r. 1682-1706

SUMMARY OF EVENT

The Christian kingdom of Ethiopia, ruled by the once-powerful Solomonid Dynasty since the thirteenth century, had barely recovered from a debilitating Muslim invasion of the sixteenth century when it was engulfed by a new wave of population movements that threw the country into crisis and led to its decline. Propelled by ecological and demographic forces, Cushitic-speaking groups from the southern fringes of the empire burst into the highlands from several directions.

Of special significance was the migration of the Oromo, a pastoral community that originated from the Bale region in southeastern Ethiopia. The sudden upsurge of the Oromo and their rapid expansion into the southern and central plateau as well as northward into the rich highlands of Ethiopia and eastward into Harar dramatically altered the demographic features of the country. As they advanced farther into the interiors of Ethiopia, the Oromo absorbed other Cushitic-speaking peoples in the area and significantly boosted their numbers and strength within a short time. More and more areas slipped out of the control of the central government and fell into the hands of the advancing Oromo. Although they never succeeded in constituting themselves into a single political entity, the various segments of the Oromo-speaking communities became a major cultural and political force in Ethiopia.

Still reeling from the Muslim onslaught of the sixteenth century, the Solomonid rulers of Ethiopia were slow to address the new threat. The frontier garrisons on which the central government had relied for centuries to guard the periphery of the empire were already destroyed by the Muslim invasion. Lacking the resources to protect the outlying provinces, the Solomonid kings increasingly abandoned the effort to reclaim lost territories and instead focused on repositioning their forces to defend and stabilize the core region of the empire in the north. The Solomonid rulers of the seventeenth century also had to wrestle with an increasingly restive nobility.

Since the loss of the border provinces had drastically shrunk the revenue base available for the ruling elite at the center, there ensued fierce competition between the monarchy and the regional nobility for control of the limited resources of the northern region. The imperial regiments that were key instruments of Solomonid authority could no longer be relied upon to play their traditional role of protecting the center. The personal troops of the kings intervened frequently to settle succession issues to their favor—in one instance elevating a seven-year-old boy to the throne. The early decades of the seventeenth century witnessed such succession crises and numerous uprisings led by the nobility and army commanders. Two of the emperors, Za Dengel and Yacob (r. 1604-1606), were killed in battle by a coalition of disgruntled generals and noblemen.

The introduction of Catholicism and the growing influence of European Jesuit missionaries in the Ethiopian court added further complication to the many challenges facing the Christian polity. Impressed by the discipline and hierarchy of the Catholic establishment, and desiring to secure the support of Western Christendom against his numerous rivals in the center and the periphery, the Ethiopian emperor Susenyos was converted to Catholicism in 1622. Susenyos set out to change the age-old tradition of the Ethiopian church and aggressively moved to force it to conform to Catholic doctrine and practice. This, however, created more rift in the country. Ecclesiastics and laypeople joined hands in defense of the national Orthodox church and fiercely resisting the king's effort to impose Catholicism over the country. Susenyos spent the next decade trying to suppress one uprising after another, only to discover that the rebellion and the bloodshed grew worse from year to year. Finally, he realized the futility of his policy and abdicated in favor of his son, Fasilides. Fasilides restored the Ethiopian Orthodox Church and banned Catholicism from the country. Jesuit missionaries were expelled, and further contact with Europe was discontinued.

Fasilides used his newly won prestige as defender of the national faith to revive imperial power and to stabilize the kingdom. Although efforts to reestablish authority over the old geographic framework proved impossible, Fasilides brought a measure of peace and order to the country. He founded a new capital at Gondar, which soon grew into a sophisticated city of splendid palaces and churches, a center of high culture and learning not seen in the country's history since the fall of Axum about one thousand years earlier. The flourishing of Gondar as a major political and cultural center promoted the growth of trade and the resumption of Ethiopia's commercial contacts with the "outside" world.

Fasilides's successors, John I and Iyasu I the Great, continued the drive to strengthen the monarchy and unify the core area of the kingdom. Iyasu in particular was determined to establish the absolute supremacy of the Crown over the regional lords and to build a powerful military that would reassert its authority over the lost provinces. He carried out reforms in the military and administration and conducted several campaigns in the south that reestablished, briefly, imperial authority over many Oromo settled areas. However, Iyasu's forceful policy of national integration and royal supremacy encountered serious resistance from the regional nobility and the church establishment.

Torn by sectarian conflict initially triggered by disputes over the nature of Christ, the Ethiopian Orthodox church, which for centuries had served as the ideological arm of the Solomonid Dynasty, turned into a source of strife in the latter half of the seventeenth century. Iyasu's efforts to impose unity among the dissident clergy backfired, as those who felt disfavored by the emperor joined the ranks of his enemies. The regional nobility that was threatened by Iyasu's centralizing drive moved eagerly to exploit the religious controversy against the emperor. In the end, a coalition of the nobility and dissident clergymen succeeded in persuading Iyasu's son to depose and assassinate his father. The removal of this powerful monarch marked the triumph of centrifugal forces in Ethiopia. For the next century and a half, the Solomonid kings virtually remained captives of the nobility.

SIGNIFICANCE

The Solomonid Dynasty's rulers who were instrumental in the creation of the mighty Ethiopian Christian empire of the medieval period became shadows of their former selves by the end of the seventeenth century. Although they were allowed to nominally occupy the throne, their authority never extended outside the confines of the palace in Gondar. The usurpation of real power by the regional lords destroyed central authority in the country, and Ethiopia entered into what is popularly known as the Era of Princes, a period of disorder and anarchy that lasted for more than a century and a half.

—Shumet Sishagne

FURTHER READING

Abir, Mordecai. "Ethiopia and the Horn of Africa." In *The Cambridge History of Africa*. Vol. 4. New York: Cambridge University Press, 1975. A remarkably succinct presentation of the political history of the Horn of Africa in the seventeenth century.

_______. *Ethiopia and the Red Sea: The Rise and Decline of the Solomonic Dynasty and Muslim-European Rivalry in the Region*. London: Cass, 1980. A detailed account of the saga of the Solomonic Dynasty and its impact in shaping the political landscape in northeastern Africa.

Beckingham, Charles F., and G. W. B. Huntingford, eds. *Some Records of Ethiopia, 1593-1648*. London: Hakluyt Society, 1954. An extremely useful work on seventeenth century Ethiopia that contains extracts from royal chronicles and other primary sources.

Crummey, Donald. *Land and Society in the Christian Kingdom of Ethiopia: From the Thirteenth to the Twentieth Century*. Urbana-Champaign: University of Illinois Press, 1999. One of the best works on the political and social history of the highland Christian society of Ethiopia.

Haberland, Eike. "The Horn of Africa." In *General History of Africa: Africa from the Sixteenth to the Eighteenth Century*. Vol. 5. Berkeley, Calif.: UNESCO, 1992. A brief outline of the history of the Horn of Africa region with helpful information on the massive population movements of the sixteenth and seventeenth centuries.

Marcus, Harold. *A History of Ethiopia*. Berkeley: University of California Press, 1994. One of the best standard works on the history of Ethiopia by a well-respected historian.

SEE ALSO: c. 1625: Formation of the Kuba Kingdom; Aug. 26, 1641-Sept., 1648: Conquest of Luanda; 1644-1671: Ndongo Wars; Late 17th cent.: Rise of Buganda.

RELATED ARTICLE in *Great Lives from History: The Seventeenth Century, 1601-1700:* Njinga.

1682
FRENCH COURT MOVES TO VERSAILLES

The French court isolated the government from the people when it moved from the Louvre to the newly built palace at Versailles, serving as a means to control the French nobility and becoming the symbol of King Louis XIV's dominance in France and France's supremacy in Europe.

LOCALE: Paris and Versailles, France
CATEGORIES: Government and politics; architecture

KEY FIGURES

Louis XIV (1638-1715), king of France, r. 1643-1715

Anne of Austria (1601-1666), queen of France, r. 1615-1643, queen regent, r. 1643-1651, and mother of Louis XIV

Jules Mazarin (1602-1661), succeeded Cardinal de Richelieu as chief minister in 1643 and was retained by Anne of Austria until his death

Louis Le Vau (1612-1670), French architect who played a major role in planning the construction of Versailles

SUMMARY OF EVENT

Cardinal de Richelieu, the chief minister of France, died in 1642. Six months later, the five-year-old Louis XIV inherited his father's throne, and during his minority, his mother, Anne of Austria, served as regent of France. In this turbulent period, the power of the state was in the hands of Cardinal Jules Mazarin, a favorite of the Queen Mother and a protégé of Richelieu, who attempted to continue the diplomatic policies of his predecessor. In domestic affairs, Mazarin continued efforts to consolidate power in the hands of the central government.

In the final half century of the reign of the House of Valois, the French nobility had strengthened their position during the civil and religious wars, but Henry IV, founder of the House of Bourbon, strengthened the monarchy and placed it on a sound economic basis. Under Henry's son, Louis XIII, Richelieu moved against the nobility. He strengthened the position of the intendants at the expense of the provincial nobility, he forbade private warfare (including dueling) he dismantled fortified castles that could not be of any use in defending French frontiers, and he pensioned old army officers. Upon his death, Richelieu left a nobility that was seriously wounded, though not dead. Richelieu was succeeded by an Italian opportunist, a small boy, and the boy's mother—an unimpressive trio that caused the nobility to believe that the time had come for them to reverse the trend toward centralization.

The civil wars called the Wars of the Fronde (1648-1653), which marked the minority of Louis XIV, taught the young king to distrust the nobility of France and to fear the people of Paris, who generally supported the opponents of Mazarin. At the height of the civil disorder, the Queen Mother fled from the capital to Saint-Germain, taking with her the impressionable eleven-year-old uncrowned monarch. Louis XIV always remembered this flight; he never forgave the city of Paris for the insult, and he never felt safe in the city thereafter.

When Cardinal Mazarin died in 1661, the king assumed full power. He accelerated the weakening of the power of the nobility, and he brought the concept of absolute monarchy to its zenith in France. Paris did not allow the degree of aloofness that he required, so Louis XIV had a palace built at Versailles, some eleven miles southwest of the capital, in a marshy area where a favorite royal hunting lodge was situated. To build the new royal residence, Louis Le Vau and other top architects, artists, engineers, landscapers, and gardeners were employed, along with tens of thousands of laborers. Work was begun in 1661, and construction costs proved to be astronomical.

In 1682, as soon as he could, Louis XIV moved to Versailles with his entire court. Versailles provided him with the opportunity to escape Paris and its unruly population, and it also allowed him to hunt daily, a sport for which he had developed a passion. He was following the example of Spanish monarchs in the sixteenth century, who spent most of their time at El Escorial. Yet Louis had many original purposes for Versailles as well. Versailles was intended as a monument to the Sun King himself, to his absolutist dominance of France, and to France's political and cultural supremacy in European civilization. State receptions at the palace did overwhelm foreign visitors, while court culture and the palace itself became a standard-setter for European monarchies.

For Louis, Versailles also was a place to keep the semi-independent high nobility under a watchful eye and to transform them into dependent creatures, kept too busy with minutia and entertainment to seriously involve themselves with practical political matters. Housed in tiny and crowded quarters, and impoverished by the move, the expenses of court life, and continuous gambling at court, many became dependent on royal favor. This meant involvement in the complicated daily activity of the king, his dressing and undressing, his meals and snacks, his rising and retiring. If properly bowing to the passing of the king's food or moving up in a line of courtiers in a royal dressing line meant recognition and royal favor, then these things became matters of paramount importance. In institutionalizing and domesticating the high nobles, Versailles served a very practical end. Unfortunately, while King Louis XIV's daily routine involved long and hard work, and he escaped being victim to his own creation, his successors appear to have been overwhelmed by the inanities of court life at Versailles, producing serious problems in a system that ran by competent absolutist rule.

SIGNIFICANCE

For the following century, no French king resided in Paris, and Versailles came to be synonymous with the Bourbon monarchy. The return of Louis XVI to Paris in October of 1789 was the result of the Women's March on Versailles, when the unruly population of the capital forced its king to abandon the isolation of his two predecessors and become a prisoner of the people of Paris.

The isolation of the kings of France during the eighteenth century undoubtedly contributed to the French Revolution of 1789. The kings were cut off from their subjects. Misunderstandings and suspicion between the royal government and the masses of people led to a credibility gap that paved the way for revolution. The causes

A photograph of one of the many elaborate halls of the palace at Versailles. (George L. Shuman)

King Louis XIV holds court. (Hulton|Archive by Getty Images)

of the French Revolution were deeper and more complex than the move to Versailles, but the isolation of the king, the court, and the royal administration ultimately led to the execution of Louis XVI and the overthrow of the monarchy.

—*John G. Gallaher and Irwin Halfond*

Further Reading

Berger, Robert W. *A Royal Passion: Louis XIV as Patron of Architecture*. New York: Cambridge University Press, 1994. The work surveys Versailles and other buildings closely associated with Louis to explain why these structures, gardens, and decorations were so important to him and how they represented his absolute authority.

Bluche, François. *Louis XIV*. Translated by Mark Greengrass. New York: Franklin Watts, 1990. A comprehensive study of the Sun King's reign, with significant detail of court life.

Edmunds, Martha Mel Stumberg. *Piety and Politics: Imagining Divine Kingship in Louis XIV's Chapel at Versailles*. Newark: University of Delaware Press, 2002. An analysis of Louis's royal chapel, constructed as a dynastic shrine and consecrated to his ancestor, King Louis IX.

Lossky, Andrew. *Louis XIV and the French Monarchy*. New Brunswick, N.J.: Rutgers University Press, 1994. An excellent political biography of the Sun King.

Norton, Lucy, ed. and trans. *Saint-Simon at Versailles*. London: H. Hamilton, 1958. Reprint. New York: Harmony Books, 1980. An account of life at Versailles during the last twenty years of the king's reign, by a highly perceptive, though not always objective, court noble.

Pérouse de Montclose, Jean-Marie. *Versailles*. New York: Abbeville Press, 1991. A lavishly illustrated, large-format study of the entire project at Versailles, Le Vau's early role and designs, and the accommodations to them made by later architects and contractors.

Rubin, David L., ed. *Sun King: The Ascendancy of French Culture During the Reign of Louis XIV*. Cranbury, N.J.: Associated University Presses, 1992. A collection of papers presented at a major symposium on Louis, court life, and the cultural and intellectual developments in France during his reign.

Walton, Guy. *Louis XIV's Versailles*. Chicago: University of Chicago Press, 1986. A thorough study of social and cultural life at Versailles during Louis's reign.

Weiss, Allen S. *Mirrors of Infinity: The French Formal Garden and Seventeenth Century Metaphysics*. New York: Princeton Architectural Press, 1995. A concise intellectual history of the function and meaning of Versailles and other French formal gardens.

See also: 1661: Absolute Monarchy Emerges in France; 1673: Renovation of the Louvre.

Related articles in *Great Lives from History: The Seventeenth Century, 1601-1700:* Anne of Austria; Jean-Baptiste Colbert; André Le Nôtre; Louis Le Vau; Louis XIV; Madame de Maintenon; François Mansart; Jules Hardouin-Mansart; Jules Mazarin; Madame de Sévigné.

August, 1682-November, 1683
Rye House Plot

Beginning as early as the summer of 1682, two unrelated groups, one radical Whigs and the other disgruntled republicans, planned to prevent a Roman Catholic accession by assassinating Charles II and James, duke of York. Their conspiracies are known collectively as the Rye House Plot, and their failure led to the execution of a number of prominent Whigs and old Cromwellians.

Locale: London and Hertfordshire, England
Categories: Government and politics; religion and theology

Key Figures

Charles II (1630-1685), king of England, r. 1660-1685
James, Duke of York and Albany (1633-1701), Roman Catholic brother of Charles, heir presumptive, and king of England as James II, r. 1685-1688
Duke of Monmouth (James Scott; 1649-1685), the eldest of Charles II's illegitimate sons
First Earl of Shaftesbury (Anthony Ashley Cooper; 1621-1683), leader of the Exclusion effort in Parliament and founder of the Whigs
Lord Russell (William Russell; 1639-1683), a leader of the Parliamentary Whig faction
Algernon Sidney (1623-1683), political philosopher implicated in the Rye House Plot
First Earl of Essex (Arthur Capel; 1632-1683), a leading Whig politician and conspirator
John Hampden (1653-1696), republican politician and participant in the plot

Summary of Event

Historians are still divided on the question of whether the Rye House Plot was actually an attempt to assassinate Charles II and his brother, James, duke of York, or a cleverly contrived government effort to destroy the leadership of the exclusionary faction. This faction, which had acquired the nickname "Whigs" and would later evolve into a formal political party of that name, sought to remove the Catholic James from the line of succession. They feared that if he became Supreme Head of the Church of England, James would turn England into a Catholic nation. Charles, who had no desire to remove his brother from the succession, had motive to fabricate a false plot. However, the behavior of James Scott, duke of Monmouth, before and after the crisis supports those who contend that the plot was genuine.

There were actually two plots, and the link between them was Monmouth. Anthony Ashley Cooper, first earl of Shaftesbury, who had managed the failed Parliamentary attempt to exclude James, was living in exile. Before his death, like a skilled puppet master, Shaftesbury used Monmouth, Lord Russell, the first earl of Essex, Algernon Sidney, Lord Howard of Escrick, and John Hampden to formulate a plan for a general insurrection, which centered on kidnapping the king and his brother. The "Council of Six," as they called themselves, could not agree what to do if they succeeded in this bold venture. Although they began discussing their insurgency as early as the summer of 1682, their plan never quite matured.

Meanwhile, a small group of republican fanatics led by a former Cromwellian soldier, Colonel John Rumsey, and including Richard Rumbold, who had stood guard at the execution of Charles I, began planning a much bolder solution to the possibility of a Roman Catholic succession. Beginning as early as February, 1683, Rumsey and his associates began to discuss the possibility of assassinating Charles II and the duke of York. Every year, the king attended the spring race meeting at Newmarket, in Hertfordshire. The republicans planned to ambush the royal brothers at Rye House, an isolated spot near the village of Ware on the road to London. Charles II enjoyed evading his bodyguard, so the attack could be made and the murders accomplished before the soldiers caught up with the royal coach. Monmouth, who could easily be controlled by the heirs of Shaftesbury, would then be proclaimed king, and the Whig faction would assume control of the government. Robert Ferguson, one of the conspirators, informed Monmouth of the assassination plot. He was one of Shaftesbury's henchmen, and when the first arrest warrants were issued on June 23, he was able to flee abroad.

Once the duke of York became King James II, he took his revenge upon the duke of Monmouth for his role in the Rye House Plot. Monmouth is shown here begging James for mercy. (Francis R. Niglutsch)

On March 22, a disastrous fire in Newmarket destroyed a large portion of the town, including the royal lodging. As a result, Charles II and the duke of York returned to the capital ahead of schedule. The assassins did not have an alternative plan, and thus they were caught off guard by the conflagration and the royal escape. The failure of this conspiracy threw the aristocratic plotters into a quandary, and their plans had to be postponed. The whole affair might have been forgotten save for the fact that some of the participants began to talk too freely to individuals who were actually government agents.

Early in the summer of 1683, the accusations began. Terrified by the possibility of suffering the full penalty for treason, Josiah Keeling, a Baptist oil merchant, turned informer. William Carstares confessed under torture and implicated a number of individuals. Among those arrested were Russell, Essex, Howard, Sidney, Hampden, Captain Thomas Walcott, who was rumored to have been the executioner of Charles I, Nathaniel Wade and Robert West, who were lawyers, and James Holloway, a linen merchant from Bristol. The Tories (the Royalist faction in Parliament, which would evolve into the party opposed to the Whig Party) had been crippled by the witch-hunt conducted against Catholics during the Popish Plot (1678-1681). They now sought their revenge. The king personally questioned the Whig lords when they were brought before the Privy Council.

The state trials began in early July, 1683, but unlike the trials of the Catholic peers during the Popish Plot, the outcomes were not predictable. The grand jury handed down indictments against twenty-one persons including the duke of Monmouth. Lord Howard of Escrick, who had been a close associate of Shaftsbury, was pardoned, because he had given evidence against his fellow conspirators. Walcott was convicted and executed on July 20, but William Blague was acquitted. Lord Russell, John Rouse, William Hone, James Holloway, and Algernon Sidney were executed for treason, but John Hampden, the nephew of a famous Civil War Parliamentarian, was fined and sentenced to prison. The earl of Essex was not brought to trial; he committed suicide in his cell in the Tower of London. Charles II was particularly distressed at news of Essex's death, because his father had been executed for his devotion to the Royalist cause, and the king would probably have commuted his sentence to imprisonment if he had been convicted of treason.

As the evidence was assembled during the investigation and the trials, it became apparent that there was no nationwide plot, despite the fact that the Whig lords had tried to involve a group of dissident Scots. This was a disappointment for the duke of York, who felt that his brother had exercised too much restraint in punishing the traitors who had sought to take his life. When he ascended the throne as James II on February 6, 1685, however, he would have the opportunity to complete the process begun in 1683 and in particular to punish his nephew, Monmouth.

When the arrests of the Rye House conspirators began, Monmouth went into hiding, fearing that he might be charged with treason for plotting the overthrow of the government as well as knowing of the plan to murder his father. Despite the fact that his eldest natural son was as guilty as many of those executed for their participation in the plots, Charles II forgave Monmouth. His uncle James was not so merciful. When Monmouth sought to seize the throne after his father's death, James II did not hesitate to send him to the block. Thus, in 1685, the severed head of the so-called Protestant Hope would join what remained of his fellow traitors still rotting on the spikes above Tower Bridge.

SIGNIFICANCE

The Rye House Plot was the last crisis in the reign of Charles II, and its resolution in favor of the Crown ensured the undisputed succession of the duke of York in 1685. James actually garnered some degree of popularity from the Rye House affair, and he mounted the throne with a great deal of public goodwill—which he soon squandered. The execution of a number of the more radical Whigs ensured the ascendancy of the moderate wing of the faction and its return to power after the Glorious Revolution of 1688.

—Clifton W. Potter, Jr.

FURTHER READING

Coote, Stephen. *Royal Survivor: The Life of Charles II.* New York: St. Martin's Press, 2000. A study of the political sagacity of Charles II as he faced and survived the various crises of his reign.

Fraser, Antonia. *King Charles II.* London: Phoenix Press, 2002. The most balanced biography of the king, it places the events of the Rye House Plot in their proper context.

Greaves, Richard L. *Secrets of the Kingdom: British Radicals from the Popish Plot to the Revolution of 1688-1689.* Stanford, Calif.: Stanford University Press, 1992. It links the successive attempts to alter the nature of the English government, which finally ended with the Glorious Revolution. It is the most complete modern work on the Rye House Plot.

Harris, Tim. *London Crowds in the Reign of Charles II: Propaganda and Politics from the Restoration Until the Exclusion Crisis.* Cambridge, England: Cambridge University Press, 1987. An in-depth study of the component that made the city of London unstable.

Jones, J. R. *The First Whigs: The Politics of the Exclusion Crisis, 1678-1683.* London: Oxford University Press, 1961. A thorough study of the men who failed to alter the legitimate succession.

SEE ALSO: Nov. 5, 1605: Gunpowder Plot; Nov. 3, 1640-May 15, 1641: Beginning of England's Long Parliament; 1642-1651: English Civil Wars; May, 1659-May, 1660: Restoration of Charles II; Aug. 13, 1678-July 1, 1681: The Popish Plot; Nov., 1688-Feb., 1689: The Glorious Revolution.

RELATED ARTICLES in *Great Lives from History: The Seventeenth Century, 1601-1700:* Charles II (of England); James II; Mary II; Duke of Monmouth; First Earl of Shaftesbury; William III.

July 14-September 12, 1683
Defeat of the Ottomans at Vienna

The defeat of the Ottoman Turks by an allied European army at Vienna heralded the beginning of the Ottoman retreat from Central Europe and the rise of Austria as a powerful Danubian state.

Locale: Vienna, Austria
Categories: Wars, uprisings, and civil unrest; government and politics

Key Figures

Innocent XI (Benedetto Odescalchi; 1611-1689), Roman Catholic pope, 1676-1689
John III Sobieski (1629-1696), king of Poland, r. 1674-1696, and commander in chief of the allied army relieving Vienna
Merzifonlu Kara Mustafa Paşa (1634/1635-1683), grand vizier of the Ottoman Empire, 1676-1683
Leopold I (1640-1705), Holy Roman Emperor, r. 1658-1705, king of Hungary, r. 1655-1687, and hereditary ruler of Habsburg domains of Austria and Bohemia
Charles V Leopold (1643-1690), duke of Lorraine, commander of Habsburg forces
Mehmed IV Avci (1642-1693), Ottoman sultan, r. 1648-1687
Count Ernst Rüdiger von Starhemberg (1635-1701), Austrian field marshal defending Vienna
Imre Thököly (1657-1705), Hungarian nationalist and claimant to the Hungarian throne

Summary of Event

By the mid-seventeenth century, few Europeans perceived Ottoman decline. Originating as a fierce, expansionist warrior state reaching its high point under Süleyman the Magnificent, who ruled from 1520 to 1566, the Ottoman Empire still dominated the Middle East and the Balkans. Various complex internal changes had taken place, however, including a decline in quality of the sultans, or rulers; deterioration in the *tīmār* system of fiefs; support of the traditional Turkish cavalry, the *sipahi*; and erosion of obedience and discipline within state service by the admission of other subjects to the positions formerly monopolized by a slave class recruited from the famous "boy tax" on Christian villagers in the Balkans.

Dramatic population increase and rampant inflation fueled the growth of banditry and civil disorder. An overextended empire posed logistical problems, and years of warfare in Persia and southeastern Europe burdened the state. Reformers, culminating in the Köprülü family of grand viziers, attempted to restore the bases of traditional Ottoman rule while once again embarking upon an aggressive military policy in Europe.

Since the conquest of most of Hungary during Süleyman the Magnificent's reign, only a portion remained under Habsburg control. Further Ottoman advance into Habsburg Hungary stopped in 1664 after the Battle of Szentgotthárd (Saint Gotthard), and an uneasy peace of almost twenty years prevailed until Merzifonlu Kara Mustafa Paşa, a Köprülü protégé, became grand vizier. The ambitious vizier saw opportunity when discontented Hungarian nationalists, resentful over Emperor Leopold's policy of centralization and Counter-Reformation religious conformity, rose in revolt under Imre Thököly. Upon Thököly's acceptance of Turkish suzerainty, the sultan recognized him as king of Hungary.

The French encouraged Ottoman militancy, hoping to keep the Austrians distracted in the east. Long preoccupied with their historic struggle against the French in western Europe, the Habsburgs at first did not perceive the seriousness of the Turkish threat and hoped to negotiate with the Ottomans. Kara Mustafa Paşa, fortified by French assurances not to come to the assistance of the Austrians and by Thököly's success in northern Hungary, decided to attack the Habsburgs. The sultan attended a grand military review of one hundred thousand troops on May 13, 1683, in Belgrade, where he proclaimed a jihad, or holy war, and handed his vizier the sacred standard of the Prophet Muḥammad (c. 570-632). An even larger Ottoman host led by Kara Mustafa Paşa marched across Hungary toward Vienna.

Emperor Leopold retreated first to Linz and then to Passau, where he sought to build up a Christian alliance against the Turks. With money and encouragement from Pope Innocent XI, Leopold was able to secure support from the dukes of Bavaria and Saxony as well as John Sobieski, king of Poland, who had already won fame by fighting the Turks in the Ukraine. It took time, however, for the allied army to gather its forces and relieve the city.

Leopold placed Count Ernst Rüdiger von Starhemberg in charge of Vienna's defenses. Starhemberg, an energetic and experienced commander, concentrated the city's artillery at the point of Ottoman attack, organized companies of firefighters to combat incendiary bombs, and commanded the troops who made sorties and defended the city walls. His personal courage and his sense

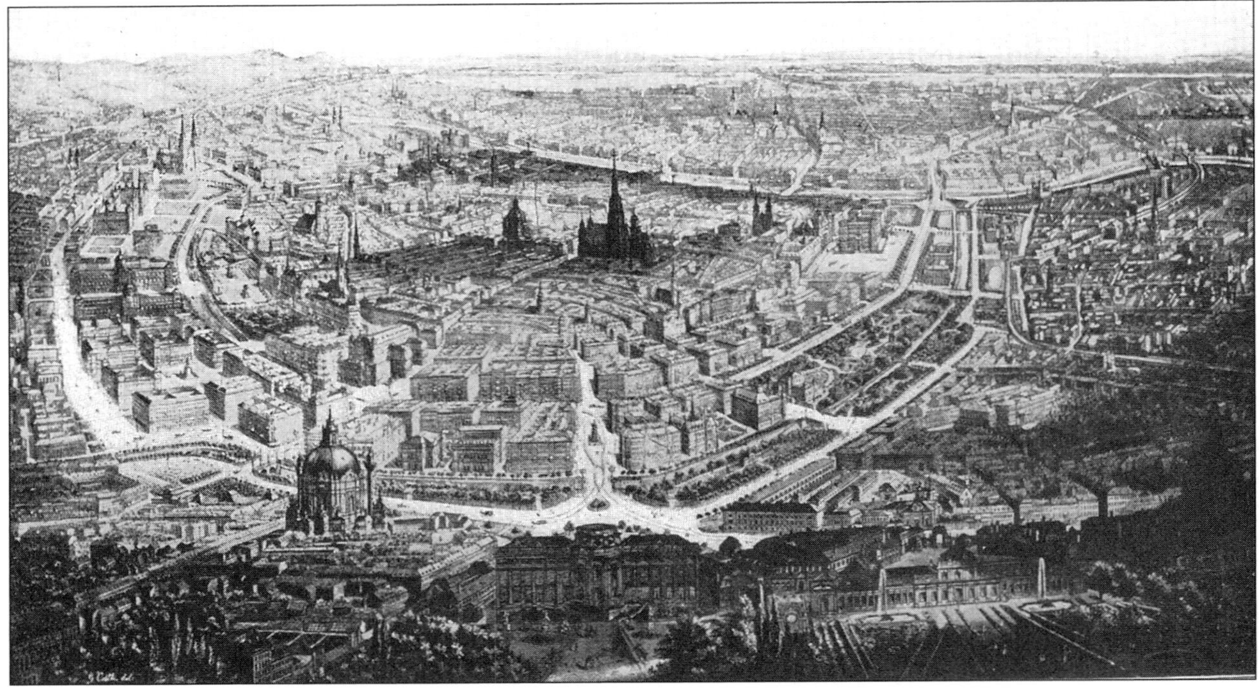

A panoramic view of Vienna, stronghold of the seventeenth century Austrian Habsburg Dynasty. (George L. Shuman)

of discipline earned him his heroic image as Vienna's defender.

Like many cities of the time, Vienna adopted early modern fortification methods, encircling its bastion-reinforced city walls with ravelins (triangular stone outworks), moats, and counterscarps on the outer rim of the moat projecting toward the enemy. These fortifications had begun in the 1560's at the time of an earlier siege and had been added to during the seventeenth century. Starhemberg hurried last-minute reinforcements before the siege.

The Turks relied upon two tactics: artillery and mining. Logistics problems prevented them from bringing their largest artillery across the Balkans, so they contented themselves with pieces of smaller caliber, which did not inflict significant damage to the fortifications. The Ottoman forces primarily relied upon the traditional method of taking a besieged town: digging a series of ever closer parallel trenches so that mines could be placed to breach the enemy walls. The Turks perfected such tactics while taking Candia in Crete in 1669. By the end of August, mines had breached several walls but hastily erected barriers and hard fighting temporarily stopped the Ottoman advance. Desperation set in by early September: Vienna had lost half its defenders and was running short of supplies. It was only a matter of time before the Turks entered the city.

The coalition of Austrians, Germans, and Poles spent the summer assembling troops. John III Sobieski arrived with twenty-one thousand experienced Polish warriors, about one-third of the total allied army of perhaps sixty-five thousand (estimates vary). They marched through the hilly upcountry of the Viennese Woods without difficulty, for Kara Mustafa Paşa had failed to secure the approach to the city. Refusing to abandon the siege when victory was so close, the grand vizier split his troops: 10,000 stayed in the trenches, while perhaps 63,500 confronted the allied army. While the two armies were roughly equal in size, the allies had more field cannon. On September 12, the Battle of Kahlenberg took place west of Vienna. The allies under the command of Sobieski advanced, with Charles V Leopold and the Austrians on the left wing, Germans in the center, and the Poles on the right wing. The decisive charge of the Polish cavalry broke the Ottoman ranks, and Kara Mustafa Paşa and the Turkish army fled in confusion. The Turks retreated to Belgrade, where Kara Mustafa Paşa ordered numerous executions to excuse his own failure, but he was removed from office and strangled upon the sultan's orders.

Significance

Numerous German and Polish accounts celebrated the "Christian" triumph over Islam. After 1683, the Ottoman Empire ceased to be a serious threat to Europe. The Turkish defeat at Vienna began a series of military reverses that marked the Turkish retreat from great-power status. Leopold made a pivotal decision. He continued to pursue the Turks down the Danube River instead of confronting Louis XIV in western Europe. Leopold made a truce with the French king, the Peace of Ratisbon (Regensburg), which recognized prior French annexations in Germany for the next twenty years. The Austrians used the time wisely. Pope Innocent XI encouraged a Holy League committing Austria, Poland, and Venice against the Turks. In 1686, the Austrians captured Buda, the capital of Turkish Hungary, and seized Belgrade in 1688. The Treaty of Karlowitz (1699) formally recognized Austria's possession of Hungary and Transylvania, although the Turks kept Belgrade. Austria emerged as the major power in central Europe. Its position as a powerful Danubian monarchy enabled it to maintain itself as one of the great powers.

John III Sobieski hoped to use the victory to protect Polish territory, strengthen his own rule, and secure the elective Polish crown for his son. Sobieski was ultimately disappointed. He continued fighting against the Turks but he experienced no great success. Unable to translate his prestige into dominance over the powerful Polish nobility, he never established a dynasty. He was the last strong native Polish monarch.

—*Douglas Clark Baxter*

Further Reading

Ackerl, Isabella. *Three Hundred Years Ago: The Second Turkish Siege, Vienna, 1683*. Vienna: Federal Press Service, 1982. A brief Austrian commemorative monograph that summarizes the siege from an Austrian perspective.

Barker, Thomas M. *Double Eagle and Crescent: Vienna's Second Turkish Siege and Its Historical Setting*. Albany: State University of New York Press, 1967. This detailed and well-organized account by an American historian is especially strong on the larger international background.

Goffman, Daniel. *The Ottoman Empire and Early Modern Europe*. New York: Cambridge University Press, 2002. This study describes Ottoman-Habsburg relations during the seventeenth century.

Hoskins, J. W. *Victory at Vienna: The Ottoman Siege of 1683*. Washington, D.C.: Library of Congress, European Division, 1983. A concise account supported by an extended reading list.

Ingrao, Charles W. *The Habsburg Monarchy, 1618-1815*. 2d ed. New York: Cambridge University Press, 2000. Traces the emergence of the Habsburg Empire as a military and cultural power. Chapter 3, "Facing East: Hungary and the Turks, 1648-1699," describes the empire's relations with the Ottoman Turks.

Leitsch, Walter. "1683: The Siege of Vienna." *History Today* 33 (July, 1983): 37-40. A brief interpretative overview of the siege's significance by a leading Austrian scholar.

Morton, J. B. *Sobieski, King of Poland*. London: Eyre & Spottiswoode, 1932. An older but serviceable biography of John III Sobieski.

Parvev, Ivan. *Habsburgs and Ottomans Between Vienna and Belgrade, 1683-1739*. Boulder, Colo.: Eastern European Monographs, 1995. This work examines relations between the Habsburg and Ottoman Empires from the Siege of Vienna through the Treaty of Belgrade.

Stoye, John. *The Siege of Vienna*. London: Collins, 1964. A vivid and well-researched narrative of the siege by a British historian.

Sturdy, David J. *Fractured Europe, 1600-1721*. Oxford, England: Blackwell, 2002. Chapter 7 of this overview of European history describes the relations of Central and Southern Europe with the Ottoman Empire from 1648 through 1720.

See also: Nov. 11, 1606: Treaty of Zsitvatorok; Aug. 22, 1645-Sept., 1669: Turks Conquer Crete; 1656-1676: Ottoman Empire's Brief Recovery; Summer, 1672-Fall, 1676: Ottoman-Polish Wars; 1677-1681: Ottoman-Muscovite Wars; 1684-1699: Holy League Ends Ottoman Rule of the Danubian Basin; Beginning 1687: Decline of the Ottoman Empire; Jan. 26, 1699: Treaty of Karlowitz.

Related articles in *Great Lives from History: The Seventeenth Century, 1601-1700:* Innocent XI; John III Sobieski; Merzifonlu Kara Mustafa Paşa; Leopold I; Louis XIV.

1684-1699
HOLY LEAGUE ENDS OTTOMAN RULE OF THE DANUBIAN BASIN

Following the failed Ottoman Siege of Vienna in 1683, a Christian counterattack ended Ottoman rule in much of the Danubian basin, leading ultimately to the decline of the Ottoman Empire.

LOCALE: Balkans
CATEGORIES: Wars, uprisings, and civil unrest; religion and theology; organizations and institutions

KEY FIGURES

Leopold I (1640-1705), Holy Roman Emperor, r. 1658-1705
John III Sobieski (1629-1696), king of Poland, r. 1674-1696
Charles V Leopold (1643-1690), duke of Lorraine, imperial commander, 1675-1690
Louis William I (Ludwig Wilhelm; 1655-1707), margrave of Baden and imperial general
Eugene of Savoy (François-Eugène, prince of Savoie-Carignan; 1663-1736), imperial commander, 1696-1697
Merzifonlu Kara Mustafa Paşa (1634/1635-1683), Ottoman grand vizier, 1676-1683
Köprülü Fazıl Mustafa Paşa (1637-1691), Ottoman grand vizier, 1689-1691
Amcazade Hüseyin Paşa (1644-1702), Ottoman grand vizier, 1697-1702

SUMMARY OF EVENT

The failure of the Ottoman grand vizier Merzifonlu Kara Mustafa Paşa to take Vienna in September, 1683, provoked a formidable Christian counterattack. During that year of crisis, Pope Innocent XI (1676-1689) brought Holy Roman Emperor Leopold I and Polish king John III Sobieski into a military alliance to which the pope transferred massive funds to subsidize Sobieski's forces.

The Polish king led an allied force of 64,000 men, including imperial units under Duke Charles V Leopold of Lorraine and the electors of Bavaria, Saxony, and Brandenburg, to the Danube. On September 12, 1683, the Ottoman army was decisively routed. The allies, thereafter, pursued the defeated Ottoman army, part of which was destroyed by Sobieski and Charles V at Parkany, near Esztergom (October 9, 1683). Sobieski had made his last appearance in the campaign. The majority of Poles were preoccupied with the affairs of Sweden and Brandenburg, the Baltic and Muscovy. Sobieski had been acclaimed as "the last crusader," but it was doubtful that he could continue to maintain a Polish army so far from home. In any case, the emperor strongly disapproved of Sobieski's meddling in Transylvania and Moldavia.

Meanwhile, Merzifonlu Kara Mustafa Paşa, in Buda, sought to rally what was left of the defeated Ottoman forces. He was already planning a second attempt on Vienna once the winter was over, but his numerous enemies had the ear of the sultan. Only on reaching Belgrade did he learn of the order for his execution (December 25, 1683).

The quick Ottoman collapse presented the allies with unanticipated opportunities. In March of 1684, Pope Innocent founded a new Holy League, consisting of the Holy Roman Emperor, the Polish king, and the Venetian Republic (eager to avenge the loss of Crete in 1669). Later, in 1686, Muscovy, under its regent Sophia, half sister of the future czar Peter the Great, joined the alliance. The league's aim was to liberate Ottoman-controlled Christian territory, and it proved to be one of the most effective coalitions in early modern Europe.

In 1684 and 1685, the commander of the imperial forces, Charles V Leopold, recaptured upper Hungary. The main imperial army then proceeded down the Danube River to Buda, where, after a bloody two-and-a-half month siege and after 145 years of Turkish occupation, the city fell (1686). A decisive battle, close to the historic field of Mohacs (scene of the Hungarian disaster of 1526), ensued in 1687, which opened Sclavonia to imperial forces. In April of 1688, Elector Maximilian II Emmanuel (1679-1726) of Bavaria captured Belgrade. By the close of the year, imperial armies were operating along the line of the Drava and the Danube from Sclavonia to Walachia, but the French king, Louis XIV, could not allow his Ottoman allies to collapse if he were to achieve his own ambitions in the West. In August, therefore, the French crossed the Rhine River, and Leopold was forced to move his best troops and his best commanders, including Charles V, to the west. The Ottomans had breathing space.

In Constantinople, news of the defeat at Mohacs and the loss of Belgrade brought mutiny and mayhem. Köprülü Fazıl Mustafa Paşa, son of the great Köprülü Mehmed Paşa, engineered the deposition of the long-reigning Sultan Mehmed IV Avci and replaced him with his brother, Süleyman İbrahim II (r. 1687-1691), whose premature death led to the accession of his half brother, the dropsical and no-less-inert Ahmed II (r. 1691-1695).

Mustafa Paşa became grand vizier in 1689 and began his reform of the army. He planned a major riposte to the advancing imperialists, and mustered a formidable force with which he recaptured Nish and Belgrade in 1690. Vienna, however, was alerted to the threat, and the second of Leopold's great generals, Louis William I, was sent to meet the challenge. Louis William I confronted the Ottomans at Slankaman, just north of Belgrade, in one of the bloodiest engagements of the entire war. By the end of the day, Mustafa Paşa and most of his commanders were dead on the field, but the victorious imperialists had thirty thousand casualties, mortal and wounded (August 20, 1691), and Belgrade remained in Ottoman hands. This marked the end of the Ottoman counteroffensive, but Leopold was now preoccupied with war with France (1689-1697). Louis William (called Türkenlouis) was needed in the West, and thereafter, the imperial armies made blunder after blunder under the incompetent elector of Saxony, Frederick Augustus I (1694-1733), who was later king of Poland as Augustus II (r. 1697-1704).

Meanwhile, the Venetian Republic, which had joined the Holy League in 1684, the league's first year, enjoyed considerable success. In Bosnia and Dalmatia, it is true that little was achieved, but farther south, under the former defender of Crete, Venetian captain general Francesco Morosini (1618-1694), the Venetians captured Morea (Peloponnese) and pressed on to Athens (September, 1687), where they accidently blew up the Parthenon before moving on to Lepanto. In 1692, however, they failed to retake Crete, and in 1694, they captured Chios but lost it almost immediately, because their rule proved so heavy-handed that they were ejected by a popular uprising. The long decline in Sobieski's health left Poland a half-hearted member of the league, although in 1692 and 1694, Polish raiders reached the upper Dniester River. Sophia launched two unsuccessful expeditions against the Ottomans' vassal, the khan of the Crimea, in 1687 and 1689. Subsequently, her half brother, Peter the Great, captured Ottoman Azov in 1696.

Sultan Ahmed II died in 1695 and was succeeded by Mustafa II (r. 1695-1703), a son of Mehmed IV. Twenty-one years old and brought up in a freer environment than his immediate predecessors, he yearned to emulate the warrior sultans of the past. In August, he led his army to Belgrade, crossed the Danube, and took Lippa by storm (September 7, 1695). In the following year, he crossed the Danube at Semlin and the two armies met in a bloody although inconclusive engagement. Thereafter, Leopold was able to recall the elector with the bait of the Polish throne, and he appointed his best general, Prince Eugene of Savoy, to command the badly demoralized imperial forces in Hungary.

So far, Mustafa had been fortunate that, for two campaigning seasons (1695-1696), he had been pitted against an inferior commander. This time, although he did not know it, he was facing a military genius. The Ottomans reached Belgrade on August 10, 1697, and the main army crossed the Danube, heading for Transylvania. Eugene barred their way at the Tisza River and the sultan turned back toward the Banat region of Temesvár (now in Romania). Eugene's skillful countermarching forced an engagement at Zenta (Senta) in September. It was brilliantly orchestrated, but it also was more of a massacre than a battle. Out of an army of around fifty thousand, Eugene's losses were a mere two thousand. On the other side, the grand vizier and many of his commanders perished; much of the army, and the sultan (minus his baggage and treasure), fled to Temesvár. This was the crowning victory in thirteen years of war.

In January, 1698, the sultan accepted the good offices of the British ambassador to Turkey, Lord William Paget, to negotiate a general peace. The result was the Treaty of Karlowitz (1699), perhaps the most disastrous treaty in Ottoman history, in which sultan and people acquiesced only through the insistence of the new grand vizier, Amcazade Hüseyin Paşa, another Köprülü and a nephew of Fazıl Mustafa Paşa.

Significance

The Holy League of 1684-1699 could be described as the last of the crusades, a grand alliance willed into being by the Papacy to meet the challenge of Islam. For Ottoman history, for the history of the Muslim world as a whole, the Treaty of Karlowitz was overwhelmingly negative, for it initiated the political and military decline of Islam and the Ottomans and the beginning of an epoch of European military superiority, which would lead to the end of the Ottoman Empire and the colonial subservience of most of the Islamic world.

The Treaty of Karlowitz enlarged the Habsburg monarchy greatly and gave it a Danubian as much as a German identity, with Hungary and Transylvania, except for the Banat of Temesvár, passing under Habsburg rule. Venice gained parts of the Dalmatian coast and, briefly, the Morea. Poland recovered Podolia, and Muscovy acquired Azov by a separate treaty of 1700. No less important, the drawn-out war, despite incalculable devastation, gave Emperor Leopold the opportunity, even before the peace was concluded, to establish the future patterns of Habsburg rule in the newly acquired lands. The map of much of the Danubian basin had been completely redrawn.

—*Gavin R. G. Hambly*

FURTHER READING

Davies, Norman. *God's Playground: A History of Poland.* 2 vols. New York: Columbia University Press, 1982. An excellent set on Sobieski's role.

Ingrao, Charles. *The Habsburg Monarchy, 1618-1815.* New York: Cambridge University Press, 1994. A well-written narrative of the period from the perspective of the Holy League.

McKay, Derek. *Prince Eugene of Savoy.* London: Thames & Hudson, 1977. McKay provides a detailed account of Eugene's military career.

Shaw, Stanford J. *History of the Ottoman Empire and Modern Turkey.* 2 vols. Cambridge, England: Cambridge University Press, 1976. An excellent narrative of the period from the Ottoman standpoint.

Spielman, John P. *Leopold I of Austria.* London: Thames & Hudson, 1977. Detailed account of imperial policies.

Stoye, John. *Marsigni's Europe, 1680-1730.* New Haven, Conn.: Yale University Press, 1994. A fascinating history of an Italian officer in the imperial service, surveying the reconquered Danubian basin.

SEE ALSO: Aug. 22, 1645-Sept., 1669: Turks Conquer Crete; Summer, 1672-Fall, 1676: Ottoman-Polish Wars; July 14-Sept. 12, 1683: Defeat of the Ottomans at Vienna; Beginning 1687: Decline of the Ottoman Empire; 1697-1702: Köprülü Reforms of Hüseyin Paşa; Jan. 26, 1699: Treaty of Karlowitz.

RELATED ARTICLES in *Great Lives from History: The Seventeenth Century, 1601-1700:* John III Sobieski; Merzifonlu Kara Mustafa Paşa; Leopold I; Louis XIV; Sophia.

1685
LOUIS XIV REVOKES THE EDICT OF NANTES

King Louis XIV's revocation of the Edict of Nantes removed the remaining guarantees of religious freedom granted to Huguenots in France by King Henry IV eighty-seven years earlier.

LOCALE: France

CATEGORIES: Government and politics; laws, acts, and legal history; religion and theology

KEY FIGURES

Duke de Sully (Maximilien de Béthune; 1559-1641), Henry IV's finance minister

Frederick William, the Great Elector (1620-1688), elector of Brandenburg, r. 1640-1688

Henry IV (1553-1610), Protestant king of Navarre who became a Catholic and king of France, r. 1589-1610

Louis XIV (1638-1715), king of France, r. 1643-1715

Marquis de Louvois (François-Michel Le Tellier; 1639-1691), succeeded his father Michel Le Tellier as minister of war in 1666, reorganized the French army, and became chief adviser to Louis XIV

Michel Le Tellier (1603-1685), French minister of war, 1643-1666, made chancellor in 1677, and an enemy of the Huguenots

Madame de Maintenon (Françoise d'Aubigné; 1635-1719), second wife of Louis XIV, former royal governess

François de Marillac (fl. 1681), intendent of Poitou Province who implemented the first Dragonnades in 1681

Cardinal de Richelieu (Armand-Jean du Plessis; 1585-1642), chief minister of Louis XIII, 1624-1642

SUMMARY OF EVENT

Following the Wars of Religion that tore France asunder during the second half of the sixteenth century (1565-1598), Henry Bourbon, king of Navarre and cousin of the last Valois kings, was accepted as king of France. Henry (now Henry IV) had been a Protestant and leader of the Huguenots during the last phase of the civil wars. To make himself acceptable to most of the nation, he became a Catholic.

Nevertheless, he did not abandon his former comrades in arms. Not only did he make the duke de Sully, a Huguenot, his chief minister, but also, to prevent future persecution of the Protestant minority in France after his death, Henry also issued on April 13, 1598, the Edict of Nantes, an explanation of the edict he had issued at Nantes in 1591. This edict confirmed the rights of Huguenots as recorded in the enactments of his predecessors: They could not be persecuted for their beliefs and could worship wherever they had done so in 1591, including at least one town in every district and in the homes of nobility above a certain rank; provisions were also made for the equal treatment of the Huguenots in the courts and in appointments to office. In addition to these provisions, the Edict of Nantes increased the number of Huguenot safe havens from ten to one hundred, threw open government offices to men of all faiths, and created courts with a mixed religious membership to try cases involving Huguenots.

The Edict of Nantes was a negotiated political treaty between the Catholic king of France and a minority religious group within his kingdom. It provided for a state within a state by giving the Huguenots political and military control over certain sections of the kingdom to ensure them their religious and political rights. Yet it was a settlement that could hardly be expected to survive many years after the death of its chief negotiator. During the reign of Louis XIII, Cardinal de Richelieu, who exercised real control of the state, destroyed the political power of the Huguenots in a civil war that culminated in the siege of La Rochelle in 1628. Richelieu did not, however, move against the freedom of religion that had been granted by the Edict of Nantes. It was not until well into the reign of Louis XIV that such action was taken.

Louis XIV took his title of "Most Christian Majesty" literally. He believed that it was his duty to God to see that all his subjects adhered to the one true religion, and in his own mind there was no doubt but that this religion was Catholicism. Furthermore, in waging war with the predominantly Protestant states of northern Europe, particularly the Netherlands, he believed that the French Huguenots were real, or at best potential, sympathizers with the enemies of the Crown. The elimination of Calvinism in France, which he viewed as an offense against God and himself, would serve a dual purpose. By the 1680's, increasing influence was being exerted upon the king by his fanatically Catholic second wife, Madame de

A public official announces French king Louis XIV's revocation of the Edict of Nantes. (Francis R. Niglutsch)

ON THE REVOCATION OF THE 1598 EDICT OF NANTES

King Louis XIV infuriated many in France when he revoked the Edict of Nantes, which had been signed by King Henry IV in 1598. The edict gave the French Protestant Huguenots certain religious and political rights and also ended the French Wars of Religion (1562-1598). Louis's court historian, the duc de Saint-Simon (1675-1755), gives an account of how the revocation profoundly affected France and the rest of Europe.

The revocation of the Edict of Nantes, without the slightest pretext or necessity, and the various proscriptions that followed it, were the fruits of a frightful plot, in which the new spouse [Madame de Maintenon] was [believed by some to be] one of the chief conspirators, and which depopulated a quarter of the realm; ruined its commerce; weakened it in every direction; gave it up for a long time to the public and avowed pillage of the dragoons; authorized torments and punishments by which many innocent people of both sexes were killed by the thousands; ruined a numerous class; tore in pieces a world of families; armed relatives against relatives, so as to seize their property and leave them to die of hunger; banished our manufacturers to foreign lands; made those lands flourish and overflow at the expense of France, and enabled them to build new cities; gave to the world the spectacle of a prodigious population proscribed without crime, stripped, fugitive, wandering, and seeking shelter far from their country; sent to the galleys nobles, rich old men, people much esteemed for their piety, learning, and virtue, people carefully nurtured, weak, and delicate;—and all solely on account of religion.

Source: Louis de Rouvroy, duc de Saint-Simon, *Mémoires* (pb. 1829-1830), excerpted in *Readings in European History*, edited by James Harvey Robinson (Boston: Atheneum Press, 1906), pp. 382-383.

Maintenon. A widow, she had come to court as governess to the royal children, and because of her common origins, King Louis had married her in a private ceremony. She continually urged the king to develop a tougher policy toward the Huguenots.

The king first tried the velvet glove. He encouraged conversions by the exemption of new converts from personal taxes, and he granted them six livres in a recently established "conversion fund." Yet, as the great majority of the more than one million Huguenots in France were prosperous merchants, manufacturers, and well-to-do farmers, they ridiculed the offer of "pieces of silver." By 1670, the king had decided that it would be necessary to use the iron hand. He began by merely closing Huguenot places of worship and harassing and arresting their clergy. When this move failed to produce the desired result, the king gave the marquis de Louvois, his war minister, carte blanche in dealing with the problem. François de Marillac, the royal intendent in charge of Poitou in 1681, devised a method of forcing conversions by billeting Catholic troops in Protestant homes. Because of the prominence of dragoon units in Poitou, the practice was termed a "Dragonnade."

Soldiers quartered upon the Huguenots were virtually given a free hand outside the law. The military reign of terror that followed is one of the most shameful acts in the annals of French history. Nevertheless, it also failed to produce the desired results. Finally, the king took the ultimate step. In 1685, at the urging of his chancellor Michel Le Tellier, father of the minister of war, the king revoked the Edict of Nantes, and Protestantism became illegal in France. Louis XIV persecuted the Huguenots most cruelly by forbidding escape into exile, by driving them under torture to the Mass, and by separating families.

SIGNIFICANCE

The mass flight of French Huguenots that followed proved to be a severe blow to the state. Approximately 200,000 well-educated bourgeoisie, prosperous merchants, military and naval personnel, and skilled artisans took refuge in England, the Netherlands, Prussia, Scandinavia, Switzerland, Russia, North America, and South Africa. The departure of this large percentage of shrewd capitalists and skilled workers caused a noticeable decline in the French economy. Not only did production drop off in France, but the stimulus the Huguenots gave to the industries of the nations that welcomed them also led to a decline in the demand for French goods.

International condemnation of the revocation was widespread; even Pope Innocent XI denounced Louis's actions. Brandenburg's Frederick William, the Great Elector, indignantly protested and issued his own Edict of Potsdam (1686), whereby he officially encouraged refugee Huguenots to settle in his domains.

From the military point of view, the defection of seasoned infantry, particularly engineers, as well as naval officers into the armed forces of Louis's enemies (notably England, the Netherlands, and Brandenburg) contributed significantly to France's major setbacks during the Wars of the League of Augsburg (1689-1697) and the

Wars of the Spanish Succession (1701-1714).

Many thousands of Protestants, however, had chosen to remain in France, sometimes outwardly professing Catholicism, but secretly holding Protestant services. This practice became known as the Church of the Desert. Persistent harassment by royal officials often aggravated a violent response, the most bloody of which was a guerrilla struggle known as the Camisard Uprising, which occurred in southern France from 1702 to 1705.

—*John G. Gallaher and Raymond Pierre Hylton*

FURTHER READING

Benedict, Philip. *The Faith and Fortunes of France's Huguenots, 1600-1685*. Burlington, Vt.: Ashgate, 2001. A social and religious history of the French Huguenot community from the time the Edict of Nantes was issued until Louis's revocation.

Bernier, Olivier. *Louis XIV: A Royal Life*. New York: Doubleday, 1987. The author takes an extremely sympathetic view of Louis, portraying him as having been deceived about the Huguenot issue by Louvois, and thereby revoking the Edict of Nantes on the basis of misinformation.

Gwynn, Robin D. *Huguenot Heritage: The History and Contributions of the Huguenots in Britain*. London: Routledge & Kegan Paul, 1985. An excellent study of the overseas effects of the revocation. Gwynn makes a good case in favor of Louis XIV's action in revoking the Edict of Nantes as having contributed to his subsequent military defeats.

Holt, Mack P. *The French Wars of Religion, 1562-1629*. New York: Cambridge University Press, 1995. A comprehensive account of French sectarian conflict, a unique account that ties in the seventeenth century war with the better-known wars of the sixteenth century.

Mentzer, Raymond A., and Andrew Spicer, eds. *Society and Culture in the Huguenot World, 1559-1685*. New York: Cambridge University Press, 2002. A collection of essays about Huguenot culture and identity in France from the mid-sixteenth century until the revocation of the Edict of Nantes. Examines the Huguenot's religious and social institutions and their interactions with French state and society.

Ogg, David. *Europe in the Seventeenth Century*. New York: Collier, 1962. Argues that the revocation was deliberately planned as a key element in Louis XIV's policy—a major blunder that had the effect of consigning France to absolutism.

Smith, David L. *Louis XIV*. New York: Cambridge University Press, 1992. Smith takes no particular position in this biography, but uses primary source documents to illustrate the pros and cons of the major issues of Louis's reign.

Wolf, John B. *Louis XIV*. New York: W. W. Norton, 1968. Wolf sees Louis as a victim of his own flawed vision of total unity, which included uniformity of worship.

SEE ALSO: 1625-Oct. 28, 1628: Revolt of the Huguenots; Mar. 6, 1629: Edict of Restitution; 1661: Absolute Monarchy Emerges in France.

RELATED ARTICLES in *Great Lives from History: The Seventeenth Century, 1601-1700:* Frederick William, the Great Elector; Innocent XI; Jacob Leisler; Louis XIII; Louis XIV; Madame de Maintenon; Marie de Médicis; Cardinal de Richelieu; Friedrich Hermann Schomberg; Duke de Sully.

1686
HALLEY DEVELOPS THE FIRST WEATHER MAP

Edmond Halley's weather map illustrated a theory that accounted for major features of Earth's atmospheric circulation, including trade winds and monsoon winds. He based his map on common elements that he abstracted from vast, diffuse particulars, including those derived from newly invented meteorological instruments such as the thermometer and the barometer.

LOCALE: London, England
CATEGORIES: Science and technology; inventions; cultural and intellectual history; astronomy; physics; mathematics

KEY FIGURES

Edmond Halley (1656-1742), an English astronomer and mathematician, the first to determine the elliptical orbits of comets and the first to develop a meteorological map

Sir Isaac Newton (1642-1727), an English mathematician and philosopher, best known for his formulation of the law of universal gravitation and laws of motion

Robert Hooke (1635-1703), an English physicist and inventor, who extended the number and range of instruments to measure physical nature

Robert Boyle (1627-1691), Irish chemist, who was the first to distinguish between an element and a compound, also defined chemical reaction and analysis and formulated a law relating to gases

SUMMARY OF EVENT

Edmond Halley, who was the first to determine the elliptical orbits of comets, especially of the one that bears his name, also developed the first weather map, which he included in his work "Historical Account of the Trade Winds, and Monsoons, Observable in the Seas Between and Near the Tropics, with an Attempt to Assign the Physical Cause of Said Winds." The paper appeared in the *Philosophical Transactions*, a scholarly journal of the Royal Society of London, formed in 1662 to advance the sciences, notably their practical applications.

Halley edited and financed the publication of his friend Sir Isaac Newton's *Philosophiae naturalis principia mathematica* (pb. 1687; *The Mathematical Principles of Natural Philosophy*, 1729; best known as the *Principia*), perhaps the greatest book in the history of science. Halley believed that the underlying order of nature, its component parts and forces, and their changing relationships, interactions, movements, and transformations, could be expressed in mathematical form.

Halley's contributions to meteorology and mapmaking, as well as to many other scientific fields, grew out of his lifelong study of motion: the movement of objects or bodies through time and space, their dimensions or qualities, the effects of their movement, and their changing locations or distances. He often rendered his studies through charts and maps of the earth and sky. He produced terrestrial maps and sky charts, both of which were closely related at the time. Although they differed in method, subject, or purpose, Halley's maps and charts organized and correlated enormous amounts of information through inductive methods.

In 1676, Halley left Queen's College, Oxford, and traveled to Saint Helena Island, off the southwest coast of Africa, to produce an astronomical map of the brighter southern stars. English astronomer John Flamsteed (1646-1719) had produced a map of the brighter northern stars. Halley's *Catalogus stellarum Australium* (pb. 1679; catalog of the southern stars) contained a circular chart of the southern sky, the first catalog made with a telescope. He determined the direction of 341 stars from Earth and from each other, boldly suggesting that since ancient times the stars had shifted positions. He thus offered the first proof that stars moved in endless space.

Halley's skills as an observer and interpreter of natural phenomena were honed from his experience with sea navigation, geography, astronomy, and Newton's mathematics. His work on planetary wind belts involved the study of weather (a set of atmospheric conditions as they occur) and climate (prevailing atmospheric conditions during a given period of time), thus developing a kind of global meteorology. The term "meteorology" comes from the Greek *meteora*, meaning "things in the sky," and was part of the English language by about 1620. For Halley, meteorology studied the result of actions over the entire Earth (and possibly even the entire solar system), events that include solar heating of Earth's surface, atmospheric pressure, temperature, humidity, wind, cloud type, precipitation, and Earth's rotation.

Prior to Halley's time, the ideas of Greek philosopher Aristotle (384-322 B.C.E.) dominated the study of meteorology. Historically, Aristotle's theories had been paramount, but there were many who still believed that sky gods controlled the weather. Others customarily accepted the weather as it came, learning to cope with its constant changes through astrological prediction or the folklore presented in almanacs. Aristotle, in his treatise *Meteorologica* (wr. c. 340 B.C.E.; *Meteorology*, 1812), interpreted weather and climate in terms of four "elements" that he believed made up the material universe—fire, air, water, and earth—and their properties—hot, cold, moist, and dry. His explanations for observed phenomena eventually were proved inadequate, but not until the sixteenth and seventeenth centuries, indicating the revolutionary nature of the ideas of Halley and Galileo (1564-1642), whose work inspired Halley.

Galileo is thought to have initiated the scientific study of weather. In 1593, he invented a thermometer, and in 1638, he conceived of a barometer, with temperature and air pressure being key meteorological components. Like Galileo, Halley believed that accurate scientific knowledge could be obtained only through direct observation, experimentation, and mathematical proof, believing empirical knowledge superior to the traditional knowledge of the ancients, including Aristotle.

For his weather map, Halley drew upon the work of other scientists, including Gerardus Mercator (1512-1594), a Flemish geographer, mathematician, and cartographer known for his method of cylindrical map projection (1568), and Robert Hooke, who developed a mercury-based barometer to determine air pressure. The principle behind this thermometer was discovered by the Italian physicist Evangelista Torricelli (1608-1647). Also, Halley drew upon the work of Robert Boyle. In 1662, improving the instrument Hooke developed to study air, Boyle discovered the law that connects the volume and pressure of a quantity of air or other gas. In 1686, Halley developed a mathematical law linking air pressure to height above sea level, and he explored interactions of wind, temperature, air pressure, moisture, and Earth's rotation. Moreover, Halley's affiliation with the Royal Society of London, beginning in 1678, kept him at the forefront of scientific and technological developments in Britain and continental Europe.

To create his worldwide weather map of winds, Halley employed technical inventions that grew logically from those currently in use or that could be developed from currently accepted theories. Also, he devised ingenious experiments to extract theories from diffuse, interacting, and highly variable data. Halley's weather map, printed from a line engraving on copper, measured 19.25 by 5.75 inches, and was a Mercator projection. It focused on the equator and approximately 30 degrees of latitude north and south, ocean areas where wind belts developed best, atmospheric conditions being more uniform over oceans than over continents.

The map extended 90 degrees west of the prime meridian, which passes through Greenwich, England, and 150 degrees east of it. Its system of reference lines combined 15-degree longitude lines with 10-degree latitude lines, producing rectangles that differ in proportion to latitude. The map, representing about half of Earth's surface, included tapered lines that indicated movement of the trade winds, the steady winds near the equator, and also shorter, thicker arrows that indicated movement of the monsoons. By identifying complex patterns of atmospheric motion that caused those winds, Halley determined, for instance, that the trade winds resulted from the unequal heating of Earth's surface by the sun, one consequence of the 23.5 degree tilt of Earth's axis. Warm air moved outward from the tropics, and cold air moved outward from the poles. Halley realized, however, that earth's rotation from west to east affected the winds moving toward the equator and those moving toward the poles. It caused them to blow from the northeast in the northern hemisphere and from southeast in the southern hemisphere.

In addition, Halley traced the course of the monsoon winds of the Indian Ocean and the western and southern Pacific Ocean. Temperature variations arising from the distribution of landmasses caused the monsoon winds, a seasonal reversal of the trade winds. Monsoons blow from the southwest from April to October and from the northeast between November and March.

Significance

Edmond Halley's weather map, though untitled, became known as "Halley's Chart of the Trade Winds," a chart being a map designed for a specific purpose. In this case, Halley's map aided sea navigation, which was dependent upon ocean winds.

Even though Halley's theories were tentative and provisional, he was able to visually demonstrate—with his maps—fundamental and comprehensive qualities of physical nature. Mapping winds had never before been done. His weather map initiated scientific weather forecasting well in advance of its sporadic appearance in the eighteenth century and its international establishment in the nineteenth century.

—*Timothy C. Miller*

Further Reading

Armitage, Angus. *Edmond Halley*. London: Thomas Nelson and Sons, 1966. A biography that focuses on Halley's many scientific achievements.

Cook, Alan. *Edmond Halley: Charting the Heavens and the Seas*. Oxford, England: Clarendon Press, 1998. A comprehensive account of Halley's life and science.

Ipsen, David Carl. *Edmond Halley: More than a Man with a Comet*. Philadelphia: Xlibris, 2004. Ipsen summarizes Halley's explorations and discoveries.

MacPike, Eugene Fairfield. *Correspondence and Papers of Edmond Halley*. London: Taylor and Francis, 1937. A collection of Halley's correspondence that includes a memoir of Halley by a contemporary.

See also: 1601-1672: Rise of Scientific Societies; 1643: Torricelli Measures Atmospheric Pressure; Summer, 1687: Newton Formulates the Theory of Universal Gravitation.

Related articles in *Great Lives from History: The Seventeenth Century, 1601-1700:* Robert Boyle; Galileo; Edmond Halley; Robert Hooke; Sir Isaac Newton; Evangelista Torricelli.

June, 1686-April, 1689
Dominion of New England Forms

The creation of the Dominion of New England represented the British crown's first major effort to centralize control over the American colonies.

Locale: New England colonies, New York, and the Jerseys

Categories: Government and politics; colonization

Key Figures

Edmond Andros (1637-1714), governor of the Dominion of New England

James II (1633-1701), king of England, r. 1685-1688

Jacob Leisler (1640-1691), merchant and militia captain who assumed control of the New York government in 1689

Edward Randolph (1632-1703), royal collector of customs and secretary of the Dominion of New England

William III (1650-1702), king of England, r. 1689-1702

Summary of Event

Only after the restoration of the Stuart monarchy in 1660, when England recognized the advantages of bringing the American colonies into its expanding commercial system, did the lack of an adequate colonial policy become apparent. By then, however, it was too late. England had permitted its colonies a large measure of local self-government and had demanded little of them. The governments in the American colonies, which had never experienced direct royal control, had become accustomed to independence and wanted no interference, even from a relatively liberal mother country. Massachusetts, the most independent and rebellious of the colonies, not only violated the Navigation Acts and refused to cooperate with Edward Randolph (whom the Crown had appointed collector and surveyor of customs in 1678) but also usurped powers not granted by its corporate charter and denied that the laws of Parliament applied in the Massachusetts Bay Colony. The Crown had no choice but to declare the colony's charter null and void, and it did so in 1684.

By this time, it had become evident that revocation of the colonial charters was necessary for the development of England's commercial plans. The lords of trade issued writs of *quo warranto* ("by what authority?") to Connecticut, Rhode Island, the Jerseys, Pennsylvania, Maryland, the Carolinas, Bermuda, and the Bahamas, in preparation for nullifying their charters. Because the establishment of royal governmental machinery in each colony would have been too expensive, a plan for three unions was devised, one for New England, one for the Middle Colonies, and one for the South.

Only the New England union materialized. It began in the fall of 1685 as a provisional government for Massachusetts, Maine, New Hampshire, and the Narragansett Bay region, and it was supposed to last until a royal governor could be commissioned and sent to America. On December 20, 1686, Sir Edmond Andros arrived to assume the governorship and to organize the Dominion of New England. Rhode Island was incorporated into the union almost immediately, and Connecticut was brought in within a year. New York and the Jerseys entered in 1688.

The commission and instructions drafted for Andros by the lords of trade provided for a governor and council appointed by the king and a representative assembly chosen by the people, but James II had eliminated the provision for an assembly. The governor was empowered to appoint all officials, and, with the council, he was to legislate, levy taxes, establish courts, and sit as a supreme court. All laws were to be sent to England for approval.

Until a committee for codification could develop a uniform body of laws consistent with those of England, each colony was to operate in accordance with its old laws. In the absence of any revenue acts in effect in Massachusetts, the governor and council enacted increased customs, import and tonnage duties, excises, and land and poll taxes. The Puritans habitually had ignored or nullified laws that they disliked, and although the new taxes represented only a small increase, the selectmen of Ipswich led a revolt against them, claiming that they were an instance of taxation without representation.

The matter of taxation was one of several areas of conflict between the Dominion government and the Puritans. In an effort to achieve conformity in the method of granting land and to make the new government self-supporting, the king had ordered that quitrents be collected on all new land granted and that fees be charged for the compulsory confirmation of all old titles. The New Hampshire and Maine colonists welcomed the opportunity to ensure their titles, but the Puritans could not understand why the land was not theirs by right. Because Andros enforced the hated Navigation Acts, New England trade dropped off drastically. The continuing need for English manufactured goods created a drain on the colonies' hard currency.

When the Dominion government attempted to make the administration of justice conform to English law, the Puritans resented the change. Jurors no longer had to be chosen from among the landowners, eliminating some of the power of the leaders of the theocracy. Even more alarming to the Puritans was the Declaration of Liberty of Conscience of April 4, 1687, granting liberty of conscience to all the king's subjects. No longer were the Puritan ministers and schools supported by the taxes of the entire population. When Andros appropriated one of Boston's Congregational churches for Anglican worship, the Puritans began to fear that the Church of England would become established in the colonies.

The Puritans regarded themselves as God's chosen people and interpreted the interference of the English government as a divine punishment upon the younger generation for having slipped from the straight and narrow path. Thus, they anticipated their eventual deliverance from the oppressors. In the spring of 1688, Increase Mather, the influential Puritan clergyman, traveled to England to petition for an assembly and other reforms. When James II was forced to publish a proclamation restoring rights to corporations, Mather and his fellow agents interpreted this concession to include colonial corporations. Mather gained the favor of the attorney general, and the lords of trade agreed to promote a new charter granting more powers to the colonists.

The Dominion of New England, 1686-1689

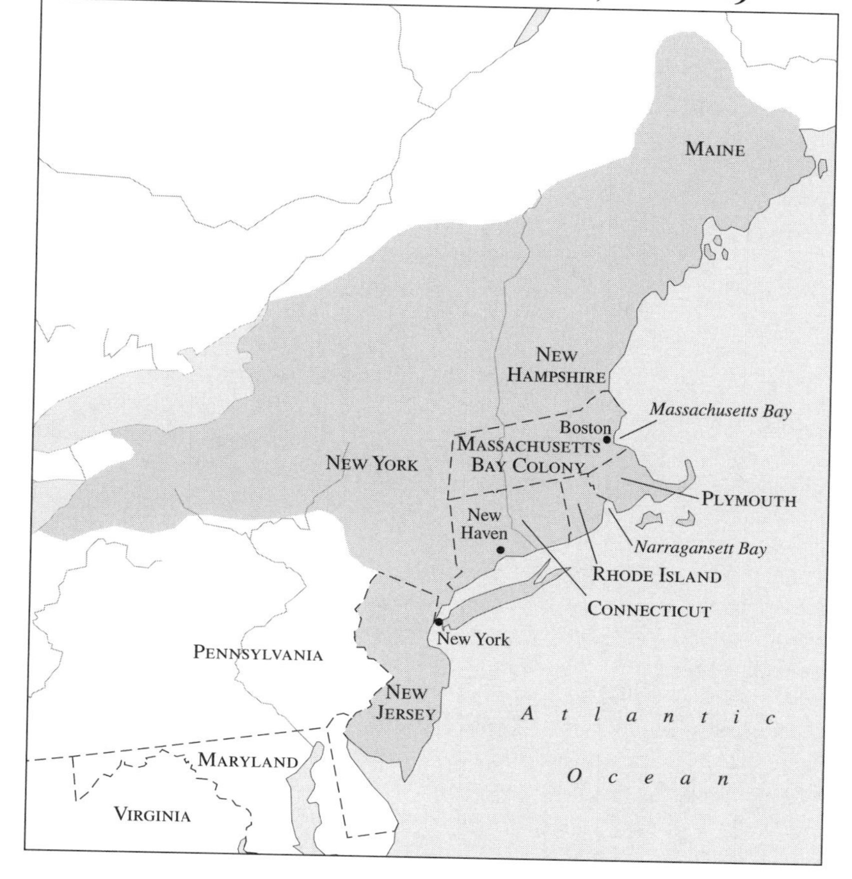

The Glorious Revolution of 1688 and the accession of William III and Mary II in 1689 embodied the sign of deliverance that the Puritans had been expecting. The lords of trade recommended, however, that the Dominion of New England be continued, with two commissioners replacing Andros. In an effort to create the impression that the Puritans were allied with William and Mary against the Dominion and the deposed James, Mather suggested to the Massachusetts Puritans that they overthrow Andros in the name of the new sovereigns.

On April 18, 1689, when troops who had mutinied on the Maine frontier marched into Boston, insurrection broke out, and Andros was imprisoned. Within a month, all the colonies had overthrown the Dominion government. In New York, where Francis Nicholson served as Andros's deputy, the Long Island militia rose in revolt and was joined by the New York City militia, while Nicholson abandoned the province and returned to England. Jacob Leisler, a New York City merchant and militia captain, proclaimed William III and Mary II the sovereigns of England and assumed the position of commander in chief of the province for the next two years. Leisler's Rebellion was driven by a number of complex motives, including Dutch resentment toward English rule and the dominant elite of Anglo-Dutch merchants and landowners, anti-Catholicism, and genuine fear of a French invasion.

On May 9, a convention of delegates from the New England colonies voted to restore the governments and laws of 1686. Once back in power, the Puritan officials of Massachusetts Bay returned to their authoritarian policies, evoking many complaints from non-Puritans. Both pro- and anti-Dominion forces pleaded their cases before William and Mary on the question of New England's future government. King William was more concerned about gaining the Puritans' support for his war with the French than with colonial policy. Thus, a new charter for Massachusetts was sealed on October 7, 1691.

Significance

The new charter allowed for a governor appointed by the Crown, but it also provided for an elected assembly and a council chosen by that assembly. New Hampshire became a separate royal colony, Maine and Plymouth were annexed to Massachusetts, and Connecticut and Rhode Island operated under their old charters. Massachusetts had gained a charter, but new policies ensuring religious freedom and broadening the franchise had destroyed the Puritan oligarchy. In New York, Leisler and his son-in-law, Jacob Melburne, had resisted turning the government over to the new governor sent by William and Mary. They were hanged for treason at the behest of their political enemies, the Anglo-Dutch elite that Leisler had so resented and harassed while in authority. William and Mary did call for elections to a legislative assembly for New York, its first permanent one, but politics in the province remained bitterly divided over Leisler's Rebellion for the next twenty years.

The Dominion of New England, then, while extremely short-lived, had long-term effects upon the governments of all of the colonies within New England, as well as New York. It resulted in the charters of some colonies ultimately being confirmed at a time when they had been in jeopardy, and it resulted in new charters being created for other colonies. The Dominion represented the first attempt of the English crown to make the American colonies resemble England, and its failure incorporated the first formal if halting steps toward defining a distinctively American form of government.

—*Warren M. Billings and Ronald W. Howard*

Further Reading

Andrews, Charles M., ed. *Narratives of the Insurrections, 1675-1690*. New York: Barnes and Noble, 1959. Includes descriptions of the revolt against Andros in Boston and materials related to Leisler's Rebellion in New York.

Barnes, Viola. *The Dominion of New England: A Study in British Colonial Policy*. New York: Frederick Ungar, 1960. Dated but comprehensive study emphasizing the reasons why the Dominion was established and why it failed.

Bremer, Francis J. *The Puritan Experiment: New England Society from Bradford to Edwards*. Rev. ed. Hanover, N.H.: University Press of New England, 1995. Chapter 12 contains information about Andros and the Dominion of New England.

Hall, Michael G. *Edward Randolph and the American Colonies, 1676-1703*. Chapel Hill: University of North Carolina Press, 1960. Focuses on Randolph, a dedicated public servant and England's foremost expert on the colonies, and the role he played in the formation and government of the Dominion.

________. *The Last American Puritan: The Life of Increase Mather*. Middletown, Conn.: Wesleyan University Press, 1988. Demonstrates the important role this remarkable Puritan leader played in both the overthrow of Andros and the acquisition of the royal charter for Massachusetts Bay.

Lusting, Mary Lou. *The Imperial Executive in America: Sir Edmund Andros, 1637-1714*. Madison, N.J.: Fairleigh Dickinson University Press, 2002. Readable recent biography. Refutes the view that Andros was an autocratic tyrant and credits his achievements in administering New York.

Miller, Perry. *From Colony to Province*. Vol. 2 in *The New England Mind*. Cambridge, Mass.: Harvard University Press, 1953. Discusses the decline of Puritan power in the years following the Restoration.

Sosin, J. M. *English America and the Revolution of 1688: Royal Administration and the Structure of Provincial Government*. Lincoln: University of Nebraska Press, 1982. Takes a comprehensive view of the American colonies during the Restoration era. Emphasizes the social and economic tensions behind the political upheavals inspired by the Glorious Revolution in England.

Voorhees, David Williams. "The 'Fervent Zeale' of Jacob Leisler." *William and Mary Quarterly* 51 (July, 1994): 447-472. A provocative interpretation that stresses the religious motivation of Leisler amid the ethnic and economic antagonism in New York.

See also: May 14, 1607: Jamestown Is Founded; July 30-Aug. 4, 1619: First General Assembly of Virginia; Dec. 26, 1620: Pilgrims Arrive in North America; July, 1625-Aug., 1664: Founding of New Amsterdam; May, 1630-1643: Great Puritan Migration; Fall, 1632-Jan. 5, 1665: Settlement of Connecticut; June, 1636: Rhode Island Is Founded; Nov., 1641: Massachusetts Recognizes Slavery; Sept. 8, 1643: Confederation of the United Colonies of New England; Apr. 21, 1649: Maryland Act of Toleration; Oct., 1651-May, 1652: Navigation Act Leads to Anglo-Dutch Wars; Sept. 13, 1660-July 27, 1663: British Navigation Acts; Mar. 24, 1663-July 25, 1729: Settlement of the Carolinas; Mar. 22, 1664-July 21, 1667: British Conquest of New Netherland; Apr., 1670: Charles Town Is Founded; 1688-1702: Reign of William and Mary; Nov., 1688-Feb., 1689: The Glorious Revolution.

Related articles in *Great Lives from History: The Seventeenth Century, 1601-1700:* James II; Jacob Leisler; Mary II; William III.

Beginning 1687
Decline of the Ottoman Empire

After the Ottoman Empire suffered a horrendous military defeat besieging the city of Vienna in 1683, the Austrians drove the Turks out of almost all their provinces north of the Danube. Repeated Ottoman attempts to regain lands during the next decade only led to more disasters for the Turks, resulting in unprecedented loss of vital territories to Austria and initiating domestic crises that corroded the government's power.

Locale: Southeastern Europe and the Middle East
Categories: Government and politics; diplomacy and international relations; wars, uprisings, and civil unrest; cultural and intellectual history

Key Figures

Mehmed IV Avci (1642-1693), Ottoman sultan, r. 1648-1687
Köprülü Fazıl Mustafa Paşa (1637-1691), Ottoman grand vizier, 1689-1691
Süleyman İbrahim II (1642-1691), Ottoman sultan, r. 1687-1691
Eugene of Savoy (François-Eugène, prince of Savoie-Carignan; 1663-1736), Austrian general
Ahmed II (1642-1695), Ottoman sultan, r. 1691-1695
Peter the Great (1672-1725), czar of Russia, r. 1682-1725

Summary of Event

In 1687, the very existence of the Ottoman Empire appeared imperiled. Four years earlier, in 1683, the Ottoman army had laid siege to Vienna, capital of Habsburg Austria. For this monumental military gamble, the Ottomans drained their subjects of men, money, and resources, deploying more than 100,000 troops, innumerable cannon, and enormous stores of food, equipment, and supplies. The gamble failed.

Exhausted by Vienna's defenses, the weary Ottomans staggered before a surprise assault by Polish relief forces. Seizing the initiative, the Austrians and Poles drove the sultan's army out of Hungary, a territory the Ottomans had occupied for 150 years. Also fallen was Belgrade, the pivotal fortress guarding the crossing of the Danube River. Simultaneously, a Russian-Polish alliance began deep raids into the Ottoman provinces of the northern Black Sea coast. Venice landed troops in Ottoman Greece and, in 1687, captured Athens. The Holy League alliance—Poland, the Venetian Republic, Russia, and the Papacy—confronted the Ottomans with a new kind of threat, an enemy alliance able to coordinate attacks simultaneously on multiple fronts.

The virtual disintegration of the Ottoman army compounded the crisis. Deserters and demobilized soldiers became bandits. Officer deaths and mutinies wrecked the command structure. Excessive food requisitions and conscription of peasants set off local famines, hoarding, food riots, and price inflations. Thousands of Muslim refugees fled south to escape the invaders. Desperate for funds, Sultan Mehmed IV Avci decreed special taxes on the salaries of government and religious employees. The sultan preferred the harem and the hunt to the business of state and war, so his exactions quickly became the focus of public fury. The grand vizier, Köprülü Fazıl Mustafa Paşa, responded immediately. Leader of the House of Köprülü, one of the great Osmanli families that included several brilliant grand viziers, he rallied the courtiers, clergy, and soldiers of Istanbul to depose Mehmed.

The reign of Ottoman sultan Ahmed II was considered disastrous for the empire, a reign remembered as the beginning of Ottoman decline. (Hulton|Archive by Getty Images)

Süleyman İbrahim II, the new sultan, assumed the throne as Istanbul lay in the grip of rioting garrison troops, deserters, and armed racketeers. At first, he seemed cowed by these factional struggles in his own streets. Then, in early 1688, he called for the soldiers to march on Belgrade and promised to cut taxes. Those who rallied to his colors became the sultan's police force, crushing the mutinies and restoring order in the capital. The grand vizier then canceled many of the offending taxes. The promised liberation of Belgrade, however, failed to materialize. In fact, the Ottomans hoped for a peace with the Austrians in order to face the Venetian threat in the south and the Russo-Polish danger in the northeast. Vienna, fearing a French invasion of Bavaria, could be persuaded. Taking control over the vast lands of Hungary, Transylvania, and Walachia meant that Habsburg Austria, too, needed stability and peace. However, the Holy League insisted that Austria remain at war so that other members might get their own piece of the Ottomans.

Revolts in Ottoman Serbia during 1689 convinced the Austrians to move south across the Danube and occupy Bosnia and northern Serbia. This conquest placed them on the road to Istanbul, a menace that Sultan Süleyman and Fazıl Mustafa Paşa used to reform and reconstitute the Ottoman military. Frictions between the Roman Catholic Austrians and the Orthodox Christians of Serbia and Bosnia also dampened the enthusiasm of the Balkan peoples for their German "liberators." As the Ottoman army grew, the Austria army shrank, having been called back to Hungary to deal with revolts and to Germany to counter French expeditions across the Rhine River. Finally, the success of the Tatars of the Crimea, allies of the Ottomans, in defending Perekop from Russian assaults meant that Austria would not receive help from the east. Thus, in the autumn of 1690, Fazıl Mustafa Paşa's expedition to Serbia quickly pushed the weakened Austrians back over the Danube and recaptured the vital fortress of Belgrade. Although Turkish raiders sometimes crossed into Transylvania, the grand vizier held off risking a real invasion.

The reforms of the sultan and the vizier seemed, at least superficially, to revive Ottoman military prowess. Habsburg Vienna, preoccupied by French threats against England, Bavaria, and the Netherlands, needed tranquility on the Danube frontiers. With the Crimean Tatars holding off the Russians, Fazıl Mustafa Paşa turned to domestic revival. Corrupt officials lost their offices, new troops joined and received rigorous training, state salaries increased, and military industries such as cannon

The Ottoman Empire c. 1700

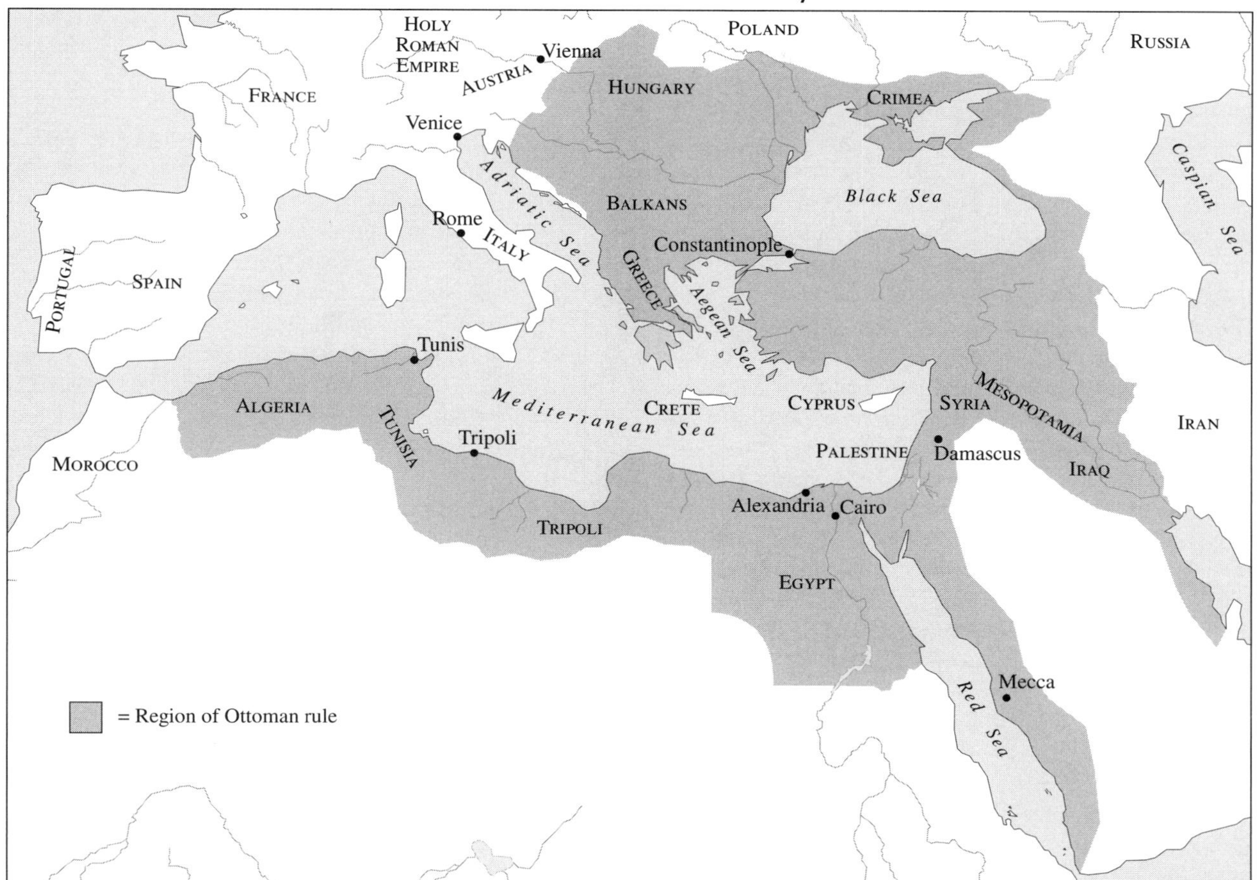

foundries and gunpowder works expanded. Such reforms, however, fit more into traditional patterns than patterns of modernization. Ottoman military manufactures, for example, produced old-style weapons already being replaced in European armies by better equipment. Price controls and commodity requisitions proved less effective in reviving agriculture and bringing down food prices. Thinking that his reforms had already succeeded, the grand vizier returned to the offensive in the summer of 1691.

Fazıl Mustafa Paşa convinced himself that the Ottomans could reclaim their Hungarian lands if they moved quickly. Austrian forces on the plains of Hungary, drawn west to face France, reportedly lacked supplies and numerical strength. Tatar chiefs promised thousands of horse warriors and weaponry. Although Süleyman died as the vizier was preparing his advance, the new sultan, Ahmed II, gave Fazıl Mustafa Paşa his eager support. Determined to surprise the enemy, Fazıl Mustafa Paşa ignored the cautions of his field commanders and led his forces up the Danube toward Karlowitz. In August, 1691, the Ottomans and Austrians clashed at the Battle of Slankamen. The better armed and better disciplined Habsburg infantry ambushed the disorganized Ottoman expedition. The grand vizier was killed after being hit by a bullet in the forehead. His carefully reconstructed army, abandoning its guns and supplies, disintegrated and fled in panic.

Shattered by the losses and bereft of his Köprülü mentor, Sultan Ahmed proved an inept and rudderless ruler. Without Fazıl Mustafa Paşa, contesting political factions soon paralyzed the state. New viziers came and left rapidly. Although the generals managed to reassemble a creditable army, these conscripts lacked the cohesion and sufficient leadership to sustain complex operations, let alone take the offensive. Corruption and venality was revived, coinage was debased, and inflation undermined the economy. Four years of angry, undeclared peace passed between Vienna and Istanbul, but it was Austria and Russia that used these years to strengthen and improve their militaries. Indeed, under a new czar, Peter the Great, Russia managed, in 1696, to capture the port of Azov and gain naval and commercial access to the Black Sea.

The death of Ahmed II in 1695 raised Mustafa II to the sultanate (until 1703). Strongly influenced by the Islamic clergy, Mustafa resolved to lead the army in person, imitating the great warrior sultans of the Ottoman past. Energetic but inexperienced, a few easy victories convinced him the army could sustain and win a massive operation against Budapest. In September, 1697, attempting to take the offensive into Hungary, the sultan began a river-crossing operation near Zenta (Senta). However, as night was falling, Commander Eugene of Savoy and his Austrian army arrived on the scene. Although outnumbered, they pounced on the startled and unprepared Ottomans and annihilated half the Turkish army. Tens of thousands of Ottoman officers and soldiers died and vast stores of supplies and equipment fell into Austrian hands. Mustafa returned to Istanbul completely demoralized, and his surviving forces scattered and mutinied.

SIGNIFICANCE

Zenta ended Istanbul's efforts to regain Hungary and the other territories they once held north of the Danube. These lands now belonged to their Austrian enemies. From this point on, the Ottoman Empire would find itself increasingly on the defensive militarily and depending more and more on the diplomacy of allies such as France to hold conquerors at bay. At the same time, the corrosion of Ottoman internal stability accelerated well into the next century until the former Terror of Europe became known as the Sick Man of Europe.

—*Weston F. Cook, Jr.*

FURTHER READING

Goffman, Daniel. *The Ottoman Empire and Early Modern Europe*. New York: Cambridge University Press, 2002. This work describes the Ottoman-Habsburg relationship of the seventeenth century.

Kinross, Lord. *The Ottoman Centuries*. New York: William Morrow, 1977. An engaging narrative history focused on the personalities of Ottoman history.

McCarthy, Justin. *The Ottoman Turks*. New York: Longman, 1997. A first-rate history of the Ottomans.

Murphey, Rhoads. *Ottoman Warfare, 1500-1700*. New Brunswick, N.J.: Rutgers University Press, 1999. This historical text is focused on the military institutions and soldiers of the empire.

Shaw, Stanford J. *History of the Ottoman Empire and Modern Turkey*. Vol. 1. Cambridge, England: Cambridge University Press, 1976. An excellent detailed analysis using primary sources.

SEE ALSO: 17th cent.: Rise of the Gunpowder Empires; 1638: Waning of the *Devshirme* System; Aug. 22, 1645-Sept., 1669: Turks Conquer Crete; Summer, 1672-Fall, 1676: Ottoman-Polish Wars; July 14-Sept. 12, 1683: Defeat of the Ottomans at Vienna; 1684-1699: Holy League Ends Ottoman Rule of the Danubian Basin; Mar. 9, 1697-Aug. 25, 1698: Peter the Great Tours Western Europe; Jan. 26, 1699: Treaty of Karlowitz.

RELATED ARTICLES in *Great Lives from History: The Seventeenth Century, 1601-1700:* Innocent XI; Merzifonlu Kara Mustafa Paşa; Leopold I; Louis XIV; John III Sobieski.

April 4, 1687, and April 27, 1688
Declaration of Liberty of Conscience

King James II issued the Declaration of Liberty of Conscience in 1687 and again in 1688 in order to promote toleration for all religions in Protestant England. However, hasty implementation and personal bias by Catholic James II actually intensified British religious conflicts, created deep wounds between the two Christian faiths, and divided Britain.

Locale: London, England
Categories: Laws, acts, and legal history; religion and theology; government and politics

Key Figures

James II (1633-1701), king of England, r. 1685-1688
William III (1650-1702), king of England, r. 1689-1702
Mary II (1662-1694), queen of England, r. 1689-1694
Louis XIV (1638-1715), king of France, r. 1643-1715
Innocent XI (Benedetto Odescalchi; 1611-1689), Roman Catholic pope, 1676-1689
Charles I (1600-1649), king of England, r. 1625-1649
Charles II (1630-1685), king of England, r. 1660-1685

Summary of Event

James, duke of York and Albany, was the third son of King Charles I, who was beheaded in 1649, during the English Civil Wars, when James was sixteen years old. After the Restoration of the Anglican (Protestant) monarchy in 1660, Charles II ruled England for twenty-five years with no legitimate offspring. His brother James, a devout Catholic, became King James II of England and Ireland and King James VII of Scotland on February 6, 1685, at the age of fifty-two.

For 132 years prior to James's reign, England had been ruled by monarchs and Parliaments who supported Protestantism within the Church of England, or Anglican Church. Throughout the seventeenth century, the Stuart monarchs, as Supreme Heads of the Church of England, had modified Anglican services to suit their own religious beliefs. Whenever these modifications had seemed to shift the tenor of Anglican services or doctrine in the direction of Catholicism, they had caused the Protestant majority in England to worry and the Catholic minority to rejoice. There was a fear on the part of many that the Catholic James might attempt to make England a Catholic nation once again, and the public supported his accession only when he declared he would uphold Protestantism as the state religion. Nevertheless, four months after James inherited the crown, the duke of Monmouth launched an unsuccessful anti-Catholic attempt to seize the crown. In reprisal, James sanctioned the execution of many insurrectionists in an episode called the Bloody Assizes, which increased the animosity of many Anglicans toward their Catholic monarch.

At the time, English law promoted and protected the Anglican state religion. The Test Acts of 1673 and 1678 prohibited the appointment of Catholics, Puritans, or other Protestant Dissenters to public office or to leadership positions within the army. The penal laws were imposed if one did not receive Communion from the Church of England. The Catholic James II wanted Parliament to repeal these laws. However, his reign had already been threatened militarily, and his largely Anglican army was growing hostile to him, making such a repeal dangerous. James also realized that, even if it were prudent to repeal the acts, Parliament simply would not agree to do so.

In 1686, therefore, James changed his policy: Rather than take the symbolic and potentially dangerous step of formally repealing the Test Acts, James simply disregarded them. He managed to pack the Court of the King's Bench with sympathetic judges, and their decisions allowed him to sidestep the Test Acts without incurring the penalties they had prescribed. Over the next two years, James doubled the size of his standing army, put Catholic officers in positions of command, appointed a Catholic as lord deputy of Ireland, and placed Catholic lords on his Privy Council. In 1686, Pope Innocent XI came to London, and James ceremoniously received the Catholic pope and celebrated Mass, which greatly angered many English Protestants, Anglican and Nonconformist alike.

On April 4, 1687, James issued the Declaration of Liberty of Conscience (also called the Declaration of Indulgence) mandating the free exercise of religion in Britain. This decree noted that the attempts of four reigns to establish one religion in England were hindering trade and depopulating England; in addition, James argued that conformity of religion was impossible to achieve given each subject's innate devotion to the faith of his or her forefathers. The declaration suspended religious penal laws and granted individuals the freedom to practice any religion or none at all. This declaration was largely popular with the people, because it gave equal social and civil rights to everyone.

James's motives in issuing the Declaration of Liberty of Conscience extended beyond Britain's borders. His

American colonies were teeming with religious discontent, threatening the Crown's security in the territories. James was fearfully aware that prevailing opinion supported republicanism. James believed he could garner popular support by including all religions in his declaration of tolerance. The declaration was met with some suspicion, however, as many suspected that his primary objective was to entrench Catholicism in England, not to promote any other religion. At home, moreover, there were fears that James might ally himself with the Catholic Louis XIV of France and become powerful enough to dissolve Parliament. Parliament refused to abolish the Test Act, rendering James's declaration somewhat toothless.

James decided to assert his supreme authority as king: He reissued the full text of his Declaration of Liberty of Conscience on April 27, 1688, and required it to be read on two consecutive Sundays in every church. At the time, the most efficient way for the head of the country to distribute a message to the people was through the nation's pulpits. The new declaration stated that James would present the declaration to the next meeting of Parliament for its confirmation but that for the interim it must be followed based upon his divine right as king. In response, the archbishop of Canterbury and six other bishops distributed thousands of copies of a petition that they had presented to James asking that the order be withdrawn. They pointed out that in 1662 and 1672, Parliament had ruled that the monarch could not suspend Parliamentary powers in ecclesiastical matters. Countering this petition, others asserted the monarch was the supreme authority and that administrative orders must be followed without question, lest dissent lead to anarchy.

Annoyed by the bishops' public distribution of the contentious petition, James charged the bishops with seditious libel for refusing to read the Declaration of Liberty of Conscience from the pulpit. When the bishops refused to post bond assuring their appearance for trial, they were committed to the Prison Tower. At the trial, two of the four justices hearing the case ruled that the petition was not maliciously false and did not constitute sedition, because the bishops had sought Parliament's intervention in an ecclesiastical matter: The judges recommended acquittal to the jury, who complied. The acquittal was praised in London, and it boosted the spirits of those who believed that a king's power should be limited by Parliament; however, James retaliated by dismissing the justices who had ruled against him.

The birth of James's son in 1688 created a Catholic heir to the throne and seemed to preclude any hope of succession by James's Protestant daughter and son-in-law, Mary and William III of Orange, leaders of the United Provinces of the Netherlands. The fear of an English Catholic Dynasty led powerful members of Parliament to act. They offered monetary and military support to William and Mary to take control of the country. Early in November, 1688, William landed in England. William's army was quickly buttressed by deserters from James's forces. Faced with violent riots in London and overwhelming desertion by even his own daughter and relatives, James fled to France on December 23, 1688. Because there was no military engagement and no loss of life, these events were dubbed the Glorious Revolution.

To ensure that Protestantism would never again be threatened, in 1689 Parliament imposed a series of penal laws that even further limited the rights of Catholics, calling the measures the Bill of Rights. This so-called Bill of Rights prohibited Catholics from living within ten miles of London and denied them ownership of land and representation in courts and Parliament. In March, 1689, Louis XIV declared war on Britain and sent French troops to help James lead a war in Ireland to regain his throne. The effort was not successful. On July 4, 1690, James returned to France, where he remained until his death in 1701.

Significance

Centuries of war in Britain proved the impossibility of peaceful coexistence when one religion is elevated over others by imposing religious oaths and tests as prerequisites to qualify for public office. In the Declaration of the Liberty of Conscience, James II called for Parliament to protect and support all religions, yet his ultimate motive was to increase state support of Catholicism. James's preference to aid one religion over another, giving special status rather than equal standing to Catholicism, led to much discontent and eventually to his downfall. James's Declaration of Liberty of Conscience was a missed opportunity to extend religious freedom to all of Britain, and its effects can still be seen in the violence between Catholics and Protestants that is endemic in Northern Ireland today.

Without complete religious toleration, there is often a backlash, as evidenced by the 1689 English Bill of Rights. The framers of the United States Constitution clearly recognized this problem as they hotly debated the topic during the Constitutional Convention of 1789. Article 6 of the Constitution prevents the federal government from requiring a religious test to qualify for a position of public office or trust. Ultimately, the concept of separation of church and state prevailed, and it is embodied in the United States

Constitution's First Amendment, which states that Congress may not establish or prohibit a religion.

—*John R. Elliott*

Further Reading

Foster, Roy F. *Modern Ireland, 1600-1972*. New York: Penguin Group, 1990. Examines how the partition of Protestants and Catholics in Ireland in the 1600's affected the Irish people. Biographical summaries in the book are helpful for understanding individuals who had important roles in Irish history.

Maguire, W. A. *Kings in Conflict*. Belfast, Northern Ireland: Blackstaff, 1990. Features the intrigues as blood-line monarchs vied for power. After Henry VIII overruled the Catholic pope and created the Protestant Church of England, succession wars occurred as religions fought for control.

Murphy, Andrew R., and William Penn. *The Political Writings of William Penn*. Indianapolis, Ind.: Liberty Fund, 2001. Penn, a seventeenth century political and religious philosopher, supported liberty of conscience and strongly encouraged its practice for developing colonial America. This volume presents complete texts of Penn's political writings.

Robbins, Caroline. *The Eighteenth-Century Commonwealthman: Studies in the Transmission, Development, and Circumstance of English Liberal Thought from the Restoration of Charles II Until the War with the Thirteen Colonies*. Indianapolis, Ind.: Liberty Fund, 2004. The author relates how the essays and arguments concerning liberty of conscience were received in America.

See also: Nov. 5, 1605: Gunpowder Plot; 1611: Publication of the King James Bible; Mar.-June, 1639: First Bishops' War; Oct. 23, 1641-1642: Ulster Insurrection; 1642-1651: English Civil Wars; Aug. 17-Sept. 25, 1643: Solemn League and Covenant; 1652-1689: Fox Organizes the Quakers; May, 1659-May, 1660: Restoration of Charles II; 1661-1665: Clarendon Code; May 19, 1662: England's Act of Uniformity; 1673-1678: Test Acts; Aug. 13, 1678-July 1, 1681: The Popish Plot; Aug., 1682-Nov., 1683: Rye House Plot; 1688-1702: Reign of William and Mary; Nov., 1688-Feb., 1689: The Glorious Revolution; Feb. 13, 1689: Declaration of Rights; May 24, 1689: Toleration Act.

Related articles in *Great Lives from History: The Seventeenth Century, 1601-1700:* Charles I; Charles II (of England); Oliver Cromwell; Innocent XI; James II; Louis XIV; Mary II; William III.

Summer, 1687

Newton Formulates the Theory of Universal Gravitation

Newton's theory of universal gravitation provided the physical basis for the Copernican revolution, establishing a mechanical universe governed by universal natural laws and thus forming the foundation for the Enlightenment.

Locale: Trinity College, Cambridge University, England

Categories: Astronomy; physics; science and technology; cultural and intellectual history

Key Figures

Sir Isaac Newton (1642-1727), professor of mathematics at Cambridge University

Galileo (1564-1642), Italian mathematician who formulated laws of motion

Johannes Kepler (1571-1630), German astronomer who formulated new laws of the planets

Robert Hooke (1635-1703), English physicist and secretary of the Royal Society

Edmond Halley (1656-1742), English astronomer who applied Newton's laws to comets

John Locke (1632-1704), English philosopher who applied Newtonian ideas to social theory

Summary of Event

The publication of Sir Isaac Newton's theory of universal gravitation in his monumental treatise *Philosophiae naturalis principia mathematica* (1687; *The Mathematical Principles of Natural Philosophy*, 1729; better known as the *Principia*) marked the culmination of the scientific revolution. This revolution began with the 1543 publication by Nicolaus Copernicus of his heliocentric (Sun-centered) system of the planets (*De revolutionibus orbium coelestium*; *On the Revolutions of the Heavenly Spheres*, 1939; better known as *De revolutionibus*). Copernicus was unable to explain how Earth could rotate on its axis and move around the Sun, however, and his system contradicted the philosophical and theological ideas of his time. Only a few astronomers began to develop his ideas, most notable of whom were Galileo and Johannes Kepler.

In 1609, Galileo began to use the telescope for astronomy and discovered four moons that orbit Jupiter in much the same way that Copernicus described planetary motion around the Sun. He also introduced the concept of inertia, which proposed that motion is the natural state of an object, and described the constant acceleration of gravity. By 1619, Kepler had completed his laws of the planets, which described and correlated the speeds, sizes, and shapes of their elliptical orbits around the Sun. He made an unsuccessful attempt to explain how the Sun could cause the motion of the planets.

The mechanical concepts of Galileo and Kepler were further developed by French philosopher and mathematician René Descartes (1596-1650) and Dutch scientist Christiaan Huygens (1629-1695), but neither was able to successfully account for planetary motion. In the latter half of the seventeenth century, Newton was able to correct and correlate these new mechanical ideas within a unified heliocentric system, but the emergence of this Newtonian synthesis involved many other scientists, and it is difficult if not impossible to assign credit properly.

Newton was born on Christmas Day of 1642 at the farm of his mother's parents near Grantham in Lincolnshire, after his father had died. He was raised by his maternal grandparents and then enrolled in Trinity College, Cambridge, in 1661, to study mathematics under Isaac Barrow (1630-1677). After completing his degree in 1665, he returned home for nearly two years to escape the plague. During this isolation, he began to formulate his ideas about universal gravitation after making a connection between the fall of an apple and the motion of the Moon. His calculations revealed that the Moon in its orbit, which is sixty times farther from the center of Earth than the apple, accelerates toward Earth about 60^2 times slower than the falling apple. Thus, if gravity extends to the Moon, it diminishes according to an inverse-square law. After returning to Cambridge, Newton received his master's degree in 1668 and became Lucasian professor of mathematics a year later on the recommendation of Barrow. For nearly two decades, much of his work remained unknown beyond Cambridge.

In the meantime, Robert Hooke was trying to develop the idea that gravity was similar to magnetic attraction. In discussing the comet of 1664 with Christopher Wren, Hooke suggested that the gravitational attraction of the Sun caused the greater curvature of the comet's orbit near the Sun. After Huygens's formula for centrifugal force appeared in 1673, several scientists, including Hooke, Wren, and Edmond Halley, showed that circular orbits could be explained by a force that varied inversely as the square of the distance from the Sun. They were unable to show, however, that such an inverse-square law could account for elliptical orbits.

In 1684, Halley visited Newton at Cambridge and posed the problem to him. Newton immediately replied that he had solved the problem, but he was unable to find his calculations. Three months later, he sent Halley a paper that successfully derived all three of Kepler's laws. Recognizing the importance of Newton's achievement, Halley returned to Cambridge and urged him to write a book on his new dynamics of the solar system. For nearly two years, Newton concentrated on writing his *Principia*, perhaps the single most important scientific treatise in the history of science.

Sir Isaac Newton. (Library of Congress)

When book 1 of three projected volumes reached the Royal Society in 1685, Hooke claimed that Newton had plagiarized his ideas. Newton was furious and proceeded to delete all references to Hooke. Although the society at first planned to publish the *Principia*, it was short of funds, so Halley agreed to pay the expenses himself. He received the completed manuscript in April, 1686, and it was published in the summer of 1687. In an introductory section entitled "Axioms or Laws of Motion," the three laws of Newton appear as the basis for his study of motion. The first two laws define inertia and force, based on the earlier work of Galileo and Descartes, while the third law introduces the idea that every force has an equal and opposite reaction.

In the first two books of the *Principia*, Newton derives a series of theorems from his three laws to describe motions for various kinds of forces. Using an inverse-square force of attraction, he derives all three of Kepler's laws. In book 3, entitled *The System of the World*, he applies the hypothetical laws of the first two books to the universe as observed. The central concept is the law of universal gravitation, which generalizes the inverse-square law to give the mutual attraction (F) between any two bodies as being proportional to the product of their masses (m and M) and inversely as the distance (R) between them. This is usually written as $F = G\ mM/R^2$ where G is the constant of universal gravitation.

Perhaps the single most important law in the history of science, the law of universal gravitation unifies terrestrial and celestial motions, assigning the same cause to the motion of projectiles and planets. Newton uses it to derive Galileo's law for falling bodies, calculates the bulge of Earth's equator due to rotation and its effect on the acceleration of gravity, gives the first satisfactory explanation of the tides, and shows the requirements for an Earth satellite. He also accounts for the motions of comets, the slow wobbling of the axis of Earth, and small deviations from Kepler's laws in the motions of the planets and the Moon.

The collapse of the geocentric view of the universe had caused consternation and confusion, compounded by the idea of a moving Earth in infinite space. The Newtonian synthesis restored confidence in reason based on experience, giving birth to a new sense of optimism and progress in the eighteenth century that was later called the Enlightenment. It produced a new picture of the world as a great machine consisting of moving bodies subjected to universal laws in perfect order and harmony. Almost immediately it began to influence social theories.

Philosopher John Locke began the task of translating Newtonian science into political and philosophical theory. He argued that individuals are the atomic units of the state, which should be structured by self-evident natural rights such as life, liberty, and property, and the democratic ideals of equality and tolerance. He also suggested that the human mind is a "blank tablet" at birth, in which simple atomic ideas gained by sensation are correlated by the laws of association and reason to form complex ideas. Since reason must be based on experience, human knowledge is limited to the natural world, and humans can know God only through God's universal laws in nature, thus initiating deism as a system of natural religion in which a clockmaker God is revealed only in nature.

Significance

The enlightened ideas of Newton and Locke were brought to France by Voltaire, who, with his mistress, wrote a popular account of Newtonian theory in 1738. In 1776, Locke's ideas were used as the basis of the American Revolution as expressed by Thomas Jefferson in the Declaration of Independence. In the same year, Scottish philosopher Adam Smith published the natural laws that govern economics. In Smith's theory of free enterprise, individuals are subject to market forces, requiring no interference because the market automatically adjusts to the forces of competition according to universal economic laws. Even the arts were affected by these mechanical ideas, giving rise to formalized literary forms and Baroque musical styles.

—*Joseph L. Spradley*

Further Reading

Alioto, Anthony. *A History of Western Science*. Englewood Cliffs, N.J.: Prentice Hall, 1993. Chapter 16, "Such a Wonderful Uniformity," gives a succinct historical account.

Aughton, Peter. *Newton's Apple: Isaac Newton and the English Scientific Revolution*. London: Weidenfeld & Nicolson, 2003. Describes Newton's life and work as part of the scientific rebirth occurring after the English Civil Wars.

Boorstin, Daniel J. *The Discoverers*. New York: Random House, 1983. Chapter 52, "God Said, Let Newton Be!" provides a brief but authoritative historical account.

Chandrasekhar, S. *Newton's "Principia" for the Common Reader*. New York: Oxford University Press, 1995. This work explains the scientific theories explored in *Principia*, including the law of gravitation, theory of the tides, and ideas about revolving orbits and comets.

Cohen, I. Bernard. *The Newtonian Revolution*. New York: Cambridge University Press, 1980. A more-extensive discussion of Newton's work and its influence.

Cohen, I. Bernard, and George E. Smith, eds. *The Cambridge Companion to Newton*. New York: Cambridge University Press, 2002. A collection of essays, including explorations of the methodology of the *Principia* and Newton's argument for universal gravitation.

Manuel, Frank. *A Portrait of Isaac Newton*. Cambridge, Mass.: Harvard University Press, 1968. A well-written scholarly biography of Newton.

Westfall, Richard S. *Never at Rest: A Biography of Isaac Newton*. New York: Cambridge University Press, 1980. Along with the work by Frank Manuel, this is one of the best biographies of Newton and his work.

SEE ALSO: 1601-1672: Rise of Scientific Societies; 1615-1696: Invention and Development of the Calculus; 1620: Bacon Publishes *Novum Organum*; 1623-1674: Earliest Calculators Appear; 1632: Galileo Publishes *Dialogue Concerning the Two Chief World Systems, Ptolemaic and Copernican*; 1637: Descartes Publishes His *Discourse on Method*; 1643: Torricelli Measures Atmospheric Pressure; Late Dec., 1671: Newton Builds His Reflecting Telescope; Dec. 7, 1676: Rømer Calculates the Speed of Light.

RELATED ARTICLES in *Great Lives from History: The Seventeenth Century, 1601-1700:* Giovanni Alfonso Borelli; Pierre de Fermat; Galileo; James Gregory; Francesco Maria Grimaldi; Edmond Halley; Robert Hooke; Christiaan Huygens; Johannes Kepler; Gottfried Wilhelm Leibniz; John Locke; Sir Isaac Newton; John Wallis; Sir Christopher Wren.

1688-1702
REIGN OF WILLIAM AND MARY

The reign of William III and Mary II saw the development of England's system of constitutional monarchy, an expansion of political and religious liberty, creation of the Bank of England, a costly war with France, and the modernization of governmental bureaucracy.

LOCALE: England, the Netherlands, Scotland, and Ireland
CATEGORY: Government and politics

KEY FIGURES

William III (1650-1702), king of England, Scotland, and Ireland, r. 1689-1702
Mary II (1662-1694), joint monarch with William III, r. 1689-1694
James II (1633-1701), king of England, Scotland, and Ireland, r. 1685-1688
Charles Montagu (1661-1715), English statesman and financial leader, Baron Halifax, 1700-1714, and earl of Halifax, 1714-1715
Louis XIV (1638-1715), king of France, r. 1643-1715
Viscount Dundee (John Graham; 1649-1689), Scottish rebel loyal to James II
Sir John Fenwick (1645-1697), English politician and Jacobite conspirator

SUMMARY OF EVENT

William and Mary became joint monarchs in England's Glorious Revolution of 1688-1689. Mary was the eldest child of James II. Her education, directed by the bishop of London, was strictly Protestant. In 1677, she married her cousin, William III of Orange, the powerful and wealthy stadtholder of the Netherlands. Initially, the marriage was not very happy, and Mary was particularly dismayed by her husband's frequent infidelities. Gradually, however, the couple developed respect and affection for each other. Because William was the military commander of Dutch operations against the invading French forces from 1672 to 1678, he was famous as a heroic defender of Protestantism. In the mid-1680's, as Louis XIV appeared likely to launch another invasion of the Netherlands, William looked to England as a potential ally to help overcome the French threat.

Meanwhile in England, James II was attempting to strengthen royal powers and restore Catholicism as the established religion. The people of England had no desire to live through another civil war, however, and so long as James had no heir, their fears of his Catholicism were contained. In June of 1688, however, a son was born to James and his Catholic wife. The many opponents of the king's political and religious policies were dismayed by the birth, because it meant that his daughter Mary was no longer

Representatives of Parliament offer William and Mary the English crown. (Francis R. Niglutsch)

next in line for the throne. Instead, it seems to presage an English Catholic dynasty—an intolerable prospect for most of the king's subjects. In response to this turn of events, the bishop of London and six noblemen (called the Immortal Seven) took the initiative and invited William III of Orange to come to the island to defend Protestantism. William accepted the invitation, primarily because of his desire for English support against Louis XIV, who invaded the German Palatinate in September, 1688.

William landed at Torbay with more than fifteen thousand soldiers on November 5, 1688. Support for James rapidly evaporated, and he fled to France on December 23. A Convention Parliament gathered and proclaimed that the king's flight constituted an act of abdication, whereas Scottish leaders argued that he had forfeited his crown by his pro-Catholic policies against Scotland. Many Parliamentary leaders would have preferred to name Mary as sole monarch, with William as regent. Both she and her strong-willed husband, however, insisted on joint sovereignty.

On February 13, 1689, the Convention Parliament offered the Crown to the couple with the condition that they accept a Declaration of Rights, which required Parliamentary consent to suspend statutes, levy taxes, and maintain a standing army in peacetime. The declaration also condemned various acts of previous kings, including the prosecution of petitioners and the imposition of cruel and unusual punishments. Although William disliked some of the restrictions, he reluctantly accepted them. On April 11, William and Mary were crowned at Westminster Abbey. The following month, Parliament attempted to encourage national unity with the passage of a Toleration Act, which allowed limited religious liberty to Protestant dissidents. In December, another act of Parliament codified the principles of the Declaration of Rights into a Bill of Rights.

The new monarchs faced two interrelated challenges: They needed to establish their authority throughout the realm, and they needed to oppose Louis XIV's expansionism in northern Europe. On May 12, 1689, William joined an alliance with Louis XIV's enemies, which meant participation in the Wars of the League of Augsburg (called King William's War in America). William's most immediate threat, though, was Ireland, where

James II, with French support, remained the king. On July 1, 1690, William's army defeated the Jacobites in the Battle of the Boyne, although Irish Catholics continued to wage war until the surrender of Limerick in 1691, which was followed by the Treaty of Limerick.

Pacification of the pro-Jacobite clans in the Scottish Highlands was more difficult. In July of 1689, the Jacobites were victorious at the Battle of Killiecrankie, although the death of John Graham, Viscount Dundee, doomed their cause. In August, William's victory at Kunkeld secured his authority over most of Scotland. In 1692, after Alexander MacIan MacDonald of Glencoe failed to meet a deadline for swearing allegiance to the Crown, English troops slaughtered MacDonald and thirty-eight clan members in the infamous Glencoe Massacre, which badly stained William's name. Conspiracies to overthrow William and Mary continued. In July, 1694, the Lancashire Plot was quickly suppressed. Two years later, after Sir John Fenwick's conspiracy to assassinate William was uncovered, Parliament sentenced him to death in an act of attainder.

In the war with France, meanwhile, neither side was able to win a decisive victory. England prevailed in the naval Battle of La Hogue (1692), while French forces were victorious in the land Battle of Neerwinden (1693). Fighting dragged on until the signing of the Treaty of Ryswick in 1697, in which Louis was forced to give up most of his conquests. The war, nevertheless, was extremely costly in terms both of finance and of William's popularity at home.

Mary, who had limited interest in affairs of state, generally preferred to leave these matters to her husband. She would, however, assume the direction of government when her husband was out of the country. William, who was perceived as a cold foreigner, was never popular, but he was a competent and assertive leader, and he had the wisdom not to become excessively involved in the domestic affairs of the country.

During the reign of the dual monarchs, political parties were developing from the less cohesive political factions that had formed around the question of the royal succession in the 1670's and 1680's. The parties began especially to cohere after the Triennial Act of 1694 required that no Parliament could last longer than three years. Although most pro-royal conservatives, the Tories, had endorsed the Glorious Revolution, it was the liberal critics of royal power, the Whigs, who firmly supported William's foreign policies and thereby consolidated their position. In 1693, William appointed a ministry drawn from a group of talented Whig leaders, called the Junto, which is now regarded as the forerunner of the modern Cabinet of Ministers.

William's most famous minister, Charles Montagu, was responsible for the 1694 establishment of the Bank of England, which was considered necessary to facilitate borrowing to finance the war with France. The war also stimulated the government to modernize its bureaucracy and system of taxation. In 1695, Parliament's decision not to renew the Licensing Act represented a major step toward the freedom of the press, even though publishers and authors could still be prosecuted on charges of seditious libel. The Act of Settlement of 1701 secured the Protestant succession to the throne and required the monarch to seek the consent of Parliament before engaging in foreign wars for the defense of possessions not belonging to the English crown.

After Mary died childless of smallpox in December, 1694, William showed signs of severe depression, and he became more unpopular than ever. In March, 1702, he died from complications resulting from a fall while riding his horse at Hampton Court. He was succeeded by Mary's younger sister, Anne.

Significance

The reign of William and Mary is remembered primarily for the revolutionary settlement of 1689, which was an important landmark in the development of Britain's system of constitutional monarchy. The royal autocracy of the Stuart Dynasty came to an end, and the practical supremacy of Parliament over legislation and taxation would never again be successfully challenged. In addition, the Toleration Act and the Bill of Rights significantly expanded individual liberties in both England and the English colonies of North America. In America, the impact of the revolutionary settlement can be seen in the Declaration of Independence and the United States Constitution with its first ten amendments.

William and Mary successfully contained the territorial expansion of Louis XIV, while at the same time they defeated their Jacobite opponents in Ireland and Scotland. During their reign, political parties in England began to take their modern form. Several reforms, moreover, promoted the process of modernization, including reorganization in the system of taxation, greater rationalization of the bureaucracy, creation of the Bank of England, and a significant growth in military power.

—Thomas Tandy Lewis

Further Reading

Burnet, Gilbert. *History of His Own Time*. Rutland, Vt.: Charles E. Tuttle, 1992. The only narrative source written by an important observer of the period.

Erickson, Carolly. *Royal Panoply: Brief Lives of the English Monarchy*. New York: History Book Club, 2003. Interesting and useful summaries of about ten pages each, dealing primarily with personal lives of the monarchs.

Hamilton-Philips, Martha, and Robert Maccubbin, eds. *Age of William the Third and Mary the Second: Power, Politics, and Patronage, 1688-1702*. Williamsburg, Va.: College of William & Mary Press, 1989. A collection of scholarly essays about the politics, science, and culture of the period.

Hoak, Dale, and Mordechal Feingold, eds. *The World of William and Mary: Anglo-Dutch Perspectives on the Revolution of 1688-1689*. Stanford, Calif.: Stanford University Press, 1996. Anti-Whigish essays that minimize the importance of constitutional changes and emphasize the theme of modernization.

Kenyon, John P. *Revolution Principles: The Politics of Party, 1689-1720*. New York: Cambridge University Press, 1990. A scholarly study of the ideologies of the Whig and Tory parties of the period.

Macaulay, Thomas. *History of England from the Accession of James II*. Reprint. New York: E. P. Dutton, 1958. A classic nineteenth century narrative written from the Whig perspective—detailed, interesting, and still useful.

Miller, John. *The Stuarts*. London: Hambledon, 2004. An introductory narrative of the dynasty that ruled England from 1603 to 1714.

Van der Kiste, John. *William and Mary*. New York: Sutton, 2003. A concise and interesting dual biography that includes private acts, personalities, politics, and international relations.

Van der Zee, Henri, and Barbara Van der Zee. *William and Mary*. New York: Alfred A. Knopf, 1973. A widely available dual biography that is detailed, scholarly, and readable.

See also: Mar. 24, 1603: James I Becomes King of England; 1642-1651: English Civil Wars; May, 1659-May, 1660: Restoration of Charles II; 1685: Louis XIV Revokes the Edict of Nantes; Apr. 4, 1687, and Apr. 27, 1688: Declaration of Liberty of Conscience; Nov., 1688-Feb., 1689: The Glorious Revolution; 1689-1697: Wars of the League of Augsburg; Feb. 13, 1689: Declaration of Rights; May 24, 1689: Toleration Act; July 27, 1694: Bank of England Is Chartered; May 3, 1695: End of Press Censorship in England.

Related articles in *Great Lives from History: The Seventeenth Century, 1601-1700:* Charles I; Charles II (of England); Oliver Cromwell; James I; James II; First Duke of Leeds; Louis XIV; Mary II; William III.

1688-1704
Genroku Era

Tokugawa urban culture thrived during the Genroku era, financially sustained by the merchant class. Merchants and samurai in Edo, Kyōtō, and Ōsaka patronized the Bunraku and Kabuki theaters and the licensed urban quarters. Literature and art flourished as well, but government repression and fiscal irresponsibility created serious social problems.

Locale: Edo (Tokyo), Kyōtō, and Ōsaka, Japan
Categories: Cultural and intellectual history; literature; theater; art; trade and commerce; government and politics

Key Figures

Higashiyama (1675-1710), emperor of Japan, r. 1687-1709
Matsuo Bashō (1644-1694), haiku poet
Ihara Saikaku (1642-1693), novelist
Chikamatsu Monzaemon (1653-1725), playwright
Hishikawa Moronobu (1618-1694), artist and illustrator
Tokugawa Tsunayoshi (1646-1709), shogun of Japan, r. 1680-1709
Yanagisawa Yoshiyasu (1659-1714), Tsunayoshi's chamberlain, 1688-1709
Sakata Tōjurō (1647-1709), Kabuki actor
Ichikawa Danjūrō I (1660-1704), Kabuki actor
Ogata Kōrin (1658-1716), painter
Ogata Kenzan (1663-1743), painter and potter

Summary of Event

Genroku was the name of Emperor Higashiyama's period of reign in Kyōtō. Emperors had limited authority, since the de facto ruler of Japan was the shogun in Edo. The shogun at this time, Tokugawa Tsunayoshi, became shogun in 1680 through the sponsorship of powerful aristocrats such as Hotta Masatoshi, but after Hotta's assassination four years later, Tsunayoshi assumed full control over the government and nation. He took advice from an altruistic thinker, the distinguished Confucian scholar Hayashi Hōkō (1644-1732), and from Yanagisawa Yoshiyasu, originally Tsunayoshi's obsequious personal attendant, who became the shogun's official chief adviser, or chamberlain. Hayashi counseled thrift and good government, while Yanagisawa catered to Tsunayoshi's whims and had a reputation as a self-promoting schemer.

Because of contradictory advice from aides and his own erratic nature, Tsunayoshi promoted austerity among the people, harshly curtailed the authority of regional lords, and allowed favored court officials to do as they pleased. To make matters more difficult, Tsunayoshi prohibited the killing of living things, including fish, trying to force the entire nation to become vegan. He believed also that he had a strong zodiacal kinship with dogs because he was born in the Year of the Dog. So he ordered special facilities created around Japan for the protection of dogs. These measures made Tsunayoshi very unpopular, earning him the whispered epithet *Inukubō*, the dog shogun.

At the same time, Tsunayoshi and his retinue put in effort and money to promote learning, literature, and the arts, especially among the urban intelligentsia. Though it may not have been Tsunayoshi's intention, his combination of lavish government spending and purchases, the growing demand for interest-bearing commercial loans by aristocrats impoverished by confiscatory government policies, and lax actual enforcement of regulations in the cities assisted the rise of the merchant class.

The result was a relatively affluent society, particularly in the big cities. Entertainers, artists, and writers prospered, catering to the wants of the shogunate, the urban merchants, and the favored aristocrats, and Genroku culture was born. Genroku culture flourished in the three great urban centers of Edo (modern Tokyo), Ōsaka, and Kyōtō, largely consisting of popular art forms that flourished in the entertainment areas of these three cities.

In Edo, Yoshiwara was sanctioned by the shogunate as the sole area that permitted prostitution and its associated cabarets. There were similar entertainment districts in Ōsaka and Kyōtō. The ambiance of these districts was known as *ukiyo* (floating world), in which no commitments were permanent and only the pleasure of the moment counted. This ambiance served as the basis of a variety of popular art and entertainment forms originating in the Genroku Era.

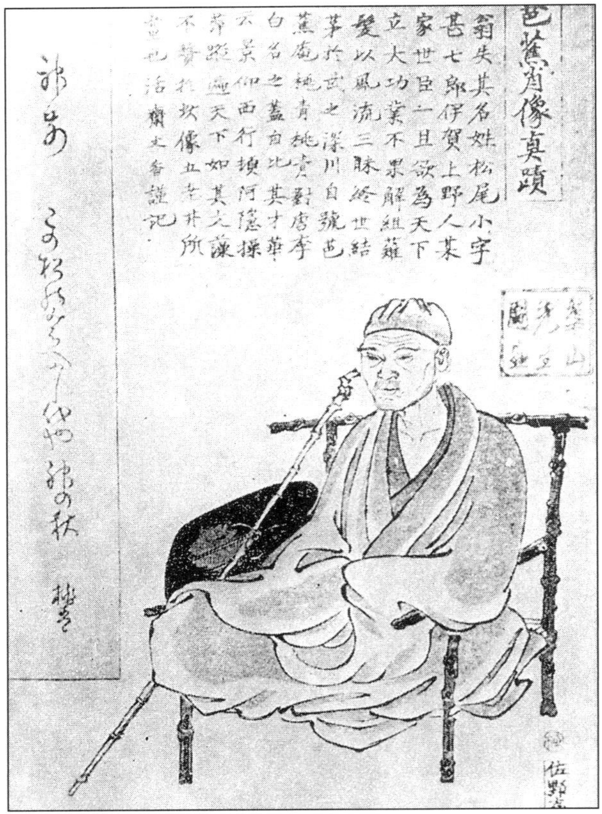

The Tokugawa shogunate thrived culturally during the Genroku era in Japan. Edo poet Matsuo Bashō, a master of haiku, is depicted on a scroll painting. (The Granger Collection)

Two main forms of theater, Bunraku puppet plays and Kabuki musical dramas, were popular in the entertainment areas of all three cities, though the leading Bunraku theater, the Takemoto-za, was in Ōsaka. This puppet theater was established and managed by Takemoto Gidayū, whose troupe of puppet masters and reciters performed many plays written for their theater by Chikamatsu Monzaemon.

Chikamatsu also wrote scripts for the famous Kabuki performer Sakata Tōjurō, who performed in Ōsaka and Kyōtō. Chikamatsu's well-developed plots inspired more realistic action in Sakata's performances, which had previously focused on dance moves, for the most part. This Kabuki style prevalent in Ōsaka and Kyōtō was known as *nuregoto* (poignant performance) because it emphasized pathos in romance. In Edo, the Kabuki actor

Ichikawa Danjūrō I developed a new assertive style of his own: *aragoto* (bold performance), which focused on samurai behavior, giving Edo Kabuki a developmental lead. This *aragoto* approach soon came to characterize Edo Kabuki in general.

Also in Edo, the classically trained painter Hishikawa Moronobu explored new artistic media, developing woodblock prints, depicting popular Kabuki performers and Yoshiwara courtesans in black and white, with coloring painted in by hand. This form, known as *ukiyo-e*, was later printed in color. Moronobu also excelled in making book illustrations for literary classics and for topical albums of his own creation.

The Edo poet Matsuo Bashō developed the seventeen-syllable haiku into a classical poetic form, used mainly in spontaneous sequential compositions at social literary gatherings. Influenced by Zen Buddhism, Bashō imbued his poems with many philosophical and aesthetic elements. He created his own school of haiku composition, spending his later years traveling around Japan, teaching the writing of haiku to regional groups of followers.

Ihara Saikaku began his career in Ōsaka as a poet, famous for long tour de force chains of linked haiku, composed extemporaneously at public gatherings. Saikaku subsequently switched to fiction, writing episodic picaresque novels, spiced with erotic elements and with characters from the merchant or samurai classes. These novels were successful and lucrative prototypes of the popular Edo novel form known as *ukiyozoshi*, the "floating world" narratives of the less-decorous aspects of merchant and samurai life.

Ogata Kōrin and his brother Ogata Kenzan were Kyōtō artists who flourished in the nurturing climate of the Genroku era. Their family had an exclusive textile and kimono business, and their father Sōken's customers included the shogun's family in faraway Edo. Sen learned painting and calligraphy from famous Kyōtō masters, but Kōrin and Kenzan were the first family members to become professional artists. Kōrin worked as a painter of multipanel pictures, mostly of landscapes, birds, or flowers, which were mounted on standing screens, establishing the Rinpa, or Kōrin school of screen painting. His younger brother Kenzan, who later moved to Edo, was an outstanding potter, making unique porcelain objects known as Kenzan-yaki (Kenzan-fired pieces).

The Genroku era concluded with a series of tragedies and disasters that symbolically and materially signaled a leveling of the flourishing artistic and literary cultures. The suppression of the Asano clan and the confiscation of all its property in Kansai by Tsunayoshi's close associates triggered a murderous attack on the Edo mansion of one of Yanagisawa's cronies by clan warriors in December, 1702, followed by the mass suicide of the Asano warriors in February, 1703. On November 22, 1703, an earthquake and tsunami damaged Edo and nearby areas, followed a week later by a firestorm that destroyed most of what remained of Edo.

SIGNIFICANCE

As the Genroku era came to a close, one year after the Asano incident, the Kabuki star Ichikawa was stabbed to death by a disgruntled musician during a performance. Chikamatsu, who was moved by the bravery of the members of the Asano clan in the face of repression and injustice, wrote the play *Kiban Taiheiki* in 1706 to honor them. It was well received by a public weary of Tsunayoshi's regime and was followed by later plays on the same theme, notably Takeda Izumo's *Kanadehon Chūshingura* in 1748.

There were more Chūshingura plays over the years, followed by motion pictures and television series in the twentieth century.

Whereas the great cultural achievements of the Genroku era remain highly valued, Shogun Tsunayoshi and his advisers and associates gained little or no credit for these achievements, being consistently portrayed as villains on stage and in historical fiction. Popular resentment of Tsunayoshi contributed significantly to the public devaluation of succeeding shoguns, making it easier for the Tokugawa shogunate to be overthrown in 1867-1868, which restored the authority of the Meiji emperor.

—*Michael McCaskey*

FURTHER READING

American Haiku Archives. *The Floating World: An Evocation of Old Japan*. New York: Universe Books, 1989. A collection of Edo period poetry. Illustrated with *ukiyo-e* prints.

Bell, David. *Chūshingura and the Floating World: The Representation of Kanadehon Chūshingura in Ukiyo-e Prints*. Richmond, Surrey, England: Japan Library, 2001. A detailed examination of the Chūshingura story in *ukiyo-e* prints and on stage in eighteenth century Japan. Includes a bibliography of further reading.

Bodart-Bailey, Beatrice, ed. *Kaempfer's Japan: Tokugawa Culture Observed*. Honolulu: University of Hawaii Press, 1999. A firsthand description of Tsunayoshi's Japan by Engelbert Kaempfer (1651-1716), a German physician and natural scientist who visited Edo.

Drake, Christopher. "Collision of Traditions in Saikaku's Haikai." *Harvard Journal of Asiatic Studies* 52, no. 1 (June, 1992): 5-75. A good starting place to review Saikaku's achievements as a poet and literary innovator. Includes a detailed comparison of Saikaku and Bashō.

Gerhart, Karen M. *The Eyes of Power: Art and Early Tokugawa Authority*. Honolulu: University of Hawaii Press, 1999. Focuses on art patronage by the Tokugawa shogunate in the seventeenth century.

Kita, Sandy, et al., eds. *The Floating World of Ukiyo-e: Shadows, Dreams, and Substance*. New York: Harry N. Abrams, 2001. This illustrated catalog showcases *ukiyo-e* works archived at the Library of Congress in Washington, D.C. Bibliography.

McClain, James L., and Wakita Osamu, eds. *Osaka: The Merchant's Capital of Early Modern Japan*. Ithaca, N.Y.: Cornell University Press, 1999. A social and cultural history of early modern Ōsaka, with emphasis on the Genroku era.

Totman, Conrad. *Early Modern Japan*. Berkeley: University of California Press, 1993. The most readable and authoritative full-scale account in English of three centuries of Tokugawa history.

Traganou, Jilly. *The Tokaidō Road: Traveling and Representation in Edo and Meiji Japan*. New York: Routledge Curzon, 2004. A history of travel on the old Tokaidō Road between Edo and Kyōtō, recorded in literature and art, with related studies of cartography, transportation, and communication in Tokugawa and Meiji Japan.

Ueda, Makoto. *Bashō and His Interpreters: Selected Hokku with Commentary*. Stanford, Calif.: Stanford University Press, 1992. A chronologically organized anthology of 255 of Bashō's poems, each accompanied by the original Japanese text (transliterated into Western characters) and literal translations. Also includes commentary by Japanese poets and critics from the late seventeenth to the late twentieth centuries.

See also: 1603: Tokugawa Shogunate Begins; 1603-1629: Okuni Stages the First Kabuki Dance Dramas; Beginning 1607: Neo-Confucianism Becomes Japan's Official Philosophy; 1615: Promulgation of the *Buke shohatto* and *Kinchū narabini kuge shohatto*; 1617: Edo's Floating World District; 1680-1709: Reign of Tsunayoshi as Shogun.

Related articles in *Great Lives from History: The Seventeenth Century, 1601-1700:* Hishikawa Moronobu; Ihara Saikaku; Matsuo Bashō; Tokugawa Ieyasu; Tokugawa Tsunayoshi.

November, 1688-February, 1689
The Glorious Revolution

Responding to the birth of an heir to Catholic king James II and the possibility of a Catholic dynasty being founded in England, members of Parliament invited the Protestant William and Mary to seize control of the country. The resulting Glorious Revolution resulted in the decisive institution of constitutionally limited monarchy in England, as well as maintaining the nation's Protestant identity.

Locale: England
Category: Government and politics

Key Figures

William III of Orange (1650-1702), stadtholder of the United Provinces of the Netherlands, r. 1672-1702, and king of England as William III, r. 1689-1702

Mary Stuart (1662-1694), Protestant eldest daughter of James II, wife of William III of Orange, and queen of England as Mary II, r. 1689-1694

James II (1633-1701), king of England, r. 1685-1688

James Edward (1688-1766), son of James II and Mary of Modena

Louis XIV (1638-1715), king of France, r. 1643-1715

Summary of Event

A watershed event in modern English constitutional history, the Glorious Revolution of 1688 was the culmination of the battles between the Parliament and the Crown that had been waged for most of the seventeenth century. The struggle between the proponents of absolutism and constitutional monarchy had begun in earnest during the reign of Charles I, and had resulted in the outbreak of the English Civil Wars in 1642. In 1649, Oliver Cromwell had abolished both kingship and Parliament, at least in their traditional forms. This transformation of the English constitution did not long survive Cromwell's death in 1658, but it did bequeath to the restored government the idea that the Crown no longer had absolute power and that it must rule through Parliament. During his long reign, Charles II conceded this arrangement, although he resisted it when he could and consolidated his royal authority to the extent possible. However, his brother James, who succeeded him as James II in 1685, quickly alienated Parliament, precipitating the crisis that led to the Glorious Revolution.

James II came to the throne a devout Roman Catholic and upholder of the divine right of kings. There was at first, however, no fervor to depose him for such shortcomings, particularly as the already fifty-two-year-old James seemed unlikely to leave a male heir who would perpetuate Catholic rule. James had two Protestant daughters, Mary and Anne, by his first wife, Anne Hyde, daughter of the first earl of Clarendon, so a Protestant succession seemed to be assured. Most English subjects preferred a temporary period of Catholic rule to another era of protracted civil war.

After alienating much of the country by brutally suppressing two weak rebellions, however, James stirred up additional opposition by pursuing his major goal: the restoration of Roman Catholicism in England. It is not clear whether he believed that he could restore Catholicism to its pre-Reformation status, but his first steps were in that direction. He tried to persuade Parliament to repeal the Test Acts of 1673 and 1678, which required officeholders to take Communion according to the rites and ceremonies of the Church of England, contrary to the conscience of devout Catholics.

William III of Orange is told that James II has produced a Catholic male heir. (R. S. Peale and J. A. Hill)

When Parliament refused to repeal the Test Acts, James packed the Court of the King's Bench with new judges, thus securing a decision that permitted him to use his royal prerogative to dispense with penalties incurred under the Test Acts. Parliament bitterly opposed the court's decision because it placed the king above the law. Moreover, James used the court's decision to appoint Catholics to posts not only in government but also in the Church, army, and universities.

Despite mounting opposition, James did not retreat from his pro-Catholic position. In April, 1687, he issued a Declaration of Liberty of Conscience (also known as the Declaration of Indulgence), which suspended all penal laws against Dissenters and Roman Catholics and granted both freedom to worship. James sought the support of Nonconformist Protestants while at the same time furthering the Catholic cause, but he found himself opposed strongly by all Protestants. Undaunted, he issued a second Declaration of Liberty of Conscience on April 27, 1688, and stipulated that all Church of England clergy should read it in their churches in May. When all but a few clergy refused, James arrested and tried seven bishops who had petitioned him to rescind the order, charging them with publishing a seditious libel.

The Glorious Revolution

In June of 1688, two events finally united the country against James: The seven bishops were acquitted, and the king's second wife gave birth to a Catholic heir, James Edward. The unexpected appearance of a male Catholic heir, whose claim would take precedence over the hitherto secure female Protestant succession, threatened the precarious political legacy of Charles II. Anglicans and Dissenters might despise one another, and Whigs and Tories might quarrel, but they all united in rejecting a resurgence of Stuart tyranny, especially when exercised by a "popish" prince.

This unity of purpose among all members of the opposition was reflected in a secret letter sent by seven prominent Whig and Tory leaders to William III of Orange, stadtholder of the Netherlands, on June 30, 1688—the same day that the seven bishops were acquitted. The letter invited William to come to England to save the country from Catholic despotism and to replace James II as king. William was a logical choice: He had a double claim as a Protestant grandson of Charles I and as the husband of James II's daughter Mary. Concerned about departing for England on the eve of war between Louis XIV of France and the League of Augsburg, of which the Netherlands was a member, William had to delay his acceptance until he could be sure that Louis would not attack Holland. He gained this assurance when, on September 2, 1688, Louis invaded the Rhenish Palatinate. With the French army tied down on German soil, William landed in England in early November; by mid-December, he had triumphed in an essentially bloodless struggle, forcing James to flee to France.

As England was now without a government, William called for the election of a Convention. This body, which met on January 22, 1689, was for all practical purposes a Parliament. For three weeks, the representatives debated how power was to be transferred lawfully from James to William. Finally, on February 13, the Convention Parliament formally bestowed the crown jointly upon William III and Mary II. This bestowal was a revolutionary act since the Convention Parliament, which had not been called by royal writ, now became the source of royal power. In a similar fashion, William and Mary were also recognized as joint sovereigns in Scotland. Ireland did not acknowledge their sovereignty until 1690,

James II is told that William III of Orange has invaded England. (Francis R. Niglutsch)

following William's defeat of James II at the Battle of the Boyne.

The offer of joint rule to William and Mary was accompanied by a Declaration of Rights. This declaration, later enacted as the Bill of Rights, was the cornerstone of a body of legislation enacted between 1689 and 1701 known collectively as the revolutionary, or constitutional, settlement. The Bill of Rights of 1689 stated nothing new; instead, it enumerated all the rights claimed by Parliament in its struggle with the Stuarts since 1603. All subsequent legislation in the era of the constitutional settlement attested to and buttressed this shift in power.

Among the other major acts passed by the Settlement Parliaments were the Mutiny Act (1689), by which Parliament exercised control over the king's use of the army; the Act of Toleration (1689), which granted freedom of conscience to all subjects except Catholics, Unitarians, and atheists; the Triennial Act (1694), which required Parliament to be summoned every three years, with no Parliament to last longer than that period; the Treasons Act (1696), which narrowed the definition of treason to an overt act witnessed by two persons, thus preventing the king from eliminating his political opponents simply by accusing them of that crime; and the Act of Settlement (1701), which readjusted the succession of the throne as laid down in the Bill of Rights, because neither Mary, nor her sister Anne, the next in line, had any issue. In the event of Anne's death without issue, the act stipulated that the throne would pass to Sophia of Hanover, granddaughter of James I, and her heirs. Only a Protestant could henceforth sit upon the English throne.

Significance

The Glorious Revolution and the ensuing constitutional settlement had several important consequences. Domestically, a constitutional balance was established between the Crown and Parliament, and measures were enacted to prevent a return to royal absolutism. The revolution thus finally resolved political tensions that had been present in British politics, both overtly and covertly, for more than eighty years.

Internationally, it played a different role. Whereas the Puritan Revolution took place in relative isolation from the Continent, the Glorious Revolution was inextricably bound to affairs in Europe. Eager to advance French aims on the Continent, Louis XIV believed William's arrival in England would initiate a long civil war there that would eliminate Dutch and English interference in his imperial project. Instead, England and the Dutch Republic, united under William and Mary, proceeded to make war against Louis XIV. This outbreak marked the beginning of a century-long conflict between England and France, a struggle fought intermittently until 1815 on the European continent and in the New World and punctuated by French support for Catholic Stuart claims to the English throne.

—*Edward P. Keleher and Wendy Sacket*

Further Reading

Ashley, Maurice. *The Glorious Revolution of 1688*. New York: Charles Scribner's Sons, 1967. Written by a noted historian of the Stuart period, this work provides a concise, balanced account of the year in which James II was deposed.

Hoak, Dale, and Mordechai Feingold, eds. *The World of William and Mary: Anglo-Dutch Perspectives on the Revolution of 1688-1689*. Stanford, Calif.: Stanford University Press 1996. Collection of essays examining the Glorious Revolution within the context of British, Dutch, and European history.

Horowitz, Henry. *Parliament, Policy, and Politics in the Reign of William III*. Newark: University of Delaware Press, 1977. Although somewhat challenging for laypersons, this study provides an indispensable narrative of English politics during the reign of William and Mary.

Jones, George Hilton. *Convergent Forces: Immediate Causes of the Revolution of 1688 in England*. Ames: Iowa State University Press, 1990. A historian of Restoration politics presents fresh perspectives on the events leading up to the deposition of James II.

Jones, J. R. *The Revolution of 1688 in England*. New York: W. W. Norton, 1972. A fine study of the Glorious Revolution that is particularly useful for explaining the motivation for William's involvement in English affairs.

_______, ed. *Liberty Secured? Britain Before and After 1688*. Stanford, Calif.: Stanford University Press, 1992. Collection of essays about history, politics, and constitutional rights before and after the Glorious Revolution. Essayists maintain the Glorious Revolution did not give birth to a more liberal Great Britain, but was part of long process of liberalization that occurred in the late seventeenth century.

Schwoerer, Lois G., ed. *The Revolution of 1688-1689: Changing Perspectives*. New York: Cambridge University Press, 1992. Reflecting contemporary perspectives on the Glorious Revolution, this collection includes scholarly essays presented at a 1989 conference held in Washington, D.C.

SEE ALSO: Mar. 24, 1603: James I Becomes King of England; Nov. 5, 1605: Gunpowder Plot; Mar., 1629-1640: "Personal Rule" of Charles I; 1642-1651: English Civil Wars; Dec. 6, 1648-May 19, 1649: Establishment of the English Commonwealth; Dec. 16, 1653-Sept. 3, 1658: Cromwell Rules England as Lord Protector; May, 1659-May, 1660: Restoration of Charles II; 1661-1665: Clarendon Code; May 19, 1662: England's Act of Uniformity; Apr. 6, 1672-Aug. 10, 1678: French-Dutch War; 1673-1678: Test Acts; Aug. 13, 1678-July 1, 1681: The Popish Plot; Aug., 1682-Nov., 1683: Rye House Plot; 1685: Louis XIV Revokes the Edict of Nantes; Apr. 4, 1687, and Apr. 27, 1688: Declaration of Liberty of Conscience; 1688-1702: Reign of William and Mary; 1689-1697: Wars of the League of Augsburg; Feb. 13, 1689: Declaration of Rights; May 24, 1689: Toleration Act.

RELATED ARTICLES in *Great Lives from History: The Seventeenth Century, 1601-1700:* Charles I; Charles II (of England); Oliver Cromwell; James I; James II; Louis XIV; Mary of Modena; Mary II; William III.

Beginning 1689
REFORMS OF PETER THE GREAT

Peter the Great instituted a series of reforms designed to Westernize the Russian military, economy, religious institutions, bureaucracy, and political and social structures. These reforms helped Russia develop into a major European power, with the strength, the clout, and the will to intervene in international affairs involving the traditional powers of Western Europe.

LOCALE: Russia
CATEGORIES: Government and politics; social issues and reform; economics

KEY FIGURES

Peter the Great (1672-1725), czar of Russia, r. 1682-1725
Alexis Kurbatov (d. 1721), influential financial adviser to Peter
François Lefort (1656-1699), close friend and associate of Peter
Aleksandr Danilovich Menshikov (1673-1729), close companion of Peter who helped reform the Russian army
Patrick Gordon (1635-1699), Scottish soldier of fortune who helped reform the Russian army
Alexis Petrovich (1690-1718), son of Peter the Great who opposed his father's reforms

SUMMARY OF EVENT

The reign of Peter the Great marked the emergence of a decisive Russian influence in European affairs, an influence that would last into the twenty-first century. It was Peter who inaugurated modern Russia's vigorous and aggressive foreign policy against its three neighboring states, Sweden, Poland, and the Ottoman Empire. Through the Great Northern War (1700-1721), he decisively broke Sweden's supremacy in the Baltic, while his wars against the Ottoman Turks and his interference in the internal affairs of Poland set precedents that later Russian rulers would follow in subsequent decades. These great strides made by Russia in Eastern Europe were to a considerable extent the result of Peter's extensive program of reforms, which touched all facets of Russian life.

Many of the reforms undertaken by Peter the Great were influenced by his contacts with Western Europe. As a young man, his companions included a number of Westerners, including Patrick Gordon, a Scottish adventurer who sought his fortune at the czar's court, and the German François Lefort. The transfer of Russia's capital to the new city of St. Petersburg symbolized the Western orientation of Peter's reign, and the number of foreigners in Russian service increased significantly after his celebrated journey to Western Europe in 1697-1698. Largely as a result of this journey, Peter decided to undertake a selective Westernization of his country, especially in financial and political administration, foreign and domestic trade, the military, the church, education, and society in general. Gordon and Lefort, for example, were recruited to work with Aleksandr Danilovich Menshikov, one of Peter's closest advisers and friends, in order to modernize the obsolete Russian army.

The reforms that Peter brought about were designed not only to strengthen Russia as a nation but also to strengthen his rule over that nation. He sought practical Western techniques and skills, rather than theory and philosophy, that could be applied directly to improve Russia's political system, economy, and military forces.

When these techniques were introduced into Russia, the result was a country half European and half Russian. This contradiction can be seen in the financial reforms carried out by Alexis Kurbatov, one of Peter's leading advisers, who substantially increased government revenues by imposing new taxes and increasing existing ones. Such policies added to the misery and hardship of the general population. Peter's political reforms produced an expanded bureaucratic structure, which was clearly designed to be more efficient and augment the autocratic power of the czar.

Queen regent Sophia was forcibly seized and whisked off to a convent at the start of Peter the Great's reign. Sophia was the czar's half sister. (Francis R. Niglutsch)

Peter improved Russia's domestic and foreign trade with the West, using mercantilist theories of extensive state control over goods to be shipped abroad. Primary emphasis was given to the development of industry, including mining and the manufacture of military equipment such as cannons. Substantial funds were provided for Russia's industrial growth. Peter sought to make his nation more independent in meeting its own essential needs, especially for his numerous military campaigns.

The size of the Russian military was increased, training was provided by Western officers brought to Russia for that purpose, and the quality of Russian weapons was improved. A new policy of raising military forces through an expanded conscription system provided the sizable forces Peter needed for his campaigns. He also established the first Russian navy of note.

Among other reforms, Peter abolished the patriarchate of the Russian Orthodox Church and placed religious affairs under the control of a government department. He ordered the establishment of technical schools to provide the needed skills for government officials and military officers. Less significant but still often noted reforms include the elimination of the old Russian calendar in favor of the Julian calendar and the adoption of Western dress for the upper classes of society. The Russian alphabet was also simplified.

Peter's policies had the broad effect of creating a larger urban population, which was somewhat better educated than previously. New skills were needed among large segments of the population, especially in industry. The institution of serfdom remained essentially the same, however, as far as the daily lives of individual peasants were concerned. Peter's efforts to reach his objectives led to the creation of a table of ranks of military and government officials: Persons of lower social status could climb higher on this table on the basis of merit and service to the state. Possessed of a violent temper, Peter demanded total loyalty from his subordinates, and he punished those who fell into disfavor or were suspected of disloyalty.

Peter the Great. (R. S. Peale and J. A. Hill)

Such a range of reforms obviously meant changes in the traditional Russian way of life, and they provoked discontent and resistance. A serious serf rebellion broke out but was crushed by Peter's military forces. By 1710, some of the remaining opposition to Peter found a champion in the czar's disgruntled son Alexis Petrovich. As the years passed, Peter's suspicion of his son's activities increased. The final break between the two came in 1718, when Peter, suspecting Alexis of involvement in a plot to repeal the reforms and cooperate with Russia's foreign enemies, forced him to renounce his succession to the throne. Not satisfied with this, the czar cast him into prison where, in June, 1718, he died from repeated tortures.

SIGNIFICANCE

Peter's methods notwithstanding, his reforms had an undeniable impact upon Russian history, causing Russia to emerge from its Byzantine-Asiatic medieval past. The Petrine framework of modern Russia, particularly its governmental and social structure, remained relatively intact until the Revolution of 1917. Although the country, like its geography, was half European and half Asian, the domestic transformation of Russia strengthened it to the point where it could henceforth play a significant role in the international affairs of Europe.

One of the major controversies in the field of Russian historiography has been the true significance of Peter's reforms. To some scholars, the importance of these reforms simply cannot be overemphasized; to others, their significance has been greatly exaggerated. Most scholars who study the Petrine period conclude that, while some of Peter's reforms were relatively limited in their impact or actually began under his predecessors, the impact of his economic and military policies in particular was decisive. Moreover, the forceful methods he employed to generate change are noteworthy, even if they were not always admirable or even successful.

—*Edward P. Keleher and Taylor Stults*

FURTHER READING

Anderson, M. S. *Peter the Great.* 2d ed. New York: Longmans, Green, 1995. Balanced and comprehensive account, emphasizing aspects of continuity during Peter's reign.

Anisomov, E. V. *The Reforms of Peter the Great: Progress Through Coercion in Russia.* Armonk, N.Y.: M. E. Sharpe, 1993. This Russian historian interprets Peter as a conservative seeking to strengthen the autocratic system.

Cracraft, James. *The Petrine Revolution in Russian Culture.* Cambridge, Mass.: The Belknap Press of Harvard University Press, 2004. Third of three books examining how Peter the Great's reforms profoundly altered Russian culture. In this volume, Carcraft describes the changes in publishing, literature, and the Russian language. His two previous books examine architecture and the visual arts.

_______. *The Revolution of Peter the Great.* Cambridge, Mass.: Harvard University Press, 2003. Cracraft emphasizes the revolutionary nature of Peter's reforms, maintaining Peter's policies created a cultural revolution that changed how Russians perceived their world.

_______, ed. *Peter the Great Transforms Russia.* 3d ed. Lexington, Mass.: D. C. Heath, 1991. Excellent collection of essays assessing Peter's leadership and achievements; detailed and comprehensive.

De Jonge, Alex. *Fire and Water: A Life of Peter the Great.* New York: Coward, McCann & Geoghegan, 1980. Positive view of Peter's successes in moving Russia away from its old ways, thanks to his insatiable curiosity, dynamic energy, and sweeping authority.

Hughes, Lindsey. *Russia in the Age of Peter the Great.* New Haven, Conn.: Yale University Press, 1998. Hughes, a professor of Russian history at the University of London, provides a detailed description of Peter's attempts to modernize Russia.

Kliuchevskii, Vasili. *Peter the Great*. New York: St. Martin's Press, 1961. A noted Russian historian interprets Peter as a restless reformer, without a master plan to fulfill.

Massie, Robert K. *Peter the Great*. New York: Alfred A. Knopf, 1980. Detailed sympathetic biography, focusing on Peter's dynamic leadership and the creation of a major European power. Reprinted in paperback in 1986.

Oliva, L. J. *Russia in the Era of Peter the Great*. Englewood Cliffs, N.J.: Prentice-Hall, 1969. Comprehensive account (under two hundred pages) of Peter's rule and significance.

SEE ALSO: Feb. 7, 1613: Election of Michael Romanov as Czar; Jan. 29, 1649: Codification of Russian Serfdom; 1652-1667: Patriarch Nikon's Reforms; Apr., 1667-June, 1671: Razin Leads Peasant Uprising in Russia; Mar. 9, 1697-Aug. 25, 1698: Peter the Great Tours Western Europe.

RELATED ARTICLES in *Great Lives from History: The Seventeenth Century, 1601-1700:* Alexis; Ivan Stepanovich Mazepa; Nikon; Michael Romanov; Sophia.

1689-1694
FAMINE AND INFLATION IN FRANCE

The economic downturn that began in France with the Wars of the League of Augsburg in 1688 was capped by a great famine. Killing up to one-tenth of the population, the famine, combined with expensive warfare, helped to empty the French treasury. It also convinced the Crown to step up its incarceration of the poor and of vagrants, and it exposed the weaknesses of the French economy and its tax system.

LOCALE: France
CATEGORIES: Economics; natural disasters; government and politics

KEY FIGURES

Louis XIV (1638-1715), king of France, r. 1643-1715
François Salignac de La Mothe-Fénelon (1651-1715), archbishop of Cambrai
Madame de Maintenon (Françoise d'Aubigné; 1635-1719), an educator and queen consort of Louis XIV

SUMMARY OF EVENT

The famine of 1693-1694 has seared itself into the social imagination as one of the worst events in French history. The weather had changed, marked by colder than usual temperatures for several years. It was the beginning of what historians have labeled a "mini-ice age," when mean summer temperatures dropped by about 1 degree centigrade.

Beginning in 1692, however, a series of wet, cool summers and shorter growing seasons devastated the grain harvest. Wheat especially was left rotting or unripened in the fields, and the previous year's wheat supply was barely sufficient to hold off famine. The harvest of 1692 was terrible, and that of 1693 catastrophic. In Normandy, travelers and royal officials described corpses lying unburied along the roads, with those still alive subsisting on acorns and grass. With a weakened population and unhealthy food sources, intestinal disorders, infections, and various pestilences sickened and killed many of the survivors. Between 1.3 million and 2 million men, women, and children, roughly one-tenth of the population, perished in less than 3 years. Historian Joël Félix has pointed out that the deaths were equivalent to the losses sustained by the French in World War I.

The regional, and even local, nature of subsistence crises like those of 1693-1694 cannot be overemphasized. France during the *ancien régime* was a collection of local economies, each circumscribed by the lack of transportation, roads, and regional markets. It was not unusual to find one village plunging into famine, while another scarcely thirty miles away was virtually unscathed. Subsistence crises in France were typically wheat crises. They were often less severe in areas such as coastal Brittany or the Mediterranean littoral, where fish made up a significant part of the diet, or in regions where buckwheat or chestnuts could be used for bread flour. Where wheat was dominant, though, especially in the cereal plains of the north, the crises could be fearsome. The more generalized crises of 1660-1661 and of 1693-1694 thus left some regions relatively untouched, while devastating others. Lower Languedoc and Brittany fared better than Normandy during the great famine of 1693-1694. Paris, with its powerful state officials and developed transportation system, did far better than many small cities and towns.

The economic crises of 1688-1694 and the great famine were also knit into larger demographic patterns in the seventeenth century. Since the Black Death of the fourteenth century had devastated the European population, subsistence crises and full-scale famines had recurred at irregular intervals. Population and resources remained in precarious balance, even though the long-term trend was one of slow population growth. The seventeenth century was, on balance, far worse than the sixteenth century had been. There had already been a previous, widespread famine at the outset of King Louis XIV's personal reign in 1661-1662. There were poor harvests and serious food shortages at the outbreak of the Wars of the Fronde (1648-1653), and yet another in 1698.

The subsistence crises provoked by nature were exacerbated, however, by human-made crises. The disorders and violence of the Fronde devastated large swaths of the French countryside. Steeply rising taxation from Louis XIV's wars placed increasing burdens on the peasantry, who paid the vast majority of French taxes through the taille, or hearth tax. Between 1688 and 1697, the Wars of the League of Augsburg stretched French finances and the tax burden to the breaking point. The league pitted the combined forces of the Habsburgs, the Dutch, and the English against French claims to new territory. The costs of prosecuting a war against so many opponents forced the king to collect tax revenues in advance from future years' taxation. The consequences in the countryside were plain to see. Increasing numbers of peasants fell into the class of landless or nearly landless laborers, while a few wealthy peasants concentrated more land into their hands.

The spiraling price of bread by 1692 also had a domino effect on the entire French economy. A typical family spent 50 percent to 60 percent of its income on bread alone; and when the supply failed, bread prices doubled and then quadrupled in many areas. As food prices escalated, the sale of cloth dropped off dramatically, throwing textile workers out of production. From cottage spinners and weavers to the urban workshops of dyers, drapers, and finishers, their looms and workshops went silent. Since textiles and agriculture were the mainstays of the French economy, the ripple effect spread into other crafts and mercantile operations as well. This set off two apparently contradictory movements in the economy. When inflation struck bread prices, deflationary trends set into other sectors. Prices fell as demand fell for goods other than bread, and the economy as a whole became depressed. Deflationary, rather than inflationary, prices marked most of the reign of Louis, until after his death in 1715.

Ordinary people were far from passive in the face of recession, famine, and death. Local court records show that poaching increased in the countryside, along with food theft and begging; and both urban and rural commoners took to the streets in riots that alarmed authorities everywhere. The food riot was the most characteristic form of popular disturbance in early modern Europe. More than one hundred of them were recorded in 1690's France, in which women played prominent roles. These often took the form of angry mobs gathering at bakeries or mills, where they would insist that grain or bread be sold at what they considered a fair price.

The French state was more aware of the scale of the catastrophe than contemporaries gave them credit for, but their tools were limited. State charity scarcely existed in seventeenth century France, and private charity was insufficient to meet the crisis. François de Salignac de La Mothe-Fénelon, soon to be archbishop of Cambrai, sent a famous letter in 1694 to Louis XIV's second wife, Madame de Maintenon, for the king to see. "All of France is no more than a huge hospital," he wrote, "desolate and without provision." On October 20, 1693, the king had published an ordinance requiring each community to feed its poor, but wealthier residents often resisted the large contributions that were expected of them.

In the provinces, *parlements* issued decrees requiring bakers to sell bread, and they organized massive almsgiving to calm the food riots that were breaking out in every quarter. Nearly one-third of the population of Rouen received daily alms and thousands more begged at the height of the crisis. In Paris, the Louvre palace courtyard was converted into an enormous outdoor bakery, producing 100,000 loaves per day to be distributed to the poor. In their urgency to supply the cities and prevent widescale urban disorder, however, officials stripped bare many rural areas and left the villagers to starve. One northern village recorded the deaths of 60 percent of its inhabitants in 1694 alone. The state's most permanent response was to incarcerate what it called the deserving poor and vagrants in state hospitals, reportedly to prevent disorder and theft.

SIGNIFICANCE

The famine of 1693-1694, and the subsequent losses to the French treasury from peasants who could no more afford to pay the taille than they could afford to feed themselves, added to the French state's fiscal woes. The mounting costs of the Wars of the League of Augsburg finally became insupportable. In September, 1697, the French and the Dutch negotiated the Treaty of Ryswick, ending the Nine Years' War. Louis XIV gave up many of his territorial conquests of the past thirty years, although he kept Strasbourg. The double burden of war and famine had proved too much for even Europe's largest state to sustain.

While famine stalked parts of France again in 1709-1710 (the famously cold winter in which it was said that wine froze in the king's glass at Versailles) and in 1740-1741, the years 1693-1694 saw the last great famine mortality in France. Population growth resumed, lands were brought back into cultivation, and communities slowly reconstructed themselves. Within a decade, the demographic losses had been recouped. However, the possibilities for disorder during food crises never were far from the minds of officials. French ministers were fitfully mindful of the need to build more roads and canals and to better understand the distribution of population and food, but there were too many other pressing demands upon state revenue in the eighteenth century. The poor harvest of 1788 would again help fuel popular unrest and bread riots in 1789, and would become one of many streams of discontent flowing into the French Revolution.

—Zoë A. Schneider

Further Reading

Collins, James B. *The State in Early Modern France*. New York: Cambridge University Press, 1995. The best modern study of the French state in this period, revising many old assumptions about seventeenth century government and the economy in particular.

Felix, José. "The Economy." In *Old Regime France, 1648-1788*, edited by William Doyle. New York: Oxford University Press, 2001. An excellent chapter addressing the nature and limitations of the French economy and tax system.

Kettering, Sharon. *French Society, 1589-1715*. New York: Oxford University Press, 2001. This work describes the human consequences of plagues, famines, and the French economy in villages and towns.

Treasure, Geoffrey. *The Making of Modern Europe, 1648-1780*. New York: Methuen, 1985. Treasure places the French experience in the context of the European economy and climate of the time.

See also: 17th cent.: Birth Control in Western Europe; 17th cent.: England's Agricultural Revolution; June, 1648: Wars of the Fronde Begin; 1661: Absolute Monarchy Emerges in France; 1661-1672: Colbert Develops Mercantilism; 1689-1697: Wars of the League of Augsburg; Sept. 20, 1697: Treaty of Ryswick.

Related articles in *Great Lives from History: The Seventeenth Century, 1601-1700:* Jean-Baptiste Colbert; François Salignac de La Mothe-Fénelon; Louis XIV; Madame de Maintenon.

1689-1697
Wars of the League of Augsburg

The Wars of the League of Augsburg launched a global conflict involving a coalition of European powers against France. The wars produced little territorial change and failed to resolve major issues that were revisited in subsequent wars.

Locale: Western Europe, the British Isles, North America, the Caribbean, Africa, Asia

Categories: Wars, uprisings, and civil unrest; expansion and land acquisition; government and politics

Key Figures

James II (1633-1701), king of England, r. 1685-1688

Leopold I (1640-1705), Holy Roman Emperor, r. 1658-1705

Louis XIV (1638-1715), king of France, r. 1643-1715

Mary II (1662-1694), eldest daughter of James II, Protestant wife of William of Orange, and queen of England, r. 1689-1694

Victor Amadeus II (1666-1732), duke of Savoy-Piedmont, 1675-1730

William III of Orange (1650-1702), Protestant leader of the United Provinces of the Netherlands, and king of England, Scotland, and Ireland as William III, r. 1689-1702

Summary of Event

The Wars of the League of Augsburg is also known as the Nine Years' War and, in North America, King William's War. It involved a coalition of European powers—the League of Augsburg (Emperor Leopold I and German princes), Sweden, Spain, the Netherlands, Savoy, and England—fighting against France. King Louis XIV of France had been pursuing an aggressive foreign policy since the 1660's, attacking the Spanish Netherlands in the War of Devolution (1667-1668) and waging war against the Dutch (1672-1678), earning the lifelong enmity of William of Orange, Protestant leader of the Netherlands. William was to become king of England as William III after his successful invasion of England and after the Glorious Revolution (1688).

Several issues brought the major powers into conflict, including the French desire for territory and influence within the Holy Roman Empire, Leopold I's goal of maintaining control in the empire and securing territory from the Spanish Succession, and William III wanting to protect the Netherlands and prevent French hegemony in western Europe.

This war was the first in a series of global conflicts between the European powers who attacked each other's colonies in Asia, Africa, the Caribbean, and North America in addition to action in the British Isles and western Europe. The Treaties of Nijmegen (1678-1679), which ended the French-Dutch War and hostilities between other European nations, had given France stronger borders, but King Louis XIV continued to add territory (Lorraine and German areas), through the so-called reunion policy and use of his army of 340,000. The Peace of Ratisbon (1684; also known as the Peace of Regensburg), which was to last twenty years, recognized territories that were seized by the reunions and French control of Strasbourg and Luxembourg.

Such aggressive actions caused Leopold I and German princes to form the League of Augsburg in 1686 to uphold the territorial arrangements of the Peace of Westphalia (1648) and Treaties of Nijmegen and to provide a quota of troops. Although religious factors were not as important as they were in the Thirty Years' War (1618-1648), Louis XIV's revocation of the Edict of Nantes in 1685, which stripped French Protestants of their limited religious and political rights, was viewed as an aggressive act.

The military action began in September, 1688, when the French army attacked Philippsburg in the Palatinate of the empire to try to make the Peace of Ratisbon a treaty and force the emperor to accept it within three months and to influence the election of the archbishop of Cologne. Louis XIV sought to retain influence within the empire. The movement of the French army away from the Netherlands allowed William of Orange to launch his invasion of England, which initiated the Glorious Revolution. William sought to gain the English throne to use England's military resources against the French. James II was overthrown by William, who was his son-in-law, and by Mary II (Mary Stuart), James's daughter, and the two became joint rulers of England.

James II fled to France, where he received assistance in his attempt to control Ireland for use as a springboard for regaining the English throne. An Anglo-French naval action at Bantry Bay, Ireland, was inconclusive in May of 1689, but William III's victory over James II at the Battle of the Boyne in July, 1690, kept Ireland under English Protestant control. The Treaty of Limerick signed in October, 1691, provided for a general amnesty, religious toleration for Catholics, and transport of Irish soldiers to France. However, these provisions were rendered ineffectual by measures passed by Ireland's Protestant-dominated legislature. Supporters of James II were also defeated in Scotland. Warfare in the British Isles produced the most decisive results of the entire war.

William III formally declared war on Louis XIV in May, 1689, and the Grand (Triple) Alliance was formed. It included Leopold I, the League of Augsburg, the Dutch, England, Sweden, Spain, and Savoy. The alliance's mandate was to return France to its borders as defined by the Peace of Westphalia and the Treaty of the Pyrenees (1659). The French army devastated the Palatinate in the winter of 1688-1689, France declared war on the Netherlands in November, 1688, and this area was the scene of major engagements with the French winning victories at Fleurus (July, 1690), Mons (April, 1691), Steenkerk (August, 1692), and Neerwinden (July, 1693). Failure to follow up these victories, however, allowed the allies to remain in the field. After the French defeat at Namur (September, 1695), neither side held an advantage in the Netherlands.

France had scored a major naval victory over an Anglo-Dutch fleet at Beachy Head (July, 1690) in the English Channel, but the French did not press their advantage and the allies regained naval control by defeating the French navy at Barfleur-La Hogue (June, 1692), thus preventing any future French-supported invasions of the British Isles by James II. During the course of the war, the English navy established a presence in the Mediterranean.

In northern Italy, the French invasion of Savoy caused the duke of Savoy-Piedmont, Victor Amadeus II, to join the anti-French coalition. A major French victory at Marsaglia in October, 1693, however, led Savoy to seek terms with France, producing the secret Treaty of Turin (June, 1696) whereby Savoy left the Grand Alliance, thus allowing French troops to concentrate their efforts on Catalonia in Spain and besiege Barcelona, which fell on August, 1697, causing Leopold I to seek peace.

In fighting outside Europe, the Dutch captured Pondicherry in India in September, 1693. Along the African coast, France regained Gorée and the River Senegal. Military action in the Caribbean was inconclusive, as the French repulsed English attempts to capture French possessions. In North America, the French and English raided each other's colonies and were supported by their American Indian allies, thus establishing a pattern for subsequent Anglo-French conflicts.

In 1695, Louis XIV began to negotiate with the allies separately, hoping to break up the Grand Alliance. Several factors led to the Treaty of Ryswick, negotiated in September-October, 1697, which ended the war: war weariness, economic pressure, French desire to secure some territorial gains, William III's worries about the stability of the Grand Alliance, Leopold I's concern about the failing health of King Charles II of Spain (1665-1700), and possible division of the Spanish empire.

In September of 1697, the English, Dutch, and other powers came to terms with the French; Leopold I and Louis XIV concluded their agreement in October, 1697. The major provisions involved French evacuation of Catalonia; French retention of forts seized from Spain, including Luxembourg; French abandonment of territory seized east of the Moselle River; French retention of Alsace, including Strasbourg; and France yielding in the disputes over Cologne and the Palatinate. Lorraine was restored to its duke, and Louis XIV recognized William III as king of England but refused to expel James II from France as William III demanded.

The Dutch gained an extensive commercial treaty with France. In North America, conquests were restored to the original "owners," and the question of control of Hudson Bay in Canada was referred to a group of commissioners.

SIGNIFICANCE

The extensive peace terms produced no great advantages for any country, although recognition of William III allowed England to emerge as a major power, as did Leopold I's Austria. Tensions elsewhere in Europe erupted into major wars within a few years: the Great Northern War (1700-1721) and the Wars of the Spanish Succession (1701-1714). The vast military undertakings on a global scale resulted in tremendous expenditures, which escalated greatly in future wars. England's establishment of the Bank of England in 1694 provided funds for subsequent conflicts through which England acquired a worldwide empire.

—Mark C. Herman

FURTHER READING

Baxter, Stephen B. *William III and the Defense of European Liberty, 1650-1702*. New York: Harcourt, Brace & World, 1966. Baxter covers the lifelong struggle of William of Orange against French aggression, highlights William's plans for the invasion of England, and examines William's military actions in the war.

Black, Jeremy. *European Warfare, 1660-1815*. New Haven, Conn.: Yale University Press, 1994. The author, who has published extensively on military and diplomatic history, places this struggle within a broader chronological context and describes weaponry, tactics, and strategy.

Childs, John. *The Nine Years' War and the British Army, 1688-1697: The Operations in the Low Countries*. New York: Manchester University Press, 1991. In addition to discussing the political and diplomatic context of the war, Childs provides a detailed account of British and allied war efforts in the Netherlands.

Rose, Craig. *England in the 1690's: Revolution, Religion, and War*. Oxford, England: Blackwell, 1999. Rose describes how the war transformed England by uniting rival Whigs and Tories against a common enemy, accustoming the country to new levels of taxation and returning the country to the larger arena of European affairs.

Spielman, John P. *Leopold I of Austria*. New Brunswick, N.J.: Rutgers University Press, 1977. This biography of one of the main protagonists in the war examines Leopold's policy and military actions in western Europe and his protracted struggles in eastern Europe.

Symcox, Geoffrey. *Victor Amadeus II: Absolutism in the Savoyard State, 1675-1730*. Berkeley: University of California Press, 1983. Symcox focuses on the implications of the war for southern Europe and Savoy's struggles against the French, an often neglected aspect of other studies.

Troost, Wouter. *William III, the Stadholder-King: A Political Biography*. Translated by J. C. Grayson. Burlington, Vt.: Ashgate, 2004. A comprehensive biography by a Dutch historian that includes information about the war and the formation of the Grand Alliance.

Wolf, John B. *Louis XIV*. New York: W. W. Norton, 1968. This excellent biography analyzes Louis XIV's foreign and military policy prior to and during the war.

See also: 1617-1693: European Powers Vie for Control of Gorée; May, 1640-Jan. 23, 1641: Revolt of the Catalans; July, 1643-Oct. 24, 1648: Peace of Westphalia; Nov. 7, 1659: Treaty of the Pyrenees; Mar. 22, 1664-July 21, 1667: British Conquest of New Netherland; May 24, 1667-May 2, 1668: War of Devolution; Jan. 23, 1668: Triple Alliance Forms; Apr. 6, 1672-Aug. 10, 1678: French-Dutch War; Aug. 10, 1678-Sept. 26, 1679: Treaties of Nijmegen; 1685: Louis XIV Revokes the Edict of Nantes; 1688-1702: Reign of William and Mary; Nov., 1688-Feb., 1689: The Glorious Revolution; July 27, 1694: Bank of England Is Chartered; Sept. 20, 1697: Treaty of Ryswick.

Related articles in *Great Lives from History: The Seventeenth Century, 1601-1700:* Charles II (of Spain); James II; Leopold I; Louis XIV; Mary II; William III.

February 13, 1689
Declaration of Rights

The Declaration of Rights installed William III and Mary II as joint rulers of Britain and settled the question of the royal succession. It established both a constitutional monarchy for Britain and a list of the rights of British subjects, and it formed the basis for the later English Bill of Rights.

Locale: London, England
Categories: Laws, acts, and legal history; government and politics; social issues and reform

Key Figures

William III (1650-1702), king of England, r. 1689-1702
Mary II (1662-1694), queen of England, r. 1689-1694
James II (1633-1701), king of England, r. 1685-1688
John Somers (1651-1716), chairman of the Declaration of Rights committee and later chief minister to William III, 1696-1700
Henry Powle (1630-1692), speaker of the House of Commons in 1689
First Marquess of Halifax (George Savile; 1633-1695), speaker of the House of Lords in 1689
Anne (1665-1714), daughter of James II and later queen of England, r. 1702-1707, and of Great Britain, r. 1707-1714

Summary of Event

In the mid-1680's, England under James II was rendered unstable by the monarch's suspension both of Parliament and of anti-Catholic legislation, as well as by widespread fears that his marriage to Mary of Modena would produce a Catholic heir. On June 10, 1688, the feared heir was born and named James Edward. On June 30, a group of prominent Englishmen invited William III of Orange, husband of James's daughter Mary, to bring an army to defend English liberties against tyranny. After William's army arrived on November 5, James soon felt forced to flee to France. By January 22, 1689, a Parliament convened to settle the question of James II's deposition and the royal succession.

The Parliament that generated the Declaration of Rights was presided over by Henry Powle, speaker of the House of Commons, and George Savile, first marquess of Halifax, speaker of the House of Lords. Powle, Halifax, and the Whig attorney John Somers were the lead negotiators with William and Mary in the process of offering them the English crown. Somers played a crucial role in convincing Parliament to determine, on January 28, 1689, that the throne had been abdicated by James II. The Declaration of Rights, which resulted from months of negotiations in Westminster, was approved by Parliament on February 12, 1689, and was formally accepted by William and Mary the following day, at Whitehall Palace. In exchange for agreeing to the Declaration of Rights issued by what became known as the Convention Parliament of 1689, William and Mary would become the jointly ruling monarchs of England, Scotland, and Ireland.

The declaration not only created the monarchs William III and Mary II but also settled the question of succession: If William and Mary failed to produce children together, the line would pass to Anne, daughter of James II and his first wife Anne Hyde, and her direct descendants. Failing an heir in Anne's line, the crown could pass to a child of William III by a wife other than Mary.

Besides settling the royal succession, the Declaration of Rights asserted the "rights and liberties of the subject." It opened with a list of criminal deeds committed by James II that were claimed to be contrary both to English law and to "freedom." Citing such actions as James's suspension of Parliament, his abuse of the legal system, and his maintenance of a standing army, the declaration concluded that James sought to root out both Protestantism and traditional "laws and liberties" from the realm of England, Scotland, and Ireland.

After citing James's tyrannical behavior, the declaration described the Convention Parliament's establishment by William III of Orange and its principal task of "vindicating and asserting" the "ancient rights and liberties" of the realm of England, Scotland, and Ireland. The declaration then included a list of assertions accepted by William and Mary, a number of which delineated basic rights of British subjects. Somers presided over the drafting of what would later become known as the English Bill of Rights.

The declaration outlawed the levying of excessive bail and fines, as well as "cruel and unusual punishments," and took steps to reform the jury system. The right of citizens to petition the king was declared to be inviolable. Reflecting the religious tensions between Catholics and Protestants during the period, the declaration also asserted that Protestant citizens could legally bear arms for self-defense.

The majority of the declaration's assertions of British rights, however, focused on protecting Parliamentary power, effectively creating a constitutional system of monarchy. The declaration outlawed royal suspension of legislation, disallowing any attempt at absolute rule by the monarchy. The declaration also required that elections to the legislature be free and that freedom of speech in Parliament be protected, ensuring that its proceedings would not be compromised by royal intervention. Standing armies were held to be dependent upon Parliamentary consent. Parliament was declared the sole authorizing body for royal revenue generation and spending. Finally, the declaration stipulated that Parliaments were to be held "frequently."

Through patently anti-Catholic propositions, the Declaration of Rights revealed the anxiety that had been created by James II's Catholicism and the resulting ascendancy of Protestant forces in the English government. The declaration included new forms for the oaths of allegiance required by officers and legislators. The belief that a British ruler might be deposed because of excommunication by papal authority was specifically outlawed, and office holders were required to affirm that no foreign ruler had any jurisdiction within the realm of England.

Though the Declaration of Rights settled the issue of William and Mary's joint rule immediately after its formal acceptance, it soon was revised and expanded as the Bill of Rights Act. Significant additions to the Declaration of Rights included a formal declaration that England was a Protestant nation and that no Catholic could succeed to the English throne; however, much of the text of the Bill of Rights follows that of the earlier declaration. Somers, for his work in negotiating with Parliament and in drafting the declaration's list of rights, was rewarded by William and Mary with the position of solicitor general; he would go on to be a key player in William and Mary's administration, becoming lord chancellor and Baron Somers of Evesham in 1697.

The Bill of Rights was read to William III and Mary II at their coronation, which took place in Westminster Abbey on April 11, 1689. Immediately afterward, the Bill of Rights passed through Parliament. It was not until December 16, 1689, when William and Mary gave the bill royal assent, that the liberties and reforms originally asserted by the Declaration of Rights became law.

SIGNIFICANCE

The Declaration of Rights led to the transformation of British government, destroying the notion of the divine right of kings. The declaration set in motion the formation of a system of constitutional monarchy, in which royal power was contingent upon Parliamentary consent. The Declaration of Rights was thus the first and most critical strike in the Parliamentary moves against absolute monarchy that have come to be known as the Glorious Revolution.

The Declaration not only set up William III and Mary II as joint rulers of England, Scotland, and Ireland but also settled the question of succession, ensuring that Anne would rule after William. The declaration, especially in its revised form as the Bill of Rights, decisively defined Britain as a Protestant state, excluding Catholics from the throne. It also profoundly affected constitutional development elsewhere, particularly in the United States. The Declaration of Independence (1776) follows the model of the Declaration of Rights, opening with a list of tyrannical acts by the government of King George III (r. 1760-1820), while also including a set of assertions of the basic rights of citizens. The U.S. Bill of Rights (1791) is clearly indebted to the list of fundamental rights embedded with the 1689 declaration.

—*Randy P. Schiff*

Further Reading

Ashley, Maurice. *The Glorious Revolution of 1688.* London: Hodder and Stoughton, 1966. Exhaustive analysis of the circumstances surrounding the parliamentary removal of James II, with an emphasis on political and legal traditions.

Cruickshanks, Eveline. *The Glorious Revolution.* London: Palgrave-Macmillan, 2000. Historical analysis of the years of political and religious crisis immediately preceding the declaration. Offers a revised view of James II as a revolutionary leader.

Rakove, Jack N. *Declaring Rights: A Brief History with Documents.* New York: St. Martin's Press, 1997. Presents seventeenth century English legal history, placing the American Bill of Rights in the context of English common law. Provides the texts of numerous primary sources, including the 1689 Declaration.

Schwoerer, Lois G. *The Declaration of Rights, 1689.* Baltimore: Johns Hopkins University Press, 1981. Detailed analysis of the declaration and the historical circumstances in which it was composed, with special emphasis on legal precedents and legislative tradition.

Smith, David L. *The Stuart Parliaments, 1603-1689.* New York: Oxford University Press, 1999. Presents an exhaustive description of the structure and functions of Parliament, with separate essays on the key assemblies that shaped seventeenth century legislation in England. Includes appendices with detailed information on parliamentary representatives and acts.

See also: Dec. 18, 1621: The Great Protestation; May 6-June 7, 1628: Petition of Right; Mar., 1629-1640: "Personal Rule" of Charles I; Nov. 3, 1640-May 15, 1641: Beginning of England's Long Parliament; 1642-1651: English Civil Wars; May, 1659-May, 1660: Restoration of Charles II; 1661-1665: Clarendon Code; May 19, 1662: England's Act of Uniformity; 1673-1678: Test Acts; 1679: Habeas Corpus Act; Apr. 4, 1687, and Apr. 27, 1688: Declaration of Liberty of Conscience; 1688-1702: Reign of William and Mary; Nov., 1688-Feb., 1689: The Glorious Revolution; May 24, 1689: Toleration Act.

Related articles in *Great Lives from History: The Seventeenth Century, 1601-1700:* James II; Mary of Modena; Mary II; William III.

April 18-July 31, 1689
Siege of Londonderry

Londonderry, a Protestant town that supported William III and Mary II, was besieged by Royalist forces loyal to King James II during the War of the Two Kings. Williamite ships eventually broke the boom on the River Foyle and relieved the city.

Locale: Ulster, Ireland
Category: Wars, uprisings, and civil unrest

Key Figures

James II (1633-1701), king of England, r. 1685-1688

William III (1650-1702), stadtholder of the United Provinces of the Netherlands, r. 1672-1702, and king of England, r. 1689-1702

Richard Talbot (1630-1691), earl of Tyrconnel, 1685-1691, lord deputy of Ireland, 1687-1689, and titular duke of Tyrconnel, 1689-1691

George Walker (1645/1646-1690), Anglican Protestant clergyman and co-governor of Londonderry, April-July, 1689

Alexander MacDonnell (1615-1699), third earl of Antrim and Jacobite military commander

Sir William Stewart (1653-1692), first Viscount Mountjoy and commander of troops originally garrisoned in Londonderry

Robert Lundy (d. before 1717), governor of Londonderry, December, 1688-April, 1689

Percy Kirke (d. 1691), British military commander

Friedrich Hermann Schomberg (1615/1616-1690), commander in chief of the Williamite army in Ireland

Baron de Pointis (Jean-Bernard-Louis Desjean; 1645-1705), French naval engineer who designed the boom across the River Foyle

Summary of Event

The events of 1688-1689 in England threw Ireland into a state of uncertainty. In the Glorious Revolution of 1688, William III of Orange, stadtholder of the United Provinces of the Netherlands, had invaded England at the invitation of powerful members of Parliament, and King James II had fled from England to France. William III and his wife Mary II, daughter of the deposed king, had been declared joint sovereigns of England, Scotland, and Ireland by the Declaration of Rights in February of 1689. The lord deputy of Ireland, Richard Talbot, earl of Tyrconnel, was known to have been a favorite of the Catholic King James, but most of the Protestant population, especially in Ulster, preferred the Protestant William and Mary. After Parliament passed the declaration and formally endorsed the Glorious Revolution, Tyrconnel openly threw in his lot for King James.

During November to December of 1688, however, positions had not yet been made clear, and there was a great deal of confusion and lack of direction among the people of Ireland. In order to strengthen his position—come what may—Tyrconnel decided to shift some of the military units under his command. He ordered that the Protestant detachments commanded by Sir William Stewart, Viscount Mountjoy, be dispatched from Londonderry to Dublin. A Catholic unit under the seventy-three-year-old Alexander MacDonnell, third earl of Antrim, was sent to take up their Londonderry post. Londonderry was one of the more significant garrison towns in Ulster. Before the seventeenth century, it had been a Catholic Irish town, Derry, but the Protestant plantations of Lowland Scots and some Welsh and English settlers who migrated there had turned it into a Protestant stronghold. Heavily subsidized by merchant investors from London, the town had been renamed Londonderry.

Antrim was tardy in getting organized, and the plan went awry when Mountjoy lost patience and set out for Dublin on November 23, 1688, before Antrim's arrival. Londonderry was awash in rumors, and the population on the verge of panic. A letter purported to have been found on the streets of the town of Comber in County Tyrone claimed to provide evidence that a massacre of Protestants by Catholics similar to one perpetrated in 1641 was being planned. The Comber Letter turned out to be a forgery, but, in the heat of the moment, many supposed it to be genuine. Thus, as Antrim's Catholic force approached, the townspeople were divided: Anglican bishop Ezekiel Hopkins counseled calm and submission, but on December 7, 1688, as Scottish highlander units dubbed Redshanks advanced to within less than 100 yards (91 meters) of the city, thirteen youthful apprentices (memorialized in Protestant legend as the Apprentice Boys) shut the gates and refused the troops admittance.

Mountjoy returned to Londonderry to arrange a compromise: The city would be regarrisoned by some of his Protestant units under the direction of Colonel Robert Lundy, who was appointed governor. Thus, despite the efforts of the earl of Tyrconnel, Londonderry remained in Protestant hands. By March 12, 1689, when King James II landed at Kinsale, Ireland, Tyrconnel had secured all of Ireland for his sovereign except for some pockets in the North. Londonderry was one of these pockets. By this time, most Irish residents had declared themselves to either be Jacobite (that is, supportive of King James) or Williamite in sympathy.

With Jacobite forces advancing on Londonderry early in April, Colonel Lundy believed that resistance was futile and urged capitulation. However, he was overruled by more militant Protestant elements led by the Reverend George Walker, the Anglican rector of Donoughmore in County Tyrone, who had taken refuge within the city walls. Lundy was deposed and replaced by co-governors: George Walker and Major Henry Baker. The colonel was then ordered out and escaped the city dressed as a common soldier. In later Protestant legend, he has been rather unjustly denounced as a traitor, and the annual celebrations commemorating the siege have always included the effigy-burning of "the traitor Lundy."

On April 18, 1689, King James himself advanced to the city wall and, allegedly to the cries of "No Surrender!" from the defenders, was fired upon. James returned to Dublin to leave the siege operations to his generals, Jacques Fontanges, marquis de Maumont, who was shortly afterward killed in battle, and Richard Hamilton. Even though the Londonderry garrison was small, the walls proved extraordinarily difficult to breach. The most determined attack, that of Donough Maccarthy, Lord Clancarty, at the Butcher's Gate on June 28, was repelled with great loss of life. It seemed more promising to starve out the defenders; to prevent relief supplies from arriving via the River Foyle, the French engineer Jean-Bernard-Louis Desjean, baron de Pointis, constructed a boom to prevent the passage of ships.

As the siege dragged on, Londonderry's population was being reduced by starvation and disease, living on the flesh of horses, dogs, and cats and on tallow. Major Henry Baker was among those who succumbed to an epidemic; he was replaced by as co-governor of the town by Colonel John Mitchelburn. The defense of Londonderry at last engaged William III's attention, and a relief force was sent under command of Major-General Percy Kirke. Kirke hesitated, wary of the boom erected by Pointis, but was ordered by William's commander in chief, Friedrich Hermann Schomberg, to attempt an attack. Thus, on July 28, 1689, three vessels—the *Mountjoy*, the *Phoenix*, and the *Dartmouth*—ventured toward the boom. Captain

Micaiah Browning of the *Mountjoy* first broke through and was killed in the process. However, supplies were unloaded, and having failed to maintain their stranglehold on the city, Jacobite forces withdrew. The Siege of Londonderry had lasted for 105 days and cost the defenders some twenty-eight hundred casualties.

Significance

Though not significant in the minds of William III and James II, both of whom set greater priority elsewhere, the Siege of Londonderry significantly lifted the morale of Protestants in Ireland and was, conversely, a humiliating setback for the Irish Jacobite cause. Perhaps, however, its most lasting significance lies in its subsequent glorification into a legendary epic victory for the Protestant cause. The siege is still re-enacted as part of an annual Ulster Protestant ritual (the so-called Marching Season). This has often sparked unhappy consequences, such as the 1969 Catholic Bogside uprising, which occurred in reaction to an "Apprentice Boys" march through Londonderry.

—*Raymond Pierre Hylton*

Further Reading

Gray, Tony. *"No Surrender!" The Siege of Londonderry, 1689*. London: Macdonald and Jane's, 1975. Older work, but as far as blow-by-blow narration goes, one of the more comprehensible.

Kelly, William, ed. *The Sieges of Derry*. Dublin: Four Courts Press, 2001. Series of essays by different scholars that tend to deal more with the siege's mythical significance than with the events themselves.

Simms, J. G. *Jacobite Ireland, 1685-1691*. London: Routledge and Kegan Paul, 1969. Still the most scholarly account of this period; tends to emphasize the military over the political history of the event.

Stewart, A. T. Q. *The Narrow Ground: Patterns of Ulster History*. Belfast: Pretani Press, 1977. The author emphasizes how the actual events became transformed into an heroic legend of endurance and deliverance for the Protestant community in Northern Ireland and how it affects current events there.

Tanner, Marcus. *Ireland's Holy Wars: The Struggle for a Nation's Soul, 1500-2000*. New Haven, Conn.: Yale University Press, 2001. This recent study parallels its account of the events of 1689 with an attempt to place them into a contemporary context.

See also: Mar.-June, 1639: First Bishops' War; Oct. 23, 1641-1642: Ulster Insurrection; 1642-1651: English Civil Wars; Aug. 17-Sept. 25, 1643: Solemn League and Covenant; Mar. 12-14, 1655: Penruddock's Uprising; May, 1659-May, 1660: Restoration of Charles II; Aug. 13, 1678-July 1, 1681: The Popish Plot; 1688-1702: Reign of William and Mary; Nov., 1688-Feb., 1689: The Glorious Revolution; Feb. 13, 1689: Declaration of Rights.

Related articles in *Great Lives from History: The Seventeenth Century, 1601-1700:* James II; Mary II; Friedrich Hermann Schomberg; William III.

May 24, 1689
Toleration Act

An outgrowth of the constitutional and religious conflicts that culminated in the Glorious Revolution of 1688-1689, the Toleration Act provided a limited degree of religious freedom to Protestant sects, but it did not apply directly to Catholics or Unitarians.

Locale: London, England

Categories: Laws, acts, and legal history; government and politics; religion and theology; social issues and reform

Key Figures

Second Earl of Nottingham (Daniel Finch; 1647-1730), Tory politician who introduced the bill

William III (1650-1702), king of England, Scotland, and Ireland, r. 1689-1702

Mary II (1662-1694), joint monarch with William III, r. 1689-1694

James II (1633-1701), king of England, Scotland, and Ireland, r. 1685-1688

John Locke (1632-1704), English philosopher

Gilbert Burnet (1643-1715), influential cleric who favored toleration

Summary of Event

As in most places in seventeenth century Europe, religious dissidents in England suffered from oppressive laws. Following the restoration of the Stuart monarchy in 1660, the Anglican Church regained its monopolistic privileges as the established religion of the nation. All persons were required by law to attend its services.

The Act of Uniformity of 1662, which was part of the repressive Clarendon Code, required all ministers to be ordained according to Anglican rites and to subscribe to every doctrine in the Thirty-nine Articles of Religion. Additional statutes prohibited Dissenters from assembling for religious worship. The Test Act of 1673 excluded from military and political office anyone refusing to take the oaths of supremacy or refusing to receive Communion in the established Church. In the early 1680's, more than two thousand religious dissidents—Catholics, Presbyterians, Congregationalists, Baptists, Quakers, among others—were sent to prison for disobeying these restrictive penal laws.

In this context, King James II attempted to utilize religious toleration as a means of restoring Catholicism as the dominant religion. In March, 1686, he issued a general pardon for imprisoned dissidents, and some twelve hundred Quakers were released. His Declaration of Liberty of Conscience of 1688 granted broad toleration to both English Catholics and Protestant Dissenters, and he imprisoned seven bishops who petitioned against the reading of the declaration. The resulting conflict was a primary cause of James's deposition in the Glorious Revolution of 1688. When the Convention Parliament offered the Crown to William and Mary in February, 1689, its leaders recognized the need to seek the united support of Protestants in order to counter the threat from Rome. In addition, the Parliament contained about thirty Dissenters, and William, having come from the relatively tolerant Netherlands, made it clear that he strongly supported an expansion of religious liberty.

On February 28, 1689, the second earl of Nottingham, a devout High Anglican with a powerful following, introduced two bills in the Convention Parliament. The first bill would have revised Anglican doctrines in order to make them acceptable to Presbyterians, a proposal called "Comprehension." The second bill allowed limited toleration for the Protestant sects. Because of strong protests from influential church leaders, the Comprehensive bill was dropped, but on May 24, both houses of Parliament overwhelmingly passed Nottingham's second bill, which was entitled "An Act for Exempting Their Majesties' Protestant Subjects Dissenting from the Church of England from the Penalties of Certain Laws."

The statute contained specific provisions for particular groups. Protestant Dissenters were allowed to meet separately in unlocked meeting houses provided that they took an oath to William and Mary, swore that the pope had no jurisdiction over England, and abjured the Roman Catholic doctrine of Communion, called transubstantiation. Dissenting ministers who subscribed to most of the Thirty-nine Articles of the Anglican Church were exempted from the penalties and limitations of the Clarendon Code. Baptist ministers, moreover, were exempted from Article 27, which mandated support for infant baptism. Quakers, who were opposed to taking oaths, were allowed to substitute affirmations for oaths in civil trials, although not in criminal trials.

The Toleration Act, however, had many important limitations. Its benefits did not extend to Roman Catholics, atheists, or any person who denied the doctrine of the Trinity. Dissenters continued to be required to pay tithes to the Anglican Church, and persons not attending services of a Dissenting group were required to attend Anglican services. Another limitation was that Dissenting churches had to petition local officials for permission to hold meetings, a requirement that gave Anglican officials a veto over which groups would be recognized. The Test Acts, moreover, continued to be binding, which meant that Protestant Dissenters were still not allowed to hold political or military office. Although King William urged Parliament to repeal the Test Acts, the majority in the Parliament refused to follow his suggestion.

As a result of the Toleration Act, more than twenty-five hundred Dissenting places of worship were licensed by 1710. Although conservative Anglicans feared that the law would encourage the growth of Dissent, the number of Dissenters in the country actually declined. Whereas they constituted about 5 percent of the population in 1670, their numbers declined to about 2 percent by 1710.

In passing the Toleration Act, Parliament was cautiously moving in the direction of liberal policies that were increasingly common among English aristocrats. Gilbert Burnet and other Anglican Latitudinarians, for example, favored doctrinal flexibility, condemned intolerance, and emphasized the benevolent morality of Christianity. In 1689, philosopher John Locke published his *Epistola de Tolerantia* (1689; *A Letter Concerning Toleration*, 1689), which advocated considerably more freedom than the statute allowed, but even Locke approved of legislation against Catholicism and atheism, both of which he considered harmful to the public interest. There is no evidence that his essay had any direct influence on either the framing or the passage of the statute, although it is entirely possible that some members of Parliament were familiar with its content.

SIGNIFICANCE

The Toleration Act, the first statute to give legal recognition to Protestant Dissenters in England, has often been called the Great Charter of religious liberty. By allowing orthodox Dissenters the freedom to worship in their own way, the statute was a great milestone in the gradual evolution of religious liberty. Although the act did not directly extend to Catholics, it nevertheless meant that church attendance could no longer be made compulsory, which allowed Catholics to establish discreet meeting places for private worship. By taking away the Anglican Church's monopoly over the religious life of the nation, the act made it difficult for Anglicans to enforce ecclesiastical discipline. Although the Church of England continued to be established by law, it was no longer the only lawful church in the country.

The limitations of the statute should be well recognized, however. The intention of the act was not to create full religious equality for Dissenting Protestants, and the act did not give them any political rights. Like other European countries, England remained committed to the policy of maintaining the special status of the established church. Only with passage of the Indemnity Act of 1727 were Nonconformists finally permitted to hold public office, and the Test Act officially remained on the books until 1828.

In North America, the Toleration Act had considerable influence, except in Pennsylvania, Rhode Island, and New Jersey—three colonies that already guaranteed more religious liberty than the act required. In Massachusetts, where the Congregational Church was established, a new charter of 1691 granted "liberty of conscience" to all Christians except Roman Catholics. In Virginia, the legislature recognized the application of the Toleration Act to the colony in 1699, and the legislatures of Maryland and Connecticut grudgingly allowed Dissenting sects to hold religious services in 1700 and 1702.

—*Thomas Tandy Lewis*

FURTHER READING

Burnet, Gilbert. *History of His Own Time*. Rutland, Vt.: Charles Tuttle, 1992. Memoirs of William III's chaplain, who encouraged passage of the Toleration Act.

Coffey, John. *Persecution and Toleration in Protestant England, 1558-1689*. New York: Longman, 2000. Scholarly account of how diverse voices of the Puritan Revolution combined with liberal intellectuals to promote the idea of toleration. Highly recommended.

Crait, Gerald. *Puritanism in the Period of the Great Persecution, 1660-1688*. New York: Russell & Russell, 1971. Chapter 9, entitled "On the Threshold of Toleration," provides a good discussion of the background to the law.

Henriques, Ursula. *Religious Toleration in England, 1787-1833*. London: Routledge & Kegan Paul, 1961. A standard account of the growth of religious freedom from James II's first Declaration of Indulgence until the beginning of the Oxford Movement.

Macaulay, Thomas. *History of England from the Accession of James II*. New York: E. P. Dutton, 1958. This classic work by a famous nineteenth century Whig historian includes a detailed discussion of the act and its background.

Murphy, Andrew. *Conscience and Community: Revisiting Toleration and Religious Dissent in Early Modern England and America*. University Park: Pennsylvania University Press, 2001. A non-Whig interpretation that emphasizes the ambiguities and limitations of toleration in the seventeenth century.

Schochet, Gordon. "The Act of Toleration and the Failure of Comprehension." In *The World of William and Mary*, edited by Dale Hoak and Mordechai Feingold. Stanford, Calif.: Stanford University Press, 1996. An anti-Whig and one-sided argument that the creators of the act intended to perpetuate the disabilities of Nonconformists.

Vernon, Richard. *The Career of Toleration: John Locke, Jonas Proust, and After*. Montreal: McGill-Queens University Press, 1997. A study of two important writers of the time who had radically different ideas about religious liberty.

Watts, Michael. *The Dissenters: From the Reformation to the French Revolution*. Oxford, England: Clarendon Press, 1978. An excellent history of dissident groups, demonstrating that the Toleration Act did indeed benefit Protestant Dissenters.

Zagorin, Perez. *How the Idea of Toleration Came to the West*. Princeton, N.J.: Princeton University Press, 2003. Historical account that celebrates how religious toleration gradually developed as a result of liberal writers, religious conflicts, and growing diversity.

SEE ALSO: Nov. 5, 1605: Gunpowder Plot; Mar.-June, 1639: First Bishops' War; 1642-1651: English Civil Wars; Aug. 17-Sept. 25, 1643: Solemn League and Covenant; May, 1659-May, 1660: Restoration of Charles II; 1661-1665: Clarendon Code; May 19,

1662: England's Act of Uniformity; 1673-1678: Test Acts; Aug. 13, 1678-July 1, 1681: The Popish Plot; Aug., 1682-Nov., 1683: Rye House Plot; Apr. 4, 1687, and Apr. 27, 1688: Declaration of Liberty of Conscience; 1688-1702: Reign of William and Mary; Nov., 1688-Feb., 1689: The Glorious Revolution; Feb. 13, 1689: Declaration of Rights.

Related articles in *Great Lives from History: The Seventeenth Century, 1601-1700:* James II; John Locke; Mary II; William III.

August 29, 1689

Treaty of Nerchinsk Draws Russian-Chinese Border

The Treaty of Nerchinsk ended several decades of military confrontation between Russia and China on the Amur River and established a border and trade relations between the two countries. The treaty was China's first agreement with a European power.

Locale: Nerchinsk, in Chita region, Transbaikalia, Russia

Categories: Diplomacy and international relations; expansion and land acquisition

Key Figures

Fyodor Alekseyevich Golovin (1650-1706), Russian count, diplomat, and naval commander

Suoetu (fl. late seventeenth century), Manchu prince and imperial commissioner

Sophia (1657-1704), Russian regent, r. 1682-1689

Kangxi (K'ang-hsi; 1654-1722), Chinese emperor, r. 1661-1722

Vasily Poyarkov (d. 1668), Russian explorer

Yerofey Khabarov (fl. seventeenth century), Russian trader

Summary of Event

In Manchuria in the beginning of the seventeenth century, the Tungusic-speaking Juchen tribes (called Manchus after 1636) were united into the Later Jin state by a warlord named Nurhaci. The Juchen economy at the time was based largely upon fur trade with the tribes of the Amur River region. With the weakening of the Chinese Ming Dynasty, the Juchens began to play a mediating role between the peoples of the Amur region and the Chinese fur market. Gradually, the Juchens extended their influence on the Sungari River and the Middle Amur. Other Tungusic-speaking tribes, the Duichers and Daurs, were subdued in the 1630's and paid them tribute in furs. However, not only furs attracted the Manchus' attention to the region: Subdued tribes were forcibly mobilized and included in the Eight Banner system, the Manchu military first instituted by Nurhaci. The Manchus conquered northern China, and in 1644 their troops entered Beijing, instituting the Manchu Qing Dynasty.

Meanwhile, the nascent Russian peoples were beginning to push east. The conquest of the Siberian Khanate, one of the remnants of the Golden Horde, at the end of the sixteenth century opened the way for Russia to colonize Siberia, and Russian explorers, traders, and Cossack troops advanced into eastern Siberia, through the weakly populated but fur-rich taiga and tundra regions. The lucrative fur trade was a basic impetus of early Siberian colonization. In 1632, the town of Yakutsk was founded on the Lena River, and it soon became the base of Russian expansion on the Amur River and to the Pacific Ocean. The indigenous peoples of Siberia paid to the Russians a tribute in furs referred to as a *yasak*.

In the middle of the seventeenth century, some Russian pioneers attempted to annex the Amur region in order to develop it economically. The region, however, was inhabited by tribes related to the Manchus. In 1644, the first Russian Cossacks, under Vasily Poyarkov, descended the Amur, bringing back news of the "great river Amur," inhabited by flourishing agricultural tribes, where cattle and abundant stocks of sable were to be found. The Cossacks were the first Europeans to reach and descend the Amur River. In 1649, Yerofey Khabarov, a trader and adventurer, recruited a band of Cossacks and appeared at the Amur River, burning to ashes villages down the river and killing hundreds of local people.

On the banks of the Amur, the Russians encountered not only desperate resistance by indigenous peoples but also punitive Chinese military expeditions, which had been sent to eliminate the "unknown Amur tribe" (as the local Manchu authorities first referred to the Russians). The Qing considered the appearance of Russians in the Amur region a threat to their own fur revenues, as well as their sovereign territory, and they decided to use scorched-earth tactics in response: In order to deprive the Russian expeditions of their food supply and tributary population, they removed practically all inhabitants of the middle Amur, far inland of Manchuria. For nearly four decades, the Amur Valley became the stage for a series of armed collisions between the Russians and the Manchu rulers of China.

Enlarging the sphere of their influence in the Amur region, the Russians at the same time undertook a number of steps toward the establishment of official relations with China: From the 1650's through the 1670's, several diplomatic and commercial missions were dispatched to Beijing. The main purpose of these missions was to open regularized, state-controlled trade between China and Russian. In contrast to the Qing, during the diplomatic negotiations Russian representatives did not press toward the stabilization of the situation in the Amur region. They wished to leave open the possibility of further extending Russian influence in the area.

The Chinese emperor, Kangxi, eventually became dissatisfied with diplomatic efforts to solve the Amur question. Diplomacy, he believed, was also failing to yield results in a number of other areas, including the problem of the return of Duarian Prince Gantimur, who had defected with his people to the Russians. Kangxi therefore decided to exclude the Russians from the upper Amur region by force. After suppressing the revolt of the Three Feudatories in 1681, the Qing concentrated their forces against Russia.

In 1682-1683, Chinese troops annihilated Russian settlements in the basin of the Zeia and Selemja Rivers; at the same time, preparations for an attack on the Russian fort of Albazin began. The siege of the fort and its 450 defenders by the 15,000-man Manchu army began on June 12, 1685. After one month's siege, the Manchus forced the Cossacks into an honorable surrender. However, by autumn the settlers had already restored the fort, to the Manchus' complete surprise. The second siege of the fort, in which one thousand defenders resisted eleven thousand Manchus, continued until the signing of the Treaty of Nerchinsk. The number of defenders had decreased from one thousand to sixty-six people, including children, by spring of the following year. The Manchus suffered enormous losses as well.

Facing further escalation of military conflict on the Amur, Princess Sophia's government finally decided to bring the Amur question to the negotiation table. Fyodor Alekseyevich Golovin was appointed the great and plenipotentiary ambassador for the negotiation of a peaceful settlement with the Qing. The Russian-Qing negotiations started in Nerchinsk (a Russian fort on the Nercha River, founded in 1653) on August 12, 1689. In spite of the fact that the Qing's great ambassador Prince Suoetu arrived in Nerchinsk at the head of an imposing fifteen thousand-man army in forty-seven ships (Golovin had about two thousand men), on the whole the circumstances were favorable to the Russian party, since in June of the same year Russia's ally, the khan of Dzungaria Galdan, had crushed the Qing's allies, the Khalkha Mongols.

The signing of the treaty took place two weeks later, on August 29. Territorial demarcation between Russia and China was determined in the first and second articles; a border was established along the Argun and Gorbitsa Rivers and the Stanovoi Range toward the Sea of Okhotsk. Some territories in the basin of the Uda River in the eastern frontier remained undefined. Thus, Russia agreed to significant territorial concessions: 600,000 square miles (1.5 million square kilometers) of the Amur region became part of the Qing Empire. According to the third article, the fort of Albazin had to be destroyed, and the Russians were excluded from the Amur. The fourth article determined the conditions of mutual extradition of defectors; the article had no retroactive effect, so Gantimur and his peoples remained in Russia. While making some territorial concessions, Russia at the same time could achieve one aim it had held for many decades, the establishment of permanent diplomatic relations and trade connections with China (articles 5 and 6).

Thus, the Treaty of Nerchinsk concluded several decades of military confrontation between Russia and the Qing. It differentiated the spheres of influence of Russia and the Qing and promoted a normalization of the relations between the two countries and the establishment of trade relations.

Significance

The Treaty of Nerchinsk was a result of compromises on both sides and therefore reflected the interests of both China and Russia. It constituted China's first agreement with a European power. Concluded on an equal basis, it regulated the relations between the two countries until 1858, when the Aigun Treaty superceded it.

In Nerchinsk, the Qing succeeded not only in obtaining a buffer zone with Russia (the Amur region) but also acquired a powerful lever in further dealings with Russia by assuming control of caravan trade. The treaty considerably strengthened the geopolitical position of China in Central Asia, since it guaranteed Russia's neutrality in China's war with Dzungaria, and as a result, Galdan Khan was finally defeated in 1696. The treaty completed the formation of a Chinese system of "nominal vassalage," in which some peoples of the Lower Amur and

Sakhalin recognized their vassal dependence upon the Qing and obtained the formal status of provincial nations.

The treaty opened the door to China for Russian trade caravans and brought to Russia immediate mercantile benefits. At the time it was signed, then, it was advantageous to the Russian government, but in the long term, the treaty critically hampered the development of Siberia and the Russian Far East for the next 160 years, as Russia lost easy access to the Pacific via the Amur. Russia's efforts to regain access to the Amur without harming its trade relationship with China determined the duality and inactivity of Russian policy in the Far East up to the middle of the nineteenth century.

—*Anatolii Trekhsviatskyi*

Further Reading

Chen, Vincent. *Sino-Russian Relations in the Seventeenth Century*. The Hague, the Netherlands: Martinus Nijhoff, 1966. Detailed description of Sino-Russian relations based on Chinese and Russian historical sources.

Evans, John L. *Russian Expansion on the Amur, 1848-1860: The Push to the Pacific*. New York: Edwin Mellen Press, 1999. A detailed overview of the Russian expansion on the Pacific Ocean and especially the occupation of the Amur River Valley; chapter 1 focuses on the Treaty of Nerchinsk and Sino-Russian relations in the seventeenth century.

Stephan, John J. *The Russian Far East: A History*. Stanford, Calif.: Stanford University Press, 1994. The first comprehensive history of the Russian Far East in English. Part One is useful in explaining the historical context of the Treaty of Nerchinsk. Maps.

See also: 1616-1643: Rise of the Manchus; Dec., 1639: Russians Reach the Pacific Ocean; Apr. 25, 1644: End of the Ming Dynasty; June 6, 1644: Manchus Take Beijing; Feb. 17, 1661-Dec. 20, 1722: Height of Qing Dynasty; Dec., 1673-1681: Rebellion of the Three Feudatories.

Related articles in *Great Lives from History: The Seventeenth Century, 1601-1700:* Alexis; Michael Romanov; Sophia.

Early 1690's
Brazilian Gold Rush

An influx of gold seekers followed the discovery of extensive gold deposits in Brazil's interior. The gold rush led to Portuguese settlement of the region and contributed to the stagnation of Brazil's sugar economy. The gold riches helped monetize the world economy and facilitate European trade with East Asia.

Locale: Minas Gerais, Mato Grosso, and Góias provinces of eastern Brazil

Categories: Economics; geology; trade and commerce; exploration and discovery; expansion and land acquisition

Summary of Event

The discovery of gold and silver in Spanish America encouraged the Portuguese to explore the Brazilian interior in hope of finding mineral riches. Mixed-race *bandeirantes*, of indigenous Brazilian and Portuguese descent, had found a few small gold deposits but no major strikes. Brazil consequently developed as an agricultural economy, producing dyewoods (especially brazilwood), tobacco, and sugar for export. The Portuguese first bartered with the indigenous population for brazilwood, but after the introduction of sugarcane, the indigenous and then Africans were enslaved by the Portuguese, providing the labor for the plantations. Brazil's sugar plantations and refineries were clustered along the coast, particularly in the northeast, and the early colonial capital was established in that zone at Salvador da Bahia.

In the early 1690's, the *paulista* prospectors (the *bandeirantes* from São Paulo) discovered bonanza after golden bonanza, first in the province of Minas Gerais (general mines) and later in Goiás, Mato Grosso, Ceará, Sergipe, and Bahia. With these rich strikes along the alluvial plains, thousands of hopeful miners rushed to the region. Many made the arduous trek across the mountains from Rio de Janeiro and São Paulo, and others followed the São Francisco River south from Bahia into the mining zones. They took with them thousands of black slaves. As word reached Europe of the discoveries, men from Portugal and its Atlantic islands, such as the Azores and Madeira, also thronged to Minas Gerais.

The *bandeirantes* who had made the discoveries were frontiersmen, accustomed to the harsh conditions of the Brazilian interior, but many of the would-be miners were ill-suited and poorly equipped to survive at the diggings. They reached the mines with little food and even less intention of using their slaves to grow crops when the chattels could be panning for gold. It took two months for foodstuffs to be transported to the mining region from Bahia, and during the early years there were reports of starvation and widespread malnutrition. Eventually, entrepreneurs earned great profits by supplying the mine operators and their workers with basic necessities; gold was plentiful but food and clothing were scarce. Gold also caused inflation in the coastal areas by driving up the price for imports, foodstuffs, and other merchandise there.

It took several years for the Portuguese crown to recognize the significance of the discovery and respond to the gold rush. The monarchy initially assumed that the strikes would be of short duration, as had been the case with those made earlier. Indeed, the Crown began to respond in a significant way only when it received complaints from the sugar planters that they were suffering a labor shortage: Many slaves had been shipped to the mines and the miners had the gold to outbid the planters for chattels arriving from Africa. The monarchy worried that the drain of men to the mines would leave Brazil defenseless and that it would destroy the tobacco and sugar industries. In 1701, the Crown consequently prohibited further migration to the mines. Such decrees had little effect, however, and Lisbon had to revise its gold-rush policy. It eventually became clear that the *bandeirantes* had struck a fabulous bonanza and that the government needed to regulate the miners if it hoped to garner its share of the profits.

Yet oversight of the mining districts proved difficult. With its high value and small volume, gold was easy to smuggle, and the officials had trouble collecting the royal fifth on the miners' production. The government's reluctance to pay for officials to regulate the mining provinces added to the disorder and tumult that reigned on the frontier. The scarce royal officials could do little to prevent the civil war that broke out in October, 1708, between the *paulistas* and the *emboabas*, a derisive term for what the *bandeirantes* considered Portuguese and Bahian interlopers. Yet the numerical superiority of the *bandeirantes* enabled them to drive the *paulistas* out of many of their claims before royal officials managed to mediate a truce in December of 1709. By 1720, miners were exploiting the main gold deposits of Minas Gerais, Mato Grosso, and Goiás. Townships had emerged in the backlands, along with the basic institutions of government. Royal assay and smelting houses, established at Taubaté and Parati, lay some distance from the gold fields, however, impeding the efficient collection of mining taxes.

African and Afro-Brazilian slaves provided nearly all the labor for the gold mines. Masters particularly sought workers from the Bight of Benin, because many of them had experience in mining and refining gold in Africa. Indeed, they often had more expertise than their Portuguese masters. The gold rush provoked a large migration of Africans to the Brazilian interior. By 1700, about 2,600 slaves arrived in Minas Gerais each year, and four decades later, the quantity had grown to 7,000 annually. This meant that Minas Gerais soon had more slaves than any of Brazil's other provinces, including the old sugar regions.

The slaves were occupied in two main processes of gold mining. The first were large enterprises that handled relatively large amounts of earth on hillsides and rechanneled rivers to get at the gold-bearing alluvium. Sluices separated the gold from what had been dug up. Operations generally had gangs of slaves, laboring under a close supervision that kept the workers from stealing gold nuggets and ensuring that they kept working. The size of the operator's claim generally depended on the number of slaves he had. Although inhumane and brutal, it often made economic sense to work the slaves as hard as possible, even if it endangered their health or their lives, in order to extract as much gold as possible before the arrival of competitors.

The second principal method of gold production required less investment and fewer slaves. Prospector-slaves worked with considerable independence from their owners. Masters demanded that the prospector-slaves (*faiscadores*) produce a stipulated amount of gold, perhaps a few grams, each week. If they managed to pan more, they were allowed to keep the surplus. A number of *faiscadores* managed to save enough to buy their own freedom. Some masters agreed to free productive *faiscadores* after a specified number of years of service. Other slaves simply escaped to the *quilombos* (independent villages that were culturally African and made of runaway slaves) that grew in the interior. By the final decades of the eighteenth century, more than 75 percent of the population of Minas Gerais was Afro-Brazilian and 40 percent were free rather than slaves.

Gold production grew until the middle of the eighteenth century, reaching its high point probably between 1730 and 1755, with an annual output of 18 to 20 tons. The exact amount is impossible to ascertain, however, given the widespread smuggling and the Portuguese exchequer's feeble control over the mining industry. It has been estimated that the state managed to tax only one-third of Brazilian gold output. During the 1700's, Brazil may have produced as much as one thousand tons of gold. By way of comparison, Europe's entire stock of gold around 1500 amounted to around 3,500 tons. Brazil far surpassed the amount of gold yielded by Spanish America, whose mines chiefly produced silver.

SIGNIFICANCE

The gold rush of the 1690's opened the Brazilian southwest to settlement, eventually transformed social relations within the mining provinces, and played a major role in world economic development. It also stimulated economic activity in other parts of Brazil, which supplied the mines with foodstuffs and other daily necessities. The gold flowed out of Brazil as tax revenues and as payment for imported merchandise. Many of those goods were English, for the English had gained access to the Portuguese Empire under provisions of the Treaty of Metheun (1703). In fact, Portuguese political economists complained that the English derived more benefit from Brazilian gold than did Portugal. Nonetheless, Brazil's gold was crucial to monetizing the European economy, and it helped pay for the spices, silks, and porcelain imported from Asia.

—*Kendall W. Brown*

FURTHER READING

Bethell, Leslie, ed. *Colonial Brazil*. New York: Cambridge University Press, 1984. Chapter 5, "The Gold Cycle, c. 1690-1750," is an excellent survey of the economic implications of the gold rush and its effects on slave labor.

Boxer, Charles R. *The Golden Age of Brazil, 1695-1750: The Growing Pains of a Colonial Society*. Berkeley: University of California Press, 1962. An early work with chapters on the gold rush and development of Minas Gerais by one of the most eminent historians of Portuguese expansion.

Cardozo, Manoel. "The Brazilian Gold Rush." *Americas* 3, no. 2 (October, 1946): 137-160. A basic overview and narrative of the gold strikes in the Brazilian interior and the ensuing rush to exploit them.

Higgins, Kathleen J. *"Licentious Liberty" in a Brazilian Gold-Mining Region: Slavery, Gender, and Social Control in Eighteenth-Century Sabará, Minas Gerais*. University Park: Pennsylvania State University Press, 1999. Higgins shows how conditions in the mining regions affected slavery and particularly how gender issues influenced the evolution toward greater autonomy for the slaves.

Russell-Wood, A. J. R. *Slavery and Freedom in Colonial Brazil*. Oxford, England: Oneworld, 2002. A new edition of the author's *The Black Man in Slavery and Freedom in Colonial Brazil* (1982), which contains a wealth of information on the gold mines and labor system.

SEE ALSO: 1609: Bank of Amsterdam Invents Checks; 1630-1660's: Dutch Wars in Brazil; 1654: Portugal Retakes Control of Brazil; Beginning 1680's: Guerra dos Bárbaros.

RELATED ARTICLES in *Great Lives from History: The Seventeenth Century, 1601-1700:* Piet Hein; Abel Janszoon Tasman.

Beginning 1690's
Movement to Reform Manners

The Society for the Reformation of Manners developed during a time when social problems were thought to come from idleness, irreligion, and immoral impulses. The organization believed that arrests, prosecutions, and convictions could eradicate bad behavior and reform society. Although the society served its goals, its methods led to a predictable backlash.

Locale: England
Categories: Social issues and reform; religion and theology; laws, acts, and legal history; cultural and intellectual history; organizations and institutions

Key Figures

Edward Stillingfleet (1635-1699), bishop of Worcester
Josiah Woodward (1660-1712), one of the society's most vocal sermonizers
Jeremy Collier (1650-1726), clerical foe of the London stage

Summary of Event

Following the Glorious Revolution of 1688, poverty and crime were becoming endemic in the greater London area, leading to outrageous corruption and a perceived breakdown in public order. London's population had increased by 76 percent in forty years because of an influx of the impoverished. With few opportunities for subsistence, many of the poor resorted to vagrancy, begging, and prostitution, from the city of London to the West End. Bawdy houses, gambling houses, and so-called Molly houses (venues for homosexual activity, considered lewd at the time), were opening everywhere, while the streets seemed rampant with drunkenness, theft, blasphemy, and riotous behavior. Many feared that the ecclesiastical courts had abdicated their traditional role of upholding public morality. Many residents called for official action.

Founding members of the Society for the Reformation of Manners (SRM), including Edward Stillingfleet and Anthony Horneck, believed that an individual was condemned to eternal damnation not only through sin and vice but also through failure to act against their spread, which were believed to resemble contagious diseases. God's wrath could destroy the community, and Christian "soldiers" were needed to keep individuals in a state of moral and physical health, to keep the economy in financial and moral order, to move society into equilibrium, and to keep England safe from destruction and the machinations of Rome and the pope.

Justices initiated numerous arrests in 1689, after church officials of St. Martin's-in-the-Field petitioned the justices of Westminster for action against brothels. The SRM campaigns began soon after an October 30, 1690, pamphlet, *A Proclamation for Apprehending Robbers on the Highway*, was distributed, which described such criminals as "lewd, disorderly, and wicked persons." The proclamation argued also that the elimination of prostitution would result in the elimination of related crimes. The SRM, with its roots in Puritanism, formed with the meeting of a group of evangelical Christians at Tower Hamlets in the East End of London. They documented their program in *Antimoixeia: Or, The Honest and Joynt Design of the Tower Hamblets for the General Supression of Bawdy Houses* (1691).

The movement gained royal sanction: In 1691, Queen Mary II wrote to the justices of the peace of Middlesex to enforce laws against "drunkenness, uncleanness, swearing, cursing, profanation of the Lord's day, etc."; in 1692, King William's royal proclamation condemned such behavior and others considered "dissolute, immoral or disorderly," which would include sodomy, printing obscene matter, attending masquerades and fairs, and participating in the purported "sin pits" of the theaters. The SRM's *Proposals for a National Reformation of Manners* (1694)—containing summaries of laws and rulings, the queen's letter to the magistrates, and their reply—also condemned theaters as venues for "delight in idleness, excessive vanity, revellings, luxury, wantonness, lasciviousness [and were] whoredoms." Frequenting theaters was thought to lead to a decline in "the natural vigour and manliness, prowess, and valour of our kingdom."

In his *A Short View of the Immorality and Profaneness of the English Stage* (1698), Jeremy Collier fulminated against the Restoration stage, denouncing, among others, the plays of Sir John Vanbrugh, William Congreve, and John Dryden for debauching public morals. So effective was Collier's propaganda that Vanbrugh had difficulty securing a license for his theater in the Haymarket. An anonymous *Account of the Societies for the Reformation of Manners in London and Westminster, and Other Parts of the Kingdom . . . for Effecting a National Reformation* (1699) included Queen Mary's letter, King William's proclamation of February 24, 1697, an address to the king by the House of Commons, and a listing of penal laws, sample warrants, and registers.

Members of the SRM varied in social status, from craftspeople and tradesmen to constables, members of Parliament, and justices of the peace. The Bristol society was made up of mostly gentlemen. Although not uniform in emphasis, society chapters generally believed that correct behavior provided a model for the roughest classes to imitate, which would result in their leading lives of civility through piety; that those not yet fallen into disgrace could be kept from it through education and honest work. Theologically, they believed that a vengeful Old Testament God was in perpetual conflict with Satan; that sin, according to one of the most vocal of the SRM's speakers, Josiah Woodward, kept people from living in a rational state; that the eternal struggle between God and Satan was played out within the individual soul; and that "neutrality" was indicative of Satanic collusion. Salvation depended upon grace, given by God not through predestination but through rejecting earthly pleasures, and by serving as active Christian warriors.

To achieve its goals, the SRM carried out a campaign of informing on alleged criminals and enforcing vice laws through criminal courts rather than through church courts. SRM informants met with special agents, who were paid to hear them and complete warrants against the alleged criminal parties; the warrants were presented to justices of the peace, who delivered them to constables, who then served them by carrying out arrests. Alleged criminals were arraigned and sentenced by the justice of the peace. "Black lists" were published from 1693 to 1707, noting the crimes that had been prosecuted. By 1725, the number of public prosecutions neared 100,000. Meanwhile, there had been a split between, on one hand, reform movements that concentrated on charity schools and the workhouse movement, and, on the other hand, the SRM, which had shifted its focus from that of enforcing a pious life to prosecuting social miscreants.

SIGNIFICANCE

The Society for the Reformation of Manners' most active days were over by 1738, by which time it had seen an upsurge in attacks on informers, arresting officers, and SRM members as well. It was reconstituted two decades later for a short while. John Wesley, sermonizing in 1763, stressed the damage the theater had done "to the Faith and Morals of the Nation" as "Schools of Vice, and Nurseries of Profaneness and Lewdness," where lurked moral disease and contagion. By this time, however, the bawdry of the Restoration stage was long gone. The society's final days came in 1766 with a falsely obtained indictment in the Court of King's Bench.

Also, social changes decreased the perceived need for the SRM's activities. Whereas female prostitutes traditionally had been considered perpetrators, they came to be considered victims, in part because of the increased perception of male libertinism in the eighteenth century. As early as 1711, Joseph Addison described in the *Spectator* a "loose Tribe of Men" on the prowl in London, searching out "unfortunate Females" to seduce. The SRM's campaign against the sexual double standard took root and grew in the eighteenth century in the idea that only the chaste husband was a respectable member of the middle class. In 1736, Sir John Gonson's efforts in passing the Gin Act eventually contributed to the decline of the SRM through reaction against the use of informers. Also, intellectual worldviews changed. The Enlightenment, with its widespread notions grounded in reason and its belief that society and nature functioned independently of divine intervention, had little room for the SRM and its mandates.

The legacy of the SRM pursued a meandering course through English social life. Negatively, it fed into that deleterious tradition of censoriousness and regulation in sexual matters, which partly determined, up to the 1960's, what the English could read and what they could see in theaters. Positively, however, it fed a broad humanitarian and compassionate stream that, beginning with Joseph Addison and Sir Richard Steele in the *Spectator* seeking the improvement of manners, flowed throughout the eighteenth century into philanthropic and charitable concerns. Thus, in one direction, the SRM pursued a tradition of social reform exemplified by such projects as the Foundling Hospital, established by Thomas Coram, himself a member of the Society for Promoting Christian Knowledge (one of the many offshoots of the SRM); John Howard and Elizabeth Fry's penal reforms; and societies such as those created for the prevention of cruelty to children and animals.

In another direction, the dissenting tradition of Wesley and Methodism combined the objectives of attaining both spiritual grace and social amelioration. By the turn of the century, its course included the Abolitionist movement and the missionary Evangelicalism of Exeter Hall and the Clapham Sect.

—*Donna Berliner*

FURTHER READING

Curtis, T. C., and W. A. Speck. "The Societies for the Reformation of Manners: A Case Study in the Theory and Practice of Moral Reform." *Literature and History* 3 (1976): 45-64. An excellent foundation for the study of the SRM. Draws on archival material and seventeenth and eighteenth century SRM sermons.

Dillon, Patrick. "The Roots of Reform." *History Today* 53, no. 4 (July, 2003): 44-46. Focuses on 1754, but gives information concerning the SRM's founding, the Gin Act, and the movement toward social reform.

Hurl-Eamon, Jennine. "Policing Male Heterosexuality: The Reformation of Manners Societies' Campaign Against the Brothels in Westminster, 1690-1720." *Journal of Social History* 37, no. 4 (Summer, 2004): 1017-1035. Discusses the SRM's activity in prosecuting male clients of prostitutes. Hurl-Eamon's study looks at prosecution according to class, information drawn from contemporary Westminster recognizances.

Meadley, T. D. "Society for the Reformation of Manners." *London Quarterly Review* 6, no. 2 (January/October, 1951): 144-148. Discusses the development of the SRM and outlines Wesley's sermon.

Shoemaker, Robert. "Reforming the City: The Reformation of Manners Campaign in London, 1690-1738." In *Stilling the Grumbling Hive*, edited by Lee Davison et al. New York: St. Martin's Press, 1992. Provides statistical data from the London SRM annual reports and other sources, and argues that SRM activity had social rather than religious motivations.

See also: 1688-1702: Reign of William and Mary; Nov., 1688-Feb., 1689: The Glorious Revolution.

Related articles in *Great Lives from History: The Seventeenth Century, 1601-1700:* Richard Baxter; Mary II; Madeleine de Scudéry; James Shirley.

c. 1690
Extinction of the Dodo Bird

The flightless Dodo bird was the first animal whose extinction was known to have been caused by human beings. With its tragic disappearance occurring less than a century after its first encounter with humans, the Dodo has become a cultural icon and symbol of endangered species.

Locale: Mauritius, Mascarene Islands, Indian Ocean
Categories: Environment; biology

Key Figures

Wybrant van Warwijck (1569-1615), Dutch vice-admiral who traveled to Mauritius Island

Roelandt Savery (1576-1639), Flemish artist

Jan Savery (1589-1654), Flemish artist and nephew of Roelandt Savery

Volquard Iverson (fl. 1662), survivor of a shipwrecked Dutch vessel, who reported seeing a dodo bird in 1662

John Tradescant (1608-1662), English botanist and royal gardener

Thomas Herbert (1606-1682), English traveler and author

Summary of Event

Dodos (*Raphus cucullatus*) were flightless birds of the pigeon family. They were native inhabitants of Mauritius, the largest of three volcanic islands known as the Mascarene Islands, located east of Madagascar in the Indian Ocean. These islands were discovered in the early fifteenth century by Arab seamen, whose ships had been blown off course by storms. In the early sixteenth century, Portuguese expeditions explored this area as well, but the Portuguese never created settlements on the islands. They stopped there to restock their ships with food. In September of 1598, the first Dutch ships arrived in Mauritius, and in less than a century the dodo bird became extinct.

The commander of this first fleet of five ships from Holland was Vice-Admiral Wybrant van Warwijck, who claimed Mauritius as a Dutch possession. His report about this trip contained the first known account of the dodo. Warwijck's narrative, and his illustrations of the dodo, were published in *True Report of the Gainefull, Prosperous, and Speedy Voyage to Java in the East Indies* (1599?) and *Het tweede boeck: Journael oft dagh-register* (1601; later published in *De tweede schipvaart der Nederlanders naar Oost-Indië onder Jacob Cornelisz. van Neck en Wybrant Warwijck, 1598-1600*, five volumes, 1938-1951). These first descriptions of the dodo depicted large-headed but thin, swift birds as big as swans. In place of wings, dodos had small quills. They were grey, with thick bowed beaks and long legs.

The exact origin of the name "dodo" is unknown. One possibility is the Portuguese word *duodo*, which means "foolish" or "idiot." The dodo had lived in a predator-free environment before the arrival of humans, so it was easily captured. The bird's innocence might have appeared to be stupidity. A more commonly accepted origin is *dodoor*, the Dutch word for "sluggard" (lazy).

For more than forty years, the Dutch used Mauritius, with its fresh water and food supplies, as a call (or restocking) station for ships of the Dutch East India Company.

Dutch sailors hunted dodos for food, but written accounts indicate that dodo meat was tough, not very tasty, difficult to digest, and even nauseating. On his return voyage from Persia in 1629, the English traveler and author Sir Thomas Herbert visited Mauritius. He described the dodo in his celebrated travel book, *A Relation of Some Yeares Travaile, Begvnne anno 1626 into Afrique and the Greater Asia* (1634; *A Relation of Some Yeares Travaile into Afrique, Asia, Indies*, 1971), which includes fine drawings.

The dodo bird, native to Mauritius Island off the coast of Africa near Madagascar, became extinct not long after coming into contact with humans, who used the island first as a restocking station for trade ships and then a settlement. (Hulton|Archive by Getty Images)

Besides being a source of food on Mauritius Island, live dodos were taken to Europe for entertainment purposes. Live birds in cages were used for touring exhibitions. The dodo's unusual habit of eating stones, probably to help digestion, fascinated the public. The dodo also fascinated European artists. The Flemish painter Roelandt Savery produced numerous paintings of the dodo from life. In 1651, his nephew, Jan Savery, created the well-known dodo painting now at the Ashmolean Museum of Art and Archaeology in Oxford, England. Unlike the illustrations of sailors and others who saw the dodos in Mauritius, the European paintings depict plump, immobile, and apparently "stupid" dodos, portrayals of the dodo that have become the bird's popular image. There is speculation that the "exhibition" dodos in Europe had been overfed or that many of the paintings were based on stuffed specimens instead of live birds.

With the destruction and exploitation of the dodo in both Mauritius and Europe, the bird became rare by 1640. In 1644, the Dutch colonized Mauritius. The new settlers brought to the island cats, dogs, rats, chickens, swine, cattle, and monkeys. Since dodos could not fly, their nests were built on the ground. Many of the new animals destroyed dodo nests and ate the eggs or young dodos. With the introduction of the new predators, the extinction of the dodo was inevitable.

The exact date of the dodo bird's extinction is not known. Traditionally, 1662 was believed to be the year of the last known encounter with a dodo, recorded by the sailor Volquard Iverson, a survivor of the shipwrecked Dutch vessel, the *Arnhem*. Stranded on Mauritius, Iverson and several other sailors were searching for food when they discovered several dodos on a coastal islet offshore. Another accepted date of extinction was 1681, when Benjamin Harry, the first mate on the ship *Berkley Castle*, reported a dodo sighting.

However, other records and analyses have supported a later extinction date of 1690. Seventeenth century archives in The Hague and in Cape Town indicate that live dodos existed in 1689. In 2003, using a statistical test based on the last ten recorded sightings by sailors and others, zoologists David Roberts of Britain's Royal Botanical Gardens and Andrew Solow of the Woods Hole Oceanographic Institution in Massachusetts concluded that the actual extinction date of the dodo most likely was 1690. They determined that in the case of a species

HABITAT OF THE DODO BIRD

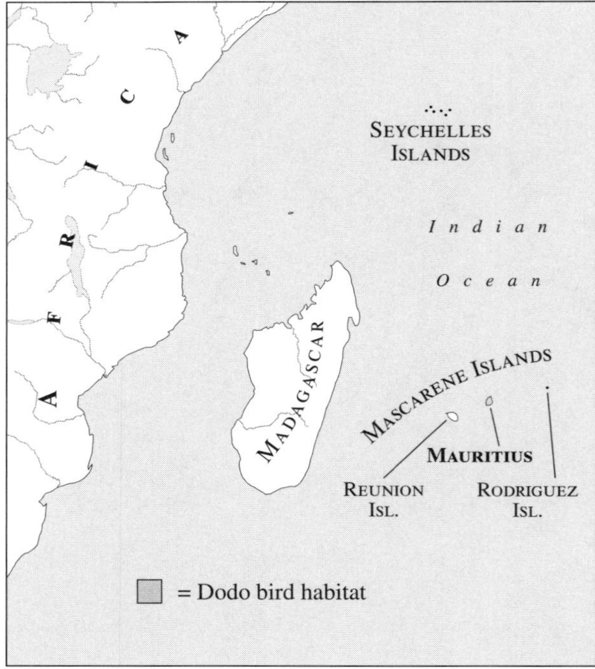

whose sightings become increasingly sporadic, species members might exist unseen for years; the last sighting does not necessarily indicate the date of extinction.

John Tradescant, a renowned naturalist and traveler, stuffed the last dodo specimen. The bird had been brought to Europe for exhibition. When Tradescant died in 1662, his unique collection of plants and other curiosities were bequeathed to Elias Ashmole (1617-1692), who then donated the collection, among other items, to Oxford University, creating the Ashmolean Museum (1683). This was the last intact, complete dodo specimen in the world. Unfortunately, the condition of the stuffed dodo continued to deteriorate and decompose until most of it was burned as a discarded item in 1755. A curator was able to save a head and the right foot, both with skin, the only known surviving soft tissues of a dodo. The specimens are now at the Oxford University Museum of Natural History.

Some skeletal remains of the dodo, most of which come from Mare aux Songes, a four-acre swamp near the southeast coast of Mauritius, were discovered in 1865 by George Clark, a naturalist and teacher. He found enough bones to reconstruct a complete dodo skeleton, which can be found at the Natural History Museum of Mauritius.

SIGNIFICANCE

The dodo painting by Savery and dodo pieces at the Ashmolean Museum inspired Victorian author Lewis Carroll. His 1885 *Alice's Adventures in Wonderland* featured "Dodo," a character illustrated by the English caricaturist Sir John Tenniel (1820-1914). This popular book gave the dodo it first widespread recognition and prominence. Subsequently, the dodo appeared in various cartoons, advertisements, and newspapers.

The dodo has become Mauritius's national symbol. On August 25, 1906, Mauritius's coat of arms was granted, depicting the dodo. Countless successful commercial enterprises in Mauritius revolve around the dodo image, which appears on souvenirs, woodcarvings, textiles, and other popular products.

The first known animal to disappear because of human intervention, the dodo rivals the dinosaurs as the most "famous" extinct animal. Surrounded by mythology, the dodo has become a cultural icon, appearing in literature, the arts, and popular culture. There are dodo posters and illustrations, music boxes, toys, jewelry, tea towels, cookie jars, and even a clothing company label. Children's books include Lynne and Brian Edward's *Dead as the Dodo* (1973) and *In Search of the Last Dodo* (1989) by Ann and Reg Cartwright. In 1985, *Sesame Street* produced a movie called *Follow That Bird*, in which "Big Bird" lives with the "Dodo family." In 1996, Dick King-Smith and Nigel Lambert composed a musical for children called "Dodos Are Forever," in which a pair of dodos named "Beatrice" and "Berty" dream of their future happy life together on an island in the Indian Ocean. The two are oblivious to the ship anchored in the harbor.

—*Alice Myers*

FURTHER READING

Fuller, Errol. *Dodo: A Brief History*. New York: Universe, 2002. This comprehensive, scholarly study of the Dodo bird provides the complete history and mythology of this creature and discusses how it became a cultural icon. Beautifully illustrated throughout, with a bibliography of both primary and secondary sources.

Hachisuka, Masauji. *The Dodo and Kindred Birds: Or, The Extinct Birds of the Mascarene Islands*. London: H. F. & G. Witherby, 1953. An excellent resource providing the historical and pictorial evidence for the Dodo, its habits, and extinction. Includes maps, drawings, color plates, and a bibliography.

Moree, Perry. *A Concise History of Dutch Mauritius, 1598-1710*. London: IIAS/Kegan Paul International, 1998. Moree discovered records showing that there were living dodos in 1689, which proved that their extinction was decades later than previously estimated. Includes illustrations and a bibliography.

Pinto-Correia, Clara. *Return of the Crazy Bird: The Sad, Strange Tale of the Dodo*. New York: Copernicus Books, 2003. This illustrated work describes the discovery, history, and legacy of the dodo bird, plus the rise of "dodology." Includes a bibliography.

Quammen, David. *The Song of the Dodo: Island Biogeography in an Age of Extinction*. New York: Scribner, 1996. This scientific analysis of the distribution of species on islands and their extinction discusses the slaughter of the dodo bird. Includes a glossary source notes, maps, and a bibliography.

SEE ALSO: Mar. 20, 1602: Dutch East India Company Is Founded; Beginning Spring, 1605: Dutch Dominate Southeast Asian Trade; 1642 and 1644: Tasman Proves Australia Is a Separate Continent.

1690
LOCKE PUBLISHES *TWO TREATISES OF GOVERNMENT*

Locke's Two Treatises of Government *argued against the divine right of kings, promoted individual rights, argued that sovereignty lay ultimately with the people, and created a body of political theory that would strongly influence the framers of the United States Constitution and all other Western theorists of democracy.*

LOCALE: England
CATEGORIES: Philosophy; literature

KEY FIGURES

John Locke (1632-1704), political theorist, philosopher, and founder of British empiricism
First Earl of Shaftesbury (Anthony Ashley Cooper; 1621-1683), Parliamentary opposition leader and founder of the Whigs
Mary II (1662-1694), queen of England, r. 1689-1694
William III (1650-1702), stadtholder of the Netherlands, r. 1672-1702, and king of England, r. 1689-1702
James II (1633-1701), king of England, r. 1685-1688

SUMMARY OF EVENT

From an early age, John Locke acquired a firsthand, practical knowledge of politics that was to influence the writing of his *Two Treatises of Government* (1690). For much of Locke's life, England was involved in political and religious strife and reform. The country was torn between those who wanted to strengthen the power of Parliament and limit the power of monarchs and those who sought to uphold royal prerogatives as a matter of divine right.

In 1667, shortly after Locke received a master of arts degree from Christ Church College, Oxford University, his medical license afforded him the opportunity of becoming the personal secretary, physician, and friend of Anthony Ashley Cooper, later lord chancellor of England and the first earl of Shaftesbury. Shaftesbury—the satirical object of John Dryden's poem *Absalom and Achitophel, Part I* (1681)—was influential in court circles. He led the opposition to King Charles II in Parliament, and he is credited with founding what came to be known as the Whig faction. Shaftesbury led the attempt to exclude the king's Roman Catholic brother, the duke of York and Albany (later James II), from the succession to the English throne.

As a result of his association with Shaftesbury, Locke became personally involved in politics, obtained minor government posts, and was fortunate enough to make many influential contacts. In 1669, at Shaftesbury's request, he wrote a constitution for the American colony of Carolina (later separated into North and South Carolina). Locke observed the political machinations that forced his mentor Shaftesbury to flee England for Holland, seeking political asylum after being charged with high treason. In 1675, Locke himself was suspected of disloyalty and fled to France, where he studied the doctrines of the philosopher René Descartes, who had held views similar to those featured by Locke in his classic *An Essay Concerning Human Understanding* (1690).

While in France, Locke also played a vital role in the plans to depose the Catholic James II and crown the Protestant William III of Orange and Princess Mary in his stead. Indeed, scholars argue that Locke's teachings provided justification for the overthrow of the monarchy. He returned to England in 1688, the year of the Glorious Revolution, escorting the future Queen Mary II of England.

Locke's observation of and his involvement in the politics of England had far-reaching effects. In continental Europe at this time, divine right—the idea that kings and queens were the natural-born rulers of society, reigning in God's name and with his absolute authority—still held sway. England, however, was moving toward a constitutional monarchy, in which the people retained rights with which the monarchy could not interfere, including the right to be represented by a legislative body that was equal in power to the throne. The institutionalization of constitutional monarchy had taken most of the seventeenth century to accomplish, but it was finally cemented by the Glorious Revolution and the measures passed by Parliament in the wake of that revolution.

Locke's Second Treatise, the more popular of the *Two Treatises of Government*, was written in defense of the Glorious Revolution. A foundational work in modern theories of democracy, the treatise advocates religious tolerance and rights to personal property. In chapter 2, Locke declares that human beings are all born into a natural state of perfect freedom and goodness—free "to order [their] actions," in any way they see fit. Locke calls this state the law of nature. He believes that according to natural law, individuals should not have to ask anyone, for example, to be able to dispose of their own possessions. People are part of a "great and natural community," he writes, whose common interests are established by natural law. Every individual has the right to enforce the law of nature and to assist others to enforce it in the best interests of preserving humankind. People are free and equal in the state of nature and possess natural rights. Entrance into civil society, for Locke, entails ceding a small portion of one's natural rights (primarily the right to judge and punish others), but the rights of individuals in the state of nature remain the benchmark by which civil rights are to be judged.

John Locke. (Library of Congress)

Individuals, Locke states, should live under natural law—the law enacted by God, "a wise Maker"—which guarantees the right to life, liberty, and property. It is each individual's responsibility, "which obliges everyone," to enact the law of nature, which requires that they preserve peace and not harm one another. According to Locke, the law of nature ordains that individuals should respect and love God, obey their superiors, keep their promises, tell the truth, be mild and pure in character, maintain a friendly disposition, and love their neighbors. Acts such as murder, theft, and rape are "altogether forbidden" by this natural law. Rulers are necessary to rule justly. All this, he believes, is for the "public good."

Locke declares that rulers secure power from the consent of the people. In his seventh essay on natural law, Locke explains the obligations of rulers. The government should be a contract, or a "compact," as Locke calls it, between rulers and subjects. On one hand, sovereigns must rule justly and fulfill the purpose for which they were created—to preserve property—or lose their power. In other words, if the ruler violates the rights of the people or aspires to absolute power, then it becomes the responsibility of the representatives of the people to dismiss the ruler in question and find a replacement. On the other hand, people must sacrifice certain rights in return for just rule—they must obey the government in order for civil society to function.

Locke maintains that, although individuals may not deliberately enter consensual "compacts" with the government, their behavior nevertheless suggests that they "tacitly" consent to existing governmental laws: Anyone "that hath any possession or enjoyment of any part of the dominions of any government doth thereby give his tacit consent, and is as far forth obliged to obedience to the laws of that government." To clarify, if people take advantage of governmental services, by calling for assistance from

Locke on Tyranny

John Locke's Two Treatises of Government *was a fundamental influence upon the American Declaration of Independence and the notion that a tyrannical government is an illegitimate government. His treatises also provided the clearest seventeenth century articulation of a theory of the limits of power, in contradistinction to absolutist theories based in the divine right of kings. The passage below defines tyranny as a function of the rightful limits of power and the willful exercise of power in excess of those limits.*

As usurpation is the exercise of power, which another hath a right to; so tyranny is the exercise of power beyond right, which no body can have a right to. And this is making use of the power any one has in his hands, not for the good of those who are under it, but for his own private separate advantage. When the governor, however intitled, makes not the law, but his will, the rule; and his commands and actions are not directed to the preservation of the properties of his people, but the satisfaction of his own ambition, revenge, covetousness, or any other irregular passion.

Source: From section 199 of *Two Treatises of Government*, by John Locke (London: Millar, Woodfall, et al., 1764). http://oregonstate.edu/instruct/phl302/texts/locke/locke2/2nd-contents.html. Accessed April 19, 2005.

the fire department, asking for police protection, or even using the highways, they are consenting to a contract with the government and are therefore obliged to obey the law.

Significance

The *Two Treatises of Government* had a tremendous effect on the history of Western political philosophy. Locke was, after all, a radical and revolutionary thinker. Many considered his argument against the divine right of kings and his sanctioning of rebellion to be a call to revolution, or even to anarchy. In the American colonies during the eighteenth century, Locke's writings were to influence such patriots as Thomas Jefferson and Thomas Paine. Jefferson mirrored Locke's political doctrine in the Declaration of Independence (1776), when he wrote that government rests on popular consent and people should rebel when their rights are threatened.

The roots of American democracy are to be found in Locke's concept of natural laws, which Jefferson too expounded: "the will of the majority, the Natural law of every society, is the only sure guardian of the rights of man." Indeed, Locke's rights to "Life, Liberty and Property" foreshadow the rights to "Life, Liberty and the Pursuit of Happiness" enshrined in the Declaration of Independence. Locke's idea of the equality of people was also the inspiration of the popular aphorism "All men are created equal." In addition, radical writer Thomas Paine culled Locke's philosophy for inspiration in his popular pamphlet *Common Sense* (1776). In France, Locke's work in combination with Jean-Jacques Rousseau's *Du contrat social: Ou, Principes du droit politique* (1762; *Treatise on the Social Contract: Or, The Principles of Politic Law*, 1764) played a vital role in launching the French Revolution in 1789 and inspired many of the guarantees included in the French Constitution established in 1871.

During his lifetime, Locke published his political works anonymously in an effort to keep them apart from his classic *An Essay Concerning Human Understanding*, the bedrock of empiricism, in which he sought to examine the nature of knowledge free from any political considerations. Locke retired to Essex in 1691, where, as one of the seventeenth century's most influential men, he continued to exercise great political sway. His philosophical and political theories had influenced the work of such later philosophers as George Berkeley, David Hume, John Stuart Mill, and Bertrand Russell. Nobel Prize-winner Russell described Locke as "the most fortunate of philosophers, because his philosophical and political views were widely understood."

—*M. Casey Diana*

Further Reading

Ashcraft, Richard, ed. *Locke's "Two Treatises of Government."* London: Allen & Unwin, 1987. Seven essays provide a strong critical analysis of Lockean scholarship and a comprehensive evaluation of these secondary works.

Colman, John. *John Locke's Moral Philosophy*. Edinburgh: Edinburgh University Press, 1983. Scholarly examination of the philosophy behind Locke's political theories.

Cranston, Maurice. *John Locke: A Biography*. 1957. Reprint. New York: Oxford University Press, 1985. Comprehensive biography of Locke that includes insights into the British political workings leading up to the publication of *Two Treatises of Government*.

Dunn, John. *Political Thought of John Locke*. Reprint. New York: Oxford University Press, 1983. Extensive analysis and interpretation of the thought behind *Two Treatises of Government*.

Harpham, Edward. *John Locke's "Two Treatises of Government": New Interpretations*. Lawrence: University Press of Kansas, 1992. Scholarly but approachable account of how the interpretation of John Locke's political doctrine has changed over time. Includes a strong analysis of the religious and economic backgrounds of the time and a comprehensive bibliography.

Locke, John. *Two Treatises of Government*. Edited by P. Laslett. Cambridge, England: Cambridge University Press, 1960. John Locke's original classic. Like most works from this era, general readers will find this challenging to digest, but it is quite lucid in sections, and certainly worth the effort.

_______. *"Two Treatises of Government" and "A Letter Concerning Toleration."* Edited by Ian Shapiro. New Haven, Conn.: Yale University Press, 2003. Reprints two works in which Locke expresses his political theories. Also includes essays by historians Shapiro, John Dunn, and Ruth Grant that place these works in their historical, biographical, and intellectual contexts, describe the democratic elements of Locke's political theory, and explain Locke's views on women and the family.

See also: 1637: Descartes Publishes His *Discourse on Method*; 1651: Hobbes Publishes *Leviathan*; Nov., 1688-Feb., 1689: The Glorious Revolution; Feb. 13, 1689: Declaration of Rights; May 24, 1689: Toleration Act; May 3, 1695: End of Press Censorship in England.

Related articles in *Great Lives from History: The Seventeenth Century, 1601-1700:* Charles II (of England); René Descartes; Thomas Hobbes; James II; John Locke; Mary II; First Earl of Shaftesbury; William III.

June 2, 1692-May, 1693
Salem Witchcraft Trials

Growing hysteria over the possibility of witches living among them led Massachusetts colonists to try, convict, and execute a number of people, now believed to have been innocent, for the capital crime of witchcraft.

Locale: Salem, Massachusetts

Categories: Laws, acts, and legal history; religion and theology; social issues and reform

Key Figures

Samuel Parris (1653-1720), Puritan pastor of Salem Village

Tituba (1648?-1692), West Indian slave in the Parris household

William Phips (1651-1695), royal governor of Massachusetts, 1692-1694

Simon Bradstreet (1603-1697), provisional governor of Massachusetts after the fall of the Dominion of New England

William Stoughton (1631-1701), deputy governor and presiding justice at the witch trials

Samuel Sewall (1652-1730), Massachusetts magistrate and a judge at the witch trials

John Hathorne (1641-1717), assistant of the Massachusetts General Court who conducted examinations of accused witches

Jonathan Corwin (fl. 1692-1693), Massachusetts General Court examiner and judge

Nicholas Noyes (1647-1717), Puritan pastor of Salem Town

Increase Mather (1639-1723), pastor of the Boston Puritan church and president of Harvard College

Cotton Mather (1663-1728), Puritan minister who both criticized and defended the judges at the trials

Sarah Good and *Sarah Osborne*, two of the women accused of witchcraft

Summary of Event

Early in 1692, a circle of young girls began to meet in the home of Samuel Parris, the Puritan pastor of Salem Village. The minister's nine-year-old daughter, Betty, and Betty's eleven-year-old cousin, Abigail Williams, were fascinated by the voodoo-like tales and tricks of the family's Barbados slave, Tituba, and soon they began to invite their friends to share in the entertainment. Before long, some of the girls in the circle began to behave strangely, complaining of physical maladies, reporting visions, lapsing into trances, and trembling and babbling without restraint.

Among the Puritans, inexplicable afflictions were customarily attributed to the work of the devil, so most of the inhabitants of Salem Village believed the young girls when they charged that Tituba and two village women of doubtful respectability were practicing witchcraft upon them. Two assistants of the Massachusetts General Court, John Hathorne and Jonathan Corwin, were called upon to conduct a legal examination of the accused women. Placing no store in lawyers, the Puritans were governed essentially by Old Testament law. When they found a statement in the Scriptures that witches must not be allowed to live, their duty became clear. The two magistrates conducted their examination more like prosecuting attorneys than impartial investigators. They accepted the dreams and fancies of the young girls as positive evidence and concluded that a "strange tit or wart" on the body of one of the women was a "witches' tit," at which the devil and his familiars, or messengers, sucked the blood of the witch.

As in any system of law, the identity of the accused was essential to the Salem proceedings. One method of identification was a search of the accused's body for physical signs left behind by the devil. These bodily searches were performed on the woman accused by matrons and midwives, by order of the sheriff. The first six women to be identified as witches through this method were executed. Ironically, women who had knowledge of medicine and who used astrology (an acceptable form of prediction in certain cultures) to forecast illness were historically the victims of accusation themselves. As early as 1441, the duchess of Gloucester had been accused of witchcraft for her "uncanny knowledge of medicine and astrology."

Parris had planned to implicate Tituba as a witch and force her into naming others. When Tituba confessed her own connection with the devil, she implicated the other accused witches, and on March 7, all three were sent to prison. Tituba later said that Parris beat her into a confession, claiming that her accusations of Sarah Good and Sarah Osborne, as well as two other women, were the result of his abuse.

Although many of the villagers were skeptical of the claims of the girls, the examiners, supported by Parris and Nicholas Noyes, his colleague in Salem Town, called upon other ministers of the area to consult with them. More accusations—this time against respectable, pious women of the community—came almost immediately, and it seemed that the devil was carrying out his deception by possessing seemingly innocent persons. The

A woman condemned for witchcraft is burned at the stake. (Gay Brothers)

panic soon enveloped not only the residents of Salem but also those of neighboring towns. The trials would begin in Salem Village, but most of the accused resided in Andover.

Warrants for three Salem Village women were issued on February 29, 1692. The timing of the accusations had greatly increased their impact upon the populace, as the Massachusetts Bay Colony was still quite agitated over the loss of its charter in 1684 and the overthrow of the Dominion of New England in 1689. The weak provisional government, headed by the ailing governor Simon Bradstreet, was merely awaiting the arrival of a new governor and did nothing to avert the crisis. When Sir William Phips, royal governor of Massachusetts, arrived in May, 1692, with the new Massachusetts charter, he decided immediately that proper courts must be established for the trying of witches. On the last Wednesday in May, the Governor's Council set up a general court, which promptly appointed seven judges to constitute a special Court of Oyer and Terminer to convene on June 2.

The witchcraft fever continued to spread, but the accused were confident that the distinguished judges Bartholomew Gedney, Samuel Sewall, John Richards, William Sergeant, Wait Winthrop, Nathaniel Saltonstall (later replaced by Jonathan Corwin), and Presiding Justice William Stoughton represented some of the best minds in the colony and would deal justly with the witchcraft problem. The court, however, accepted the testimony gathered at the examination as proven fact. At the trials, the judges simply heard new evidence, and a jury decided the prisoners' fate. On June 8, the General Court revived an old law making witchcraft a capital offense. Two days later, Bridget Bishop, the first condemned witch, went to the gallows.

A schism among the judges over the validity of spectral evidence necessitated a delay in the proceedings while they sought the advice of clergy of the Boston area. Although the ministers urged caution in the handling of spectral evidence, they praised the judges and encouraged further prosecution of the witches. As the summer brought more hangings, the remaining prisoners began to fear for their lives and several managed to escape. The judges, as good Puritans, accepted confession as evidence of possible regeneration and were merciful to those who would confess their dealings with the devil and repent, but few of the accused, as staunch Puritans, were willing to lie, even to save their lives.

On July 15, Martha Carrier, a resident of Andover, was arrested after being accused by several of the afflicted girls from Salem. Carrier's courage and defiance during her legal examination may have been considered malicious and imprudent by the seventeenth century audience. Testimony by her neighbors may suggest why she first came under suspicion: ". . . and there happening some difference betwixt us she gave forth several threatening words, as she often used to do," testified one male neighbor. According to religious faith during this time, such threats were considered a curse. The Court of Oyer and Terminer condemned Carrier on August 5, 1692. Five days later, her children—Thomas Jr., ten years of age, and Sarah, age seven—were imprisoned and tricked by magistrate Hathorne into naming their

SARAH GOOD IS INDICTED FOR WITCHCRAFT

After she was named by the slave Tituba and examined by the magistrates, Sarah Good faced three indictments for the crime of witchcraft. Reproduced below is the first of the three indictments.

The jurors for our sovereign lord and lady, the king and queen, present that Sarah Good, wife of William Good of Salem Village in the county of Essex, husbandman, [on] the second day of May in the fourth year of the reign of our sovereign lord and lady, William and Mary, by the grace of God, of England, Scotland, France, and Ireland king and queen, defenders of the faith, etc., and [on] diverse other days and times, as well before as after, certain detestable arts called witchcrafts and soceries wickedly and feloniously hath used, practiced, and exercised, at and within the township of Salem in the county of Essex aforesaid, in, upon, and against one Sarah Vibber, wife of John Vibber of Salem aforesaid, husbandman, by which said wicked arts, she the said Sarah Vibber, [on] the said second day of may in the fourth year abovesaid and [on] diverse other days and times, as well before as after, was and is tortured, afflicted, pained, consumed, wasted, and tormented, and also for sundry other acts of witchcraft by said Sarah Good committed and done before and since that time against the peace of our sovereign lord and lady, the king and queen, their crown and dignity, and against the form of the statute in that case made and provided.

Source: From the University of Virginia Salem Witch Trials Documentary Archive and Transcription Project. http://etext.virginia.edu/salem/witchcraft/texts/transcripts.html. Accessed February 18, 2005. Orthography and punctuation modified by the editors.

mother. The court further abused all four of her children in hopes that she would confess, but she never did. On August 19, 1692, Martha Carrier was hanged at Salem.

By the time the last of the twenty convicted witches had been executed on September 22, public support for the trials was waning. There were numerous reasons for this change: Several of those who were executed in August died calmly, forgiving their accusers and judges and protesting their innocence to the end; the court's procedures seemed to be aggravating the witchcraft problem rather than alleviating it; and as the witch hunt spread, persons were being accused who no one could believe were guilty. The panic had been confined almost exclusively to Essex County, and ministers from outside the immediate area began taking a stand against continuing the trials. Increase Mather, the great Boston divine, warned against reliance on spectral evidence and traveled to Salem to investigate the method of obtaining confessions. A petition from Andover was the first of many to call for release of the remaining prisoners and to denounce the accusing girls. On October 29, Governor Phips dismissed the Court of Oyer and Terminer. Its end marked the end of the witch hunt.

While some people were disappointed to see the trials end, most were relieved to return to their long-neglected work. Blaming Parris for allowing the death of innocent relatives and friends, the congregation of the Salem church voted to void his salary. In the ensuing years, many of the accusers of the condemned repented, and in 1709 and 1711, the Massachusetts General Court restored to many of those who had been accused of being witches, as well as the children of the executed victims, their good names. Those families were awarded compensation for financial losses. The names of some, however, were never cleared.

During the Salem witchcraft trials, both Increase and Cotton Mather expressed their doubts about the proceedings, especially concerning the use of spectral evidence. Increase Mather insisted that the special Court of Oyer and Terminer be terminated because it might be guilty of shedding innocent blood. Cotton Mather, one of the most cogent critics of the court's methods while it was sitting, afterward offered a strongly partisan defense of the judges. Because of this defense, historians have incorrectly presented Cotton Mather as the instigator of the witchcraft trials. He was, in fact, guilty of not opposing the trials vigorously enough. Although the Salem trials were not the last, because of the Massachusetts authorities' actions in discovering, acknowledging, and disowning their errors, the Salem experience helped to end witchcraft trials in Western civilization.

Significance

The tragedy of Salem extended beyond the people who were executed. Added to the list of victims should be Sarah Good's nursing infant, who died while Good was incarcerated; Roger Toothaker, who was murdered in prison; Lydia Dustin, who was found innocent but never released and died in prison in 1693; and many others, including slaves who suffered not only from bondage but also from witchcraft accusations. By acts of the General Court of November 23 and December 16, special sessions of the Superior Court of Judicature were ordered to complete the trials. The new circuit court was composed largely of the same judges as the recently dissolved court, but it now held spectral evidence to be inadmissible. Fifty-two accused witches came to trial early in January, 1693, and forty-nine were released immediately for lack of evidence. The governor soon reprieved the others, and by May, all the remaining prisoners had been discharged.

A number of reasons have been offered to explain this tragic period in colonial history: Generational, racial, and sexual hostility, opposition to law, social stresses, and food poisoning all have been advanced as the causes of anxiety and hysteria in Salem during this time. However, the causes were complex and no single explanation is sufficient in itself. Whatever their causes, the Salem witchcraft trials have taken on an iconic role in American history, and an unjust search for scapegoats is now commonly referred to as a "witch hunt." Indeed, when Senator Joseph McCarthy conducted his search for Communists in the United States government and in Hollywood in the 1950's, playwright Arthur Miller responded by writing *The Crucible* (pr., pb. 1953), a play about the Salem witchcraft trials.

—*Warren M. Billings and Kimberly Manning*

Further Reading

Fox, Sanford J. *Science and Justice: The Massachusetts Witchcraft Trials*. Baltimore: Johns Hopkins University Press, 1968. Describes the role of science in prosecuting the accused witches. Examines the scientific awareness, attitudes, and ethos at the time of the trials.

Goodbeer, Richard. *The Devil's Dominion: Magic and Religion in Early New England*. New York: Cambridge University Press, 1992. Examines the inconsistencies of folk magic as practiced by ordinary men and women in early New England. Focuses on the similarities between Puritanism and magic that enabled even church members to switch from one to the other without questioning their actions. Chapter 5 is devoted to the witch hunt of 1692.

Hill, Frances. *A Delusion of Satan: The Full Story of the Salem Witch Trials*. New York: Da Capo Press, 1995. Well-written and well-researched popular account of the trials, examining them within the social, religious, economic, and political climate of seventeenth century Massachusetts.

Hoffer, Peter Charles. *The Salem Witchcraft Trials: A Legal History*. Lawrence: University Press of Kansas, 1997. Recounts the events of the trials, describing how the desolation of New England life—Indian wars, disease, severe weather, and challenges to Puritan power—created an atmosphere of paranoia that spurred the persecution of alleged witches.

Norton, Mary Beth. *In the Devil's Snare: The Salem Witchcraft Crisis of 1692*. New York: Alfred A. Knopf, 2002. Norton contends the witchcraft trials must be understood in relation to the Second Indian War (King William's War), because colonists' religious interpretation of the war created an environment in which the trials could take place.

Robinson, Enders A. *The Devil Discovered: Salem Witchcraft, 1692*. New York: Hippocrene Books, 1991. Begins with a chronological sequence of events and concludes by analyzing the lives of the first seventy-five accused witches. Tables, illustrations, and maps clarify the intricate relationships of the accusers and accused.

Rosenthal, Bernard. *Salem Story: Reading the Witch Trials of 1692*. New York: Cambridge University Press, 1993. Investigates the assumptions surrounding the trials, the mythologizing of the event, and the stereotyping of witches regarding gender and age. Uses surviving documentation to illustrate that many of the accusers used logic and reason, rather than hysteria, to charge their victims.

Weisman, Richard. *Witchcraft, Magic, and Religion in Seventeenth Century Massachusetts*. Amherst: University of Massachusetts Press, 1984. Contends that the cultural response to the witch hunts of 1692 was aided, in part, by a lack of consensus over how to define and deal with witchcraft. Addresses political and legislative issues.

SEE ALSO: 1610-1643: Reign of Louis XIII; Dec. 26, 1620: Pilgrims Arrive in North America; May, 1630-1643: Great Puritan Migration; Sept. 8, 1643: Confederation of the United Colonies of New England; June 30, 1680: Spanish Inquisition Holds a Grandiose *Auto-da-fé*; June, 1686-Apr., 1689: Dominion of New England Forms.

RELATED ARTICLES in *Great Lives from History: The Seventeenth Century, 1601-1700:* John Alden; Charles II (of Spain); Robert Fludd; Matthew Hale; Johannes Kepler; The Mancini Sisters; Rebecca Nurse.

June 8, 1692
CORN RIOTS IN MEXICO CITY

Food shortages and racial resentment contributed to colonial Mexico's most violent and damaging riot, as the large mixed-race and Indian racial elements of the capital went on a rampage that destroyed many government buildings and businesses.

LOCALE: Mexico City, New Spain (now in Mexico)
CATEGORIES: Wars, uprisings, and civil unrest; social issues and reform; economics; agriculture

KEY FIGURES

Gasper de la Cerda Sandoval Silva y Mendoza (1653-1697), conde de Galve and viceroy of New Spain, 1688-1696

Francisco de Aguiar y Seijas (d. 1698), archbishop of Mexico, 1680-1698

Carlos de Sigüenza y Góngora (1645-1700), Spanish intellectual and chronicler of the riots

SUMMARY OF EVENT

In 1692, Mexico City, capital of the large Viceroyalty of New Spain, experienced its second major riot of the century. Both disturbances, or *tumultos*, involved the city's sizeable population of underprivileged mestizos, blacks, and Indians, who took to the streets and wrought considerable destruction.

By the seventeenth century, Mexico City contained large numbers of persons on the extreme margins of society who were a potentially volatile force in times of cultural stress. This situation stemmed from the racial policies and laws of the Spanish colonial system, which imposed the dominance of an elite European minority that made up less than 20 percent of the population over a large, racially diverse society. After the conquest, intermarriage (or at least child bearing) between Spaniards and Indians created a new mixed-race element, the mestizos. The ethnic situation was further complicated by the presence of African slaves and freemen, as well as a few Asians, resulting in further diversity and racial mixing. Furthermore, the dominant European group itself eventually became divided into those born in Spain (*peninsulars*), who were especially favored by the Crown, and a larger, American-born creole population.

Europeans embraced the concept of *limpieza de sangre* (an untainted pure bloodline) as a rationalization for keeping the increasing numbers of nonwhites in check and maintaining for themselves exclusive control over political and economic institutions and many professions. Creoles, whose bloodlines were often considered "suspect" by the *peninsulars*, were particularly responsible for the creation of a complicated, hierarchal system of racial classification containing from sixteen to forty possible categories, ranked according to the degree and type of racial mixture.

To simplify matters, all those who did not qualify as pure Spaniard or pure Indian under this system were ultimately referred to as *castas*. Government positions, private land ownership, higher education, mercantile trades, and the more prestigious artisan crafts became the monopoly of Spanish- or American-born whites, through laws that defined the rights and status of each of the various racial groups. Residents of New Spain who fell into the nonwhite categories were, with minor exceptions, effectively relegated to being unskilled laborers, peasants, and household servants. Many were unemployed or underemployed.

Although some enterprising *castas* and Indians did manage to become artisans, their situation was nevertheless unstable and volatile. In general, people of color lived in miserable conditions. The Spanish elite's restrictions on socioeconomic activities and possibilities for advancement of the other racial groups created great urban slums and barrios whose disadvantaged inhabitants included many desperate beggars and indigent persons living by their wits outside the law as pickpockets and thieves. Meanwhile, the ruling classes viewed the debased conditions of these marginalized peoples as proof of their inferiority, immorality, treachery, and debased criminal nature.

Although the complicated hierarchal racial classifications proved rather difficult to maintain in a strict, rigid sense, the colonial masters also effectively used a system of patronage to control or subordinate the majority, nonwhite population. This practice enforced dependency on upper class benefactors and manipulated the lower classes by using favoritism in unevenly dispensing rewards, playing one group against another, and co-opting the more successful *castas*.

The Mexico City riots of 1624 and 1692, had several common elements. The later *tumulto*, however, exploded into a more serious challenge to Spanish authority. A combination of economic, social, and political circumstances contributed to the uprising. In 1691, severe rains and floods were followed by rot, blight, and failure of the maize and wheat crops. Shortages soon led to skyrocketing prices, and in 1692, maize prices reached their highest level in a century. Although Viceroy Gaspar de la Cerda Sandoval Silva y Mendoza, conde de Galve, and other leaders made some efforts to increase the supply of grain in the capital, these measures were not sufficient. Also, their decision not to impose price controls in hopes that a free market would lead to more supply only exacerbated the desperate situation of the poor. Food prices tripled in 1692, pushing many toward starvation. In addition, commoners believed that the authorities were guilty of corruption and mismanagement.

The situation became volatile on June 8, when rumors spread that officials had killed or mortally injured a poor Indian woman who was part of a group assembled at the city's *alhóndiga* (granary). A small angry group of Indians appeared at the archbishop's palace in the afternoon to complain and demand justice. Archbishop Don Francisco de Aguiar y Seijas told the petitioners to seek out the viceroy with this request. Shortly after 5:30 P.M. at the viceregal palace in the city's main plaza, known as the Zócalo, the group, now numbering around 150 to 200 people, was again turned away and denied access to authority. With these channels of communication and safety valves denied, the crowd's hitherto semi respectful attitude toward Spanish authority degenerated into contempt. The palace guards became objects of taunts and insults. By six o'clock, a riot had broken out. As the Indians began to throw stones and the word spread, both the size and the racial diversity of the mob increased. Soon, the rioters numbered in the thousands, including some lower-class whites.

After the palace came under attack, the undermanned contingent of guards charged the crowd but was turned back. The guards' efforts to barricade the doors only prompted the mob to set those doors ablaze, and flames soon poured from every side of the doomed edifice. Crowds also burned the public gibbet and stocks, as well as the viceroy's carriage. In a series of other spontaneous actions and separate chaotic scenes, rioters in the plaza torched the municipal buildings, including the offices of city government, the archives, and the granary. Finally, nearly three hundred stalls and shops around the plaza's marketplace were looted and burned. Clothing, weapons, and alcoholic beverages, such as *pulque*, figured prominently among the stolen goods.

According to witnesses, an indescribable, menacing, raucous, earsplitting din filled the plaza. In this tumult, various threatening slogans and insults were reportedly shouted: "Long live the king and death to bad government!" "Down with the Spaniards and the Gachupines (an insulting term for peninsular Spaniards) . . . who are eating up our corn!" "Death to the viceroy and his wife!" "Death to the *corregidor* (governor)!" "Long live the king and death to his cuckold!" In using the latter term, the crowds insulted the manliness of the Spaniards and thereby their right to command respect. As the riot unfolded, Spaniards moved through the crowd to escape and many hid behind the bolted doors of their homes. An attempt by the archbishop to appeal to the crowd's conscience failed. Other efforts by churchmen had mixed success but saved a few important buildings.

The riot's momentum began to dissipate during the final stage of looting. The crowd soon started to thin out as participants headed for home with their prizes. While people dispersed, armed Spaniards began to enter the plaza after seven o'clock, killing and wounding many of those still present. By ten o'clock, the square was empty except for the bodies of the dead and wounded.

Spanish authorities quickly and brutally restored order. Roughly sixty individuals received sentences ranging from gruesome executions to whipping and public humiliation. Military forces were strengthened and new restrictions placed on Indians, who apparently made up the majority of rioters. Interestingly, many of the Indian and *casta* participants were artisans and represented the higher ranks of their racial categories whose position had become extremely precarious in the economic crisis.

SIGNIFICANCE

The 1692 uprising was the most destructive *tumulto* in the history of colonial New Spain. Damage totaled an astronomical two million pesos. Reconstruction of some buildings was not complete until 1720. Scores of people were killed and many times that number injured. Moreover, in the riot's initial stage, the rioters became a unified social and political force, threatening the control of the ruling Spaniards. This unity of purpose and revolutionary fellowship revealed the limits of Spanish efforts at racial control and the fragility of Spanish authority. However, without discipline, leadership, and planning, the uprising degenerated into a looting spree in which each person acted only for herself or himself; it was therefore easily extinguished.

The rioters lacked the vision and means to construct an alternative to Spanish rule. In the aftermath, many fearful commoners collaborated with the authorities by revealing participants in hopes of avoiding punishment. Within a relatively short time, when it became apparent that order was effectively restored, many of the government's strict measures were relaxed. Nothing was done to address the real causes of this destructive and traumatic event, however. Spaniards preferred to interpret the unsettling episode not as a spontaneous uprising of economically distressed masses but as a planned conspiracy with key leaders. Carlos de Sigüenza y Góngora, New Spain's most prestigious intellectual and scientist, witnessed part of the rebellion and wrote an account. Don Carlos's interpretation reflected a typical elite viewpoint in citing drunkenness and natural moral perversity of the so-called "lesser breeds" as important factors.

—*David A. Crain*

FURTHER READING

Cope, R. Douglas. *The Limits of Racial Domination: Plebeian Society in Colonial Mexico City, 1660-1720.* Madison: University of Wisconsin Press, 1994. The most complete analysis available of the Mexico City riot of 1692. A well-researched and informative treatment of racial policy and race relations.

Guthrie, Chester L. "Riots in Seventeenth-Century Mexico City: A Study of Social and Economic Conditions." In *Greater America: Essays in Honor of Herbert Eugene Bolton*. Reprint. Freeport, N.Y.: Books for Libraries Press, 1968. Analysis and interpretation of these events that confirms the spontaneous nature of the 1692 riot.

"Tumult and Shouting." In *Many Mexicos*, edited by Leslie B. Simpson. Berkeley: University of California Press, 1959. This chapter in a well-written monograph describes and analyzes the riots of 1624 and 1692 in Mexico City.

See also: 1604-1680: Rise of Criollo Identity in Mexico; Nov. 28, 1607: Martin Begins Draining Lake Texcoco; 1615: Guamán Poma Pleas for Inca Reforms; Feb. 22-27, 1632: Zuñi Rebellion; Mar. 31, 1650: Earthquake Destroys Cuzco; Beginning 1680's: Guerra dos Bárbaros; Aug. 10, 1680: Pueblo Revolt.

Related article in *Great Lives from History: The Seventeenth Century, 1601-1700:* Sor Juana Inés de la Cruz.

1693
Ray Argues for Animal Consciousness

Contrary to René Descartes and other thinkers, natural historian, philosopher, and theologian John Ray argued that animals indeed are conscious beings.

Locale: England

Categories: Biology; philosophy; religion and theology

Key Figures

John Ray (1627-1705), an English natural historian and natural theologian

René Descartes (1596-1650), a French philosopher and mathematician

Henry More (1614-1687), an English scientist and theologian

Nicolas Malebranche (1638-1715), a French mathematician and philosopher

Summary of Event

John Ray's reaction to the denial of consciousness in animals by René Descartes's theory of animal automatism must be viewed in the context of the differences between the philosophies of Ray and Descartes. Descartes had several reasons to deny consciousness in animals. First, he started with a definition of the soul that entailed a strict mind-body dualism. Matter, extended substance, was fundamentally different and separate from soul, or thinking substance. Moreover, the properties of matter explained the phenomena of life in all organisms, including humans.

It is in part 5 of *Discours de la méthode* (1637; *Discourse on Method*, 1649) that Descartes formally denies that animals have consciousness. He argues that whereas the presence of a soul is not necessary for life, it *is* necessary for consciousness, that is, the soul is necessary for the awareness of sensation. It is also by possession of the soul that human beings have the capacity to reason. Thus, consciousness in animals would entail the presence of a soul with its capacity to reason, a presence that would be the case for all animals, including oysters, worms, and sponges—an idea Descartes found ridiculous.

In addition to this deductive argument, Descartes proposed two tests to distinguish human beings from mere machines, or automatons. According to the language test, machines cannot express thoughts or intentions through language (through speech or sign). For example, Descartes dismissed the mimicking of language by the parrot, who seems to "speak," because its words do not originate from its own mental state or from its own thoughts; its words were not meant to communicate, as do the words of humans. The parrot, then, merely mimics, and is therefore an automaton.

The second test, the action test, claims that although machines can do some things as well or even better than humans, they nevertheless would fail at others, therefore proving they cannot "adjust" their actions according to what they know. Descartes believed that this fact proved that the machine did not act through understanding, but only through the composition of its internal "physical" or "mechanical" structures.

In a 1649 letter to Henry More, cited by Ray in his *Synopsis animalium quadrupedum et serpentini generis* (1693; synopsis of the types of quadrupedal animals and serpents), Descartes wrote that the action test was the main reason to reject animal thought. By these two arguments, Descartes concluded that animals are not rational and that their behavior is analogous to that of a clock (a mechanism).

Ray's beliefs in the matter fall squarely within the natural theology tradition. He believed that the role of God in nature could not simply be to form matter, divide it into parts, and apply laws of nature, as Descartes had thought. The works of nature were too complicated to come from natural law alone; they required design. Ray devoted *The Wisdom of God Manifested in the Works of Creation* (1691) to an exposition of God's fitting of the various means in nature to their ends. In the work, Ray presented illustrations showing animal behavior that was thought-based. He used the example of a dog who, arriving at a fork in the road before his keeper, waited to see which road the keeper chose before proceeding himself.

In another example, a dog, wanting to jump onto a high table, used a chair as a step. In yet another example, Ray illustrated the case of birds who kept track of their young so that no chick would be missed in feeding, a feat Ray asserted could not be performed by a machine. In *Synopsis*, he described how blind beggars were helped by dogs and how horses performed various tricks. In *Wisdom of God*, Ray argued that God had made creatures so that they could enjoy life. That is, one of God's purposes for creating the "lesser" beings included experiences that required consciousness.

Ray rejected Descartes's views on the soul and accepted the traditional Aristotelian doctrine of three souls to account for life: the vegetative soul for nutrition and growth, the sensitive soul for sensation and movements, and the rational soul for reasoning, present in humans. Ray believed that animals had a sensitive soul, that they were fully conscious of sensations, and that the sensitive soul was not material. Furthermore, he asserted that he would rather attribute low-grade reason to animals than have them considered simply machines or automatons. The possession of an immaterial soul did not entail immortality for animals, however. Descartes had explicitly rejected the Aristotelian conception of the soul and had perhaps been driven to develop his concept of soul in reaction to it.

Ray provided a list of reasons to support consciousness in animals. One, he observed that people sympathize with the pain and suffering of animals. Two, he invoked Proverbs 10:12, in which God instructed people to be kind to animals, an admonition that would not make sense, he insisted, if animals were only machines. Third, Ray suggested that God would not make animals mere machines solely to mock the actions of human beings.

In *Synopsis* Ray argued that if consciousness in animals were a property of matter, then why not also reason? Reason and perception (cognition) were separate, he said, and sensation was separate from intelligence and reason. Thus, animals could have true sensation without having reason or intelligence. He also pointed out that animals and humans share similar nerves, bones, muscles, and so forth, and that similar causes of actions should entail similar results. In contrast, Descartes believed that all these "parts" simply operated mechanically.

Significance

John Ray's views on the soul formed only one part of his rejection of René Descartes's philosophical system. He also rejected Descartes's denial of final causes and his cosmological and ontological proofs for the existence of God, based as they were on innate ideas, as Ray put it. In short, Ray rejected Descartes's rationalism.

Descartes's theory of animal automatism contradicted what most likely was common to the human experience of animals, and the shortcomings of his particular arguments have been exposed. In so doing, Descartes seemed forced to argue that the apparent experience of sensation in animals was analogous to the mechanical contrivances that imitated the living. In contrast, Ray emphasized experience, both in finding evidence for God's existence and in providing several pages of descriptions of intelligent behavior in various animals in *Wisdom of God*.

Ray shared his approach to nature with other English scientists and philosophers of his time, notably Robert Boyle, who had written a tract on final causes in nature. Moreover, Ray's views tended toward vitalism, insisting that life was caused by immaterial souls, and he clearly attacked mechanism and materialism, both of which he associated with Descartes's philosophy. While Descartes's views created quite a furor, he, too, had defenders, such as Nicolas Malebranche, who argued that animals did not sense pain because God would be unjust if he let innocents (animals) suffer. One story tells of how, after Malebranche kicked a pregnant dog (which had then cried out in pain) to "prove" his point, he replied to the reproaches of a bystander who witnessed the incident by saying that the dog did not feel the kick.

—*Kristen L. Zacharias*

Further Reading

Graukroger, Stephen. *Descartes: An Intellectual Biography*. Oxford, England: Clarendon Press, 1995. A thorough treatment of the development of Descartes's ideas. Useful for understanding his views on dualism.

Kinghorn, A. M. "'In Doubt to Deem Himself a God, or Beast.'" *Journal of European Studies* 21 (1991): 129-144. A brief history of the philosophical problem of animal automatism, starting with the ideas of Descartes.

Newman, Lex. "Unmasking Descartes's Case for the Bete Machine Doctrine." *Canadian Journal of Philosophy* 31 (2001): 389-426. A technical analysis of Descartes's arguments denying consciousness to animals and a critique of several interpretations of his position.

Radner, Daisie, and Michael Radner. *Animal Conscious-*

ness. New York: Prometheus Books, 1989. The authors present Descartes's views and seventeenth century responses, with the author's critique of the validity of the arguments. The second half of the book treats contemporary theories.

Raven, Charles E. *John Ray, Naturalist: His Life and Works*. Cambridge, England: Cambridge University Press, 1950. Still the only book-length biography of Ray, useful for descriptions of his works, though outdated methodologically. Emphasizes Ray's natural theology.

Walker, Stephen. *Animal Thought*. London: Routledge & Kegan Paul, 1983. Walker provides a history of the problem of animal thought and covers late twentieth century research in animal psychology.

See also: 1601-1672: Rise of Scientific Societies; 1617-1628: Harvey Discovers the Circulation of the Blood; 1637: Descartes Publishes His *Discourse on Method*.

Related articles in *Great Lives from History: The Seventeenth Century, 1601-1700:* Giovanni Alfonso Borelli; René Descartes; Jean de La Fontaine; John Ray; Tokugawa Tsunayoshi.

July 27, 1694
Bank of England Is Chartered

The chartering of the Bank of England created a central bank that provided financial support to the British government and consolidated control of its financial systems.

Locale: London, England
Categories: Economics; government and politics; organizations and institutions; trade and commerce

Key Figures

William Paterson (1658-1719), Scottish-born creator of the concept of the Bank of England

Charles Montagu (1661-1715), earl of Halifax, commissioner of the treasury who championed the plan for the bank

John Houblon (1632-1711), first director of the Bank of England

Summary of Event

One of the oldest of the European national banks, the Bank of England was chartered in 1694, establishing a trend followed by most major Western nations during the subsequent three hundred years. Sweden had created its own "central" bank, the Riksbank, almost fifty years before the Bank of England, but neither it nor the other European government-originated banks, such as the Bank of Amsterdam in Holland, created in 1609, truly had *central* banking powers. Technically, a central bank not only acts as a lender of last resort to the private sector and furnishes loans to the government but also regulates the financial system through its use of reserves. No European bank possessed that capability, well into the 1800's.

The Bank of England originated with the seizure of merchants' funds by King Charles I, after the funds had been deposited in the Tower of London. The merchants had intended to use the money to pay overseas debts, but Charles needed it to cover expenses arising from his Scottish wars. Although the king gave back the money—in return for a loan of forty thousand pounds—the outraged merchants knew they no longer could leave deposits at the tower, choosing instead to keep the funds in their stores under the authority of their employees. After the English Civil Wars erupted, however, the clerks started to lend the money to local goldsmiths at four pence a day. The goldsmiths proved trustworthy and inspired confidence in the business community.

As with most national banks, however, the true impetus for creating such an institution came from the government's chronic need for funds. William Paterson, a Scottish promoter, part-time merchant, and full-time adventurer, had hatched three separate ideas to provide the Crown with money. Under his plans, Paterson and his fellow merchants received interest, while the king had his loan. In the context of defending the bank concept, Paterson wrote a pamphlet outlining the necessity for a bank. In 1693, Paterson put forth his third scheme along with a group of London merchants, to lend the government 1.2 million pounds at 8 percent interest. Ultimately, Charles Montagu, later the earl of Halifax, championed the concept. The lords of the treasury, after considering several plans, found Paterson's the most appealing.

Actually establishing the bank proved rather easy: The bank was created under the authority of sixteen sections of the Tunnage Act of 1694, for the purpose of paying into the exchequer the sum of 1.2 million pounds. Commissioners received subscriptions, and the institution was chartered as The Governor and Company of the Bank of England. No individual could subscribe for more than twenty thousand pounds. The bank could deal in bills of exchange, could buy and sell bullion, and sell commodities deposited as securities for loans that were not redeemed at the agreed upon date (or three months thereafter). Sir John Houblon was the first bank governor, and William Paterson one of the twenty-four directors. A second bank act increased the bank's original capital from 1.2 million pounds to more than 2.3 million pounds. Although the official name was the Bank of England, people often referred to the bank in its first one hundred years generally as the Bank of London.

The government attempted to give the bank a monopoly, but its charter's prohibitory enactments did not curtail private corporations from conducting banking activities. Consequently, in 1709, the bank's partial monopoly was tightened, with Parliament making it illegal for any group of people to "borrow, owe, or take up any sum or sums of money on their bills or notes, payable at demand, at any less time than six months from the borrowing." The bank paid interest on deposits, and could issue its own notes (paper money).

By the Wars of the Spanish Succession (1701-1714), the English government became totally dependent on the bank and its loans for funding, with Parliament providing six short-term renewals between 1696 and 1781. Every renewal involved fighting a war or paying for the results of one. Developing a banking policy out of a string of crises gave the Bank of England neither a clear definition nor a role. As a result, it lagged far behind the major banks of Holland, Germany, and Sweden. The bank's focus differed substantially from the policies of Alexander Hamilton, whose program as first U.S. Secretary of the Treasury almost a century later resulted in the creation of the Bank of the United States (BUS). Hamilton's financial design emphasized providing a stable money supply and solid credit rating for the United States, while the Bank of England's major role remained the financial support of government.

Over time, however, the Bank of England found that it had to discount bills, secure deposits, and act as a lender of last resort, forcing some discipline on the bank itself. The state-oriented nature of the bank stifled the development of a healthy private-sector banking system as had emerged in neighboring Scotland. In Scotland, there evolved a system of "free banks," which had no monopoly over note issue and thus had to compete with each other's money. The Bank of England not only slowed the appearance of private banking but also found itself as dependent on the state as the state was on it. Most advances to the English treasury, for example, were in the form of interest-bearing loans; in return, the bank received charter extensions. Yet as joint-stock companies started to appear, they made direct payments to the government for monopoly privileges, leading many to think that the state

The Bank of England, founded at the Royal Exchange in London, would play an instrumental role in the development of a global English empire. (Hulton|Archive by Getty Images)

had not gained as much from its relationship with the bank as it could have. As with any monopoly, the bank also raised suspicions that it wielded undue political influence. Other corporations in London complained that the situation encouraged the bank to meddle in domestic politics. The Bank of England, as did the later Bank of the United States, soon came under fire for its cozy connections with the government, while the government was charged with being controlled by the monied interests.

Each charter renewal expanded the bank's capital and its power. The capital rose from 1.2 million pounds in 1694 to 10.7 million pounds in 1742. Loans to the government, however, grew even faster. By 1749, the government owed the bank 11.6 million pounds. English finance, therefore, was born and continued to live in a borrowing mode. Again, that stood in contrast to the American financial structure, devised by treasury secretary Hamilton, who had made it a priority to limit the amount of debt the U.S. Congress could incur by creating a sinking fund in which old debt had to be retired before new debt could be assumed. In that context, the reason for creating the Bank of the United States was to help eliminate all the old debts.

The Bank of England's monopoly over note-issue functions in England made it impossible for the private sector to instill discipline on the financial sector. Not only had the 1709 act virtually prohibited private banks from printing money, but it made the bank substantially different from the Continental banks and the Bank of the United States, all of which had to compete at some level. In the United States, for example, each state had its own chartering process in which banks were granted the authority to issue notes. Consequently, the Bank of the United States could not issue notes indiscriminately, or their value would drop relative to the value of the state notes.

Yet the Bank of England enjoyed the confidence of the London merchants because the government did not underwrite the bank's revenues directly. The paper it issued for circulation and the paper it provided to the government technically remained separate, although foreigners found it difficult to distinguish between the two. London merchants had found the bank generally reliable, not subject to runs, and therefore did not hesitate to place their deposits there. The bank's monopoly position enhanced its accumulation of deposits, which in turn provided the basis for mercantile, as well as government, credit. Thus, despite the lack of competition, the bank remained sound throughout the 1700's and its stock remained above par for fifteen of the bank's first twenty years. In addition, the bank kept a sharp focus on the commercial activities in and around London, and refrained from underwriting ambitious development or overseas projects, further adding to local confidence.

Significance

Private business dealings remained a small portion of the bank's overall activities, however. It discounted local notes and serviced the needs of merchants, but was careful not to emit too many notes. It kept a bullion-to-paper ratio of as little as 19.7 percent; in one year—1763—the bank's reserves fell so low that it had only seven ounces of gold for every one hundred pounds in circulation. Yet the bank proved so cautious in its lending that from 1694 to 1788, it lost only sixty-eight thousand pounds in bad paper. It did not see its role primarily as a lender of last resort to other banks, and when the Scottish Ayr Bank pleaded for funds in 1772, the Bank of England only offered the strictest terms, which the Scottish bank could not pay, and it subsequently failed. Investors and London merchants, however, viewed such actions as positive signs that the Bank of England was solid and solvent.

The Bank of London made the transition to a true national bank, the Bank of England, in the 1800's, when it began to extend its influence over the economy as a whole. After the Napoleonic wars, for example, the bank's directors engaged in a discussion about the conditions under which it would resume cash payments for paper. Even then, the directors argued simultaneously for more authority and less control from the government, and yet resisted the notion that the bank had any responsibility for the economy. The government reviewed the entire banking policy and the relationship between the bank and the government. Out of those 1819 discussions, the Bank of England's functions changed more toward that of a central bank in the modern sense, with greater control over the economy but also greater political control.

—*Larry Schweikart*

Further Reading

Andreades, A. *History of the Bank of England, 1640-1903*. 1909. Reprint. New York: Augustus M. Kelley, 1966. This source contains substantial material on the early history and environment of the Bank of England. Based upon early primary-source documentation.

Calomiris, Charles. "Alexander Hamilton." In *The Encyclopedia of American Business History and Biography: Banking and Finance to 1913*, edited by Larry

Schweikart. New York: Facts On File, 1990. This biographical sketch provides a good comparison to the conceptual framework of central banking. Calomiris argues that Hamilton—considered usually as pro-big government—established constraints on government growth in the way he structured the borrowing powers and the national bank.

Clapham, John. *The Bank of England: A History*. Cambridge, England: Cambridge University Press, 1944. The classic work on the Bank of England. Although some of the modern debates over the role of "free banking" or competitive note issue are absent, this work remains a standard source.

Dickson, P. G. M. *The Financial Revolution in England: A Study in the Development of Public Credit, 1688-1756*. New York: St. Martin's Press, 1967. Excellent for understanding the political side of the bank's origins.

Forrester, Andrew. *The Man Who Saw the Future: William Paterson's Vision of Free Trade*. New York: Thomson/Texere, 2004. In the first modern biography, Forrester argues that Paterson's vision of world commerce was far ahead of its time.

Richards, R. D. *The Early History of the Bank of England*. New York: Augustus M. Kelley, 1965. Richards provides excellent early material, and reprints the text of entire documents, including letters and the bank's balance sheets. Unfortunately, Richards's work suffers from the absence of any modern discussions of central bank theories.

Roberts, Richard, and David Kynaston, eds. *The Bank of England: Money, Power, and Influence, 1694-1994*. Oxford, England: Clarendon Press, 1995. A modern series of essays, this collection examines all aspects of the bank, citing updated scholarship. Especially useful is H. V. Bowen's introductory history, "The Bank of England During the Long Eighteenth Century, 1694-1820," which analyzes the bank's political relationships.

Smith, Vera C. *The Rationale of Central Banking*. London: P. S. King, 1936. An early, but still useful overview of the principles of central banking from the perspective of Depression-era England.

White, Lawrence. *Free Banking in Britain: Theory, Experience, and Debate, 1800-1845*. New York: Cambridge University Press, 1984. The best work on the system that developed within Scotland and stood in stark contrast to the monopoly in England. White argues that private, competitive note issue provided a sound alternative to government control over money supply.

SEE ALSO: 1609: Bank of Amsterdam Invents Checks; 1688-1702: Reign of William and Mary.

RELATED ARTICLES in *Great Lives from History: The Seventeenth Century, 1601-1700:* William Paterson; Gerrard Winstanley.

May 3, 1695
END OF PRESS CENSORSHIP IN ENGLAND

The lapse of the Licensing Acts in 1695 ended government restrictions on and licensing of printed materials and printers. This lapse permitted printed material—imported books, pamphlets from outside the city of London, foreign and unlicensed newspapers—to inundate the English market.

LOCALE: London, England

CATEGORIES: Laws, acts, and legal history; social issues and reform

KEY FIGURES

John Locke (1632-1704), English philosopher and prominent intellectual

Edward Clarke (1649/1651-1710), Whig member of Parliament who led the opposition to renewal of the Licensing Acts

SUMMARY OF EVENT

Printing in seventeenth century England was restricted by a series of Licensing Acts. In Restoration England, the initial law renewing press censorship was the Licensing Act of 1662, which was renewed several times during the next three decades in Licensing Acts of 1664, 1665, 1685, 1692, and 1693. The 1662 act comprehensively controlled the production of printed material, either as works in production or as volumes imported from overseas. It controlled domestic print production in four ways. First, print production was geographically restricted to the cities of London and York and to the universities of Cambridge and Oxford.

Second, the Stationers' Company, the printer's guild of the day, was permitted to designate only twenty master printers, other than those in the king's or university's service, to print works. Third, the Stationers' Company, acting for the government, set the number of printers, apprentices, journeymen, and physical presses. Fourth, all manuscripts intended for publication had to receive prepublication approval from a licensing office. Works from overseas were controlled by import destination; they could only be brought into London.

The Licensing Acts, then, permitted an extraordinary range of government control over printed materials. The 1685 act was initially due to expire at the end of the 1692-1693 Parliamentary session, but it was extended twice. Each extension was for one year and then to the end of the next Parliament, so it was finally scheduled to lapse at the end of the 1694-1695 Parliament. Each extension, in the 1692-1693 session and then in the 1693-1694 session, revealed more constituent concerns about the Licensing Act, so its lapse in 1695 should be seen as a result of deliberate inaction by the House of Commons.

Each extension of the Licensing Acts brought forth explicit political debate on the topic. For example, in 1693, many pamphlets were written about censorship. In 1694, John Locke wrote a memorandum on the Licensing Acts, in which he systematically commented upon each point of the law. Although he was familiar with John Milton's *Areopagitica* (1644), instead of arguing for an abstract freedom of the press in his memorandum, Locke highlighted the restraints on publishing that had resulted from the Licensing Acts. He also pointed out that the press did not need to be controlled, so long as printed materials bore the name of the responsible printer or publisher. That way, if anything in the works violated the common laws of England, such as those against libel, Locke believed the printer, publisher, or author could be held liable.

These ideas were not unique to Locke; they had been expressed in several pamphlets distributed around the time of the first proposed extension to the 1685 act, in the 1692-1693 Parliamentary session. Locke's memorandum, though, was directed personally to Edward Clarke, the member of Parliament for Taunton. Clarke and Locke were friends; in fact, Clarke was a member of Locke's College, a private political discussion group he sponsored.

On November 30, 1694, the House of Commons appointed a committee to examine laws that had expired or were about to expire. On January 9, 1695, the committee reported that it had resolved to renew the Licensing Act yet again. However, the House of Commons deferred acting on this report until February 11, 1695. The Commons then rejected the option of renewing the act. Instead, it appointed another committee, this one to prepare a revised bill that would allow for better control over print.

The Stationers' Company noticed the delays in the House of Commons. Intent on maintaining the status quo—that is, perpetual copyright on a work once it was entered into the Company Register and profitable monopolies on reprints of old authors—the company lobbied the Commons as well but to less effect than Locke's efforts. The new bill proposed by the ad-hoc committee of February 11 permitted printers outside of London, York, and the universities, as well as exempting works on medicine, science, the arts, and heraldry from licensure. It also lifted restrictions on importing books.

However, the revised bill failed, because it did not limit copyright—even the works of Aesop (c. 620-c. 560 B.C.E.), for example, were considered to be under copyright by the Licensing Acts, and the proposed revision did nothing to alter the situation. It also failed, because although more people would be able to print works under the revised bill, anyone who did so would have to follow a detailed set of rules. These rules would require that printers refrain from printing anything that contradicted the laws or religion of the land and that they deliver a copy of every book published to the king's and universities' libraries before any copies could be sold.

Edward Clarke introduced this revised bill in the House of Commons on March 2, 1695, and he believed it permitted nearly anything to be printed. However, the bill was strongly opposed by three significant court groups, the nobles and peers, the bishops, and the Stationers' Company. Their concerns were grounded in the limited requirements for licensing manuscripts and in the possibility that presses could be opened up around the country. Locke objected to it as well, because it did not contain a copyright clause. Locke was also concerned about the vagueness of the requirement that the work not contradict the laws or religion of the land.

Finally, by early April, it became clear that the revised bill would not pass out of the committee evaluating it. Therefore, the other house of Parliament, the House of Lords, acted. The House of Lords inserted a clause renewing the Licensing Act for another year and a session, just like the prior two extensions, into a bill to revive several pieces of legislation. When this renewing bill was put before the Commons, they passed it but struck out the clause relating to the Licensing Act. In a joint conference to reconcile the differences on the bill, Clarke explained why the Commons would not accept the Licensing Act clause.

The House of Commons presented four reasons to the House of Lords for its refusal to extend the Licensing Act. First, the act had not fulfilled its purpose. Second, the common law of the land already protected against excessive liberty of the press. Third, the fees for licensing were unspecific. Fourth, the "offensive" books banned by the act were an undefined category. The House of Lords was unable to overcome these objections and therefore accepted the removal of the Licensing Act clause from the bill it had sent to the Commons.

Thus, when Parliament ended its session on May 3, 1695, the Licensing Act expired. In the next session of Parliament, variations of the Licensing Act were considered. Once again, though, no bill overcame the objections raised against it, and prepublication censorship ended in England.

SIGNIFICANCE

Immediately after the Licensing Act lapsed, printers began to publish a range of works, such as newsletters, pamphlets, and even novels. Chaos ensued as they attempted to secure particular, profitable works by certain authors, and this confusion led ultimately to the Copyright Act of 1709. The lapse of the act also permitted the freer distribution of works such as controversial theological texts: Whether imported from the Continent or printed outside of London or York, works containing diverse religious ideas began to circulate more widely.

Finally, the lapse of the law controlling printing eventually expanded the English print culture. Printers moved outside London to escape its saturated markets and began to publish in the provinces. They published news and opinions from the court, from London, and from within their home province. Within ten years, London alone had twenty periodicals that were published at least weekly; one was even published daily. In addition to the London periodicals, the major provincial centers had their own weeklies.

The government would later respond to the explosion of print culture with the Stamp Acts in the eighteenth century. These represented an attempt to make publication prohibitively expensive and thereby to silence voices unpopular to the government. However, the British government never regained the control it once had under the Licensing Acts. The lapse of those acts therefore constituted a watershed moment for media, politics, and the people.

—Clare Callaghan

FURTHER READING

Astbury, Raymond. "The Renewal of the Licensing Act in 1693 and Its Lapse in 1695." *The Library*, 5th ser. 33 (4): 296-322. Examines the specific political machinations behind the Licensing Act's last renewal and then its lapse.

Black, Jeremy. *The English Press in the Eighteenth Century*. London: Croom Helm, 1987. The introduction examines the seventeenth century roots of the eighteenth century press.

Cranfield, G. A. *The Press and Society: From Caxton to Northcliffe*. New York: Longman, 1978. Reviews the first centuries of printing in England.

O'Gorman, Frank. *The Long Eighteenth Century: British Political and Social History, 1688-1832*. New York: Arnold, 1997. Places the Licensing Act and subsequent attempts at press censorship in the context of the long eighteenth century.

Sommerville, C. John. *The News Revolution in England: Cultural Dynamics of Daily Information*. New York: Oxford University Press, 1996. Examines the development of the reading audiences of newspapers.

Sutherland, James. *The Restoration Newspaper and Its Development*. London: Cambridge University Press, 1986. Investigates newspapers published between 1660-1720.

SEE ALSO: 1662-May 3, 1695: England's Licensing Acts; Nov., 1688-Feb., 1689: The Glorious Revolution; Feb. 13, 1689: Declaration of Rights; May 24, 1689: Toleration Act; 1690: Locke Publishes *Two Treatises of Government*.

RELATED ARTICLES in *Great Lives from History: The Seventeenth Century, 1601-1700:* John Locke; Mary II; William III.

1697-1702
Köprülü Reforms of Hüseyin Paşa

The fifth Ottoman grand vizier of the Köprülü family, Köprülü Amcazade Hüseyin Paşa, negotiated the Treaty of Karlowitz in 1699 and tried to shore up the crumbling Ottoman Empire by instituting far-reaching reforms.

Locale: Ottoman Empire

Categories: Government and politics; social issues and reform; wars, uprisings, and civil unrest

Key Figures

Köprülü Amcazade Hüseyin Paşa (d. 1702), Ottoman grand vizier, 1697-1702

Mezemorta Hüseyin Paşa (d. 1701), Ottoman grand admiral, 1695-1701

Feyzullah Efendi (1638-1703), *sheyhülislam*, or chief judge, and former tutor of Mustafa II

Summary of Event

From 1656 to 1702, the fortunes of the Ottoman Empire were linked with those of the Albanian Köprülü family of grand viziers. It was during the long reign of the inept Sultan Mehmed IV Avci (r. 1648-1687) that the first two Köprülü grand viziers, Mehmed Paşa (1656-1661) and Fazıl Ahmed Paşa (1661-1676), expanded the frontiers of the empire to their greatest extent and introduced reforms in the army and the civil administration.

Upon Fazıl Ahmed Paşa's death, his foster brother and brother-in-law, Merzifonlu Kara Mustafa Paşa, became grand vizier, but his administration (1676-1683) ended with the failed Siege of Vienna in 1683 and his own execution. Following further military disasters in the Danubian provinces, a palace coup led to the deposition of Mehmed IV and the accession of his younger brother, Süleyman II (1687-1691).

Another Köprülü grand vizier, Fazıl Mustafa Paşa, younger brother of Fazıl Ahmed, served as grand vizier from 1689 until 1691. Demonstrating that extraordinary resilience of which the Ottomans were still capable, he recaptured Nish and Belgrade but was defeated and killed in battle at Slankamen (Serbia) on August 19, 1691. Following additional defeats, Mehmed IV's eldest son, Mustafa II (r. 1695-1703), appointed Köprülü Hüseyin Paşa as grand vizier (in 1697). Hüseyin Paşa was a nephew of Mehmed Paşa and a cousin of Fazıl Ahmed Paşa (who nicknamed him Amcazade, meaning "uncle's son"), and Fazıl Mustafa Paşa.

Not much is known about Hüseyin Paşa's birth date or place, or his early life. He served on the Vienna campaign of 1683 and in various posts subsequently: governor of Shehrizor in Iraq; military governor (*muhafiz*) of Chardak, opposite Gallipoli; and, in 1689, *muhafiz* of Seddulbahr at the entrance to the Dardanelles. He served briefly as *kaymakan* (deputy vizier), during January-February of 1692 and again between January and June, 1694.

In December of 1694, Hüseyin Paşa was appointed *kapudan-i derya* (grand admiral). He was ordered to retake Chios, which the Venetians had recently occupied. In February, 1695, he won two naval engagements against the Venetians off Chios, leading to their prompt evacuation of the island; he became *muhafiz* of Chios in May, 1695, but was later transferred to Belgrade (September-October, 1696).

The armies of the Holy League had been approaching the Danube River, and the Ottomans could barely slow their advance. In August, 1697, at a council of war in Belgrade, Hüseyin Paşa advocated speedy negotiations before things would deteriorate, but he was overruled. Then followed Prince Eugene's overwhelming victory at Zenta (September 11, 1697), witnessed by the horrified sultan from across the Tisza River. The defeated Janissary corps mutinied and murdered the grand vizier, Elmas Mehmed Paşa. Shortly thereafter, the sultan summoned Hüseyin Paşa to succeed Elmas Mehmed Paşa.

Few grand viziers assumed office in more unfavorable circumstances. Peace and breathing space were absolute necessities, but the new grand vizier also needed the support of the sultan and the weakened military establishment, as well as the compliance of the enemy. Plenipotentiaries met at Karlowitz, near Peterwardein, with Sir William Paget, the English ambassador, and his Dutch colleague, as mediators. The Ottomans were represented by Mehmed Rami Efendi, a future grand vizier, and by an experienced Phanariot Greek, Count Alexander Mavrocordato (1641-1709), who became the Holy Roman Empire's secretary of state.

Hüseyin Paşa moved to Belgrade with what was left of the army in case negotiations broke down. After seventy-two days, agreement was reached on the basis of *uti possidetis*, meaning that the Holy League's members kept their recent acquisitions: the Austrian Habsburgs regained Transylvania and most of Hungary (except the Banat of Temesvar); the Venetians acquired the Morea;

and Poland got Podolia. The Treaty of Karlowitz had been the Ottomans' greatest humiliation. A formerly all-conquering Islam had been thrown into a defensive mode by its Christian foes. It was for Hüseyin Paşa to persuade sultan, army, and empire that there was no alternative to these terms, which were eloquently defended by the leading Ottoman historian, Mustafa Naima (1655-1716).

Perhaps no member of the Köprülü family did more for the empire than Hüseyin Paşa in persuading his contemporaries to accept the inevitable. One circumstance greatly assisted the grand vizier. This was the support he received from the outstanding naval commander, Mezemorta Hüseyin Paşa, nicknamed Mezemorta, which is Turkish for "half-dead," as a result of near-fatal wounds incurred in his youth in a naval battle with the Spaniards. A brilliantly successful Algerian corsair, from 1689 he commanded fleets on the Danube, in the Black Sea, and in the Aegean Sea. He fought beside Hüseyin Paşa in the naval engagements off Chios, and, in 1695, he replaced Hüseyin Paşa as *kapudan-i derya*.

Between September, 1695, and September, 1698, Mezemorta Hüseyin Paşa defeated the Venetians in a series of battles in the Aegean, although Western sources dispute some of these victories. However, in a period characterized by dismal Ottoman performance on land, victories at sea greatly strengthened the grand vizier's hand. Moreover, the admiral implemented a reform program that mirrored that of the grand vizier: the introduction of sail-driven galleons alongside oared galleys; and the division of the fleet into squadrons, each commanded by a *derya bey* (bey of the sea), who was responsible for the men, ships, ammunition, and supplies in each squadron. A clear command hierarchy was instituted throughout the service, with officers and men paid regularly and in receipt of pensions on retirement, and the fleet was to be governed by a wide-ranging code of regulations (*kanun-nama*). Unfortunately, the admiral died in 1701 and was buried on Chios. His death deprived the grand vizier of an invaluable ally in his reform program.

Military reforms were Hüseyin Paşa's highest priority. Scrutinizing the *kapi kulu* lists (lists of the palace slaves, including the household troops), he dismissed those unfit for service, replacing them with trained Anatolian peasants. Part-time soldiers in the Janissary corps were also dismissed, and the overall size of the corps was reduced to approximately 34,000. However, he also improved conditions of service, constructed new barracks, and repaired fortresses. The *sipahi* (feudal cavalry) were overhauled, and new recruits were drawn from nomadic Anatolian tribes and from *sipahi* expelled from Hungary. Their commanders, the *sanjak beys*, were closely supervised, and abuses in the *timars* (cavalry fiefs), many of which had passed to landholders who performed no military services, were eliminated.

In general, the empire's economy was in desperate straits. Famine and conditions ideal to famine were widespread, with an accompanying breakdown of law and order. In Anatolia, the peasantry was abandoning the land to migrate to the capital or to embark upon a life of peripatetic brigandage. Hüseyin Paşa sought to settle nomadic tribes on agricultural land that had fallen out of cultivation. He was particularly concerned for the Christian *reaya* (peasantry) in the Balkan provinces, who had suffered so much from the passage of armies and from fiscal and commissarial exactions. In urban centers, he endeavored to reduce or abolish illegal taxes on items such as coffee, tobacco, oil, and soap. He also sought to protect handicrafts from competition from imported European goods by setting up local workshops.

In all this, he was opposed by vested interests, and especially by the highly conservative *sheyhülislam*, Feyzullah Efendi, who was influential because he had been the sultan's tutor. Faced with bitter opposition and in declining health, the grand vizier resigned in September of 1702 (he had lost his ally, Mezemorta Hüseyin Paşa, in the previous year) and retired to his estate at Silivri on the Sea of Marmora, dying on September 22. He was buried in the mosque and religious college (madrasa) complex that he had founded in Sarajhana in the capital. His splendid *yali* (waterside residence) at Kapica, north of Anadolu Hisar on the Bosporus, still survives, and his library is preserved in the Süleymaniye complex.

Significance

It was entirely appropriate that both the peace negotiations and the abortive reforms that brought the Ottoman seventeenth century to a close should be the work of the last Köprülü grand vizier. Indubitably, the Treaty of Karlowitz ushered in a period of Ottoman decline, but Köprülü Amcazade Hüseyin Paşa probably negotiated the best terms possible under the circumstances, although he had to bear the opprobrium for having "sold out."

As for his failed reforms and the unwillingness of the Ottoman establishment to see them implemented, if it meant loss of power or profit, that was already, by the end of the century, an old story: Shrewd and perspicacious minds had long identified the systemic weaknesses of the empire, but no reformer had gone beyond tinkering with the problems, not even the first two Köprülü grand viziers. Hüseyin Paşa was an intelligent statesman, but the post-Karlowitz years and his declining health prevented him from confronting the vested interests that had so long put personal gain before public necessity.

—*Gavin R. G. Hambly*

Further Reading

Argenti, P., ed. *The Occupation of Chios by the Venetians, 1694*. London: Cambridge University Press, 1966. This work is crucial for understanding the Venetian role in this period.

Kurat, Akdes Nimet. "The Retreat of the Turks, 1683-1730." Vol. 6 in *The New Cambridge Modern History*. New York: Cambridge University Press, 1970. An excellent account of Hüseyin Paşa's administration.

Murphey, Rhoads. *Ottoman Warfare, 1500-1700*. New Brunswick, N.J.: Rutgers University Press, 1999. A useful work that examines seventeenth century Ottoman military campaigning.

Rifat, A. Abou El-Haj. "Ottoman Diplomacy at Karlowitz." *Journal of the American Oriental Society* 87 (1967): 498-512. An extremely useful article for background to the peacemaking.

Shaw, Stanford J. *History of the Ottoman Empire and Modern Turkey*. Vol. 1 in *Empire of the Gazis: The Rise and Decline of the Ottoman Empire, 1280-1808*. New York: Cambridge University Press, 1996. A classic, scholarly history, with integrated treatment of Ottoman governmental developments.

Sugar, Peter F. *Southeastern Europe Under Ottoman Rule, 1354-1804*. Seattle: University of Washington Press, 1977. Sugar's work is generally very good on the Köprülü period in the Balkans.

See also: 1623-1640: Murad IV Rules the Ottoman Empire; Aug. 22, 1645-Sept., 1669: Turks Conquer Crete; 1656-1676: Ottoman Empire's Brief Recovery; Summer, 1672-Fall, 1676: Ottoman-Polish Wars; 1677-1681: Ottoman-Muscovite Wars; July 14-Sept. 12, 1683: Defeat of the Ottomans at Vienna; 1684-1699: Holy League Ends Ottoman Rule of the Danubian Basin; Beginning 1687: Decline of the Ottoman Empire; Jan. 26, 1699: Treaty of Karlowitz.

Related articles in *Great Lives from History: The Seventeenth Century, 1601-1700:* John III Sobieski; Merzifonlu Kara Mustafa Paşa; Bohdan Khmelnytsky; Kösem Sultan; Leopold I; Murad IV.

March 9, 1697-August 25, 1698
Peter the Great Tours Western Europe

Peter the Great made a trip to Western Europe incognito, the first Russian monarch to leave Russia since the tenth century. His exposure to Western technologies led him to selectively modernize Russia, and he returned with hundreds of European artisans, shipbuilders, and other skilled professionals.

Locale: Livonia, Courland, Brandenburg-Prussia, Hanover, Holland, England, Saxony, Prague, and Vienna

Categories: Diplomacy and international relations; social issues and reform; cultural and intellectual history

Key Figures

Peter the Great (1672-1725), czar of Russia, r. 1682-1725

François Lefort (1656-1699), Swiss émigré, confidant of Peter the Great, and official leader of the trip to Western Europe

William III (1650-1702), stadtholder of the Netherlands, r. 1672-1702, and king of England, r. 1689-1702, who hosted Peter in Holland and England

Summary of Event

Born to Czar Alexis by his second wife Natalya Naryshkina in 1672, Peter was three years old when his father died. The death of his elder half brother Fyodor III in 1682 brought Peter and his weak half brother Ivan to the throne as joint heirs. However, for seven years his elder half sister Sophia actually ruled Russia. During this time Peter taught himself tactics, sailing, and mathematics, and foreign friends introduced him to Western ideas. In 1689, Peter confined Sophia in a convent and asserted his personal rule. Ivan V's death in 1696 gave him undisputed sovereignty, and he decided to experience Western Europe himself.

In March of 1697, Peter left Russia with an entourage of about 250 individuals. Choosing to travel incognito, he took the name Peter Mikhailov. The Grand Embassy, as the tour was called, was led by his friend and mentor

General-Admiral François Lefort along with two professional diplomats. Peter's companions were ordered to not treat him as the czar nor to admit that the czar was part of the embassy; to do so would mean punishment by death. These efforts were fruitless, however. In an age when the average man was about five feet, six inches tall, it was well known that the czar was a six-foot-seven-inch "giant." Traveling as Peter Mikhailov gave Peter the Great more freedom to do as he wished, including avoiding many of the ceremonial functions he disliked, but his size and abrupt mannerisms meant that he was noticed, stared at, and followed, circumstances which at times annoyed and even enraged him.

After leaving Russia, the Grand Embassy passed through Riga in Swedish Livonia, the duchy of Courland, the cities of Königsberg and Berlin, and the electorate of Hanover. Though well received and lavishly entertained along the way, Peter was anxious to reach Holland, which was among the most prosperous states in Europe and which had the second largest navy in the world. Seafaring was one of Peter's passions, so at the Zaandam shipyards, and later in Amsterdam, he took the role of a carpenter and forced some of his companions to work as well. Even though he was able to speak Dutch, his tenure as a workman in Zaandam was brief, partly because of the relentless crowds that followed him everywhere.

In Amsterdam, efforts were made to shield Peter from gatherings of the curious. He visited military, educational, and commercial sites and was able to recruit several hundred specialists for the Russian military. He also met the European ruler he most admired, Stadtholder William of Orange (William III), who happened to be in Holland, which he much preferred to his English kingdom.

After nearly five months in Holland, Peter crossed to England in January of 1698 with a few companions, leaving most of the embassy with Lefort and the ambassadors, who were negotiating a treaty with the Dutch. While in London, Peter visited Parliament and the Royal Society and was entertained by King William III and various members of the nobility. His natural curiosity

Peter the Great's trip to Western Europe included a highly anticipated visit to Holland in the Dutch Republic to learn the art of shipbuilding. (Francis R. Niglutsch)

PETER THE GREAT'S GRAND EMBASSY, 1697-1698

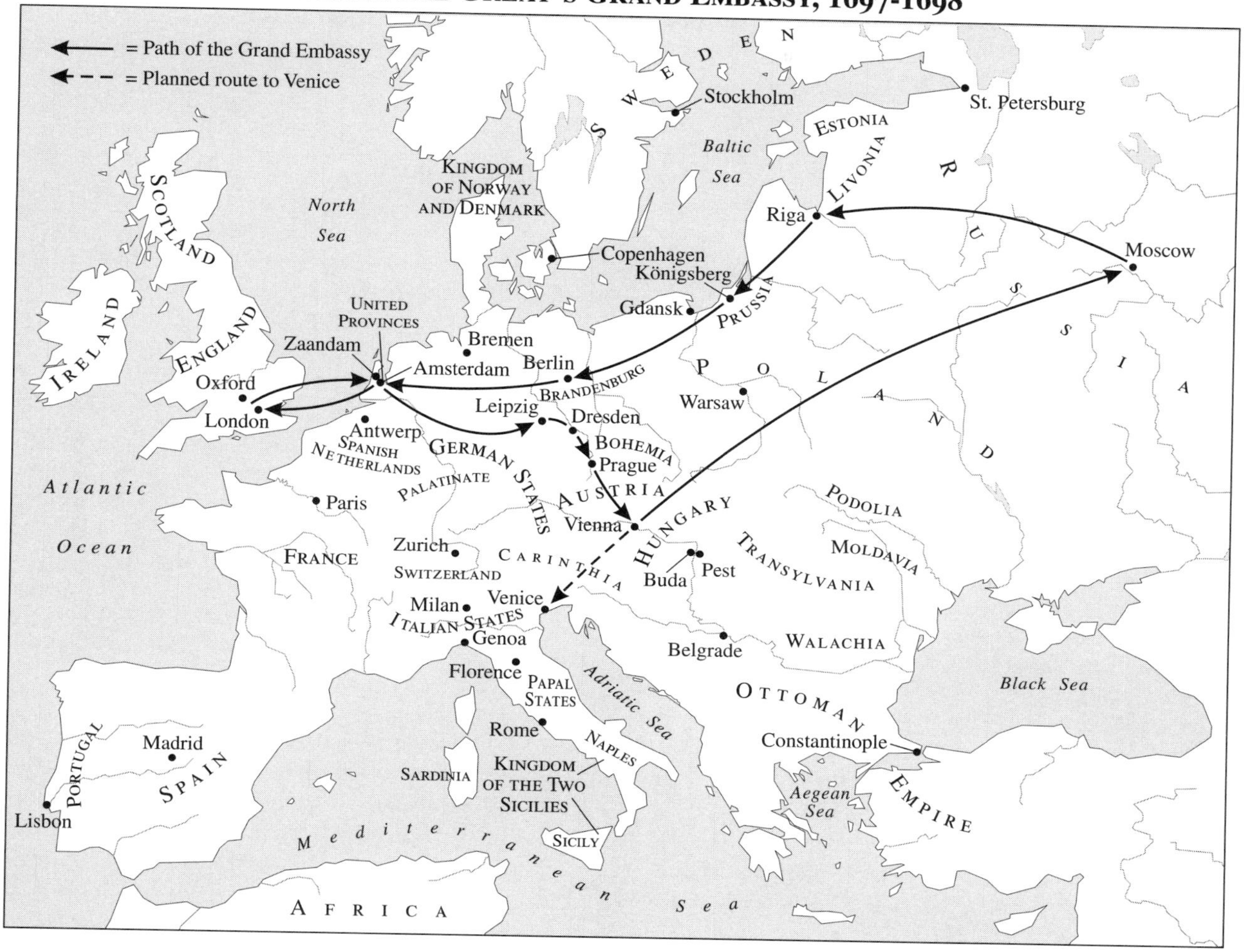

led him to become interested in the Society of Friends, or Quakers. He met William Penn, with whom he conversed in Dutch, and attended several Quaker meetings. Peter also received a delegation of Anglican clergy, who tried, unsuccessfully, to convert him, and visited the University of Oxford and admired its Bodlean Library.

Peter disliked London's crowds and was intensely interested in shipbuilding, so he was loaned an elegant townhouse, which belonged to the noted English author John Evelyn, near the Deptford shipyards. Unfortunately, Peter and his comrades had no appreciation for Evelyn's elegant townhome. They destroyed the house's interior, breaking windows, burning the furniture, and tearing up Evelyn's prized garden, obliging William III's government to later reimburse Evelyn for his losses. Such raucous behavior, coupled with the Russians' wild drinking bouts, confirmed the belief of many that Peter and his companions were brutes and savages.

As a young man, Peter had learned to smoke tobacco, despite the disapproval of the Orthodox Church. While in England, he negotiated a contract for Britain to sell tobacco in Russia. His new friend, a ship designer and drinking companion, paid to facilitate the monopoly, and British merchants were delighted at this new market. The mounting costs of the Grand Embassy were somewhat alleviated by this transaction.

In May of 1698, Peter left London in a twenty-gun yacht presented to him by William, and he returned to Amsterdam to rejoin the members of the embassy who had waited for him there. The party then traveled to Leipzig, Dresden, and Prague. During a two weeks' stay in Vienna, Peter met with Emperor Leopold I, but while feted by the Austrian court was unable to achieve his objective: Austria's promise to continue its campaign against the Turks. Instead, the Austrians were preparing to make peace. Frustrated by this, Peter prepared to go to Venice. However, in July, he learned that four regiments of the *streltsy*, the conservative, volatile Kremlin guards, had revolted and proclaimed his eight-year-old son Alexis czar. Abruptly, he jettisoned his remaining itinerary and returned to Moscow.

Shortly after arriving in Moscow in August, Peter brutally ended the revolt and personally executed some of the rebels. Distrust of the West among the nobles and the serfs ran deep in Russia. As the effects of Peter's reforms extended into all segments of society, rumors persisted that the true czar had died somewhere in Europe and that the man who came back to Russia was an imposter, if not the Antichrist. Peter ignored but sometimes crushed all forms of opposition, and he then continued through sheer strength of will to turn Russia into a modern militaristic state.

Significance

Peter the Great's tour of Western Europe, the first by a Russian sovereign since the tenth century trip to Constantinople by the princess of Rus, Saint Olga, was abruptly terminated by the *streltsy* revolt, but still, he was able to return to Russia with a wealth of knowledge and hundreds of professional workers. He modernized the Russian army and navy and built weapons' factories. He decreed compulsory education for children of the nobility and altered the nobility's social customs. Men, for example, had to cut their beards (symbols of male salvation) and dress in Western style, and women and girls had to give up their traditional seclusion and learn to dance, gamble, and live like Western European women.

Of the places he visited, Peter preferred Holland and England for their naval superiority and mastery of commercial matters. The informality of English and Dutch society pleased him as well, as it helped him put aside the constraints of monarchy and associate with men of all ranks, whose technical expertise he valued. When he began to build his new capital, St. Petersburg, in 1703, it was modeled on the city of Amsterdam.

Despite Peter's efforts, however, the westernization of Russia was somewhat of a veneer; the lives of the upper classes were profoundly and positively changed by his edicts, but the majority of Russia's population—the serfs—experienced few benefits from his reforms. Practically, Peter's trip officially introduced Western Europe to Russia.

—*Dorothy Potter*

Further Reading

Cracraft, James. *The Petrine Revolution in Russian Culture*. Cambridge, Mass.: Belknap Press, 2004. An extensive study of more than 500 pages of Peter and his transformation of Russian's traditional lifestyles.

De Jonge, Alex. *Fire and Water: A Life of Peter the Great*. New York: Coward, McCann & Geoghegan, 1980. A concise biography, offering a good introduction to Peter's life and reign for general readers.

Hughes, Lindsey. *Peter the Great: A Biography*. New Haven, Conn.: Yale University Press, 2002. Among the better studies of Peter, this work reflects updated scholarship on the enigmatic czar and his ties to the people whom he governed with an iron hand.

Massie, Robert K. *Peter the Great: His Life and World*. New York: Alfred A. Knopf, 1980. This book of more than 900 pages is detailed and vividly written. It explores not only Peter and Russia but also his European contemporaries.

Piotrowski, Harry. "Peter the Great." In *Great Leaders, Great Tyrants: Contemporary Views of World Leaders Who Made History*, edited by Arnold Blumberg. Westport, Conn.: Greenwood Press, 1995. A succinct comparison of the positive and negative aspects of Peter's rule.

Riasanovsky, Nicholas V. *The Image of Peter the Great in Russian History and Thought*. New York: Oxford University Press, 1985. This work examines the changing image of Peter as a symbolic and mythical personality represented in eighteenth through twentieth century history and thought.

See also: 17th cent.: Rise of the Gunpowder Empires; 1652-1667: Patriarch Nikon's Reforms; 1672-c. 1691: Self-Immolation of the Old Believers; Beginning 1687: Decline of the Ottoman Empire; Jan. 26, 1699: Treaty of Karlowitz; Nov. 30, 1700: Battle of Narva.

Related articles in *Great Lives from History: The Seventeenth Century, 1601-1700:* Alexis; John Evelyn; Leopold I; William III.

September 20, 1697
TREATY OF RYSWICK

The Treaty of Ryswick ended the hostilities of the Wars of the League of Augsburg and proved to be a peace signed out of exhaustion more than a concrete settlement of the issues. Neither side offered much in the way of significant concessions and many problems, most notably the question of who would inherit the Spanish Habsburg Empire, were unsettled.

LOCALE: Ryswick, United Provinces (now in the Netherlands)

CATEGORIES: Diplomacy and international relations; wars, uprisings, and civil unrest; government and politics; expansion and land acquisition

KEY FIGURES

Louis XIV (1638-1715), king of France, r. 1643-1715

William III (1650-1702), stadtholder of the Netherlands, 1672-1702, and king of England, r. 1689-1702

Leopold I (1640-1705), Holy Roman Emperor, r. 1658-1705

James II (1633-1701), king of England, r. 1685-1688

William Bentinck (1649-1709), first earl of Portland, longtime confidant of William III, and special peace envoy

Louis-François (1644-1711), duke of Boufflers, marshal of France, and special peace envoy

Henri de Massue (1648-1720), first earl of Galway, former deputy-general of the Huguenots in France, and lord justice of Ireland

SUMMARY OF EVENT

During the nine years of the Wars of the League of Augsburg (1689-1697), contending armies from a variety of nations marched over and through Germany, Flanders, Ireland, Savoy, North America, and India and had yielded very little advantage to either Louis XIV of France or to the coalition aligned against him. This coalition, which was variously known as the League of Augsburg, or the Grand Alliance, was organized and sustained mainly by William III, Dutch stadtholder and king of England, and had included England, the Netherlands, the Holy Roman Empire, Savoy, and Spain, among the major powers.

On both sides, sentiment grew to break the deadlock and bring the hostilities to a close. William III was ultimately won over to the idea of arriving at a settlement by the defection of Victor Amadeus II, duke of Savoy, who negotiated a separate peace with Louis XIV at Turin. William feared that France could now deploy free troops from the Italian front to use against his armies in Flanders and perhaps achieve a breakthrough in that sector of operations. He hoped to forestall this potential disaster by initiating peace talks, and Louis XIV, himself anxious to end the incessant warfare, agreed to the idea of a peace conference mediated by Sweden and taking place at the Dutch town of Ryswick, which at that time lay halfway between the two opposing armies.

Long-standing mutual suspicion and enmity prevented Louis and William, the two most crucial individuals involved, from even sustaining meaningful negotiations, and the talks soon reached an impasse. However, in an unusual move, special representatives from either side were hand-picked to meet informally and lay the basis for further discussion. The two who were chosen to break the log jam were Marshal Louis-François, duke of Boufflers, and William Bentinck, first earl of Portland. They were old friends, and both enjoyed the trust of their respective monarchs: Boufflers had gained international notice for his tenacity and skill at the Battle for Namur in 1695, and Portland had been William III's childhood companion and served his sovereign as a diplomat and as a lieutenant-general of cavalry.

Boufflers and Portland began meeting in June of 1697 and had soon resolved the more prickly details surrounding the major issues. The primary bone of contention was over recognition of William III's claim to be king of England. In 1688, William had landed in England and deposed his father-in-law, James II. James had fled to France, where he received the support of Louis XIV, who had allowed him to maintain a court in exile at Saint-Germain. The military and financial assistance tendered to James by King Louis had continuously nettled William, who also faced at home a strong Jacobite (pro-James II) sentiment that he could not afford to ignore. Boufflers and Portland proposed that Louis XIV should recognize William and agree to give no further assistance to the Jacobite cause, and also to prohibit James's subjects from giving such assistance. Louis, however, refused to expel James and his family from France, though he stopped insisting that William grant a pardon to exiled Jacobite sympathizers. These conditions proved to be mutually acceptable, and formal exchanges resumed.

Paramount issues included the status of border regions seized by Louis XIV during his 1680's "reunions," the fate of the exiled Huguenots, and the controversy over the principality of Orange. On the sensitive issues over territorial claims, a compromise was reached, whereby France agreed to suspend such claims in the German states and to restore nearly all the lands seized on Germany's eastern and northern borders that had not been specified as French in the Treaties of Nijmegen, with the significant exception of Strasbourg, and virtually the whole of Alsace with it. Lorraine was to be reconstituted as an independent duchy under the former ducal family. Though Holland gained no land, Dutch forces were permitted to deploy at various key locations in the Spanish Netherlands. Spain was accordingly confirmed in its possession of the southern Netherlands, the grand duchy of Luxembourg, and the province of Catalonia, following the withdrawal of French troops. Colonial transfers of territory included the cession by Spain to France of the western part of the island of Hispaniola, as the colony of Haiti, and the return of French colonial possessions in India and North America, which had been taken by allied forces during the course of the war.

Henri de Massue, first earl of Galway, was a former deputy-general of the French Calvinists at the court of Louis XIV and the titular leader-in-exile of some 200,000 Huguenots who had been forced to flee from France under persecution. Massue had high hopes that King Louis would relent and agree to take the Calvinist refugees back under a contract guaranteeing religious freedom. Now an English peer who had been an ardent participant in the military and diplomatic efforts against Louis, Galway was at the height of his influence. However, on this deeply religious matter, Louis—who was becoming more fanatically Catholic as he grew older—absolutely refused to budge and William did not press the issue. The principality of Orange, King William's ancestral home, which was nestled inside southern France, was allowed to revert to him, but under the strict condition that it would not be the site of any activity against Louis and would never become a haven for Huguenots—in fact, no Huguenots were to dwell there at all.

Though Louis XIV and William III readily agreed to the conditions of the pact, Spain and the Holy Roman Empire at first raised objections. By September 20, 1697, though, the government of Spain had yielded, and it joined France, England, and the Netherlands for the official signing of the treaty. The lone holdout was Emperor Leopold I, who resented the loss of Strasbourg, but energetic diplomacy on the part of King William persuaded the emperor to finally come to terms on October 30, 1697.

Significance

Though the Treaty of Ryswick reflected the indecisive nature of the conflict that it ended, it did provide all concerned with much-needed breathing space and a relief from nearly a decade of fighting. The question of the Spanish Succession, the most daunting of the controversies facing the signatories of the Treaty of Ryswick, was deferred for further discussion.

In the final analysis, the Treaty of Ryswick was a reasonably solid agreement, and its provision cannot be blamed for bringing about the Wars of the Spanish Succession in 1701. The succession war can be more accurately attributed to the failure of the sovereigns and statesmen to arrive at a viable formula for peace in the years between.

—*Raymond Pierre Hylton*

Further Reading

Churchill, Winston S. *Marlborough: His Life and Times*. Book 1. Reprint. Chicago: University of Chicago Press, 2002. The author submits that Ryswick was a great triumph for King William III, and it marked the height of his international prestige.

Ladurie, Emmanuel Leroy. *The Ancien Regime: A History of France, 1610-1774*. Translated by Mark Greengrass. Cambridge, Mass.: Blackwell, 1996. Assigns great importance to the Ryswick Pact as marking a significant realignment in the European balance of power away from overwhelming domination by France.

Lynn, John A. *The Wars of Louis XIV*. New York: Longman, 1999. This volume is strong as far as providing the historical background to the Ryswick talks but falls a bit short in providing actual details of the diplomatic process.

McKay, Derek, and H. M. Scott. *The Rise of the Great Powers, 1648-1715*. New York: Longman, 1983. Offers a fairly detailed analysis of the factors propelling the Ryswick negotiations and the domestic difficulties faced by Louis and William that factored in the final settlement.

Wolf, John B. *Toward a European Balance of Power, 1620-1715*. Chicago: Rand McNally, 1970. A highly useful account of the major diplomatic and military efforts of the time. The Treaty of Turin and the Boufflers-Portland meetings are considered to be historically critical.

SEE ALSO: May, 1640-Jan. 23, 1641: Revolt of the Catalans; Mar. 4, 1665-July 31, 1667: Second Anglo-Dutch War; Aug. 10, 1678-Sept. 26, 1679: Treaties of Nijmegen; 1689-1694: Famine and Inflation in France; 1689-1697: Wars of the League of Augsburg; Oct. 11, 1698, and Mar. 25, 1700: First and Second Treaties of Partition.

RELATED ARTICLES in *Great Lives from History: The Seventeenth Century, 1601-1700:* James II; Leopold I; Louis XIV; William III.

July 25, 1698
SAVERY PATENTS THE FIRST SUCCESSFUL STEAM ENGINE

Steam power, especially when produced by burning coal in place of wood, made the Industrial Revolution of the eighteenth century possible. Savery's invention showed how steam power could be used to do important industrial work, but it would take many incremental improvements before an efficient and effective steam engine would be produced.

LOCALE: England
CATEGORIES: Science and technology; inventions; engineering; economics

KEY FIGURES

Thomas Savery (c. 1650-1715), English inventor
Thomas Newcomen (1663-1729), English inventor and follower of Savery
Otto von Guericke (1602-1686), German physicist and engineer
Robert Boyle (1627-1691), Irish chemist and physicist
Denis Papin (1647-c. 1712), French physicist and inventor
Francis Bacon (1561-1626), English scientist, philosopher, and politician

SUMMARY OF EVENT

Behind the religious politics that took center stage in the first half of the seventeenth century, a revolution was occurring in the way people thought about the world around them. In some respects, this revolution began with Francis Bacon, who challenged the deductive reasoning that had been the hallmark of medieval scholastic thought. The leading thinkers of the latter half of the seventeenth century challenged the old style of reasoning in other ways as well, notably by insisting that facts as they were observed in nature should be the basis of one's understanding of reality.

Underlying the successful development of the steam-propelled pump was the realization that the atmosphere has weight and that its weight causes it to surround Earth. The creation of an airless vacuum would therefore create a force sufficient to pull water into the airless space to fill up the vacuum. Linked to this understanding was the realization that water turned into steam would take up more space than would the same amount of water in its liquid state. Thus, when a closed cylinder was filled with water that was then boiled to make steam, the pressure resulting from the expanding water vapor in the container would force outward any vessel in which it was contained. If the steam were then turned back into water, it would leave a vacuum that could be used to power a water pump but with the limitation that the force could only be as strong as that of the atmosphere seeking to fill the vacuum.

The first person to build a successful air pump was Otto von Guericke, an official of the German city of Magdeburg, in 1650. Robert Boyle, seventh son of the earl of Cork, who had learned of Guericke's accomplishment, also built one in 1659. Boyle demonstrated his device to the Royal Society, the collection of scientific luminaries established by Charles II, king of England, in 1662. Thus, the concept of a pump whose force was derived from the vacuum in a closed vessel was becoming widely known at the time that Thomas Savery began his experiments.

An exiled French Huguenot, Denis Papin, who worked in close collaboration with Robert Boyle, built a cylinder-and-piston device in the 1690's that provided the basic concept that was used in the Savery engine, but for reasons unknown, did not pursue this idea further. Some of his ideas may have been incorporated in Savery's engine, which Savery demonstrated before the Royal Society in 1699.

A factor that played an important part in stimulating the work of men like Savery was the severe shortage of wood fuel in seventeenth century England. To replace wood, men turned to the use of coal, and England's coal deposits were aggressively mined to supply the demand, but as coal near the surface was mined out, men had to dig deeper into the earth to get the coal, and this posed a problem, because the deeper mines tended to fill with water. To make possible continued exploitation of the mines, it was highly desirable to find an efficient way to pump the water out of them, and this was the primary use envisaged for a workable steam-powered pump.

However, for the system to work effectively, a sealed vessel had to be created capable of holding a vacuum sufficient to act as the propulsive force in such pumps. Engineering skills in the late seventeenth century were relatively limited, and it was extremely difficult for Savery and others to make two metal vessels that would fit tightly together, as would be necessary to create a pump vessel with a piston inside it. This limit in engineering technology limited in turn the amount of power that could be created: It was well understood that if the steam power could be increased, the pull of the vacuum could also be increased, but all the early attempts to do this foundered, because inventors could not create a containing vessel capable of withstanding the higher pressures they desired to harness. Many explosions resulted from their attempts.

The concept embodied in Savery's pump was of a containing cylinder with a piston inside it. The water in the cylinder was heated and the steam pushed the piston up in the cylinder. Then the steam was cooled by pouring cold water over the cylinder, and the pressure of the air seeking to fill the vacuum thus created provided the propulsive force to bring water up in a pipe. It was intended that this method would be used to bring up the water gathering in the bottom of coal mines. However, the application turned out to have limited value, because it soon became clear that the force of the atmosphere could pull up water in a contained pipe only 32 feet (10 meters). Dual pipes could double that figure, but it was not enough to pump water out of mines that were 100 feet (30 meters) deep and more.

A number of Savery's pumps were installed following their development, and they enjoyed a wide reputation. Well-documented use of them in mines is, however, lacking. The pump appears to have been used chiefly on a number of gentlemen's estates to create water displays, highly popular at the time. Nevertheless, the combination of cylinder and piston was the basis of all steam-powered mechanical devices that provided artificial power that could be used wherever natural sources, such as wind (as in the Dutch windmills) or water (as in waterfalls on streams and rivers) were not available. It was the availability of this artificial power source, particularly as improved by Thomas Newcomen, who began working with Savery in the first decade of the eighteenth century, that made the Industrial Revolution possible.

SIGNIFICANCE

Because Savery's pump was protected by a patent that ran until 1733, Thomas Newcomen was obliged to work with him in developing his own steam engine. Newcomen's engine, however, provided significant improvements over Savery's. In particular, Newcomen separated the pump from the propulsive part of the engine, using a series of valves to transfer the vacuum to the pump. By this means, he was able to avoid having to cool the steam in the cylinder back to water to create the necessary vacuum. Although a number of Savery pumps were built, even after Newcomen had produced his improvements, it was the idea of using fire and steam propulsion that constituted the giant leap forward that was embodied in Savery's invention.

—*Nancy M. Gordon*

FURTHER READING

Briggs, Asa. *The Power of Steam*. Chicago: University of Chicago Press, 1982. With profuse illustrations, this book lays out the progress of steam propulsion from Savery onward.

Lynch, William T. *Solomon's Child: Method in the Early Royal Society of London*. Stanford, Calif.: Stanford University Press, 2001. Makes clear the central role played by the Royal Society in developing empirical science, without which many of the technical advances of the next century would have been impossible.

Rolt, L. T. C. *Thomas Newcomen: The Prehistory of the Steam Engine*. London: David & Charles, 1963. Contains a clear description of Savery's pump, as well as descriptions of the work of contemporaries who contributed ideas that played a part in developing the pump. It must, however, be used with caution as it contains a number of factual inaccuracies.

Sandfort, John F. *Heat Engines*. Garden City, N.Y.: Anchor Books, 1962. Describes the scientific background to the development of the steam engine, complete with drawings of some early pumps.

Schafer, Simon, and Stever Shapen. "'*Leviathan*' and the Air-Pump: Hobbes, Boyle, and the Experimental Life." In *Science in Europe, 1500-1800*, edited by Malcolm Oster. New York: Palgrave, 2002. Depicts the role of Boyle in creating, in the Royal Society, in effect a modern scientific laboratory.

SEE ALSO: 1601-1672: Rise of Scientific Societies; Sept., 1608: Invention of the Telescope; 1612: Sanctorius Invents the Clinical Thermometer; 1620: Bacon Publishes *Novum Organum*; 1623-1674: Earliest Calculators Appear; 1643: Torricelli Measures Atmospheric Pressure; 1660's-1700: First Microscopic Observations; 1660-1692: Boyle's Law and the Birth of Modern Chemistry.

RELATED ARTICLES in *Great Lives from History: The Seventeenth Century, 1601-1700:* Robert Boyle; Charles II (of England); Otto von Guericke; Denis Papin; Thomas Savery.

October 11, 1698, and March 25, 1700
FIRST AND SECOND TREATIES OF PARTITION

The treaties of partition were attempts by the king of France and the king of England, Scotland, and Ireland to maintain a balance of power in Europe and avoid war by dividing the vast Spanish Empire in anticipation of the death of the last Spanish Habsburg ruler of Spain.

LOCALE: France and England
CATEGORIES: Diplomacy and international relations; expansion and land acquisition

KEY FIGURES

Charles II (1661-1700), king of Spain, r. 1665-1700
Charles III (1685-1740), king of Spain, r. 1700-1711, and Holy Roman Emperor as Charles VI, r. 1711-1740
Joseph Ferdinand (1692-1699), electoral prince of Bavaria
Leopold I (1640-1705), Holy Roman Emperor, r. 1658-1705
Louis XIV (1638-1715), king of France, r. 1643-1715
Maximilian II Emmanuel (1662-1726), elector of Bavaria, 1679-1726
Philip of Anjou (1683-1746), second son of French dauphin, and king of Spain as Philip V, r. 1700-1746
William III (1650-1702), king of England, Scotland, and Ireland, r. 1689-1702, and stadtholder of the United Provinces, r. 1672-1702

SUMMARY OF EVENT

In the second half of the seventeenth century, the Spanish Habsburg Dynasty was represented by Charles II, who suffered serious physical and mental disabilities. He was not expected to live long, and the major European powers feared that a war would erupt over the spoils of the Spanish Empire. This concern led to the extraordinary circumstance in which European countries, including France, Austria, and England negotiated to partition Spain.

As early as January 19, 1668, French king Louis XIV and the Austrian Habsburg emperor Leopold I executed a secret treaty to partition the Spanish Empire. This was the only partition treaty to which Leopold agreed, for he was convinced of the legality of the claims of the Austrian Habsburgs to the Spanish Empire and the inevitability of Austrian Habsburg acquisition of Spanish territories. The treaty's terms stipulated that Louis XIV would gain the Spanish Netherlands, Naples, Franche-Comté, Navarre, and the Philippines. Leopold I would gain Spain, Milan, and the colonies in the Americas if Charles II were to die without heirs.

Louis XIV and William III, king of England, Scotland, and Ireland and leader of the Netherlands, were enemies during France's war against the Dutch (1672-1678) and during the Wars of the League of Augsburg (1689-1697). The two leaders took advantage of the tenuous balance of power established by the Treaty of Ryswick (1697) to begin negotiations to prevent a European war over the disposition of the Spanish Empire. There were assumptions underlying these negotiations, including that the Spanish Empire, upon the death of Charles II, would be kept intact and given to one candidate, or that it could be divided among rivals. In either case, a union of the Spanish Empire with either the French monarchy or Austrian Empire would be prevented.

Urgency was the order of the day when Charles II became seriously ill in February-March, 1698, as Louis XIV began talks with the English ambassador in France, William Bentinck, first earl of Portland, and then sent French ambassador Camille Tallard to England to negotiate with William III personally in late March of 1698. After several months of discussions in England, Bentinck and Tallard traveled to France in August. Louis sought a peaceful resolution to the Spanish Succession problem because France had suffered a serious financial burden in the wake of Louis's wars and major crop failures in the 1690's. William was concerned because the English army had been drastically reduced in size, and he believed that France was in a position to acquire the Spanish Empire by military action.

The negotiations were tedious and moved slowly,

given the many proposals and counterproposals. Spain, its colonies, the Spanish Netherlands, and Sardinia would go to Joseph Ferdinand, the electoral prince of Bavaria and son of Maximilian II Emmanuel of Bavaria and Maria Antonia, oldest daughter of Leopold I and niece of Charles II. Maria Antonia earlier had renounced her claim to the Spanish throne. Furthermore, if the young Joseph Ferdinand died, his father, Maximilian II Emmanuel, would succeed him, and Milan would go to Charles III (later Holy Roman Emperor Charles VI), second son of Leopold I. Louis, the French dauphin, would receive Naples, Sicily, Tuscan ports, and the Spanish province Guipuzcoa. Dutch troops would occupy a series of fortresses in the Spanish Netherlands as a barrier against possible French aggression. The First Partition Treaty was signed by England and France on September 8, 1698, and officially ratified on October 11, 1698.

This treaty proved satisfactory to William and Louis but outraged the Spanish, who would not countenance the division of their empire. Charles II named Joseph Ferdinand as his heir by will on November 14, 1698. Leopold rejected the First Partition Treaty and asserted his claim to the entire Spanish Empire on behalf of Charles III. Historians note that if Charles II had died in late 1698, Joseph Ferdinand would have ascended the throne supported by both the First Partition Treaty and Charles II's will; however, the unexpected death of Joseph Ferdinand on February 6, 1699, at the age of six, threw diplomacy into chaos, leaving only two alternatives for the Spanish throne: an Austrian of the Habsburg Dynasty or a French member of the Bourbon Dynasty.

Louis and William negotiated a Second Partition Treaty and framed a preliminary agreement on June 11, 1699, to be presented to the Dutch and to Leopold for their approval. Leopold's rejection and some dissension among the Dutch delayed ratification until March 25, 1700. The provisions involved Charles III's inheriting Spain, the Spanish colonies, and the Spanish Netherlands. The French dauphin Louis would inherit Naples, Sicily, and Lorraine, while the duke of Lorraine would obtain Milan as compensation for relinquishing Lorraine. Naples and Sicily would be exchanged for Piedmont-Savoy. The Spanish rejected the treaty, leading to a fierce struggle within the Spanish court over whether the Austrian or French candidate should inherit the empire intact. Charles II's queen, Maria Anna of Bavaria-Neuburg, pushed for Charles III. The Spanish clergy supported the French and eventually convinced Charles II to make a will on October 2, 1700, designating the dauphin's second son, Philip of Anjou, as heir to the entire Spanish Empire, provided he relinquish his claim to the French throne. If Philip did not accept the Crown, it would be offered to the Austrian Habsburgs.

Spanish policy was consistent in maintaining the empire's territorial integrity, and a calculation of military might indicated that France would be in the best position to defend the empire. Charles II died on November 1, 1700, and Louis had to determine whether to adhere to the Second Partition Treaty or to Charles II's will. The English and Dutch believed that Leopold would now accept the Second Partition Treaty, as would Louis, since France would gain Piedmont-Savoy through the treaty, whereas, by accepting the will, France would gain nothing. Louis nevertheless accepted the will on November 16, 1700, and the sixteen-year-old Philip of Anjou began his journey to Spain to become its king—to reject the will would give the Spanish Empire to Charles III. On November 18, 1700, Leopold ordered his military advisers to begin planning an attack on Milan.

Significance

The Second Treaty of Partition paved the way for the Wars of the Spanish Succession (1701-1714). Philip of Anjou arrived in Madrid on February 18, 1701, to be crowned King Philip V. He brought with him French military advisers. Aggressive actions by Louis upset the English and Dutch; French troops expelled Dutch troops from the barrier fortresses in the Spanish Netherlands; Louis recognized Philip V's right to the French throne; Philip V awarded the lucrative slaving contract, the *asiento*, to the French for ten years. Smaller European powers began to gravitate toward France. Maximilian II Emmanuel of Bavaria entered into a military alliance with France in March of 1701. Europe was lurching toward the war so many had worked so hard to avoid.

Hostilities began in Italy on June 19, 1701, as the French tried to block an Austrian advance into Milan. England, Austria, and the Dutch signed the Grand Alliance to fight for a partition of the Spanish Empire in early September, and, in late September, Louis recognized James, the so-called Pretender and the son of King James II (r. 1685-1688), as king of England, an extremely provocative action.

The Grand (Triple) Alliance officially declared war on France on May 15, 1702, with the following aims: Spain and France were not to be ruled by the same monarch, and there would be compensation for Leopold with Italian territory and commercial concessions for the English and Dutch. The war ended with the Treaty of Utrecht (1713) and the Treaties of Rastatt and Baden

(1714), which partitioned the Spanish Empire. Holy Roman Emperor Charles VI, the former King Charles III of Spain, received Naples, Sardinia, Milan, Tuscan ports, and the Spanish Netherlands. Philip V renounced claims to the French throne and retained the remainder of the Spanish Empire, except for Gibraltar, which England had conquered during the war.

—*Mark C. Herman*

Further Reading

Baxter, Stephen B. *William III and the Defense of European Liberty, 1650-1702*. New York: Harcourt, Brace and World, 1966. This analytical biography discusses William's negotiations during the formation of the Partition Treaties in chapter 26, "Armed Truce."

Bromley, J. S., ed. *The Rise of Great Britain and Russia*. Vol. 6 in *The New Cambridge Modern History*. Cambridge, England: Cambridge University Press, 1970. Numerous chapters in this comprehensive survey deal with the Partition Treaties and the international background, especially chapters 11-13.

Frey, Linda, and Marsha Frey, eds. *The Treaties of the War of the Spanish Succession*. Westport, Conn.: Greenwood Press, 1995. An excellent resource with short reference entries on the Partition Treaties, the rulers, diplomats, and the subsequent Wars of the Spanish Succession.

Grimblot, Paul, ed. *The Letters of William III and Louis XIV and Their Ministers*. London: Longman, Brown, Green, and Longmans, 1848. A valuable collection of the correspondence between the two monarchs in the years 1697-1700. Essential for understanding the foreign policy of this period.

Spielman, John P. *Leopold I of Austria*. New Brunswick, N.J.: Rutgers University Press, 1977. This biography presents the Austrian Habsburg position on the Spanish Succession and the partition treaties.

Wolf, John B. *Louis XIV*. New York: W. W. Norton, 1968. Louis's aggressive foreign policy, his participation in the diplomacy that produced the partition treaties, and his rationale for accepting Charles II's will are all discussed in this biography.

See also: Mar. 4, 1665-July 31, 1667: Second Anglo-Dutch War; May 24, 1667-May 2, 1668: War of Devolution; Apr. 6, 1672-Aug. 10, 1678: French-Dutch War; Aug. 10, 1678-Sept. 26, 1679: Treaties of Nijmegen; 1688-1702: Reign of William and Mary; 1689-1697: Wars of the League of Augsburg; Sept. 20, 1697: Treaty of Ryswick.

Related articles in *Great Lives from History: The Seventeenth Century, 1601-1700:* Anne of Austria; Charles II (of Spain); James II; John of Austria; Leopold I; Louis XIV; Marie-Thérèse; Philip IV; William III.

1699
British Establish Trading Post in Canton

The British East India Company established a post at Canton, China, to trade primarily for tea, a commodity that had acquired a great deal of value and would exert significant influence upon the world markets, leading ultimately to the American Revolutionary War in the eighteenth century and the Opium Wars between England and China in the nineteenth.

Locale: Guangzhou (Kuang-chou or Canton), China
Categories: Economics; trade and commerce

Key Figures

Charles II (1630-1685), king of England, r. 1660-1685
Elizabeth I (1533-1603), queen of England, r. 1558-1603
James I (1566-1625), king of England, r. 1603-1625, and king of Scotland as James VI, r. 1567-1625
Qianlong (1711-1799), emperor of China, r. 1735-1796

Summary of Event

At the very end of the seventeenth century, the British East India Company established a trading post in Guangzhou (Canton), China. Although the post had little immediate impact, within a short time it came to play a major role in world events. However, an overview of the company's history is necessary to grasp the significance of its establishment of a permanent trading post in China.

On the last day of the sixteenth century, December 31, 1600 England's Queen Elizabeth I granted a royal charter to the British East India Company, or as it was formally known, the Governor and Company of Merchants of London Trading into the East Indies. The company was given exclusive rights to trade in the East Indies for fifteen years. The "John Company," or simply the "Company," as it came to be popularly called, was founded by a group of businessmen willing to take great financial risk. Initially, the organization made headway into India, which was soon to be called the Jewel in the Crown. The profits generated were so enormous that back in England, King James I once again signed an exclusive, unrestricted charter with the company.

The British East India Company grew quickly and became so powerful that in time it acquired governmental and military functions that overshadowed its commercial activities. So great was its supremacy that it exceeded the Portuguese and the Dutch in the trade of cotton, silk, indigo, saltpeter, and tea. After the Restoration of the monarchy in 1660, the English king Charles II gave the company the right to annex territories, to mint money, to raise native armies, and even to declare war. In short, as a commercial enterprise, the John Company became a nation unto itself.

This was how the situation stood when, in 1699, the *Macclesfield*, one of the company's new fast-sailing galley supercargo ships, sailed from London in six months and moored in Whampoon Harbor to establish a trading post in Guangzhou, China—which the English promptly named Canton—to trade silk, porcelain, and, most important, tea for silver. Canton was the major port in southern China. It took less than one hundred years for China to outstrip India in profits for the company.

Significance

During the seventeenth century, tea became a powerful economic factor by providing large sources of government revenue. From its arrival in Europe, taxes on tea provided a means of enriching the royal coffers. It quickly became a mass-produced staple and eventually accounted for one-tenth of the British tax income. Indeed, in England the demand for tea increased to such proportions that by the late 1700's, the drink accounted for more than 60 percent of the company's total trade. However, the company found it difficult to sell its products, primarily woolen goods, in China and so experienced a deficit in Chinese trade until the early nineteenth century.

Unlike many other Eastern nations, China set itself apart from the rest of the world. While trade was certainly allowed, European traders were not allowed to remain on Chinese soil. In 1773, Lord McCartney, the first envoy of Britain to China, arrived with a large British delegation on board a sixty-four-gun man-of-war. His meeting with Emperor Qianlong during his diplomatic mission to the Celestial Empire in time ended China's isolationist policy and brought about the beginning of a relaxation of China's restrictive trading policies.

Two years later, Britain lost its American colonies (1775) and experienced a sudden and severe loss of silver. However, by this time, the British demand for Chinese tea was insatiable and the company was forced to look around for a different good to trade for tea. It found the solution in the form of opium. The company began to pay for its tea with opium grown in its Indian colonies and smuggled to China in the company's ships. Indeed, the start of a large-scale trade in opium from the British East India company in India to China reversed the imbalance of trade, as it created widespread addiction among the Chinese population and ultimately led to the Opium Wars between England and China.

Meanwhile, in 1773, the New England colonists rebelled against the "tea tax" imposed upon them without their consent, and angry patriots boarded the company's ships, where they threw 342 chests of tea into Boston Harbor. In time, this came to be known as the Boston Tea Party. As a result, British king George III closed Boston Harbor and royal troops occupied the city. The colonial leaders came together to resist the occupation, and the American Revolution was underway.

The British East India company was arguably the largest trading power of all time. Its influence stretched from London to China and later to Australia. For more than two centuries, it controlled half of the world's trade and established the largest empire the world has ever known. Indeed, without the company, there simply would have been no British Empire.

—M. Casey Diana

Further Reading

Hanes, William Travis, et al. *The Opium Wars: The Addiction of One Empire and the Corruption of Another*. New York: Sourcebooks, 2002. Succinctly illustrates how the British dependence on tea and the loss of its American colonies in 1775 led to Britain's turn to opium and the subsequent ruin of China and the emergence of Hong Kong and Singapore.

Keay, John. *The Honourable Company: A History of the English East India Company*. New York: Macmillan, 1991. Beginning in 1600, Keay uses the journals of British East India Company officers to illustrate the rise and ultimate demise of the greatest trading power of all time. Comprehensive coverage of Britain's first venture into Canton, China, in 1699.

Pettigrew, Jane. *A Social History of Tea*. London: National Trust, 2002. Explores tea's enormous influence on society and history. Includes accounts of the British East India Company and its influence in China, the Boston Tea Party, smuggling, and the Opium Wars.

Wilbur, Marguerite. *The East India Company and the British Empire in the Far East*. London: Russell & Russell, 1970. Approachable account of the British East India Company, its might and right, and its quest for profits in the East, especially in China.

SEE ALSO: 17th cent.: Age of Mercantilism in Southeast Asia; 17th cent.: The Pepper Trade; 17th cent.: Rise of the Gunpowder Empires; Mar. 20, 1602: Dutch East India Company Is Founded; Beginning Spring, 1605: Dutch Dominate Southeast Asian Trade; 1609: China Begins Shipping Tea to Europe; May, 1659-May, 1660: Restoration of Charles II.

RELATED ARTICLES in *Great Lives from History: The Seventeenth Century, 1601-1700:* Charles II (of England); James I.

January 26, 1699
TREATY OF KARLOWITZ

The Treaty of Karlowitz ended the Ottoman Empire's expansion in Europe, liberated Hungary from the Turks, and marked the consequent ascendancy of Habsburg Austria.

LOCALE: Karlowitz, Hungary
CATEGORIES: Diplomacy and international relations; wars, uprisings, and civil unrest

KEY FIGURES

Eugene of Savoy (François-Eugène, prince of Savoie-Carignan; 1663-1736), Austrian general
Innocent XI (Benedetto Odescalchi; 1611-1689), Roman Catholic pope, 1676-1689
John III Sobieski (1629-1696), king of Poland, r. 1674-1696
Merzifonlu Kara Mustafa Paşa (1634/1635-1683), Ottoman grand vizier, 1676-1683
Leopold I (1640-1705), Holy Roman Emperor, r. 1658-1705, and princely ruler of the Habsburg Austrian possessions
Louis XIV (1638-1715), king of France, r. 1643-1715
Mehmed IV Avci (1642-1693), Ottoman sultan, r. 1648-1687
Mustafa II (1664-1703), Ottoman sultan, r. 1695-1703

SUMMARY OF EVENT

The signing of the Treaty of Karlowitz in 1699 was significant in at least four ways. It marked the termination of the major wars between the Austrians and the Ottoman Turks, liberated Hungary from the Turks, led to Habsburg ascendancy on the lower Danube River at the expense of the receding Ottoman Empire, and marked the genesis of the so-called Eastern Question that involved the decline of the Ottoman Empire for the following two hundred years. Simultaneous with Ottoman decline was a growing Austro-Russian antagonism that would have worldwide repercussions.

The Austrians and Ottomans had fought intermittently since the early sixteenth century. Austria's position throughout this last major struggle was complicated by continuing French aggression against the Holy Roman Empire in the Rhineland, and by King Louis XIV's promise to the Turks that he would not render military assistance to the Habsburgs in defense of Vienna. Hence, throughout this period, Leopold I, in his capacity as Holy Roman Emperor and princely ruler of Austria, and in his role as the defender of the western and eastern boundaries of the Holy Roman Empire, was faced both with actual war as well as the threat of war on two fronts. To dilute the strength of his adversaries, especially the Turks, Leopold, on March 31, 1683, entered into an alliance with King John III Sobieski of Poland, an alliance arranged by Pope Innocent XI. On the same day, Mehmed IV Avci led a huge Turkish host, which by summer would swell to around 250,000 men, on a march north from Adrianople (Edirne) toward Vienna At Belgrade, Mehmed transferred command to the grand vizier, Merzifonlu Kara Mustafa Paşa, who would conduct military operations.

The second Siege of Vienna, which began in mid-July, 1683, marked the opening of the longest of the Austro-Turkish wars; it would be terminated only in 1699 with the Treaty of Karlowitz. For two months, some twenty thousand defenders repulsed six great assaults directed against the walls of the Habsburg citadel. On September 12, when the city was in imminent danger of falling, relief contingents of German and Polish troops arrived. The Turks were forced to break off the siege and commence a retreat that would ultimately take them back to Belgrade, where Kara Mustafa Paşa was executed on the orders of Mehmed IV, who had retired to Edirne.

Anxious to follow up this success, Leopold signed an alliance in the following year with Poland and Venice, again arranged by Innocent XI, an alliance called the Holy League. In addition, Leopold entered into a truce with Louis XIV, which enabled Austria, at least temporarily, to concentrate its energies solely against the Turks. During the first two years of the war, Austrian forces made only limited progress, but they won spectacular victories during the next three years, including the Second Battle of Mohács (1687) and the capture of Belgrade (1688). Hungary was thereby completely liberated. Venice, meanwhile, had captured Athens.

When the Habsburgs seemed to have victory in their grasp, Louis XIV began the Wars of the League of Augsburg in the west to bolster the fighting spirit of the faltering Ottoman Empire, which had recently proposed peace. The Turks, encouraged by the French move, renewed hostilities and had recaptured Belgrade by 1690. Leopold, despite the Ottoman recovery, was obliged to devote most of his attention to the war in the west. Only in 1697, as this contest with Louis XIV drew to a close, was Austria's foremost general and recently appointed commander in chief, Prince Eugene of Savoy, able to inflict a decisive defeat at Zenta. Here, Turkish forces, led by Sultan Mustafa II, were caught while crossing the Tisza River. The Turks now had no choice but to sue for peace.

The Treaty of Karlowitz sealed the fate of the Ottomans, as the empire began its decline as a regional power. Before the treaty was signed, Ottoman grand vizier Merzifonlu Kara Mustafa Paşa failed to take Vienna from the Habsburgs in 1683. He was soon executed by officers of Sultan Mehmed IV Avci. (Francis R. Niglutsch)

The ensuing peace settlement, mediated by the British and Dutch, was drawn up on January 26, 1699, in the devastated village of Karlowitz after negotiations that had opened November 13 of the previous year. Separate treaties were signed by the Turkish representatives with Austria, Poland, and Venice. Negotiations with Russia (whose czar, Peter the Great, had been at war with the Ottoman Empire since 1695) continued until June, 1700, when the Treaty of Constantinople was concluded. Under the most important provision of the Treaty of Karlowitz, Austria received Slavonia, Transylvania, territory east of the Tisza River, and most of Hungary with the exception of the Banat of Temesvár, which remained under Ottoman rule. Poland kept Podolia, Kamieniniec, the western Ukraine, and a strip east of the Dniester River. Venice gave up Athens, but retained the Morea, the island of Santa Maura, and Albanian and Dalmatian territories. The Russians retained only Azov and adjoining districts. They signed a treaty for only two years, in contrast with those of twenty-five or more years signed by the other powers.

Ottoman failure in the seventeenth century resulted from an inability to modernize administrative structures, military tactics, and armaments. Their rapid expansion had resulted from superior armaments, especially artillery, a social organization offering a better life to European feudal serfs, and shared Islamic ideology. They were unable, however, to organize a trained civil service, a professional military, or an educational system matching that of the European nation-states. They also discouraged technical innovation, and thus, their military equipment became obsolete.

Significance

The Treaty of Karlowitz is an important milestone in the history of the Balkans, with far-reaching implications for all Europe. Austria replaced the Ottoman Empire as the dominant power in the lower Danube region. Whereas Europe had been faced with an aggressive and powerful Ottoman Empire before 1699, henceforth the Continent would be confronted by the opposite problem, the steady decline of Turkish power. This decline of the Ottoman Empire between 1699 and 1914 historically has been referred to as the Eastern Question.

The Turkish decline created a power vacuum in the Balkans. Austria took an important step toward filling the western half of this vacuum by conquering Hungary. Subsequently, before the end of the eighteenth century, Russia began to assert influence over the eastern half of the Balkans. The continuing clash of Austrian and Russian Balkan interests during the nineteenth century, always at Ottoman expense, contributed greatly to the unrest of that area and to the outbreak of World War I in 1914.

—*Edward P. Keleher and Ralph L. Langenheim, Jr.*

FURTHER READING

Goffman, Daniel. *The Ottoman Empire and Early Modern Europe*. New York: Cambridge University Press, 2002. Goffman describes Ottoman-Habsburg relations during the seventeenth century.

Hertz, Frederick. *The Age of Enlightenment*. Vol. 2 in *The Development of the German Public Mind: A Social History of German Political Sentiments, Aspirations, and Ideas*. London: Allen & Unwin, 1962. Examines the Treaty of Karlowitz from the Austrian point of view.

Hoskins, J. W. *Victory at Vienna: The Ottoman Siege of 1683*. Washington, D.C.: Library of Congress, European Division, 1983. A concise account supported by an extended reading list.

Kinross, Lord. *The Ottoman Centuries: The Rise and Fall of the Turkish Empire*. New York: William Morrow, 1977. Kinross discusses the events from the second Siege of Vienna through the Treaty of Karlowitz from an Ottoman perspective.

Ogg, David. *Europe in the Seventeenth Century*. 9th ed. London: A. and C. Black, 1971. A general account of events leading to the Treaty of Karlowitz.

Parvev, Ivan. *Habsburgs and Ottomans Between Vienna and Belgrade, 1683-1739*. Boulder, Colo.: Eastern European Monographs, 1995. Parvev examines relations between the Habsburg and Ottoman empires from the Siege of Vienna through the Treaty of Belgrade.

Stavrianos, L. S. *The Balkans Since 1453*. New York: Holt, Rinehart and Winston, 1963. A discussion emphasizing the impact of the Treaty of Karlowitz on the Ottoman Empire.

Stoye, John. *The Siege of Vienna*. London: Collins, 1964. An extended account of the Siege of Vienna.

Sturdy, David J. *Fractured Europe, 1600-1721*. Oxford, England: Blackwell, 2002. Chapter 7 of this overview of European history describes the relations of Central and Southern Europe with the Ottoman Empire from 1648 through 1720.

Wolf, John B. *The Emergence of the Great Powers, 1695-1713*. Vol. 7 in *The Rise of Modern Europe*, edited by William J. Langer. New York: Harper & Row, 1951. A comprehensive discussion of the Austrian offensive against the Turks within the international context of the late seventeenth century.

SEE ALSO: Aug. 22, 1645-Sept., 1669: Turks Conquer Crete; 1656-1676: Ottoman Empire's Brief Recovery; Summer, 1672-Fall, 1676: Ottoman-Polish Wars; July 14-Sept. 12, 1683: Defeat of the Ottomans at Vienna; 1684-1699: Holy League Ends Ottoman Rule of the Danubian Basin; Beginning 1687: Decline of the Ottoman Empire; 1689-1697: Wars of the League of Augsburg; 1697-1702: Köprülü Reforms of Hüseyin Paşa; Mar. 9, 1697-Aug. 25, 1698: Peter the Great Tours Western Europe; Nov. 30, 1700: Battle of Narva.

RELATED ARTICLES in *Great Lives from History: The Seventeenth Century, 1601-1700:* Innocent XI; John III Sobieski; Merzifonlu Kara Mustafa Paşa; Leopold I; Louis XIV.

March 30, 1699
Singh Founds the Khalsa Brotherhood

The creation of the Khalsa brotherhood, an order of militant ascetics, inaugurated social reform, instituted a religious-political bond, and instilled a martial spirit among certain Sikhs in India who joined the order as a form of self-defense against a reviving orthodox Islam.

Locale: Anandpur, Punjab (India)
Categories: Religion and theology; organizations and institutions; social issues and reform

Key Figures

Gobind Singh (1666-1708), founder of the Khalsa brotherhood and tenth Sikhguru, r. 1675-1708
Arjun (1563-1606), fifth Sikhguru, r. 1581-1606
Tegh Bahādur (1621-1675), ninth Sikhguru, r. 1644-1675
Jahāngīr (1569-1627), Mughal emperor of India, r. 1605-1627
Shah Jahan (1592-1666), Mughal emperor of India, r. 1628-1658
Aurangzeb (1618-1707), Mughal emperor of India, r. 1658-1707

Summary of Event

The creation of the Khalsa, or the Brotherhood of the Militant Ascetics (Saint-Soldiers) by the tenth and the last Sikhguru Gobind Singh was the culmination of the evolutionary process of the Sikh *oikoumene*, or the *Panth*, dating from the days of the fifth Sikhguru, Arjun. Arjun's achievements included the development of the *masand* system, in which deputies of the guru were in charge of collecting voluntary contributions—similar to tithe from a parish flock); finalizing the foundation of the Sikh headquarters at Amritsar and the temple of God, Harimandir; and the compilation in 1604 of the *Guru Granth Sahib*, the sacred scripture of the Sikhs containing 5,894 hymns composed by saints of the twelfth through the seventeenth centuries.

These developments were instrumental in articulating a distinct Sikh identity toward the closing years of Emperor Akbar's reign (r. 1556-1605). Akbar's reign also witnessed an orthodox Islamic revivalist movement responding to his founding of an eclectic religion called Din-i-Ilahi (Divine Faith) in 1580. The Sikh community came to be seen not only as a non-Islamic sect but also as a separate polity—resembling an *imperium et imperio*—within the Mughal Empire. Guru Arjun's complicity with the rebellion of the Mughal crown prince Khusru in 1606 quickly led to his execution by Emperor Jahāngīr. Arjun's death forced the peace loving Sikhs to transform themselves into a militant community (*waza-i-sipahiana*) for self-defense. His death was seen as martyrdom, and, according to tradition, it led directly to a deliberate arming of the community and the Mughal government's apprehension. A common threat thus united the Sikhs in a common faith.

The word *khalsa* appears to have been derived from the Persian *khalisa*, which designated Crown lands in Mughal India. In "panthic" parlance, *khalisa* became synonymous with the pure Sikh community, the Khalsa, who were initiated by their guru and who owed their offerings to him (instead of to the *masands*). These offerings resembled the revenue from the Crown lands (*khalisa*) that were paid directly to the emperor's revenue collectors. Guru Gobind sought to unify the Sikhs who had divided into different factions or sects. The dissidents were known as *minas*, rival lineages claiming guruship beginning with the elder brother of Guru Arjun. The *minas* were supported by the *masands*, who needed to be segregated and suppressed. This "cleansing" operation was necessary because of the rising Mughal hostility that began during the reign of Emperor Shah Jahan and reached a climax with Guru Tegh Bahādur's execution in 1675, discussed below.

During the reign of the sixth guru (Arjun's son Hargobind, 1606-1644) and the seventh guru (Har Rāi, 1644-1661), who actually retired to Kiratpur in the Kahlur hills following the outbreak of hostilities with the Mughal headquarters of the Punjab at Lahore, relations between the Sikhs and the imperial Mughals were more or less uneventful. It was during the reign of the ninth guru, Tegh Bahādur (who had moved to the plains) that hostilities resumed between the *Panth* and the imperial administration. Eventually, Tegh Bahādur was executed by Emperor Aurangzeb. Like the execution of the fifth guru, Arjun, the death of Tegh Bahādur was interpreted by the *Panth* as martyrdom, which provided strong motivation for the consolidation of "panthic" cohesion. It was this cohesion that led to the creation of the Khalsa.

According to tradition, Guru Gobind founded the Khalsa Order at Anandpur on Baishakhi Day, 1699, the first day of the Indian astronomical year (which corresponds to March 30, 1699). In the early morning hours, Gobind entered a specially constructed canopy, where a huge congregation of Sikhs had gathered to celebrate the spring festival. Behind the canopy was a small tent with a single opening for entry. Gobind delivered a fiery sermon, listing the atrocities of the Mughal rulers and the inaction of numerous Hindu sects. He exhorted his listeners to safeguard their secular and spiritual rights and endeavor to organize collectively to redress the wrongs inflicted on them as a community.

Also during his sermon, he sang paeans to the sword: "God subdues enemies, so does the sword, therefore Sword is God and God is the sword." After his oration, he sang, "I salute arrows and gun. O Sword! You are powerful and relentless, I salute thee." He then brandished a sword and declared that dharma (religion or duty) demanded sacrificial blood. He then asked for a volunteer who was willing to be sacrificed. Five men offered their heads: a man of the *khatri* (trader class), a farmer, a *dhobi* (washerman), a *kahar* (water-carrier), and a *nai* (barber). Even though the congregation saw the five men enter the tent one by one and saw the guru emerge five times with a blood-smeared sword, the volunteers were spared their lives for their loyalty and courage. In their place, five goats were beheaded by the guru. The volunteers came to be known as the "five beloved," or the Panj Pyare—the five original Khalsa.

The guru baptized the chosen five with a double-edged sword (*khande di pahul*) and was in turn baptized by the five, thereby establishing the tradition of guru as disciple and disciple as Guru (*ape Gur Chela*). Following the baptismal ritual (*pahul*), they all took the surname Singh, which means "lion." The guru then announced the *rahit*, which all initiated members of the Khalsa were to observe henceforth. The *rahit*, a series of instructions and injunctions for the lifestyle of the initiated, declared, among other things, that every initiated Sikh was to wear a *kachha* (undershorts), *kirpan* (dagger or sword), *kesh* (uncut hair), *kangha* (comb), and *kara* (steel bracelet). The *rahit* is also known as the five K's. The initiates also were forbidden to touch meat that was slaughtered in the Muslim manner (*kuttha*) and instead consume *jhatka* meat from an animal decapitated with one stroke. There was to be no idolatry, and the guru's hymns should be read or sung daily. The initiates at all times were to avoid the company of nonbelievers, to confine their matrimonial relations within the families of the initiated, and to not beg, accept gifts, practice slavery, lie, boast, or steal. The prescribed professions for the Khalsa included farming, trade, warfare, and any work with the pen.

Significance

The importance of this brotherhood for the Sikh community lies primarily in the fact that the Khalsa became a political entity as contrasted with the pre-Khalsa *panth*. This development was a major factor behind the revolt of Banda Singh Bahādur (1670-1716), who established for some time a veritable Khalsa *rāj* (a Khalsa state or rule). Later, the Khalsa emerged as a highly politicized community with a distinct political goal developed since Guru Gobind's days: The Khalsa will rule (*raj karega khalsa*).

It must be noted, however, that not all Khalsa Sikhs were Singhs. Even in Guru Gobind's days baptism of the double-edged sword was voluntary. The Singhs thus baptized came to be known as *keshdharis* (bearing uncut hair) and the non-Singhs as *sahajdharis* (slow-adopters, or the easygoing) Khalsa. The latter came to be seen as somewhat inferior to the former and were encouraged to observe the five K's of the *rahit*. Eventually, the Khalsa Singhs acquired the distinction of representing Sikh identity.

—*Narasingha P. Sil*

Further Reading

Banerjee, Anil Chandra. *The Khalsa Raj*. New Delhi: Abhinav, 1985. This work examines the achievements of the Sikhs to the period ending in 1849.

Banerjee, Himadri, ed. *The Khalsa and the Punjab: Studies in Sikh History to the Nineteenth Century*. New Delhi: TulikaBooks, 2002. This edited volume provides up-to-date analyses by distinguished Indian experts.

Banerjee, Indubhusan. *Evolution of the Khalsa*. 2 vols. Calcutta: A. Mukherjee, 1947-1963. A pioneering history by an acknowledged master of Sikh history of Calcutta University.

Kapoor, Sukhbir S. *The Creation of the Khalsa: The Saint Soldier*. New Delhi: Hemkunt Press, 1999. An anthology of specialized articles, mostly by Sikh scholars.

Kohli, Surindar S. *The Life and Ideas of Guru Gobind Singh, Based on Original Sources*. New Delhi: Munshiram Manoharlal, 1986. Contains an important excerpt from the English translation of Guru Gobind's autobiography, *Bachittar Natak* (wondrous drama).

Loehlin, Clinton E. *The Granth of Guru Gobind Singh and the Khalsa Brotherhood*. Lucknow, India: Lucknow Publishing House, 1971. A succinct analytical survey.

McLeod, Hew. *Exploring Sikhism: Aspects of Sikh Identity, Culture, and Thought*. New York: Oxford University Press, 2000. A solid general survey useful for students as well as general readers.

_______. *Sikhism*. New York: Penguin, 1997. Explores how Sikhism emerged from the Hindu background of the times and examines the splitting off of a number of separate sects.

_______. *Sikhs of the Khalsa: A History of the Khalsa Rahit*. New York: Oxford University Press, 2003. A magisterial analysis of the Khalsa and their *rahit*.

SEE ALSO: 1658-1707: Reign of Aurangzeb; c. 1666-1676: Founding of the Marāthā Kingdom.

RELATED ARTICLES in *Great Lives from History: The Seventeenth Century, 1601-1700:* Aurangzeb; Jahāngīr; Shah Jahan; Śivājī.

May 1, 1699
FRENCH FOUND THE LOUISIANA COLONY

France's successful establishment of a Louisiana colony negated Spain's claims to the lower Mississippi Valley and blocked England's plans to expand into the region.

LOCALE: Southern Mississippi River Valley and the Gulf Coast (now in Mississippi, Alabama, and Louisiana)

CATEGORIES: Expansion and land acquisition; colonization; exploration and discovery; government and politics

KEY FIGURES

Pierre Le Moyne d'Iberville (1661-1706), Canadian-born explorer, French naval officer, and founder of the Louisiana colony

Jean-Baptiste Le Moyne (sieur de Bienville; 1680-1767), Iberville's brother, fellow explorer, governor of Louisiana, 1701-1713, and founder of New Orleans and Mobile

Sieur de La Salle (René-Robert Cavelier; 1643-1687), French explorer who claimed Louisiana for France

Henri de Tonty (1650?-1704), Italian-born explorer, lieutenant of La Salle and later of Iberville

Louis XIV (1638-1715), king of France, r. 1643-1715

SUMMARY OF EVENT

By founding the Louisiana Colony in 1699, France supported its previous claim to the Mississippi Valley, which was also coveted by Spain and by England.

In the sixteenth century, Spanish explorers based in Florida discovered the Gulf Coast and the Mississippi River, but they did not found a colony there. More than a century later, after the French had established a colony in Quebec, Canada, explorers and fur traders venturing south and west began exploring the upper reaches of the Mississippi River. Early in 1682, René-Robert Cavelier, sieur de La Salle, a prominent French Canadian explorer, and his longtime lieutenant, Henri de Tonty, organized an expedition whose goal was to reach the mouth of the Mississippi at the Gulf of Mexico. They were successful, and on April 9, 1682, La Salle claimed the Mississippi Valley for France, naming the territory Louisiane, in honor of Louis XIV, the French king.

However, when La Salle attempted to return two years later with a boatload of colonists, he mistakenly ended up in Texas. His colony there failed, and La Salle was murdered by his own men. Nevertheless, his project was not forgotten. Tonty's book about La Salle's final expedition, published in 1697, drew the attention of French readers to Louisiana, and about the same time, Louis XIV was informed that the English were making plans to seize the Mississippi Valley. It was decided that a French expedition to establish a colony in Louisiana should be organized immediately and that the best person to lead it was Pierre Le Moyne d'Iberville, a native Canadian, who as a French naval officer had gained fame for his victories against the British.

On October 24, 1698, Iberville sailed from Brest, France, with four ships, carrying a crew of three hundred. His second-in-command was his brother, Jean-Baptiste Le Moyne. At Santo Domingo, Iberville took the precautionary measure of adding the warship *François* to his little fleet, but when they reached Mobile Bay without sighting any English ships, he sent the *François* back to Santo Domingo. After exploring the Mobile Bay area, Iberville sailed west, anchoring beside Ship Island, near what is now Biloxi, Mississippi.

Iberville's next project was to select a site for his colony. Loading some fifty crew members into two longboats, Iberville and his brother set off through the marshy islands, searching for the mouth of the Mississippi. They reached their goal on March 2, 1699, and then spent two and a half weeks moving up the river, visiting several Indian tribes, until they separated into two parties for further explorations before returning to their ships. Iberville was now convinced that it would be most wise to place the first French settlement in Louisiana on the Gulf Coast, where large ships could anchor, rather than in a less accessible place upriver. He settled on a site on the eastern side of Biloxi Bay. There he directed his men to build a small square fort, which he named Fort Maurepas (now Ocean Springs, Mississippi), in honor of the French prime minister. On May 9, Iberville set off for France, leaving the fort and the seventy men who remained behind in charge of the sieur de Sauvole, with Bienville as second-in-command.

When Iberville returned in December, 1699, bringing additional colonists, he learned that several months previously Bienville had encountered an English ship on the Mississippi not far from what is now New Orleans. When Bienville convinced the British captain that there was a French fleet just up the river, the captain turned around and sailed away, abandoning his plan to establish a British settlement on the Mississippi River. Realizing that he needed a second fort, one that could command the river itself, Iberville dispatched his brother to find a suitable site and construct a fort there. The result was Fort de la Boulaye, situated on the west bank of the river, 50 miles (80 kilometers) north of its mouth.

Unfortunately, the men Iberville brought over from France were not farmers and had no interest in raising crops, nor did they have any prior experience that would equip them for frontier life. They depended for their very existence on supply ships from France. Many of them became ill and died; some actually starved to death. A contingent of colonists whom Tonty brought down from

French Louisiana, 1702

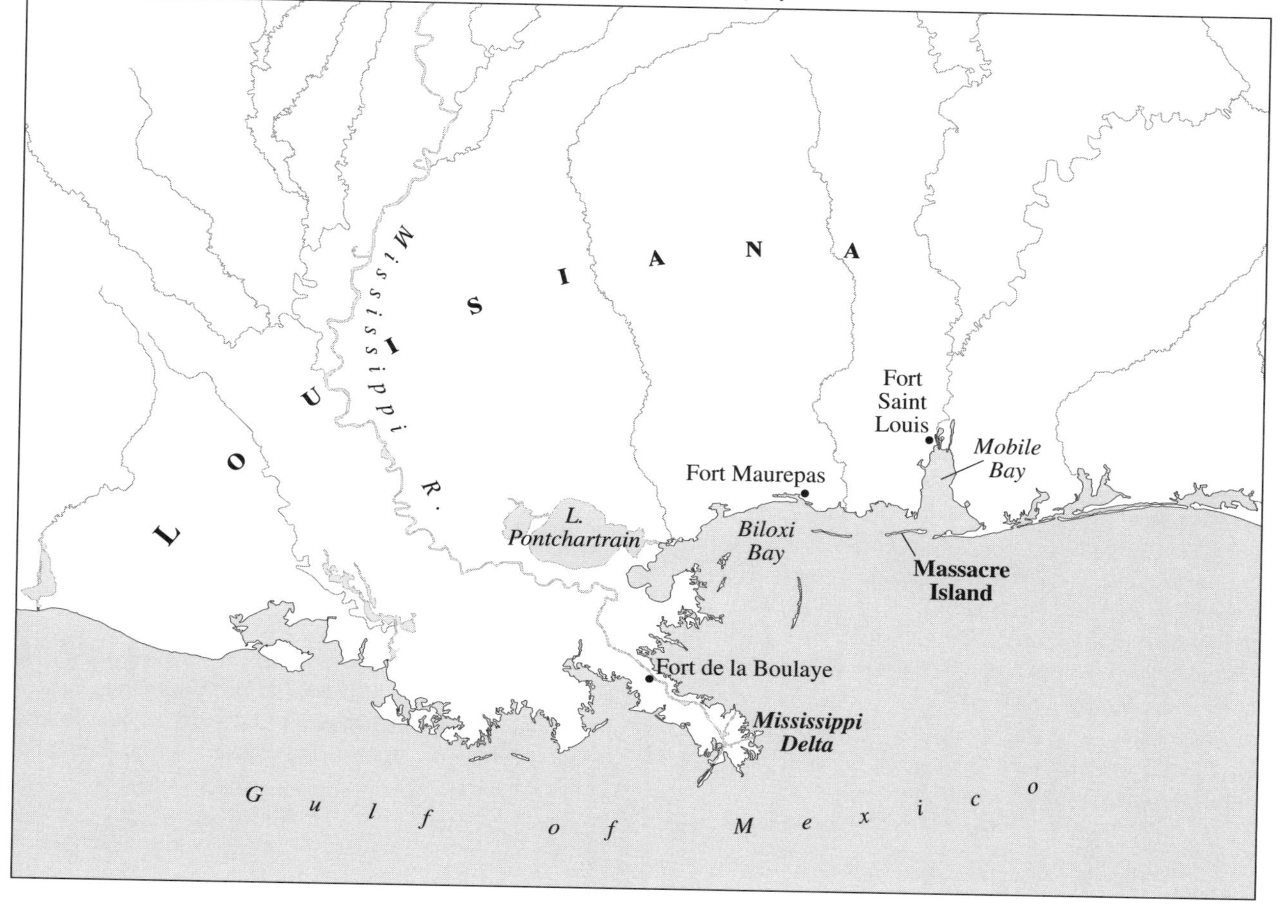

Canada fared better, for they had the skills that life on the frontier demanded; their presence among the settlers was invaluable.

When Iberville came back from France in December, 1701, he decided to move most of the colonists from Fort Maurepas to a temporary home on Massacre Island, now Dauphin Island, and then to a third settlement on the western side of Mobile Bay. There, he had Bienville build a fort much larger and more substantial than the other two. He intended Fort Saint Louis de la Mobile to be the administrative center of the Louisiana colony.

Iberville left Louisiana for the last time in April, 1702; four years later, he died of yellow fever. Tonty fell victim to the same disease in 1704. After the death of Sauvole in 1701, Bienville became governor of the colony. He is credited with holding it together during the yellow fever epidemics of 1701 and 1704 and also with insisting that the settlers raise the crops that would ensure their survival when supply ships were not forthcoming.

Significance

Instead of the easy wealth that they expected to acquire in the New World, the French colonists found only hardship, misery, illness, disease, and, in many cases, an untimely death. The survival of the Louisiana colony was due in large part to the efforts of three indomitable men, Iberville, Bienville, and Tonty. Although Iberville's dream of a French inland empire or even of a French continent would never be realized, the southern Mississippi Valley and the Gulf Coast still reflect the culture of the nation that first colonized the area.

Had the French not successfully established the Louisiana colony, the history of the United States would have been altogether different. If Spain had followed up that early claim and placed settlements in the area, it might have become another Mexico rather than a part of the United States. If the British had colonized the area and taken control of the southern coast, the outcome of the American Revolution might well have been very different. In any case, it was only because the French had taken possession of Louisiana that the United States was able to buy it from them in 1803, thus acquiring an area that extended from the Mississippi River to the Rocky Mountains and from Canada to the Gulf of Mexico. Without the Louisiana Purchase, it would never have been possible for the United States of America to become a land that stretches "from sea to shining sea."

—Rosemary M. Canfield Reisman

Further Reading

Brasseaux, Carl A., trans. and ed. *A Comparative View of French Louisiana, 1699 and 1762: The Journals of Pierre Le Moyne d'Iberville and Jean-Jacques-Blaise d'Abbadie*. USL History Series 13. Lafayette: Center for Louisiana Studies, University of Southwestern Louisiana, 1979. Contains Pierre Le Moyne d'Iberville's personal account of his first journey to the Gulf Coast. Maps, illustrations, and notes.

Crouse, Nellie M. *Lemoyne D'Iberville: Soldier of New France*. Reprint. Baton Rouge: Louisiana State University Press, 2001. A reprint of the 1954 standard biography, with a new introduction by Daniel H. Usner.

Davis, Edwin Adams. *Louisiana: The Pelican State*. Baton Rouge: Louisiana State University Press, 1959. A good starting point for the study of Louisiana history. Illustrated.

Giraud, Marcel. *The Reign of Louis XIV, 1698-1715*. Vol. 1 in *A History of French Louisiana*, translated by Joseph C. Lambert, revised and corrected by the author. Baton Rouge: Louisiana State University Press, 1974. A major scholarly work. Useful maps and charts.

Hauck, Philomena. *Bienville: Father of Louisiana*. Lafayette: Center for Louisiana Studies, University of Southwestern Louisiana, 1998. A biographical study of the governor credited with permanently establishing the Louisiana colony.

McGinty, Garnie William. *A History of Louisiana*. 5th ed. New York: Exposition Press, 1951. Almost half of this work is devoted to the exploration and settlement of Louisiana.

See also: Mar. 15, 1603-Dec. 25, 1635: Champlain's Voyages; Spring, 1604: First European Settlement in North America; Apr. 27, 1627: Company of New France Is Chartered; May, 1642: Founding of Montreal; Aug., 1658-Aug. 24, 1660: Explorations of Radisson and Chouart des Groseilliers; Beginning 1673: French Explore the Mississippi Valley; Dec., 1678-Mar. 19, 1687: La Salle's Expeditions.

Related articles in *Great Lives from History: The Seventeenth Century, 1601-1700:* Samuel de Champlain; Pierre Le Moyne d'Iberville; Louis Jolliet; Sieur de La Salle; Louis XIV; Jacques Marquette; Pierre Esprit Radisson.

November 30, 1700
Battle of Narva

The Battle of Narva marked the decisive victory of Sweden over Peter the Great and the Russian army.

Locale: Narva, a fortress in Swedish Estonia on the Gulf of Finland

Categories: Wars, uprisings, and civil unrest; expansion and land acquisition; government and politics

Key Figures

Augustus II (1670-1733), elector of Saxony as Frederick Augustus, r. 1694-1733, and king of Poland, r. 1697-1704, 1710-1733

Charles XII (1682-1718), king of Sweden, r. 1697-1718, and leader of the Swedes during most of the Great Northern War

Frederick IV (1671-1730), king of Denmark, r. 1699-1730

Peter the Great (1672-1725), czar of Russia, r. 1682-1725

Summary of Event

The Battle of Narva constituted one of the first major episodes in the Great Northern War, which began earlier in 1700 as the result of military operations by Denmark, Poland, and Russia against King Charles XII of Sweden. Each of the allied powers had good reason to make war on Charles because of his continued expansion in northern Europe. Sweden had wrested extensive territories from Poland and Russia in the eastern Baltic during the seventeenth century, and in the west had seized the southern part of the Scandinavian peninsula from Denmark. Moreover, Sweden gained the valuable district of western Pomerania by the terms of the Peace of Westphalia at the end of the Thirty Years' War (1618-1648). By the mid-seventeenth century, Sweden was the strongest power in northern Europe; the Baltic Sea in effect became a Swedish lake.

Sweden's neighbors, however, were unwilling to accept their defeats as final, and competition for power and territory continued in the region surrounding the Baltic during the latter seventeenth century. When Charles XII became the king of Sweden in 1697, he was only fifteen years old; it seemed an opportune time for Denmark, Poland, and Russia to recover some if not all of their losses. Accordingly, in the fall of 1699, Frederick IV, king of Denmark; Augustus II (Frederick Augustus), elector of Saxony and king of Poland; and Peter the Great, czar of Russia, created a secret military alliance against Sweden. When the Great Northern War broke out in early 1700, Frederick, anxious to eliminate Swedish influence in Holstein-Gottorp, concentrated his forces against the German provinces of Sweden.

Simultaneously, Polish-Saxon forces attacked Swedish positions in Livonia in the eastern Baltic. Easy victories were anticipated on both fronts, but the unexpected landing of Charles XII in northern Denmark with eleven thousand men resulted in Frederick IV's capitulation by August 8, 1700, in the Peace of Travendal. Meanwhile, Russia finally entered the Great Northern War on August 9 because of protracted peace negotiations with the Turks arising out of the War of Azov. In effect, Russia took the place of defeated Denmark. Peter the Great and Augustus, impressed by the Danish defeat, offered to negotiate with Charles, but the confident boy king haughtily rejected their overtures. Hence, for the next three months the Russians had no choice but to assist their Polish-Saxon allies in attempting to conquer Swedish territories along the coastline of the Gulf of Finland.

Most of Russia's efforts during the fall of 1700 were directed against the Swedish fortress of Narva, located in Estonia on the Gulf of Finland. For two months, beginning in September, approximately 35,000 Russian troops invested the fortress in an unsuccessful siege. Shortages of artillery ammunition and lack of a coherent plan of action, however, hindered Russian success. When Charles finally landed in the area in October with the original intention of lifting the Polish siege of Riga to the south, he found that the enemy there had withdrawn. As a result, he decided instead to deal with the potentially more serious Russian threat at Narva.

After making necessary preparations, Charles set out on November 13 with an army of 8,000 veteran soldiers to attack the raw Russian recruits encamped before Narva. Reaching the area on November 19, he launched his assault on November 20 in the middle of a snowstorm. The Swedes broke through the Russians' center line, while their cavalry fled in panic. Several Russian units fought doggedly to hold their positions, but they could not stem the onslaught of Charles's veterans. By the end of the battle, the Swedes had won a complete victory, capturing all the Russian artillery and ending the siege. Swedish losses are estimated at no more than 2,000 casualties, compared with approximately 8,000 killed and wounded on the Russian side. Thousands of

Russian soldiers surrendered to Charles's forces, although precise figures vary widely. Ten generals were among the Russian captives.

Peter the Great had left Narva on the eve of the battle, and interpretations disagree whether he was absent primarily because of fear in the face of imminent battle or because of a search for reinforcements and ammunition. In any case, the problems arising from his absence were compounded by other factors. The duke de Croy, appointed to command the Russian army after Peter's departure, surrendered to the Swedes during the battle with some of his key officers. A combination of poor leadership, inadequately trained conscript troops, and a determined enemy proved fatal to the Russians, who suffered one of the most infamous defeats in their history. All this occurred at the hands of the eighteen-year-old Swedish monarch, whose reputation quickly increased as a result.

SIGNIFICANCE

The Swedish victories over Denmark and over the Russians at Narva led to a far longer and bloodier war than was envisioned by those states that attacked Sweden in 1700. Charles curiously did not press his advantage against Russia in 1700, when he had the opportunity, but turned his attention toward other opponents to the west. In the aftermath of his Narva victory, for example, Charles succeeded in ousting Augustus as king of Poland before again turning his attention to Russia in 1707. Meanwhile, Peter the Great used this welcome respite to develop a modern army in size, weaponry, and training. In 1703, he also established his new capital city of Saint Petersburg on Swedish territory, which he had recently captured.

Several years later, in 1709, Russian forces under Peter decisively defeated Charles at the Battle of Poltava to the south. Charles now was unable to stem the slow but steady Russian advance against his eastern Baltic strongholds. Peter's conquests of these areas, including Livonia, Estonia, Ingria, and part of Karelia, were confirmed in the Treaty of Nystadt of August 30, 1721. This agreement with Sweden brought the Great Northern War to an end. Charles's death in battle in 1718 further weakened the Swedish cause, and Russia consequently emerged for the first time as both a Baltic and European power.

—*Edward P. Keleher and Taylor Stults*

FURTHER READING

Anderson, M. S. *Peter the Great*. New York: Longman, 1995. A broad interpretation of Peter's significant impact on Russia.

De Jong, Alex. *Fire and Water: A Life of Peter the Great*. New York: Coward, McCann & Geoghegan, 1980. A clear account of the Narva campaign in the context of Russo-Swedish competition.

Duffy, Christopher. *Russia's Military Way to the West: Origins and Nature of Russian Military Power, 1700-1800*. London: Routledge & Kegan Paul, 1981. Duffy interprets the impact of Peter's military reforms and wars.

Englund, Peter. *The Battle That Shook Europe: Poltava and the Birth of the Russian Empire*. New York: I. B. Tauris, 2003. Englund recounts the decisive battle in 1709 that changed the course of the Great Northern War. Compares Poltava to the earlier Battle at Narva.

Frost, Robert I. *The Northern Wars: War, State, and Society in Northeastern Europe, 1558-1721*. New York: Longman, 2000. Frost examines the Great Northern War's impact on the social and political systems of Sweden, Russia, Denmark, and Poland-Lithuania. Discusses how and why Russia emerged victorious.

Fuller, William C., Jr. *Strategy and Power in Russia, 1600-1914*. New York: Free Press, 1992. Fuller traces the growth of military and economic systems developed to support Russia's foreign policy objectives.

Grey, Ian. *Peter the Great: Emperor of All Russia*. New York: J. B. Lippincott, 1960. Solid coverage of the Great Northern War, including the Battle of Narva.

Kirby, David. *Northern Europe in the Early Modern Period: The Baltic World, 1492-1772*. London: Longman, 1990. Kirby examines Sweden's role as a major political power, and the country's eventual decline. Also discusses the evolving political and social systems of the Baltic states.

Massie, Robert K. *Peter the Great*. New York: Alfred A. Knopf, 1980. A detailed biography, including extensive coverage of the Narva campaign and Great Northern War.

SEE ALSO: July, 1643-Oct. 24, 1648: Peace of Westphalia; July 10, 1655-June 21, 1661: First Northern War; Mar. 9, 1697-Aug. 25, 1698: Peter the Great Tours Western Europe; Jan. 26, 1699: Treaty of Karlowitz.

RELATED ARTICLES in *Great Lives from History: The Seventeenth Century, 1601-1700:* Alexis; Charles X Gustav; Christina; Frederick William, the Great Elector; Gustavus II Adolphus; John III Sobieski; Leopold I.

Great Events from History

Appendices

TIME LINE

The time line below includes the events and developments covered in the essays in this publication (appearing in SMALL CAPITAL *letters) as well as more than 250 other important events and developments. Each event is tagged by general region or regions, rather than by smaller nations or principalities, which changed significantly over the century covered in this publication; by this means, the time line can be used to consider general trends in the same region over time. However, because many events, although occurring in one or two regions, nevertheless had a global or cross-regional impact, they have been left in strict chronological order to facilitate a better understanding of simultaneous events and their occasional interaction. The abbreviation "c." is used below to stand for both "circa" (when it precedes the date) and "century" or "centuries" (when it follows the date).*

DATE	REGION	EVENT
Early 17th c.	Europe	REVENGE TRAGEDIES BECOME POPULAR IN ENGLAND
Early 17th c.	Africa	RISE OF RWANDA
17th c.	World	ADVANCES IN MEDICINE
17th c.	Southeast Asia	AGE OF MERCANTILISM IN SOUTHEAST ASIA
17th c.	Europe	BIRTH CONTROL IN WESTERN EUROPE
17th c.	Africa	EMERGENCE OF LUBA GOVERNANCE
17th c.	Europe	ENGLAND'S AGRICULTURAL REVOLUTION
17th c.	Europe	EUROPE ENDORSES SLAVERY
17th c.	Southeast Asia	THE PEPPER TRADE
17th c.	Europe	RISE OF PROTO-INDUSTRIAL ECONOMIES
17th c.	World	RISE OF THE GUNPOWDER EMPIRES
17th c.	Africa	SONGHAI EMPIRE DISSOLVES
1601	Europe	Caracci finishes the Galleria ceiling of the Palazzo Farnese
1601	Europe	ELIZABETHAN POOR LAW
c. 1601	Europe	EMERGENCE OF BAROQUE MUSIC
c. 1601	Africa	EMERGENCE OF THE MERINA KINGDOM
Beginning c. 1601	Africa	EXPANSION OF THE OYO KINGDOM
1601	Europe	Foundation of the Academy of the Lynxes
c. 1601-1606	Europe	APPEARANCE OF THE FALSE DMITRY
c. 1601-1613	Europe	SHAKESPEARE PRODUCES HIS LATER PLAYS
c. 1601-1620	Europe	EMERGENCE OF BAROQUE ART
1601-1672	Europe	RISE OF SCIENTIFIC SOCIETIES
c. 1601-1682	Europe	SPANISH GOLDEN AGE
Feb. 7-19, 1601	Europe	ESSEX REBELLION
July 5, 1601-Apr., 1604	Europe	SIEGE OF OOSTENDE
Dec., 1601	Southeast Asia	DUTCH DEFEAT THE PORTUGUESE IN BANTAM HARBOR
1602	Europe	Caccini publishes *The New Music*
1602	Europe	Caravaggio paints *The Taking of Christ*
1602	Europe	Ulster submits to England
1602-1613	East Asia	JAPAN ADMITS WESTERN TRADERS
1602-1639	Middle East	OTTOMAN-ṢAFAVID WARS
Mar. 20, 1602	South Asia	DUTCH EAST INDIA COMPANY IS FOUNDED
Nov., 1602	Europe	FIRST MODERN LIBRARIES IN EUROPE
1603	Africa	Death of the last Saʿdian sultan
1603	East Asia	TOKUGAWA SHOGUNATE BEGINS
1603-1617	Middle East	REIGN OF SULTAN AHMED I
1603-1629	East Asia	OKUNI STAGES THE FIRST KABUKI DANCE DRAMAS
Mar. 15, 1603-Dec. 25, 1635	North America	CHAMPLAIN'S VOYAGES
Mar. 24, 1603	Europe	JAMES I BECOMES KING OF ENGLAND

DATE	REGION	EVENT
1604	Europe	First Enclosure Act passed by English parliament
1604	Europe	King James I publishes *A Counterblaste to Tobacco*
1604	Europe	Treaty of London
1604-1680	North America	RISE OF CRIOLLO IDENTITY IN MEXICO
Spring, 1604	North America	FIRST EUROPEAN SETTLEMENT IN NORTH AMERICA
1605	North America	French found Acadia
1605	East Asia	Tokugawa Ieyasu passes the title of shogun to his son
c. 1605-1606	Europe	First production of Shakespeare's *King Lear*
1605 and 1615	Europe	CERVANTES PUBLISHES *DON QUIXOTE DE LA MANCHA*
1605-1627	South Asia	MUGHAL COURT CULTURE FLOURISHES
Beginning Spring, 1605	Southeast Asia	DUTCH DOMINATE SOUTHEAST ASIAN TRADE
Sept., 1605	Africa	EGYPTIANS REBEL AGAINST THE OTTOMANS
Nov. 5, 1605	Europe	GUNPOWDER PLOT
1606	Southeast Asia	Dutch and Portuguese first battle for control of Malacca
1606-1674	South Asia	EUROPEANS SETTLE IN INDIA
Apr. 29, 1606	Australia	FIRST EUROPEAN CONTACT WITH AUSTRALIA
Sept., 1606-June, 1609	Middle East	GREAT JELĀLĪ REVOLTS
Nov. 11, 1606	Europe	TREATY OF ZSITVATOROK
Beginning 1607	East Asia	NEO-CONFUCIANISM BECOMES JAPAN'S OFFICIAL PHILOSOPHY
1607	Europe	Scrooby Congregation emigrates to the Netherlands
1607	Europe	Ulster's nobility flees to the Continent
Feb. 24, 1607	Europe	FIRST PERFORMANCE OF MONTEVERDI'S *LA FAVOLA D'ORFEO*
May 14, 1607	North America	JAMESTOWN IS FOUNDED
Nov. 28, 1607	North America	MARTIN BEGINS DRAINING LAKE TEXCOCO
1608	Europe	Establishment of the Evangelical Union
1608	Latin America	JESUITS FOUND PARAGUAY
1608	North America	Quebec is founded
Sept., 1608	Europe	INVENTION OF THE TELESCOPE
1609	Europe	BANK OF AMSTERDAM INVENTS CHECKS
1609	East Asia/Europe	CHINA BEGINS SHIPPING TEA TO EUROPE
1609	East Asia	Dutch traders establish factory on Hirado Island, Japan
1609	Europe	Establishment of the Catholic League
1609	Europe	Kepler publishes his *New Astronomy*
1609	Europe	Spain expels the Moriscos
1609-1617	Middle East	CONSTRUCTION OF THE BLUE MOSQUE
1609-1619	Europe	KEPLER'S LAWS OF PLANETARY MOTION
1610	North America	Franciscans found a mission in Santa Fe
1610	Europe	GALILEO CONFIRMS THE HELIOCENTRIC MODEL OF THE SOLAR SYSTEM
1610-1614	Europe	Rubens paints his triptychs of Christ on the Cross
1610-1617	Europe	Regency of French queen Marie de Médicis
1610-1643	Europe	REIGN OF LOUIS XIII
Beginning June, 1610	North America	HUDSON EXPLORES HUDSON BAY
1611	South Asia	British East India Company establishes a factory at Masulipatam
1611	Europe	PUBLICATION OF THE KING JAMES BIBLE
1611-1630's	North America	JESUITS BEGIN MISSIONARY ACTIVITIES IN NEW FRANCE
1612	North America	INTRODUCTION OF TOBACCO FARMING IN NORTH AMERICA
1612	Africa	RISE OF THE ARMA IN TIMBUKTU
1612	Europe	SANCTORIUS INVENTS THE CLINICAL THERMOMETER
Aug., 1612	Europe	Expulsion of Polish forces from Moscow
Feb. 7, 1613	Europe	ELECTION OF MICHAEL ROMANOV AS CZAR
June 29, 1613	Europe	BURNING OF THE GLOBE THEATRE

Date	Region	Event
July-Nov., 1613	North America	Captain Samuel Argall, admiral of Virginia, destroys French settlements at Port Royal, Saint Croix, and Saint Sauveur
1614-1615	East Asia	Siege of Ōsaka Castle
Jan. 27, 1614	East Asia	Japanese Ban Christian Missionaries
July-Nov., 1613	North America	Captain Samuel Argall, admiral of Virginia, destroys French settlements at Port Royal, Saint Croix, and Saint Sauveur
Beginning c. 1615	Europe	Coffee Culture Flourishes
1615	Europe	The Inquisition condemns the Copernican model of the solar system
1615	Latin America	Guamán Poma Pleas for Inca Reforms
1615	Europe	Polish landowners invade Ottoman Moldavia
1615	East Asia	Promulgation of the *Buke shohatto* and *Kinchū narabini kuge shohatto*
1615-1696	Europe	Invention and Development of the Calculus
1616	South Asia	Danish East India Company is founded
1616	East Asia	Nurhaci founds the Hou Jin Dynasty
1616-1643	East Asia	Rise of the Manchus
1617	Africa	Dutch purchase Gorée Island
1617	East Asia	Edo's Floating World District
1617-1619	Southeast Asia	Sultan of Banten besieges Dutch headquarters at Jacatra (Jakarta)
1617-1628	Europe	Harvey Discovers the Circulation of the Blood
1617-1693	Africa	European Powers Vie for Control of Gorée
1617-c. 1700	North America	Smallpox Epidemics Kill Native Americans
Mar., 1617	Europe	Spain and the Habsburgs agree to cooperate in Catholic military ventures
1618-1648	Europe	Thirty Years' War
May 23, 1618	Europe	Defenestration of Prague
Beginning c. 1619	North America	Indentured Servitude Becomes Institutionalized in America
1619-1622	Europe	Jones Introduces Classicism to English Architecture
1619-1633	Europe	Filaret, patriarch of the Russian Orthodox Church, rules Russia alongside Michael
1619-1636	Central Asia	Construction of Samarqand's Shirdar Madrasa
1619-c. 1700	Americas/Africa	The Middle Passage to American Slavery
May, 1619	Southeast Asia	Jacatra is destroyed and renamed Batavia
July 30-Aug. 4, 1619	North America	First General Assembly of Virginia
Aug. 20, 1619	North America	Africans Arrive in Virginia
1620	Europe	Bacon Publishes *Novum Organum*
1620	Middle East	Construction of the Lab-i Haws
July, 1620-Sept., 1639	Europe	Struggle for the Valtelline Pass
July 3, 1620	Europe	Treaty of Ulm
Nov. 8, 1620	Europe	Battle of White Mountain
Dec. 26, 1620	North America	Pilgrims Arrive in North America
1621	Southeast Asia	Dutch invade Banda Islands
1621	Caribbean	Dutch West India Company is founded
1621	Europe	Siege of Khotin
Mar. 31, 1621-Sept. 17, 1665	Europe	Reign of Philip IV
Apr., 1621	Europe	Treaty of Madrid
Dec. 18, 1621	Europe	The Great Protestation
1622	East Asia	The Great Martyrdom: Fifty-five Japanese Christians are executed
Jan., 1622	Middle East	Ṣafavids take Hormuz from the Portuguese
Mar. 22, 1622-Oct., 1646	North America	Powhatan Wars
Apr. 25, 1622	Europe	Battle of Wiesloch

DATE	REGION	EVENT
May 19, 1622	Middle East	JANISSARY REVOLT AND OSMAN II'S ASSASSINATION
1623	Southeast Asia	Dutch massacre English traders at Amboina
1623	Europe	Publication of Shakespeare's First Folio
1623-1624	Middle East	ʿAbbās the Great invades Iraq
1623-1640	Middle East	MURAD IV RULES THE OTTOMAN EMPIRE
1623-1674	Europe	EARLIEST CALCULATORS APPEAR
1624	Europe	Donne publishes *Devotions upon Emergent Occasions*
1624	Latin America	Dutch launch naval strikes against Salvador
1624	Europe	English parliament abolishes monopolies
1624	Middle East	Oman expels Portuguese and establishes Al-Yaʿruba Dynasty
1624	North America	Virginia becomes a royal colony
1624-1627	East Asia	Imperial eunich Wei Zhongxian acts as de facto dictator of China
1624-1640's	East Asia	JAPAN'S SECLUSION POLICY
1625	Africa/Americas	Dutch enter the transatlantic slave trade
c. 1625	Africa	FORMATION OF THE KUBA KINGDOM
1625	Europe	GROTIUS ESTABLISHES THE CONCEPT OF INTERNATIONAL LAW
c. 1625	Europe	Strozzi paints *The Cook*
1625-Oct. 28, 1628	Europe	REVOLT OF THE HUGUENOTS
May 14, 1625-1640	Caribbean	ENGLISH DISCOVER AND COLONIZE BARBADOS
July, 1625-Aug., 1664	North America	FOUNDING OF NEW AMSTERDAM
Oct., 1625-1637	Africa	DUTCH AND PORTUGUESE STRUGGLE FOR THE GUINEA COAST
1626	Europe	Treaty of Monzon
1626-1673	Southeast Asia	CIVIL WAR RAVAGES VIETNAM
Apr. 10-21, 1626	Europe	Battle of Dessau Bridge
May 6, 1626	North America	ALGONQUIANS "SELL" MANHATTAN ISLAND
Aug. 26, 1626	Europe	Battle of Lutter
1627	Europe	Cardinal de Richelieu reforms French colonial policy
Apr. 27, 1627	North America	COMPANY OF NEW FRANCE IS CHARTERED
Aug. 10, 1627-Oct. 28, 1628	Europe	Siege of La Rochelle
1628-1631	Europe	War of Mantuan Succession
May-July, 1628	Europe	Siege of Strasund
May 6-June 7, 1628	Europe	PETITION OF RIGHT
1629	Europe	Grace of Alais
1629	East Asia	Japan bans women from the stage
1629	Middle East	ṢAFAVID DYNASTY FLOURISHES UNDER ʿABBĀS THE GREAT
Mar., 1629-1640	Europe	"PERSONAL RULE" OF CHARLES I
Mar. 6, 1629	Europe	EDICT OF RESTITUTION
May 22, 1629	Europe	Peace of Lübeck
1630's-1694	Latin America	SLAVES RESIST EUROPEANS AT PALMARES
1630	Europe	Stelluti publishes the first drawings of insects as seen through a microscope
1630	Europe	Treaty of Cherasco
1630-1648	Europe	DESTRUCTION OF BAVARIA
1630-1654	Latin America	Dutch establish New Holland in northeastern Brazil
1630-1660's	Latin America	DUTCH WARS IN BRAZIL
May, 1630-1643	Europe/North America	GREAT PURITAN MIGRATION
July-Nov., 1630	Europe	Electoral assembly at Regensburg
July 6, 1630	Europe	Swedish army arrives in Pomerania
Nov. 10, 1630	Europe	THE DAY OF DUPES
1631	East Asia	Siege of Dalinghe
1631-1645	East Asia	LI ZICHENG'S REVOLT
Feb. 24, 1631	Europe	WOMEN FIRST APPEAR ON THE ENGLISH STAGE
May 20, 1631	Europe	Fall of Magdeburg

DATE	REGION	EVENT
Sept. 17, 1631	Europe	First Battle of Breitenfeld
1632	Central Asia	Cossacks establish Yakutsk
1632	Europe	GALILEO PUBLISHES *DIALOGUE CONCERNING THE TWO CHIEF WORLD SYSTEMS, PTOLEMAIC AND COPERNICAN*
1632	North America	Powhatan Indians negotiate a peace treaty with English settlers
1632	North America/Europe	Treaty of Saint-Germain-en-Laye reestablishes French sovereignty over Acadia, Nova Scotia, and Quebec
1632-c. 1650	South Asia	SHAH JAHAN BUILDS THE TAJ MAHAL
1632-1667	Europe	POLISH-RUSSIAN WARS FOR THE UKRAINE
Feb. 22-27, 1632	North America	ZUÑI REBELLION
Apr., 1632	Europe	Battle of Lech
Fall, 1632-Jan. 5, 1665	North America	SETTLEMENT OF CONNECTICUT
Nov. 16, 1632	Europe	Battle of Lützen
1633	Europe	Trial of Galileo
1633-1638	Europe	Van Dyck paints his portraits of Charles I
Sept. 2, 1633	Middle East	GREAT FIRE OF CONSTANTINOPLE AND MURAD'S REFORMS
1634	Africa/Americas	French enter the transatlantic slave trade
Feb. 25, 1634	Europe	Wallenstein is assassinated
June, 1634	Europe	Peace of Polianovka
Sept. 6, 1634	Europe	Battle of Nördlingen
1635	North America	Jesuits found a college in Quebec
1635	East Asia	Manchus establish a capital at Mukden
1635	Europe	Velázquez paints the *Surrender of Breda*
May, 1635-Dec., 1638	Middle East	Murad IV invades Iraq
May 30, 1635	Europe	PEACE OF PRAGUE
Oct. 9, 1635	North America	Massachusetts Bay Colony orders Roger Williams to leave its territory
1636	East Asia	Abahai renames Hou Jin Dynasty as Qing Dynasty and declares himself first Qing emperor of China
Jan., 1636	North America	Williams flees Massachusetts
June, 1636	North America	RHODE ISLAND IS FOUNDED
July 20, 1636-July 28, 1637	North America	PEQUOT WAR
Oct. 4, 1636	Europe	Battle of Wittstock
1637	Europe	DESCARTES PUBLISHES HIS *DISCOURSE ON METHOD*
1637	Europe	Archbishop Laud and Charles I attempt to impose a Book of Common Prayer on Scotland
Oct., 1637-Apr. 15, 1638	East Asia	SHIMABARA REVOLT
1638	North America	FIRST PRINTING PRESS IN NORTH AMERICA
1638	North America	New Haven is founded
1638	Middle East	WANING OF THE *DEVSHIRME* SYSTEM
1638-1639	Central Asia	URGA BECOMES THE SEAT OF THE LIVING BUDDHA
1638-1669	Europe	SPREAD OF JANSENISM
Mar. 2, 1638	Europe	Battle of Rheinfelden
1639	Caribbean	Barbados holds its first Parliament
1639	North America	Framing of the Fundamental Orders of Connecticut
1639-1640	South Asia	BRITISH EAST INDIA COMPANY ESTABLISHES FORT SAINT GEORGE
Mar.-June, 1639	Europe	FIRST BISHOPS' WAR
Spring, 1639	North America	Pocasset (Portsmouth) is founded
April 22, 1639	Europe	Pope Urban VIII issues a bull outlawing slavery in the New World
May, 1639	Middle East	Treaty of Kasr-I Shirin
June 19, 1639	Europe	Pacification of Berwick
Sept., 1639	Europe	Capitulation of Milan

DATE	REGION	EVENT
Dec., 1639	East Asia	RUSSIANS REACH THE PACIFIC OCEAN
1640	Africa	FOUNDATION OF THE DARFUR SULTANATE
1640	East Asia	Portugal sends a diplomatic mission to reopen relations with Japan; most of the crew is executed
1640-1641	Europe	Diet of Regensburg
1640-1641	Europe	Publication of Jansen's *Augustinus*
1640-1688	Europe	REIGN OF FREDERICK WILLIAM, THE GREAT ELECTOR
Apr. 13-May 5, 1640	Europe	England's Short Parliament
May, 1640-Jan. 23, 1641	Europe	REVOLT OF THE CATALANS
June, 1640	Europe	Pope Urban VIII issues a bull condemning the enslavement of Native American peoples
June-Aug., 1640	Latin America	*BANDEIRANTES* EXPEL THE JESUITS
Nov. 3, 1640-May 15, 1641	Europe	BEGINNING OF ENGLAND'S LONG PARLIAMENT
Dec., 1640	Europe	Portugal asserts its independence from Spain
1641	Europe	Descartes publishes *Meditations on First Philosophy*
1641	East Asia	Dutch trade in Japan is confined to Dejima Island, Nagasaki Harbor
1641-1645	North America	Kieft's War
Jan. 14, 1641	Southeast Asia	CAPTURE OF MALACCA
Feb. 8, 1641	Europe	Parliamentary debate begins on England's Root and Branch Petition
Feb. 16, 1641	Europe	England's Triennial Act
Aug. 26, 1641-Sept., 1648	Africa	CONQUEST OF LUANDA
Oct. 23, 1641-1642	Europe	ULSTER INSURRECTION
Nov., 1641	North America	MASSACHUSETTS RECOGNIZES SLAVERY
1642	South Asia	French East India Company is founded
1642	Central Asia	Gushri Kahn installs the Dalai Lama as religious and secular ruler of Tibet
1642	Europe	Rembrandt paints *The Night Watch*
1642 and 1644	Australia	TASMAN PROVES AUSTRALIA IS A SEPARATE CONTINENT
1642-1651	Europe	ENGLISH CIVIL WARS
1642-1666	Middle East	REIGN OF SHAH ʿABBĀS II
1642-1684	North America	BEAVER WARS
1642-1700	North America	WESTWARD MIGRATION OF NATIVE AMERICANS
May, 1642	North America	FOUNDING OF MONTREAL
Sept. 2, 1642	Europe	CLOSING OF THE THEATERS
Oct. 23, 1642	Europe	Battle of Edgehill
Nov. 2, 1642	Europe	Second Battle of Breitenfeld
Nov. 12, 1642	Europe	Battle of Turnham Green
1643	Europe	Fall of Olivares as Spain's chief minister
1643	Europe	TORRICELLI MEASURES ATMOSPHERIC PRESSURE
1643	Southeast Asia	Vietnam defeats small Dutch fleet near Da Nang
Nov. 24-25, 1643	Europe	Battle of Tuttlingen
1643-1645	Europe	Swedish-Danish War
1643-1715	Europe	Louis XIV rules France
June 30, 1643	Europe	Battle of Adwalton Moor
July, 1643-Oct. 24, 1648	Europe	PEACE OF WESTPHALIA
July 5, 1643	Europe	Battle of Lansdown Hill
July 13, 1643	Europe	Battle of Roundway Down
Aug. 17-Sept. 25, 1643	Europe	SOLEMN LEAGUE AND COVENANT
Sept. 8, 1643	North America	CONFEDERATION OF THE UNITED COLONIES OF NEW ENGLAND
Sept. 20, 1643	Europe	First Battle of Newbury
Oct. 11, 1643	Europe	Battle of Winceby

Date	Region	Event
Dec. 12, 1643	Europe	Battle of Alton
1644	Europe	The Globe Theatre is demolished
1644-1654	Europe	Reign of Queen Christina of Sweden
1644-1671	Africa	Ndongo Wars
Apr. 18, 1644	North America	Powhatan Indians massacre five hundred English settlers
Apr. 25, 1644	East Asia	End of the Ming Dynasty
June 6, 1644	East Asia	Manchus Take Beijing
July 2, 1644	Europe	Battle of Marston Moor
Aug. 31-Sept. 2, 1644	Europe	Battle of Lostwithiel
Sept., 1644	North America	Providence, Portsmouth, and Newport are united by royal patent
Oct. 27, 1644	Europe	Second Battle of Newbury
c. 1645-1652	Europe	Bernini sculpts the *Ecstasy of Saint Theresa*
1645-1683	East Asia	Zheng Pirates Raid the Chinese Coast
Spring, 1645-1660	Europe	Puritan New Model Army
Apr., 1645	Europe	English parliament passes the Self-Denying Ordinance, purging all of its members except Cromwell from the army
June 14, 1645	Europe	Battle of Naseby
July 10, 1645	Europe	Battle of Langport
Aug. 22, 1645-Sept., 1669	Europe	Turks Conquer Crete
1646-1649	Europe	Levellers Launch an Egalitarian Movement
1647	East Asia	Russians found Pacific port of Okhotsk
Mar. 14, 1647	Europe	Truce of Ulm
1648	Middle East	ʿAbbās II drives the Mughals out of Iran
1648	North America	Cult of the Virgin of Guadalupe
1648	East Asia/North America	Dezhnyov and Alekseyev navigate the Bering Strait
1648	Europe	Spain recognizes Dutch independence; end of the Eighty Years' War
1648-1654	Europe	Dnieper Cossacks rebel against Poland
Spr., 1648-1649	Middle East	Venetian fleet blockades Constantinople
May 17, 1648	Europe	Battle of Zusmarshausen
June, 1648	Europe	Wars of the Fronde Begin
Aug. 18, 1648	Latin America	Portuguese Brazil takes Dutch Brazilian stronghold at São Paulo
Aug. 20, 1648	Europe	Battle of Lens
Dec. 6, 1648	Europe	Pride's Purge
Dec. 6, 1648-May 19, 1649	Europe	Establishment of the English Commonwealth
1649	North America	Cambridge Platform unifies church and state in the Massachusetts Bay Colony
1649	Europe	Treaty of Reuil
Jan. 29, 1649	Europe	Codification of Russian Serfdom
Jan. 30, 1649	Europe	Charles I is beheaded
Apr. 21, 1649	North America	Maryland Act of Toleration
Aug., 1649	Europe	Lilburne is tried and acquitted of treason
Mid-17th c.	Europe	Dutch School of Painting Flourishes
Mid-17th c.	Africa	Emergence of the Guinea Coast States
1650	North America	Connecticut recognizes slavery
1650	Europe	Guericke invents the air pump
1650	Middle East	Oman takes Muscat
1650-1698	Middle East/Africa	Wars for the Red Sea Trade
Mar. 31, 1650	Latin America	Earthquake Destroys Cuzco
May 30-31, 1650	North America	First College in North America
Sept. 3, 1650	Europe	Battle of Dunbar
1651	Europe	Hobbes Publishes *Leviathan*
1651	Europe	Scotland recognizes King Charles II in exile

DATE	REGION	EVENT
1651-1652	East Asia	EDO REBELLIONS
1651-1680	East Asia	IETSUNA SHOGUNATE
Sept. 3, 1651	Europe	Battle of Worcester
Oct., 1651-May, 1652	Europe	NAVIGATION ACT LEADS TO ANGLO-DUTCH WARS
1652	East Asia	Japan bans young boys from the stage
1652-1667	Europe	PATRIARCH NIKON'S REFORMS
1652-1689	Europe	FOX ORGANIZES THE QUAKERS
Apr., 1652	Africa	DUTCH BEGIN TO COLONIZE SOUTHERN AFRICA
May, 1652	Europe	George Fox has a revelation on Pendle Hill
Oct. 13, 1652	Europe	Barcelona surrenders to Spain
Dec. 16, 1653-Sept. 3, 1658	Europe	CROMWELL RULES ENGLAND AS LORD PROTECTOR
1654	Europe	Abdication of Sweden's Queen Christina
1654	Europe	PASCAL AND FERMAT DEVISE THE THEORY OF PROBABILITY
1654	Latin America	PORTUGAL RETAKES CONTROL OF BRAZIL
1654-1667	Europe	Thirteen Years' War
Summer, 1654-1656	North America	FIRST JEWISH SETTLERS IN NORTH AMERICA
1655	North America	Pequot nation is relocated onto two reservations on Mystic River
1655-1663	Europe	GRIMALDI DISCOVERS DIFFRACTION
1655-1664	North America	Peach Wars
Mar. 12-14, 1655	Europe	PENRUDDOCK'S UPRISING
May 10, 1655	Caribbean	ENGLISH CAPTURE OF JAMAICA
July 10, 1655-June 21, 1661	Europe	FIRST NORTHERN WAR
1656	Europe	POPULARIZAITON OF CHOCOLATE
1656	Europe	Velázquez paints *Las Meninas*
1656-1657	Europe	Publication of Pascal's *The Provincial Letters*
1656-1662	Middle East	PERSECUTION OF IRANIAN JEWS
1656-1667	Europe	CONSTRUCTION OF THE PIAZZA SAN PIETRO
1656-1676	Middle East	OTTOMAN EMPIRE'S BRIEF RECOVERY
Feb., 1656	Europe	HUYGENS IDENTIFIES SATURN'S RINGS
June, 1656	Middle East	Venetian fleet destroys the Ottoman fleet at the Dardanelles
1657	East Asia	WORK BEGINS ON JAPAN'S NATIONAL HISTORY
1657-1667	Europe	Italian Academy of Experiments meets
Jan. 18-20, 1657	East Asia	MEIREKI FIRE RAVAGES EDO
Sept., 1657	Europe	Treaty of Wehlau
1658	South Asia	Dutch drive Portuguese out of Ceylon
Beginning 1658	Europe	FIRST NEWSPAPER ADS APPEAR
1658-1659	East Asia	Zheng Chenggong invades central China
1658-1707	South Asia	REIGN OF AURANGZEB
June 19, 1658	Europe	Battle of Konotop
Aug., 1658-Aug. 24, 1660	North America	EXPLORATIONS OF RADISSON AND CHOUART DES GROSEILLIERS
Sept. 16, 1658	Europe	Treaty of Hadiach
1659	Africa	EXPANSION OF THE ALAWIS
May, 1659-May, 1660	Europe	RESTORATION OF CHARLES II
Nov. 7, 1659	Europe	TREATY OF THE PYRENEES
1660's-1700	Europe	FIRST MICROSCOPIC OBSERVATIONS
1660	Europe	English theaters reopen
1660	Europe	Marcello Malpighi discovers capillaries
1660-1665	Africa	Oman occupies Mombasa
1660-1677	Africa	A JIHAD IS CALLED IN SENEGAMBIA
1660-1692	Europe	BOYLE'S LAW AND THE BIRTH OF MODERN CHEMISTRY
Sept. 13, 1660-July 27, 1663	Europe/North America	BRITISH NAVIGATION ACTS
1661	Europe	ABSOLUTE MONARCHY EMERGES IN FRANCE
1661	East Asia	Zheng Chenggong seizes control of Taiwan from the Dutch

DATE	REGION	EVENT
1661-1665	Europe	CLARENDON CODE
1661-1672	Europe	COLBERT DEVELOPS MERCANTILISM
Feb. 17, 1661-Dec. 20, 1722	East Asia	HEIGHT OF QING DYNASTY
Mar., 1661-1705	North America	VIRGINIA SLAVE CODES
June 23, 1661	South Asia	PORTUGAL CEDES BOMBAY TO THE ENGLISH
1662	Europe	English Quaker Act
1662	North America	HALF-WAY COVENANT
1662-May 3, 1695	Europe	ENGLAND'S LICENSING ACTS
Mar. 18, 1662	Europe	PUBLIC TRANSPORTATION BEGINS
May 3, 1662	North America	Connecticut secures a royal charter
May 19, 1662	Europe	ENGLAND'S ACT OF UNIFORMITY
July 15, 1662	Europe	Royal Society of London is chartered
1663	North America	Maryland recognizes slavery
1663	North America	New France becomes a royal colony
1663	Europe	Ruisdael paints *The Jewish Cemetary*
1663	East Asia	Tokugawa Ietsuna outlaws *Junshi*, or ritual suicide by samurai upon the death of their lord
Mar. 24, 1663-July 25, 1729	North America	SETTLEMENT OF THE CAROLINAS
July 18, 1663	North America	Rhode Island receives a royal charter codifying its policy of freedom of conscience
1664 and 1670	Europe	English Conventicle Acts
1664	Caribbean	French West India Company is established
1664	Europe	Hals paints *Regentesses of the Old Men's Almshouse*
1664	Europe	MOLIÈRE WRITES *TARTUFFE*
1664	North America	New York and New Jersey recognize slavery
1664	Europe	WILLIS IDENTIFIES THE BASAL GANGLIA
Mar. 22, 1664-July 21, 1667	North America	BRITISH CONQUEST OF NEW NETHERLAND
July 13, 1664	Europe	TRAPPIST ORDER IS FOUNDED
Aug., 1664	Europe	Battle of Szentgotthárd
Aug. 10, 1664	Europe	Treaty of Vasvár
1665	Europe	CASSINI DISCOVERS JUPITER'S GREAT RED SPOT
1665-1681	Europe	CONSTRUCTION OF THE LANGUEDOC CANAL
Jan., 1665	Middle East	SHABBETAI TZEVI'S MESSIANIC MOVEMENT BEGINS
Jan. 5, 1665	North America	Connecticut annexes New Haven
Mar. 4, 1665-July 31, 1667	Europe	SECOND ANGLO-DUTCH WAR
Spring, 1665-Fall, 1666	Europe	GREAT PLAGUE IN LONDON
Oct. 29, 1665	Africa	BATTLE OF MBWILA
c. 1666	Europe	STRADIVARI MAKES HIS FIRST VIOLIN
1666-1667	Europe	Vermeer paints *Allegory of Painting*
c. 1666-1676	South Asia	FOUNDING OF THE MARĀTHĀ KINGDOM
Sept. 2-5, 1666	Europe	GREAT FIRE OF LONDON
December 22, 1666	Europe	Paris Academy of Sciences is established
1667	North America	CONSECRATION OF THE FIRST CATHEDRAL IN MEXICO
1667	Europe	Foundation of France's Royal Observatory
1667	Europe	MILTON PUBLISHES *PARADISE LOST*
1667	Europe	PUFENDORF ADVOCATES A UNIFIED GERMANY
1667	North America	Virginia Assembly declares that religious conversion is not grounds for slaves to be freed
Jan., 1667	Europe	Treaty of Andrusovo
Apr., 1667-June, 1671	Europe	RAZIN LEADS PEASANT UPRISING IN RUSSIA
May 24, 1667-May 2, 1668	Europe	WAR OF DEVOLUTION
Dec. 19, 1667	Europe	IMPEACHMENT OF CLARENDON
1668	Europe	Redi demonstrates the source of maggots in rotting flesh

DATE	REGION	EVENT
1668	Europe	Vermeer paints *The Astronomer*
Jan. 23, 1668	Europe	TRIPLE ALLIANCE FORMS
Feb. 13, 1668	Europe	SPAIN RECOGNIZES PORTUGAL'S INDEPENDENCE
Oct. 8, 1668	Europe	Peace of the Church
1669	East Asia	Japanese Ainu stage a rebellion
1669	Europe	STENO PRESENTS HIS THEORIES OF FOSSILS AND DYNAMIC GEOLOGY
Feb., 1669-Jan., 1677	Europe	JOHN OF AUSTRIA'S REVOLTS
1670	Europe	Bushnell's Case
c. 1670	East Asia/Middle East	FIRST WIDESPREAD SMALLPOX INOCULATIONS
1670	Europe	POPULARIZATION OF THE GRAND TOUR
1670	East Asia	PROMULGATION OF THE SACRED EDICT
1670-1699	Africa	RISE OF THE ASANTE EMPIRE
Apr., 1670	North America	CHARLES TOWN IS FOUNDED
May 2, 1670	North America	HUDSON'S BAY COMPANY IS CHARTERED
June 1, 1670	Europe	France and England sign the Treaty of Dover in secret
Summer, 1670	Europe	Razin takes Saratov and Samara
July 8, 1670	Caribbean	Treaty of Madrid
Beginning 1671	North America	AMERICAN INDIAN SLAVE TRADE
Nov. 29, 1671	Africa	Portuguese sack Ndongo's capital and kill its ruler
Late Dec., 1671	Europe	NEWTON BUILDS HIS REFLECTING TELESCOPE
1672	Africa	England's Royal African Company is founded
1672	Europe	Plague breaks out in Lyon
1672-1684	Europe	LEEUWENHOEK DISCOVERS MICROSCOPIC LIFE
1672-c. 1691	Europe	SELF-IMMOLATION OF THE OLD BELIEVERS
Apr. 6, 1672-Aug. 10, 1678	Europe	THIRD ANGLO-DUTCH WAR
Summer, 1672-Fall, 1676	Europe/Middle East	OTTOMAN-POLISH WARS
Aug. 27, 1672	Europe	Ottomans take Kamieniec Podolski
Oct., 1672	Europe/Middle East	Treaty of Buczacz
c. 1673	Europe	BUXTEHUDE BEGINS HIS ABENDMUSIKEN CONCERTS
Beginning 1673	North America	FRENCH EXPLORE THE MISSISSIPPI VALLEY
1673	Europe	HUYGENS EXPLAINS THE PENDULUM
1673	Europe	Louis XIV strips *parlement* of the right to remonstrate against his edicts
1673	Africa	Nāṣir al-Dīn establishes a foothold in Senegal
1673	Europe	RENOVATION OF THE LOUVRE
1673-1678	Europe	TEST ACTS
Dec., 1673-1681	East Asia	REBELLION OF THE THREE FEUDATORIES
1674	South Asia	French East India Company establishes a base at Pondicherry
Late 17th c.	Africa	DECLINE OF BENIN
Late 17th c.	Africa	RISE OF BUGANDA
Late 17th c.	Australia	SULAWESI TRADERS MAKE CONTACT WITH AUSTRALIAN ABORIGINES
1675-1708	Europe	WREN SUPERVISES THE REBUILDING OF ST. PAUL'S CATHEDRAL
June 20, 1675	North America	METACOM'S WAR BEGINS
June 28, 1675	Europe	Battle of Fehrbellin
1676	Europe	SYDENHAM ADVOCATES CLINICAL OBSERVATION
May 10-Oct. 18, 1676	North America	BACON'S REBELLION
Dec. 7, 1676	Europe	RØMER CALCULATES THE SPEED OF LIGHT
1677	Africa	Akwamu captures Greater Accra
1677-1681	Middle East/Europe	OTTOMAN-MUSCOVITE WARS
Nov. 1, 1677	Africa	France seizes Gorée Island
Feb. 18, 1678	Europe	BUNYAN'S *THE PILGRIM'S PROGRESS* APPEARS

Date	Region	Event
Aug. 10, 1678-Sept. 26, 1679	Europe	Treaties of Nijmegen
Aug. 13, 1678-July 1, 1681	Europe	The Popish Plot
Dec., 1678-Mar. 19, 1687	North America	La Salle's Expeditions
1679	Europe	Habeas Corpus Act
1679	Europe	Treaty of St. Germain
1679-1709	South Asia	Rājput Rebellion
Beginning 1680's	Latin America	Guerra dos Bárboros
1680-1709	East Asia	Reign of Tsunayoshi as Shogun
June 30, 1680	Europe	Spanish Inquisition Holds a Grandiose *Auto-da-Fé*
Aug. 10, 1680	North America	Pueblo Revolt
1681	Europe	Oil street lights are first used in London
Mar. 4, 1681	North America	"Holy Experiment" Establishes Pennsylvania
Beginning c. 1682	Africa	Decline of the Solomonid Dynasty
1682	Europe	French Court Moves to Versailles
1682	North America	South Carolina recognizes slavery
1682-1725	Europe	Peter the Great rules as Czar of Russia
Aug., 1682-Nov., 1683	Europe	Rye House Plot
July-Oct., 1683	East Asia	Qing forces defeat of the Zheng pirates
July 14-Sept. 12, 1683	Europe	Defeat of the Ottomans at Vienna
1684	East Asia	China annexes Taiwan
1684-1699	Europe	Holy League Ends Ottoman Rule of the Danubian Basin
June 21, 1684	North America	Massachusetts Bay Colony's charter is revoked by Charles II
1685	North America	First printing press in Philadelphia
1685	Europe	Louis XIV Revokes the Edict of Nantes
1686	Southeast Asia	Dutch take control of Banten's pepper trade
1686	Europe	Halley Develops the First Weather Map
1686	Europe	Perpetual Peace (Treaty of Moscow) is signed
June, 1686-Apr., 1689	North America	Dominion of New England Forms
1687	South Asia	British East India Company moves its headquarters to Bombay
1687	South Asia	Mughal Empire defeats Golconda sultanate and annexes southeastern India
Beginning 1687	Middle East	Decline of the Ottoman Empire
Apr. 4, 1687, and Apr. 27, 1688	Europe	Declaration of Liberty of Conscience
Summer, 1687	Europe	Newton Formulates the Theory of Universal Gravitation
1688	South Asia	Madras becomes first city in India to receive an English royal charter
1688-1702	Europe	Reign of William and Mary
1688-1704	East Asia	Genroku Era
Nov., 1688-Feb., 1689	Europe	The Glorious Revolution
1689	Middle East	Grand Vizier Kara Mustafa begins to reform Ottoman army
1689	North America	Leisler's Rebellion
1689	Africa	Morocco takes Al-Araish
Beginning 1689	Europe	Reforms of Peter the Great
1689-1694	Europe	Famine and Inflation in France
1689-1697	Europe	Wars of the League of Augsburg
Feb. 13, 1689	Europe	Declaration of Rights
Mar., 1689	Europe	Louis XIV declares war on William and Mary and sends troops to Ireland to support James II
Apr. 18, 1689	North America	Mutinous troops lead an insurrection in Boston
Apr. 18-July 31, 1689	Europe	Siege of Londonderry
May 24, 1689	Europe	Toleration Act
July, 1689	Europe	Battle of Killiecrankie

DATE	REGION	EVENT
Aug. 21, 1689	Europe	Battle of Dunkeld
Aug. 29, 1689	East Asia	TREATY OF NERCHINSK DRAWS RUSSIAN-CHINESE BORDER
Early 1690's	Latin America	BRAZILIAN GOLD RUSH
Beginning 1690's	Europe	MOVEMENT TO REFORM MANNERS
c. 1690	Africa	EXTINCTION OF THE DODO BIRD
1690	Europe	LOCKE PUBLISHES *TWO TREATISES OF GOVERNMENT*
1690	Europe	Scottish Parliament ratifies Westminster Confession of Faith and Presbyterian Polity
1690-1698	South Asia	Siege of Jinji
July 1, 1690	Europe	Battle of the Boyne
1691	North America	Massachusetts Bay Colony annexes Plymouth Colony
Mar. 10, 1691	Europe	Treaty of Limerick
Aug. 20, 1691	Europe	Battle of Slankaman
June 2, 1692-May, 1693	North America	SALEM WITCHCRAFT TRIALS
June 8, 1692	North America	CORN RIOTS IN MEXICO CITY
1693	Africa	England temporarily gains control of Gorée Island
1693	Europe	RAY ARGUES FOR ANIMAL CONSCIOUSNESS
July 27, 1694	Europe	BANK OF ENGLAND IS CHARTERED
May 3, 1695	Europe	END OF PRESS CENSORSHIP IN ENGLAND
Mar., 1696-Dec. 14, 1698	Africa	Siege of Fort Jesus
1697-1702	Middle East	KÖPRÜLÜ REFORMS OF HÜSEYIN PAŞA
Mar. 9, 1697-Aug. 25, 1698	Europe	PETER THE GREAT TOURS WESTERN EUROPE
Sept. 20, 1697	Europe	TREATY OF RYSWICK
1698	Africa	Oyo invades Weme and Allada
1698	Africa	Royal African Company loses its monopoly on the English slave trade
July 25, 1698	Europe	SAVERY PATENTS THE FIRST SUCCESSFUL STEAM ENGINE
Oct. 11, 1698, and Mar. 25, 1700	Europe	FIRST AND SECOND TREATIES OF PARTITION
Dec. 14, 1698	Africa	Mombasa falls to Oman
1699	Africa	Oman wrests control of Swahili Coast north of Mozambique from Portugal
1699	East Asia	BRITISH ESTABLISH TRADING POST IN CANTON
Jan. 26, 1699	Europe	TREATY OF KARLOWITZ
Mar. 30, 1699	South Asia	SINGH FOUNDS THE KHALSA BROTHERHOOD
May 1, 1699	North America	FRENCH FOUND THE LOUISIANA COLONY
c. 1700	Europe	Bank of Amsterdam invents system to provide payment anywhere in the world
1700	North America	Carolina Supreme Court is established
c. 1700	Africa	Introduction of *ndop* sculpture in Kuba kingdom
c. 1700	Africa	King Mwine Kadilo begins expansion of Luba kingdoms
1700	North America	Pennsylvania and Rhode Island recognize slavery
June, 1700	Middle East/Europe	Treaty of Constantinople
July 11, 1700	Europe	Foundation of the Berlin Academy of Science
Aug. 8, 1700	Europe	Peace of Travendal
Nov. 30, 1700	Europe	BATTLE OF NARVA

Glossary

Abbey: A self-sufficient religious community of monks or nuns or both, run by an abbot or abbess and sometimes subject to a higher secular authority through feudal obligation. Abbots and abbesses occupied posts that were socially, politically, and spiritually important and powerful. *See also* Monastery, Monk, Nun, Nunnery.

ʿAbd: Arabic for "slave," often seen in proper names combined with other words referring to Allah ("slave of God"), one of Allah's attributes ("servant of the Merciful"), or royalty ("servant of the king").

Alaafin: A king of the Oyo in Nigeria, Africa.

Alchemy: A science and speculative philosophy first practiced during the Middle Ages and promoted in the seventeenth century by scientists such as Jakob Böhme. Alchemists attempted, among other things, to transform common substances, such as base metals, into less common ones, such as gold.

Allegory: A story, literary work, or play in which characters in the narrative personify abstract ideas or qualities and so give a second level of meaning to the work.

Amir: *See* Emir.

Apostate: One who renounces religious orders or other duties, considered a serious breach of faith.

Asantehene: A head of the Asante state in West Africa.

Auto-da-fé: The public pronouncement of a sentence by a religious court of the Inquisition, followed by the public execution, usually by burning, of that sentence by secular authorities. *Auto-da-fé* means not only "act of faith" but also "judicial sentence." *See also* Heresy, Heretic, Inquisition.

Baconian method: A method proposed by Francis Bacon in which knowledge is gained by making inferences from observations of particular, concrete facts, and then by making generalizations and hypotheses based on those observations. Also, the Baconian method calls for *testing* hypotheses through more observations and experiments.

Baroque: A style of art, architecture, literature, and music that flourished in seventeenth and early eighteenth century Europe. Baroque is defined especially by its monumental, dynamic, exuberant, grandiose, and theatrical style; its complex and ornate forms; its illusionism; and its tension. *See also* Classicism, Genre painting, Gongorism, Gothic, Mannerism, Still life.

Bey: The governor of a province of the Ottoman Empire. Also called "beg." *See also* Sultan, Vizier.

Beylerbey: The governor-general of a province of the Ottoman Empire. *See also* Bey, Sultan, Vizier.

Bishop: The highest-ranking priest within a diocese, responsible for its administration and the guidance of its clergy.

Boyar: A Russian noble—of the landed military aristocracy—ranking just below a ruling prince.

Boyle's Law: The inverse relationship between a gas's pressure and volume; a "law" developed by Irish chemist and physicist Robert Boyle, whose theoretical ideas were published as *The Sceptical Chymist* in 1661. *See also* Corpuscular philosophy.

Bull: A formal papal letter or document issuing an authoritative statement or policy. Named after the pope's lead seal, or *bulla*.

Bunn: Coffee beans, which were crushed then eaten, especially before coffee beans were brewed and consumed starting around the early fifteenth century along the Arabian Peninsula. *See also* Kiraathane, Marqaḥa, Qahwa.

Burgher: In Germanic regions, a townsperson.

Bushido: The code of conduct of the Japanese warrior class, stressing martial prowess, honor and fearlessness in battle, and unwavering loyalty to one's lord. *See also* Ronin, Samurai, Shogun.

Calculus: A central branch of mathematics first developed during ancient times in Greece and theorized by seventeenth century mathematicians such as Gottfried Wilhelm Leibniz, René Descartes, and Sir Isaac Newton. Calculus is concerned, in part, with determining volumes and areas of curved surfaces, with determining the lengths of curved lines, with problems of slopes and areas, and so forth.

Caliph: Islamic ruler claiming both spiritual and secular authority as the successor of the Prophet Muḥammad. *See also* Islam.

Calvinism: The theology based on the teachings of John Calvin in the sixteenth century, which places supreme faith in God and believes in human fallibility and predestination. *See also* Catholicism, Presbyterian, Protestantism.

Canon law: The system of governing the Roman Catholic Church, its bishops, clerics, and laypersons.

Cardinal: A high official in the Roman Catholic Church, second only to the pope in authority. Cardinals are appointed by the pope, and the college of cardinals is the body that elects a new pope.

Castle: A fortification with a variety of architectural features designed for safety and defense.

Cathedral or cathedral church: The central church in a diocese, the seat of a bishop's cathedra, or throne.

Catholicism: From the Greek *catholicos*, meaning "universal," Catholicism is a branch of Christianity organized in a strict hierarchy and subscribing to a complex body of religious dogma, including belief in transubstantiation, in papal infallibility, and in justification by faith in combination with good works. The two Catholic Churches are the Roman Catholic Church and the Eastern Orthodox Church. *See also* Calvinism, Eastern Orthodox Church, Islam, Judaism, Presbyterian, Protestantism.

Chamber: The personal quarters or sleeping rooms of a noble or king, overseen by a chamberlain.

Chamberlain: The officer in a royal household responsible for overseeing the king's chamber and private household.

Chancellor: The head of the Chancery, an officer in a royal household, often a bishop familiar with law, who served as the king's secretary and was responsible for domestic and foreign affairs.

Charter: A document issued by a lord or king, addressed to the public, in which title to property was recorded or, in a charter of franchise, freedom from servitude of a serf or a town.

Chattel: An item, such as furniture and other personal effects, that could be moved with its owner. Excluded real estate and, for example, buildings part of real property. Also, chattel could be a person considered property, as slaves and, in some cultures, women and girls.

Chivalry: The culture and ethic of the noble knight, whose life was devoted to his lord, the defense of the weak, and the honor of his lady.

Christianity: The religion derived from the teachings of Jesus Christ and from the words of the Bible, which is considered sacred scripture. Christianity is practiced by Roman Catholic, Protestant, and Eastern Orthodox bodies. *See also* Catholicism, Eastern Orthodox Church, Islam, Judaism, Presbyterian, Protestantism.

Church: When used alone in the context of the seventeenth century, "Church" is generally capitalized in reference to the universal Catholic Church. The term is not capitalized when it refers to the building or complex that hosts services. *See also* Cathedral.

Classicism: A style of art based on the classical period of the Greeks and Romans. Classicism is marked by its simplicity, proportion and harmony, and restraint. The composition of a work of art or the design of a building is meant to be balanced and harmonious, and the representation of a given "object," especially the human body, is meant to strike a balance between the conflicting demands of realism (the body should look like a "real" body) and idealism (the body should be represented in an ideal, or beautiful, form). *See also* Baroque, Mannerism, Naturalism, Realism.

Clerics or clergy: A general term for all members of the Church, including abbots, monks, priests, friars, bishops, archbishops, cardinals, and others.

Colonialism: The control and subjugation by one power, such as a country or empire, over an area made up of those who become dependent upon that power. *See also* Chattel, Colony.

Colony: A territory taken, usually by force, and occupied by peoples of a different, usually distant nation (mostly countries of Western Europe).

Commerce: The exchange, buying, and selling of commodities, usually on a large scale and between multiple locations. The seventeenth century witnessed increased commerce because of an unprecedented rise in trade between countries and regions of the world, mostly by sea. *See also* Colonialism, Commodity, Consumption, Mercantilism.

Commodity: Any good that circulates as an article of exchange in a money economy. *See also* Commerce, Consumption, Mercantilism.

Commoner: One who is not a member of the clergy or of a noble or royal family. *See also* Peasant, Serf.

Commonwealth: The English state from King Charles I's execution in 1649 to the beginning of the Restoration in 1660. The Commonwealth, planned as a representative democracy and a country without a monarch, was the first modern republic to be founded upon the trial and execution of a king. *See also* Protector, Protectorate, Restoration, Royalist, Tory, Whig.

Congregational: Of, or relating to, the Protestant churches that developed in seventeenth century England that affirmed the critical importance and autonomy of local congregations. Final authority in church matters rested with each congregation. "Congregationalism" is the practice of those who believe in Congregational administration and worship. *See also* Episcopacy, Presbyterian, Protestantism.

Consort: A spouse; when used in conjunction with a royal title, consort becomes the title of a royal spouse, such as queen consort, prince consort, and so forth.

Consumption: Satisfying wants and desires through purchasing and using goods and services. The use of these goods results in their transformation, deterioration, or destruction, which ensures that individuals will continue to purchase new goods, thereby maintaining an economy.

Convent: *See* Nunnery.

Corpuscular philosophy: An atomic theory of matter devised by Irish chemist and physicist Robert Boyle.

Cossack: The term "cossack" comes from the Turkic for "free warriors." The Cossacks, frontier warriors in southern Russia, lived as free persons. Slaves and peasants fleeing serfdom often would join them. *See also* Hetman, Peasant, Serf.

Count: From the Latin *comes* (companion) and the Middle French *comte*, the French or Continental equivalent of an earl. The office became a noble title, ranked below duke.

Counter-Reformation: A movement within the Catholic Church in the sixteenth and seventeenth centuries, designed both to defeat the external threat of the Protestant Reformation and to institute reforms to respond to internal issues that gave rise to Protestantism. *See also* Protestantism, Reformation.

Court: The group of officials, councillors, and hangers-on assembled at the official residence of a monarch or other ruler. European courts contained a mixture of those who wielded real power, those who served the ruler or the ministers, an entourage of people who merely desired to be near power, and practitioners of the arts who enjoyed the patronage of their ruler.

Courtier: A member of a ruler's entourage at court.

Covenanter: One who adhered to the Scottish National Covenant of 1638, which denounced and rebelled against English king Charles I's institution in Scotland of the Scottish Prayer Book, similar to the Book of Common Prayer used by the Anglicans in England. Also, a signer of the covenant.

Creed: A formal statement of belief, often religious or theological.

Crown: A term meaning "regal" or "imperial power," as in the French crown, or monarchy.

Czar: A Russian or other Slavic emperor. The word "czar" is derived from the Roman title "caesar" and suggests a ruler of equal stature to the emperors of imperial Rome.

Deacon: A member of the clergy ranking just below priest in the Roman Catholic, Anglican, and Eastern Orthodox Churches. In Roman Catholicism, the deacon is the middle rank of the three major orders, falling between priest and subdeacon in the hierarchy.

Deccan: Region of India between the Narmada and Krishna Rivers. After the fourteenth century, the Deccan was populated by Muslims and was largely conquered by the Mughal Empire in the seventeenth century.

Defenestration: To throw something or someone out of a window. In 1618, Protestant nobles, expressing their opposition to the Holy Roman Emperor's attempt to re-Catholicize Bohemia, threw two imperial commissioners (who were Catholics) from a window of Prague Castle. The defenestration marked the start of revolts leading to the Thirty Years' War between Protestants and Catholics in Europe. *See also* Catholicism, Protestantism.

Devshirme: A levy of Christian boys, enslaved for training and recruitment to serve in various parts of the administration of the Ottoman Empire. The recruits formed the Janissary corps and also served in the sultan's household. *See also* Janissaries.

Diocese: The basic administrative and territorial unit of the Catholic Church. Each diocese is governed by a bishop. *See also* Bishop, Cathedral.

Divine right: The concept that God bestowed the right to rule upon kings.

Dogma: The body of beliefs and doctrines formally held and sanctioned by a church.

Dualism: In philosophy, at minimum, two definitions: One, the perspective of René Descartes in the seventeenth century that held that humans are made of two separable and distinct substances: body (physical and mechanical) and soul (sensing, thinking, emoting). Two, the belief that bodies and minds (compare with the Cartesian "soul") are distinct, mainly because bodies are not simply material entities. Also, dualism is a world view that has typified several religions, holding that the world is divided and controlled by good and evil and by the material and the spiritual.

Duke, duchess: From Roman *dux*, a governor, especially of a military jurisdiction; later, a member of nobility who was lord over several counties (headed by "counts"), who could pass the title duke or duchess to offspring. *See also* Count.

Dynasty: A line of rulers who succeed one another based on their familial relationships. *See also* Colonialism, Colony, Empire.

Eastern Orthodox Church: A group of self-governing Catholic churches, such as the Russian Orthodox Church, that split from the Roman Catholic Church in 1054. While the patriarch, or leader, of each branch of Orthodoxy is ranked hierarchically in relation to the others, each branch is essentially self-governing, and the relationship among the various branches is that of a loose federation. *See also* Catholicism, Christianity, Old Believers.

Ecclesiastical: Of, or relating to, a church.

Edict: An order, command, or proclamation with legal authority.

Emir: A general title given to Islamic military commanders, rulers, and governors.

Empire: A large realm, ruled by an emperor or empress, which consists of previously distinct political units joined together under a ruler's central authority. *See also* Colonialism, Colony, Dynasty.

Episcopacy: A system of church governance in which the bishops hold all authority. *See also* Congregational, Presbyterian, Protestantism.

Estates-General: The governing body, or national assembly, of the Netherlands. Also called "States-General."

Fairy tale: A narrative form of folk literature and oral tradition, which tells the story of a hero or heroine and his or her fortunate and unfortunate adventures. Fairy tales are often fantastical and magical, and they usually end with the protagonist living "happily ever after." French writer Charles Perrault's seventeenth century fairy tale collection, *Tales of Mother Goose*, is considered by many the first work in the fairy tale genre.

Fatwa: A legal opinion or ruling issued by an Islamic legal scholar, or mufti. *See also* Mufti.

Flank: The side of a military formation.

Genre painting: Painting that represents scenes from everyday life, such as a domestic interior or a village or outdoor market. Dutch painters Jan Vermeer and Rembrandt, Flemish painter Frans Hals, and others of the seventeenth century perfected genre painting. *See also* Mannerism, Naturalism, Realism, Still life.

Gold Coast: Coastal area of West Africa, corresponding roughly with the coast of modern-day Ghana. *See also* Ivory Coast, Slave Coast, Transatlantic slave trade.

Gongorism: A highly stylized form of writing influenced by Spanish writer Luis de Góngora y Argote and marked as baroque, intricate, mythological, Latinized, ornamental, artful, affective, and ostentatious. *See also* Baroque, Classicism.

Gothic: A style of European architecture between the twelfth and sixteenth centuries, especially, characterized by ornateness, strong vertical lines, and pointed arches. The Gothic style greatly influenced seventeenth century Baroque style. *See also* Baroque, Classicism.

Governor: The proxy representative of an emperor or central government who rules over a colony or an imperial territory.

Grand duke: The ruler of a sovereign territory called a grand duchy.

Grand prince: The ruler of a Russian city-state.

Haiku: A Japanese verse form developed in the sixteenth century but perfected by Matsuo Bashō in the seventeenth century. Haiku expresses profound simplicity—a seeming contradiction—of thought, imagination, or feeling in three lines of seventeen syllables total.

Heresy: Making a statement or holding a belief that contradicts established church dogma. Heresy against the Roman Catholic Church constituted a serious crime subject to severe punishment and even death. *See also* Auto-da-fé, Heretic, Inquisition.

Heretic: Someone judged to have committed heresy. *See also* Auto-da-fé, Heresy, Inquisition.

Hetman: A Cossack leader. *See also* Cossack.

Homophony: Music characterized by melodies that are "in step," having sounds or voices in rhythm, to form a harmonious compositional whole. *See also* Baroque, Madrigal, Polyphony.

House: A royal or noble family.

Huguenots: Originally, one who adhered to a Swiss political movement of the mid-sixteenth century. The term is most commonly associated with the French Protestants of the late sixteenth century and the seventeenth century.

Humanism: Born in fourteenth century Italy and embraced by subsequent centuries, a world view that centralizes humankind, human values, and human achievements. In contrast, supernatural or religious world views often consider humanity to be inferior or intrinsically depraved. Humanism led to individualism, secularism, rational critical thought, and the notion that humankind could triumph over nature. As Humanism blossomed, so did science, revealing physical laws that explained natural phenomena and seemed at odds with biblical and theological explanations of the universe. Humanism also was characterized by a return to classic Greek and Latin (pre-Christian) literature. *See also* Classicism, Humanistic, Renaissance.

Humanistic: Relating to a broad concern with the values or tenets associated with Humanism; "humanistic" applies to more general and less systematic beliefs and practices than does "Humanist." *See also* Humanism, Renaissance.

Humors: In medicine prior to the seventeenth century, the humors were the four bodily fluids—blood, phlegm, yellow bile, and black bile—any excess of which created a distortion or imbalance of personality; by extension, the term came to mean "mood" or "disposition." Advances in medicine and medical knowledge in the seventeenth century led to the eventual demise of the term's usage and authority.

Imam: An Islamic religious and political leader. Also, an Islamic ruler in East Africa. *See also* Sultan.

Indigenous: Someone or something native to a particular region. "Indigenous" has replaced the terms "Indian" or "American Indian" in many contexts that refer to the early peoples of North America and Central America.

Infidel: One who does not believe in a particular religion.

Inquisition: A Roman Catholic court of religious inquiry charged with discovering and punishing heresy. *See also* Auto-da-fé, Heresy, Heretic.

Islam: The religion founded by the Prophet Muḥammad, which, after his death in 632, began to spread throughout the world. The resulting clash of Islamic and, especially, Christian cultures—spurred by the movement of Muslims into traditionally Christian lands and of Christians into the Holy Land—contributed to military conflict, starting with the Crusades of the eleventh and twelfth centuries and continuing into the twenty-first century, most notably with the Iraq War. The spread of Islam, however, has also contributed to intellectual advancement and the blending of the arts. A person who practices Islam is a Muslim. *See also* Catholicism, Christianity, Judaism, Protestantism.

Ivory Coast: Coastal area of West Africa, corresponding roughly with the coast of the modern-day Republic of Côte d'Ivoire. *See also* Gold Coast, Slave Coast, Transatlantic slave trade.

Janissaries: From the Turkish for "new corps," an elite corps of non-Muslim children, usually Christians from the Balkans, recruited as slaves of the sultan. The Janissaries played a key role in the rise of the Ottoman Empire, with some holding high governmental positions. *See also* Devshirme.

Jesuits: Members of the Roman Catholic Society of Jesus, founded in the mid-sixteenth century, who devote their lives to educational and missionary work. *See also* Abbey, Catholicism, Mission, Missionary, Monastery, Monk.

Jihad: A holy "war" waged by Muslims against those who do not follow Islam, considered by many Muslims a duty imposed by holy law.

Judaism: The religion characterized by belief in one transcendent God who has revealed himself to Abraham, Moses, and the Hebrew prophets. Judaism is practiced in accordance with Scriptures and rabbinic traditions. *See also* Catholicism, Christianity, Eastern Orthodox Church, Islam, Protestantism.

Kabaka: A king of Buganda in Uganda, Africa.

Kabuki: A popular Japanese drama developed in the seventeenth century by Izumo no Okuni, which combines song, dance, and other varieties of performance. Elaborate, detailed, and ornately costumed and designed, Kabuki plays are based on not only legends and myths but also historical subjects.

Khamr: Wine, prohibited by the Qurʾān. How it is defined varies among the schools of Islam. *See also* Qahwa.

Khan: Beginning in the tenth century and extending into the 1600's, the title of a Turkish, Central Asian, or Mongol ruler who reigned over a group of tribes or territories.

King: A male monarch who ruled a large region and under whom ruled subordinate lords. A king's title was usually hereditary and most often for life. *See also* Queen, Sultan.

Kiraathane: Literally, "reading room," a neighborhood coffee or tea house, most common in Turkey. *See also* Bunn, Marqaḥa, Qahwa.

Latitude: The distance between a given point on Earth and the Earth's equator, expressed in angular degrees.

Levellers: A group of Protestant radicals that rose to prominence during the English Civil War, demanding legal equality and religious toleration. Many Levellers later adopted Quakerism. *See also* Huguenots, Old Believers, Protestantism, Quakerism.

Longitude: The distance between a given point on Earth and a line (called the prime meridian) that extends from the North Pole to the South Pole, expressed in angular degrees.

Madrigal: A short lyric set to music and sung by more than one person. Themes include love, satire, and the pastoral. *See also* Baroque, Homophony, Polyphony.

Manikongo: A king of Kongo in Angola, Africa.

Mannerism: A style of art preceding that of the Baroque, in which painters expressed often highly emotional subjects through distorted and exaggerated forms and with vivid colors. *See also* Baroque, Classicism, Naturalism, Realism.

Marqaḥa: Literally, "coffee euphoria." Beginning in the sixteenth century, the term was used by Arabic speakers but is probably of Ethiopian origin. The term is used to describe coffee's mental and physical effects. *See also* Bunn, Khamr, Kiraathane, Qahwa.

Masque: An elaborate combination of poetic drama, song, dance, music, and sumptuous costuming presented as entertainment at court. English playwright Ben Jonson, along with English architect Inigo Jones, created the best forms of the genre in the seventeenth century, with Jones producing elaborate sets that would influence the work of William Shakespeare and many other playwrights.

Mercantilism: An economic theory first known as "Colbertisme" (after its early proponent Jean-Baptiste Colbert of France) that emerged during the seventeenth century. Mercantilism at the time advocated governmental leadership in guiding a nation's economy toward prosperity. *See also* Colonialism, Commodity, Consumption.

Metaphysical poetry: A form of poetry marked by wit, originality, directness, shock, argument, and paradox, all in a style resembling, most often, actual speech. The Metaphysical poets, especially Englishman John Donne, used forms of knowledge from countless, seemingly antithetical, traditions to show parallels and similarities between things that seemed dissimilar.

Mission: A colonial ministry whose task is to convert indigenous peoples to Christianity. *See also* Catholicism, Christianity, Colonialism, Missionary.

Missionary: An agent of the Catholic Church commissioned to travel to a colony or other "distant" location to gain converts. *See also* Catholicism, Christianity, Colonialism, Mission.

Monastery: A place where monks or nuns lived a religious life, frequently including a chapter house for meetings as well as sleeping quarters and various other facilities depending on the work of the monastery. *See also* Abbey, Monk, Nun, Nunnery.

Monk: A man who has taken religious vows of self-privation, and who lives in seclusion or semiseclusion from the material world in a monastery or abbey. *See also* Jesuits, Monastery, Nun, Trappists.

Mufti: A specialist in Islamic law who is not a public official but a private scholar who functions as a consultant. *See also* Fatwa, Imam.

Muscovy: Moscow; former name for Russia, first used in the early sixteenth century.

Muslim: One who practices the religion of Islam. *See also* Islam.

Mwami: A king of Rwanda, Africa.

Mysticism: The practice of many religious faiths, including Christianity and Islam, which emphasize the nonrational, spiritual, and felt rather than intellectual aspects of religious truth as an emotional or transcendent experience. *See also* Sufism.

Naturalism: An artistic style emphasizing the realistic portrayal of an object as it appears in nature. "Realism" is often used as a synonym for naturalism. *See also* Baroque, Genre painting, Mannerism, Realism.

Noble: A member of the landed aristocracy.

Nun: A woman who has taken religious vows of self-privation, and who lives in seclusion or semiseclusion from the material world. *See also* Abbey, Monastery, Monk, Nunnery.

Nunnery: A home for nuns or other persons living in accordance with religious vows. *See also* Abbey, Monastery, Nun.

Oba: A ruler of Benin in West Africa.

Old Believers: Conservative members of the Russian Orthodox Church who were labeled dissidents for opposing church reforms. *See also* Eastern Orthodox Church, Heresy, Heretic, Huguenots, Inquisition, Levellers, Patriarch.

Ottomans: Turkish rulers of the Islamic world who ruled as sultans from roughly 1281 to 1922. Their conquest in 1453 of the seat of the Byzantine Empire and Eastern Christian Orthodoxy, Constantinople, marked their ascendant power. *See also* Ṣafavids, Sultan.

Palatinate: A county or principality ruled by a lord whose rights included those of a king, such as the right to coin money or appoint judges. Also, in Germany, the proper name of a principality. *See also* Palatine.

Palatine: The term "palatine" referred to the lord of a palatinate or a resident of the (German) Palatinate. *See also* Palatinate.

Papal States: A sovereign Italian city-state, which was based in Rome and ruled by the pope and served as the spiritual seat of his papacy. *See also* Catholicism, Pope.

Parliament: An assembly of representatives, usually a mix of nobles, clergy, and commoners, which functions as a legislative body serving under the sovereignty of a monarch.

Paşa: The highest title of rank or honor in the Ottoman Empire. The title evolved to include governors of foreign territories and to viziers of a domestic government.

Pasha: A man of high rank in northern Africa. *See also* Imam, Paşa.

Pashalik: A state formed in Mali, northwest Africa, by the Arma, a military caste descended from Moroccan soldiers.

Patriarch: The head of one of the self-governing branches of the Eastern Orthodox Church. *See also* Eastern Orthodox Church.

Patron: One who financially or materially supports an artist, composer, poet, or other creative individual.

Peasant: The lowest rank of commoner, who works the land in order to subsist. *See also* Commoner, Serf.

Persia: A term used by Westerners until the early twentieth century to describe the region always known as Iran to Iranians.

Plague: A contagious disease caused by a bacterium, which becomes epidemic and causes a high rate of mortality. Called the Black Death during the Middle Ages, it took more than seventy thousand lives in London in the mid-seventeenth century. *See also* Humors.

Polyphony: Music characterized by the juxtaposition of independent melodies—many sounds or many voices—to form a harmonious compositional whole. *See also* Baroque, Homophony, Madrigal.

Pope: The spiritual leader of the Roman Catholic Church and temporal ruler of the Papal States. *See also* Catholicism, Christianity.

Presbyterian: A Protestant Christian church that is mostly Calvinistic in doctrine. "Presbyterianism" is a system of church governance favored as more democratic than Episcopalianism because it is characterized by a graded system of representative ecclesiastical bodies. *See also* Calvinism, Catholicism, Christianity, Congregational, Ecclesiastical, Episcopacy, Presbytery, Protestantism.

Presbytery: The ruling body in Presbyterian churches. Also, the part of a church reserved for clergy who officiate. *See also* Presbyterian.

Pretender: Someone who falsely claims to be a rightful ruler. Since the "right" of a ruler was often asserted and defended by force, a pretender who succeeded in overthrowing a sitting monarch was no longer a pretender.

Privateer: A pirate or pirate ship commissioned or licensed by a government to raid the ships of other nations. Privateers also participated in the slave trade of the seventeenth century.

Protector: Title sometimes given to a regent, signifying that he is both the protector of a young monarch and the protector of the realm during a monarch's youth. A "Protector" or "Lord Protector" also was the title of the executive head of the Commonwealth of England in the mid-seventeenth century. *See also* Commonwealth, Protectorate, Regent.

Protectorate: In the mid-seventeenth century, the English government—the Commonwealth of England—under the Cromwells. *See also* Commonwealth, Protector.

Protestantism: A branch of Christianity, incorporating many different churches, which "protests" and rejects Catholic tradition, especially its doctrine of papal infallibility, and believes instead in a religion of all believers who read the Bible for themselves rather than having it interpreted to them by clergy. *See also* Calvinism, Catholicism, Christianity, Ecclesiastical, Episcopacy, Presbyterian, Quakerism.

Puritan: In sixteenth and seventeenth century Protestant England and New England, one who opposed the ceremonial worship and prelacy of the Church of England. "Puritanism" is the belief and practice of Puritans. *See also* Calvinism, Catholicism, Christianity, Presbyterian, Protestantism, Quakerism.

Qahwa: Coffee; a term believed to be of Iranian origin. Also spelled *qahva*. *See also* Bunn, Khamr, Kiraathane, Marqaḥa.

Quakerism: A Protestant group that began in seventeenth century England, which rejected ritualized forms of worship. Traditional Quaker worship services are not led by ordained ministers and do not involve the recitation of a religious creed. Women play a major role in Quakerism, since Quakers believe that men and women are equally suited to preach the word of God. Quaker religious beliefs are egalitarian and humanitarian. *See also* Levellers, Protestantism, Puritan.

Queen: A female monarch who ruled a large region. A queen's title, unlike that of the king's—which was usually hereditary—was often gained upon marriage to a king. Some wives of kings were called "consorts," or "queen consorts," instead of "queens." Also, queens would become "regents" if they lived after the death of their husband-kings and were pronounced virtual rulers during the minority of monarchs to be. *See also* Consort, King, Queen-Mother, Regent.

Queen-Mother: A former queen who is the mother of a current ruler. *See also* Queen, Regent.

Quietism: In religion, quietism refers to a mysticism that teaches, among other things, suppression of the will to obtain spiritual peace and perfection. Politically, quietism is the withdrawn or passive attitude or policy toward world affairs.

Realism: In art, the attempt to depict objects, human figures, or scenes as they appear in real life; that is, without distortion or stylization. "Naturalism" is often used as a synonym for realism. *See also* Genre painting, Mannerism, Naturalism.

Rector: A religious leader. In some Protestant churches, the leader of a parish; in the Roman Catholic Church, the head of a church that has no pastor or a cleric who shares duties with a pastor. *See also* Catholicism.

Recusant: An English Roman Catholic, especially of the sixteenth through eighteenth centuries, who refused to obey the teachings of and participate in the services of the Church of England, thereby committing a statutory offense. *See also* Catholicism, Protestantism, Remonstrant.

Reformation: The Protestant movements that swept through Europe during the Renaissance and into the seventeenth century, ending Catholicism's claim as the sole form of Christianity. *See also* Catholicism, Christianity, Protestantism.

Regent: One who temporarily governs in place of a monarch or other ruler who is too young or infirm to govern for him- or herself. Oftentimes, a regent is the monarch's mother. *See also* Queen, Queen-Mother.

Remonstrant: One who vigorously opposes some form of incorporated change. During the seventeenth century, remonstrants could be those who refused to accept a monarch's call for his or her subjects to practice one particular religion over another. *See also* Recusant.

Renaissance: A general term for the resurgence of cultural production in a given area. Renaissance also refers to the specific flourishing of art and culture during the transition from medieval to modern political, economic, and social structures in Western Europe in the two centuries immediately preceding the seventeenth century. *See also* Humanism, Humanistic.

Republic: A political unit not ruled by a monarch, especially one governed by a group of representatives chosen by and responsible to its citizens. *See also* Parliament.

Restoration: The restoration of the Stuart monarchy in England in 1659-1660, a time in which King Charles II gained power and the Royalist tradition was revived. The Restoration also marked the end of the failed experiment of the Commonwealth, which began in 1648. *See also* Commonwealth, Protector, Protectorate, Royalist.

Ronin: A masterless samurai. Because serving one's master well was the central value of the samurai code of *bushido*, *ronin* were usually considered dishonorable, either because they had failed their lord or because they had willfully rejected the code. *See also* Bushido, Samurai, Shogun.

Royalist: One who favors monarchical government and the power of a ruler. *See also* Commonwealth, Restoration, Tory, Whig.

Rump Parliament: A parliament that conducts the business of government after the expulsion or departure of a large number of its original members. *See also* Parliament.

Ṣafavids: An Islamic empire in Iran (Persia), founded in 1501 and ended in 1722. The Ṣafavid Empire was, along with the Ottoman Empire, one of the most powerful of the seventeenth century. Shīʿite Islam, developed by the early Ṣafavids, continues to be the dominant religion of Iran into the twenty-first century.

Salon: An informal social gathering of artists, writers, and other intellectuals who met at a private home. Salons were popular in the seventeenth century, namely in France. Famous salons of Paris included those of the marquise de Rambouillet and madame de Scudéry. *See also* Humanism, Humanistic.

Samurai: A member of the Japanese warrior caste, especially a warrior who serves a daimyo and who subscribes to a strict code of conduct called *bushido*. *See also* Bushido, Ronin, Shogun.

Satire: A literary style that uses wit, sarcasm, humor, and such to point out human vices, follies, and immoralities. Notable satirists of the seventeenth century include Ben Jonson, John Dryden, John Donne, Molière, and Nicolas Boileau-Despréaux. *See also* Humanism, Humanistic, Salon.

Schism: A split or division within a formerly unified entity, especially a formal split within a church or other religious institution. One major schism in the seventeenth century was that between the Russian Orthodox Church and the Old Believers. *See also* Eastern Orthodox Church, Old Believers.

Secular: Nonreligious, either in content or in context. Thus, secular can be a simple antonym of "religious," but it can also refer to members of the clergy who live and act in the public sphere rather than spending their lives in religious seclusion in a monastery or abbey.

Serf: A peasant bound to the land through contract. Serfs were given a parcel of land on which to live and work, but any surplus they produced was owed to their landlord as rent, tax, or tribute. In Russia, serfdom was codified into law in 1649. *See also* Commoner, Peasant.

Shabbetism: A messianic movement led by Jewish mystic Shabbetai Tzevi, who emphasized inner union with the divine, a symbolic approach to Jewish law, and women's equality. *See also* Judaism.

Sharia: Islamic holy law. *See also* Islam.

Sharif: A Muslim who claims descent from the Prophet Muḥammad. *See also* Islam.

Shia: The Muslims of the Shīʿite branch of Islam. *See also* Imam, Shīʿite, Sunni.

Shīʿite: The branch of Islam that believes that Ali and the imams are the only rightful successors of Muḥammad and that the last imam will someday return. *See also* Imam, Shia, Sunni.

Shogun: A Japanese military ruler. *See also* Bushido, Ronin, Samurai.

Siege: A military operation in which a city or other territory is cut off from the outside world in order to compel its surrender when food and other supplies are exhausted.

Slave Coast: Coastal region of West Africa along the Bight of Benin and along the coasts of modern-day Nigeria, Benin, and Togo. The area was a major center for the slave trade among African rulers and European nations, from about 1500 to the late eighteenth century. The seventeenth century saw an increase in the trade of slaves, thus the region's moniker. *See also* Gold Coast, Ivory Coast, Transatlantic slave trade.

Spice Islands: The group of islands that make up the easternmost part of Indonesia. The Spice Islands are so named because the area was the center of the European spice trade. *See also* Mercantilism.

Stadtholder: A provincial governor of the Netherlands. The stadtholders were initially viceroys of Burgundy and of the Habsburgs, but after the Dutch Revolt that ended in the early seventeenth century, the offices became elective. *See also* Estates-General, State.

State: An autonomous, self-governing, sovereign political unit. *See also* Estates-General, Parliament.

Still life: An arrangement of inanimate objects, such as fruit in a bowl or a vase with flowers, depicted in a setting not "natural" but indoors. Objects are isolated on a table, for example, and not part of a larger composition, as they were in earlier forms of the painting of objects. Still life painting began with the Dutch and Flemish artists of the sixteenth and seventeenth centuries. *See also* Baroque, Genre painting, Naturalism, Realism.

Succession: The passing of sovereign authority from one person or group to another person or group, or the rules governing that process.

Sufism: Islamic mysticism. A Sufi is one who practices Sufism. *See also* Islam, Mysticism.

Sultan: Beginning in the eleventh century, any political and military ruler of an Islamic state or emirate (as opposed to the caliph, the religious authority of the Islamic state). Applied mostly to Ottoman rulers. *See also* Caliph.

Sunni: Muslims who adhere to the orthodox tradition of Islam, which acknowledges the first four caliphs, the religious authorities of Islam, as rightful successors of the Prophet Muḥammad. *See also* Imam, Shia, Shīʿite.

Tory: In England, the Royalist party that was opposed to the Whigs. *See also* Commonwealth, Royalist, Whig.

Tragicomedy: A drama that combines elements of tragedy and of comedy, brings together characters from tragedies (usually the upper classes) and those from comedies (the middle and lower classes), and presents a plot with a seemingly tragic end but ends with a reversal of fortune for the protagonist, leading to a happy ending. John Fletcher, Francis Beaumont, William Shakespeare, Pierre Corneille, and Molière wrote tragicomedy in the seventeenth century.

Transatlantic slave trade: The trade in slaves, mostly from Africa, that crossed the Atlantic Ocean from and between East Africa, Europe, North America, and South America. *See also* Slave Coast.

Trappists: Members of a branch of the Catholic Church seeking monastic reform. The Trappist Order was founded in 1664 at the monastery of La Trappe, France. *See also* Jesuits, Monastery, Monks.

Treaty: An agreement or arrangement between, especially, two nations and made by negotiation.

Tsar: *See* Czar.

Vernacular: That which characterizes a people, period, or place. Often applied to things—and people—considered common and ordinary. Also used to define "common language," as opposed to learned or foreign language, and local architecture.

Vizier: Title given to high officials of Islamic nations. In the Ottoman Empire beginning around 1453, the viziers were specifically ministers to the sultan. The chief minister was known as the grand vizier, and members of the council that assisted and filled in for the grand vizier were called dome viziers. Use of the title was later expanded to include other important domestic officials, as well as provincial governors. *See also* Bey, Beylerbey, Islam, Sultan.

Whig: In seventeenth century England, a political party opposed to absolute royal authority and favoring increased parliamentary power. *See also* Commonwealth, Parliament, Royalist, Tory.

—Desiree Dreeuws

Bibliography

CONTENTS

General Studies, Surveys, and Reference Works

Bergin, Joseph, ed. *The Short Oxford History of Europe—The Seventeenth Century: Europe, 1598-1715.* New York: Oxford University Press, 2001.

Cameron, Euan, ed. *Early Modern Europe: An Oxford History.* New York: Oxford University Press, 1999.

Cook, Jacob Ernest, ed. *Encyclopedia of the North American Colonies.* 3 vols. New York: Charles Scribner's Sons, 1993.

Dewald, Jonathan, ed. *Europe, 1450-1789: Encyclopedia of the Early Modern World.* 6 vols. New York: Charles Scribner's Sons, 2004.

Munck, Thomas. *Seventeenth Century Europe: State, Conflict, and the Social Order in Europe, 1598-1700.* New York: St. Martin's Press, 1990.

Ogg, David. *Europe in the Seventeenth Century.* 9th ed. London: A. C. Black, 1971.

Pennington, D. H. *Europe in the Seventeenth Century.* 2d ed. London: Longman, 1989.

Sauer, Carl O. *Seventeenth Century North America.* Berkeley, Calif.: Turtle Island, 1980.

Scott, H. M., ed. *The European Nobilities in the Seventeenth and Eighteenth Centuries.* 2 vols. London: Longman, 1995.

Thackeray, Frank W., and John E. Findling, eds. *Events That Changed the World in the Seventeenth Century.* Westport, Conn.: Greenwood Press, 1999.

Winks, Robin W., and Lee Palmer Wandel. *Europe in a Wider World, 1350-1650.* New York: Oxford University Press, 2003.

Africa

Barry, Boubacar. *Senegambia and the Atlantic Slave Trade.* Translated by Ayi Kwei Armah. New York: Cambridge University Press, 1998.

Ehret, Christopher. *The Civilizations of Africa: A History to 1800.* Charlottesville: University of Virginia Press, 2002.

Fage, J. D., and William Tordoff. *A History of Africa.* 4th ed. New York: Routledge, 2002.

Falola, Toyin, ed. *African History Before 1885.* Vol. 1 in *Africa.* Durham, N.C.: Carolina Academic Press, 2000.

Gilliomee, Herman. *The Afrikaners: Biography of a People.* London: C. Hurst, 2003.

Hunwick, John O. *Timbuktu and the Songhay Empire.* Boston: Brill, 1999.

McCaskie, T. C. *State and Society in Pre-colonial Asante.* New York: Cambridge University Press, 1995.

Marcus, Harold. *A History of Ethiopia*. Berkeley: University of California Press, 1994.

Ogot, B. A., ed. *Africa from the Sixteenth to the Eighteenth Century*. Vol. 5 in *General History of Africa*. Berkeley: University of California Press, 1999.

Ogunmola, M. O. *A New Perspective to Oyo Empire History, 1530-1944*. Ibadan, Nigeria: Vantage, 1997.

Page, Willie F., ed. *Encyclopedia of African History and Culture*. 3 vols. New York: Facts On File, 2001.

Terreblanche, Sampie. *A History of Inequality in South Africa, 1652-2002*. Pietermaritzburg, South Africa: University of Natal Press, 2002.

Thompson, Leonard. *A History of South Africa*. 3d ed. New Haven, Conn.: Yale University Press, 2001.

Vansina, Jan. *Antecedents to Modern Rwanda: The Nyiginya Kingdom*. Madison: University of Wisconsin Press, 2004.

Wrigley, Christopher. *Kingship and State: The Buganda Dynasty*. New York: Cambridge University Press, 1996.

Art and Architecture

Alpers, Svetlana. *The Art of Describing: Dutch Art in the Seventeenth Century*. Chicago: University of Chicago Press, 1983.

Asher, Catherine. *Architecture of Mughal India*. New York: Cambridge University Press, 1992.

Beach, Milo Cleveland. *Mughal and Rajput Painting*. New York: Cambridge University Press, 1992.

Blair, Sheila A. S., and Jonathan Bloom. *The Art and Architecture of Islam, 1250-1800*. New Haven, Conn.: Yale University Press, 1994.

Blunt, Anthony. *Art and Architecture in France, 1500-1700*. 5th ed. Revised by Richard Beresford. New Haven, Conn.: Yale University Press, 1999.

_______, et al. *Baroque and Rococo Architecture and Decoration*. New York: Harper & Row, 1978.

Canby, Sheila R. *The Golden Age of Persian Art: 1501-1722*. New York: Harry N. Abrams, 2000.

Gardner, Helen, et al. *Gardner's Art Through the Ages*. 11th ed. Fort Worth, Tex.: Harcourt College, 2001.

Gaskell, Ivan. *Seventeenth Century Dutch and Flemish Painting*. New York: Rizzoli, 1990.

Grimm, Claus. *Frans Hals: The Complete Work*. Translated by Jürgen Riehle. New York: Harry N. Abrams, 1990.

Hopkins, Andrew. *Italian Architecture: From Michelangelo to Borromini*. New York: Thames & Hudson, 2002.

Janson, H. W., and Anthony F. Janson. *History of Art*. 6th ed. 2 vols. New York: Harry N. Abrams, 2001.

Lillehoj, Elizabeth, ed. *Critical Perspectives on Classicism in Japanese Painting, 1600-1700*. Honolulu: University of Hawaii Press, 2004.

Morrissey, Jake. *The Genius in the Design: Bernini, Borromini, and the Rivalry That Transformed Rome*. New York: Morrow, 2005.

Mowl, Timothy, and Brian Earnshaw. *Architecture Without Kings: The Rise of Puritan Classicism Under Cromwell*. New York: St. Martin's Press, 1995.

Norberg-Schulz, Christian. *Baroque Architecture*. 1971. Reprint. London: Phaidon Press, 2003.

Olson, Todd P. *Poussin and France: Painting, Humanism, and the Politics of Style*. New Haven, Conn.: Yale University Press, 2002.

Oppenheimer, Paul. *Rubens: A Portrait*. New York: Cooper Square Press, 2002.

Paine, Robert Treat, and Alexander Soper. *The Art and Architecture of Japan*. Rev. ed. Baltimore: Penguin Books, 1975.

Powell, Nicolas. *From Baroque to Rococo: An Introduction to Austrian and German Architecture from 1580 to 1790*. London: Faber & Faber, 1959.

Sadao, Tsuneko S., and Stephanie Wada. *Discovering the Arts of Japan: A Historical Overview*. New York: Kodansha International, 2003.

Schama, Simon. *Rembrandt's Eyes*. New York: Alfred A. Knopf 1999.

Stratton-Pruitt, Suzanne L., ed. *The Cambridge Companion to Velázquez*. New York: Cambridge University Press, 2002.

Summerson, John. *Inigo Jones*. New Haven, Conn.: Yale University Press, 2000.

Tinniswood, Adrian. *His Invention So Fertile: A Life of Christopher Wren*. New York: Oxford University Press, 2001.

Visonà, Monica Blackmun, et al. *A History of Art in Africa*. New York: Harry N. Abrams, 2001.

Welch, Anthony. *Shah ʿAbbās and the Arts of Isfahan*. New York: Asia Society, 1973.

Witkower, Rudolf, Joseph Connors, and Jennifer Montagu. *Art and Architecture in Italy, 1600-1750*. 6th ed. New Haven, Conn.: Yale University Press, 1999.

Australia

Day, Alan Edwin. *Historical Dictionary of the Discovery and Exploration of Australia*. Lanham, Md.: Scarecrow Press, 2003.

Estensen, Miriam. *Discovery: The Quest for the Great South Land*. New York: St. Martin's Press, 1999.

Flannery, Tim F., ed. *The Explorers: Stories of Discovery and Adventure from the Australian Frontier*. New York: Grove, 2000.

Welsh, Frank. *Great Southern Land: A New History of Australia*. London: Allen Lane, 2004.

China

Clements, Jonathan. *Pirate King: Coxinga and the Fall of the Ming Dynasty*. Phoenix Mill, Gloucestershire, England: Sutton, 2004.

Crossley, Pamela Kyle. *The Manchus*. Malden, Mass.: Blackwell, 2002.

Crozier, Ralph C. *Koxinga and Chinese Nationalism: History, Myth, and the Hero*. Cambridge, Mass.: East Asian Research Center, Harvard University, 1977.

Ebrey, Patricia Buckley. *The Cambridge Illustrated History of China*. New York: Cambridge University Press, 1996.

Fairbank, John King, and Merle Goldman. *China: A New History*. Enlarged ed. Cambridge, Mass.: Harvard University Press, 1998.

Hummel, Arthur W., ed. *Eminent Chinese of the Ch'ing Period, 1644-1912*. 2 vols. Washington, D.C.: Government Printing Office, 1943-1944.

Mungello, D. E. *The Great Encounter of China and the West, 1500-1800*. Lanham, Md.: Rowman & Littlefield, 1999.

Peterson, Willard J. *The Ching Empire to 1809*. Vol. 9 in *The Cambridge History of China*. New York: Cambridge University Press, 2002.

Wakeman, Frederic, Jr. *The Great Enterprise: The Manchu Reconstruction of Imperial Order in Seventeenth-Century China*. 2 vols. Berkeley: University of California Press, 1985.

Colonial North America

Alves, Abel A. *Brutality and Benevolence: Human Ethology, Culture, and the Birth of Mexico*. Westport, Conn.: Greenwood Press, 1996.

Balesi, Charles John. *The Time of the French in the Heart of North America, 1673-1818*. Chicago: Alliance Française Chicago, 1992.

Bennett, Herman L. *Africans in Colonial Mexico: Absolutism, Christianity, and Afro-Creole Consciousness, 1570-1640*. Bloomington: Indiana University Press, 2003.

Berkin, Carol. *First Generations: Women in Colonial America*. New York: Hill and Wang, 1996.

Berkin, Carol, and Leslie Horowitz, eds. *Women's Voices, Women's Lives: Documents in Early American History*. Boston: Northeastern University Press, 1998.

Billings, Warren M., John E. Selby, and Thad W. Tate. *Colonial Virginia: A History*. White Plains, N.Y.: KTO Press, 1986.

Canny, Nicholas, and Alaine Low, eds. *The Origins of Empire: British Overseas Enterprise at the Close of the Seventeenth Century*. Vol. 1 in *The Oxford History of the British Empire*, edited by William Roger Lewis. New York: Oxford University Press, 1998.

Dillon, Francis. *The Pilgrims*. Garden City, N.Y.: Doubleday, 1975.

Eccles, William John. *Canada Under Louis XIV, 1663-1701*. London: Oxford University Press, 1964.

_______. *France in America*. Rev. ed. East Lansing: Michigan State University Press, 1998.

Foster, Lynn V. *A Brief History of Mexico*. New York: Facts On File, 2004.

Francis, R. Douglas, Richard Jones, and Donald B. Smith. *Origins: Canadian History to Confederation*. 5th ed. Scarborough, Ont.: Nelson Canada, 2004.

Hambleton, Else L. *Daughters of Eve: Pregnant Brides and Unwed Mothers in Seventeenth Century Massachusetts*. New York: Routledge, 2004.

James, Sidney V. *Colonial Rhode Island: A History*. New York: Charles Scribner's Sons, 1975.

Knight, Alan. *The Colonial Era*. Vol. 2 in *Mexico*. New York: Cambridge University Press, 2002.

Krugler, John D. *English and Catholic: The Lord Baltimores in the Seventeenth Century*. Baltimore: Johns Hopkins University Press, 2004.

McInnis, Edgar, with Michael Horn. *Canada: A Political and Social History*. 4th ed. Toronto: Holt, Rinehart, and Winston Canada, 1982.

Mays, Dorothy A. *Women in Early America: Struggle, Survival, and Freedom in a New World*. Santa Barbara, Calif.: ABC-CLIO, 2004.

Miller, Perry. *The New England Mind: The Seventeenth Century*. Cambridge, Mass.: Harvard University Press, 1954.

Moogk, Peter. *La Nouvelle France: The Making of French Canada—A Cultural History*. East Lansing: Michigan State University Press, 2000.

Nash, Gary B. *Quakers and Politics: Pennsylvania, 1681-1726*. New ed. Boston: Northeastern University Press, 1993.

Poole, Stafford. *Our Lady of Guadalupe: The Origins and Sources of a Mexican National Symbol, 1531-1797*. Tucson: University of Arizona Press, 1995.

Price, David. *Love and Hate in Jamestown: John Smith, Pocahontas, and the Heart of a New Nation*. New York: Knopf, 2003.

Shorto, Russell. *The Island at the Center of the World: The Epic Story of Dutch Manhattan, the Forgotten Colony That Shaped America*. New York: Doubleday, 2004.

Simonian, Lane. *Defending the Land of the Jaguar: Natural History of Mexico*. Austin: University of Texas Press, 1996.

Treckel, Paula A. *To Comfort the Heart: Women in Seventeenth-Century America*. New York: Twayne, 1996.

Van Kirk, Sylvia. *Many Tender Ties: Women in Fur-Trade Society*. Norman: University of Oklahoma Press, 1983.

England, Scotland, and Ireland

Ashley, Maurice. *Charles I and Oliver Cromwell: A Study in Contrasts and Comparisons*. London: Methuen, 1987.

_______. *The Glorious Revolution of 1688*. New York: Charles Scribner's Sons, 1967.

Barnard, Toby. *The Kingdom of Ireland, 1641-1760*. New York: Palgrave Macmillan, 2004.

Bucholz, Robert, and Newton Key. *Early Modern England, 1485-1714: A Narrative History*. New York: Oxford University Press, 2003.

Canny, Nicholas. *Making Ireland British, 1580-1640*. New York: Oxford University Press, 2001.

Capp, B. S. *When Gossips Meet: Women, Family, and Neighbourhood in Early Modern England*. New York: Oxford University Press, 2003.

Coward, Barry. *Cromwell*. New York: Longman, 2000.

_______, ed. *A Companion to Stuart England*. Malden, Mass.: Blackwell, 2003.

Crawford, Patricia. *Women in Religion in England, 1500-1720*. New York: Routledge, 1993.

Crawford, Patricia, and Laura Gowing, eds. *Women's Worlds in Seventeenth-Century England*. London: Routledge, 2000.

Daybell, James. *Women and Politics in Early Modern England, 1450-1700*. Burlington, Vt.: Ashgate, 2004.

Erickson, Amy Louise. *Women and Property in Early Modern England*. New York: Routledge, 1993.

Fitzpatrick, Brendan. *Seventeenth Century Ireland: The War of Religions*. Totowa, N.J.: Barnes and Noble Books, 1989.

Fraser, Antonia. *The Weaker Vessel: Woman's Lot in Seventeenth-Century England*. New York: Vantage Books, 1984.

Frith, Valerie, ed. *Women and History: Voices of Early Modern England*. Concord, Ont.: Irwin, 1997.

Gardiner, Samuel Rawson. *The First Two Stuarts and the Puritan Revolution, 1603-1660*. New York: Longmans, Green, 1876. Reprint. New York: Thomas Y. Crowell, 1970.

Gregg, Pauline. *King Charles I*. London: J. M. Dent and Sons, 1981.

Haynes, Alan. *The Gunpowder Plot: Faith in Rebellion*. Stroud, Gloucestershire, England: Sutton, 1994.

Hill, Christopher. *The Century of Revolution, 1603-1714*. New York: Norton, 1980.

_______. *Change and Continuity in Seventeenth Century England*. Rev. ed. New Haven, Conn.: Yale University Press, 1991.

Hunt, Tristram. *The English Civil War at First Hand*. London: Weidenfeld & Nicolson, 2002.

Laurence, Anne. *Women in England, 1500-1760: A Social History*. New York: St. Martin's Press, 1994.

Lee, Maurice, Jr. *The "Inevitable" Union and Other Essays on Early Modern Scotland*. East Linton, East Lothian, Scotland: Tuckwell Press, 2003.

Macinnes, Alan I., and Jane Ohlmeyer, eds. *The Stuart Kingdoms in the Seventeenth Century: Awkward Neighbours*. Portland, Oreg.: Four Courts Press, 2002.

Mack, Phyllis. *Visionary Women: Ecstatic Prophecy in Seventeenth-Century England*. Berkeley: University of California Press, 1992.

Ohlmeyer, Jane H., ed. *Ireland from Independence to Occupation, 1641-1660*. New York: Cambridge University Press, 1995.

Peters, Christine. *Women in Early Modern Britain, 1450-1640*. New York: Palgrave Macmillan, 2004.

Rose, Craig. *England in the 1690's: Revolution, Religion, and War*. Malden, Mass.: Blackwell, 1999.

Smith, Lacey Baldwin. *This Realm of England, 1399 to 1688*. Vol. 2 in *A History of England*, edited by Lacey Baldwin Smith. 7th ed. Lexington, Mass.: D. C. Heath, 1996.

Solt, Leo F. *Church and State in Early Modern England, 1509-1640*. New York: Oxford University Press, 1990.

Exploration

Allen, Oliver E. *The Pacific Navigators*. Alexandria, Va.: Time-Life Books, 1980.

Balesi, Charles John. *The Time of the French in the Heart of North America, 1673-1818*. Chicago: Alliance Française Chicago, 1992.

Champlain, Samuel de. *Algonquians, Hurons, and Iroquois: Champlain Explores America, 1603-1616*. Translated by Annie Nettleton Bourne, edited by Edward Gaylord Bourne. Dartmouth, N.S.: Brook House Press, 2000.

Coulter, Tony. *Jacques Cartier, Samuel de Champlain, and the Explorers of Canada*. New York: Chelsea House, 1993.

Dampier, William. *A Voyage to New Holland: The English Voyage of Discovery to the South Seas in 1699*. 2 vols. London: James Knapton, 1703-1709. Rev. ed. Stroud, Gloucestershire, England: Sutton, 1981.

Goodman, Edward J. *The Explorers of South America*. Norman: University of Oklahoma Press, 1992.

Hanbury-Tenison, Robin, ed. *The Oxford Book of Exploration*. New York: Oxford University Press, 1993.

La Salle, Nicolas de. *The La Salle Expedition on the Mississippi River: A Lost Manuscript of Nicolas de La Salle, 1682*. Translated by Johanna S. Warren, edited by William C. Foster. Austin: Texas State Historical Association, 2003.

Slot, B. J. *Abel Tasman and the Discovery of New Zealand*. Amsterdam: O. Cramwinckel, 1992.

France

Bannister, Mark. *Condé in Context: Ideological Change in Seventeenth-Century France*. Oxford, England: European Humanities Research Centre, 2002.

Berce, Yves Marie. *The Birth of Absolutism: A History of France, 1598-1661*. Translated by Richard Rex. New York: St. Martin's Press, 1996.

Bergin, Joseph. *The Rise of Richelieu*. New Haven, Conn.: Yale University Press, 1991.

Bergin, Joseph, and Laurence Brockliss, eds. *Richelieu and His Age*. Oxford, England: Clarendon Press, 1992.

Duindam, Jeroen. *Vienna and Versailles: The Courts of Europe's Dynastic Rivals, 1550-1780*. New York: Cambridge University Press, 2003.

Dunlop, Ian. *Louis XIV*. New York: St. Martin's Press, 2000.

Holt, Mack P. *The French Wars of Religion, 1562-1629*. New York: Cambridge University Press, 1995.

Levi, Anthony. *Cardinal Richelieu and the Making of France*. New York: Carroll & Graf, 2000.

_______. *Louis XIV*. New York: Carroll & Graf, 2004.

Lossky, Andrew. *Louis XIV and the French Monarchy*. New Brunswick, N.J.: Rutgers University Press, 1994.

Mentzner, Raymond A., and Andrew Spicer, eds. *Society and Culture in the Huguenot World, 1559-1685*. New York: Cambridge University Press, 2002.

Ranum, Orest. *The Fronde: A French Revolution*. Baltimore: Johns Hopkins University Press, 1993.

Sturdy, David J. *Richelieu and Mazarin: A Study in Statesmanship*. New York: Palgrave Macmillan, 2004.

Treasure, G. R. R. *Mazarin: The Crisis of Absolutism in France*. New York: Routledge, 1995.

_______. *Seventeenth Century France*. 2d ed. London: J. Murray, 1981.

Germany and Austria

Brook-Shepherd, Gordon. *The Austrians: A Thousand Year Odyssey*. New York: Carroll & Graf, 1996.

Duindam, Jeroen. *Vienna and Versailles: The Courts of Europe's Dynastic Rivals, 1550-1780*. New York: Cambridge University Press, 2003.

Evans, R. J. W. *The Making of the Habsburg Monarchy, 1550-1700: An Interpretation*. 3d ed. New York: Oxford University Press, 1991.

Fichtner, Paula Sutter. *The Habsburg Monarchy, 1490-1848: Attributes of Empire*. New York: Palgrave Macmillan, 2003.

Frey, Linda, and Marsha Frey. *Frederick I: The Man and His Times*. Boulder, Colo.: East European Monographs, 1984.

Fulbrook, Mary. *A Concise History of Germany*. 2d ed. New York: Cambridge University Press, 2004.

Gagliardo, John G. *Germany Under the Old Regime, 1600-1790*. London: Longman, 1991.

Hughes, Michael. *Early Modern Germany, 1477-1806*. Philadelphia: University of Pennsylvania Press, 1992.

Ingrao, Charles W. *The Habsburg Monarchy, 1618-1815*. New York: Cambridge University Press, 1994.

McKay, Derek. *The Great Elector: Frederick William of Brandenburg-Prussia*. New York: Longman, 2001.

Schindler, Norbert. *Rebellion, Community, and Custom in Early Modern Germany*. Translated by Pamela E. Selwyn. New York: Cambridge University Press, 2002.

Shennan, Margaret. *The Rise of Brandenburg-Prussia*. New York: Routledge, 1995.

Wilson, Peter H. *From Reich to Revolution: German History, 1558-1806*. New York: Palgrave Macmillan, 2004.

India

Athar Ali, M. *The Mughal Nobility Under Aurangzeb*. Rev. ed. New York: Oxford University Press, 1997.

Gordon, Stewart. *The Marathas, 1600-1818*. New York: Cambridge University Press, 1993.

Hallissey, Robert C. *The Rajput Rebellion Against Aurangzeb: A Study of the Mughal Empire in Seventeenth Century India*. Columbia: University of Missouri Press, 1977.

Keay, John. *India: A History*. New York: Atlantic Monthly Press, 2000.

Raj Kumar, ed. *India Under Shah Jahan*. New Delhi, India: Anmol, 2000.

Richards, John F. *The Mughal Empire*. New York: Cambridge University Press, 1993.

Wolpert, Stanley. *A New History of India*. New York: Oxford University Press, 2000.

Invention and Technology

Asimov, Isaac. *Eyes on the Universe: A History of the Telescope*. Boston: Houghton Mifflin, 1975.

Aspray, William, ed. *Computing Before Computers*. Ames: Iowa State University Press, 1990.

Bedino, Silvio A. *The Pulse of Time: Galileo Galilei, the Determination of Longitude, and the Pendulum Clock*. Florence, Italy: L. S. Olschki, 1991.

Febvre, Lucien, and Henri-Jean Martin. *The Coming of the Book: The Impact of Printing, 1450-1800*. Translated by David Gerard, edited by Geoffrey Nowell-Smith and David Wooter. London: Foundations of History Library, 1997.

Fournier, Marian. *The Fabric of Life: Microscopy in the Seventeenth Century*. Baltimore: Johns Hopkins University Press, 1996.

King, Henry C. *The History of the Telescope*. Mineola, N.Y.: Dover, 2003.

Middleton, W. E. Knowles. *The History of the Barometer*. Baltimore: Johns Hopkins University Press, 2003.

Misa, Thomas J. *Leonardo to the Internet: Technology and Culture from the Renaissance to the Present*. Baltimore: Johns Hopkins University Press, 2004.

Ruestow, Edward G. *The Microscope in the Dutch Republic: The Shaping of Discovery*. New York: Cambridge University Press, 1996.

Struik, Dirk J. *The Land of Stevin and Huygens: A Sketch of Science and Technology in the Dutch Republic During the Golden Century*. Boston: D. Reidel, 1981.

Italy

Black, Christopher F. *Early Modern Italy: A Social History*. New York: Routledge, 2001.

Dandelet, Thomas James. *Spanish Rome, 1500-1700*. New Haven, Conn.: Yale University Press, 2001.

Holmes, George, ed. *The Oxford Illustrated History of Italy*. New York: Oxford University Press, 2001.

Marino, John A., ed. *Early Modern Italy, 1550-1796*. New York: Oxford University Press, 2002.

Martin, John, and Dennis Romano, eds. *Venice Reconsidered: The History and Civilization of an Italian City-State, 1297-1797*. Baltimore: Johns Hopkins University Press, 2000.

Sella, Domenico. *Italy in the Seventeenth Century*. London: Longman, 1997.

Japan

Bowring, Richard, and Peter Kornicki, eds. *The Cambridge Encyclopedia of Japan*. New York: Cambridge University Press, 1993.

Gordon, Andrew. *A Modern History of Japan: From Tokugawa Times to the Present*. New York: Oxford University Press, 2003.

Hall, John W., Nagahara Keiji, and Kozo Yamamura, eds. *Japan Before Tokugawa: Political Consolidation and Economic Growth, 1500 to 1650*. Princeton, N.J.: Princeton University Press, 1981.

Jansen, Marius B. *The Making of Modern Japan*. Cambridge, Mass.: Harvard University Press, 2000.

Massarella, Derek. *A World Elsewhere: Europe's Encounter with Japan in the Sixteenth and Seventeenth Centuries*. New Haven, Conn.: Yale University Press, 1990.

Merton, Linda K., Noren W. Lush, Eileen H. Tamura, and Chance I. Gusukuma. *The Rise of Modern Japan*. Honolulu: University of Hawaii Press, 2003.

Murdoch, James. *A History of Japan During the Century of Early Foreign Intercourse, 1542-1651*. Vol. 2 in *A History of Japan*. Reprint. New York: Routledge, 1996.

Jewish Diaspora

Faber, Eli. *A Time for Planting: The First Migration, 1654-1820*. Vol. 1 in *The Jewish People in America*. Baltimore: Johns Hopkins University Press, 1992.

Gurock, Jeffrey S., ed. *The Colonial and National Periods, 1654-1820*. Vol. 1 in *American Jewish History*. New York: Routledge, 1998.

Hershkowitz, Leo. "Judaism." In *Encyclopedia of the North American Colonies*, edited by Jacob Ernest

Cook. Vol. 3. New York: Charles Scribner's Sons, 1993.

Israel, Jonathan I. *European Jewry in the Age of Mercantilism, 1550-1750*. 3d ed., rev. and updated. London: Vallentine Mitchell, 1998.

Kaplan, Yosef. *An Alternative Path to Modernity: The Sephardi Diaspora in Western Europe*. Leiden, the Netherlands: Brill, 2000.

Marcus, Jacob R. *The Colonial American Jew, 1492-1776*. 3 vols. Detroit, Mich.: Wayne State University Press, 1970.

Nadler, Steven. *Rembrandt's Jews*. Chicago: University of Chicago Press, 2003.

Ruderman, David B. *Essential Papers on Jewish Culture in Renaissance and Baroque Italy*. New York: New York University Press, 1992.

Sutcliffe, Adam. *Judaism and Enlightenment*. New York: Cambridge University Press, 2003.

Swetschinski, Daniel M. *Reluctant Cosmopolitans: The Portuguese Jews of Seventeenth Century Amsterdam*. London: Vallentine Mitchell, 2000.

LITERATURE

Applebaum, Robert. *Literature and Utopian Politics in Seventeenth-Century England*. New York: Cambridge University Press, 2002.

Bloom, Harold, ed. *Cervantes' Don Quixote*. Philadelphia: Chelsea House, 2000.

_______. *John Donne and the Seventeenth Century Metaphysical Poets*. New York: Chelsea House, 1986.

Carey, John. *John Donne: Life, Mind, and Art*. New ed. Boston: Faber and Faber, 1990.

Cascardi, Anthony, ed. *The Cambridge Companion to Cervantes*. New York: Cambridge University Press, 2002.

Corns, Thomas, ed. *The Cambridge Companion to English Poetry: Donne to Marvell*. New York: Cambridge University Press, 1993.

Fowler, Alastair, ed. *The New Oxford Book of Seventeenth Century Verse*. New York: Oxford University Press, 2002.

Fumaroli, Marc. *The Poet and the King: Jean de La Fontaine and His Century*. Translated by Jane Marie Todd. Notre Dame, Ind.: University of Notre Dame Press, 2002.

Gillespie, Katherine. *Domesticity and Dissent in the Seventeenth Century: English Women Writers and the Public Sphere*. New York: Cambridge University Press, 2004.

Hager, Alan, ed. *The Age of Milton: An Encyclopedia of Major Seventeenth-Century British and American Authors*. Westport, Conn.: Greenwood Press, 2004.

Hammond, Nicholas. *Creative Tensions: An Introduction to Seventeenth Century French Literature*. London: Duckworth, 1997.

Hill, Christopher. *A Tinker and a Poor Man: John Bunyan and His Church*. New York: W. W. Norton, 1990.

Hutner, Heidi, ed. *Rereading Aphra Behn: History, Theory, and Criticism*. Charlottesville: University Press of Virginia, 1993.

Kanning, Douglas. *The Romanticism of Seventeenth Century Japanese Poetry*. Lewiston, N.Y.: E. Mellen Press, 1998.

Keeble, N. H., ed. *The Cambridge Companion to Writing of the English Revolution*. New York: Cambridge University Press, 2001.

Keene, Donald. *World Within Walls: Japanese Literature of the Pre-modern Era, 1600-1867*. New York: Holt, Rinehart, and Winston, 1976.

Lewalski, Barbara Kiefer. *The Life of John Milton: A Critical Biography*. Malden, Mass.: Blackwell, 2000.

McGrath, Alister E. *In the Beginning: The Story of the King James Bible and How It Changed a Nation, a Language, and a Culture*. New York: Anchor Books, 2002.

Merrim, Stephanie. *Early Modern Women's Writing and Sor Juana Inéz de la Cruz*. Nashville, Tenn.: Vanderbilt University Press, 1999.

Parente, James A., Jr., Richard Erich Schade, and George C. Schoolfield. *Literary Culture in the Holy Roman Empire, 1555-1720*. Chapel Hill: University of North Carolina Press, 1991.

Reid, David. *The Metaphysical Poets*. Harlow, Essex, England: Longman, 2000.

Sagarra, Eda, and Peter Skrine. *A Companion to German Literature: From 1500 to the Present*. Malden, Mass.: Blackwell, 1997.

Ueda, Makoto. *Bashō and His Interpreters: Selected Hokku with Commentary*. Stanford, Calif.: Stanford University Press, 1992.

Wilson, Douglas. *Beyond Stateliest Marble: The Passionate Femininity of Anne Bradstreet*. Nashville: Highland Books, 2001.

Wynne-Davies, Marion. *Sidney to Milton, 1580-1660*. New York: Palgrave Macmillan, 2003.

MATHEMATICS

Alexander, Amir R. *Geometrical Landscapes: The Voyages of Discovery and the Transformation of Mathe-*

matical Practice. Stanford, Calif.: Stanford University Press, 2002.

Bell, E. T. *Men of Mathematics*. 1937. Reprint. New York: Simon and Schuster, 1986.

Burton, David M. *The History of Mathematics: An Introduction*. 5th ed. Boston: McGraw-Hill, 2003.

Dunham, William. *Journey Through Genius: The Great Theorems of Mathematics*. New York: Wiley, 1990.

_______. *The Mathematical Universe: An Alphabetical Journey Through the Great Proofs, Problems, and Personalities*. New York: Wiley & Sons, 1994.

Mancosu, Paolo. *Philosophy of Mathematics and Mathematical Practice in the Seventeenth Century*. New York: Oxford University Press, 1996.

Neal, Katherine. *From Discrete to Continuous: The Broadening of Number Concepts in Early Modern England*. Boston: Kluwer Academic, 2002.

Simmons, George F. *Calculus Gems: Brief Lives and Memorable Mathematics*. New York: McGraw-Hill, 1992.

Struik, Dirk J. *A Concise History of Mathematics*. New York: Dover, 1967.

MEDICINE

Bono, James J. *The Word of God and the Languages of Man: Interpreting Nature in Early Modern Science and Medicine*. Madison: University of Wisconsin Press, 1995.

Debus, Allen G. *The Chemical Philosophy: Paracelsian Science and Medicine in the Sixteenth and Seventeenth Centuries*. Mineola, N.Y.: Dover, 2002.

_______. *Chemistry and Medical Debate: Van Helmont to Boerhaave*. Canton, Mass.: Science History, 2001.

Frank, Robert G., Jr. *Harvey and the Oxford Physiologists: A Study of Scientific Ideas*. Berkeley: University of California Press, 1980.

French, Roger. *Ancients and Moderns in the Medical Sciences: From Hippocrates to Harvey*. Brookfield, Vt.: Ashgate, 2000.

_______. *William Harvey's Natural Philosophy*. New York: Cambridge University Press, 1994.

Pagel, Walter. *Joan Baptista van Helmont: Reformer of Science and Medicine*. Cambridge, England: Cambridge University Press, 1982.

Woolley, Benjamin. *Heal Thyself: Nicholas Culpeper and the Seventeenth Century Struggle to Bring Medicine to the People*. New York: HarperCollins, 2004.

Zimmer, Carl. *Soul Made Flesh: The Discovery of the Brain and How It Changed the World*. New York: Free Press, 2004.

MUSIC

Abraham, Gerald, ed. *The Age of Humanism, 1540-1630*. Vol. 4 in *The New Oxford History of Music*. New York: Oxford University Press, 1968.

_______. *Concert Music, 1630-1750*. Vol. 6 in *The New Oxford History of Music*. New York: Oxford University Press, 1986.

Anthony, James R., et al., eds. *The New Grove French Baroque Masters: Lully, Charpentier, Lalande, Couperin, Rameau*. New York: Norton, 1986.

Arnold, Alison, ed. *South Asia, The Indian Subcontinent*. Vol. 5 in *Garland Encyclopedia of World Music*. New York: Garland, 2000.

Arnold, Denis, et al., eds. *The New Grove Italian Baroque Masters: Monteverdi, Frescobaldi, Cavalli, Corelli, A. Scarlatti, Vivaldi, D. Scarlatti*. New York: W. W. Norton, 1984.

Campbell, Margaret. *Henry Purcell: Glory of His Age*. New York: Oxford University Press, 1995.

Fabbri, Paolo. *Monteverdi*. Translated by Tim Carter. New York: Cambridge University Press, 1994.

Hanning, Barbara Russano. *Concise History of Western Music*. 2d ed. New York: Norton, 2002.

Lewis, Anthony, and Nigel Fortune, eds. *Opera and Church Music: 1630-1750*. Vol. 5 in *The New Oxford History of Music*. London: Oxford University Press, 1975.

Parker, Roger, ed. *The Oxford Illustrated History of Opera*. New York: Oxford University Press, 2001.

Powell, John S. *Music and Theatre in France, 1600-1680*. New York: Oxford University Press, 2000.

Rifkin, Joshua, et al., eds. *The New Grove North European Baroque Masters: Schütz, Froberger, Buxtehude, Purcell, Telemann*. New York: Norton, 1985.

Sadie, Stanley, ed. *The New Grove Dictionary of Music and Musicians*. 2d ed. 29 vols. New York: Grove, 2001.

Smallman, Basil. *Schütz*. New York: Oxford University Press, 2000.

Stone, Ruth M., ed. *Africa*. Vol. 1 in *Garland Encyclopedia of World Music*. New York: Garland, 1998.

NATIVE AMERICANS

Adorno, Rolena. *Guaman Poma: Writing and Resistance in Colonial Peru*. 2d ed. Austin: University of Texas Press, 2000.

Allen, Paula Gunn. *Pocahontas: Medicine Woman, Spy, Entrepreneur, Diplomat*. San Francisco, Calif.: HarperSanFrancisco, 2003.

Bourne, Russell. *The Red King's Rebellion: Racial Politics in New England, 1675-1678*. New York: Atheneum, 1990.

Cave, Alfred. *The Pequot War*. Amherst: University of Massachusetts Press, 1996.

Drake, James David. *King Philip's War: Civil War in New England, 1675-1676*. Amherst: University of Massachusetts Press, 1999.

Josephy, Alvin M., Jr. *Five Hundred Nations: An Illustrated History of the North American Indians*. New York: Alfred A. Knopf, 1994.

Price, David. *Love and Hate in Jamestown: John Smith, Pocahontas, and the Heart of a New Nation*. New York: Knopf, 2003.

Rountree, Helen C. *Pocahontas' People: The Powhattan Indians of Virginia Through Four Centuries*. Norman: University of Oklahoma Press, 1990.

Waters, Frank. *Brave Are My People: Indian Heroes Not Forgotten*. Santa Fe, N.Mex.: Clear Light, 1993.

NETHERLANDS

Dash, Mike. *Tulipomania: The Story of the World's Most Coveted Flower and the Extraordinary Passions It Aroused*. New York: Crown, 1999.

Israel, Jonathan. *The Dutch Republic: Its Rise, Greatness, and Fall, 1477-1806*. Oxford, England: Clarendon Press, 1995.

Price, J. L. *The Dutch Republic in the Seventeenth Century*. New York: St. Martin's Press, 2002.

Schama, Simon. *The Embarrassment of Riches: An Interpretation of Dutch Culture in the Golden Age*. New York: Vintage, 1997.

OTTOMAN EMPIRE AND THE MIDDLE EAST

Eskandar Beg Monshi. *The History of Shah ʿAbbās the Great*. 2 vols. Translated by Roger M. Savory. Boulder, Colo.: Westview Press, 1978.

Imber, Colin. *The Ottoman Empire, 1300-1650: The Structure of Power*. New York: Palgrave, 2002.

Jackson, Peter, and Laurence Lockhart, eds. *The Cambridge History of Iran*. Vol. 6 in *The Timurid and Safavid Periods*. New York: Cambridge University Press, 1986.

McCarthy, Justin. *The Ottoman Turks*. New York: Longman, 1997.

Melville, Charles, ed. *Safavid Persia: The History and Politics of an Islamic Society*. New York: St. Martin's Press, 1996.

Murphey, Rhoads. *Ottoman Warfare, 1500-1700*. New Brunswick, N.J.: Rutgers University Press, 1999.

Savory, Roger M. *Iran Under the Safavids*. Cambridge, England: Cambridge University Press, 1980.

Somel, Selcuk Aksin. *Historical Dictionary of the Ottoman Empire*. Lanham, Md.: Scarecrow Press, 2003.

PHILOSOPHY

Bordo, Susan, ed. *Feminist Interpretations of René Descartes*. University Park: Pennsylvania State University Press, 1999.

Broad, Jacqueline. *Women Philosophers of the Seventeenth Century*. New York: Cambridge University Press, 2002.

Chappell, Vere, ed. *The Cambridge Companion to Locke*. New York: Cambridge University Press, 1994.

_______. *Seventeenth Century British Philosophers*. New York: Garland, 1992.

Cottingham, John, ed. *The Cambridge Companion to Descartes*. New York: Cambridge University Press, 1992.

Dunn, John. *Locke: A Very Short Introduction*. Rev. ed. New York: Oxford University Press, 2003.

French, Peter A., Howard K. Wettstein, and Bruce Silver, eds. *Renaissance and Early Modern Philosophy*. Malden, Mass.: Blackwell, 2002.

Garrett, Don, ed. *The Cambridge Companion to Spinoza*. New York: Cambridge University Press, 1996.

Gaukroger, Stephen. *Francis Bacon and the Transformation of Early Modern Philosophy*. New York: Cambridge University Press, 2001.

Gaukroger, Stephen, John Schuster, and John Sutton, eds. *Descartes's Natural Philosophy*. New York: Routledge, 2000.

Hammond, Nicholas, ed. *The Cambridge Companion to Pascal*. New York: Cambridge University Press, 2003.

Hunter, Ian. *Rival Enlightenments: Civil and Metaphysical Philosophy in Early Modern Germany*. New York: Cambridge University Press, 2001.

Israel, Jonathan I. *Radical Enlightenment: Philosophy and the Making of Modernity, 1650-1750*. New York: Oxford University Press, 2001.

Knott, Sarah, and Barbara Taylor, eds. *Women, Gender, and Enlightenment, 1650-1850*. New York: Palgrave Macmillan, 2005.

Moriarty, Michael. *Early Modern French Thought: The Age of Suspicion*. New York: Oxford University Press, 2003.

Smith, Steven B. *Spinoza's Book of Life: Freedom and Redemption in the "Ethics."* New Haven, Conn.: Yale University Press, 2003.

Sorrell, Tom, ed. *The Cambridge Companion to Hobbes*. New York: Cambridge University Press, 1996.

Tuck, Richard. *Hobbes: A Very Short Introduction*. New York: Oxford University Press, 2002.

Political Science

Harrison, Ross. *Hobbes, Locke, and Confusion's Masterpiece: An Examination of Seventeenth-Century Political Thought*. New York: Cambridge University Press, 2003.

Sullivan, Vickie B. *Machiavelli, Hobbes, and the Formation of a Liberal Republicanism in England*. New York: Cambridge University Press, 2004.

Tuck, Richard. *Philosophy and Government, 1572-1651*. New York: Cambridge University Press, 1993.

Wolin, Sheldon. *The Politics of Vision: Continuity and Innovation in Western Political Thought*. Expanded ed. Princeton, N.J.: Princeton University Press, 2004.

Religion and Theology

Adair, John. *Puritans, Religion, and Politics in Seventeenth Century England and America*. Stroud, Gloucestershire, England: Sutton, 1998.

Bailey, Richard. *New Light on George Fox and Early Quakerism: The Making and Unmaking of a God*. San Francisco, Calif.: Edwin Mellen Press, 1992.

Baron, Samuel H., and Nancy Shields Kollman, eds. *Religion and Culture in Early Modern Russia and Ukraine*. De Kalb: Northern Illinois University Press, 1995.

Benedict, Philip. *The Faith and Fortunes of France's Huguenots, 1600-1685*. Burlington, Vt.: Ashgate, 2001.

Bremer, Francis J. *John Winthrop: America's Forgotten Founding Father*. New York: Oxford University Press, 2003.

_______, ed. *Puritanism: Transatlantic Perspectives on a Seventeenth-Century Anglo-American Faith*. Boston: Massachusetts Historical Society, 1993.

Bushkovitch, Paul. *Religion and Society in Russia: The Sixteenth and Seventeenth Centuries*. New York: Oxford University Press, 1992.

Byrd, James P., Jr. *The Challenges of Roger Williams: Religious Liberty, Violent Persecution, and the Bible*. Macon, Ga.: Mercer University Press, 2002.

Carden, Allen. *Puritan Christianity in America: Religion and Life in Seventeenth-Century Massachusetts*. Grand Rapids, Mich.: Baker Book House, 1990.

Como, David R. *Blown by the Spirit: Puritanism and the Emergence of an Antinomian Underground in Pre-Civil-War England*. Stanford, Calif.: Stanford University Press, 2004.

Conn, Marie A. *Noble Daughters: Unheralded Women in Western Christianity, Thirteenth to Eighteenth Centuries*. Contributions to the Study of Religion 60. Westport, Conn.: Greenwood Press, 2000.

Cotton, John. *John Cotton on the Churches of New England*. Edited by Larzer Ziff. Cambridge, Mass.: Harvard University Press, 1968.

Crawford, Patricia. *Women and Religion in England, 1500-1720*. New York: Routledge, 1993.

Doran, Susan, and Christopher Durston. *Princes, Pastors, and People: The Church and Religion in England, 1500-1700*. 2d ed. London: Routledge, 2002.

Hall, David D. *Puritans in the New World: A Critical Chronology*. Princeton, N.J.: Princeton University Press, 2004.

Ingle, H. Larry. *First Among Friends: George Fox and the Creation of Quakerism*. New York: Oxford University Press, 1994.

Knoppers, Laura Lunger, ed. *Puritanism and Its Discontents*. Newark: University of Delaware Press, 2003.

Lossky, Nicholas. *Lancelot Andrewes the Preacher, 1555-1626: The Origins of the Mystical Theology of the Church of England*. Translated by Andrew Louth. New York: Oxford University Press, 1991.

McClain, Lisa. *Lest We Be Damned: Practical Innovation and Lived Experience Among Catholics in Protestant England, 1559-1642*. New York: Routledge, 2004.

Mack, Phyllis. *Visionary Women: Ecstatic Prophecy in Seventeenth-Century England*. Berkeley: University of California Press, 1992.

Mentzer, Raymond A., and Andrew Spicer, eds. *Society and Culture in the Huguenot World, 1559-1685*. New York: Cambridge University Press, 2002.

Phillips, Henry. *Church and Culture in Seventeenth-Century France*. New York: Cambridge University Press, 1997.

Scholem, Gershom. *Sabbatai Sevi: The Mystical Messiah*. New York: Littman, 1997.

Spurr, John. *English Puritanism, 1603-1689*. New York: St. Martin's Press, 1998.

Weddle, Meredith Baldwin. *Walking in the Way of Peace: Quaker Pacifism in the Seventeenth Century*. New York: Oxford University Press, 2001.

Wilcox, Catherine M. *Theology and Women's Ministry in Seventeenth-Century English Quakerism: Handmaids of the Lord*. Lewiston, N.Y.: E. Mellen Press, 1995.

Russia and Poland

Anderson, M. S. *Peter the Great*. 2d ed. New York: Longman, 1995.

Cracraft, James. *The Revolution of Peter the Great*. Cambridge, Mass.: Harvard University Press, 2003.

Davies, Norman. *God's Playground: A History of Poland*. 2 vols. New York: Columbia University Press, 1982.

Dunning, Chester S. L. *Russia's First Civil War: The Time of Troubles and the Founding of the Romanov Dynasty*. University Park: Pennsylvania State University Press, 2001.

Hughes, Lindsey. *Russia in the Age of Peter the Great*. New Haven, Conn.: Yale University Press, 1998.

Kotilaine, Jarmo, and Marshall Poe, eds. *Modernizing Muscovy: Reform and Social Change in Seventeenth Century Russia*. London: Routledge Curzon, 2004.

Lukowski, Jerzy, and Hubert Zawadzki. *A Concise History of Poland*. New York: Cambridge University Press, 2001.

Perrie, Maureen. *Pretenders and Popular Monarchism in Early Modern Russia: The False Tsars of the Time of Troubles*. New York: Cambridge University Press, 1995.

Riasanovsky, Nicholas V., and Mark D. Steinberg. *A History of Russia*. 7th ed. New York: Oxford University Press, 2004.

Soloviev, Sergei M. *The First Romanov: Tsar Michael, 1613-1645*. Edited and translated by G. Edward Orchard. 2 vols. Gulf Breeze, Fla.: Academic International Press, 1991-1995.

Ure, John. *The Cossacks: An Illustrated History*. New York: Penguin, 2002.

Science

Albanese, Denise. *New Science, New World*. Durham, N.C.: Duke University Press, 1997.

Aughton, Peter. *Newton's Apple: Isaac Newton and the English Scientific Revolution*. London: Weidenfeld & Nicolson, 2003.

Bennett, Jim, et al. *London's Leonardo: The Life and Work of Robert Hooke*. New York: Oxford University Press, 2003.

Chappell, Vere, ed. *Seventeenth-Century Natural Scientists*. New York: Garland, 1992.

Connor, James A. *Kepler's Witch: An Astronomer's Discovery of Cosmic Order Amid Religious War, Political Intrigue, and the Heresy Trial of His Mother*. San Francisco, Calif.: HarperSanFrancisco, 2004.

Dear, Peter Robert. *Revolutionizing the Sciences: European Knowledge and Its Ambitions, 1500-1700*. Princeton, N.J.: Princeton University Press, 2001.

Dijksterhuis, Fokko Jan. *Lenses and Waves: Christiaan Huygens and the Mathematical Science of Optics in the Seventeenth Century*. Dordrecht, the Netherlands: Kluwer, 2004.

Drake, Stillman. *Galileo at Work: His Scientific Biography*. Mineola, N.Y.: Dover, 2003.

Feingold, Michael. *The Newtonian Moment: Isaac Newton and the Making of Modern Culture*. New York: Oxford University Press, 2004.

Ferguson, Kitty. *Tycho and Kepler: The Unlikely Partnership That Forever Changed Our Understanding of the Heavens*. New York: Walker, 2002.

Fermi, Laura, and Gilberto Bernardini. *Galileo and the Scientific Revolution*. Mineola, N.Y.: Dover, 2003.

Fournier, Marian. *The Fabric of Life: Microscopy in the Seventeenth Century*. Baltimore: Johns Hopkins University Press, 1996.

Gleick, James. *Isaac Newton*. New York: Pantheon Books, 2003.

Henry, John. *Knowledge Is Power: How Magic, the Government, and an Apocalyptic Vision Inspired Francis Bacon to Create Modern Science*. Cambridge, England: Icon, 2004.

Jacob, James R. *The Scientific Revolution: Aspirations and Achievements, 1500-1700*. Atlantic Highlands, N.J.: Humanities Press, 1998.

Jowitt, Claire, and Diane Watt, eds. *The Arts of Seventeenth Century Science: Representations of the Natural World in European and North American Culture*. Burlington, Vt.: Ashgate, 2002.

Kelly, Jason M., ed. *Looking Up: Science and Observation in the Early Modern Period*. New York: Legas, 2002.

Machamer, Peter, ed. *The Cambridge Companion to Galileo*. New York: Cambridge University Press, 1998.

Palmerino, Carla Rita, and J. M. M. H. Thijssen, eds. *The Reception of the Galilean Science of Motion in Seventeenth Century Europe*. Boston: Kluwer Academic, 2004.

Renn, Jürgen. *Galileo in Context*. New York: Cambridge University Press, 2001.

Selin, Helaine, ed. *Encyclopedia of the History of Science, Technology, and Medicine in Non-Western Cultures*. Boston: Kluwer Academic, 1997.

Windelspecht, Michael. *Groundbreaking Scientific Experiments, Inventions, and Discoveries of the Seventeenth Century*. Westport, Conn.: Greenwood Press, 2002.

South America

Abreu, João Capistrano de. *Chapters of Brazil's Colonial History, 1500-1800*. Translated from the Portuguese by Arthur Brakel. New York: Oxford University Press, 1997.

Adorno, Rolena. *Guaman Poma: Writing and Resistance in Colonial Peru*. 2d ed. Austin: University of Texas Press, 2000.

Cohen, Thomas M. *The Fire of Tongues: António Vieira and the Missionary Church in Brazil and Portugal*. Stanford, Calif.: Stanford University Press, 1998.

Fisher, John R., ed. *Peru*. Santa Barbara, Calif.: ABC-CLIO, 1990.

Hunefeldt, Christine. *A Brief History of Peru*. New York: Facts On File, 2004.

Klarén, Peter Flindell. *Peru: Society and Nationhood in the Andes*. New York: Oxford University Press, 2000.

Meade, Teresa A. *A Brief History of Brazil*. New York: Facts On File, 2003.

Reiter, Frederick J. *They Built Utopia: The Jesuit Missions in Paraguay, 1610-1768*. Potomac, Md.: Scripta Humanistica, 1995.

Russell-Wood, A. J. R. *Society and Government in Colonial Brazil, 1500-1822*. Brookfield, Vt.: Variorum, 1992.

Smith, Joseph, and Francisco Vinhosa. *A History of Brazil, 1500-2000: Politics, Economy, Society, Diplomacy*. New York: Longman, 2002.

Spain and Portugal

Anderson, James M. *The History of Portugal*. Westport, Conn.: Greenwood Press, 2000.

Birmingham, David. *A Concise History of Portugal*. New York: Cambridge University Press, 2003.

Carr, Raymond, ed. *Spain: A History*. New York: Oxford University Press, 2000.

Dandelet, Thomas James. *Spanish Rome, 1500-1700*. New Haven, Conn.: Yale University Press, 2001.

Kamen, Henry. *Empire: How Spain Became a World Power, 1492-1763*. New York: HarperCollins, 2003.

_______. *Spain, 1469-1714: A Society in Conflict*. 2d ed. Harlow, England: Longman, 1991.

Lynch, John. *The Hispanic World in Crisis and Change, 1598-1700*. Malden, Mass.: Blackwell, 1992.

Russell-Wood, A. J. R. *The Portuguese Empire, 1415-1808: A World on the Move*. Baltimore: Johns Hopkins University Press, 1998.

Stradling, R. A. *Spain's Struggle for Europe, 1598-1668*. London: Hambledon Press, 1994.

Sweden

Frost, Robert I. *The Northern Wars: War, State, and Society in Northeastern Europe, 1558-1721*. New York: Addison Wesley Longman, 2000.

Kirby, David. *Northern Europe in the Early Modern Period: The Baltic World, 1492-1772*. New York: Longman, 1995.

Lockhart, Paul Douglas. *Sweden in the Seventeenth Century*. New York: Palgrave Macmillan, 2004.

Moberg, Vihelm. *A History of the Swedish People: From Renaissance to Revolution*. Translated by Paul Britten Austin. New York: Dorset Press, 1989.

Oakley, Stewart P. *War and Peace in the Baltic, 1560-1790*. Cambridge, England: Cambridge University Press, 1986.

Roberts, Michael. *The Early Vasas: A History of Sweden, 1523-1611*. Cambridge, England: Cambridge University Press, 1986.

_______. *Gustavus Adolphus*. 2d ed. London: Longman, 1992.

_______. *Swedish Imperial Experience, 1560-1718*. Cambridge, England: Cambridge University Press, 1979.

Theater

Banham, Martin, ed. *A History of Theatre in Africa*. New York: Cambridge University Press, 2004.

Bowers, Faubion. *Japanese Theatre*. 1952. Reprint. Westport, Conn.: Greenwood Press, 1976.

Brandon, James R., ed. *The Cambridge Guide to Asian Theatre*. New York: Cambridge University Press, 1997.

Brandt, George W., ed. *German and Dutch Theatre, 1600-1848*. New York: Cambridge University Press, 1993.

Brereton, Geoffrey. *French Comic Drama From the Sixteenth to the Eighteenth Century*. London: Methuen, 1977.

Brockett, Oscar, and Franklin J. Hildy. *History of the Theatre*. 9th ed. Boston: Allyn and Bacon, 2003.

Carlin, Claire L. *Pierre Corneille Revisited*. New York: Twayne, 1998.

Fei, Faye Chunfang, ed. and trans. *Chinese Theories of Theater and Performance from Confucius to the Present*. Ann Arbor: University of Michigan Press, 1999.

Fisk, Deborah Payne, ed. *The Cambridge Companion to English Restoration Theatre*. New York: Cambridge University Press, 2000.

Ganelin, Charles, and Howard Mancing, eds. *The Golden Age Comedia: Text, Theory, and Performance*. West Lafayette, Ind.: Purdue University Press, 1994.

Gurr, Andrew. *The Shakespearean Stage, 1574-1642*. 3d ed. New York: Cambridge University Press, 1992.

Harp, Richard, and Stanley Stewart, eds. *The Cambridge Companion to Ben Jonson*. New York: Cambridge University Press, 2000.

Hochman, Stanley, ed. *McGraw-Hill Encyclopedia of World Drama: An International Reference Work in Five Volumes*. 2d ed. New York: McGraw-Hill, 1984.

Howe, Elizabeth. *The First English Actresses: Women and Drama, 1660-1700*. New York: Cambridge University Press, 1992.

Kerr, David. *African Popular Theatre: From Pre-colonial Times to the Present Day*. Portsmouth, N.H.: Heinemann, 1995.

Leach, Robert, and Victor Borovsky, eds. *A History of Russian Theatre*. New York: Cambridge University Press, 1999.

Leiter, Samuel L., ed. *A Kabuki Reader: History and Performance*. Armonk, N.Y.: M. E. Sharpe, 2002.

McKendrick, Melveena. *Theatre in Spain, 1490-1700*. Cambridge, England: Cambridge University Press, 1989.

Mackerras, Colin, ed. *Chinese Theater: From Its Origins to the Present Day*. Honolulu: University of Hawaii Press, 1988.

Maraniss, James E. *On Calderón*. Columbia: University of Missouri Press, 1978.

Owen, Susan J. *Restoration Theatre and Crisis*. New York: Oxford University Press, 1996.

Powell, John S. *Music and Theatre in France, 1600-1680*. New York: Oxford University Press, 2000.

Scott, Virginia. *Molière: A Theatrical Life*. New York: Cambridge University Press, 2000.

Tobin, Ronald W. *Jean Racine Revisited*. New York: Twayne, 1991.

TRADE AND COMMERCE

Andrews, Kenneth R. *Trade, Plunder, and Settlement: Maritime Enterprise and the Genesis of the British Empire, 1480-1630*. Cambridge, England: Cambridge University Press, 1984.

Blackburn, Robin. *The Making of New World Slavery: From the Baroque to the Modern, 1492-1800*. London: Verso, 1997.

Bowen, H. V., Margarette Lincoln, and Nigel Rigby, eds. *The Worlds of the East India Company*. Rochester, N.Y.: D. S. Brewer, 2002.

Brewer, John, and Roy Porter, eds. *Consumption and the World of Goods*. London: Routledge, 1993.

Brown, Jennifer S. H. *Strangers in Blood: Fur Trade Company Families in Indian Country*. Norman: University of Oklahoma Press, 1996.

Ekelund, Robert, Jr., and Robert D. Tollison. *Politicized Economies: Monarchy, Monopoly, and Mercantilism*. College Station: Texas A&M University Press, 1997.

Farrington, Anthony. *The English Factory in Japan, 1613-1623*. London: British Library, 1991.

_______. *Trading Places: The East India Company and Asia, 1600-1834*. London: British Library, 2002.

Klein, Herbert S. *The Atlantic Slave Trade*. New York: Cambridge University Press, 1999.

Lawson, Philip. *The East India Company: A History*. London: Longman, 1993.

Loades, David. *England's Maritime Empire: Seapower, Commerce, and Policy, 1490-1690*. New York: Longman, 2000.

Marks, Robert B. *Tigers, Rice, Silk, and Silt: Environment and Economy in Late Imperial South China*. New York: Cambridge University Press, 1998.

Mathee, Rudolph P. *The Politics of Trade in Safavid Iran: Silk for Silver, 1600-1730*. New York: Cambridge University Press, 1999.

Middleton, Arthur Pierce. *Tobacco Coast: A Maritime History of Chesapeake Bay in the Colonial Era*. Baltimore: Johns Hopkins University Press and the Maryland State Archives, 1984.

Overton, Mark. *Agricultural Revolution in England: The Transformation of the Agrarian Economy, 1500-1850*. New York: Cambridge University Press, 1996.

Prakash, Om. *The Dutch East India Company and the Economy of Bengal, 1630-1720*. Princeton, N.J.: Princeton University Press, 1985.

_______. *European Commercial Enterprise in Pre-colonial India*. New York: Cambridge University Press, 1998.

Price, Jacob M. *Tobacco Atlantic Trade: The Chesapeake, London, and Glasgow, 1675-1775*. Brookfield, Vt.: Variorum, 1995.

Reese, Ted. *Soft Gold: A History of the Fur Trade in the Great Lakes Region and Its Impact on Native American Culture*. Bowie, Md.: Heritage Books, 2001.

Stein, Stanley J., and Barbara Stein. *Silver, Trade, and War: Spain and America in the Making of Early Mod-*

ern Europe. Baltimore: Johns Hopkins University Press, 2003.

Thomas, Hugh. *The Slave Trade: The Story of the Atlantic Slave Trade, 1440-1870*. New York: Simon & Schuster, 1997.

Tuck, Patrick, ed. *Britain and the China Trade, 1635-1842*. London: Routledge, 2000.

Wild, Antony. *The East India Company: Trade and Conquest from 1600*. London: HarperCollins, 1999.

Wills, John E., Jr. *Pepper, Guns, and Parleys: The Dutch East India Company and China, 1662-1681*. Cambridge, Mass.: Harvard University Press, 1974.

Winius, George D., and Marcus P. M. Vink. *The Merchant-Warrior Pacified: The VOC (The Dutch East India Company) and Its Changing Political Economy in India*. New York: Oxford University Press, 1991.

WARFARE

Asch, Ronald G. *The Thirty Years' War: The Holy Roman Empire and Europe, 1618-1648*. New York: St. Martin's Press, 1997.

Black, Jeremy. *European Warfare, 1660-1815*. New Haven, Conn.: Yale University Press, 1994.

Chase, Kenneth. *Firearms: A Global History to 1700*. New York: Cambridge University Press, 2003.

Childs, John. *Warfare in the Seventeenth Century*. Washington, D.C.: Smithsonian Books, 2004.

Croxton, Derek. *Peacemaking in Early Modern Europe: Cardinal Mazarin and the Congress of Westphalia, 1643-1648*. Selinsgrove, Pa.: Susquehanna University Press, 1999.

Fissel, Mark Charles. *English Warfare, 1511-1642*. New York: Routledge, 2001.

Graff, David A., and Robin Higham, eds. *A Military History of China*. Boulder, Colo.: Westview Press, 2002.

Hogg, Ian V. *The History of Fortification*. London: Orbis, 1981.

Lee, Stephen J. *The Thirty Years' War*. New York: Routledge, 1991.

Lynn, John A. *The Wars of Louis XIV, 1667-1714*. London: Longman, 1999.

Parker, Geoffrey. *The Cambridge Illustrated History of Warfare*. New York: Cambridge University Press, 2000.

_______, ed. *The Thirty Years' War*. 2d ed. London: Routledge, 1997.

Perrin, Noel. *Giving Up the Gun: Japan's Reversion to the Sword, 1543-1879*. Boston: David R. Godine, 1979.

Powell, John, ed. *Magill's Guide to Military History*. 5 vols. Pasadena, Calif.: Salem Press, 2001.

_______. *Weapons and Warfare*. 2 vols. Pasadena, Calif.: Salem Press, 2002.

Turnbull, Stephen R. *Samurai: The World of the Warrior*. London: Osprey Books, 2003.

Wedgwood, C. V. *The Thirty Years' War*. New Haven, Conn.: Yale University Press, 1939. Reprint. New York: Methuen, 1981.

WOMEN'S STUDIES

Berkin, Carol. *First Generations: Women in Colonial America*. New York: Hill and Wang, 1996.

Berkin, Carol, and Leslie Horowitz, eds. *Women's Voices, Women's Lives: Documents in Early American History*. Boston: Northeastern University Press, 1998.

Bordo, Susan, ed. *Feminist Interpretations of René Descartes*. University Park: Pennsylvania State University Press, 1999.

Capp, B. S. *When Gossips Meet: Women, Family, and Neighbourhood in Early Modern England*. New York: Oxford University Press, 2003.

Conn, Marie A. *Noble Daughters: Unheralded Women in Western Christianity, Thirteenth to Eighteenth Centuries*. Contributions to the Study of Religion 60. Westport, Conn.: Greenwood Press, 2000.

Crawford, Patricia. *Women and Religion in England, 1500-1720*. New York: Routledge, 1993.

Crawford, Patricia, and Laura Gowing, eds. *Women's Worlds in Seventeenth-Century England*. London: Routledge, 2000.

Daybell, James. *Women and Politics in Early Modern England, 1450-1700*. Burlington, Vt.: Ashgate, 2004.

Erickson, Amy Louise. *Women and Property in Early Modern England*. New York: Routledge, 1993.

Fraser, Antonia. *The Weaker Vessel: Woman's Lot in Seventeenth-Century England*. New York: Vantage Books, 1984.

Frith, Valerie, ed. *Women and History: Voices of Early Modern England*. Concord, Ont.: Irwin, 1997.

Hambleton, Else L. *Daughters of Eve: Pregnant Brides and Unwed Mothers in Seventeenth Century Massachusetts*. New York: Routledge, 2004.

Knott, Sarah, and Barbara Taylor, eds. *Women, Gender, and Enlightenment, 1650-1850*. New York: Palgrave Macmillan, 2005.

Laurence, Anne. *Women in England, 1500-1760: A Social History*. New York: St. Martin's Press, 1994.

Mack, Phyllis. *Visionary Women: Ecstatic Prophecy in Seventeenth-Century England.* Berkeley: University of California Press, 1992.

Mays, Dorothy A. *Women in Early America: Struggle, Survival, and Freedom in a New World.* Santa Barbara, Calif.: ABC-CLIO, 2004.

Mikesell, Margaret, and Adele Seeff, eds. *Culture and Change: Attending to Early Modern Women.* Newark: University of Delaware Press, 2003.

Moore, Dorothy. *The Letters of Dorothy Moore, 1612-1664: The Friendships, Marriage, and Intellectual Life of a Seventeenth-Century Woman.* Compiled by Lynette Hunter. Burlington, Vt.: Ashgate, 2004.

Peters, Christine. *Women in Early Modern Britain, 1450-1640.* New York: Palgrave Macmillan, 2004.

Treckel, Paula A. *To Comfort the Heart: Women in Seventeenth-Century America.* New York: Twayne, 1996.

Van Kirk, Sylvia. *Many Tender Ties: Women in Fur-Trade Society.* Norman: University of Oklahoma Press, 1983.

Wilcox, Catherine M. *Theology and Women's Ministry in Seventeenth-Century English Quakerism: Handmaids of the Lord.* Lewiston, N.Y.: E. Mellen Press, 1995.

Williams, Selma R., and Pamela Williams Adelman. *Riding the Nightmare: Women and Witchcraft from the Old World to Colonial Salem.* New York: HarperPerennial, 1992.

—Rebecca Kuzins

ELECTRONIC RESOURCES

WEB SITES

The permanence of the URL's for the sites listed below cannot be guaranteed. However, long-standing sites—such as those of university departments, national organizations, and government agencies—generally maintain links when sites move or upgrade their offerings.

GENERAL

Avalon Project at Yale Law School
http://www.yale.edu/lawweb/avalon/avalon.htm
A collection of digitized documents that are relevant to the fields of law, history, economics, politics, diplomacy, and government. The documents are organized chronologically, with a separate page entitled "Pre-Eighteenth-Century Documents" that includes many digitized items from the seventeenth century. Among these items are charters and constitutions for American colonies, the Articles of Confederation of the United Colonies of New England, the English Bill of Rights, and the Treaty (or Peace) of Westphalia.

The Catholic Encyclopedia
http://www.newadvent.org/cathen/
The electronic version of this reference book contains more than eleven thousand alphabetically arranged articles exploring the entire range of Catholic interests. The encyclopedia is particularly good for information about religion, with articles about Puritans, Calvinists, Jansenists, Quakers, Huguenots, and other religious groups. It also contains an article about the Thirty Years' War and information about Catholics who have played important roles in history, such as Louis XIV, Cardinal de Richelieu, and Cardinal Jules Mazarin, and other prominent seventeenth century figures.

Development of Western Civilization: World History, Baroque
http://history.evansville.net/baroque.html#Introduction
This page about the Baroque era is part of a Web site that Nancy Mautz, a professor at the University of Evansville, designed for her Western Civilization course. The page contains links to relevant information on people, places, events, art, architecture, literature, drama, music, dance, and daily life.

History World International
http://history-world.org/
This recently revised site contains a wealth of historical information covering the Neolithic period to the present. Users can access the "Contents A-Z" page for a list of pages on the Americas; art and architecture; Asia and the Middle East; Africa, Australia, and the Sea Islands; Europe; science; world religions; and other general topics. The "Europe" section includes pages on European absolutism and power politics, Louis XIV, and the Iberian Golden Age; the science section includes pages about Galileo and Sir Isaac Newton, while the arts and architecture section contains a page about the Baroque era.

Internet Modern History Sourcebook
http://www.fordham.edu/halsall/mod/modsbook.html
Paul Halsall of Fordham University has compiled a collection of primary source materials from various regions and eras. This site on modern history offers pages headed "Early Modern World," "Everyday Life," "Absolutism," "Constitutionalism," and "The Scientific Revolution," which feature primary documents relevant to the seventeenth century.

Seventeenth Century Net.Net: Gateway to the Renaissance and Seventeenth Century on the Net
http://www.17thcenturynet.net/
This site is a collection of thousands of links to information about seventeenth century British literature and history, as well as Western art, music, architecture, philosophy, and witchcraft. There also are links to Web sites for e-journals, societies, and organizations.

WebChron: Web Chronology Project
http://campus.northpark.edu/history/webchron/
The Web Chronology Project was created by the History Department of North Park University in Chicago. It includes a series of hyperlinked time lines for use in

history classes and chronologies of developments in Africa, China, India, East Asia, and Southern Asia, as well as in Islam, Christianity, and Judaism. Also, there are time lines for art, music, literature, and speculative thought in the Western tradition.

Africa

Internet African History Sourcebook
http://www.fordham.edu/halsall/africa/africasbook.html
This page of the Internet History Sourcebook features primary source materials about African history, including documents regarding African societies, the impact of slavery, and European imperialism.

Slavery @ the Cape
This site about slavery at the Cape of Good Hope in Dutch and British South Africa is part of the Dutch East India Company Web site described in the "Trade and Commerce" section (below).

Art and Architecture

Art History Resources on the Web
http://witcombe.sbc.edu/ARTHLinks.html
Chris Witcombe, a professor of art history at Sweet Briar College in Virginia, has compiled this extensive list of art history Web sites. One section specifically deals with seventeenth century Baroque art, and there are links to sites on Asian art and to art museums and galleries around the world.

A Digital Archive of Architecture
http://www.bc.edu/bc_org/avp/cas/fnart/arch/17arch_europe.html
Professor Jeffery Howe of Boston College has designed this slide collection of architecturally significant buildings. The site contains five examples of seventeenth century European architecture, including Versailles, near Paris and the Château de Vaux-le-Vicomte near Melun, France. There are also photographs of Rembrandt's house in Amsterdam, Peter Paul Rubens's house in Antwerp, and the Church of St. Charles Borromeo in Antwerp, which Rubens helped design.

A Digital Archive of American Architecture
http://www.bc.edu/bc_org/avp/cas/fnart/fa267/fa267.html
Another Web site by Jeffery Howe, this one specializes in American architecture and features photographs of seventeenth century houses, churches, and industrial buildings.

Metropolitan Museum of Art: Time Line of Art History
http://www.metmuseum.org/toah/splash.htm
The museum's Web site describes itself as "a chronological, geographical, and thematic exploration of the history of art from around the world, as illustrated especially by the Metropolitan Museum of Art's collection." Time lines contain photographs of artworks, maps, and chronologies for specific eras and areas of the world. There also are numerous pages devoted to specific topics, including European art in the Baroque and Rococo, African art, Asian art, and Islamic art.

Renaissance and Baroque Architecture: Architectural History 102
http://www.lib.virginia.edu/dic/colls/arh102/
This collection of images is a project of the University of Virginia Library Digital Image Center. The site contains photographs of art and architecture in Italy and other European countries from the fifteenth through seventeenth centuries.

World Art Treasures
http://www.bergerfoundation.ch/
A collection of more than 100,000 slides compiled by art historian Jacques-Édouard Berger. The site includes pages containing slides of seventeenth century art as well as slides of paintings by Rembrandt, Peter Paul Rubens, Jan van Eyck, Jan Vermeer, and other artists.

Asia

Internet East Asian History Sourcebook
http://www.fordham.edu/halsall/eastasia/eastasiasbook.html
One of the highly regarded "sourcebook" projects of Fordham University, maintained by Paul Halsall. This site has historical and cultural information on China, Japan, and Korea, and it also features information about European exploration of East Asia and the activities of the private European companies that mounted trade expeditions and exploited the region.

Manas
http://www.sscnet.ucla.edu/southasia/index.html
Vinay Lal, associate professor of history at the University of California, Los Angeles, has created this Web site with a vast array of information about the history, politics, and culture of India. The section titled "British India" includes information about the origins of the East India Company and its activities in India. The section on architecture features photos and information about the Taj Mahal.

Tokugawa Japan, 1603-1868
http://www.wsu.edu:8080/~dee/TOKJAPAN/TOKJAPAN.HTM
This Web site, created by Professor Richard Hooker of Washington State University for his world civilization course, describes Tokugawa Japan and covers Tokugawa Ieyasu, daily life during this period, Neo-Confucianism, and kabuki.

Colonial America

Internet Modern History Sourcebook: Colonial North America
http://www.fordham.edu/halsall/mod/modsbook07.html
A collection of links to primary source materials, featuring documents from seventeenth century colonies in Quebec, Virginia, New England, and Maryland. Also includes a selection of documents written by John Winthrop, Anne Bradstreet, and William Penn.

The Pilgrim Story
http://www.pilgrimhall.org/museum.htm
Pilgrim Hall Museum in Plymouth, Massachusetts, offers a Web site about the Puritans and the Plymouth Colony. This page of the site contains links with information about the Pilgrims' history in Europe, their voyage on the *Mayflower*, and the founding and demise of their colony. The site also describes the colonists' relations with the Native Americans, including a page about King Philip's (Metacom's) War.

The Plymouth Colony Archive Project
http://etext.lib.virginia.edu/users/deetz/
This collection of searchable texts is continually updated and contains a range of documents regarding the Plymouth Colony between the years 1620 and 1691. Court records, colony laws, seventeenth century journals and memoirs, probate inventories, wills, town plans, maps, and fort plans are among the documents included. There also are biographical profiles of some of the colonists and information about the colony's architecture.

Salem Witch Trials: Documentary Archive and Transcription Project
http://jefferson.village.virginia.edu/salem/home.html
A compendium of primary sources and other information about the infamous witch trials, held from February, 1692, through April, 1693. The site provides transcriptions of court records of the trials, with an index of names that allows users to find specific references to people cited in the transcripts. There also are records and files of the quarterly courts of Essex County from 1636 through 1686, additional court records from various archives, and the record books from Salem Village and the Salem Village Church. In addition to these primary sources, the site contains maps and biographies of people associated with the trials.

U-S-History.Com
http://www.u-s-history.com/pages/eras.html#colonial
An overview of American history, including information about the colonial era. There are pages about each of the original thirteen colonies, with information about Native Americans, exploration and settlement, and the colony's role in the American Revolution. The site also contains information about the New England Confederation, the Dominion of New England, mercantilism, and Native American wars.

Virtual Jamestown
http://www.virtualjamestown.org/siteindex.html
This history of the Jamestown colony includes an interactive flash map that allows users to re-create John Smith's voyages to Chesapeake Bay. It also contains original maps of the colony, public records, and registers of indentured servants who were sent from England to foreign plantations between 1654 and 1686. These registers are searchable, allowing users to hunt for information about individual servants.

Economics

The History of Economic Thought Website
http://cepa.newschool.edu/het/
Created by the Department of Economics at the New School for Social Research, this site offers user-

friendly information about economics. It features information about more than five hundred economists, including such seventeenth century natural law philosophers as John Locke, Thomas Hobbes, Samuel von Pufendorf, and Hugo Grotius. An alphabetical index of economists allows users to access bibliographies, selections from written works, and overviews of economic theory for a specific economist. The site also contains pages of information about schools of economic thought and links to other Web sites regarding economics.

Exploration

Age of Exploration

http://www.mariner.org//educationalad/ageofex/intro.php

This collection of materials about exploration from ancient times through 1768 was compiled by The Mariners' Museum in Newport News, Virginia. The site provides information on Henry Hudson, Samuel de Champlain, Sieur de La Salle, and other explorers.

European Discovery: South Pacific and Indo-West Pacific

http://www.muffley.net/pacific/default.htm

An overview of European exploration in Australia and New Zealand, containing pages about the seventeenth century Dutch landfall discoveries of Australia and the voyages of Abel Janszoon Tasman and William Dampier.

Virtual Museum of New France

http://www.civilization.ca/vmnf/vmnfe.asp

A project of the Canadian Museum of Civilization, this site focuses on French exploration and settlement of North America. It includes information on the expeditions of Samuel de Champlain, Jacques Marquette, Louis Jolliet, Sieur de La Salle, and other French explorers, as well as maps, glossaries, and information about the education of children in New France.

France

Château de Versailles

http://www.chateauversailles.fr/en/

The official site of the Château de Versailles provides a great deal of information about life in Louis XIV's France. The site describes the château and other places related to it, including the Trianon and the park designed by André Le Nôtre. In addition, there is a description of life at Louis's court, including his daily schedule, court politics, and entertainment. Additional pages provide biographies of Louis XIV and other historical figures. The information on the site is available in English, French, Spanish, and Japanese.

France 1610 to 1715

http://www.historylearningsite.co.uk/france_1610_to_1715.htm

This is one of the pages contained in History Learning Site, a Web site created by British history teachers to provide students with Web-based materials. The page about seventeenth century French history includes information about Louis XIII, religion during Louis XIII's reign, Marie de Médicis, and Cardinal de Richelieu.

Germany

Frederick William, the Great Elector

http://www.historylearningsite.co.uk/frederick_william1.htm

Another page from the History Learning Site, featuring information about Frederick William of Brandenburg-Prussia and his son, Frederick I. The site describes Frederick William's attempts to modernize Brandenburg-Prussia, his army, and his foreign policy.

Great Britain

British Civil Wars, Commonwealth, and Protectorate, 1638-1660

http://www.british-civil-wars.co.uk/

A Web-based overview of this period in British history, containing time lines, biographies, and military history. The site also has a useful list of links to other Web resources.

English Civil War

http://www.spartacus.schoolnet.co.uk/CivilWar.htm

Provides a wide range of information about the battles, events, and issues in the war, as well as biographies of military leaders. The site also places the war within the context of English society, with biographies of political and religious figures, writers, and artists, and information about social movements, such as the Diggers and the Levellers. A separate section of the site contains information about religious groups that were prominent in this period, including the Puritans, Quakers, and Anabaptists.

Monarchs of Britain
http://www.britannia.com/history/h6f.html
This informative, easy-to-use site contains biographies and portraits of the queens and kings who have ruled England since 829. There are also pages of information about the governments of Oliver Cromwell and Richard Cromwell.

The Oliver Cromwell Website
http://www.olivercromwell.org/
A wealth of Cromwelliana, compiled by the Cromwell Association and the Cromwell Museum. The site includes a time line of Oliver Cromwell's life, a brief biography, quotations by Cromwell, and information about the Protectorate and the 1654 Union of Scotland with England.

Time Traveler's Guide to Stuart England
http://www.channel4.com/history/microsites/H/history/guide17/part01.html
An extremely comprehensive review of seventeenth century British history, compiled by British television's Channel 4. The site includes an extensive time line of events occurring from 1603 until 1714, with a separate page of information about each event based on the book *A Century of Troubles: England in the Seventeenth Century*, by Stevie Davies. Other pages contain a time line of the Civil War; biographies of prominent political figures; and information about the arts, science, religion, and politics.

LITERATURE

The Cambridge History of English and American Literature: An Encyclopedia in Eighteen Volumes
http://www.bartleby.com/cambridge/
An exhaustive examination of all forms of writing in Great Britain and the United States, including literature, legal and church writing, journalism, pamphlets, and philosophy. Volumes 4 through 8 contain articles about various aspects of seventeenth century literature and drama. Volume 7 includes an article about John Milton. Volume 15 focuses on literature from the colonial United States.

Luminarium: Early Seventeenth Century (1603-1660)
http://www.luminarium.org/sevenlit/
Created by Anniina Jokinen in 1996 and continually updated since, this site includes the literature of John Milton, John Donne, Ben Jonson, Lancelot Andrewes, and many others. A collection of essays and articles concerning the literature of this period, information about the Metaphysical and Cavalier poets, and links to Web sites about English literature and history are also included.

The Milton Reading Room
http://www.dartmouth.edu/~milton/reading_room/index.shtml
Designed by Thomas Luxon and his students, of Dartmouth University's English Department, this site contains the works of John Milton, including *Paradise Lost*, *Paradise Regain'd*, and shorter poems and prose. The site is fully annotated, including definitions of words and phrases and background about the works. There is also an extensive bibliography.

Voice of the Shuttle: Literatures (Other than English)
http://vos.ucsb.edu/browse.asp?id=2719
This site is a page from Voice of the Shuttle, a collection of Web resources about the humanities compiled by professors at the University of California, Santa Barbara. The page links to a wide assortment of sites about world literature in general, as well as to more specific sites about literature in Arabic, Chinese, French, German, Italian, Japanese, Persian, Spanish, and other languages.

Voice of the Shuttle: Renaissance & Seventeenth Century
http://vos.ucsb.edu/browse.asp?id=2749
Another page from the excellent Voice of the Shuttle, this site contains links to English-language essays, literary criticism, and examples of prose, poetry, and drama from a long list of authors.

MATHEMATICS

The MacTutor History of Mathematics Archive
http://www-groups.dcs.st-and.ac.uk/~history/
A comprehensive Web site, created and maintained by the school of mathematics and statistics at the University of St. Andrews, Scotland, that features bi-

ographies of prominent mathematicians. These can be accessed by either an alphabetical or a chronological index. The site also contains information about the history of mathematics, with separate pages explaining important mathematical discoveries and concepts.

Mathematicians of the Seventeenth and Eighteenth Centuries
http://www.maths.tcd.ie/pub/HistMath/People/RBallHist.html
This page, part of a Web site maintained by the school of mathematics at Trinity College in Dublin, Ireland, links to biographical information about prominent mathematicians of these two centuries. The biographies are adapted from *A Short Account of the History of Mathematics* by W. W. Rouse Ball (4th ed., 1908). René Descartes, Pierre de Fermat, Blaise Pascal, Christiaan Huygens, Marin Mersenne, Evangelista Torricelli, Sir Isaac Newton, Gottfried Wilhelm Leibniz, the Bernoulli family, and Colin Maclaurin are among the mathematicians covered.

Military History

Military History Encyclopedia on the Web
http://www.rickard.karoo.net/main.html
Compiled by three British professors, this Web-based encyclopedia features articles about wars and battles throughout history. The information can be assessed with several indexes, including alphabetical listings of biographies; wars, campaigns, and treaties; battles; weapons, equipment, and units; and countries. The Thirty Years' War and the three Anglo-Dutch Wars are included.

The Thirty Years' War
http://www.pipeline.com/%7Ecwa/TYWHome.htm
A narrative of the war, including information about its causes, the various phases and battles, and the Treaty (or Peace) of Westphalia. The site also features a bibliography and a listing of Web resources.

Music

Baroque Music: Composers
http://baroque-music.com/frames/info/composers.shtml
This page from a Web site on Baroque music has biographical information on thirty-six composers, including Johann Sebastian Bach, Heinrich Schütz, Arcangelo Corelli, Claudio Monteverdi, and Henry Purcell.

The Classical MIDI Connection: The Baroque Period
http://www.classicalmidiconnection.com/cmc/baroque.html
A collection of MIDI (musical instrument digital interface) files, which enable people to listen to music with most Web browsers. The site has an alphabetized list of composers with links to MIDI files of their music and a separate page devoted to music of Baroque era composers, including Jean-Baptiste Lully, Arcangelo Corelli, Johann Pachelbel, and Henry Purcell.

Essentials of Music
http://www.essentialsofmusic.com/
Built around Sony's Essential Classics music series, the site includes an overview of Baroque music from 1600 to 1750, and biographies of five Baroque composers: Claudio Monteverdi, Henry Purcell, Johann Sebastian Bach, Antonio Vivaldi, and Georg Frederick Handel. It also contains about two hundred musical excerpts from the classics music series in RealPlayer format.

Music at UCC: Web Resources for Research in Music
http://www.music.ucc.ie/wrrm/index.html
University College, Cork, Ireland, has produced this comprehensive list of links to Web sites about music. There is a separate page about seventeenth century music, with links to sites about Heinrich Schütz, Henry Purcell, and other composers, as well as links to information about types of repertories, such as ballads, songs, and liturgical music. The site also contains a separate page with links to information about seventeenth and eighteenth century opera and theater music.

Music History 102: A Guide to Western Composers and Their Music from the Middle Ages to the Present
http://www.ipl.org/div/mushist/#baro
This site, part of the Internet Public Library's authoritative collection of Web links, provides an overview of music in six eras, including the Baroque age. It features sound files that provide a sample of representative music for the era. The section on Baroque

music includes information about harpsichord music, Claudio Monteverdi, Johann Sebastian Bach, and Antonio Vivaldi.

Philosophy

Internet Encyclopedia of Philosophy

http://www.utm.edu/research/iep/

A collection of articles written by philosophy professors, including information about René Descartes, Baruch Spinoza, John Locke, and Thomas Hobbes. An alphabetical list of article subjects helps users find information quickly.

EpistemeLinks.com

http://www.epistemelinks.com

EpistemeLinks.com contains about 16,500 cataloged links to philosophy Web sites. It links to pages describing the philosophy of specific historical eras, including a page about philosophy of the early modern era with links to information about René Descartes, Baruch Spinoza, Thomas Hobbes, John Locke, Gottfried Wilhelm Leibniz, Blaise Pascal, Marin Mersenne, Sor Juana Inés de la Cruz, and others.

Studia Spinoziana

http://www.mtsu.edu/~rbombard/RB/spinoza.new.html

This page is part of the Web site that Professor Ron Bombardi created for his philosophy courses at Middle Tennessee State University. The page contains links to information about Baruch Spinoza's life, times, and philosophy. In addition, there are numerous links to information about seventeenth and eighteenth century studies, including Web sites about Pierre Bayle, Antoni van Leeuwenhoek, Jan Vermeer, René Descartes, and Gottfried Wilhelm Leibniz.

Religion

America as a Religious Refuge: The Seventeenth Century

http://www.loc.gov/exhibits/religion/re101.html

This information about the seventeenth century is contained in "Religion and the Founding of the American Republic," a Web site accompanying an exhibit at the Library of Congress. The exhibit examined how the colonies that eventually became the United States of America were founded by deeply religious settlers, who emigrated to the New World in order to practice their faiths freely. The site describes religious persecution in Europe and colonial America and explains how Puritans, Jews, Quakers, Roman Catholics, and others established New World communities.

Divining America: Religion and National Culture

http://www.nhc.rtp.nc.us:8080/tserve/divam.htm

TeacherServe, an organization that helps teachers design lesson plans, created this site to give students a better understanding of the role religion played in developing the United States. Although the site contains instructions for teachers, it also features a great deal of historical information and links to related Web sites. The section on the seventeenth and eighteenth centuries features pages on Native American religion, Puritanism, witchcraft in Salem, religious pluralism in the Middle Colonies, the role of the Church of England in colonial America, and American colonial women and family life.

Russia

E-Museum @ Minnesota State University, Mankato

http://www.mnsu.edu/emuseum/history/russia/timeoftroubles.html

http://www.mnsu.edu/emuseum/history/russia/romanov.html

The university has created a collection of Web sites with information on a wide range of subjects, including Russian history. Two of the site's pages describe the Time of Troubles and the origins and reign of the Romanov Dynasty.

Peter the Great

http://www.historylearningsite.co.uk/peter_the_great.htm

The History Learning Site's pages about Peter the Great provide biographical information, as well as a discussion of his military, domestic, and government reforms.

Science, Technology, and Medicine

Eric Weisstein's World of Science

http://scienceworld.wolfram.com/

This online reference source has been compiled by a research scientist and former professor of astronomy. It contains comprehensive encyclopedias of astronomy, chemistry, mathematics, and physics, as well as brief biographies and pictures of noteworthy scientists.

The Galileo Project
http://galileo.rice.edu/
Created and maintained by Rice University, this site provides information about the life and work of Galileo and the science of his time. The site includes a searchable database with information about 631 prominent scientists from the sixteenth and seventeenth centuries, discussions of specific inventions and discoveries, a time line of Galileo's life, maps, a glossary, a bibliography, and links to related Web pages.

History of Western Biomedicine
http://www.mic.ki.se/West.html#West3
Compiled by Sweden's Karolinska Institutet, this site contains links to information about medical history. The section entitled "Modern Period, 1601-" offers links to sites about seventeenth century medicine, including information about blood circulation, optics, Antoni van Leeuwenhoek, and the Jesuits and the sciences.

Seventeenth Century Inventions, 1600-1699
http://inventors.about.com/library/inventors/b11600's.htm
About.com has created a time line of inventions, with links to additional information about some of the inventions and inventors of the century. Hans Lippershey's telescope, Otto von Guericke's air pump, and Evangelista Torricelli's barometer are among the inventions covered.

Sweden

Sweden from 1611 to 1718
Http://www.historylearningsite.co.uk/sweden_1611_to_1718.htm
This History Learning Site page focuses on seventeenth and early eighteenth century Swedish history, with information about Gustavus II Adolphus, Axel Oxenstierna, Queen Christina, Sweden and the Thirty Years' War, and the Great Northern War.

Theater

Renaissance Drama from Its Medieval Origins to the Closing of the Theatres
http://athena.english.vt.edu/~jmooney/renmats/drama.htm
A brief overview of English theater from the Middle Ages until the Puritans closed the theaters in 1642, compiled by a professor of English at Virginia Polytechnic Institute and State University. The site includes information about the plays and lives of Ben Jonson, Francis Beaumont, and John Fletcher.

Theatre Database: Seventeenth Century Theatre
http://www.theatredatabase.com/17th_century/
A comprehensive set of links to information about theater history, this site features a page devoted to the seventeenth century. Included are links to information about Lope de Vega Carpio, Pedro Calderón de la Barca, Pierre Corneille, John Dryden, Ben Jonson, Molière, and Jean Racine. The site also offers articles about Spanish drama, the origins of opera, the closure of the English theaters in 1642, and theater in Restoration England.

Trade and Commerce

Dutch East India Company (Verenigde Oostindishe Compagnie)
http://batavia.rug.ac.be/
This site, in English and Dutch, offers valuable information about the history of the Dutch East India Company, including a virtual tour with images of Europe and the East Indies in the seventeenth and eighteenth centuries. Most impressive is its lengthy section titled "Slavery @ the Cape," containing information about slavery at the Cape of Good Hope in Dutch and British South Africa. Included here is a copy of the Cape Slave Code, a time line of developments in South African history, demographic statistics about slavery, and a list of archival information on the slave trade in South Africa.

Women

A Celebration of Women Writers: Writers Living Between 1601 and 1700
http://digital.library.upenn.edu/women/_generate/1601-1700.html
Mary Mark Ockerbloom has spent years compiling this compendium of women's literature. The site includes a separate page listing women writers of the seventeenth century, with links to works by some of the writers, including Anne Bradstreet, Margaret Cavendish, Marie-Catherine Hortense Desjardins, and Sor Juana Inés de la Cruz. The site can be searched by an author's name, type of literature, country, and the authors' ethnicity.

Seventeenth Century Women Poets
http://www.uni-koeln.de/phil-fak/englisch/kurse/17c/index.htm
Created for a course at the University of Köln (Cologne), Germany, this site features biographical information and poetry from several women, including Anne Bradstreet and Aphra Behn. The site also contains articles, essays, and links to other resources about this period.

The Sor Juana Inés de la Cruz Project
http://www.dartmouth.edu/~sorjuana/
This site, sponsored by the department of Spanish and Portuguese at Dartmouth College, is a self-described celebration of "the greatest poet the American continent produced in the seventeenth century." It contains the full texts of Sor Juana Inés de la Cruz's plays, poetry, and prose, as well as a chronology of her life and a bibliography.

Women Artists: Renaissance and Baroque Painters, Sculptors, and Engravers
http://womenshistory.about.com/library/weekly/aa021230a.htm
This page, part of About.com's Women's History Guide, contains brief biographies of seventeenth century women artists. The site also provides links to other Web resources.

Women Artists: Self-Portraits & Representations of Womanhood from the Medieval Period to the Present
http://www.csupomona.edu/%7Eplin/women/womenart.html
California State University, Pomona, sponsors this Web site about women artists and their depiction of women. The site features portraits, brief biographies, and bibliographies of women artists. The information is arranged chronologically, with two pages devoted to the sixteenth and seventeenth century and to the seventeenth and eighteenth century artists.

SUBSCRIPTION WEB SITES

The following sites are Web based but are available to paying subscribers only. Many public, college, and university libraries subscribe to these sources. Readers are encouraged to ask reference librarians if these resources are available at their local or school libraries.

General

Oxford Reference Online
http://www.oxfordreference.com
A virtual reference library of more than one hundred dictionaries and reference books published by Oxford University Press, *Oxford Reference Online* contains information about a broad range of subjects, including art, architecture, military history, science, religion, philosophy, political and social science, and literature. The site also features English-language and bilingual dictionaries, as well as collections of quotations and proverbs.

Oxford Scholarship Online
www.oxfordscholarship.com
Oxford Scholarship Online currently contains the electronic versions of more than 750 books about economics, finance, philosophy, political science, and religion that are published by Oxford University Press. The site features advanced searching capabilities and links to other online sources.

Art

Grove Art Online
www.groveart.com
This authoritative and comprehensive site provides information about the visual arts from prehistory to the present. In addition to its more than 130,000 art images, the site contains articles on fine arts, architecture, China, South America, Africa and other world cultures, as well as biographies and links to hundreds of museum and gallery Web sites.

History

Greenwood Daily Life Online
http://dailylife.greenwood.com/
The site focuses on what its creator, Greenwood Publishing Group, describes as "the billions of anonymous men and women too often forgotten by historical studies, but without whose lives human history would be meaningless." It contains information from *The Greenwood Encyclopedia of Daily Life* and other sources describing religious, domestic, economic, intellectual, and educational life. Maps, illustrations, time lines, and teacher lesson plans are also included.

Music

Classical Music Library
http://www.classical.com/
This streaming music service contains more than thirty-five thousand music tracks, with about two thousand tracks added monthly. It also features program notes, images, playlists, and links to biographical and humanities databases.

Grove Music Online
www.grovemusic.com
This online version of the highly regarded *The New Grove Dictionary of Music and Musicians* features thousands of articles on musicians, instruments, musical techniques, genres, and styles. In addition to its articles and biographies, the site provides more than five hundred audio clips of music, and links to images, sound, and related Web sites.

Science

Access Science: McGraw-Hill Encyclopedia of Science and Technology Online
http://www.accessscience.com
This site, an online version of *McGraw Hill Encyclopedia of Science and Technology*, contains all articles found in the most recent edition of that reference book. The site includes biographies of scientists, definitions of scientific terms, bibliographies, and links to related Web sites.

ELECTRONIC DATABASES

Electronic databases usually do not have their own URLs. Instead, public, college, and university libraries subscribe to these databases and add them to their Web sites, where they are available only to library card holders or specified patrons. Readers can check library Web sites to see if these databases are available, or they can ask reference librarians about database availability.

General

Gale Virtual Reference Library
The database contains more than eighty-five reference books, including encyclopedias and almanacs, allowing users to find information about a broad range of subjects.

Biography

Biography Resource Center
The database includes biographies of more than 320,000 prominent people from throughout the world and from a wide range of disciplines.

Wilson Biographies Illustrated
This database offers more than ninety-five thousand biographies and obituaries, and more than twenty-six thousand photographs, of prominent people.

History

History Reference Center
The *History Reference Center* is a comprehensive world history database. It contains the contents of more than 650 encyclopedias and other books, the full text of articles published in about sixty history periodicals, and thousands of historical documents, biographies, photographs, and maps.

MagillOnHistory
Set to launch in 2006 on the EBSCO platform, Salem Press's *MagillOnHistory* will offer the full contents of its Great Lives from History series as well as its ongoing Great Events from History series and entries from its many history and social science encyclopedias,

such as *Ready Reference: American Indians* and its decades series, *The Fifties*, *The Sixties*, and *The Seventies*. Full-length essays numbering in the thousands are designed to cross-link coverage of events and biographies of history's movers and shapers, from ancient times to the twenty-first century.

World History FullTEXT

This database provides a global view of history with information on a wide range of topics, including anthropology, art, culture, economics, government, heritage, military history, politics, regional issues, and sociology.

World History Online

This reference database of world history features biographies, time lines, maps, charts, and other information.

LITERATURE

Literature Resource Center

The *Literature Resource Center* includes biographies, bibliographies, and critical analyses of authors from a wide range of literary disciplines, countries, and eras. The database also features plot summaries, the full text of articles from literary journals, critical essays, plot summaries, and links to Web sites.

MagillOnLiteraturePlus

Containing more than 160 volumes of information, Salem Press's comprehensive integrated literature database incorporates the full contents of its many title- and author-driven sets, and is growing as new titles are added. As of spring, 2005, these included *Masterplots* (series I and II), *Cyclopedia of World Authors*, *Cyclopedia of Literary Characters*, *Cyclopedia of Literary Places*, *Critical Surveys of Literature*, *Magill's Literary Annual*, *World Philosophers and Their Works*, and *Magill Book Reviews*. Updated quarterly, the database examines more than thirty-five thousand works and more than ten thousand writers, poets, dramatists, essayists, and philosophers. Most essays are several pages in length, and nearly all feature annotated bibliographies for further study. Essays feature critical analyses as well as plot summaries, biographical essays, character profiles, and authoritative listings of authors' works and their dates of publication.

—*Rebecca Kuzins*

Chronological List of Entries

1600's

1610's

1620's

1630's

1640's

1650's

1656-1667: Construction of the Piazza San Pietro
1656-1676: Ottoman Empire's Brief Recovery
Feb., 1656: Huygens Identifies Saturn's Rings
1657: Work Begins on Japan's National History
Jan. 18-20, 1657: Meireki Fire Ravages Edo
Beginning 1658: First Newspaper Ads Appear
1658-1707: Reign of Aurangzeb
Aug., 1658-Aug. 24, 1660: Explorations of Radisson and Chouart des Groseilliers
1659: Expansion of the Alawis
May, 1659-May, 1660: Restoration of Charles II
Nov. 7, 1659: Treaty of the Pyrenees

1660's

1660's-1700: First Microscopic Observations
1660-1677: A Jihad Is Called in Senegambia
1660-1692: Boyle's Law and the Birth of Modern Chemistry
Sept. 13, 1660-July 27, 1663: British Navigation Acts
1661: Absolute Monarchy Emerges in France
1661-1665: Clarendon Code
1661-1672: Colbert Develops Mercantilism
Feb. 17, 1661-Dec. 20, 1722: Height of Qing Dynasty
Mar., 1661-1705: Virginia Slave Codes
June 23, 1661: Portugal Cedes Bombay to the English
1662: Half-Way Covenant
1662-May 3, 1695: England's Licensing Acts
Mar. 18, 1662: Public Transportation Begins
May 19, 1662: England's Act of Uniformity
Mar. 24, 1663-July 25, 1729: Settlement of the Carolinas
1664: Molière Writes *Tartuffe*
1664: Willis Identifies the Basal Ganglia
Mar. 22, 1664-July 21, 1667: British Conquest of New Netherland
July 13, 1664: Trappist Order Is Founded
1665: Cassini Discovers Jupiter's Great Red Spot
1665-1681: Construction of the Languedoc Canal
Jan., 1665: Shabbetai Tzevi's Messianic Movement Begins
Mar. 4, 1665-July 31, 1667: Second Anglo-Dutch War
Spring, 1665-Fall, 1666: Great Plague in London
Oct. 29, 1665: Battle of Mbwila
c. 1666: Stradivari Makes His First Violin
c. 1666-1676: Founding of the Marāthā Kingdom
Sept. 2-5, 1666: Great Fire of London
1667: Consecration of the First Cathedral in Mexico
1667: Milton Publishes *Paradise Lost*
1667: Pufendorf Advocates a Unified Germany
Apr., 1667-June, 1671: Razin Leads Peasant Uprising in Russia
May 24, 1667-May 2, 1668: War of Devolution
Dec. 19, 1667: Impeachment of Clarendon
Jan. 23, 1668: Triple Alliance Forms
Feb. 13, 1668: Spain Recognizes Portugal's Independence
1669: Steno Presents His Theories of Fossils and Dynamic Geology
Feb., 1669-Jan., 1677: John of Austria's Revolts

1670's

c. 1670: First Widespread Smallpox Inoculations
1670: Popularization of the Grand Tour
1670: Promulgation of the Sacred Edict
1670-1699: Rise of the Asante Empire
Apr., 1670: Charles Town Is Founded
May 2, 1670: Hudson's Bay Company Is Chartered
Beginning 1671: American Indian Slave Trade
Late Dec., 1671: Newton Builds His Reflecting Telescope
1672-1684: Leeuwenhoek Discovers Microscopic Life
1672-c. 1691: Self-Immolation of the Old Believers
Apr. 6, 1672-Aug. 10, 1678: Third Anglo-Dutch War
Summer, 1672-Fall, 1676: Ottoman-Polish Wars
c. 1673: Buxtehude Begins His Abendmusiken Concerts
Beginning 1673: French Explore the Mississippi Valley
1673: Huygens Explains the Pendulum
1673: Renovation of the Louvre
1673-1678: Test Acts
Dec., 1673-1681: Rebellion of the Three Feudatories

1680's

1690's

Geographical Index

List of Geographical Regions

Africa

American Colonies

American Southwest

Angola

Australia

Austria

Balkans

Belgium

Benin

Bohemia

Brazil

Canada

Caribbean

China

Ghana

Hungary

India

Indonesia

Iran

Ireland

Italy

Jamaica

Japan

Category Index

List of Categories

Agriculture

Architecture

Art

ASTRONOMY

BIOLOGY

COLONIZATION

Communications

Cultural and intellectual history

Diplomacy and international relations

ECONOMICS

EDUCATION

ENGINEERING

ENVIRONMENT

Expansion and land acquisition

Exploration and discovery

Geology

Government and politics

Health and medicine

Mathematics

Music

Natural disasters

Organizations and institutions

Philosophy

Physics

Religion and theology

Science and technology

Social issues and reform

Theater

Trade and commerce

Transportation

Wars, uprisings, and civil unrest

Great Events from History

Indexes

Personages Index

Subject Index